Lucent's

General Knowledge

UPSC Civil Services, Combined Defence Services (CDS), National Defence Academy (NDA), Railway Recruitment Boards (RRBs), Special Class Railway Apprentices (SCRA), Indian Forest Services (IFS), Indian Economic Services (IES), Combined Engineering Services, Bank Probationary Officers (P.O. / T.O. / A.O.), L.I.C., G.I.C. (A.A.O.), R.B.I. Grade 'A' and 'B', other Administrative Officers Examinations, MBA, MCA, BCA, BBA entrance tests.

Every genuine copy of this book has a 3–D Hologram Sticker on the cover. To verify genunity scratch lower part of the sticker, Lucent Publication in BOLD will appear.

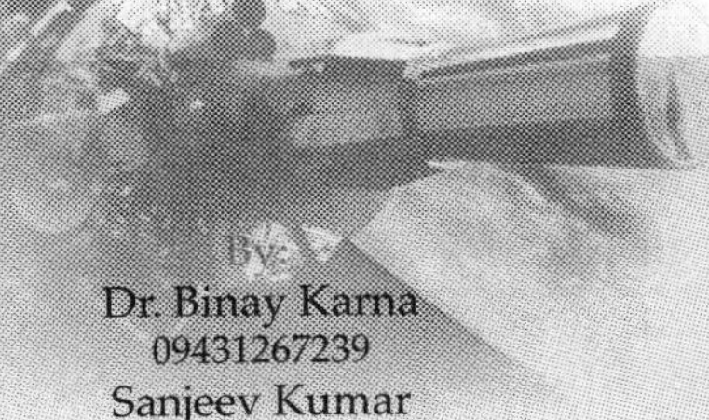

By:
Dr. Binay Karna
09431267239
Sanjeev Kumar
09801129674
Manwendra Mukul
R. P. Suman
Renu Sinha

Lucent Publication
New Bypass Road, Ashochak
Patna-800 016 (Bihar)

Publisher : *Lucent* Publication
New Bypass Road, Ashochak
Patna-800 016 (Bihar)
Phone : 09934016609

Marketing Office : 07766913350, 07766913352, 07766913353

Mail at : info@lucentpublication.com
Web : www.lucentpublication.com

1st Edition : 2007
5th Edition : 2014

ISBN : 978-81-929335-6-6

Price : ₹ **180.00**

Printed at : Jai Hind Press, Patna

Every genuine copy of this book has a 3–D Hologram Sticker on the cover. To verify genunity scratch lower part of the sticker, Lucent Publication in BOLD will appear.

Preface to the Latest Revised Edition

We have a great pleasure to present the latest revised edition of Lucent's General Knowledge within a year. It indicates general acceptance of the book by the readers, especially the candidates taking competitive exams.

General Knowledge is one of the fastest changing subject as the pace of development is very quick, and a knowledge can become stale within a short-period. That's why, the present edition of the book has been thoroughly revised. Each section of the book has been revised in accordance with the questions asked in recent examinations. Besides, some more useful information and material have been appended in History, Geography, Indian Polity and Constitution, Indian Economy, Miscellany etc.

We are grateful to our esteemed readers, some of whose suggestions have been incorporated in this edition. We would welcome still more suggestions for further improvement in the book.

Writers

Preface to the First Edition

We have a great pleasure in presenting this book Lucent's General Knowledge according to the new trends of various competitive exams. This book covers a wide range of general knowledge in a single concise volume. Apart from extensive coverage, we have recognised three main priorities : accurate & up-to-date information; concise & lucid language; and a clear-cut presentation.

The book is divided into 6 sections, namely :

1. Indian History, 2. Geography, 3. Indian Polity and Constitution, 4. Indian Economy, 5. General Science and 6. Miscellany.

Each section of the book has been compiled with utmost care by well informed persons and specialist of the subject matter. We are quite confident that this book will cater to the needs of a wide range of readers.

Despite having taken all care, some printing errors might be there in the book. Hence valuable suggestions and comments of the readers, teachers and wellwishers are solicited. The feedback will certainly helps us in further improving the book in subsequent editions.

We are thankful to our publisher who has taken great pains to bring out this book. We also express our sincere gratitude to our friends, family members and all our wellwishers for their useful suggestions, sincere support and kind co-operation.

Buddha Purnima
May 02, 2007

Writers

CONTENTS

★★★

INDIAN HISTORY 1

Ancient India

1. Harappan/Indus Civilization (2500 BC-1750 BC)

- The oldest name—Indus Civilization.
- According to archaeological tradition, the most appropriate name—Harappan Civilization (Harappa–the first discovered site).
- According to geographical point of view, the most suitable name—Inuds–Saraswati Civilization (the largest concentration of settlement–along the Indus–Saraswati river valley; 80% settlement along the Saraswati).
- The most accepted period—2500 BC–1750 BC (by Carbon-14 dating).
- *John Marshall* was the first scholar to use the term 'Indus Civilization'.
- The Indus Civilization belongs to Proto-Historic Period (Chalcolithic Age / Bronze Age).
- The Indus Civilization was spread over Sindh, Baluchistan, Punjab, Haryana, Rajasthan, Gujarat, Western U.P. and Northern Maharashtra.
- Scholars generally believe that Harappa-Ghaggar–Mohenjodaro axis represents the heartland of the Indus Civilization.
- The Northern-most site of Indus Civilization—*Ropar* (Sutlej) / Punjab (Earlier); *Manda* (Chenab) / Jammu-Kashmir (Now).

  The Southern-most site of Indus Civilization—*Bhagatrav* (Kim) / Gujarat (Earlier); *Daimabad* (Pravara) / Maharashtra (Now).

  The Eastern-most site of Indus Civilization—*Alamgirpur* (Hindon) / Uttar Pradesh.

  The Western-most site of Indus Civilization—*Sutkagendor* (Dashk) / Makran Coast, Pakistan–Iran Border.
- Capital Cities—Harappa, Mohenjodaro

  Port Cities—Lothal, Sutkagendor, Allahdino, Balakot, Kuntasi

Site	River	District	State / Province	Country	Excavators
Harappa	Ravi	Sahiwal	Punjab	Pakistan	Daya Ram Sahni (1921), Madho Swaroop Vatsa (1926), Wheeler (1946)
Mohenjodaro (Nakhlistan i.e. Oasis of Sindh)	Indus	Larkana	Sindh	Pakistan	Rakhal Das Bannerji (1922), Mackay (1927) Wheeler (1930)
Chanhudaro	Indus	Nawabshah	Sindh	Pakistan	Mackay (1925), N.G. Mazumdar (1931)
Lothal	Bhogava	Ahmedabad	Gujarat	India	S.R. Rao (1954)
Kalibanga (i.e. the bangles of black colour)	Ghaggar	Hanumangarh	Rajasthan	India	Amalanand Ghosh (1951), B.V. Lal and B.K. Thapar (1961)
Banawali	Ghaggar	Fatehabad	Haryana	India	R. S. Bist (1973)
Dholavira	Luni	Kutchh	Gujarat	India	J.P. Joshi (1967-68)

Site	Archaeological Finds
Harappa	6 Granaries in row, Working floors, Workmen's quarters, Virgin-Goddess (seal), Cemetery (R-37, H), Stone symbols of Lingam (male sex organ) and Yoni (female sex organ), Painted pottery, Clay figures of Mother Goddess, Wheat and Barley in wooden mortar, Copper scale, Crucible for bronze, Copper-made mirror, Vanity box, Dice.
Mohenjodaro	Great Granary, Great Bath (the largest building of civilization), Assembly hall, Shell strips, Pashupati Mahadeva / Proto-Shiva (seal), Bronze Image of a nude woman dancer, Steatite image of bearded man, Human skeltons huddled together, Painted seal (Demi-God), Clay figures of Mother Goddess, A fragment of woven cotton, Brick Kilns, 2 Mesopotamian seals, 1398 seals (56% of total seals of civilization), Dice.
Chanhudaro	City without a citadel, Inkpot, Lipstick; Metal-workers', shell-ornament makers' and bead-makers' shops; Imprint of dog's paw on a brick, Terracotta model of a bullock cart, Bronze toy cart.
Lothal	Dockyard, Rice husk; Metal-workers', shell-ornament makers' and bead-makers' shopes; Fire altars, Terracotta figurine of a horse, Double burial (burying a male and a female in a single grave), Terracotta model of a ship, Dying vat, Persian / Iranian seal, Baharainean seal, Painted jar (bird and fox).
Kalibanga	Ploughed field surface (Pre-Harappan), 7 Fire altars, Decorated bricks, Wheels of a toy cart, Mesopotamian cylindrical seal.
Banawali	Lack of chess-board or gridiron pattern town planning, Lack of systematic drainage system, Toy plough, Clay figures of Mother Goddess.
Dholavira	A unique water harnessing system and its storm water drainage system, a large well and a bath (giant water reservoirs), Only site to be divided into 3 parts, Largest Harappan inscription used for civic purposes, A stadium.
Surkotada	Bones of horse, Oval grave, Pot burials.
Daimabad	Bronze images (Charioteer with chariot, ox, elephant and rhinoceros)

➢ *Mohenjodaro* – the largest site of Indus Civilization, *Rakhigarhi*—The largest Indian site of Indus Civilization.

➢ **Common Features of Major Cities :** 1. Systematic town-planning on the lines of 'grid system' 2. Use of burnt bricks in constructions 3. Underground drainage system (giant water reservoirs in *Dholavira*) 4. Fortified citadel (exception–Chanhudaro).

➢ *Surkotada* (Kutchh district, Gujarat) : the only Indus site where the remains of a horse have actually been found.

- **Main Crops :** Wheat and Barely; Evidence of cultivation of rice in *Lothal* and *Rangpur* (Gujarat) only. **Other Crops :** Dates, mustard, sesamum, cotton etc. Indus people were the first to produce cotton in the world.
- **Animals** : Sheep, goat, humped and humpless bull, buffalo, boar, dog, cat, pig, fowl, deer, tortoise, elephant, camel, rhinoceros, tiger etc.
- Lion was not known to Indus people. From *Amari*, a single instance of the Indian rhinoceros has been reported.
- There was extensive inland and foreign trade. Foreign trade with *Mesopotamia or Sumeria* (Modern Iraq), *Bahrain* etc. flourished.

Imports	From
Gold	Kolar (Karnataka), Afghanistan, Persia (Iran)
Silver	Afghanistan, Persia (Iran), South India
Copper	Khetri (Rajasthan), Baluchistan, Arabia
Tin	Afghanistan, Bihar
Lapis Lazuli and Sapphire	Badak-shan (Afghanistan)
Jade	Central Asia
Steatite	Shaher-i-Sokhta (Iran), Kirthar Hills (Pakistan)
Amethyst	Maharasthtra
Agate, Chalcedonies and Carnelians	Saurashtra and West India

- **Exports :** Agricultural products, cotton goods, terracotta figurines, pottery, certain beads (from *Chanhudaro*), conch-shell (from *Lothal*), ivory products, copper etc.
- A very interesting feature of this civilization was that *Iron was not known to the people*.
- The Sumerian texts refer to trade relations with '*Meluha*' which was the name given to the Indus region.
- *Shatughai* and *Mundigaq* were the Indus sites found in Afghanistan.
- The Sumerian texts also refer to two intermediate stations—*Dilmun* (Bahrain) and *Makan* (Makran coast). *Susa* and *Ur* are Mesopotamian places where Harappan seals were found.
- The Harappans were the earliest people to produce cotton (It was called '*Sindon*' by the Greeks).
- As there is no evidence of coins, barter is assumed to have been the normal method of exchange of goods.
- *Lothal* was an ancient port of Indus civilization.
- The Indus Civilization was primarily urban.
- There is no clear-cut evidence of the nature of polity, but it seems that the ruling authority of Indus Civilization was a class of merchants.
- The Harappan people didn't worship their gods in temple. No temple in fact has been unearthed. An idea of their religion is formed from the statues and figurines found.

- ➢ The most commonly found figurine is that of Mother-Goddess *(Matridevi or Shakti)*. There is evidence of prevalence of *Yoni* (female sex organ) worship.
- ➢ The chief male deity was the *'Pasupati Mahadeva'* i.e. the lord of Animals (Proto-Shiva) represented in seals as sitting in yogic posture; he is surrounded by four animals (elephant, tiger, rhino and buffalo) and two deer appear at his feet. There was the prevalence of Phallic *(lingam)* worship.
- ➢ Thus *Shiva-Shakti* worship, the oldest form of worship in India, appears to have been part of the religious belief of Harppan people (esp. humped bull).
- ➢ The remains and relics also reveal that zoolatry i.e. animal worship and tree worship (esp. peepal) were in vogue in those days.
- ➢ There is the evidence of pictographic script, found mainly on seals. The script has not been deciphered so far, but overlap of letters on some of the potsherds from *Kalibanga* show that writing was boustrophedon or from right to left and from left to right in alternate lines. It has been referred to as Proto-Dravidian.
- ➢ Steatite was mainly used in the manufacture of seals.
- ➢ Humpless bull is represented in most of the Indus seals.
- ➢ Inhumation or complete burial was the most common method of disposal of the dead.
- ➢ The origin of the *'Swastika'* symbol can be traced to the Indus Civilization.
- ➢ 'Indra is accused of causing the decline of Indus Civilisation'—*M. Wheeler*.
- ➢ The Rigveda speaks of a battle at a place named *'Hariyumpia'* which has been identified with *Harappa*.
- ➢ The majority of scholars believe that the makers of this civilization were Dravidian.
- ➢ Contemporary civilizations of Indus Civilization—*Mesopotamia, Egypt and China*.

2. Vedic Culture (1500 BC-600 BC)

Original Home of the Aryan

- ➢ The location of the original home of the Aryans still remains a controversial point. Some scholars believe that the Aryans were native to the soil of India and some other scholars believe that the Aryans were migrated from outside [Central Asia *(Max Muller)*/ Europe / Arctic region *(B. G. Tilak)*].
- ➢ According to popular belief, the Aryans are supposed to have migrated from Central Asia into the Indian subcontinent in several stages or waves during 2000 BC–1500 BC.
- ➢ *Boghazkai Inscription* (Asia Minor, Turkey), which mentions 4 vedic gods *Indra, Varuna, Mitra* and *Nasatyas*, proves Central Asian Theory as their homeland.

- The group that came to India first settled in the present Frontier Province and the Punjab – then called *Sapta Sindhu* i.e. region of seven rivers. They lived here for many centuries and gradually pushed into the interior to settle in the valleys of the Ganges and the Yamuna.

Vedic Literature (1500 BC-600 BC)

- It is presumed that the Rig Veda was composed while the Aryans were still in the Punjab.
- Vedic Literature comprises of four literary productions : 1. *The Samhitas or Vedas* 2. *The Brahamans* 3. *The Aranyakas* 4. *The Upanishads*.
- Vedic Literature had grown up in course of time and was really handed down from generation to generation by word of mouth. Hence these are called *Shruti* (to hear).
- The most important of Vedic Literature are *Vedas*. *Vedas* are called *Apaurasheya* i.e. not created by man but God-gifted and *Nitya* i.e. existing in all eternity.
- There are four Vedas–*Rig Veda, Sama Veda, Yajur Veda* and *Atharva Veda*. The first three Vedas are jointly called *Vedatrayi* i.e. trio of Vedas.
- Of the four Vedas, the *Rig Veda* (Collection of lyrics) is the oldest text in the wold, and therefore, is also known as 'the first testament of mankind'. The Rig Veda contains 1028 hymns, divided into 10 mandalas. Six mandalas (from 2nd to 7th mandalas) are called *Gotra/ Vamsha Mandalas (Kula Granth)*. The 1st and 10th mandalas are said to have been added later. The 10th mandala contains the famous *Purushasukta* which explains the 4 Varnas – Brahmana, Kshatriya, Vaishya and Shudra. The hymns of Rig Veda were recited by *Hotri*.
- The *Sama Veda* (book of chants) had 1549 hymns. All hymns (excluding 75) were taken from the Rig Veda. The hymns of the Sama Veda were recited by *Udgatri*. This Veda is important for Indian music.
- The *Yajur Veda* (book of sacrificial prayers) is a ritual veda. Its hymns were recited by *Adhvaryus*. It is divided into two parts–*Krishna Yajur Veda* and *Shukla Yajur Veda*. In contrast to the first two which are in verse entirely, this one is in both verse and prose.
- The *Atharva Veda* (book of magical formulae), the fourth and the last one, contains charms and spells to ward off evils and diseases. For a very long time it was not included in the category of the Vedas.
- The *Brahmans* explain the hymns of the Vedas. They are written in prose and ritualistic in nature. *Brahma* means 'sacrifice'. The various sacrifices and rituals have been elaborately discussed in the Brahamanas. Every Veda has several Brahamanas attached to it :

  Rig Veda—*Aitareya* and *Kaushitiki/Sankhyan*.

  Sam Veda—*Panchvisha (Tandya Maha Brahamana), Shadvinsh, Chhandogya* and *Jaiminaya*.

  Yajur Veda—*Shatapatha* (the oldest and the largest Brahamana) and *Taittariya*.

  Atharva Veda—*Gopatha*.

➢ The word *Aranya* means 'the forest'. The 'forest texts' were called *Aranyaka*, because they were written mainly for the hermits and the students living in jungles. The Aranyaka are the concluding portions of the Brahamanas.

➢ The *Upanishadas* are philosphical texts. They are generally called *Vedanta*, as they came towards the end of the Veda. There are 108 Upanishadas. *Vrihadaranyak*a is the oldest Upanishada.

Literature of Vedic Tradition (600 BC-600 AD)

➢ Literature of Vedic Tradition (*Smriti* i.e. rememberance literature) comprises of 6 literary works : 1. Vedangas/Sutras 2. Smritis Dharmashastras 3. Mahakavyas (Epics) 4. Puranas 5. Upvedas 6. Shad-Dharshanas.

➢ There are six *Vedangas* :

(i) **Shiksha** (Phonetics) : *'Pratishakhya'*–the oldest text on phonetics.

(ii) **Kalpa Sutras** (Rituals) : a. *Shrauta Sutras/Shulva Sutras*–deal with the sacrifices, b. *Grihya Sutras*—deal with family ceremonies, c. *Dharma Sutras*—deal with Varnas, Ashramas etc.

(iii) **Vyakarana** (Grammar) : *'Ashtadyayi' (Panini)*–the oldest grammar of the word.

(iv) **Nirukta** (Etymology) : 'Nirukta' *(Yask)* based on *'Nighantu' (Kashyap)*–a collection of difficult vedic words—*('Nighantu'—the oldest word-collection of the world; 'Nirukta'—the oldest dictionary of the world).*

(v) **Chhanda** (Metrics) : *'Chhandasutras' (Pingal)*–famous text.

(vi) **Jyotisha** (Astronomy): *'Vedanga Jyotisha' (Lagadh Muni)*–the oldest Jyotisha text.

➢ There are six famous *Smritis* : (i) *Manu Smriti* (Pre-Gupta Period)—the oldest Smriti text; Commentators : *Vishwarupa, Meghatithi, Gobindraj, Kulluk Bhatt.* (ii) *Yajnvalkya Smriti* (Pre-Gupta Period)—Commentators : *Vishwarupa, Vijnyaneshwar, Apararka* (a king of Shilahar Dynasty) (iii) *Narad Smriti* (Gupta period), (iv) *Parashara Smriti* (Gupta period), (v) *Brihaspati Smriti* (Gupta period), (vi) *Katyayana Smriti* (Gupta period).

➢ There are mainly two *Mahakavyas* (Epics) :

(i) **The Ramayana** *(Valmiki)* : It is known as *'Adi Kavya'* (the oldest epic of the world). At present, it consists of 24,000 shlokas i.e. verses (Originally 6,000, Later – 12,000, Finally – 24,000) in 7 Kandas i.e. sections. 1st and 7th Kandas were the latest additions to the Ramayana.

(ii) **The Mahabharata** *(Ved Vyasa)* : The longest epic of the world. At present, it consists of 1,00,000 shlokas i.e. verses (Originally–8,800-Jay Samhita, Later–24,000-Chaturvinshati Sahastri Samhita/Bharata, Finally–1,00,000-Shatasahastri Samhita/Maha Bharata) in 18 Parvans i.e. chapters, plus the Harivamsa supplement. *Bhagavad Gita* is extracted from Bihshma Parvan of Mahabharata. Shanti Parvan is the largest parvan (chapter) of the Mahabarata.

➢ The *Purana* means 'the old'. There are18 famous 'Puranas'. The *Matsya Purana* is the oldest Puranic text. The other important Puranas are the *Bhagavata, The Vishnu, The Vayu and The Brahamnda*. They describe genealogies of various royal dynasties.

➢ *The Upavedas* ***(the auxiliary vedas)*** were traditionally associated with vedas :

	Upavedas	Associated with
(i)	*Ayurveda* i.e. Medicine	Rig Veda
(ii)	*Gandharvaveda* i.e. Music	Sama Veda
(iii)	*Dhanurveda* i.e. Archery	Yajur Veda
(iv)	*Shilpveda / Arthaveda* i.e. the science of craft / wealth (Vishwakarma)	Atharva Veda

➢ There are 6 schools of Indian philosophy known as *Shad-Darshanas.*

	Darshana	Founder	Basic Text
(i)	Sankhya Darshana	Kapila	Sankhya Sutra
(ii)	Yoga Darshana	Patanjali	Yoga Sutra
(iii)	Nyaya Darshana	Akshapada Gautama	Nayaya Sutra
(iv)	Vaishesika Darshana	Uluka Kanada	Vaishesika Sutra
(v)	Mimansa / Purva-Mimansa	Jaimini	Purva Mimansa Sutra
(vi)	Vedant / Uttara-Mimansa	Badarayana	Brahma Sutra / Vedant Sutra

Rig Vedic/Early Vedic Period (1500 BC–1000 BC)

Geographical Area

➢ Rig Veda is the only source of knowledge for this period.

➢ From the names of rivers, mountains *(Himvant* ***i.e. Himalaya,*** *Munjavant* ***i.e. Hindukush)*** and ocean in Rig Veda we have a clear idea of the geographical area inwhich Rigvedic people lived.

➢ Rig Veda mentions 40 rivers. The *Nadisukta* hymn of the Rig Veda mentions 21 rivers which include the Ganges in the east and the Kubha (Kabul) in the west.

➢ Rigvedic people, who called themselves Aryans, were confined in the area which came to be known as *Sapta Sindhu* i.e. land of the seven rivers. Sapta Sindhu comprises *Sindhu* and their five tributaries – *Vitasta, Asikani, Vipas, Parushni & Sutuadri* and *Saraswati*.

➢ According to the Rig Veda, the most mentioned river—Sindhu, the most pious river—Saraswati, mention of the Ganges–1 time, mention of Yamuna–3 times.

➢ **The Dasrajan War** (The Battle of Ten Kings)

According to Rig Veda, the famous Dasrajan war was the internecine war of the Aryans. The Dasrajan war gives names of ten kings who participated in a war against *Sudas* who was *Bharata* king of *Tritsus* family. The ten kings were of the states of Purus, Yadus, Turvasas, Anus and Druhyus along with five others viz. Alinas, Pakhtas, Bhalanas, Sibis and Vishanins. The battle was fought on the bank of Parushni (Ravi) in which *Sudas* emerged victorious.

Rigvedic Name	Modern Name	Region
Sindhu	Indus	Punjab
Vitasta	Jhelum	Punjab
Asikani	Chenab	Punjab
Vipas	Beas	Punjab
Parushni	Ravi	Punjab
Sutudri	Sutlej	Punjab
Saraswati	Sarsuti	Rajasthan
Drishadvati	Ghaggar	Rajasthan
Kubha	Kabul	Afghanistan
Suvastu	Swati	Afghanistan
Krumu	Kurram	Afghanistan
Gomati	Gomal	Afghanistan

Polity

- *The Kula (the family)* was the basis of both social and political organisations. Above the Kula were *the Grama, the Vis, the Jana* and *the Rashtra*. A group of Kula *(families)* formed a Grama (the village) and so on.

Unit	Head
Kula (the family)	Kulapa
Grama (the village)	Gramani
Vis (the clan)	Vispati
Jana (the people)	Gopa/Gopati
Rashtra (the country)	Rajan

- Regarding the form of government it was of patriarchal nature. Monarchy was normal, but non-monarchical polities were also there.
- The Rashtra was ruled by a King or Rajan and the royal descent was by hereditary based on the law of primogeniture. Probably elective monarchy was also known.
- Very little is known about ministers of the king. *The Purohita* or domestic priest was the first ranking official. He was the king's preceptor, friend, philosopher and guide. Other important royal officials were *Senani* (army chief) and *Gramani (head of village).*
- The army consisted of foot-soldiers and charioteers. Wood, stone, bone and metals were used in weapons. Arrows were tipped with points of metal or poisoned horn. References are made to the moving fort *(Purcharishnu)* and a machine for assaulting strongholds.
- The king had religious duties also. He was the upholder of the established order and moral rules.
- Rig Veda speaks of assemblies such as the *Sabha, Samiti, Vidath, Gana*. Sabha was committee of few privileged and important

individuals. Two popular assemblies, Sabha and Samiti, acted as checks on the arbitrary rule of kings. Later Vedas record that the Sabha functioned as a court of justice.

- Theft, burglary, stealing of cattle and cheating were some of the then prevent crimes.

Society

- The Rigvedic society comprised four varnas, namely *Brahmana*, *Kshatriya*, *Vaisya* and *Shudra*. This classification of society was based on the professions or occupations of the individuals.
- Teachers and priests were called *Brahamanas*; rulers and administrators were called *Kshatriyas*; farmers, merchants and bankers were called *Vaishyas*; and artisans and labourers were reckoned as *Shudras*.
- These vocations were followed by persons according to their ability and liking, and the occupations had not become hereditary as they became later on.
- Members of the same family took to different professions and belonged to different varnas as well illustrated by a hymn of the Rig Veda. In this hymn a person says : *'I am a singer; my father is a physician, my mother is a grinder of corn.'*
- The unit of society was family, primarily monogamous and patriarchal.
- Child marriage was not in vogue.
- A widow could marry the younger brother of her deceased husband (*Niyoga*).
- The father's property was inherited by son.
- Right to property existed in respect of moveable things like cattle, horse, gold and ornaments and also in respect of immovable property like land and house.
- The home of the teacher was the school where he taught the particular sacred texts.
- Milk and its products–curd, butter and ghee–formed an important part of the diet. There is also the mention of grain cooked with milk *(Kshira-pakamodanam)*.
- The meat of fish, birds and animals was eaten.
- The cow was already deemed *Aghanya* i.e. not to be killed.
- Rig Veda prescribes a penalty of death or expulsion from the kingdom to those who kill or injure cows.
- Alcoholic drinks, *Sura* and *Soma* were also consumed.
- Aryans were primarily agricultural and pastoral people who reckoned their wealth in terms of cows.
- Amusements included music, dancing, chariot-racing and dicing. One stanza in the Rig Veda known as the gambler's lament says : 'My wife rejects me and her mother hates me'.

Religion

➢ During the Rigvedic time the gods worshipped were generally the personified powers of Nature. It was believed that divine powers were capable of conferring both boons and punishments on man. Fire was sacred as it was regarded to be the intermediary between man and God.

➢ There were nearly 33 gods. Later day tradition classified them into 3 categories of terrestrial *(prithvisthana)*, aerial or intermediate *(antarikshasthana)* and celestial *(dyusthana)* god.

(i) **Terrestrial** *(Prithvisthaniya)* : *Prithivi, Agni, Soma, Brihaspati* and rivers.

(ii) **Aerial/Intermediate** *(Antarikshasthaniya)*: *Indra, Rudra, Vayu-Vata, Parjanya.*

(iii) **Celestial** *(Dyusthaniya)* : *Daus, Surya* (In 5 forms : *Surya, Savitri, Mitra, Pushan, Vishnu*), *Varuna, Aditi, Usha* and *Asvin.*

➢ *Indra, Agni* and *Varuna* were the most popular deities of Rigvedic Aryans.

Indra or *Purandara* (destroyer of fort) : The most important god (250 Rigvedic hymns are devoted to him); who played the role of warlord and was considered to be the rain god.

Agni : The second most important god (200 Rigvedic hymns are devoted to him); fire god was considered to be the intermediary between the gods and the people.

Varuna : Personified water; was supposed to uphold *'Rita'* or the natural order *('Ritasyagopa')*.

➢ *Surya* (Sun) was worshiped in 5 forms : *Surya, Savitri, Mitra, Pushan* and *Vishnu.*

Surya (Sun) : God who used to drive daily across the sky in his chariot driven by seven horses.

Savitri (the god of light) : The famous *Gayatri Mantra* is addressed to her.

Mitra : A solar god.

Pushan : The god of marriage; main function–guarding of roads, herdsmen and straying cattle.

Vishnu : A god which covered earth in three steps (*Upakrama*).

➢ *Soma* : Originally a plant producing a potent drink during courses of *Agnishtoma* sacrifice, could be hemp / *bhang*, called king of plants; identified later with the moon. The 9th mandala of Rig Veda, which contains 114 hymns, is attributed to the *Soma*. That's why it is called 'the *Soma Mandala*'.

➢ Other Gods / Goddesses : *Rudra* (the god of animals), *Dyaus* (the oldest god and the father of the world), *Yama* (the god of death). *Ashwin*/ *Nastya* (the god of health, youth and immortality); *Aditi* (the great mother of gods), *Sindhu* (river goddess).

➢ Sometimes gods were visualised as animals but there was no animal worship.

- The nature of Rigvedic religion was Henotheism i.e. a belief in many gods but each god standing out in turns as the highest.
- Their religion primarily consisted of the worship of gods with a simple ceremonial known as *Yajna* or sacrifice. Sacrifices consisted of offerings of milk, ghee, grain, flesh and soma.

Economy

- The Aryans crossed the nomadic stage. Yet, great importance was attached to herds of cattle. Various animals were domesticated.
- The vedic people were probably not familiar with cat and camel. Tiger was not known, but the wild animals like lion, elephant and boar were known to them.
- In all probability, very little of trade was there.
- Money and markets were known but they were not extensively used. Cows and gold ornaments of fixed value were the media of exchange. Coins were not known.
- Complexity in producing goods made its appearance. Men of various professions like carpenters, smiths, tanners, weavers, potters and grinders of corn were there.
- The art of healing wounds and curing diseases were in existence. There were experts in surgery. Along with herbs and drugs charms and spells were regard as equally potential in healing diseases.
- OCP (Ochre Coloured Pottery) Culture : 1500 BC-1000 BC.

Later Vedic Period : 1000 BC - 600 BC

Geographical Area

- During the later Vedic Period, the Aryan settlements covered virtually the whole of Northern India *(Aryavarta)*.
- The centre of culture now shifted from Saraswati to Ganges *(Madhya desa)*.
- There was mention of more rivers such as *Narmada, Sadanira* (modern Gandak), *Chambal* etc.
- The expansion of people towards the east is indicated in a legend of *Satapatha Brahamana*–how *Videha Madhava* migrated from the Saraswati region, crossed Sadanira and came to the land of Videha (modern Tirhut).
- Emergence of *Janapadas—Kuru* (Combination of *Purus* and *Bharatas*), *Panchala* (Combination of *Turvashas* and *Krivis*), *Kashi* etc. in Doab region.
- Later Vedic literatures mention Vindhya mountain (Southern mountain).
- Reference to the territorial divisions the later Vedas gives three broad divisions of India, viz. *Aryavarta* (Northern India), *Madhya desa* (Central India) and *Dakhinapath* (Southern India).

Polity

- Large kingdoms and stately cities made their appearance in the later Vedic Period.
- In *Taittariya Brahmana* we notice the theory of the divine origin of kingship.
- The governmental machinery became more elaborate than before, as a sequel to the growth of the power of the king. New civil functionaries, besides the only civil functionary of the Rigvedic period the purohita came into existence. These were : the *Bhagadudha* (Collector of taxes), the *Suta/Sarathi* (the Royal herald or Charioteer), the *Khasttri* (Chamberlain), the *Akshavapa* (Courier).
- The military officials of the Rigvedic times, the Senani (the general) and the Gramani (the head of the vilalge) continued to function.
- The period also saw the beginning of a regular system of provincial government. Thus, we find *Sthapati* being entrusted with the duty of administering outlying areas ocupied by the aboriginals and *Satapati* being put over a group of one hundred villages. *Adhikrita* was the village official. *Ugras*, mentioned in the Upanishada, was probably a police official.

12 Ratninas (Satapatha Brahamana)		
1.	Purohita	the Priest
2.	Mahishi	the Queen
3.	Yuvaraja	Crown prince
4.	Suta/Sarathi	the Royal herald / the Charioteer
5.	Senani	the General
6.	Gramani	Head of the village
7.	Kshata	Gateman/Chamberlain
8.	Sangrahitri	Treasurer
9.	Bhagadudha	Collector of taxes
10.	Akshavapa	Courier
11.	Palagala	Friend of King
12.	Govikarta	Head of forest department

- The popular control over the affairs of the kingdom was exercised through *Sabha* and *Samiti*, as in the Rigvedic period. *Vidatha* had completely disappeared by now.
- Even during the later vedic times, kings did not possess a standing army.
- Judiciary also grew. The king played a great role in administering criminal law. The killing of an embryo, homicide, the murder of a Brahmana, in particular, stealing of gold and drinking sura were regarded as serious crimes. Treason was a capital offence.

Society

- As the time passed by *Yajnas* became elaborate and complicated ceremonial leading to the emergence of learned men known as *Brahmanas*.
- And as the Aryans expanded to the east and south, group of people known as *Kshatriyas* emerged to conquer territories and administer them. The remaining Aryans formed a separate class known as *Vaishyas*,

a word derived from *Vis* meaning 'people'. The non-Aryan formed the fourth class known as *Shudras*.

➢ Neverthless, these divisons of society were not rigid.
➢ The institution of *Gotra* i.e. the clan appeared in later Vedic Period.
➢ The higher castes could marry with the lower ones, but marriage with shudras was not permitted. The idea of pollution appeared in society.
➢ The earliest reference to the 4 *Ashramas* (the stages of life)—*Brahmacharya, Grihastha, Vanprastha* and *Sanyasa*–is found in the *Jabala Upanishad*. The Ashrama system was formed to attain 4 *Purusharthas (Dharma, Artha, Kama and Moksha)*.
➢ The status of women declined. According to *Aitareya Brahamana* a daughter is the sources of misery but a son is the protector of family.
➢ According to *Maitrayani Samhita* there are three evils—liquor, woman and dice.
➢ Though monogamy (a man having one wife) was the ideal but polygamy (a man having more than one wife) was frequent.
➢ Woman were prohibited to attend the political assemblies.
➢ *Yajnavalkya–Gargi dialogue (Vrihadarnyaka Upanishada)* indicates that some women had got higher education.

Types of Hindu Marriage *(Vivaha)*

Brahma Vivaha	Giving the girl to a man with dowry.
Daiva Vivaha	Giving the girl to the priest himself in lieu of his fees.
Arsha Vivaha	Giving the girl to a man after accepting a bride-price.
Prajapatya Vivaha	Giving the girl to a man without demanding a bride-price.
Gandharva Vivaha	Love marriage.
Asura Vivaha	Marriage with a purchased girl.
Rakshasa Vivaha	Marriage with the daughter of a defeated king or with a kidnapped girl.
Paishacha Vivaha	Marriage to a girl after seducing or raping her.

➢ *Anuloma Vivaha* : marriage between a bridegroom from an upper caste and a bride from a lower caste; *Pratiloma Vivaha*–the reverse of Anuloma Vivaha.
➢ **16 Samskaras**
1. Garbhadhana 2. Pumsavana 3. Simantonnayan 4. Jatakarma 5. Namakaran 6. Nishkramana 7. Annaprashana 8. Chudakarma 9. Karnachhedana 10. Vidyarmbha 11. Upanayana 12. Vedarambha 13. Samavaratana 14. Vivaha 15. Vanprastha 16. Antyesti.

Religion

➢ The earlier divinites *Indra* and *Agni* were relegated into the background while *Prajapati* (creator of the Universe, later known as *Brahma*), *Vishnu* (Patron god of Aryans) and *Rudra* (God of animals, later identified with *Shiva/Mahesha*) rose in prominence. Now *Prajapati* became supreme God.

- *Pushana*, who protected cattle in the early Vedic Period now became the god of *Shudras*.
- *Brihadaranyaka Upanishada* was first the work to give the doctrine of transmigration *(Punarjanma/Samsara-chakra)* and deeds *(Karma)*.
- The early simple ceremonial of Rigvedic Period gave place to elaborate sacrifices requiring the services of as many as 17 priests. In the later Vedas and Brahamanas sacrifices *(Yajnas)* came into prominence.
- There were two varieties of sacrifices—
  - (i) *Laghuyajnas* (simple sacrifices) : Performed by householder e.g. *Pancha Mahayajna*, *Agnihotra, Darsha Yajna* (on *Amavasya* i.e. on the last day of the dark fortnight), *Purnamasa Yajna* (on *Purnima* i.e. on the day of full moon) etc.
  - (ii) *Mahayajnas* (Grand sacrifices) : Sacrifices that could only be udnertaken by an aristocratic and wealthy man and the king.
    - (a) *Rajasuya Yajna* : Royal consecration, which in its full form comprised a series of sacrifices lasting over a year. In later days it was replaced by simplified *Abhisheka* i.e. anointment.
    - (b) *Vajapeya Yajna* : Drink of strength, which lasted for a period of seventeen days upto full one year.
    - (c) *Asvamedha Yajna* : Horse sacrifice, which lasted for three days.
    - (d) *Agnishtoma Yajna* : Sacrifice of animals dedicated to Agni, which lasted one day, although Yajnika (performer of Yajna) and his wife spent ascetic life for a year before Yajna. On the occasion of the this Yajna, *soma rasa* was consumed.
- Towards the end of the Vedic Period, there was the emergence of a strong reaction against cults, rituals and priestly domination; Reflection of this mood is found in the *Upanishadas*.

Economy

- Agriculture began to replacle rearing of cattle. The plough was at times drawn by 24 oxen. Manure was known.
- Rice, barley, beans, sesame and wheat were cultivated.
- Production of goods advanced as indicated by new occupations like fisherman, washerman, dyers, door-keepers and footmen.
- Indicating specialisation distinction was drawn between the chariot-maker and the carpenter and the tanner and the hide-dresser.
- Considerable advance was made in the knowledge of metals. Mention of tin, silver and iron was made apart from gold and *ayas* (either copper or iron) in the Rig Veda.
- Evidence was there regarding organsiation of merchants into guilds because of reference to corporations *(Ganas)* and aldermen *(Sreshtins)*.
- PGW *(Painted Grey Ware)* Culture : 1100 BC – 600 BC.

3.1. Mahajanapada Period (600 BC-325 BC)

	16 Mahajanapadas (Modern Area)	Capital
1.	Anga (districts of Munger and Bhagalpur in Bihar)	Champa / Champanagari
2.	Magadha (districts of Patna, Gaya and Nalanda in Bihar)	Girivraj, Rajgriha / Rajgir (Bimbisara), Patliputra (Udayin), Vaishali (Shishunaga), Patliputra (Kalashok)
3.	Vajji (districts of Muzaffarpur & Vaishali in Bihar)	Videha, Mithila, Vaishali
4.	Malla (districts of Deoria, Basti, Gorakhpur and Siddharthnagar in U.P.)	Kuishinara and Pawa
5.	Kashi (district of Varanasi in U.P.)	Varanasi
6.	Kosala (districts of Faizabad, Gonda, Bahraich in U.P.)	North Kosal-Sravasti / Sahet-Mahet South Kosal-Saket / Ayodhya
7.	Vatsa (districts of Allahabad, Mirzapur etc. in U.P.)	Kausambi
8.	Chedi (Bundelkhand area)	Shaktimati / Sotthivati
9.	Kuru (Haryana and Delhi area)	Indraprastha (modern Delhi)
10.	Panchala (Ruhelkhand, Western U.P.)	North Panchal–Ahichhatra South Panchal–Kampilya
11.	Shurasena (Brajmandal)	Mathura
12.	Matsya (Alwar, Bharatpur and Jaipur in Rajasthan)	Viratnagar
13.	Avanti (Malwa)	North Avanti–Ujjayini South Avanti–Mahishmati
14.	Ashmaka (between the rivers Narmada and Godavari)	Potana / Patali
15.	Gandhara (western part of Pakistan and Afghanistan)	Taxila (near Rawalpindi, Pakistan) and Pushkalavati
16.	Kamboja (Hazara district of Pakistan)	Rajapur / Hataka

➢ Buddhist literature *(Anguttara Nikaya, Mahavastu)* and Jain literature *(Bhagavati Sutta)* present a list of 16 Mahajanapadas with minor variation of names.

➢ There were two types of states—monarchical and non-monarchical / republican. Monarchial states–Anga, Magadha, Kashi, Kosala, Vatsa, Chedi, Shursena, Matsya, Avanti, Gandhara.

Republican States–Vajji, Malla, Kuru, Panchal, Kamboja, Shakya (Kapilvastu), Koliyas (Ramgrama), Moriya (Pipplivana).

Rise of Magadha

- The political history of India from 6th century BC onwards is the history of struggle between four states–Magadha, Kosala, Vatsa and Avanti–for supremacy.
- Ultimately the kingdom of Magadha emerged to be the most powerful one and succeeded in founding an empire.
- **Causes of Magadha's success**
  (i) Magadha enjoyed an advantageous geographical position in the age of iron, because the richest iron deposits were situated not far away from Rajgir, the earliest capital of Magadha and could be used for making weapons.
  (ii) Magadha lay at the centre of the middle Gangetic plain. The alluvium, once cleared of the jungles, proved immense fertile and food surplus was thus available.
  (iii) Magadha enjoyed a special advantage in military organisation. Although the Indian states were well acquainted with the use of horses and chariots, it was Magadha which first used elephants on a large scale in its war against its neighbours.

Haryanaka Dynasty : 544 BC-412 BC

Bimbisara (Shronika) : 544 BC-492 BC

- He was the founder of Haryanka dynasty.
- Magadha came into prominence under the leadership of *Bimbisara*.
- He was a contemporary of *Gautama Buddha*.
- He married the princesses of Kosala (*Kosaldevi/Mahakosala*-sister of Kosal King Prasenjit), Lichchhavi (*Chellana*-sister of Lichchhavi Head Chetaka) and Madra (*Khema*-daughter of Madra king), which helped him in his expansionist policy.
- He gained a part of *Kashi* as the dowry in his marriage with the sister of king Prasenjit of Kosala.
- He conquered *Anga*.
- He sent a royal physician, *Jivaka* to Ujjain, when Avanti King *Pradyota* was attacked by jaundice.
- Known as *Seniya*. He was the first Indian king who had a regular and standing army.
- He built the city of New Rajagriha.

Ajatashatru (Kunika) : 492 BC - 460 BC

- Bimbisara was succeeded by his son Ajatashatru. Ajatashatru killed his father and seized the throne.
- Ajatashatru followed a more aggressive policy. He gained complete control over *Kashi* and broke the earlier amicable relations by attacking his maternal uncle Prasenjit, the king of Kosala.
- The *Vajji* confederation was Ajatashatru's next target of attack. This war was a lengthy one and tradition tells us that after a long period of

16 years, he was able to defeat the Vajji only through deceit, by sowing the seeds of discord amongst the people of Vajji.

- The three things who played important role to defeat the Vajji—(i) *Sunidha* and *Vatsakar*—Ajatashatru's diplomatic ministers, who sowed the seeds of discord amongst Vajjis, (ii) *Rathamusala*—a kind of chariot to which a mace was attached (iii) *Mahashilakantaka*—a war engine which catapulted big stones.
- In this way *Kashi* and *Vaishali* (the capital of Vajji) were added to Magadha, making it the most powerful territorial power in the Ganges Valley.
- He built the fort of *Rajagriha* and a watch-fort *(Jaladurga)* at a village calledl *Patali*, on the banks of the Ganges.

Udayin : 460 BC-440 BC

- Ajatshatru was succeeded by his son Udayin.
- His reign is important because he laid the foundations of the city of *Patliputra* at the confluence of the Son and the Ganges and shifted the capital from Rajagriha to Patliputra.
- Udayin was succeeded by *Anuruddha, Munda* and *Naga-Dasak* respectively who all were weak and parricides.

Shisunaga Dynasty : 412 BC-344 BC

- *Nag-Dasak* was unworthy to rule. So the people got disgusted and elected Shisunaga as the King, the minister of the last king.
- The most important achievement of *Shisunaga* was the destruction of the Pradyota dynasty of *Avanti*. This brought to an end the huudred year old rivalry between Magadha and Avanti. From then on Avanti become a part of the Magadha rule.
- Shisunaga was succeeded by *Kalashoka (Kakavarna)*. His reign is important because he convened *the Second Buddhists Council* in *Vaishali* (383 BC).

Nanda Dynasty : 344 BC-323 BC

- The Shisunaga dynasty was overthrown by *Mahapadma* who established a new line of kings known as the Nandas.
- Mahapadma is known as *Sarvakshatrantak* i.e. Uprooter of all the Kshatriyas (Puranas) and *Ugrasena* i.e. Owner of huge army (Pali texts).
- The Puranas call Mahapadma *Ekrat* i.e. the sole monarch. He seems to have overthrown all the dynasties which ruled at the time of Shisungas. He is often described as 'the first empire builder of Indian history'.
- Mahapadma was succeeded by his eight sons. *Dhanananda* was the last one.
- The last king Dhanananda is possibly identical with the *Agrammes* or *Xandrames* of the Greek texts.
- It was during the rule of Dhanananda that the invasion of Alexander took place in north-west India in 326 BC.

➢ According to Greek writer Curtius, Dhanananda commanded a huge army 20,000 cavalry, 200,000 infantry, 2,000 chariots and 3,000 elephants. It was the might of Dhanananda that terrorised Alexander and stopped his march to the Gangetic Valley.

➢ The Nanda dynasty came to an end about 322-21 BC and was supplanted by another dynasty known as Mauryas, with *Chandragupta Maurya* as the founder.

Foreign Invasions

I. Iranian/Persian Invasion—Darius's Invasion (518 BC)

➢ The Achaemenian rulers of Iran (Persia), who expanded their empire at the same time as the Magadhan princes, took advantage of the political disunity on the North-West Frontier of India.

➢ The Achaemenian ruler *Darius I (Darayabahu)* penetrated into North-West India in 518 BC and annexed Punjab, West of the Indus and Sindh. This area constituted the 20th province *(Kshatrapi)* of Iran, the total number of provinces in the Iranian empire being 28. This province was the most fertile area of the Iranian empire. From this province the empire received 360 talent gold as revenue.

➢ The Indo-Iranian contact lasted for about 200 years.

Effects of Iranian Invasion

1. It gave an impetus to Indo-Iranian trade and commerce.
2. Through the Iranian, the Greeks came to know about the great wealth of India and this eventually led to Alexander's invasion of India.
3. The Iranian scribes brought into India a form of writing which came to be known as the *Kharosthi* script. It was written from right to left like the Arabic.
4. Iranian influence on the Mauryan Sculpture is clearly perceptible, especially in the bell shaped capitals. Iranian influence may also be traced in the preamble of Ashoka's edicts as well as in certain words used in them.

II. Macedonian Invasion—Alexander's Invasion (326 BC)

➢ In the 4th century BC, the Greeks and the Iranian fought for the supremacy of the world. Under the leadership of Alexander of Macedonia the Greek finally destroyed the Iranian empire.

➢ Alexander succeeded his father Philip to the throne of Macedonia. He was then only 20 years of Age.

➢ From his very childhood he used to dream of world-conquest. He quickly conquered many areas.

➢ As a preliminary step to conquer India, the Kabul valley and the hilly area of North-West frontier were conquered, and he reached Ohind near Attock in 326 BC.

➢ The rulers of Taxila and Abhisara submitted but *Porus (Puru)* refused to do so.

➢ Alexander then crossed the Jhelum by a trick. Porus was defeated in the battle that followed, but Alexander treated him very generously for his bravery. (*Battle of Vitasta* i.e. modern *Jhelum*, Greek-*Hydaspes* – 326 BC).

➢ This was how the Indians were defeated because of their disunity.

➢ After a brilliant victory at Sakala, the Greek forces reached the *Beas*. Alexander had to return from this place as his soldiers refused to go any further. The battle of Jhelum and Sakla had opened their eyes and they were afraid of the great Magadhan empire across the Beas.

➢ After making administrative arrangements for the conquered territory, Alexander marched back in Sep. 325 BC.

➢ He reached Babylon in 323 BC where he died at the age of 33.

Effects of Alexander's Invasion

1. By opening up both the land and sea routes between India and Europe, it brought both of them closer to each other.
2. Indirectly this invasion made possible the establishment of Indo-Bacterian and Indo-Parthian states, which at a later stage considerably influenced Indian architecture (Gandhara school of sculpture), astronomy, coinage etc.
3. The invasion opened the eyes of Indian politicians to the necessity of creating a unified empire.
4. The date of the Invasion of Alexander is the 'first reliable date in early Indian history' and considerably helps us in solving chronological difficulties.

3.2. Religious Movements (600 BC - 400 BC)

Various religious movements viz. Buddhism, Jainism etc. were born and grew up in the Post-Vedic Period known as the Period of Second Urbanisation or the Age of Buddha (6th Century BC to 4th Century BC).

Causes of Religious Movements

1. The vedic philosophy had lost its original purity.
2. The vedic religion had become very complex and had degenerated into superstitions, dogmas and rituals.
3. Supremacy of the Brahmans created unrest in the society and Kshatriyas reacted against the Brahmanical domination.
4. Introduction of a new agricultural economy in Eastern India.
5. The desire of Vaishyas to improve their social position with the increase in their economic position due to the growth of trade.

Buddhism

Buddha's Life

➢ *Gautama Buddha*, foudner of Buddhism, was born in 563 BC (widely accepted), on the vaisakha purnima day at *Lumbinivana* in *Kapilvastu* (now situated in the foothills of Nepal) in the *Sakya Kshatriya* clan.

- His father *Suddhodhana* was the republican king of Kapilvastu and mother *Mahamaya* was a princess of Kosala dynasty.
- After his mother's early death, he was brought up by his step mother and aunt *Mahaprajapati Gautami*.
- His father married him at an early age to *Yasodhara* (Princess of Kolli dynasty) from whom he had a son *Rahul*.
- Four sights–an old man, a diseased person, a dead body and an ascetic–proved to be a turning point in his carrier.
- At the age of 29, he renounced home, this was his *Mahabhinishkramana* (great going forth) and became a wandering ascetic.
- His first teacher was *Alara Kalama* (Sankhya philosopher) from whom he learnt the technique of meditation.
- His next teacher was *Udraka Ramputra*.
- At the age of 35, under a pipal tree at *Uruvella (Bodh Gaya)* on the bank of river *Niranjana* (modern name Falgu) he attained *Nirvana* (enlightenment) after 49 days of continuous meditation; now he was a fully enlightened *(Buddha or Tathagat)*.
- Buddha delivered his first sermon at *Sarnath* (Dear park) to his five deciples, this is known as *Dharmachakra Pravartana* (Turning of the wheel of law).
- He died at the age of 80 in 483 BC at *Kushinagar* (identical with the village Kasia in Siddharthanagar Janapada of Deoria district of U.P.). This is known as *Mahaparinirvana* (Final Blowing out).

Great Events of Buddha's Life	Symbols
Janma (Birth)	Lotus and Bull
Mahabhinishkramana (Renunciation)	Horse
Nirvana/Sambodhi (Enlightenment)	Bodhi tree
Dharmachakra pravartana (First Sermon)	Wheel
Mahaparinirvana (Death)	Stupa

- *Kanthaka*–Budhha's horse, *Channa*–Buddha's charioteer, *Devadatta*–Buddha's cousin, *Sujata*–the farmer's daughter who gave him rice milk at Bodh Gaya and Other names of Buddha–Gautama (Clan name), Siddharta(Childhood name), Shakya Muni.

Doctrine of Buddhism

Chatwari Arya Satyani (Four Noble Truths)

It is the essence of Buddhism.

1. Life is full of sorrow *(Dukha)* : *Sabbam Dukkam*.
2. There are causes of sorrow *(Dukha Samudaya)* : *Dwadash Nidan*/ *Pratitya Samutpada*.
3. This sorrow can be stopped *(Dukha Nirodha)* : *Nirvana*.
4. There is a path leading to the cessation of sorrow *(Dukha Nirodha Gamini Pratipada)* : *Ashtangika Marga*.

Note : (i) Pratitya samutapada is also known as *Hetuvada* (theory of cause-effect) and *Kshanabhanga Vada* (theory of momentariness / impermanence).

(ii) Desire is root cause of sorrow.

(iii) The ultimate aim of life is to attain *nirvana*, the eternal state of peace and bliss, which means liberation from the cycle of birth and death.

(iv) *Ashtangika Marga* (Eight fold path) are : right observation, right determination, right speech, right action, right livelihood, right exercise, right memory and right meditation.

(v) *Madhya Marga/ Madhyama Pratipada* (the middle path)—Man should avoid both extremes, i.e. a life of comforts and luxury, and a life of severe asceticism.

***Triratna* i.e. Three Jwels of Buddhism**

1. *Buddha* (the enlightened) 2. *Dharma* (doctrine) 3. *Sangha* (commune)

Buddhist C.	Year	Venue	Chairman	Patron	Result
1st Buddhist Council	483 BC	Saptaparni Cave, Rajgriha	Mahakassapa	Ajatashatru (Harayanka Dynasty)	Compilation of Sutta-Pitaka and Vinaya Pitaka by Ananda and Upali respectively
2nd Buddhist Council	383 BC	Chullavanga Vaishali	Sabbakami	Kalashoka (Shisunaga Dynasty)	(i) The monks of Vaishali wanted some change in rites. (ii) Schism into Sthaviravadins and Mahasanghikas.
3rd Buddhist Council	250 BC	Ashokarama Vihar, Patliputra	Mogaliputta Tissa	Ashoka (Maurya Dynasty)	(i) Compilation of Abhidhamma Pitaka (ii) Decision to send missionaries to various parts of the world
4th Buddhist Council	98 AD	Kundala Vana, Kashmir	Chairman-Vasumitra Vice chairman-Ashvaghosa	Kanishka (Kushana Dynasty)	(i)Compilationof Mahavibha sha shastra (Sanskrti comment on Tripitaka) (ii) the division of Buddhists into Hinayanists and Mahayanists

Buddhist Literature

I. Pali Texts

Tripitaka : Pitaka literally means 'basket' and it was called so, because the original texts were written on palm-leaves and kept in baskets. *Sutta Pitaka*—Buddha's sayings, *Vinay Pitaka*—monastic code, *Abhidhamma pitaka*—religious discourses of Buddha (Abhidhamma Pitaka comprises of Dighgha Nikaya, Majhim Nikaya, Sanyukta Nikaya, Anguttar Nikaya and Khuddak / Kshudraka Nikaya).

Milindapanho (i.e. Questions of Milinda)—a dialogue between *Milinda* (identical with Indo-Greek ruler *Menander*) and Buddhist saint *Nagasena*.

Dipavamsha and *Mahavamsha*—The great chronicles of Sri Lanka.

II. Sanskrit Texts

Buddha Charita, Saundarananda, Sutralankar, Sariputra Prakaran and Vajra Suchi–*Ashwagosha*; Mahavibhasha Shastra–*Vasumitra*; Visudhamagga, Atthakathayen and Sumangalvasini–*Buddhagosha*; Madhyamika Karika and Prajnaparimita Karika–*Nagarjuna* etc.

Sects of Buddhism

Hinayana (i.e. the Lesser Vehicle) : (i) Its followers believed in the original teaching of Buddha (ii) They sought individual salvation through self-discipline and meditation. (iii) They did not believe in idol-worship. (iv) They favoured *Pali* language. (v) It is known as 'Southern Buddhist Religion', because it prevailed in the South of India, e.g. Sri Lanka, Burma (Myanmar), Syam (Thailand), Java etc. (vi) There were two subsects of Hinayana–*Vaibhasika* and *Sautantrika*.

Mahayana (i.e. the Greater Vehicle) : (i) Its followers believed in the heavenliness of Buddha (ii) They sought the salvation of all through the grace and help of Buddha and Bodhisatva (iii) They believed in idol-worship (iv) They favorued *Sanskrit* language (v) It is known as 'Northern Buddhist Religion', because it prevailed in the North of India, e.g. China, Korea, Japan, etc. (vi) There were two subsects of Mahayana—*Madhyamika / Shunyavada* (founder–Nagarjuna) and *Yogachar / Vijnanavada* (founder–Maitreyanath and his disciple Asanga).

Vajrayana : (i) Its followers believed that salvation could be best attained by acquiring the magical power, which they called *Vajra*. (ii) The chief divinities of this new sect were *the Taras*. (iii) It became popular in Eastern India, particularly Bengal and Bihar.

Bodhisattvas

(i) **Vajrapani** : like Indra, he holds a thunderbolt, foe of sin and evil.

(ii) **Avlokitesvara** (the lord who looks down) also called *Padmapani* (the lotus bearer) : kind-hearted.

(iii) **Manjushri** (Stimulator of understanding) : He holds a book describing 10 paramitas (spiritual perfections).

(iv) **Maitreya** : The future Buddha.

(v) **Kshitigriha** : guardian of purgatories.

(vi) **Amitabha/Amitayusha** : Buddha of heaven.

Sacred Shrines

➢ Lumbini, Bodh Gaya, Sarnath and Kusinagar, where the four principal events of the Buddha's life, namely Birth, Enlightenment, First Sermon and Death took place. To these are added four places Sravasti, Rajgriha, Vaishali and Sankasya–these eight places have all along been considered as the eight holy places (Ashtasthanas).

➢ Other centres of Buddhism in Ancient India–Amaravati and Nagarjunikonda in Andhra Pradesh; Nalanda in Bihar; Junagadh and Vallabhi in Gujarat; Sanchi and Bharhut in M.P.; Ajanta-Ellora in Maharashtra; Dhaulagiri in Orissa; Kannauj, Kaushambi and Mathura in U.P.; and Jagadala and Somapuri in West Bengal.

➢ Buddhist architecture developed in three forms :

(i) Stupa—relics of the Buddha or some prominent Buddhist monks are preserved

(ii) Chaitya—prayer hall

(iii) Vihara—residence

Buddhist Universities	Place	Founder
Nalanda	Badagaon, Bihar	Kumargupta I (Gupta ruler)
Odantpuri	Biharsharif, Bihar	Gopala (Pala ruler)
Vikramshila	Bhagalpur, Bihar	Dharmapala (Pala ruler)
Somapuri	North Bengal	Dharmapala (Pala ruler)
Jagadal	Bengal	Ramapala (Pala ruler)
Vallabhi	Gujarat	Bhattarka (Maitrak ruler)

Royal Patrons : Bimbisara and Ajatashatru (Magadhan ruler), Prasenjit (Kosala ruler), Udayan (Vatsa ruler), Prdyota (Avanti ruler), Ashoka and Dasharatha (Mauryan ruler), Milinda / Menander (Indo-greek ruler), Kanishka (Kushana ruler), Harshavardhana (Vardhana ruler); Gopala, Dharmapala and Rampala (Pala ruler).

Note— *(i) Ashoka, the greatest patron of Buddhism, called 3rd Buddhist council and sent mission comprises of his son Mahendra and his daughter Sanghamitra to SriLanka.*

(ii) Kanishka called 4th Buddhist council and sent mission to China, Korea and Japan.

(iii) Palas of Bengal and Bihar were last great patrons of Buddhism.

JaIninism

➢ According to Jain tradition there were 24 *Thithankaras* (literally Ford maker, across the stream of existence), the first being Rishabhadeva / Adinatha and last being Mahavira.

➢ The *Vishnu Purana* and the *Bhagavat Purana* describe Rishabha as an incarnation of Narayana.

➢ The name of two Jain Tirthankaras–*Rishabha* and *Arishtanemi*–are found in the *Rig Veda*.

➢ We have historical proof of only the last two–*Parshwanath* (23rd) and *Mahavira* (24th).

➢ *Parshwanath* was a prince of Benaras who abandoned the throne and led the life of a hermit and died at *Sammet-Shikar/ Parshwanath (Parasanath)* Hill, *Giridih, Jharkhand*. His four main teachings (*Chaturthi*) were 1. *Ahimsa* (non-injury) 2. *Satya* (non-lying) 3. *Asteya* (non-stealing) 4. *Aparigraha* (non-possession). *Mahavira* adopted all these four teachings and added one more, that is *Brahmacharya* (Chastity) to it.

24 Tirthankaras

	Name	Symbol
1.	Rishabha	Bull
2.	Ajitnath	Elephant
3.	Sambharnath	Horse
4.	Abhiaandam	Monkey
5.	Sumatinath	Curlew
6.	Padmaprabhu	Red Lotus
7.	Suparswanath	Swastik
8.	Chandraji Prabhu	Moon
9.	Suvidhinath	Crocodile
10.	Shitalnath	Srivatsa
11.	Shreganath	Rhinoceros
12.	Vasupujya	Buffalo
13.	Vimalnath	Boar
14.	Anantnath	Falcon
15.	Dharmanath	Vajra
16.	Shantinath	Deer
17.	Kuntunath	He-Goat
18.	Arnath	Fish
19.	Mallinath	Waterpot
20.	Muniswasth	Tortoise
21.	Neminath	Blue Lotus
22.	Arishtanemi	Conch Shell
23.	Parshwanath	Serpent
24.	Mahavira	Lion

Mahavira's Life

➢ Mahavira was born in 540 BC in a village *Kundgrama* near *Vaishali* in *Bihar*.

➢ His father *Siddhartha* was the head of the *Jnathrika Kshtriya* clan under Vajji of Vaishali and his mother *Trishala* was the sister of Chetaka, the king of Vaishali. Mahavira was also related to Bimbisara, the ruler of Magadha, who had married Chellana, the daughter of Chetaka.

➢ Mahavira was married to *Yashoda* (daughter of Samarvira king) and a produced a daughter *Anonja Priyadarshini* whose husband *Jamali*, became the first disciple of Mahavira.

➢ At the age of 30, after the death of his father, he renounced his family, became an ascetic and proceeded in search of truth. He was accompained by *Makkhali Gosala*, but later due to some differences Gosala left him and founded *Ajivika* sect.

➢ At the age of 42, under a sal tree at *Jambhikagrama* on the bank of river *Rijupalika,* Mahavira attained *Kaivalya* (supreme knowledge).

➢ From now onwards he was called *Kevalin* (perfect learned), *Jina* or *Jitendriya* (one who conquered his senses), *Nrigrantha* (free from all bonds), *Arhant* (blessed one) and *Mahavira* (the brave) and his followers were named jain.

➢ He delivered his first sermon at *Pava* to his 11 disciples (known as *11 Gandharas/Gandharvas*). Later, he founded a *Jain Sangha* (Jain commune) at Pava.

➢ At the Age of 72 in 468 BC, he passed away at *Pavapuri* near *Biharsharif* in *Bihar*. *Sudharma* only one of 11 Ganadharas who survived after the death of Mahavira.

Doctrines of Jainism

Triratna i.e. Three Gems of Jainism

The aim of existence is to attain through the triratna of

1. *Samyak Shradha/ Viswas* (Right faith) : It is the belief in Thirathankaras.
2. *Samyak Jnan* (Right knowledge) : It is the knowledge of the Jain creed.
3. *Samyak Karma/ Acharana* (Right action / conduct) : It is the practice of the 5 vows of Jainism.

Pancha Mahavaratas i.e. Five Vows of Jainism

Five vows of Jainism are : 1. *Ahimsa* (non-injury) 2. *Satya* (non-lying) 3. *Asteya* (non-stealing) 4. *Aparigraha* (non-possession) 5. *Brahmacharya* (chastity). The first four vows were laid down by Parshwanath. The fifth one was added by Mahavira.

Types of Knowledge

There are 5 types of knowledge : 1. *Mati jnana*–Perception through activity of sense organs, including the mind 2. *Shruta jnana*–Knowledge revealed by scriptures 3. *Avadhi jnana*–Clairvoyant perception 4. *Manahparyaya jnana*–Telepathic knowledge 5. *Keval jnana*–Temporal knowledge or Omniscience.

***Syadvada* i.e. The Theory of May Be/Perhaps :** All our judgements are necessarily relative, conditional and limited. According to Syadavada seven modes of prediction (*Saptabhangi Nayavad*) are possible. Absolute affirmation and absolute negation both are wrong. All judgements are conditional. Syadvada is also known as *Anekantvada* i.e. the theory of plurality or multi-sidedness.

The Principles of Jainism as Preached by Mahavira : 1. Rejected the authority of the Vedas and vedic rituals 2. Did not believe in the existence of God. 3. Believed in Karma and the transmigration of soul 4. Laid great emphasis on equality.

Jain Council	Year	Venue	Chairman	Patron	Result
1st	300 BC	Patliputra	Sthulabhadra	Chandragupta Maurya	Compilation of 12 Angas.
2nd	512 AD	Vallabhi	Devardhi Kshmasramana	- - -	Final compilation of 12 Angas and 12 Upangas.

Jain Literature

➢ The sacred literature of the Svetambaras is written in a type of *Prakrit* called *Ardhamagadhi Prakrit*, and may be classified as follows : (i) 12 *Angas* (ii) 12 *Upangas* (iii) 10 *Parikarnas* (iv) 6 *Chhedasutras* (v) 4 *Mulasutras* (vi) 2 *Sutra-Granthas*.

Note : *14 Purvas/Parvas–It is the part of 12 Angas and the oldest text of Mahavira's preachings.*

➢ Besides this, the important jain texts are : (i) *Kalpasutra* (in Sanskrit)—Bhadrabahu (ii) *Bhadrabahu Charita* (iii) *Parishishta Parvan* (an appendix of *Trishashthishalaka Purush*)–Hemchandra.

Sects of Jainism

➢ In 298 BC, there was a serious famine in Magadha (South Bihar) leading to a great exodus of many Jain monks to the Deccan and South India *(Shravanbelgola)* along with *Bhadrabahu* and *Chandragupta Maurya*. They returned back after 12 years. The leader of the group, which stayed back at Magadha was *Sthulabhadra*. When the Jains (Bhadrabahu and others) returned from South India, they held that complete nudity be an essential part of the teachings of Mahavira, while the monks in Magadha began to put on white clothes.

➢ Thus arose the two sects *Shvetambaras* (white clad) and *Digambaras* (sky-clad).

1. *Shvetambaras* (i.e. those who put on white robes)—*Sthulabhadra*
2. *Digambaras* (i.e. those who were stark naked)—*Bhadrabahu*.

Examples of Jain Architecture

1. Gumphas i.e. Caves e.g. Hathigumpha, Baghagumpha etc., Udaigiri and Khandagiri (Orissa)—Kharvela
2. Dilwara temples e.g. Vimalavasahi temple, Tejapala temple–Mount Abu (Rajasthan)
3. Temples—Giranar and Palitana (Gujarat)
4. Temples e.g. Pavapuri temple, Rajagriha temple–Bihar
5. Statue of *Gometeshwar/Bahubali*—Shravanbelgola (Karnataka).

Royal Patrons

I. **North India :** 1. Nandas; Bimbisar, Ajatshatru and Udayin (Haryank); Chandragupta Maurya, Bindusara and Samprati (Mauryan)–Magadha 2. Pradyota (Avanti) 3. Udayan (Sindhu-Sauvira) 4. Kharavela (Kalinga).

II. **South India :** 1. Ganga Dynasty 2. Kadamb Dynasty 3. Amoghavarsha (Rashtrakuta Dynasty) 4. Siddharaj Jai Singh and Kumarpala (Chaulukya/Solanki) – the last great patrons of Jainism.

4. Maurya Period (322 BC-185 BC)

Sources for Mauryan History

1. **Literary Sources**

➢ *Kautilya's 'Arthasastra'* : It is the most important literary source for the Mauryas. It is a treatise on government and polity. It gives a clear and methodological analysis of political and economic conditions of the Mauryan period.

➢ *Megasthenese's 'Indica'* : Megasthenese was the ambassador of Selecus Nikator in the court of Chandragupta Maurya. His 'Indica' is foremost among all the foreigners' accounts for Maurya. But its original copy is lost, and it has survived only as quotations in the text of classical Greek writers, such as *Strabo, Diodorous, Arrian, Plutarch* and Latin writers such as *Pliny* and *Justin*. It refers to Mauryan administration, 7-caste system, absence of slavary and usuary in India etc.

➢ *Visakha Datta's 'Mudra Rakshasa' :* Though it was written during Gupta Period, it describes how Chandragupta Maurya get Chanakya's assistance to overthrow the Nandas. Besides this, it gives an excellent account of the prevailing socio-economic conditions.

➢ *Puranas* : Though they are a collection of legends interspread with religious teachings, they give us the chronology and lists of Mauryan kings.

➢ *Buddhist Literature :* 1. Indian Buddhist text *Jatakas* (a part of Khuddaknikaya of Suttapitaka which describes 549 stories of Buddha's previous births) reveal a general picture of socio-economic conditions of Mauryan period. 2. Ceylonese Buddhist chronicles *Dipavamsa* and *Mahavamsa* describe the part played by Ashoka in spreading Buddhism to Sri Lanka. 3. Tibetan Buddhist text *Divyavadana* gives information about Ashoka and his efforts to spread Buddhism.

2. Archaeological Sources

➢ *Ashokan Edicts and inscriptions :* There are Rock Edicts, Pillar Edicts and Cave Inscriptions located at several places in the Indian sub-continent. Their importance came to be appreciated only after their decipheration by *James Princep* in 1837 and also the identification of Ashoka as the author of these edicts in the beginning of the 20th century. Majority of them are in the nature of Ashoka's proclamations to the public at large, and only a small group of them describe his own acceptance of Buddhism and his relationship with the Sangha (Commune). Though *Prakrit* was the language used in them, the script varied from region to region (*Kharoshti* in the North-West, *Greek* and *Aramaic* in the West and *Brahmi* in the East of India).

➢ *Other Inscriptions :* Junagadh Rock Inscription of Rudradaman, Sohgaura Copper Plate Inscription in Gorakhpur district of U.P., Mahasthan Inscription in Bogara district of Bangladesh. – All these are directly concerned with the Mauryan Period, though they are believed to be not necessarily those of Ashoka.

➢ *Material Remains :* Wooden palace of Chandragupta Maurya, Northern Black Polished Ware (NBPW), Silver and Copper punch-marked coins found in Kumharar (Patna) and other places are the material remains of the Mauryan peirod.

Ashokan Edicts and Inscriptions	Contents	Found at
I. Rock Edicts		
(i) 14 Major Rock Edicts	Various Principles of Dhamma	Manshera (Hazara, Pakistan) Shahbajgarhi (Peshwar, Pakisttan), Kalsi (Dehradun, Uttarakhand), Junagadh (Girnar, Gujarat), Sopara (Thana, Maharashtra), Yerragudi (Kurnul, Andhra Pradesh), Dhauli (Puri, Orissa), Jaugada (Ganjam, Orissa)

Ashokan Edicts and Inscriptions	Contents	Found at
(ii) 2 Kalinga Rock Edicts	New system of administration after the Kalinga war	Dauli or Tosali (Puri, Orrisa), Jaugada (Ganjam, Orissa)
(iii) Minor Rock Edicts	Personal history of Ashoka and summary of his dhamma	Sasaram (Bihar), Maski (Andhra Pradesh), Bhabru-Bairat (Rajasthan), Rupanath (MP), Gavimath, Palkig-undu, Siddhpur, Jating Rameshwar, Brahmagiri (Karnataka)
(iv) Bhabru-Bairat Rock Edicts	Ashoka' conversion to Buddhism	Bhabru-Bairat (Rajasthan)
II. Pillar Edicts		
(i) 7 Pillar Edicts	Appendix to rock Edicts	Merrut-Delhi (Chhoti Lata), Topra-Delhi (Badi Lata), Allahabad (UP); Lauriya Nandangadh, Lauriya Areraj and Rampurva (Bihar)
(ii) 4 Minor Pillar Edicts	Signs of Ashoka's fanaticism to Dhamma	Sanchi (MP), Sarnath and Allahabad (UP)
(iii) 2 Tarai Pillar Edicts	Ashoka's respect for Buddhism	Rummandei/Lumbini and Nigaliva (Tarai of Nepal)
III. Cave Edicts		
3 Barabar Cave Edicts	Ashoka's toleration	Barabar Hills (Gaya, Bihar)

Ashokan 14 Major Rock Edicts

	Contents
I.	Prohibition of animal sacrifices and festive gatherings.
II.	Measures of social welfare.
III.	Respect to Brahamanas.
IV.	Courtesy to relatives, elders, consideration for animals.
V.	Appointment of Dhamma Mahamatras and their duties.
VI.	Need for efficient organisation of administration (orders to Dhamma Mahamatras).
VII.	Need for tolerance among all religious sects.
VIII.	System of Dhamma-yatras.
IX.	Attack on meaningless ceremonies and rituals.
X.	Conquest through Dhamma instead of war.
XI.	Explanation of Dhamma-policy.
XII.	Appeal for tolerance among all religious sects.
XIII.	Kalinga war, mention 5 contemporary Hellenic (Greek) kings.
XIV.	Inspiration to spend religious life.

Origin of the Mauryas

- The Puranas describe them as *Shudras*.
- 'Mudrakshasa' of Vishakhadatta uses the terms *Vrishal/ Kulhina* (of low clan).
- The Classical writers, such as Justin, describe Chandragupta only as a man of humble origin.
- The Junagarh Rock Inscription of Rudradaman (150 AD) has some indirect evidence, suggesting that the Mauryas might have been of *Vaishya* origin.
- The Buddhist work, on the other hand, try to link the Mauryan dynasty with the *Sakya Kshatriya* clan to which Buddha belonged. According to them, the region from which the Mauryas came was full of peacocks *(Mor)*, and hence they came to be known as '*Moriyas*'. It is obvious, from this that the Buddhists were trying to elevate the social position of Ashoka (their patron) and his predecessors.
- In conclusion, we can say that the Mauryas belonged to the *Moriya* tribe and were certainly of a low caste, though it is not clear as to which low caste.

Chandragupta Maurya : 322 BC-298 BC

- Chandragupta dethroned the last Nanda ruler *Dhananand* and occupied *Patliputra* in 322 BC with the help of *Kautilya (Chankya)*.
- In 305 BC, Chandragupta Maurya defeated *Selecus Nikator*, who surrendered a vast territory including Aria (herat), Arachosia (Kandhar), Gedrosia (Baluchistan) and Paropanisade (Kabul), in return for 500 elephants. According to treaty between Chandragupta and Selecus, the Hindukush became boundry between their states.
- *Megasthenese* was a Greek ambassador sent to the court of Chandragupta Maurya by Selecus Nikator.
- Chandragupta became a jain and went to *Chandragiri Hill*, *Sravanbelgola* (Karnataka) with Bhadrabahu, where he died by slow starvation *(Kaya-Klesha/Salekhan)*.
- Under Chanragupta Maurya, for the first time, the whole of Northern India was united.
- Trade flourished, agriculture was regulated, weights and measures were standardised and money came into use.
- Taxation, sanitation and famine relief became the concerns of the state.

Bindusara : 298 BC-273 BC

- Chandragupta Maurya was succeeded by his son Bindusara.
- Bindusara, known to the Greeks as *Amitrochates* (derived from the Sanskrit word *Amitraghata* i.e. slayers of foes), is said to have carried his arms to the Deccan (upto Mysore).
- Bindusara asked *Antiochus I* of *Syria* to send some sweet wine, dried figs and a sophist. Antiochus I sent wine and figs but politely replied that Greek philosphers are not for sale.
- Bindusara patronised *Ajivikas*.

Ashoka : 273 BC-232 BC

- It appears from the available evidence (Buddhist literature mainly) that there was a struggle for the throne among the princes on the death of Bindusara.
- According to Buddhist tradition, Ashoka usurped the throne after killing his 99 brothers and spared *Tissa*, the youngest one. Radhagupta a minister of Bindusara helped him in fratricidal struggle.
- This war of succession accounts for interregnum of four years (273-269 BC), and only after securing his position on the throne, Ashoka had himself formally crowned in 269 BC.
- Under Ashoka, the Mauryan Empire reached its climax. For the first time, the whole of the sub-continent, leaving out the extreme south, was under imperial control.

Ashoka	Maski minor rock edict.
Devanampriyas Ashoka Rajas	Gurjara minor rock edict
Raja Ashoka	Nitlur minor rock edict
Raja Ashoka Dewanampiya	Udegolum minor rock edict.
Piyadassi Raja Magadh	Bhabru-Bairat minor rock edict.
Piyadassi Raja	Barabar cave inscription
Piyadassi	Kandhar major rock edict and Deepvamsa.
Ashoka Maurya	Rudradaman's Junagarh rock edict.
Ashoka Vardhan	Puranas.

- Ashoka fought the *Kalinga war* in 261 BC in 9th years of his coronation. The king was moved by the massacre in this war and therefore abandoned the policy of physical occupation in favour of policy of cultural conquest. In other words, *Bherighosa* was replaced by *Dhammaghosa*.
- Ashoka was not an extreme pacifist. He did not pursue the policy of peace for sake of peace under all conditions. Thus, he retained Kalinga after his conquest and incorporated it into his empire.
- Ashoka sent missionaries to the kingdoms of the Cholas and the Pandyas, and five states ruled by Greek kings (Antiochus II, Syria; Philadelphos Ptolemy II, Egypt; Antigonus, Mecedonia; Maggus, Syrina; Alexander, Epirus). We also know that he sent missionaries to Ceylon (Sri Lanka) and Suvarnbhumi (Burna) and also parts of South-East Asia.

Ashoka's Dhamma

- Ashoka's Dhamma cannot be regarded as a sectarian faith. Its broad objective was to preserve the social order it ordained that people should obey their parents, pay respect to Brahmanas and Buddhist monks and show mercy to slaves and servants.
- He held that if people behaved well they would attain Swarga (heaven). He did never say that they would attain Nirvana, which was the goal of Buddhist teachings.

Later Mauryas : 232 BC-185 BC

- The Mauryan dynasty lasted 137 years.
- Ashoka's death was followed by the division of the Mauryan Empire into two parts-Western and Eastern.
- The Western part came to be ruled by *Kunala* (son of Ashoka) and the Eastern part came to be ruled by *Dasaratha*.
- The last Mauryan ruler, *Brihadratha*, was assassinated in 185 BC by his commender-in-chief, *Pushyamitra Sunga*, who established his own Sunga dynasty.
- **Causes for the Decline :** 1. Highly centralised administration *(Romila Thapar)* 2. Pacific policy of Ashoka *(H.C. Raychaudhuri)* 3. Brahmanical reaction *(H.P. Sastri)* 4. The partition of the Mauryan Empire 5. Weak later-Mauryan Rulers 6. Pressure on Mauryan economy 7. Neglect of North-West Frontier.

Mauryan kings	Other names of the king	Ambassdor (Greek king)
Chandragupta	Sandrocottus–Strabo, Justin Androcottus-Arrian, Plutarch Vrishala / Kulahina(i.e. of low clan)–Vishakhadatta (Mudrarakshasa)	Megasthenese (302-298 BC) (Selecus Nikator-Persia and Babylonia)
Bindusara	Amitrochates—Greek texts Vindupala—Chinease text Sinhasena—Jain text Bhadrasara—Vayu Purana	Dimachos (Antiochus I - Syria) Dionysius (Philadelphos / Potlemy II-Egypt)

Mauryan Administration

I. Central Administration

- **The king :** The Mauryan government was a centralised bureaucracy of which the nucleus was the king. According to Kautilya / Chanakya, there are 7 elements of states *(Saptanga theory)*–*Raja* (the king), *Amatya* (the secretaries), *Janapada* (territory), *Durg* (Fort), *Kosha* (the treasure), *Sena* (Army) and *Mitra* (Friend). The king was regarded as the soul among all the seven elements of the state.
- **The Mantri Prishad :** The king was assisted by Mantri Parishad, whose members included – (i) *The Yuvaraja* (the crown prince) (ii) *The purohita* (the chief priest) (iii) *The Senapati* (the commander-in-chief) (iv) a few other ministers.

Important officials

Sannidhata	Chief treasury officer
Samaharta	The collector general of revenue
Vyavaharika (Dharmastha)	Chief Justice of Dharmasthiya Nyayalaya (Civil Court)
Pradeshta	Chief Justice of Kantakashodhan Nyayalaya (Criminal Court)

Dhamma Mahamatra	A new post created by Ashoka, empowered with the dual functions of propagating Dhamma and taking care of the common folk for their material well-being.
Rashtrapala/Kumara	The viceroys in charge of a province
Pradesika	They were the modern district magistrate
Rajukas	They were the later day Patwaris and responsible for surveying and assessing the land
Yukta	A subordinate revenue officer of the district level
Sthanika	The collecting officer directly under the control of the Pradeshika
Gopa	Responsible for accounts
Nagaraka	The officer in charge of the city administration
Akshapatala	Accountant General
Sitaadhyaksha	Supervised agriculture
Panyadhyaksha	Superintendent of commerce
Samsthaadhyaksha	Superintendent of Market
Pautavadhyaksha	Superintendent of weights and measures
Navaadhyaksha	Superintendent of ships
Sulkaadhyaksha	Collector of tolls
Akaradhyaksha	Superintendent of mines
Lohadhyaksha	Superintendent of Iron

II. Provincial Administration

Province	Capital
Uttarapatha i.e. Northern Province	Taxila
Avantirashtra i.e. Western Province	Ujjain
Prachi i.e. Eastern and Central Province	Patliputra
Kalinga i.e. Eastern Province	Toshali
Dakshinapatha i.e. Southern Province	Suvarnagiri

Note : *According to the Junagadh Rock Edict of Rudradaman, Saurashtra was governed by Pushyagupta, the vaishya, at the time of Chandragupta Maurya and by the Yavan king Tushaspa at the time of Ashoka.*

Administrative Unit	Head
Chakra (i.e. province)	Rashtrapala/Kumara
Ahar/Vishaya (i.e. District)	Pradeshika (administrative) and Rajuka (land revenue)
Sangrahana (a group of 10 villages)	Gopa
Gram (i.e. village)	Gramika

III. Municipal Administration

- Kautilya devotes a full chapter to the rules of the *Nagarak* i.e. city superintendent. His chief duty was maintenance of law and order.
- Megasthenese account of the system : 6 committees of five members each, and their functions; 1st – Industrial Arts, 2nd – Entertainment of Foreigners, 3rd – Registration of Births and Deaths, 4th – Trade and Commerce, 5th – Public sale of manufactured goods, and 6th – Collection of taxes on the articles sold (1/10th of purchase price).

IV. Army

- The most striking feature of Mauryan administration was the maintenance of a huge army. They also maintained a Navy.
- According to Megasthenese the administration of Army was carried by a board of 30 officers divided into 6 committee, each committee consisting of 5 members. They are (i) Infantry (ii) Cavalry (iii) Elephants (iv) Chariots (v) Navy (vi) Transport.
- In the Mauryan period, there were two types of *Gudhapurushas* (detectives)– *Sansthan* (Stationary) and *Sanchari* (Wandering).

Economy

- The state controlled almost all economic activities.
- Tax collected from peasants varied from 1/4 to 1/6 of the produce.
- The state also provided irrigation facilities (*Setubandha*) and charged water-tax.
- Tolls were also levied on commodities brought to town for sale and they were collected at gate.
- The state enjoyed monopoly in mining, forest, salt, sale of liquor, manufacture of arms etc.
- *Sohgaura* (Gorakhpur district, U.P.) copper plate inscription and *Mahasthana* (Bogara district, Bangladesh) inscription deal with the relief measures to be adopted during a famine.
- **Important ports :** *Bharukachch/Bharoch* and *Supara* (Western coast), *Tamralipti* in Bengal (Eastern coast).
- During Mauryan period, the punch-marked coins (mostly of silver) were the common units of transactions.

Society

- *Kautilya/Chanakya/Vishnugupta* is not as rigid on the Varna system as the earlier Smriti writers.
- Kautilya's 'Arthashastra' looked upon the *Shudras* as an Aryan community which is distinguished from Malechha or non-Aryan community.
- Reduction of gap between the *Vaishyas* (most of whom were now concentrating on trade though others continued cultivation) and the *Shudras* (quite a few of whom were now agriculturists and others being artisans).
- *Magasthenese* states that Indian society was divided into 7 classes : 1. Philosophers 2. Farmers 3. Soldiers 4. Herdsmen 5. Artisans 6. Magistrates 7. Councillors. The 'classes' mentioned above appear to have been economic than social.

➢ Though Megasthenese stated that there were no slavery in India; yet, according to Indian sources, slavery was a recognised institution during Mauryan reign. It appears that Megasthenese was thinking of slavery in full legal sense as it existed in the West.

➢ Women occupied a high position and freedom in the Mauryan society. Accoording to Kautilya, women were permitted to have a divorce or remarry. Women were employed as personal body-guards of the king, spies and in other diverse jobs.

Mauryan Art

➢ Anand Coomarswamy classified Mauryan Art into two groups :

1. **Royal/Court Art :** The Royal Palace of Chandragupta Maurya (Kumharar, Patna) and City of Patliputra, Ashokan Pillars, Caves, Stupas etc.
2. **Folk/Popular Art :** (i) Figure Sculpture of Yaksha-Yakshini etc. e.g. Yaksha of Parkham (Mathura), Yakshini of Besanagar / Vidisha (M.P.), Chanwar-bearer Yakshini of Didarganj (Patna). (ii) Terracotta objects.

➢ The Mauryas introduced stone masonry on large scale during Ashoka.

➢ Fragments of stone pillars and wooden floor and ceiling indicating the existence of an 80-pillared hall have been discovered at Kumhrar on outskirts of Patna. Seeing this *Fahien* remarks as follows : *'These palaces are so beautiful and excellent that they appear to be the creation of God rather than of men'*.

➢ The pillars represent the masterpieces of Mauryan sculpture. Each pillar is made of single piece of sandstone, only their capitals, which are beautiful pieces of sculpture in form of lion or bulls, are joined with pillar on the top.

➢ Four lion capital at Sarnath and Sanchi. Lioned capital of Sarnath was adopted as 'National Emblem' of India on 26 Jan., 1950.

➢ Single lion capital at Rampurva and Lauriya Nandangarh.

➢ Single bull capital at Rampurva.

➢ A carved elephant at Dhauli and engraved elephant at Kalsi.

➢ The Mauryan artisans who started the practice of hewing out caves from rocks for monks to live in. The earliest example are *Barabar caves* (Sudama, World Hut, Chaupada of Karna, Rishi Lomesh) in Gaya (Ashokan). The other examples are *Nagarjuni caves* in Gaya *(Dasharath)*.

➢ Stupas were built throughout the empire to enshrine the relics of Buddha. Of these, the most famous are at Sanchi and Bharhuta.

'At all times, whether I am eating, or am in the women's apartments, or in my inner apartments, or at the cattleshed, or in my carriage, or in my gardens–wherever I may be–my Mahamattar should keep me in touch with public business'.
—Rock Edict VI

'All men are my children'. *—Kalinga Rock Edict I (Dhauli)*

5.I. Post-Maurya/Pre-Gupta Period (185 BC-319 AD)

I. Native Successors of Mauryas

Sunga Dynasty : 185 BC - 73 BC **[Capital-Vidisha (M.P.)]**

- Sunga Dynasty was established by *Pushymitra Sunga*, a Brahmin Commander-in-Chief of last Mauryan ruler named Brihadratha in 185 BC.
- Pushyamitra was a staunch adherent of orthodox Hinduism. However, the great Buddhist stupa at Bharhut (in M.P.) was built during the reign of Sungas.
- Pushyamitra was succeeded by his son *Agnimitra*, the hero of Kalidasa's drama *'Malvikagnimitra'*.
- After Agnimitra, a series of weak rulers such as Vasumitra, Vajramitra, Bhagabhadra, Devabhuti, followed, leading to the decline of the dynasty.
- During their rule there was a revival of Brahminical influence. The Bhagavata religion became important.
- *Patanjali*, author of the 'Mahabhasya', was born at Gonarda in Central India. Patanjali was the priest of 2 Asvamedha Yajnas, performed by Pushymitra Sunga.
- In arts, the Bharhut Stupa is the most famous monument of the Sunga period.
- The fine gateway railing which surrounds the Sanchi stupa, built by Ashoka, constructed during the Sunga period.
- Other examples of Sunga Art : Vihar, Chaitya and Stupa of Bhaja (Poona), Amaravati Stupa, Nasika Chaitya etc.

Kanva Dynasty : 73 BC - 28 BC **[Capital - Patliputra]**

- In 73 BC, Devabhuti, the last ruler of the Sunga dynasty, was murdered by his minister *Vasudeva*, who usurped the throne and founded the Kanva dynasty.
- The period of Kanva rule came to an end in 28 BC.

Satavahana Dynasty : 60 BC - 225 AD
[Capital - Pratishtana/Paithan (Maharashtra)]

- The most important of the native successors of the Mauryas in the Deccan and Central India were the Satvahanas.
- The Satvahanas are considered to be identical with the Andhras who were mentioned in the Puranas.
- The early Satvahana kings appeared not in Andhra but in Maharashtra where most of their early inscriptions have been found.
- *Simuka* (60 BC - 37 BC) was the founder of the Satvahana dynasty.
- *Satakarni I*, its 3rd ruler, raised its power and prestige by conquests.
- *Hala*, its 17th ruler, was the author of 'Gathasaptasati' or, 'Sattasai' in Prakrit. *Gunadhya*, the author of 'Vrihat Katha' (in Prakrit), was the contemporary of Hala.

- It was *Gautamiputra Satakarni* (106 - 130 AD) who revived the Satavahana power and defeated the Saka Ksatrap Nahapana. He was the greatest Satavahan ruler (23rd Satavahana ruler).
- *Vasishthiputra Sri Satakarni*, its 24th ruler, was married to the daughter of Saka Kstrapa Rudradaman, but defeated by him twice.
- *Yajna Sri Satakarni*, its 27th ruler, was the dynasty's last great ruler.
- *Pulamavi III*, its 30th ruler, was the last Satavahana ruler.
- Satavahanas were finally succeeded by the Ikshvakus in 3rd Century AD.
- Satavahanas started the practice of donating land with fiscal and administrative immunities to Brahmanas and Buddhist monks, which eventually weakened their authority. The earliest inscriptional evidence of land grant in India belongs to 1st century BC.
- Under the Satavahanas, many Chaityas (worship halls) and Viharas (monasteries) were cut out from rocks mainly in North-West Deccan or Maharashtra. The famous examples were *Nasik, Kanheri* and *Karle*.
- Stupas (large round structure erected over a sacred relic) were seen scattered all around Ellora. The most famous of these attributed to the Satavahana period are *Amravati*, a sculptural treasure house, and *Nagarjunakonda*.
- The official language of the Satavahanas was *Prakrit*.
- The Satavahanas issued their coins in lead (mainly), copper, bronze and potin.

Cheti/Chedi Dynasty of Kalinga

- The history of Kalinga after the death of Ashoka is shrouded in obscurity. A new dynasty, known as the Cheti or Chedi dynasty, rose in the region probably in the 1st century BC.
- Our information about this dynasty is derived solely from the *Hathigumpha inscription* (near Bhubaneshwar, Orissa) of *Kharavela*, the 3rd ruler of dynasty.
- A follower of Jainism, Kharavela was liberal patron of Jain monks for whose residence he constructed caves on the *Udayagiri* hill, near Bhubaneshwar in Orissa.

II. Foreign Successors of Mauryas

The Indo-Greeks : 2nd Century BC

- Indo-Greeks (Bacterian Greeks) were the first foreign rulers of North-Western India in the Post-Maurya period.
- The most famous Indo-Greek ruler was *Menander* (165 BC-145 BC), also known as *Milinda*. He was converted to Buddhism by Nagasena or Nagarjuna.
- The Indo-Greek rule is important in the history of India because of the large number of coins which they issued.
- The Indo-Greeks were the first rulers in India to issue coins which can definitely be attributed to the kings.
- They were the first to issue gold coins.

- They introduced Hellenic i.e. Greek features in art giving rise to *Gandhar school* in the North-Western India.

The Sakas : 1st Century BC - 4th Century AD

- The *Sakas*, also known as *Scythians*, replaced the Indo-Greeks in India.
- Among the five branches of Sakas with their seats of power in different parts of India, the most important was the one which ruled in Western India till the 4th Century AD.
- The most famous Saka ruler in India was *Rudradaman* (130 AD-150 AD). He is famous not only for his military conquests (particularly against the Satavahanas) but also for his public works (he repaired the famous Sudarsan lake of the Mauryan period) and his patronage of Sanskrit (he issued the first-ever long inscription in chaste Sanskrit).
- Other important Saka ruler in India were Nahapana, Ushavadeva, Ghamatika, Chashtana etc.
- In about 58 BC a king of Ujjain - Vikramaditya - is supposed to have fought effectively against the Sakas. An era called *Vikrama Samvat* is recknoed from 58 BC.

The Parthians : 1st Century BC - 1st Century AD

- Originally the *Parthians (Pahlavas)* lived in Iran, they replaced the Sakas in North-Western India, but controlled an area much smaller than the Sakas.
- The most famous Parthian king was *Gondaphernes* in whose reign *St. Thomas* is said to have come to India for the propagation of Christianity.

The Kushans : 1st Century AD - 3rd Century AD

- The Kushans were one of the five Yeuchi clans of Central Asia.
- They replaced the Parthians in North-Western India and then expanded to the lower Indus basin and the upper and middle Gangetic basin.
- The first Kushan dynasty was founded by *Kadphises I/ Kujul Kadhphises*. The second king was *Kadphises II/ Vema Kadphises* who issued gold coins.
- The second Kushan dynasty was founded by *Kanishka*. Its kings extended the Kushan power over upper India. Their capitals were at *Peshawar (Purushapura)* and *Mathura*.
- The most famous Kushan ruler was Kanishka (78 AD - 101 AD), also known as 'Second Ashoka'. He started an era in 78 AD which is now known as the *Saka era* and is used by the Government of India.
- Kanishka was a great patron of Mahayana Buddhism. In his reign *4th Buddhist council* was held in *Kundalavana, Kashmir* where the doctrines of the Mahayana form of Buddhism were finalised.
- The last great Kushan ruler was Vasudeva I.
- The Kushans controlled famous *silk route* starting from China, passing through their empire on to Iran and Western Asia. This route was a source of great income to the Kushans.

- The Kushans were the first rulers in India to issue gold coins on a wide scale.
- In the royal court of Kanishka a host of scholars found patronage. *Parsva, Vasumitra, Asvaghosha, Nagarjuna, Charak* and *Mathara* were some of them.

Facts About Post-Mauryas

Three school of Sculpture : 1. *Amaravati* School (150 BC - 400 AD) – Satvahanas 2. *Gandhar* School (50 BC - 5th Century AD) – Saka - Kushans 3. *Mathura* School (150 AD - 300 AD) – Saka-Kushans.

Note : The influence of Greek sculpture is very evident in the Gandhar school, while Mathura school, evolved an indigenous form.

- In 46-47 AD, *Hippalus*, a greek sailor, discovered the monsoon sea-route to India from West Asia.
- **Important ports :** *Barygaza (Bharoch)* and *Barbairicum* (Western Coast); *Aricamedu* (*Podeku*-according to 'Periplus')–near Pandicheri–Eastern Coast.
- 'Bullion was flowing out of Rome to India'—*Pliny*.
- 'Geographica'—*Strabo*, 'Geography'—*Ptolemy*, 'Natural History'—*Pliny*, 'Periplus of the Erithryan Sea'–Unknown.
- India had contacts with Central Asia, China, Graceo-Roman World and South-East Asia.

5.II. The Sangam Period (1st-3rd Century AD)

Three Early Kingdoms

Kingdom	Emblem	Capital	First Ruler	Famous Ruler
The Chera	Bow	Vanjji / Karayur; Main Ports : Muzris and Tondi	Udiyangeral	Senguttuvan (Red Chera)
The Chola	Tiger	Uraiaur–Inland capital–famous centre for cotton trade; Puhar / Kaveripattanam–coastal capital-main port	Elara	Karikala
The Pandya	Fish	Madurai–Inland capital–venue of Ist and IIIrd sangam; Korkai / Colchoi–coastal capital–famous for pearls.	Mudukudumi	Nendujeliyan

The Cheras

- The Chera country occupied the portion of both Kerala and Tamil Nadu.
- The capital of Cheras was *Vanjji*.
- Its main ports were *Muzris* and *Tondi*.
- The Romans set up two regiment at *Muzris* (identical with *Cranganore*) in Chera country. They also built a temple of Augustus at Muzris.

- One of the earliest and better known among Chera rulers was *Udiyangeral*. It is said that he fed both the armies of Kurukshetra war and so earned the title Ùdiyangeral.
- The greatest of Chera king, however, was *Senguttuvan* or *Red Chera*. It is said that he invaded the North and even crossed the Ganges.
- He was also the founder of the famous *Pattini cult* related to worship of goddess of chastity–*Kannagi*.

The Cholas

- The Chola kingdom called as Cholamandalam was situated to the North-East of Pandya kingdom between Pennar and Vellar rivers.
- The Chola kingdom corresponded to the modern Tanjore and Tiruchchirap-palli districts.
- Its inland capital was *Uraiyaur*, a place famous for cotton trade. One of the main sources of wealth for Cholas was trade in cotton cloth.
- *Puhar* identical with *Kaveripattanam* was the main port of Cholas and served as alternative capital of Cholas.
- The earliest known Chola king was *Elara* who conquered Sri Lanka and ruled over it for nearly 50 years.
- Their greatest king was *Karikala* (man with charred leg) who founded *Puhar (Kaveripattanam)* and constructed 160 km of embankment along the Kaveri river with the help of 12,000 Sri Lankan slaves.
- They maintained an efficient navy.
- The Cholas were wiped out in the attack of Pallavas from the North.

The Pandyas

- The Pandyas were first mentioned by Megasthanese, who said their Kingdom was famous for pearls.
- The Pandya territory included modern districts of Tirunelvelli, Ramand and Madurai in Tamil Nadu. It had its capital at Madurai, situated on the banks of Vaigai river.
- The Pandya king profited from trade with Roman Empire and sent emissaries to Roman emperor *Augustus* and *Trojan*.
- The Pandyas find mention in the Ramayana and Mahabharata.
- The earliest known Pandyan ruler was *Mudukudumi*.
- The greatest Pandya king, *Nendujelian*, accused *Kovalan* of theft. As a result, the city of Madurai was laid under a curse by *Kannagi* (Kovalan's wife).

Sangam Administration

- The king was the centre of administration. He was called *Ko, Mannam, Vendan Korravan* or *Iraivan*.
- *Avai* was the court of the crowned monarch.
- **Important officials** *(Panchmahasabha)* : 1. *Amaichchar* (Ministers) 2. *Purohitar* (Priests) 3. *Dutar* (Envoys) 4. *Senapatiyar* (Commander) 5. *Orar* (Spies).

➢ The kingdom was divided into *Mandalam / Nadu* (Province), *Ur* (town), *Perur* (Big village), *Sirur* (Small village).

➢ *Pattinam* (Name of coastal town), *Puhar* (Harbour areas), *Cheri* (Suburb of town).

➢ **Revenue Administration** : *Karai* (Land Tax), *Irai* (Tribute paid by feudatories and booty collected in war), *Ulgu* (Custom duties), *Iravu* (Extra demand or forced gift), *Variyam* (A well known unit of territory yielding tax), *Variyar* (Tax collector).

➢ It is said that in Chola territory, watered by Kaveri, the space in which an elephant could lie down produced enough to feed seven persons. It implies the lands were very fertile with irrigation facilities.

Sangam Literature

Sl. No.	Venue	Under the Chairmanship of	Surviving Texts	Patron (Pandya Rulers)
Ist Sangam	Ten-Madurai (Old capital of Pandyas, engulfed in sea)	Agastasya (Agattiyar)	x	89
IInd Sangam	Kapatapuran/ Alvai (engulfed in sea)	Agastaya (founder chairman); Tolakapiyyar (later chairman)	only 'Tolkappiyam'	59
IIIrd Sangam	North Madurai	Nakkirar	Ettutogai, Pattu-pattu, Patinenki-lakanakku etc.	49

➢ *Sangam* was an assembly of Tamil poets held under royal patronage of Pandyan kings in Madurai. According to tradition, the assembly lasted for 9,990 years and was attended by 8,598 poets and 197 Pandyan kings.

➢ *The first Sangam* was attended by Gods and legendary sages All its works have perished.

➢ Of *the second Sangam,* the only surviving work is *Tolkappiyam*, an early work on Tamil grammar written by *Tolakapiyyar*.

➢ Of *the third Sangam*, the mostly works are surviving. These are *Ettutogai* (i.e. 8 anthologies), *Pattupattu* (i.e. 10 idylls), *Patinenkilakanakku* (i.e. 18 didactical texts) etc.

➢ Ettutogai and Pattupattu are called Melakanakku (18 major works) and narrative in form. Patinenkanakku is called Kilakanakku (18 minor works) and didactive in form.

➢ *Kural* or *Muppal*, a part of Patinenkilakanakku and written by *Tiruvalluvar* is called 'The Bible of Tamil Land'. It is treatise on polity, ethics and social norms.

The Epics : Silappadikaram, Manimekalai, Sivaga Sindamani etc.

➢ Silappadikaram *(the story of the Anklet)* : Written by *Ilango Adigal*, it deals with the story of Kovalan and Madhavi of Kaveripattinam. It is called 'Illiyad of Tamil poetry'.

- Manimekalai : Written by *Sittalai Sattanar*, it deals with the adventures of Manimekalai, the daughter born of Kovalan and Madhavi. It is a sequel of Silappadikaram and strongly tinged with Buddhism.
- Sivaga Sindamani *(Jivaka Chintamani)*: Written by Jain *Tiruttakrdevas* and strongly tinged with Jainism.
- Bharatam : Written by *Perudevanar*.

Panchtinai (five Tamil regions)	**Occupation**	**Inhabitants**
Kurinji (hilly backwoods or montane)	Hunting, Gathering	Kurvar, Vetar
Palai (Parched or arid zone)	Cattle lifting, Highway robbery	Eyinar, Maravar
Mullai (Pastoral tract)	Shifting Agriculture, Animal husbandry	Ayar, Idaiyar
Marutam (Wetland)	Plough Agriculture	Ulavar, Vellalar
Neital (littoral / coastal)	Fishing, Salt extraction	Paratavar, Valayar

6. Gupta Period (319 AD-540 AD)

- In 4th Century AD a new dynasty, the Guptas, arose in Magadha and established a large kingdom over the greater part of Northern India (though their empire was not as large as that of the Mauryas). Their rule lasted for more than 200 years.
- This period is referred as the 'Classical Age' or 'Golden Age' of ancient India and was perhaps the most prosperous era in the Indian history.
- According to epigraphic evidence, the founder of the dynasty was a person named *Gupta*. He used the simple title of Maharaja.
- Gupta was succeeded by his son *Ghatotkach*, who also inherited the title of Maharaja.

The Gupta Dynasty	
Chandragupta I	319-334 AD
Samudragupta	335-380 AD
Ramgupta	380 AD
Chandragupta II (Vikramaditya)	380-414 AD
Kumargupta (Mahendraditya)	415-455 AD
Skandagupta I	455-467 AD
Purugupta→	
Kumargupta II→	
Buddhgupta→	
Narsimhagupta→	
Kumargupta III	467-540 AD

Chandragupta I : 319-334 AD

- He was the first Gupta ruler to assume the title of *Maharajadhiraja*.
- He strengthened his kingdom by matrimonial alliance with the powerful family of Lichchhavis who were the rulers of Mithila. His marriage to Lichchhvi princess *Kumaradevi*, brought to him enormous power, resources and prestige. He took advantage of the situation and occupied the whole of fertile Gangetic Valley.
- He started the *Gupta Era* in 319-20 AD.
- Chandragupta I was able to establish his authority over Magadha, Prayaga and Saketa.
- **Original type of Gold Coins** *(Dinaras)*: Chandragupta I-Kumaradevi type.

Samudragupta : 335-380 AD

- Samudragupta was the greatest king of Gupta dynasty.
- The most detailed and authentic record of his reign is preserved in the *Prayaga Prasasti/Allahabad pillar inscription*, composed by his court poet *Harisena*.
- According to Prayaga Prasasti, he was a great conqueror.
- In the Gangetic Valley and Central India, Samudragupta annexed the territories of the defeated monarchs, but in South India he remained content with victories alone and did not annex the territories of the vanquished rulers.
- Samudragupta's military compaigns justify description of him as the *'Napoleon of India'* by *V.A. Smith*.
- The reference to his dominion over Java, Sumatra and Malaya islands in the sea shows that he had a navy.
- When he died his mighty empire bordered that of the Kushan of Western province (modern Afghanistan and Pakistan) and Vakatakas in Deccan (modern Southern Maharashtra).
- His greatest achievement was the political unification of most of India or Aryavarta into a formidable power.
- **Titles :** *Kaviraja* i.e. king of poets (Prayaga Prasasti), *Param Bhagavat* (Nalanda copper plate), *Ashvamedha–parakrama* i.e. whose might was demonstrated by the horse-sacrifice (coin), *Vikram* i.e. prowess (coin), *Sarva-raj-ochchetta* i.e. uprooter of all kings (coin) etc. Note : Only Gupta ruler had the title of *Sarva-raj-ochehhetta*.
- **Original types of Gold Coins** *(Dinars)* : Garud type, Dhanurdhari i.e. Archer type, Axe type, Ashvamedha type, Vyaghrahanan i.e. Tiger-killing type, Veenavadan i.e. lute playing type.
- Samudragupta was a Vaishnavite.
- According to the Chinese writer Wang-Hiuen-Tse, *Meghavarna*, king of Sri Lanka, sent an embassy to Samudragupta for his permission to build a monastery for Buddhist pilgrims at Bodh Gaya.

Chandragupta II 'Vikramaditya' : 380-414 AD

- According to 'Devi Chandragupta' (Vishakhadatta), Samudragupta was succeeded by *Ramgupta*. It seems Ramgupta ruled for a very short period. He was 'the only Gupta ruler to issue copper coins'.
- Ramagupta, a coward and impotent king, agreed to surrender his queen *Dhruvadevi* to Saka invader. But the prince Chandragupta II, the younger brother of the king, resolved to go to the enemy's camp in the guise of the queen with a view to kill the hated enemy. Chandragupta II succeeded in killing the Saka ruler.
- Chandragupta II also succeeded in killing Ramgupta, and not only seized his kingdom but also married his widow Dhruvadevi.
- Chandragupta II extended the limits of empire by matrimonial alliances (with the Nagas and Vakatakas) and conquests (Western India). He married *Kubernaga* of Naga dynasty and married his daughter *Prabhavatigupta* with Vakataka prince *Rudrasena II*.

- As a result of the overthrow of Saka rule in Wstern India, the Gupta empire extended upto Arabian sea. He issued silver coins in the memory of victory over Sakas. He was 'the first Gupta ruler to issue silver coins' and adopted the titles *Sakari* and *Vikramaditya*. *Ujjain* seems to have been made the second capital by Chandragupta II.
- *Mehrauli* (near Kutub Minar, Delhi) Iron Pillar inscription says that the king defeated the confederacy of Vangas and Vahilkas (Bulkh).
- ***Navaratna* (i.e. nine gems) of Chandragupta II** : 1. *Kalidasa* (Poetry–Ritusamhar, Meghadutam, Kumarsambhavam, Raghuvamshama; Dramas–Malvikagnimitra, Vikramorvashiyam, Abhijnan-Shakuntalam) 2. *Amarsinh* (Amarsinhkosha) 3. *Dhanavantri* (Navanitakam–medicine text) 4. *Varahmihira* (Panch Sidhantaka, Vrihatsamhita, Vrihat Jataka, Laghu Jataka) 5. *Vararuchi* (Vartika–a comment on Ashtadhyayi) 6. *Ghatakarna* 7. *Kshapranak* 8. *Velabhatt* 9. *Shanku*.
- It was in Chandragupta's time that the Chinese pilgrim *Fahien* visited India.
- **Titles** : *Devagupta/Devaraja/Devashri, Parama Bhagavata, Narendra Chandra, Sinh Vikram* etc.
- **Original types of Gold coins *(Dinaras)***: Ashvarohi type, Chhatradhari type, Chakra–Vikram type etc.

Kumaragupta I : 415-455 AD

- Chandragupta II was succeeded by his son Kumaragupta I.
- Towards the end of his reign, the Gupta empire was threatened from the North by the *Huns*, who were temporarily checked by his son Skandagupta.
- Kumaragupta was the worshipper of god *Kartikeya*.
- He founded the *Nalanda Mahavihara* which developed into a great centre of learning.
- **Titles** : *Mahendraditya, Mahendra Sinh* and *Ashvamedha Mahendrah* (coins) etc.
- **Original types of Gold Coins *(Dinars)*** : Khadgadhari type, Gajarohi type, Gajarohi Sinh-nihanta type, Khang-nihanta i.e. rhinoceros-slayer type, Kartikeya type, Apratigh-mudra type etc.

Skandagupta : 455-467 AD

- Skandagupta, the last great ruler of the Gupta dynasty.
- During his reign the Gupta empire was invaded by the *Huns*. He succeeded in defeating the *Huns*. Success in repelling the *Huns* seems to have been celebrated by the assumption of the title 'Vikramaditya' (Bhitari Pillar Inscription).
- The continuos attacks of the *Huns* weakened the empire and adversely affected its economy. The gold coinage of Skandagupta bears testimony to this.
- The decline of the empire began soon after his death.

➢ **Titles :** *Vikramaditya* and *Kramaditya* (coins), *Param Bhagavat* (coins), *Sharkropama* (Kahaum Pillar Inscription), *Devaraja* (Arya Manjushri Mula Kalpa) etc.

The Huns : 500-530 AD—Huns were primitive pastoralists owing herds of cattle and horses but knowing nothing of agriculture. They roamed in the Steppe in search of pasture and water. From the Oxus, the white Huns came into Afghanistan, destroyed the local power and, after establishing themselves there, began to pour into India in 458 AD. However, Skandagupta who was at the time ruling in Northern India, checkmated them effectively. Whenever the Gupta empire's resistance collapsad the Huns occupied the areas upto Central India and Malwa about 500 AD. There were two powerful Hun rulers *Toramana* and his son *Mihirkula*. They ruled during 500-530 AD. Mihirkula, a Shaivite, was a persecutor of Buddhism. In 530 AD, the Huns were uprooted by Yashodarmana of Mandsaur.

Vakatakas : 3rd Century-5thCentury AD—The Vakatakas were the most important power that held sway over parts of Deccan and Central India after the fall of the Satavahanas and before the rise of Chalukyas. The founder of the Vakataka dynasty was *Vindhyasakti* (255-75 AD). Vindhyasakti was succeeded by his son *Pravarasena I* (275-335 AD), who was the real founder of the Vakataka empire. He perfomed 4 *Ashuvamedha Yajnas*. After his death, the empire was divided. *Rudrasena I* took over the reigns of main branch i.e. Northern branch. He was the contemporary of Samudragupta. Rudrasena I was succeeded by *Prithvisen I*. He was contemporary of Chandragupta II. Chandragupta married his daughter Prabhavatigupta to the prince Rudrasena II. Prithvisena I was succeeded by his son *Rudrasena II*. Rudrasena II died after a short reign of five years, leaving behind two minor sons– *Divakarasena* and *Damodarsena*. Prabhavatigupta ruled as a regent of her son. Later, Damodarsena, became ruler, with the name *Pravarasena II*. Pravarasena II composed 'Setubandh/Ravanaho' (Poetry) in Marathi Script.

Gupta Inscriptions

Rulers	Inscriptions	Their Character
Samudragupta	Prayaga/Allahabad Stone Pillar	Prasasti
	Eran Stone Pillar	Prasasti
	Nalanda Copper Plate	Royal Charter
Chandragupta II	Mehrauli Iron Pillar	Prasasti
Skandagupta	Junagarh Rock	Prasasti
	Bhitari Pillar	Prasasti
	Indore Stone Pillar	Royal Charter (Evidence of sub-infeudation)
Buddhagupta	Paharpur Copper Plate	Royal Charter (Evidence of state ownership of land)

Administration

- Centralised control was not as fully realized under Guptas as it had been under the Mauryas.
- Guptan administration was, thus, highly decentralised, and as patrimonial bureaucracy reached its logical conclusion. In hereditary grants it reflected the quasi-feudal character of the economy.
- It comprised a network of self governing tribes and tributary kingdoms and their chiefs often served as representatives of imperial powers.
- The Gupta king took exalted titles like the Mahadhiraja, Samrat, Ekadhiraja, Chakravartin, befitting their large empire and imperial status.
- The practice of appointing the crown prince *(Kumara)* came in vogue.
- The Gupta kings were assisted by a council of ministers *(Mantriparishad/Mantrimandalam)*. The existence of such a council is implied in the Prayaga/Allahabad Pillar Inscription, which speaks of the delight of the 'Sabhyas' (members) at the selection fo Samudragupta for the throne.
- Among the high officers we may take special notice of the *Kumaramatya* and the *Sandhivigrahika*, who are not known to inscriptions of earlier period.
- The *Kumaramatyas* formed the chief cadre for recruiting high officials under the Guptas. It was from them the Mantris, Senapati, Mahadandanayaka (Minister of Jsutice) and Sandhivigrahika (Minister of peace and war) were generally chosen.
- The office of *Sandhivigrahika* first appears under Samudragupta, whose amatya *Harisena* held this title.
- Other Important officials : *Mahapratihari* (the Cheif usher of the Royal Palace), *Dandapashika* (Chief officer of Polcie Department), *Vinayasthitisthapak* (Chief Officer of Religious affairs), *Mahapilupati* (Chief of Elephant corps), *Mahashvapati* (Chief of Cavalry) etc.

Adminsitrative Unit	Head
Bhukti/Bhoga (i.e. Province)	Uparika/Bhogapati
Vishaya (i.e. District)	Vishayapati/Ayukta
Vithika/Nagar (i.e. City)	Nagarpati/Purapala
Gram (i.e. village)	Gramika

- The important *Bhuktis* (i.e. provinces) of Gupta period were : Magadha, Barddhaman, Pundra Vardhana, Teerbhukti (Northen Bihar), Eastern Malwa, Western Malwa and Saurashtra.
- The administration of city was in the hand of a council *(Paura)*, which consisted of the president of the city corporation, the chief representative of the guild of merchants, a representative of the artisans and the Chief Accountant.
- Whereas under the Mauryas, the city committee was appointed by the Maurya government, under the Guptas, it was comprised of the local representatives.

- Decentaralisation of the administrative authority began during the Gupta period.
- It was during the Gupta rule that the village headmen became more important than before.
- The Gupta military organsiation was feudal by character (though the emperor had a large standing army).
- In the Gupta period for the first time civil and criminal law were clearly defined and demarcated.
- Gupta kings depended primarily on land revenue, varying from 1/4 to 1/6 of the produce.
- In Gupta period the army was to be fed by the people whenever it passed through the countryside. This tax was called *Senabhakta*.
- The villagers were also subjected to forced labour called *vishti* for serving royal army and officials.
- The Gupta period also experienced an excess of land grants. (*Agarhara* grants, *Devagrahara* grants). Land grants included the transfer of royal rights over salt and mines, which were under the royal monopoly during the Maurya period.

Society

- The varna system begins to get modified owing to the proliferation of castes. This was chiefly due to three factors : (i) A large number of foreigners had been assimilated into the Indian society primarily and were known as *Kshatriyas* (ii) There was a large absorption of tribal people into Brahamanical society through land grants. The acculturated tribes were absorbed into the *Shudra Varna*. (iii) Guilds of craftsmen were often transformed into castes as a result of the decline of trade and urban centres and the localised character of crafts.
- The social positions of *the Shudras* seems to have improved in this period. They were permitted to listen to the epics and *Puranas* and also worship a new god called Krishna.
- From around the 3rd century onwards the practice of untouchability appears to have intensified and their number registered a rise. *Katyayana*, a smriti writer of the Gupta periods, was the first to use the expression *asprasya* to denote the untouchable.
- The position of women deteriorated further. Polygamy was common.
- Early marriages were advocated and often pre-puberty marriages took place.
- The first example of *Sati* appears in Gupta time in 510 AD in Eran in Madhya Pradesh. (*Bhanugupta's Eran Inscription* – 510 AD)
- Women were denied any right to property except for *Stridhana* in the form of jewellery and garments.
- Under the patronage of Gupta ruler, Vaishnavism became very popular.

- The gods were activated by their unions with the respective consorts. Thus, Laxmi got her association with Vishnu and Parvati got her association with Shiva.
- This was the period of evolution of Vajrayanism and Buddhist tantric cults.
- Idol worship became a common feature of Hinduism from Gupta period onwards.

Economy

- It is argued by many scholars that the state was the exclusive owner of land. The most decisive argument in favour of the exclusive state ownership of land is in the *Pahadpur Copper Plate inscription* of Buddhagupta.
- From the economic stand point, we may classify land udner the Gupta period into 5 groups : 1. *Kshetra Bhoomi*-Cultivable land 2. *Khila*– Waste land 3. *Vastu Bhoomi*–Habitable land 4. *Charagah Bhoomi*–Pasture land 5. *Aprahata Bhoomi*–Forest land.
- In the Gupta period land survey is evident from the *Poona plates of Prabhavati Gupta* and many other inscriptions.

Bhaga	King's customary share of the produce normally amounting to 1/6th of the produce, paid by all cultivators.
Bhoga	Periodic supplies of fruits, fire wood, flowers etc., which the villagers had to furnish to king.
Bali	Originally it was a voluntary offering by the people to the king, but later it became compulsory. During the Gupta period, it seems to be an additional and oppressive tax.
Uparikara	An extra tax levied on all subjects.

- An officer named *Pustapala* maintained records of all land transcations in the district.
- The Guptas issued the largest number of gold coins in ancient India, but in gold content, Gupta coins are not as pure as Kushanas.
- The Guptas also issued good number of silver coins for local exchange.
- The Gupta copper coins are very few as compared to those of Kushanas, which show that use of money did not touch common people.
- Gupta period witnessed decline in long distance trade.
- Trade with the Roman Empire declined after 3rd century AD.
- Indian merchants began to rely more heavily on the South-East Asian trade.
- The ports of the East coast– *Tamralipti, Ghantashala* and *Kandura*– handled the North-Indian trade with South-East Asia; and those of the West coast–*Bharoach, Chaul, Kalyan* and *Cambay*–traded with the Mediterranean and West Asia.

Culture

➢ The architecture of the Gupta period may be divided into three categories :

1. **Rock-cut caves :** *Ajanta* and *Ellora* Group (Maharashtra) and *Bagh* (MP).
2. **Structural Temples :** *Dasavatara temple* of Deogarh (Jhansi district, UP)–the oldest and the best, *Siva temple* of Bhumra (Nagod, MP), *Vishnu* and *Kankali temple* (Tigawa, MP), *Parvati temple* of Nanchana–Kuthwa (Panna district, MP), *Shiva temple* of Khoh (Satna, Panna, MP), *Krishna brick temple* of Bhittargaon (Kanpur, UP), *Laxman temple* of Sirpur (Raipur, MP), *Vishnu temple* and *Varah temple* of Eran (MP).
3. **Stupas :** *Mirpur khas* (Sindh), *Dhammekh* (Saranath) and *Ratnagiri* (Orissa).

➢ The art of architecture attained great heights. By evolving the *Nagara Style (Shikhar style)*, the Gupta art ushers in the history of Indian architecture. Shikhara Shrine, a Vaishnava symbol, one of the most characteristic features of temple architecture, found its fullest development during this period. The temple architecture, with its *garbha griha* (shrine room) in which the image of the god was placed, began with the Guptas.

➢ The fragmentary remains of *Dasavatara temple of Deogarh* is the example of the most ornate and beautifully composed Gupta temple building.

➢ The centres of the Gandhar sculptures declined and their places were taken by *Benaras, Patliputra* and *Mathura*.

➢ For the first time we get images of *Vishnu, Shiva* and other Gods.

➢ Among the best specimen of the images of Buddha is a *seated Buddha image of Sarnath*, which depicts the Buddha preaching the Dhamma.

➢ Of the Brahmanical images perhaps the most impressive was *the Great Boar (Varah)* carved in relief at the entrance of a cave at Udayagiri.

➢ The painting of this period are found in *Bagh* (Dhar district, MP), and *Ajanta* (Aurangabad district, Maharashtra). The frescoes of the Ajanta caves are the masterpieces of the paintings of this age.

Religious Literature

A. Hindu Texts : Some of the old religious books (viz. *Vayu Purana, Vishnu Purana, Matsya Purana; Ramayan* and *Mahabharata, Manu Smriti*) were re-written. *Narada Smriti, Parashara Smriti, Bhrihaspati Smriti* and *Katyayana Smriti* were written in this period.

B. Buddhist Texts : Abhidharma Kosha *(Dignaga)*; Vishudhimagga *(Buddhghosa)*

C. Jain texts : Nyayavartam *(Sidhsena)*

Secular Literature

Ritusamhar (first poetry), Meghadutam, Kumarasam-bhavam, Raghuvamsam; Malavikagnimitra (first drama), Vikramorvashi-yam, Abhijnana-Shakun-talam *(Kalidasa)*; Mudrarakshasa *(Visakhadatta)*; Kiratarjuniya *(Bharavi)*; Kavyadarsa, Dasa Kumar Charita *(Dandin)*; Mrichchhakatika *(Sudraka)*; Panchatantra *(Vishnu Sharma)*; Kamasutra *(Vatsyayan)*.

Scientific Literature

Aryabhatiya, Surya Sidhant *(Aryabhatta)*; Brahmasidhanta *(Brahmagupta)*; Pancha Sidhantaka, Vrihat Samhita, Vrihat Jataka, Laghu Jataka *(Varahamihira)*; Ashtanga Hridaya (medicine) *(Vagbhatta)*; Navanitakam *(Dhanvantri)*; Mahabhaskarya, Laghubhaskarya *(Bhaskara)*; Hastyayurveda *(Palkapya)*

Note : 1. *'Manusmriti' was translated in English under the title of 'Institutes of Hindoo Law' by William Jones.*

2. *'Abhijnana Shakuntalam (i.e. recognition of Shakuntala) was translated in English by William Jones.*
3. *Kalidas is known as 'the Shakespeare of India'.*
4. *'Mrichchakatika' (i.e. the clay cart), love story of a poor brahman Charudatta and virtuos courtesan Vasantasena, is notable for its realistic depiction of city life.*
5. *'Kamsutra' is the earliest book on sex.*
6. *'Brahmasidhanta' was translated in Arabic under the title of 'Sind Hind'.*

Gupta Period : Golden Age of Ancient India—Reality or Myth ?
Arguments :

For : 1. There were political units; foreign rule was completely removed and peace and prosperity prevailed 2. Enlightened character of government, i.e. taxes were light, punishment mild, etc. 3. Revival of Hinduism but there was tolerance of all other religions 4. Use of Sanskrit developed and art and literature flourished during the period 5. Great personage like Kalidasa, Amarsinha, Dhanavantri, Aryabhatta, Varahamihira etc. lived during this period.

Against : 1. Existence of too many feudatories 2. Absence of large Central army and Bureaucracy 3. Development of Feudal elements (Increasing land grants, Serfdom, Sub-infeudation etc.) 4. Decline of trade and Guilds 5. Decline of urban centres 6. Increasing Varna distinction and social disorder 7. Decline in status of women.

7. Post-Gupta Period/Vardhana Dynasty (550 AD-647 AD)

Pushyabhuti/Vardhana Dynasty

- The Pushyabhuti or Vardhana dynasty was founded at *Thaneswar* (Karnal district, Haryana) by *Pushyabhuti* probably towards the beginning of the 6th century. Pushyabhuti were the feudatories of the Guptas, but has assumed independence after the Hun invasions.
- The first important ruler of the dynasty was *Prabhakaravardhana* (580-605 AD).
- Prabhakaravardhana was succeeded by his eldest son *Rajyavardhana* (605-606 AD).
- Rajyavardhana had to face problems from the day of his succession to the throne. *Grahavarman*, the Maukhari ruler of Kannauj and husband

of *Rajyashri* (sister of Rajyavardhana) was murdered by *Deva Gupta* (the ruler of Malwa) who in alliance with *Shashanka* (ruler of Gaud or North-Western Bengal) now occupied Kannauj and imprisoned Rajyashri.

- Rajyavardhana, therefore, undertook a campaign against Deva Gupta and killed him but he was killed by Shashanka in 606 AD. In the meanwhile Rajyashri escaped into the forests of Central India.

Harshavardhana : 606-647 AD

- After the killing of Rajavardhana, his younger brother, Harshavardhana also known as *Siladitya*, ascended the Pushyabhuti throne in 606 AD and from this year started the *Harsha Era*.
- After ascending the throne Harsha first rescued his widowed sister Rajyashri, from the Vindhyan forest, where she was going to throw herself into the fire.
- Harsha drove out Shashanka from Kannauj who had occupied it after killing of Rayavardhana. He not only unified *Kannauj* with Thaneswar but also made it his new capital, which made him the most powerful king of North India.
- Harsha thereafter, proceeded towards the east against *Shashanka* with a view to avenge the death of his brother, Rajyavardhana and brother-in-law, Grahavarman. Harsha was not successful in his first expedition against Gaud, but in his second expedition towards the close of his reign, after the death of Shashanka (died in 637 AD), he conquered Magadha and Shashanka's empire.
- Harshavardhana defeated *Dhruvasena II*, the Maitraka ruler of Vallabhi. However, Harsha, in order to secure the safety of the western boundary, reinstated him and gave his daughter in marriage to Dhruvasena II. Dhruvasena II accepted the position of a feudatory vassal. It was an important diplomatic achievement of Harsha.
- The course of Harsha's conquests suffered a serious setback on his expedition towards the Deccan. *Pulkeshin II* of Chalukya dynasty of Vatapi/Vadami inflicted a decisive defeat on him at the bank of Narmada. It was the only defeat of Harsha's victorious life. The Chalukya records describe Harsha as the lord of whole of Northern country *(Sakalottarapatheshvara)*.
- The area under his control covered many parts of Northern India, Eastern Rajasthan and the Ganges Valley as far as Assam. His empire included territories of distant feudal kings too.
- Harsha maintained diplomatic relations with China. In 641 AD, he sent an envoy to Tai-Tsung, the Tang Emperor of China. Three Chinese missions subsequently visited his court. *Hiuen-Tsang*, the celebrated Chinese pilgrim, visited India during Harsha's reign. He spent about eight years (635-643 AD) in the dominions of Harsha.
- Hiuen-Tsang mentions two most celebrated events of Harsha's reign the assemblies at Kannauj and at Prayaga. The *Kannauj assembly* (643 AD)

was held in the honour of Hiuen-Tsang and to popularise Mahayana sect of Buddhism. The *Prayaga assembly* was held in 643-644 AD. In *Prayaga*, Harshavardhana used to celebrate religious festivals at the end of every five years, at the confluence of the Ganges, the Yamuna and the Saraswati. It is said that this was the beginning of *Kumbha fair*.

- Harshavardhana was a Shaiva by faith, but he showed equal respect to other sects. Hiuen-Tsang portrays him as a liberal Buddhist (Mahayana) who also honoured gods of others sects.
- According to Hiuen-Tsang, *Nalanda University*, meant for Buddhist monks, was maintained by the revenue from 200 villages which granted by Harshavardhana.
- He died in 647 AD. Harsha does not appear to have any heir to his throne, which was usurped after his death by his minister named Arunashva.
- Harshavardhana was not only a patron of learning, but was himself an accomplished author. He wrote three Sanskrit plays–*Nagananda, Ratnavali* and *Priyadarsika*. He gathered around him a circle of learned men, of whom *Banabhatta*, the author of *Harshacharita* (an important historical work narrating the incidents of the earleir part of Harsha's reign) and *Kadambari* (a poetical novel of great literary merit) and *Bhartrihari*, the author of *Niti Shataka, Shringar Shataka* and *Vairagya Shatak* (jointly called *Shatakatrayi*) are the well known.
- Harsha governed his empire on the same lines as the Guptas did, except that this administration had become more feudal and decentralised.

States of the Deccan and South India

Chalukyas of Vatapi/Vadami : 543-755 AD

- The Vakataka power was followed by Chalukyas.
- Chalukyas established their capital at Vatapi / Badami in the district of Bijapur in Karnataka.
- *Pulakesin II* (609-42 AD) was able to check Harsha's design to conquer Deccan.
- *Aihole inscription* is an eulogy written by his court poet *Ravikirti*.
- He sent an ambassador to the Persian King Khusrau II in 625 AD and also received one from him.
- The Chinese pilgrim *Hiuen-Tsang* visited his kingdom.
- Pallava ruler *Narsimhavarman 'Mammala'* invaded the Chalukya kingdom, killed Pulakesin II and captured Vatapi. He adopted the title *Vatapikonda* i.e. the conqueror of Vatapi.
- In 757 AD, Chalukyas were overthrown by their feudatories, the Rashtrakutas.

Vesara Stye/Deccan Style

- Chalukyas began the Vesara style or Deccan style in building structural temples, which however, reached culmination, only under the Rashtrakutas and the Hoyasalas.

- **Specimens of Chalukyan Temples** : 1. Vesar style–*Jinendra temple/ Meguti temple*–Aihole (Ravikirti); *Vishnu temple*–Aihole, *Ladh Khan temple* (attributed to god Surya)–Aihole, *Durga temple*–Aihole; Aihole is called a 'town of temples' because it contains about 70 temples. 2. Nagara style : *Papanatha temple*–Pattadakal 3. Dravida style : *Virupaksha temple* and *Sangamesvara temple* – Pattadakal.

Pallavas of Kanchi : 575-897 AD

- There is controversy regarding the origin of Pallavas. Possibly the Pallavas were a local tribe who established their authority in the Tondaimandalam or the land of creepers.
- They were orthodox Brahmanical Hindus and their capital was Kanchi.
- Both Chalukyas and Pallavas tried to establish their supremacy over land between Krishna and Tungabhadra.
- Pallava king *Narsimhavarman* (630-668 AD) occupied Chalukyan capital Vatapi in about 642 AD and assumed the title *Vatapikonda* i.e. conqueror of Vatapi.
- Pallavas were instrumental in spreading Indian culture in South-East Asia. Till the 8th century AD Pallava influence was predominant in Cambodia. The Pallava type of Shikhara is to be found in the temples of Java, Cambodia and Annam.

Pallava Art

- Pallavas began the Dravida stye of temple architecture, which reached culmination under the rule of Cholas.
- The development of temple architecture, particularly Dravida style, under the Pallavas can be seen in four stages :

Mahendravarmana Group	Mahendravarmana I (600-630 AD)	Temple at Bhairavkona (North Arcot Distt.), Ananteswar temple at Undavalli (Guntur Distt.)
Mammala Group	Narsimhavarmana I 'Mammala' (630-668 AD)	Mandapa temples and Ratha temples (Sapt Pagodas) at Mammalapuram (Mahabalipuram)
Rajasimha Group	Narsimhavarmana II 'Rajsimha' (680-720 AD)	Kailashnatha and Vaikunth Perumal Temple at Kanchi, Shore temple at Mammalapuram
Aparajit Group	Nandivarmana 'Aparajit' (879-897 AD)	Mukteshwar and Matangeshwar temple at Kanchi, Parshurameswar temple at Gudimallam

- The Pallavas also contributed to the development of sculpture in South India. The Pallava sculpture is indebted largely to the Buddhist tradition. It is more monumental and linear in form, thus avoiding the typical ornamentation of the Deccan sculpture. The best example is the Descent of the Ganges or Arjuna's Penance at Mammalapuram.

Gupta 'n' Post-Gupta Dynasties and Their Founders

Dynasty	Founder
The Chalukyas of Vatapi	Jayasimha
The Gangas of Talakad	Konakanivarma
The Guptas of Magadha	Shri Gupta
The Kadambas of Vanavasi	Mayurasharman
The Kingdom of Gaud	Shashanka
The Kingdom of Thaneswar	Pushyabhuti
The Later-Guptas of Magadha-Malwa	Krishnagupta
The Maitrakas of Vallabhi	Bhattarka
The Maukharis of Kannauj	Yajnavarman
The Pallavas of Kanchi	Simhavarman
The Pandyas of Madurai	Kodungon
The Vakatakas	Vindhyashakti

MEDIEVAL INDIA

8. Early-Medieval Period (650-1206)

I. North India (Rajputa Period)

After Harshavardhana, the Rajputas emerged as a powerful force in Northern India and dominated the Indian political scene for nearly 500 years from the 7th century.

10 Important Rajputa Kingdoms	Period	Capital	Founder
Chauhan/Chahaman of Delhi-Ajmer	7th Cen.-1192	Delhi	Vasudeva
Pratihara/Parihar of Kannauj	730-1036	Avanti, Kannauj	Nagabhatt I
Pawar/Parmar of Malwa	790-1150	Ujjain, Dhar	Seeak II 'Sri Harsha'
Chaulukya/Solanki of Kathiyawar	942-1187	Anihalvada	Mularaja I
Rastrakuta of Malkhand	752-973	Malkhand/ Manyakheta	Dantidurg (Danti Varman II)
Chandela of Jejakabhukti.	831-1202	Khajuraho, Mahoba, Kalinjar	Nannuk Chandela
Kalchuri/Haihaya of Chedi.	850-1211	Tripuri	Kokkala I
Gadhawal/Rathor of Kannauj	1090-1194	Kannauj	Chandradeva
Tomar of Surrounding areas of Haryana and Delhi	—	Dhillika	—
Guhilota/Sisodiya of Mewar	8th. Cen.-1930	Chittor	Bappa Rawal, Hammir I

Tripartite Struggle

- Towards the close of the 8th century AD, there were three great power in India-the *Palas* in the East, the *Gurjar-Partihara* in the North and the *Rashtrakutas* in the Deccan.
- The tripartite struggle for the supremacy among the Palas, Partiharas and the Rashtrakutas was the important event of these centuries.
- The main cause for this struggle was the desire to possess the city of Kannauj (Farrukhabad Distt., UP) Which was then a symbol of sovereinity.

The Palas : 750-1150 **Capital : Muddagiri/Munger (Bihar)**

- *Gopala* founded the Pala empire in 750 AD.
- His son *Dharmpala* (770-810) succeeded him. Dharmpala revived *Nalanda University*.
- He founded the *Vikramshila University*.
- The Pala dynasty was succeeded by *Sena dynasty* of Bengal. *Jayadeva* ('Gita Gobinda') was the great court poet of *Luxman Sen*.

The Pratiharas : 730-1036

- The Pratiharas are also called Gurjara-Pratiharas probably because they originated from Gujarat or South-West Rajasthan.
- *Bhoja/Mihir Bhoja* (836-882) was the greatest ruler of of this dynasty.
- He was a devotee of Vishnu and adopted the title of *'Adivarah'*.

The Rashtrakutas : 752-973

- *Dantidurg* (752-756), who fixed his capital at *Malkhand/Malkhed* (Gulbarga distt., Karnataka), founded the Kingdom.
- The greatest Rashtrakuta rulers were *Govinda III* (793-814) and *Amoghvarsha* (814-878). Amoghvarsha ruled for 64 years but by temperament he preferred pursuit of religion and literature to war. He was himself an author and wrote *Kavirajamarga*, the earliest Kannada book on Poetics.
- The famous rock-cut *temple of Kailash (Shiva) at Ellora* was built by one of the Rashtrakuta kings *Krishna I*.

Other Important Rulers

- **Prithviraj Chauhan (1178-92) :** He ruled over Delhi and Agra and fought two important battles, viz. *First Battle of Tarain* was fought in 1191 between the forces of Prithviraj Chauhan and Mohammad Ghori in which the latter was defeated. *Second Battle of Tarain* was fought in 1192 when Mohammad Ghori again invaded India in which Prithviraj Chauhan was defeated and captured and later on slain. The Kingdom of Delhi fell to Mohammad Ghori.

  The Battle of Tarain had great significance in the political scene as it led to the establishment of Muslim rule over North India and, subsequently, in the South for several centuries.
- **Jai Chand Gadhawal/Rathor (1169-94) :** He was the last Rajputa King who was also defeated and killed by Mohammad Ghori in the *Battle of Chandawar* (1194).

➢ **Rana Kumbha, the Sisodiya ruler of Mewar (1433-68) :** Rana Kumbha was the famous ruler of Mewar. He defeated Mohammad Khilji and erected the Tower of victory *(Vijay Stambha)* in *Chittor*. His successors *Rana Sangram Singh (Rana Sanga)* and *Rana Pratap* were also great kings of Mewar state.

➢ **Salient features of the Rajputa Kingdoms** : The country remained free of invasions but lost foreign contact. The caste system was rigid. The Rajputas were proud, warrior and people but hospitable. In the field of culture many great fortresses and temples were built by them such as *Khajuraho* (MP), *Lingaraja temple* (Bhubaneshwar, Orissa), *Sun temple* (Konarka,. Orissa), the *Jagannath temple* (Puri), *Dilwara temple* (Mount Abu).

➢ **Causes of the Decline of Rajputas** : Lack of unity and foresightedness, caste the system, and defective military organization were some of the causes for the downfall of the Rajputas.

II. South India (Cholas and Others)

The Chola Empire : 850-1279AD

Capital : Tanjore, Gangaikondacholapuram

➢ The founder of the Chola dynasty was *Vijayalaya*, who was at first a feudatory of the Pallavas. He captured Tanjore in 850 AD.

➢ The greatest Chola rulers were *Rajaraja* (985-1014AD) and his son *Rajendra I* (1014-1044AD).

➢ *Rajaraja* buit *Vrihadeshwar/Rajarajeshwar* temple (attributed to Shiva) at Tanjore.

➢ *Rajendra I* conquered Orissa, Bengal, Burma and Andaman and Nicobar islands. The Chola dynasty was at its zenith during his reign.

➢ Rajendra I assumed the title of Gangaikondachola and built a city called Gangaikondacholapuram.

➢ The last ruler of Chola dynasty was Rajendra III.

➢ The king was the head of central authority helped by a council of ministers, but the administration was democratic.

➢ The Chola empire was divided into *Mandalams* (Province) and these in turn were divided into *Valanadu* (Commissionary), *Nadu* (District) and *Kurram* (a group of villages).

➢ The arrangement of local self-government is regarded as the basic feature of the administration of Cholas.

➢ Land revenue and trade tax were the main sources of income.

➢ The style of architecture which came into vogue during this period is called Dravida e.g. *Kailashnath temple* of *Kanchipuram*.

➢ Another aspect was image-making which reached its climax in dancing figure of Shiva called *Nataraja*.

➢ *Kambana* who wrote *Ramavataram* was one of the greatest figures of Tamil poetry. His Ramayana is also known as *Kamba Ramayana*.

➢ *Kambana, Kuttana* and *Pugalendi* are considered as 'three gems of Tamil poetry'.

- In the temples, the *Vimana* or the tall pyramidal tower dominates the whole structure of the shrine and imparts an extraordinary dignity to it.
- *Gopuram* and *Garbhagriha* are the other two important structures.
- The best specimens are the temples of Vijayalaya, Choleshwara, the Nageshwara temple, the Koranganath temple and the Muvarakovitha temple.

Other Kingdoms of South

Kingdom	Capital	Real Founder
Western/Later Chalukyas (973-1200)	Kalyani, Karnataka	Tailap II
Kakatiyas (1110-1326)	Warangal, Andhra Pradesh	Prolaraja II
Yadavas (1187-1312)	Devagiri, Maharashtra	Bhillam V
Hoyasalas (1173-1342)	Dwarasamudra, Karnataka	Vittigadev 'Vishnuvardhan'

Note : *The temple of Hoyasaleshwara at Dwarasamudra (Modern Halebid) is the greatest achievement of Hoyasala art.*

9. Sultanate Period (1206-1526AD)

I. The Delhi Sultanate

The Background of Delhi Sultanate

- **First Muslim Invasion-Mohammad Bin Qasim's Invasion (712AD) :** Mohammad Bin Qasim invaded India in 712 AD and conquered Sindh which became the province of Omayyad Khilafat.
- **First Turk Invasion-Mahmud Ghaznavi's Invasion (998-1030 AD) :** Sultan Mahmud of Ghazni led about 17 expeditions to India to enrich himself by taking away the wealth from India. In 1025 he attacked and raided the most celebrated Hindu temple of Somnath that lies on the coast in the extreme south of Kathiwar. The temple was destroyed in 1026 AD.
- **Second Turk Invasion-Mohammad Ghori's Invasion (1175-1206 AD) :** Mohammad Ghori invaded India and laid the foundation of the Muslim dominion in India. He may be considered the 'founder of muslim rule' in India.
- **Reasons for the Success of Turks in India :** (i) Rajputas lacked unity and organisation and were divided by rivalries (ii) There was no central government (iii) The Rajput Kingdoms were small and scattered (iv) The Turks were better organised and took advantage of the lack of mutual co-operation among the Rajputas.

The Delhi Sultanate : 1206-1526 AD

- Mohammed Ghori's conquests became the nucleus of a new political entity in India-the Delhi Sultanate. This period can be divided into 5 distinct periods viz. (i) The Slave Dynasty (1206-90) (ii) The Khilji Dynasty (1290-1320) (iii) The Tughlaq Dynasty (1320-1414) (iv) The Sayyid Dynasty (1414-51) (v) The Lodhi Dynasty (1451-1526).

The Slave Dynasty : 1206-90 AD

Qutubuddin Aibak : 1206-10

➢ A Turkish slave by origin, he was purchased by Mohammad Ghori who later made him his Governor. After the death of Ghori, Aibak became the master of Hindustan and founded the Slave Dynasty in 1206. For his generosity, he was given the title of *Lakh Bakhsh* (giver of Lakhs).

➢ He died in 1210 while playing *Chaugan* or Polo.

➢ He constructed two mosques-*Quwat-ul-Islam* at Delhi and *Adhai din ka Jhonpra* at Ajmer. He also began the constrction of *Qutub Minar*, in the honour of famous Sufi Saint *Khwaja Qutubuddin Bakhtiyar Kaki*.

➢ Aibak was a great patron of learning and patronised writers like *Hasan-un-Nizami*, author of 'Taj-ul-Massir' and *Fakhruddin*, author of 'Tarikh-i-Mubarak Shahi'.

Shamsuddin Iltutmish : 1211-36

➢ He was a slave of Qutubuddin Aibak and occupied the throne of Delhi in 1211 after deposing *Aram Bakhsh*.

➢ He was a very capable ruler and is regarded as the 'real founder of the Delhi Sultanate'. He made *Delhi* the capital in place of Lahore.

➢ He saved Delhi Sultanate from the wrath of *Chengiz Khan*, the Mongol leader, by refusing shelter to *Khwarizm Shah*, whom Chengiz was chasing.

➢ He introduced the silver coin *(tanka)* and the copper coin *(jital)*. He organised the *Iqta System* and introduced reforms in civil administration and army, which was now centrally paid and recruited.

➢ He set up an official nobility of slaves known as *Chahalgani/ Chalisa* (group of 40).

➢ He completed the construction of *Qutub Minar* which was started by Aibak.

➢ He patronised *Minhaj-us-Siraj*, author of 'Tabaqat-i-Nasiri'.

Ruknuddin : 1236

➢ He was the son of Iltutmish and was crowned by her mother, *Shah Turkan*, after death of Iltutmish. He was deposed by Razia, daughter of Iltutmish when he was out of capital to curb a rebellion in Avadh against him.

Razia Sultana : 1236-40

➢ Though Iltutmish had nominated his daughter Razia as the successor, the nobles placed Ruknuddin Firoj on the throne. However, Razia got rid of Ruknuddin and ascended the throne.

➢ She was the 'first and only Muslim lady who ever ruled India'.

➢ She was popular among the people but was not acceptable to the nobles and theologians. She further offended the nobles by her preference for an Abyssian slave *Yakut*.

➢ Soon after her accession, the governors of Multan, Badaun, Hansi and Lahore openly revolted against her. There was a serious rebellion in Bhatinda. *Altunia*, governor of Bhatinda refused to accept suzerainity of Razia. Razia accompanied by Yakut marched against Altunia.

- However, Altunia got Yakut murdered and imprisoned Razia. Subsequently, Razia married Altunia and both of them marched towards Delhi.
- In 1240 AD, Razia became the victim of a conspiracy and was assassinated near Kaithal (Haryana).

Bahram Shah : 1240-42

- After Razia, Iltutmish's third son Bahram Shah was put on the throne by the powerful turkish council *Chalisa*.
- He was considered only as de jure ruler, while Naib-e-mamlakat (the regent) was the de facto ruler.
- Bahram Shah lost his life after his failed attempt to assert his authority once on the throne.

Masud Shah : 1242-46

- He was the son of Ruknuddin but was deposed after *Balban* and Nasiruddin Mahamud's Mother, *Malika-e-Jahan*, conspired against him and established Nasiruddin Mahamud as the new Sultan.

Nasiruddin Mahamud : 1246-66

- He was the son of Iltutmish and was known as the *Darvesi King* as he was very pious and noble. He died in 1266.

Ghiyasuddin Balban : 1266-87

- Balban ascended the throne in 1266.
- He broke the power of *Chalisa* and restored the prestige of the crown. That was his greatest contribution towards the stability of the Sultanate.
- To keep himself well-informed Balban appointed spies.
- He created a strong centralised army to deal with internal disturbances and to cheek Mongols who were posing a serious danger to Delhi Sultante.
- He established the military department *Diwan-i-Arz*.
- The Persian court model influenced Balban's conception of Kingship. He took up the title of *Zil-i-Ilahi* (Shadow of God).
- He introduced *Sijda* (prostration before the monarch) and *Paibos* (kissing the feet of monarch) as the normal forms of salutation.
- He destroyed the Mewati Rajputa brigandage in the *doab*, where forests were cut and forts built.
- In his last days he overlooked the Sultanate affairs due to the death of his eldest and most loving son, *Muhammad*, and rebellion by his closest and most loved slave, *Tughril*. Muhammad died fighting the Mongolians in 1285 while Tughril was captured and beheaded.

Kaiqubad : 1287-90

- A grandson of Balban was seated on the throne by *Fakruddin*, the Kotwal of Delhi who assumed high political authority during the last days of Balban. But Kaiqubad was killed by the Khiliji family, which saw the end of Slave dynasty and beginning of Khiliji dynasty at Delhi throne.

The Khilji Dynasty : 1290-1320 AD

Jalaluddin Khilji : 1290-96

➢ Jalaluddin Khilji founded the Khilji dynasty.

Alauddin Khilji : 1296-1316

➢ He was a nephew and son-in-law of Jalaluddin Khilji. Alauddin Khilji killed him and succeeded the throne in 1296.

➢ He was the first Turkish Sultan of Delhi who separated religion from politics. He proclaimed 'Kingship knows no Kinship'.

Alauddin's Imperialism

➢ Alauddin annexed Gujarat (1298), Ranthambhor (1301), Mewar (1303), Malwa (1305), Jalor (1311). In Deccan, Aluddin's army led by *Malik Kafur* defeated *Ram Chandra* (Yadava ruler of Devagiri), *Pratap Rudradeva* (Kakatiya ruler of Warangal), Vir *Ballal* III (Hoyasala ruler of Dwarsamudra) and *Vir Pandya* (Pandya ruler of Madurai).

Administrative Reforms

➢ In order to avoid the problems created by the nobles, Alauddin issued 4 ordinances. *The Ist ordince* aimed at the confiscation of the religious endowments and free grants of lands. By *the IInd ordinance* Alauddin reorganised the spy system. *The IIIrd ordinance* prohibited the use of wine. *The IVth ordinance* issued by Alauddin laid down that nobles should not have social gathering and they should not inter-marry without his permission.

➢ He introduced the system of *Dagh* (the branding of horse) and *Chehra* (descriptive roll of soldiers).

➢ Alauddin ordered that all land was to be measured and then the share of state was to be fixed.

➢ The post of special officer called *Mustakharaj* was created for the purpose of collection of revenue.

➢ The peasants had to pay the produce as land revenue.

➢ Alauddin sought to fix cost of all commodities. For the purpose he set up three markets at Delhi : one market for food grains, the second for costly cloth and third for horses, slaves and cattle. Each market was under the control of a high officer called *Shahna* who maintained a register of the merchants and strictly controlled the shopkeepers and the prices. The check on market was kept by two officers- *Diwan-i-Riyasat* and *Shahna-i-Mandi*.

➢ All goods for sale were brought to an open market called *Sara-i-Adal*.

➢ Many forts were built by him and the most important of them was Alai fort. He also constructed the *Alai Darwaja,* the entrance gate of Qutub Minar. He also built the Palace of thousand Pillars called *Hazar Sutun*.

➢ He was a patron of art and learning. *Amir Khusrau*, the poet-musi was his favourite court poet.

➢ In 1316, after death of Alauddin, Malik Kafur, called *Hajardina* the throne. Before Kafur died, he nominated Shihabuddin (Al year old prince) as King but imprisoned the eldest prince Mubarak Khan. Kafur was killed by the loyalists of the royal family of Alauddin.

Mubarak Khan : 1316-20

➢ After the death of Kafur, Mubarak khan was freed from prison and worked as regent for Shihabuddin. He captured the throne at the first opportunity he got, but could rule only for a years as he sank into debauchery and could not give up his dissipated lifestyle. He awarded his lover *Mubarak Hassan* authority over army and palace guards, who soon obtained full control over Sultan's palace. Mabarak Hassan was given the title Khusrau Khan by the Sultan and within months Khusrau killed Mubarak Khan and assumed the title of Nasirudin in mid-1320.

Khusrau Khan : 1320

➢ Khusrau Khan was killed by Ghazi Malik, governor of Dipalpur, when he tried to oppose a rebellion by Ghazi Malik and his son Fakhruddin Jauna. This brought the end of Khilji dynasty and established the Tughlaq dynasty on the throne of Delhi.

The Tughlaq Dynasty : 1320-1414 AD

Ghiyasuddin Tughlaq : 1320-25

➢ Khusrau Khan, the last king of the Khilji dynasty was killed by Ghazi Malik. Ghazi Malik ascended the throne assuming the title Ghiyasuddin Tughlaq.

➢ He died in an accident and his son Jauna (Ulugh Khan) succeeded him under the title Mohammad-bin-Tughlaq.

Mohammad-bin Tughlaq : 1325-51

➢ Prince *Jauna*, son of Ghiyasuddin Tughlaq ascended the throne in 1325.

➢ He tried to introduce many administrative reforms. He had 5 ambitious projects for which he became particularly debatable.

(i) Taxation in the Doab (1326) : The Sultan made an ill-advised financial experiment in the Doab between the Ganges and Yamuna. He not only increased the rate of taxation but also revived and created some additional *Abwabs* or cesses. Although the share of the state remained as in time of Alauddin, it was fixed arbitrary not on the basis of actual produce. Prices were also fixed artificially for covering the produce into money. It is said that the increase was twenty fold and to this were added *Ghari* or house tax and the *Charahi* or pasture tax. The Sultan created a new department of Agriculture called *Diwan-i-Kohi*. The main object of this department was to bring more land under cultivation by giving direct help to peasants.

(ii) Transfer of Capital (1327) : The most controversial step which Mohammad-bin-Tughlaq under took soon after his accession was the so-called transfer of capital from *Delhi* to *Devagiri*. Devagiri had been a base for the expansion of Turkish rule in South India. It appears that the Sultan wanted to make Devagiri second capital so that he might be able to control South India better. Devagiri was thus named *Daulatabad*.

After a couple of years Mohammad-bin-Tughlaq decided to abandon Daulatabad largely became he soon found that just as he could not control South India from Delhi, he could not control North from Daulatabad.

(iii) Introduction of Token Currency (1329) : Mohammad-bin-Tughlaq decided to introduce bronze coins, which were to have same value as the silver coins. Mohammad-bin-Tughlaq might have been successful if he could prevent people from forging the new coins. He was not able to do so and soon the new coins began to be greatly devalued in markets. Finally Mohammad-bin-Tughlaq decided to withdraw the token currency. He promised to exchange silver pieces for bronze coins.

(iv) Proposed Khurasan Expedition (1329) : The Sultan had a vision of universal conquest. He decided to conquer Khurasan and Iraq and mobalised a huge army for the purpose. He was encouraged to do so by Khurasani nobles who had taken shelter in his court. Moreover, there was instability in Khurasan on account of the unpopular rule of Abu Said. This project was also abandoned.

(v) Qarachil Expedition (1330) : This expedition was launched in Kumaon hills in Himalayas allegedly to counter Chinese incursions. It also appears that the expedition was directed against some refractory tribes in Kumaon-Garhwal region with the object of bringing them under Delhi Sultanate. The first attack was a success but when the rainy season set in, the invaders suffered terribly.

- ➢ His five projects led to revolts. His last days were spent in checking the revolts (altogether 36 revolts in 25 years).

1335	Mudurai became independent (Jalaluddin Ahsan Shah)
1336	Foundation of Vijayanagar (Harihar and Bukka), Warangal became independent (Kanhaiya)
1341-47	Revolts of Sada Amirs and Foundation of Bahamani in 1347 (Hasan Gangu)

- ➢ He died in *Thatta* while campaigning in Sindh against Taghi, a turkish slave.

Firoz Shah Tughlaq : 1351-88

- ➢ He was a cousin of Mohammad-bin-Tughlaq. After his death the nobles and theologians of the court selected Firoz Shah as the next Sultan.
- ➢ After his accession Firoz Tughlaq was faced with the problem of preventing the imminent break up of Delhi Sultanate. He adopted the policy of trying to appease the nobality, army and theologians and of asserting his authority over only such areas, which could be easily administered from the centre. He therefore made no attempt to re-assert his authority over South India and Deccan.
- ➢ He decreed that whenever a noble died his son should be allowed t[illegible] succeed to his position including his Iqta if he had no sons, his son-[illegible] law and in his absence his slave was be succeed.
- ➢ Firoz extended the principle of heredity to the army. Soldiers [illegible] allowed to rest in peace and to send in their place their sons. The s[illegible]

were not paid in cash but by assignments on land revenue of villages *(Vajeha)*. This novel technique of payment led to many abuses.

- Firoz tried to win over the theologians proclaiming that he was a true Muslim king and the state under him was truly Islamic. In order to keep the theologians satisfied a number of them were appointed to high offices.
- He tried to ban practices which the orthodox theologians considered as non Islamic. Thus he prohibited the practice of Muslim women going out to worship at graves of saints.
- It was during the time of Firoz that *Jizya* became a separate tax. Firoz refused to exempt the Brahmanas from payment of Jizya since this was not provided for in *Shariat*.
- The new system of taxation was according to Quran. Four kinds of taxes sanctioned by the Quran were imposed. These taxes were *Kharaj, Zakat, Jizya* and *Khams*. Kharaj was the land tax, which was equal to 1/10 of the produce of the land, Zakat was 2°% tax on property, Jizya was levied on non-Muslims and Khams was 1/5 of the booty captured during war.
- In order to encourage agriculture, the Sultan paid a lot of attention to irrigation. Firoz repaired a number of canals and imposed *Haque-i-Sharb* or *Hasil-i-Sharb* (water tax).
- He was a great builder. The cities of Fatehabad, Hisar, Jaunpur and Firozabad stand to his credit.
- The two pillars of Ashoka, one from Topra (Haryana) and other from Merrut (U.P.) were brought to Delhi.
- The Sultan established at Delhi a hospital described as *Dar-ul-Shifa*.
- A new department of *Diwan-i-Khairat* was set up to make provisions for the marriage of poor girls.
- Another step which Firoz took was both economic end political in nature. He ordered his officials that whenever they attacked a place they should select handsome and well-born young boys and send them to Sultan as slaves.
- However, his rule was marked by peace and tranquility, and the credit for it goes to his Prime Minister *Khan-i-Jahan Maqbul.*
- He died in 1388.

After Firoz Shah Tughlaq : 1388-1414

- The Tughlaq dynasty could not survive much after Firoz Shah's death. The Malwa, Gujarat and Sharqi (Jaunpur) Kingdoms broke away from the Sultanate.
- **Timur's Invasion : 1398-99**-*Timur, the lame,* a Turkish Chief and cruel conqueror from Mangolia and descendant of Chengiz Khan, invaded India in 1398 during the reign of *Muhammad Shah Tughlaq*, the last ruler of Tughlaq dynasty. Taimur's army mercilessly sacked and plundered Delhi. Timur returned to Central Asia, leaving a nominee named Khizr Khan to rule to Punjab. In 1404 he died while on his way to conquer China.

The Sayyid Dynasty : 1414-50 AD

- **Khizr Khan (1414-21) :** Timur's nominee captured Delhi and was proclaimed the new Sultan. He was the first of the Sayyid dynasty which ruled over Delhi and surrounding districts.
- **Mubarak Shah (1421-34) :** He succeeded Khizr at the throne after his successful expeditions against Mewatis, Katehars and the Gangetic Doab area. He was killed by the nobles in his own court.
- **Muhammad Shah (1434-43) :** The nobles put Muhammad Shah on the throne, but he could not survive the in-fighting among the nobles in the court. He was authorised to rule only a meagre area around 30 miles, and rest the of the Sultanate was ruled by nobles.
- **Alam Shah (1443-51) :** The last Sayyid king descended in favour of Bahlol Lodhi and retired. Thus began the Lodhi dynasty which was confined to Delhi and a few surrounding areas.

The Lodhi Dynasty : 1451-1526 AD

Bahlol Lodhi : 1451-88

- Bahlol Lodhi was one of the Afghan Sardars. He established himself in Punjab after the invasion of Timur.
- He founded the Lodhi dynasty.

Sikandar Lodhi : 1489-1517

- Sikandar Lodi was the son of Bahlol Lodhi who conquered Bihar and Western Bengal.
- He shifted his capital from Delhi to *Agra*, a city founded by him.
- Sikandar was a fanatical Muslim and broke the sacred images of the Jwalamukhi Temple at Nagar Kot and ordered the temples of Mathura to be destroyed.
- He took a keen interest in the development of agriculture. He introduced the *Gaz-i-Sikandari* (Sikandar's yard) of 32 digits for measuring cultivated fields.

Ibrahim Lodhi : 1517-26

- He was the last king of the Lodhi dynasty and the last Sultan of Delhi.
- He was the son of Sikandar Lodhi.
- The Afghan nobility was brave and freedom-loving people but it was because of its fissiparous and individualistic tendencies that the Afghan monarchy was weakened. Moreover, Ibrahim Lodhi asserted the absolute power of the Sultan. As a result, some of the nobles turned against him.
- At last Daulat Khan Lodhi, the governor of Punjab invited Babur to overthrow Ibrahim Lodhi. Babur accepted the offer and inflicted a crushing defeat on Ibrahim Lodhi in *the first battle of Panipat* in 1526. Ibrahim Lodhi was killed in the battle Normal and with him ended th Delhi Sultanate.

Causes of Decline of Delhi Sultanate

The main causes were : (i) Despotic and military type of government which did not have the confidence of the people (ii) Degeneration of Delhi Sultans (esp. the wild projects of Muhammad-bin-Tughlaq, Incompetence of Firoz Tughlaq) (iii) War of succession as there was no fixed law for succession (iv) Greed and incompetency of the nobles (v)Defective military organisation (vi) Vastness of empire and poor means of communication (vii) Financial instability (viii) Number of slaves increased to 1,80,000 in Firoz Tughlaq's time which was a burden on the treasury (ix) Invasion of Timur.

Mongolian Invasions During Delhi Sultanate

Regime of Sultan	Year	Events
Iltutmish	1221 AD	Chengiz Khan came up to the bank of Indus.
Masud	1241 AD	Tair Bahadur entered Punjab. Towards the end of the 1245 AD, Balban fought back the Mongolians and recovered Multan which was captured by the Mongols.
Balban	1279 AD	Prince Muhammad of Multan, Bughra Khan from Samana and Malik Mubarak of Delhi combined together to defeat the Mongols.
Balban	1286 AD	Tamar invaded India. Prince Muhammad was killed in the battle, and was decorated with the *Khan-i-Shahid* title.
Jalaluddin Khilji	1292 AD	Abdullah came to the Northern part of India. About 4,000 Mongols got converted to Islam and became the famous '*New Musalman*'.
Alauddin Khilji	1296-99 AD	Zafar Khan defeated the Mongols at Jalandhar and Saldi, their leader was taken prisoner.
		Zafar Khan was killed in the battle.
Alauddin Khilji	1304 AD	Ali Beg and Tash were defeated.
Muhammad- bin-Tughlaq	1329 AD	Tarmashirin Khan was able to reach the outskirts of Delhi but was defeated by Muhammad-bin-Tughlaq.

Administration under Delhi Sultanate

- ➢ The Turkish Sultan in India declared themselves Lieutenant of the faithful i.e. of the Abbasid caliphate of Baghdad and included his name in *Khutba*, it did not mean that the caliph became the legal ruler. The caliph had only a moral position.
- ➢ Political, legal and military authority was vested in the Sultan. He was responsible for administration and was also the commander-in-chief of the military forces.
- ➢ No clear law of succession developed among Muslim rulers. Thus military strength was the main factor in succession to the throne.

Central Administration

Department	Head (Founded by)
Diwan-i-Wizarat (Department of Finance)	Wazir
Diwan-i-Ariz (Military Department)	Ariz-i-Mumalik
Diwan-i-Insha (Department of Correspondence)	Dabir-i-Mumalik
Diwan-i-Risalat (Department of Appeals)	Dabir-i-Mulq
Diwan-i-Mustakharaj (Department of Arrears)	(Founded by Alauddin khilji)
Diwan-i-Riyasat (Department of Commerce)	Rais-i-Mumalik (Founded by Alauddin khilji)
Diwan-i-Kohi (Department of Agriculture)	(Founded by Md-bin-Tughlaq)
Diwan-i-Bandgan (Department of Slaves)	(Founded by Firoz Tughlaq)
Diwan-i-Khairat (Department of Charity)	(Founded by Firoz Tugulaq)
Diwan-i-Isthiaq (Department of Pensions)	(Founded by Firoz Tughloq)

Administrative Unit	Head
Iqta (i.e. Province)	Muqti or Wali
Shiq (i.e District)	Siqdar
Paragana (i.e. Taluka)	Chaudhary and Amil
Gram (i.e. Village)	Muqaddam, Khut

Art and Architecture Under Delhi Sultanate

- The new features brought by the Turkish conquerors were : (i) the dome (ii) the lofty towers (iii) the true arch unsupported by beam (iv) the vault.
- They also brought with them an expert knowledge of the use of concrete and mortar, which had hitherto been little used in India.
- *The Adhai-din ka Jhonpra* at Ajmer has a beautiful prayer hall, an exquisitely carved Mehrab of white marble and a decorative arch screen.
- The first example of true or voussoired arch is said to be the *tomb of Ghiyasuddin Balban* in Mehrauli (Delhi).
- In the Khilji period the usage of voussoired arch and dome was established and for all. Famous examples is *the tomb of Hazrat Nizamuddin Aulia* at Delhi.
- The Tughlaq buildings show stark simplicity and sobriety, probably indicating less financial resources as well as puritanical tests.Slopping walls and a dark appearance characterise the buildings. Some notable Tughlaq monuments were the fort of Tughlaquabad, the tomb of Ghiyasuddin Tughlaq which marked a new phase in Indo-Islamic architecture by serving as a model for later tombs and the fort of Adilabad.
- The Sayyid period was too short to allow construction of elaborate buildings.

➢ The construction of double domes was the main feature of Lodhi Architecture. One building worth noting is the *Moth ki Masjid* erected by the prime minister of Sikandar Lodhi.

Literature of Delhi Sultanate

Book	Author	Historical Importance
Tahqiq-i-Hind	Alberuni	Alberuni was an Arabian scholar who wrote about the Slave dynasty
Tabaqat-i-Nasiri	Minhaj-us-Siraj	Gives an account of Iltutmish's reign
Laila-Majnu	Amir Khusrau	Court poet of Alauddin Khilji
Khazain-ul-Futuh	Amir Khusrau	Describes conquests of Alauddin Khilji
Tughlaq-Nama	Amir Khusrau	Gives account of Ghiyasuddin's reign
Nuh-Siphir	Amir Khusrau	Poetic description of Alauddin Khilji
Fatawa-i-Jahandari	Ziauddin Barani	Gives an account of the Tughlaq dynasty
Tarikha-i-Firoz Shahi	Ziauddin Barani	Gives an account of Firoz Shah's reign
Fatwah-i-Firoz Shahi	Firoz Shah	Gives an account of his reign
Kitab-fi-Tahqiq	Alberuni	About Indian sciences
Qanun-e-Masudi	Alberuni	About astronomy
Jawahar-fil-Jawahir	Alberuni	About mineralogy
Qamas	Firozabadi	Arabic words dictionary
Taj-ul-Maathir	Hasan Nizami	History of Ilbaris, the slave dynasty
Chach Namah	Abu Bakr	History of Sindh region
Lubab-ul-Alab	Bhukhari	Persian anthology
Khamsah	Amir khusrau	Literature and Poems
Shah Namah	Firdausi	About Mohmud Ghazni's reign
Kitab-ul-Rehla	lbn Battutah	A travelogue with stories
Miftah-ul-Futuh	Amir Khusrau	Jalaluddin's conquest and life
Multa-ul-Anwar	Amir Khusrau	Literary masterpieces
Ayina-i-Sikandari	Amir Khusrau	Literary masterpieces
Hasht Bihisht	Amir Khusrau	Literary masterpieces
Shirin Khusrau	Amir Khusrau	Literary masterpieces
Tarik-i-Firoz Shahi	Shams-i-Shiraj Afif	History of Tughlaqs
Futuh-us-Salatin	Isami	About Bahmani Kingdom

9.II. Vijayanagar and Other Kingdoms

VIJAYANAGAR EMPIRE : 1336-1565 AD

➢ Vijayanagar kingdom and the city were founded by Harihar and Bukka (sons of Sangama) who were feudatories of Kakatiyas and later became minister in the court of Kampili.

➢ Vijayanagar kingdom lay in the Deccan, to the south of the Bahmani kingdom.

➢ Vijayanagar period can be divided into four distinct dynasties viz. Sangama, Saluva, Tuluva and Aravidu.

The Sangama Dynasty : 1336-1485 AD

➢ **Harihara I and Bukka I (1336-56) :** They laid the foundation of Vijaya-nagar. Vijayanagar-Bahamani conflict began with the foundation of kingdoms. Clash of interests in three areas : Raichur doab (between Krishna and Tungabhadra), Krishna-Godavari delta and Marathwada.

Dynasty	Period	Founder
Sangama	1336-1485	Harihar and Bukka
Saluva	1485-1505	Saluva Narsimha
Tuluva	1505-1570	Veer Narsimha
Aravidu	1570-1650	Tirumala

➢ **Bukka I (1356-79) :** Bukka I strengthened the city of Vidyanagar and renamed it Vijayanagar. He restored harmony between the warring Vaishnavas and the Jains. The Rais of Malabar, Ceylon and other countries kept ambassadors at his court.

➢ **Harihar II (1379-1404) :** Bukka I was succeeded by his son Harihar II.

➢ **Deva Raya I (1406-22) :** He was the third son of Harihara II. His greatest achievement was his irrigation works where a dam was built across the Tungabhadra, with canals leading to the city. *Nicolo de conti* visited Vijayanagar during his reign.

➢ **Deva Raya II (1423-46) :** He was the grandson of Deva Raya I. Ahmad Shah I of Bahamani invaded Vijayanagar and exacted a war indemnity. Deva Raya II began the practice of employing Muslim cavalrymen and archers in the army on large scale (Their induction had began during Deva Raya I). He was called *Praudh Deva Raya*. In his inscriptions he has the title of *Gajabetekara* (the elephant hunter). Sri Lanka paid a regular tribute to him. He had learning for Vira Shavism, yet he respected other religions. *Dindima* was the court poet, whereas *Srinatha* was given the title of 'Kavisarvabhauma'. *Abdur Razzak*, the envoy of Shah Rukh visited Vijayanagar during his reign.

The Saluva Dynasty : 1486-1505 AD

➢ **Saluva Narsimha (1486-91) :** He founded the Saluva dynasty.

➢ **Tirumal (1491) and Immadi Narasimha (1491-1505) :** Both were minors during the regency of *Narsa Nayaka*. *Vosco Da Gama* landed in Calicut during his reign in 1498.

The Tuluva Dynasty : 1505-70 AD

➢ **Vira Narsimha (1505-09) :** Vir Narsimha, the son of Narsa Nayaka, became the king after the assassination of Immadi Narsimha, the last Saluva ruler.

Krishna Deva Raya : 1509-29 AD

➢ Saluva Timma, the chief minister of Vira Narsimha, placed Krishna Deva Raya, the brother of Vira Narsimha, on the throne.

➢ Krishna Deva Raya maintained friendly relations with *Albuquerque*, the Portuguese governor, whose ambassador Friar Luis resided in Vijayanagar. He won Orissa (Gajapti kingdom) for Vijayanagar and Vijayanagar emerged strongest during his reign.

- He built the *Vijaya Mahal* (House of Victory), the *Hazara Rama temple* and the *Vithal Swami temple*.
- He took the titles of *Yavanaraja Sthapnachrya* (restorer of the Yavana kingdom i.e. Bidar kingdom) and *Abhinava Bhoja*. He is also known as *Andhra Bhoj* and *Andhra Pitamaha*.
- He was a gifted scholar in both Telugu and Sanskrit, of which only two works are extant : the Telugu work on polity *'Amuktamalyada'* and the Sanskrit drama *'Jambavati Kalyanam'*.
- His court was adorned by the 'Ashtadiggajas' (the eight celebrated poets of Telugu) : 1.*Peddana* ('Manucharitam') 2. *Timmaya* ('Parijata Apaharanama') 3. *Bhattamurthi* 4.*Dhurjati* 5. *Mallan* 6. *Raju Ramchandra* 7. *Surona* 8. *Tenali Ramkrisha* ('Panduranga Mahamatya').
- Krishna Deva Raya, a contemporary of *Babur*, was the most illustrious ruler of the Deccan.
- *Duarte Barbosa* and *Dominigo Paes*, Portuguese travellers, visited Vijaya-nagar during the time of Krishna Deva Raya.
- **Achyuta Deva Raya (1529-42) :** Krishna Deva Raya nominated his brother Achyuta Deva Raya as the successor. During his reign, *Farnao Nunij*, a Portugese horse trader, visited Vijayanagar.
- **Venkata I (1542) and Sadashiva Raya (1543-76) :** Real power was exercised by *Rama Raja/Raya* and his two brothers. The five successor states of the Bahamani empire were divided through Rama Raja's diplomacy. The *Battle of Talikota* (also called the *Battle of Rakshasa–Tangadi*) was fought on 23 Jan., 1565. Rama Raja was taken prisoner and executed by Hussain Nizam Shah I. The city of Vijayanagar, which was the pride of medieval world, was mercilessly destroyed. *Caesar Frederick*, a Portuguese traveller, visited Vijayanagar in 1567-68 during the reign of Sadashiva Raya.

The Aravidu Dynasty : 1570-1650 AD

- Tirumala Raya, the brother of Rama Raja, ruled in the name of Sadasiva Raya. On his failure to repopulate Vijayanagar, he shifted the capital to *Penugonda*. He divided his empire into three practically linguistic sections.
- The empire slowly shrunk and the Aravidu dynasty ended in 1646.

Administration

- *Nayankar System* was the special feature of provincial administration.
- *Ayngar System* was the special feature of village administration. A body of 12 functionaries, known as ayangars, conducted village affairs.
- They were granted tax free lands *'Manyams'* which they were to enjoy in perpetuity.

Administrative unit	Head
Mandalam (i.e. Province)	Mandaleswar
Nadu (i.e. District)	Naduprabhu
Gram (i.e. Village)	Gauda

- The Vijayanagar rulers issued gold coins called *Varahas* or *Pagodas*. The *Perta* was half a Varaha. *The Fanam* was one tenth of Perta. All were of gold mixed with alloy. The *Tar* was a silver coin. The *Jital* was a copper coin.

Society

➢ It was the only empire in Medieval India which employed women in the state services. Women even went to battles. Also, it was only state that promoted widow remarriage. Status of women improved during this time.

➢ Viprulu : Brahmins, Rajulu : Kshatriya, Nalavajativaru : Shudras Vipravinodins : Artisans, Kaikollas : Weavers, Sahagaman : Sati, Besabaga : Forced labour.

Architecture

➢ The Vijayanagar rulers produced a new style of architecture called as *Provida* style. The large number and prominence of pillars and piers are some of the distinct features. Horse was the most common animal on the pillars.

➢ Another important features were the *Mandapa* or open pavillion with a raised platform, meant for seating deities and *Amman Shrine*.

➢ Important temples were *Vithalswami* and *Hazara Rama Temple* at Hampi, *Tadapatri* and *Parvati temples* at Chidambaram and *Varadraja* and *Ekambarnath temples* at Kanchipuram.

➢ The Vijayanagar rulers started the practice of inscribing the stories of the Ramayana and the Mahabharata on the walls of the various temples. Vithalswami and Hazara Rama Temple are examples of this type of wall inscription.

Bahmani Kingdom

➢ **Alauddin Hasan Bahman Shah (1347-58) :** He was also known as *Hasan Gangu*. He founded the Bahmani kingdom with its capital at *Gulbarga* (First capital).

➢ **Tajuddin Firoz Shah(1397-1422) :** The greatest among them all. He was determined to make Deccan the cultural centre in India. He inducted large number of Hindus in the administration on large scale. He paid much attention to the ports of his kingdom, Chaul and Dabhol which attracted trade ships from Persian Gulf and Red Sea.

➢ **Ahmad Shah Wali(1422-35) :** Transferred the capital from Gulbarga to Bidar.

Break up of Bahmani Empire into 5 Kingdoms

5 Kingdoms	Year	Founder	Dynasty	Annexation (by)
1. Berar	1484	Fataullah Imad Shah	Imad Shahi	1574 (Ahmadnagar)
2. Bijapur	1489	Yusuf Adil Shah	Adil Shahi	1686 (Aurangzeb)
3. Ahmadnagar	1490	Malik Ahmad	Nizam Shahi	1633 (Shahjahan)
4. Golconda	1518	Quli Qutub Shah	Qutub Shahi	1687(Aurangzeb)
5. Bidar	1526-27	Amir Ali Barid	Barid Shahi	1610(Bijapur)

➢ *Ibrahim Adil Shah*, the greatest ruler of Adil Shahi dynasty, introduced *Dakhini* in place of Persian as court language.

➢ *Gol Gumbaj* was built by *Muhammad Adil Shah;* it is famous for the so-called 'Whispering Gallery'.

➢ *Quli Qutub Shah* built the famous *Golconda Fort*.

➢ *Muhammad Quli Qutub Shah* was the greatest ruler of Qutub Shahi dynasty and it was he who founded the city of *Hyderabad* originally known as *Bhagyanagar* after the name of the Sultan's favourite, Bhagyamati and he also built the famous *Charminar*.

Other Provincial Kingdoms

Kingdon	Capital	Founder
Jaunpur (Sharqui)	Jaunpur	Malik Sarwar (Khwaja Jaha)
Malwa	Dhar, Mandu	Dilawar Khan Ghori
Gujarat	Ahmadabad	Ahmad Jafar Khan Muzaffar shah
Bengal	Lakhnauti, Pandua, Ekdala	Shamsuddin Iliyas Shah
Khandesh	Burhanpur and Asirgadh	Malik Raza Faruqui

10. Religious Movements in 15th-16th Centuries

I. Bhakti Movement

➢ The Bahkti movement was based on the doctrine that the relationship between God and man is through love and worship rather than through performing any ritual or religious ceremonies.

➢ It was in South India for the first time that Bahkti movement grew from a mere religious doctrine to a broad based popular movement based on social and religious equality. It was led by popular saint poets called '*Alvars*', who represented emotional side of Vaishnavism through collective songs called *Prabandhas*. It declined after the 10th century.

➢ But it was revived as a philosophical and ideological movement by '*Acharyas*' (who represented intellectual side of Vaishnavism in the 11th century). Most important among them was *Ramanuja*, whose disciple *Ramananda* took it to North India.

➢ **Main Features** : 1. Discarded rituals and sacrifices 2. Emphasised purity of heart and mind, humanism and devotion 3. Monotheistic in nature 4. God has either form *(Saguna)* or be formless *(Nirguna)* 5. Knowledge was a constituent part 6. An egalitarian movement. Denounced casteism. 7. Best form of worship is singing Bhajans and realisation of God by personal effort. No need of priestly class 8. Saint, preached in local languages.

Philosophy	Founder
Vishishtadvaita	Ramanuj Acharya
Dvaitadvaita / Bhedabhed	Nimbark Acharya
Dvait	Madhva Acharya
Shuddhadvaita	Vishnu Swami

Bhakti Saints

➢ **Ramanuja (1017-1137)** : The Vaishnava saint from South India. The earliest exponent of Bhakti movement and *Vishitadvaita* philosophy.

➢ **Ramananda (14-15 Century)** : The first great Bhakti saint of North India who opened the doors of Bhakti without any distinction of birth, caste, creed or sex.

- **Kabir (1440-1510) :** The most radical disciple of Ramananda, who was opposed to caste, creed, image worship, unnecessary rituals and sought to remove distinction between Hindus and Muslims and believed in social unity.
- **Guru Nanak (1469-1538) :** A Nirguna Bhakti saint and social reformer. The first Sikh Guru and founder of Sikhism.
- **Chaitanya (1486-1533) :** One of the great saints of Krishna Bhakti cult and founder of *Gaudiya* or *Bengal Vaishnavism*.
- **Vidyapati (14-15th Century) :** Maithili saint-poet who wrote thousands of love-ballads on Radha-Krishna ('Padavali').
- **Purandar Das (1480-1564) :** The foremost and the most prolific Vaishnav saint-composer in Karnataka. Believed to have laid the foundations of the modern phase of Karnataka music.
- **Mirabai (1498-1546) :** The Rathor princess of Merata and daughter-in-law of Rana Sanga of Mewar. The most well-known woman Bhakti saint of the Krishna cult of Vaishnavism.
- **Vallabhacharya (1479-1531) :** A great saint of the Krishna Bhakti cult of Vaishnavism, who propounded the philosophy of *Pushti Marg*.
- **Surdas (1483-1563) :** A blind poet of Agra. He sang the glory of krishna in his *'Sursagar'*.
- **Tulsidas (1532-1623) :** The greatest saint-poet of the Ram Bhakti cult of Vaishnavism. The celebrated author of *'Ramcharitamanas'*, *'Kavitawali'* and *'Gitawali'*.
- **Shankara Deva (1449-1568) :** The founder of the Vaishnava devotional movement in Assam.
- **Dadu Dayal (1544-1603) :** A Nirguna Bhakti saint belonging to the tanner caste, who was born in Gujarat but spent his whole life in Rajasthan. Founder of the *Dadu panth*.
- **Thyagaraja (1767-1847) :** A Telugu who spent his life in Tamil Nadu. The greatest saint-composer of Karnataka music. He adorned God in the form of Rama, the incarnation of Vishnu and Hero of Valmiki's Ramayana.

Bhakti saints of Maharashtra Dharma

- **Jnanesvara/Jnanadeva (1271-1296) :** The fountain-head of the Bhakti movement in Maharashtra, founder of Marathi language and literature, wrote a long commentary on the *Bhagvad Gita*, called the *'Bhavarthadipka'*, more commonly known as *'Jnaneshvari'*.
- **Namadeva (1270-1350) :** A contemporary of Jnanesvara. He was a tailor by caste and was opposed to all caste distinctions. The object of his devotion was *Vithoba* or *Vithal* (identified with Vishnu) of Pandharpur. The cult of Vithoba or Vithal known as *Varkari* sect was founded by Namadeva.
- **Eknath (1533-1599) :** A great scholar saint from Maharashtra who wrote a commentary on the Ramayana called the *'Bhavartha Ramayana'* and another commentary on the eleventh book of the Bhagavata Purana.

➢ **Tukaram (1598-1650) :** The greatest Bhakti poet from Maharashtra, wrote devotional poems, known as *Abhangas*, which are the glory of devotional poetry.

➢ **Ramdas (1608-1681) :** The last great saint poet from Maharashtra. '*Dasabodha*' is the compilation of his writings and sermons.

II. SUFI MOVEMENT

➢ Sufism is the mystical movement in Islam. The sufis while accepting the Shariat did not confine their religious practice to formal adherence and stressed cultivation of religious experience aimed at direct perception of God.

➢ The sufi doctrine was based on union with God which can be achieved through love of God, prayers, fasts and rituals, without reference to Hindu or Muslim.

➢ **Main Features :** 1. Organised in different *Silsilas* (orders) 2. Absorbed variety of ideas and practices from Hinduism, Christianity, Buddhism and Zorastrianism. 3. Sufis aimed at service of mankind through spiritual self development 4. Eager for Hindu-Muslim unity and cultural synthesis 5. Opposed to orthodoxy, they preached faith and devotion to God. 6. Discouraged materialistic life but not in favour of complete renunciation.

Sufi Saints

➢ **Khwaja Ali Hujjwiri (11th Century) :** Also Known as *Data Ganj Baksh*, the earliest Sufi saint of eminence known to have settled in India, the author of the celebrated manual of Sufism entitled '*Kashf-ul-Mahjub*'.

➢ **Shaikh Bahauddin Zakariya (1182-1262) :** The founder of the *Suhara-wardi* order who founded the first leading *Khanqah* in India at Multan.

➢ **Khwaja Muinuddin Chisti (1141-1236) :** The founder of the *Chisti* order-the first and most popular liberal Sufi order in India. He settled down at Ajmer about 1206. Other Chisti Sufi saints who followed khwaja Muinuddin Chisti or Khwaja Ajmeri were: *Sheikh Hamiduddin Nagauri* (1192-1274); *Khwaja Qutubuddin Bakhtiyar Kaki*, (died 1236) in whose memory Qutub Minar was built by Iltutmish; *Baba Fariduddin Ganj-i-Shakar* (1175-1265) popularly known as *Baba Farid*, built his Khanqah at Ajodan (Punjab) and was the first great Punjabi poet of Sufism; *Shaikh Nizamuddin Auliya* (1236-1325) who gained the popular title *Mehboob-i-Ilahi* (the beloved of the God), built his Khanqah in Delhi and was one of the most famous Sufi saint of the Chisti Order; *Shaikh Nasiruddin Mahmud* (d.1365), the charismatic Chisti saint, who was later known as *Chirag-i-Delhi* (the Lamp of Delhi); *Syed Muhammad Gesu Daraz* (d. 1421) who settled down at Gulbarga (Karnataka) was popularly known as *Bandanawaz* (Benefactor of God's creatures) and authored more than 30 books on Sufism-he was one of the early writers and poets in Urdu.

➢ **Shaikh Badruddin Samarkandi (13 Century) :** Founded *Firdausi* order which was restricted to Bihar.

➢ **Shah Nayamatu lah Qadiri and Shah Abdullah Shuttari (15th Century) :** Shah Nayamatullah Qadiri founded the *Qadiriya* order and Shah Abdullah Shuttari (d. 1458) founded the *Shuttari* order. The former spread in Uttar Pradesh and Deccan, while the latter spread mainly in Madhya pradesh and Gujarat. *Miyan Mir* (1550-1635) was the most popular Sufi saint of the Qadiriya order.

Sufi Words	Meaning
Tasawwuf	Sufism
Shaikh/Pir/Murshid	Spiritual teacher
Murid	Disciple
Khalifah	Successor
Khanqah	The hospice
Sama	Musical recital
Raksa	Dance
Fana	Self annihlation

➢ **Khwaja Baqi Billah (1536-1603) :** Founded the *Naqsbandiah* order and its most famous saint was *Shaikh Ahmad Sirhindi* (d.1625) known as *Mujaddid Alif*.

Achievements of Bhakti and Sufi Movements

1. They influenced each other and inherited from each other 2. Bhaktism reformed Hinduism and Sufism liberalised Islam 3. Both put breaks on orthodoxy. 4. Both encouraged social reform measures 5. Atmosphere of inter-religious fraternity was created. Hindu and Muslims reconciled 6. Development of regional languages 7. A cultural synthesis took place which transformed a Muslim rule in India to a national govt. under Akbar.

11. Mughal Period (1526-40 and 1555-1857)

Babur : 1526-30

➢ The foundation of the Mughal rule in India was laid by Babur in 1526.

➢ He was a descendant of Timur (from the side of his father) and Chengiz Khan (from the side of his mother).

➢ Babur defeated *Ibrahim Lodhi* in the *first battle of Panipat* on April 21, 1526 and established Mughal dynasty which lasted till the establishment of British rule in India.

➢ In 1527, he defeated *Rana Sanga* of Mewar at *Khanwa*.

➢ In 1528, he defeated *Medini Rai* of Chaneri at *Chanderi*.

➢ In 1529, he efeated *Muhammad Lodhi* (uncle of Ibrahim Lodhi) at *Ghaghra*.

➢ In 1530, he died at Agra. His tomb is at Kabul.

➢ He adopted *Tughluma* and flanking party system and first to use gunpowder and artillery in India.

➢ He wrote his autobiography *Tuzuk-i-Baburi* in Turki in which he gives an excellent account of India and his empire. Tuzuk-i-Baburi was translated in Persian (named *Baburnama*) by *Abdur Rahim Khanekhana* and in English by *Madam Bebridge*.

➢ He compiled two anthologies of poems, *Diwan* (in Turki) and *Mubaiyan* (in Persian). He also wrote *Risal-i-Usaz* or letters of Babur.

Humayun : 1530-40 and 1555-56

➢ He was the son of Babur and ascended the throne in 1530. His succession was challenged by his brothers *Kamran, Hindal* and *Askari* alongwith the Afghans.

➢ He fought two battles against *Sher Shah* at *Chausa* (1539) and at *Kannauj/Bilgram* (1540) and was completely defeated by him.

➢ He escaped to Iran where he passed 12 years of his life in exile.

➢ After Sher Shah's death Humayun invaded India in 1555 and defeated his brothers the Afghans. He once again became the ruler of India.

➢ He died while climbing down the stairs of his library (at *Din Panah*) in 1556 and was burried in Delhi.

➢ His sister, *Gulbadan Begum*, wrote his biography *Humayunama*.

➢ He built *Din Panah* at Delhi as his second capital.

Sur Empire (Second Afghan Empire) : 1540-55

Sher Shah : 1540-45

➢ He was the son of *Hasan Khan*, the Jagirdar of Sasaram. Ibrahim Lodhi transferred his father's jagir to him.

➢ In 1527-28, he joined Babur's service and then returned to South Bihar as deputy governor and guardian of the minor king Jalal Khan Lohani, son of Bahar Khan Lohani.

➢ Sher Shah usurps throne as *Hazarat-i-Ala*. He gained Chunar by marrying *Lad Malika*, the widow of governor of Chunar Fort.

➢ In 1539, he defeated Humayun in the *battle of Chausa* and assumed the title *Sher Shah* as emperor.

➢ In 1540, he defeated Humayun in the *battle of Kannauj/Bilgram* and annexed Kannauj.

➢ As an emperor, he conquested Malwa (1542), Ranthambhor (1542), Raisin (1543), Rajputana-annexation of Marwar (1542), Chittor (1544) and Kalinjar (1545). He died in 1545 while conquesting Kalinjar.

Adminstrative Unit	Head
Iqta (i.e. Province)	Haqim and Amin
Sarkar (i.e. District)	Shiqdar-i-Shiaqdaran and Munsif-i-Munsifan
Pargana (i.e. Taluka)	Shiqdar and Munsif
Gram (i.e. Village)	Muqaddam and Amil

➢ During his brief reign of 5 years he introduced a brilliant administration, land revenue policy and several other measures to improve the economic conditions of his subjects.

➢ He issued the coin called *Rupia* and fixed standard weights and measures all over the empire.

➢ He also improved communications by building several highways. He built the *Grand Trunk Road* (G.T. Road), that runs from Calcutta to Peshawar.

➢ He set up cantonment in various parts of his empire and strong garrison was posted in each cantonments.

- He introduced the principle of local responsibility for local crimes. Muqaddams were punished for failure to find culprits.
- Land was measured and 1/3rd of the average was fixed as land tax. The peasant was given a *patta* (title deed) and a *qabuliyat* (deed of agreement) which fixed the peasant's rights and taxes. Zamindar were removed and the taxes were directly collected.
- He built *Purana Quila* at Delhi.
- He was buried in Sasaram.
- Sher Shah was succeded by *Islam Shah* (1545-54); Islam Shah by *Muhammad Adil Shah* (1554-55).

Akbar : 1556-1605

- Akbar, the eldest son of Humayun, ascended the throne under the title of *Jalaluddin Muhammad Akbar Badshah Ghazi* at the young age of 14 at *Kalanaur*, Punjab and his tutor *Bairam Khan* was appointed as the regent.
- *Second Battle of Panipat* (5 Nov., 1556) was fought between *Hemu* (the Hindu General of Muhammad Adil Shah) and Bairam Khan (the regent of Akbar). Hemu was defeated, captured and slain by Bairam Khan.
- This war ended the Mughal-Afghan contest for the throne of Delhi in favour of the Mughals and enabled Akbar to reoccupy Delhi and Agra.
- Akbar ended the regency of Bairam Khan in 1560 and at the age of 18 assumed the reigns of the kingdom.
- Akbar was under the influence of Maham Anga and Adham Khan junta from 1560 to 1562. [Petticoat Govt. : 1560-62]
- In his bid to expand his empire he conquered various provincial states.
- The Rajputa kingdom of Mewar put up a fierce defence under *Rana Uday Singh* (1537-72) and his son *Rana Pratap* (1572-97).
- Akbar tried to win over the Rajputas wherever possible and inducted Rajputa kings into Mughal service and treated them at par with Mughal nobility. By marrying *Harakha Bai*, daughter of *Bharmal/Biharimal* (Kutchhwaha Rajputa Ruler of Amer, Capital–Jaipur) in 1562. Akbar displayed his secular policy with the Hindus. Most of the Rajputa Kings recognised the supremacy of Akbar except Rana Pratap Singh and his son Amar Singh (Sisodiya Rajputas of Mewar, Capital-Chittor).
- The *Battle of Haldighati* (1576) was fought between *Rana Pratap* of Mewar and Mughal army led by *Man Singh* of Amer. Rana Pratap was defeated but he did not submit and continued the struggle.

Akbar's Conquests

Year	Province	From
1560-62	Malwa	Baz Bahadur
1561	Chunar	Afghan
1562	Merata	Jaimal
1564	Gondwana (Gadh Katanga)	Rani Durgawati (regent of Bir Narayan)

Year	Province	From
1568	Chittor	Rana Uday Singh
1569	Ranthambor	Surjan Hada
1569	Kalinjar	Ram Chandra
1570	Marwar	Chandrasena, Kalyanmal, Raj Singh, Rawal Harirai
1572	Gujarat	Bahadur Shah
1574-76	Bengal-Bihar	Daud Khan Karrani
1576	Haldighati	Rana Pratap
1581	Kabul	Mirza Hakim
1585-86	Kashmir	Yusuf Khan and Yakub Khan
1590-91	Sindh	Jani Beg Mirza
1590-92	Orissa	Kutul Khan and Nisar Khan
1591	Khandesh	Ali Khan
1595	Baluchistan	Yusufzai Tribes
1595	Kandhar	Muzaffar Husain Mirza
1597-1600	Ahmadnagar	Chand Bibi (regent of Bahadur Shah)
1601	Asirgarh	Miran Bahadur Khan

➢ As a revolt against the orthodoxy and bigotry of religious priests, Akbar proclaimed a new religion, *Din-i-Ilahi*, in 1581. The new religion was based on a synthesis of values taken from several religions like Hinduism, Islam, Jainism and Christianity. It did not recognize the prophet, *Birbal* was the only Hindu who followed this new religion. Din-i-Ilahi, however, did not become popular.

➢ Akbar built *Fatehpur Sikri*, *Agra Fort*, *Lahore Fort* and *Allahabad Fort* and *Humayun's Tomb* at Delhi. Fatehpur Sikri, place near Agra–it is said that Akbar had no son for a long time. *Sheikh Salim Chisti*, a Sufi saint blessed Akbar with a son who was named *Salim/Sheikho Baba* (Jahangir). In honour of Salim Chisti, Akbar shifted his court from Agra to Fatehpur Sikri.

Important Years of Akbar	
1562	Visited Ajmer first time
1562	Ban on forcible conversion of war-prisoners into slaves
1563	Abolition of Pilgrimage Tax
1564	Abolition of Jaziya
1571	Fondation of Fatehpur Sikri
1574	Mansabadari System introduced
1575	Ibadatkhana was built
1578	Parliament of Religions in Ibadatkhana
1579	Proclamation of 'Mazhar' (written by Faizi)
1580	Dahsala Bandobast introduced
1582	Din-i-Ilahi/Tauhid-i-Ilahi
1584	Ilahi Samvat i.e. Calender
1587	Ilahi Gaz i.e. Yard

➢ He was patron of the art and in his court many persons flourished.

- **Navaratna i.e. nine jewels of Akbar :** 1. *Birbal* (administrator) 2. *Abul Fazl* (scholar and statesman) 3.*Faizi* (scholar and statesman, brother of Abul Fazl) 4. *Todarmal* (Finance Minister, *Dahsala Bandobast/Jabti*) 5. *Bhagwandas* (Mansabdar, son of Bharmal) 6. *Man Singh* (Mansabdar, Grandson of Bharmal) 7. *Tansen* (Musician) 8. *Abdur Rahim Khanekhana* (Statesman, Hindi poet) 9. *Mulla Do Pyaja*.
- *Tulsidas* ('Ramcharitamanas') also lived during Akbar's period.
- When Akbar died, he was buried at *Sikandara* near Agra.
- Akbar is considered 'the real founder of the Mughal empire' in India.
- He was the first Mughal ruler who divorced religion from politics.
- *Birbal* was killed in the battle with Yusufzai Tribe (1586).
- *Abul Fazl* was murdered by *Bir Singh Bundela* (1601).
- Akbar gave Mughal India one official language (Persian).

Jahangir : 1605-27

- Salim, son of Akbar, came to the throne after Akbar's death in 1605. He issued 12 ordinances.
- He is known for his strict administration of justice. He established *Zanjir-i-Adal* (i.e. Chain of Justice) at Agra Fort for the seekers of royal justice.
- In 1611, Jahangir married *Mihar-un-nisa*, widow of Sher Afghan, a Persian nobleman of Bengal. Later on she was given the title *Nurjahan*. Nurjahan excercised tremendous influence over the state affairs. She was made the official *Padshah Begum*.
- Jahangir issued coins jointly in Nurjahan's name and his own.
- Jahangir also married *Manmati/Jagat Gosai/JodhaBai* of Marwar, and a Kachhwaha princess.
- In 1608, *Captain William Hawkins*, a representative of East India Company came to Jahangir's court. He was given the mansab of 400. In 1615 *Sir Thomas Roe*, an ambassador of King James I of England also came to his court. Though initially Jahangir resisted, later on he granted permission to the English to establish a trading port at Surat.
- A political triumph during Jahangir reign was the submission of *Rana Amar Singh* of Mewar (1615). Jahangir captured the strong fort of Kangara (1620). A part of Ahmadnagar was also annexed. *Malik Amber* ceded back to the Mughal the territory of Balaghat (Maharashtra).
- His reign was marked by several revolts. His son *Khusrau*, who received patronage of 5th Sikh Guru *Arjun Dev*, revolted against Jahangir (1605). Arjun Dev, was later sentenced to death for his blessing to the rebel prince (1606). During his last period, *Khurram (Shanjahan)*, son of Jahangir, and *Mahavat Khan*, military general of Jahangir also revolted (Khurram : 1622-25 and Mahavat Khan : 1626-27).
- He wrote his memoirs *Tuzuk-i-Jahangiri* in Persian.
- He was buried in Lahore.

Shahjahan : 1628-58

➢ Mother's name-*Jagat Gosai/Jodha Bai* (daughter of Raja Jagat Singh).
➢ Shahjahan ascended the throne in 1628 after his father's death.
➢ He was best known for his Deccan and foreign policies.
➢ The first thing that he had to face was revolts in Bundelkhand (Jujhar Singh Bundela of Orchha : 1628-35) and the Deccan (Khan-i-Jahan Lodhi, the governor of Deccan : 1629-31)
➢ Three years after his accession, his beloved wife *Mumtaj Mahal* (original name-*Arzumand Bano*) died in 1631. To perpetuate her memory he built the Taj Mahal at Agra in 1632-53.
➢ In 1631-32, he defeated the Portuguese.
➢ In addition to Jahangir's empire, Nizam Shahi's dynasty of Ahmadnagar was brought under Mughal control (1633) by Shahjahan. The Deccan Sultanate of Bijapur and Golconda accepted his suzreignty in 1636.
➢ He sent his army to Balkh in order to secure the defence of North-Western India (1647). Shajahan who had recovered Kandhar (Afghanistan) in 1638 from the Iranians lost it again in 1647 despite three campaigns under prince Murad, Aurangzeb and Dara.
➢ Shahjahan's reign is described by French traveller *Bernier* and *Tavernier* and the Italian traveller *Nicoli Manucci*. *Peter Mundi* described the famine that occured during Shahjahan's time.
➢ Shahjahan's reign is said to have marked the pinnacle of the Mughal dynasty and empire. He is known for the promotion of art, culture and architecture during his time. The *Red Fort, Jama Masjid* and *Taj Mahal* are some of the magnificent structures built during his reign.
➢ Shahjahan's failing health set off the war of succession among his four sons in 1657. Aurangzeb emerged the victor who crowned himself in July 1658. Shahjahan was imprisoned by his son Aurangzeb in the Agra Fort where he died in captivity in 1666. He was buried at Taj (Agra).

War of Succession		
War of Bahadurpur, near Banaras	Feb. 1658	Dara and Shah Shuja
War of Dharmat, near Ujjain	April 1658	Dara and Aurangzeb-Murad
War of Sumugarh, near Agra	May 1658	Dara and Aurangzeb-Murad
War of Khajua, near Allahabad	Dec. 1658	Aurangzeb and Shah Shuja
War of Deorai, near Ajmer	Mar. 1659	Aurangzeb and Dara

Aurangzeb : 1658-1707

➢ Aurangzeb defeated Dara at Dharmat (1658), Samugarh (1658) and Deorai in which Samugarh was decisive one and Deorai was last one.
➢ After victory, Aurangzeb was crowned at Delhi under the title *Alamgir*. He ruled for 50 years till his death in Feb., 1707 in Ahmadnagar.
➢ During the first 23 years of the rule (1658-81) Aurangazeb concentrated on North India. During this period the Marathas under *Shivaji* rose to power and were a force to reckon with.

- Aurangzeb captured *Guru Teg Bahadur*, the 9th Guru of Sikhs in 1675 and executed him when he refused to embrace Islam. The 10th and last Sikh Guru, *Guru Gobind Singh*, son of Guru Teg Bahadur, organised his followers into community of warrior called *Khalsa* to fight the Muslim tyranny and avenge the killing of his father. Guru Gobind Singh was, however assassinated in 1708 by an Afghan at Nander in Deccan. *Banda Bairagi*, a trusted disciple successor of Guru Gobind Singh continued the war against Mughals.

Revolts During Aurangzeb's reign

Revolts	Year of Beginning	Leaders	Causes
I. North India (1658-81)			
Jat	1669	Gokula, Rajaram, Churamani	Agrarian policy
Bundela	1671	Champat Rai, Chhatrasal	Political and religious
Satnami	1673	Followers of Satnami Sect	Religious suppression
Sikh	1675	Guru Teg Bahadur, Guru Gobind Singh	Religious
Rajput: Rathor (Marwar)	1678	Durgadas (General of Ajit singh)	Succession to throne of Marwar
II. South India (1682-1707)			
Annexation of Bijapur	1686	Sikandar Adil Shah	Violation of treaty
Annexation of Golconda	1687	Abul Hasan Kutub Shah	Helping attitude to Maratha
Mughal-Maratha Struggle	1689	Sambhaji, Rajaram, Tarabai	Rising aspiration of Maratha nationalism

- Aurangzeb left the North in 1682 and for the next 25 years (1682-1707) made desperate bids to crush the Marathas.
- Shivaji was the most powerful Maratha king and an arch enemy of Aurangzeb. When Aurangzeb could not eliminate him, he conspired in 1665 with Jai Singh of Amber, a Rajput, to eliminate Shivaji. On a assurance given by Jai Singh, Shivaji visited Aurangzeb's court. Shivaji was imprisoned by Aurangzeb but he managed to escape and in 1674 proclaimed himself an independent monarch. He died in 1680 and was succeeded by his son Sambhaji, who was executed by Aurangzeb in 1689. Sambhaji was succeeded by his brother Rajaram and after his death in 1700, his widow Tarabai carried on the movements.
- The mughal conquests reached a climax during Aurangzeb's reign, as Bijapur and Golconda were annexed in 1686 and 1687, respectively.
- Aurangzeb died in 1707. He was buried at Khuldabed (Daulatabad).
- He was called *Zinda Pir*, the living saint.

➢ *Jaziya* was re-introduced. However, the Hindu Mansabdars maintained their high proportion during his rule.

➢ **Decline of the Mughal Empire:** After Aurangzeb, the Mughal empire rapidly declined. Important causes of the decline were: 1. Aurangzeb's Rajputa, Deccan and religious policies 2. Weak successors who were incompetent both as administrators and generals 3. Wars of succession 4. Factionalism among nobality after Aurangzeb 5. Jagirdari crisis 6. Growth of Maratha and other regional powers in Bengal, Hyderabad, Avadh, Mysore etc. 7. Foreign invasions by *Nadir Shah* (1739) and *Abdali*. 8. British conquest of India.

Important Years of Aurangzeb's religious policy	
1659	Forbade inscription of kalama on the coins, celebration of Nauroj Festival; Appointment of *Muhatasib* (Regulator of moral character)
1663	Ban on Sati custom
1668	Ban on Hindu Festival
1669	Ban on Jharokha darshan, Forbade music in the court.
1670	Ban on Tuladan (weighing of the emperor)
1679	Re-introduction of *Jaziya.*

Later Mughals

Bahadur Shah I (1707-1712) : Original Name-*Muazzam*, Title-*Shah Alam I.*

Jahandar shah (1712-1713) : Ascended the throne with the help of Zulfikar Khan; Abolished Jaziya.

Farrukh Siyar (1713-1719) : Ascended the throne with the help of Sayyid brothers–Abduall Khan and Hussain Khan.

Muhammad Shah (1719-1748) : In 1738-39, *Nadir Shah* raided India and took away Thakht-i-Taus (the peacock throne) and Kohinoor diamond.

Ahmed Shah (1748-1754) : Ahmad shah Abdali (General of Nadir Shah) marched towards Delhi and Mughals ceded Punjab and Multan.

Alamgir II (1754-1759) : Ahmad Shah occupied Delhi. Later, Delhi was plundered by Marathas.

Shah Alam II (1759-1806) : Nazib Khan became very powerful in Delhi so much so that he could not enter Delhi for 12 years.

Akbar II (1806-1837) : Pensioner of East India Company.

Bahadur Shah II (1837-1857) : Last Mughal Emperor who was made premier during 1857 revolt. He was deported to *Rangoon* (Burma, now Mayanmar) in 1858 where he died in 1862.

Administration

➢ Mughal empire was divided into *Subas* which were further subsidvided into *Sarkar, Pargana* and *Gram.*

➢ However, it also had other territorial units as *Khalisa* (royal land), *Jagirs* (autonomous rajyas) and *Inams* (gifted lands, mainly waste lands).

➢ There were 15 Subas (provinces) during Akbar's reign, which later increased to 20 under Aurangzeb's reign.

Administrative unit	**Incharge**
Suba (i.e. Province)	Sipahsalar / Subedar / Nizam—The Head Executive Diwan-Incharge of revenue department
Sarakar (i.e. District)	Fauzdar-Administrative Head Amal / Amalguzar-Revenue collection
Pargana (i.e. Taluka)	Siqdar-Administrative Head Amin, Qanungo-Revenue officials
Gram (i.e. Village)	Muqaddam-Headman, Patwari-Accountant

- Akbar introduced Mansabdari system. The term *Mansab* indicates the rank of its holder. Mansabdari was both civil and military. Almost the whole nobility, bureaucracy and military hold Mansabs.
- The Mughal Mansab was dual i.e. *Zat* (personal rank and pay status) and *Sawar* (number of horsemen to maintain).
- Mansabadar were of 3 categories: *Mansabadars, Amirs* and *Amir-i-umda.*
- According to pay mode they were of 2 types: *Naqdi* (paid through cash) and *Jagirdar* (paid through Jagirs).
- Jahangir added *Duaspah Sih-aspah* system i.e. one's sawar rank can be raised without raising his zat rank.
- Shahjahan added *Jama-Dami* or *Mahana Zagir* (Monthly Scale) system.
- It ultimately caused Jagirdari and agrarian crisis, which was a major cause of decline of Mughals.
- There were several methods of revenue collection in practice viz. *Kankut* (estimate), *Rai* (yield per unit area) and *Zabti* (based on the yields of crops).
- *Dahsala Bandobast* or *Zabti* : A standard method of collection based on rates of crops determined after 10 years assessment. *Todar Mal* pioneered it.
- Jagirdari system was the assignment of land in proportion to a Jagirdar's salary. Hence, every Mansabdar was entitled to a jagir if he was not paid in cash.
- *Madad-i-maash* or *Suyur ghal* or *Inam* were land grants to people of fovour / religious assignment.

Mughal Culture

- Babur built two mosques, one at Kabulibagh in Panipat and the other at Sambhal in Rohilakhand.
- *Humayun's tomb* was built by his widow *Haji Begum*.
- An unusual building at Fatehpur Sikri is *Panch Mahal*. Panch Mahal has the plan of Buddhist vihara.
- The *Mariam's palace, Diwan-i-Aam, Diwan-i-khas* at Sikri are Indian in their plan.
- *Buland Darwaja* (built after Gujarat victory), formed the main entrance to Fatehpur Sikri.

➢ *Salim Chisti's tomb* (redone in Marble by Jahangir) is the first Mughal building in pure marble). *Palace of Birbal, Palace of Tansen* are also inside the Fatehpur Sikri.

➢ Akbar also began to build his own tomb at *Sikandara* which was later completed by Jahangir.

➢ The architecture of Fatehpur Sikri is known as Epic in red sand stone.

➢ Nurjahan built *Itimad-ud-daula/Mirza Ghiyas Beg's marble tomb* at Agra, which is noticable for the first use of *pietra dura* (floral designs made up of semiprecious stones) technique.

➢ Jahangir introduced vigorous use of marble instead of red sand stone and use of pietra dura for decorative purpose.

➢ Jahangir built *Moti Masjid* in Lahore and his mausoleum at *Shahdara* (Lahore).

➢ Mosque building activity reached its climax in *Taj Mahal*. Shahjahan also built the *Jama Masjid*.

➢ Some of the important buildings built by Shahajahan at Agra are *Moti Masjid* (only Mosque of marble). *Khaas Mahal, Mussmman Burz* (Jasmine Palace where he spent his last year in captivity) etc.

➢ He laid the foundations of *Shahjahanabad* in 1637 where he built the *Red Fort* and *Takht-i-Taus (Peacock throne)*.

➢ Only building by Aurangzeb in the Red Fort is *Moti Masjid*.

➢ Only monument associated with Aurangzeb is *Bibi ka Makbara* which is the tomb of his wife *Rabbia-ud-daura* in Aurangabad.

➢ Aurangzab also built the *Badshahi Masjid* in Lohore.

➢ Humayun had takan into his service two master painter *Mir Syed Ali* and *Abdus Samad*.

➢ *Daswant* and *Basawan* were two famous painters of Akbar's court.

➢ *Abdul Hassan, Ustad Mansur* and *Bishandas* were three famous painters of Jahangir's court.

➢ Jahangir claims that he could distinguish the work of each artist in a picture.

Titles given by Mughal Ruler

Title	Person	Field	Ruler
Jagat Guru	Harivijay Suri	Jain Religion	Akbar
Zari Kalam	Mohammad Husain	Literature	Akbar
Sirin Kalam	Abdus Samad	Literature	Akbar
Raj Kavi	Faizi	Literature	Akbar
Kavi Priya	Birbal	Literature	Akbar
Nadir-ul-Asra	Ustad Mansur	Painting	Jahangir
Nadir-uz-Zaman	Abdul Hassan	Painting	Jahangir
Guna Samudra	Lal khan	Music	Shahjahan
Raj Kavi	Kalim	Literature	Shahjahan
Mahakaviray	Sundardas	Literature	Shahjahan

Literature of Mughal Period

Book	Author	Contents
Tuzuk-i-Baburi	Babur	Describes military tactics and administrative organisation during Babur's reign
Qanun-i-Humayun	Khwand Amair	Describes Humayun's administration, festivities and buildings of that period
Humayun Nama	Gulbadan Begum	Biography of Humayun
Akbar Nama	Abul Fazl	Gives a history of Akbar's reign
Tobaqat-i-Akbari	KhwajahNizamuddin Ahmad Baksh	-do-
Tuzuk-i-Jahangiri	Jahangir	Memoirs of his own reign
Iqbalnama-i-Jahangiri	Muhammad Khan	History of Jahangir's reign
Chahar Chaman	Chandra Bhan Brahman	History of Shahjahan's rule
Alamgir-nama	Munshi Mirza Muhamma Kazin	Gives an account of Aurangzeb's first 10 years of rule
Massir-i-Alamgiri	Saqi Mustaid Khan	Official history of Aurangzeb's reign written after his death
Ain-i-Akbari	Abul Fazl	History of Akbar's reign
Muntakhab-ul-Tawarikh	Badauni	History of Akbar's rule
Tawarikh-i-Alfi	Mulla Daud	-do-
Nuriyya-i-Sultaniyya	Abdul Haq	Theory of Kinship during Mughal Period
Waqt-i-Hyderabad	Nimat Khan Ali	Aurangzeb's Golconda conquest
Futuhat-i-Alamgiri	Ishwar Das	Aurangzeb's history
Nuskha-i-Dilkusha	Bhimsen Saxena	Analysis of Aurangzeb's rule and character
Khulasat-ul-Tawarikh	Sujan Raj Khatri	History of Aurangzeb's rule
Padshah Namah	Abdul Hamid Lahori	History of Shah Jahan's reign
Padshah Namah	Mumahad Waris	-do-
Shahjahan Namah	Muhammad Salih	-do-
Shahjahan Namah	Inyat Khan	-do-
Hamlai-Haidri	Muhammad Rafi Khan	History of Aurangzeb's rule
Namah-e-Alamgiri	Aquil Khan Zafar	-do-

Book	Author	Contents
Sirr-i-Akbar	Dara Shikoh	Urdu translation of Upanishad
Safinat-ul-Auliya	-do-	Biographies of Sufi Saints
Majma-ul-Bahrain	-do-	Philosophical ideas discussed
Raqqat-e-Alamgiri	Aurangzeb	A compendium of his letters
Hasmat-ul-Arifin	Dara Shikoh	Religious ideas discussed

12. Maratha State (1674-1720) and Maratha Confederacy (1720-1818)

Maratha State : 1674-1720

Shivaji : 1674-80

- Born at Shivneri Fort in 1627.
- Father-*Shahji Bhonsle*, Mother-*Jija Bai*, Religious Teacher-*Samarth Ramdas*.
- Shivaji inherited the Jagir of Poona from his father in 1637.
- After the death of his guardian, *Dadaji Kondadev*, in 1647, he assumed full charge of his Jagir.
- He conquered many Forts viz. Singh Garh/Kondana (1643), Rohind and Chakan (1644-45), Toran (1646), Purandhar (1648), Rajgarh/Raigarh (1656), Supa (1656) and Panhala (1659).
- *Afzal Khan* was deputed by Adil Shah (Ruler of Bijapur) to punish Shivaji; but the later Afzal Khan was killed by Shivaji in 1659.
- *Shaista Khan*, governor of Deccan, was deputed by Aurangzeb to put down the rising power of Shivaji in 1660. Shivaji lost Poona and suffered several defeats till he made a bold attack on Shaista Khan (1663) and plundered Surat (1664) and later Ahmadnager.
- *Raja Jai Singh* of Amber was then appointed by Aurangzeb to put down Shivaji (1665). Jai Singh succeeded in beseiging Shivaji in the fort of Purandhar. Consequently the *treaty of Purandhar* (1665) was signed according to which Shivaji ceded some forts to the Mughals and paid a visit to the Mughal court at Agra.
- In 1674 Shivaji was coronated at capital Raigarh and assumed the title of *Haindava Dharmodharak* (Protector of Hinduism).
- After that *Chhatrapati* Shivaji continued the struggle with Mughals and Siddis (Janjira). He conquested Karnataka during 1677-80.

Shivaji's Administration

- Shivaji divided his territory under his rule *(Swaraj)* into three provinces, each under a viceroy. Provinces were divided into *prants* which were subdivided into *parganas* or *tarafs*. The lowest unit was village headed by *Patel* (Headman).
- Shivaji was helped by the *ashtapradhan* (eight minister) which was unlike a collective of ministers, for there was no collective responsibility; each minister was directly responsible to Shivaji.

Shivaji's Ashtapradhan

Peshwa (Mukhya Pradhan)	Finance and general administration, later he became Prime Minister and assumed great importance.
Majumdar (Amatya)	Revenue and Finance Minister
Waqenavis (Mantri)	Home Minister
Dabir (Sumant)	Foreign Minister
Surnavis (Sachiv)	Head of Royal correspondence
Pandit Rao (Sadar)	Head of religious affairs
Sar-i-Naubat (Senapati)	Military commander. This is an honorary post with no real military powers.
Nyayadhish	Justice

- Most of the administrative reforms of Shivaji were based on Malik Ambar's (Ahmadnagar) reforms.
- Assessment of land revenue was based on measurement. The *Kathi* of Malik Ambar was adopted as the unit of measurement.
- Land revenue was fixed 1/3rd i.e. 33% of the gross produce (initially), 2/5th i.e. 40% of the gross produce (after reforms).
- *Chauth* was 1/4th i.e. 25% of the land revenue was paid to the Marathas so for not being subjected to Maratha raids.
- *Sardeshmukhi* was an additional levy of 10% on those lands of Maharashtra over which the Maratha claimed hereditary rights, but which formed part of the Mughal Empire.

Sambhaji : 1680-89

- Sambhaji, the elder son of Shivaji, defeated Rajaram, the younger son of Shivaji, in the war of succession.
- He provided protection and support to *Akbar II*, the rebellious son of Aurangzeb.
- He was captured at Sangameswar by a Mughal noble and executed.

Rajaram : 1689-1700

- He succeeded the throne with the help of the ministers at Rajgarh.
- He fled from Rajgarh to Jinji in 1689 due to a Mughal invasion in which Rajgarh was captured along with Sambhaji's wife and son (Shahu) by the Mughals.
- Rajaram died at Satara, which had become the capital after the fall of Jinji to Mughal in 1698.
- Rajaram created the new post of *Pratinidhi*, thus taking the total number of minister to nine (Pratinidhi + Ashtapradhan).

Tarabai : 1700-07

- Rajaram was succeeded by his minor son Shivaji II under the guardianship of his mother Tarabai.
- Tarabai continued the struggle with Mughals.

Shahu : 1707-1749

- Shahu was released by the Mughal emperor Bahadur Shah.
- Tarabai's army was defeated by Shahu in the *battle of Khed* (1700), and Shahu occupied Satara.
- But the Southern part of the Maratha kingdom with its capital Kolhapur continued to be under the control of the descendents of Rajaram (Shivaji II and later Shambhaji II).
- Shahu's reign saw the rise of Peshwas and transformation of the Maratha kingdom into an empire based on the principle of confederacy.

Balaji Viswanath (1713-20) : The First Peshwa

- He began his carrer as a small revenue official and was given the title of *Sena Karte* (marker of the army) by Shahu in 1708.
- He became *Peshwa* in 1713 and made the post the most important and powerful as well as hereditary.
- He played a crucial role in the final victory of Shahu by winning over almost all the Maratha Sardars to the side of Shahu.
- He concluded an agreement with the Syed Brothers-King Maker (1719) by which the Mughal emperor Farrukh Siyar recognised Shahu as the king of the Swarajya.

Maratha Confederacy : 1720-1818

Baji Rao I : 1720-40

- Baji Rao, the eldest son of Balaji Viswanath, succeeded him as *Peshwa* at the young age of 20.
- He was considered the greatest exponent of guerrilla tactics after Shivaji and Maratha power reached its zenith under him.
- Under him several Maratha families became prominent and got themselves entrenched in different parts of India.
- After defeating and expelling the Siddis of Janjira from the mainland (1722), he conquered Bassein and Salsette from the Portuguese (1739).

Kingdom	Territory
The Scindia	Gwalior
The Holkar	Indore
The Pawar	Dhar
The Gaekwad	Baroda
The Bhonsle	Nagpur
The Peshwa	Poona

- He also defeated the Nizam-ul-Mulk near Bhopal and conclucled the *treaty of Doraha Sarai* by which he got Malwa and Bundelkhand from the latter (1738).
- He led innumerable successful expeditions into North India to weaken the Mughal empire and to make the Marathas the supreme power in India.
- He said about Mughals : *'Let us strike at the trunk of the withering tree and the branches will fall of themselves'*.

Balaji Baji Rao : 1740-61

- Popularly known as *Nana Saheb*, he succeeded his father at the age of 20.

- After the death of Shahu (1749), the management of all state affairs was left in his hands.
- In an agreement with the Mughal emperor Ahmad Shah, the Peshwa was to protect the Mughal empire from internal and external enemies (like Ahmad Shah Abdali) in return for Chauth (1752).
- *Third battle of Panipat (Jan 14, 1761)* resulted in the defeat of the Marathas by Ahmad Shah Abdali and the death of Viswas Rao and Sadashiv Rao Bhau. This event shocked the Peshwa Balaji Baji Rao and after six month he also died. This battle ended the Maratha power.
- **Successors of Balaji Baji Rao :** *Madhav Rao* (1761-72), *Narayan Rao* (1772-73), *Sawai Madhav Rao* (1773-95) and *Baji Rao II* (1795-1818).

Anglo-Maratha Wars

- **First Anglo-Maratha War (1775-82) :** Favouring the cause of Raghunath Rao (Raghoba) for Peshwaship, English (Hastings) came in conflict with the Marathas. On being defeated, the British had to sign the humiliating *Convention of Wadgaon* (1779).
- British later signed *Treaty of Salbai* (1782), renouncing the cause of Raghoba.
- **Second Anglo-Maratha war (1803-06) :** The Maratha Peshwa signed the *Subsidiary Alliance Treaty of Bassein* (1802).
- The Maratha confederacy, which did not like the idea challenged the British power but were defeated by the British.
- **Third Anglo-Maratha war (1817-18) :** Lord Hastings was determined to proclaim British paramountcy in India. He moved against *Pindaris* transgressed the sovereignty of the Maratha chiefs and the war began.
- The Marathas were decisively defeated.

13. The Advent of the Europeans

Company	Estb.	Head Quarter/Capital
Portugese East India company	1498	Cochin (1510-30), Goa (1530-1961)
English East India Company	1600	West coast : Surat (1608-87), Bombay (from 1687) East coast : Koromandal, Masulipattanum (1611-41), Madras (from 1641) Bengal : Under Madras (upto 1700) Calcutta (from 1700)
Dutch East India Company	1602	East coast : Koromandal, Pulicut (upto 1690), Negapattanum (from 1690); Bengal : Hugli (from 1655)
Danish East India Company	1616	Serampur (Bengal) : 1676-1845
French East India Company	1664	Surat (1668-73), Pondicherry (1673-1954)

Note : *Danish company were forced to sell all their settlements in India to the British in 1845.*

Portugese

- The Cape route was discovered from Europe to India by *Vasco da Gama*. He reached the port of Calicut on May 17, 1498 and was received by the Hindu ruler of Calicut (Known by the title of *Zamorin*).
- This led to the establishment of trading stations at Calicut, Cochin and Cannanore.
- Cochin was the early capital of the Portuguese in India. Later Goa replaced it.
- *Francisco de Almeida* was the first governor of Portuguese. Almeida (1505-09) introduced *'the policy of Blue water'*.
- *Alfonso d' Albuquerque* was the second governor of Portuguese. Albuquerque (1509-15) introduced *'the policy of Imperialism'*. He captured Goa from the ruler of Bijapur in 1510.
- *Nino da Cunha* (1529-38) transferred his capital from Cochin to Goa (1530) and acquired Diu and Bassein (1534) from Bahadur Shah of Gujarat.
- *Martin Alfonso de Souza* (1542-45) : The famous Jesuit Saint *Fransisco Xavier* arrived in India with him.
- The Portuguese power witnessed a decline by the end of the 16th century.
- They lost Hugli in 1631 after being driven out by Qasim khan, a Mughal noble of Shahjahan.
- In 1661 the King of Portugal gave Bombay to Charles II of England as dowry when he married the former's sister.
- The Marathas captured Salsette and Bassein in 1739.
- In the end they were left only with Goa, Diu and Daman which they retained till 1961.

Dutch

- Formation of the company in March, 1602, by a charter of Dutch parliyament the Dutch East India Company was formed with powers to make wars, conclude treaties, acquire territories and build fortresses.
- The Dutch set up factories at Masulipattam (1605), Pulicat (1610), Surat (1616), Bimilipatam (1641), Karaikal (1645), Chinsura (1653), Kasimbazar, Baranagore, Patna, Balasore, Negapatam (all in 1658) and Cochin (1663).
- The Dutch replaced the Portuguese as the most dominant power in European trade with the East, including India.
- Pulicat was main centre in India till 1690, after which Negapatam replaced it.
- The Dutch conceded to English after their defeat in the *battle of Bedera* in 1759.

English

- Before the English East India Company established trade in India, *John Mildenhall*, a merchant adventurer, was the first English man who arrived in India in 1599 by the over land route, ostensibly for the purpose of trade with Indian merchants.

- 'The Governor and Company of Merchants of London Trading into the East Indies', popularly known as the English East India company, was formed in 1600.
- *Captain William Hawkins* arrived at Jahangir's court (1609) to seek permission to open a factory at Surat. A Farman was issued by Jahangir permitting the English to build a factory at Surat (1613).
- *Sir Thomas Roe* came to India as ambassador of James I to Jahangir's court in 1615 to obtain the permission to trade and erect factories in different parts of the empire.
- The English East India Company acquired Bombay from Charles II on lease. *Gerald Aungier* was its first governor from 1669 to 1677.
- In 1690, *Job Charnock* established a factory at Sutanati and the zamindari of the three villages of *Sutanati, Kalikata* and *Gobindpur* was acquired by the British (1698). These villages later grew into the city of *Calcutta*. The factory at Sutanati was fortified in 1696 and this new fortified settlement was named *Fort William* in 1700.
- In 1694, the British parliament passed a resolution giving equal rights to all Englishmen to trade in the East. A new rival company, known as 'the English Company of Merchants Trading to the East Indies' was formed (1698).
- The final amalgamation of the company came in 1708 under the title of 'The united company of Merchants of England Trading to the East Indies'. This new company continued its existence till 1858.

French

- The French East India Company was formed by *Colbert* under state patronage in 1664.
- The first French factory was established at Surat by *Francois Caron* in 1668.
- A factory at Masulipatam was set up in 1669.
- The French power in India was revived under *Lenoir* and *Dumas* (governors) between 1720 and 1742. They occupied Mahe in the Malabar, Yanam in Coromandal and Karaikal in Tamil Nadu (1739).
- The arrival of *Dupleix* as French governor in India in 1742 saw the beginning of Anglo-French conflict (Carnatic Wars) resulting in their final defeat in India.

Anglo-French Conflict/Carnatic Wars

- An instance of Anglo French rivalry.
- **First Anglo-French war (1746-48) :** The French besieged Madras. At St. Thome battle the Nawab of Carnatic's army was defeated by French under Dupleix.
- The *Treaty of Aix-La-Chapelle (1748)* ended the war of Austrian succession and First Anglo-French war in India.
- **Second Anglo-French war (1749-54) :** Dupleix aligned with Muzaffar Jung (Hyderabad) and Chanda Sahib (Carnatic/Arcot). After initial reverses, Robert Clive emerged victorious.

➢ The *treaty of Pondicherry / Treaty by Godehu* (new French governor in place of Dupleix) : 1754-ended the Second Anglo-French War.

➢ Third Anglo-French war (1758-63) : French Count de Lally captured Fort St. David. French were defeated at Wandiwash (1760). It was a decisive defeat of French.

➢ The *treaty of Paris (1763)* ended the Third and Final Anglo-French war in India. Pondicherry was returned to French by this treaty.

MODERN INDIA

14. Expansion of British Power

(In the context of Bengal, Mysore, Punjab etc.)

Bengal

➢ *Murshil Quli Khan* (1717-27) : In 1717, Murshid Quli Khan was appointed as Bengal's Subedar i.e. governor by Mughal emperor Farrukh Siyar. Grant of the Governorship of Orissa also to him by Farrukh Siyar in 1719. He transferred the capital of Bengal from Dacca to *Murshidabad*.

➢ *Shujauddin* (1727-39) : He was the son-in-law of Murshid Quli Khan. He was granted the Governorship of Bihar by Mughal emperor Muhammad Shah 'Rangeela' in 1733.

➢ *Sarfaraj Khan* (1739-40) : He was the son of Shujauddin and was murdered by Alivardi Khan, the Deputy Governor of Bihar, in 1740.

➢ *Alivardi Khan* (1740-56) : Legalised his usurpation by receiving a *farman* from Mughal emperor Muhammad Shah 'Rangeela' after paying him Rs. 2 Crores. He prevented the English and the French from fortifying their factories at Calcutta and Chandranagore respectively.

Sirajuddaula : 1756-57

➢ Alivardi Khan was succeeded by his grandson Sirajuddaula.

➢ Sirajuddaula seized the English factory at Kasimbazar. On 20th June, 1756, Fort William surrendered but Robert Clive recovered Calcutta.

➢ On 2nd Jan. 1757, *Treaty of Alinagar* was signed, where by Siraj conceded practically all the demands. British then captured Chandranagore, the French settlement, on March 1757.

➢ The *Battle of Plassey* was fought on 23 June, 1757. Owing to the conspiracy, the Nawab was defeated.

➢ The following betrayed the Nawab :

Mir Jafar : Mir Bakshi

Manikchand : Officer in charge of Calcutta

Amichand : Rich Sikh merchant

Jagat Seth : Biggest banker of Bengal

Khadim Khan : Commanded a large number of Nawab's troops.

Mir Jafar : 1757-60

➢ The company was granted undisputed right to free trade in Bengal, Bihar and Orissa. It received the zamindari of 24 Parganas. Mir Jafar, however, fell into arrears and was forced to abdicate in favour of his son-in-law Mir Qasim.

Mir Qasim : 1760-64

- Mir Qasim ceded Burdwan, Midnapore and Chittagong. He shifted his capital from Murshidabad to *Munger*.
- Mir Qasim soon revolted as he was angry with the British for misusing the *dastak* (free duty passes). However, having been defeated by the British, he fled to Awadh, where he formed a confederacy with Awadh ruler Shujauddaula and Mughal emperor Shah Alam II.
- The *Battle of Buxar (1764)* : Mir Qasim, Shujauddaula and Shah Alam II were defeated by Munro.
- Mir Jafar was again placed on the throne.
- **Successors of Mir Qasim** : Mir Jafar (1764-65), Nazmuddaulah (1765-66), Saifuddaula (1766-70), Mubaraquddaula (1770-72).
- On Mir Jafar's death, his son Nazmuddaula was placed on the throne and signed a treaty on 20th Feb., 1765 by which the Nawab was to disband most of his army and to administer Bengal through a Deputy Subedar nominated by the Company.
- Clive concluded two separate *treaties of Allahabad* with Shah Alam II (12 Aug., 1765) and Shujauddaula (16 Aug., 1765).

Dual Government of Bengal : 1765-72

- Dual Government of Bengal started in 1765.
- The Company acquired both *Diwani and Nizamat* rights from Nazmuddaula, the Nawab of Bengal. But the company did not take over direct administration and revenue collection.
- Warren Hastings ended the dual system of government in 1772.

Mysore

Haidar Ali : 1761-82

- Haidar Ali began his career as a soldier in the service of the Mysore state, later he became the faujdar of *Dindigul*. He established a modern arsenal in Dindigul with the help of French.
- In 1761, he overthrowed the Nanjarajar (the powerful Prime Minister of Wodeyar king Krishraja I) and usurped power, though continuing to recognise Krishnraja I as the lawful ruler.
- **First Anglo-Mysore war (1766-69)** : Haider Ali defeated the British. The *Treaty of Madras (1769)* signed.
- **Second Anglo-Mysore war (1780-84)** : Warren Hastings attacked French port Mahe, which was in Haidar Ali's territory.
- Haidar Ali led a joint front with Nizam and Maratha and captured Arcot (Capital of Carnatic state).
- In 1781, Haidar Ali was defeated at Porto Novo by Eyrecoot.
- He died during the Second Anglo-Mysore war.

Tipu Sultan 1782-99

- Haidar Ali was succeeded by his son Tipu Sultan in 1782.
- He continued the Second Anglo-Mysore war till 1784.
- The *Treaty of Mangalore (1784)* was signed by Tipu Sultan which ended the Second Anglo-Mysore war.

- **Third Anglo-Mysore war (1790-92) :** Maratha and Nizam aided the British, Cornwallis capatured Bangalore. By the *Treaty of Seringapatnam (1792),* Tipu ceded half of his territory.
- **Fourth Anglo-Mysore war (1799) :** Lord Wellesly attacked and Tipu Sultan died.
- Tipu was the only Indian ruler who have understood the importance of economic strength as the foundation of military strength.
- Tipu established the embassies to France, Turkey, Iran and Pegu to develop foreign trade.
- Tipu planted a 'tree of liberty' at his capital Seringapatnam and became a member of Jacobian Club.

Punjab

- Guru Gobind Singh, the 10th and the last Guru of the Sikhs, transformed the religious sect into a military brotherhood.
- In the confusion and disorder that followed the invasion of Nadir Shah and Ahmad Shah Abdali, the sikhs increased their military strength and became a strong power.
- **Maharaja Ranjit Singh (1792-1839) :** He was the greatest Indian ruler of his time and founder of the Sikh rule in the Punjab. Born in 1780 at Gujranwala, he occupied *Lahore* in 1799 and made it his capital. He conquered Amritsar in 1802, occupied Ludhiana and after incessant wars, annexed Kangra, Attock, Multan, Kashmir, Hazara, Bannu, Derajat and Peshawar. He died in 1839.
- **Successors of Ranjit Singh :** *Kharak Singh* (1839-40), *Naunihal Singh* (1840), *Sher Singh* (1841-43), *Dalip Singh* (1843-49).
- The Sikh power was broken by the British after the death of Ranjit Singh.
- **First Anglo-Sikh war (1845-46) :** Sikhs were defeated in all the four battles at Mudki, Ferozshah, Aliwal and Sobraon. The *Treaty of Lahore (1846)* ended the war. Sir Henry Lawerence became the first resident.
- **Second Anglo-Sikh war (1848-49) :** Dalhousie annexed Punjab. Sir John Lawerence became the first chief commissioner of Punjab.

Kingdom	Year	Founder	Annexation
Nawab of Bengal	1713	Murshid Quli Jafar Khan	1765 (Treaty of Allahabad)
Maratha-confederacy	1720	Baji Rao I	1801 (Subsidiary Alliance)
Nawab of Carnatic/Arcot	1720	Saadatulla Khan	1801 (Subsidiary Alliance)
Nawab of Avadh	1722	Mir Muhammad Amin Saadat Khan 'Burhan-ul-Mulk'	1801 (Subsidiary Alliance), 1856 (Dalhousie)
Nizam of Hyderabad	1724	Mir Qamruddin Chin Kilich Khan 'Nizam-ul-Mulk'	1798 (Subsidiary Alliance)
Mysore	1761	Haidar Ali	1799 (Subsidiary Alliance)
Punjab	1792	Ranjit Singh	1849 (Dalhousie)

15. Economic Impact of British Rule

Three Stages of British Colonialism

First phase-The Mercantile phase (1757-1813)

- The East India Company used its political power to monopolize trade and dictate terms to traders of Bengal.
- Imposition of inflated prices of goods led to buccaneering capitalism whereby wealth flowed out of barrel of the British trader's gun.
- Revenues of Bengal were used to finance exports to England.

Second phase-The Industrial phase (1813-1858)

- India was exploited as a market for British goods.
- Act of 1813 allowed one way trade for the British, as a result the Indian markets flooded with cheap and machine-made imports. Indian traders lost foreign as well as home market.
- Indians were forced to export raw materials and import finished goods.
- Heavy import duty on Indian products to England to discourage them in the market.

Third phase-Financial phase (1860 onwards)

- The British consolidated their position in India and made India a market for manufacturers and a supplier of foodstuffs and raw materials.
- Introduction of Railways (1853), Post and Telegraph (1853), Banking System (Avadh Commercial Bank-1881).
- Heavy British investment in India and burden of public debt increases.
- Industries came into existence (Tata Iron and Steel in 1907).

Drain of Wealth

- *Dadabhai Naoroji* cited it in his book "Poverty And Un-British Rule in India" (1867). *R C Dutta* in his "Economic History of India" (1901) blamed British policies for Indian economic ills.
- Drain of Wealth theory refers to a portion of national product of India which was not available for consumption to its people.
- Constituents of drain were :
  - (i) Extortion by company servants the fortunes from rulers, zamindars, merchants and common man and sending them home.
  - (ii) Purchasing goods out of revenues of Bengal and exporting them. This was called investment.
  - (iii) Duty free trade provided to the British gave them a competitive edge over Indian traders. These subsidies were financed from Indian treasury.
  - (iv) Remittances or salaries and other incomes by company officials send to England.
  - (v) Home charges or cost of salaries and pensions of company officials in India were paid from the treasury of India.
  - (vi) Hefty interests were paid to British investors.

➢ **Effects**

(i) It stunted the growth of Indian enterprise and checked and retarded capital formation in India.

(ii) It financed capitalist development in Britain.

(iii) India was kept as a zone of free trade without allowing it to develop the ability to compete.

(iv) Plantations, mines, jute mills, banking, shipping, export-import concerns promoted a system of interlocking capitalist firms managed by foreigners. It drained resources from India.

Land Revenue Systems

Permanent Settlement/Istamarari (Sthayi) Bandobast

➢ Introduced in Bengal, Bihar, Orissa, and districts of Benaras and Northern districts of Madras by *Lord Cornwallis* in 1793.

➢ *John Shore* planned the Permanent Settlement.

➢ It declared zamindars as the owners of the land. Hence, they could keep 1/11th of the revenue collected to themselves while the British got a fixed share of 10/11th of the revenue collected. The zamindars were free to fix the rents.

➢ Assured of their ownership, many zamindars styed in towns (absentee landlordism) and exploited their tenants.

Ryotwari System

➢ Introduced in Bombay and Madras. *Munro* (Viceroy) and *Charles Reed* recommended it.

➢ In this, a direct settlement was made between the government and the *ryot* (cultivator).

➢ The revenue was fixed for a period not exceeding 30 years, on the basis of the quality of the soil and the nature of the crop. It was based on the scientific rent theory of Ricardo.

➢ The position of the cultivator became more secure but the rigid system of revenue collection often forced him into the clutches of the moneylender.

➢ Besides this, the government itself became a big zamindar and retained the right to enhance revenue at will while the cultivator was left at the mercy of its officers.

Mahalwari System

➢ Modified version of zamindari settlement introduced in the Ganges valley, NWFP, parts of Central India and Punjab.

➢ Revenue settlement was to made by village or estates with landlords. In Western Uttar Pradesh, a settlement was made with the village communities, which maintained a form of common ownership known as Bhaichare, or with Mahals, which were groups of villages.

➢ Revenue was periodically revised.

Colonial Impact of Land Revenue Systems

(i) The land settlements introduced market economy and did away with customary rights. Cash payment of revenue encouraged money-lending activity.

(ii) It sharpened social differentiation. The rich had access to the courts to defend their property.

(iii) Forcible growing of commercial crops led the peasants to buy food grains at high prices and sell cash crops at low prices.

(iv) The stability of the Indian villages was shaken and the entire set up of the rural society began to break up.

Peasant Movements

Movement	place	Year	Leaders
Indigo Revolt	Bengal	1859	Bishnu and Digambar Biswas
Pabna	Bengal	1870	Ishwar Roy, Sabu Pal, Khoodi Mollah
Deccan Riots	Maharashtra	1875	- - - -
Ramosi Movement	Maharashtra	1879	Vasudev Balwant Phadke
Bijolia	Rajasthan	1913	Sitaram Das, Vijay Pathik Singh
Champaran	Bihar	1917	Gandhiji
Kheda	Gujarat	1918	Gandhiji and Vallabh Bhai Patel
Moplah	Kerala	1921	Sayyad Ali and Sayyid Fazl
Bordoli/Borsad	Gujarat	1928	Vallabh Bhai Patel
Tebhaga	Bengal	1946	Kamparan Singh, Nyamat Ali
Punnapra-Waylar	Kerala	1946	- - - -
Telengana	Andhra P.	1946	Kumaraiya and Sundaraiya
UP Kisan Sabha	UP	1918	Indra Narayan Dwivedi and Gauri Shankar Mishra
Avadh Kisan Sabha	UP	1920	Baba Ramachandra
Eka Movement	Avadh	1921	Madari Pasi
Forest Satyagrah	South India	1931	NV Rama Naidu, N G Ranga
All India Kisan Sabha	Lucknow	1936	Sahajanada Saraswati

Tribal Revolts

Tribe	Year	Leaders	Cause
Chuar	1766-72	Raja Jagannath	Excess Revenue demand, Bengal famine
Bhills	1817	Sewaram	Agrarian hardship
Hos	1820	......	British occupation of Singhbhum
Ramosi	1822	Chittur Singh, Pratap Singh, Dattaraya Patkar	British Rule
Kolis	1824		Dismantle of forests

Tribe	Year	Leaders	Cause
Ahom	1828-33	Gomadhar Kunwar	British occupation
Khasi	1829-32	Tiruth Singh	British occupation
Kol	1831-32	Buddhu Bhagat	Land transfer to outsiders
Santhals	1855-56	Sidhu and Kanhu	British Rule
Naikda	1858	Rup Singh	For Dharma Raj against ban Joria Bhagat on grazing and timber
Bhuyan and Juang	1867-68 1891	Ratna Nayak Dharni Nayak	Installation of British protege on throne
Kacha Nagas	1882	Sambhuden	British intervention
Munda (Ulgulan)	1899	Birsa Munda	Land system, Missionary activity and forced labour
Bhills	1913	Govind Guru	A temperance and purification movement
Oraons (Tana Bhagat)	1914	Jatra Bhagat and other Bhagats	Religious Reason
Chenchus	1921-22	- - - -	British control of forests
Koyas/Rampas	1922-24	Alluri Sitaram Raju	British Rule
Naga	1932	Jadunang (1905-31) and Rani Gaidinliu	A reformist movement later directed against excess of British rule

Civil Revolts

Sanyasi (Bengal, 1780): led by religious monks against British restrictions and ruin of peasantry.

Kattabomman Revolt (1792-98) : by Vira Pandya Kattabomman against imposition of British Suzerainity.

Paik Revolt (Orissa, 1804-06) : led by Bakshi Jagabandhu against British occupation and revenue policy.

Velu Thampi (Travancore, 1805) : led by Velu Thampi against British extortions.

Kittur Revolt (Karnataka, 1824) : by Chinnama and Ryappa against British interference in Kittur.

Pagal Panthis (Maimansinh, 1825-33) : by Karam Shah and Tipu. Religious nature.

Raju (Vizag, 1827) : by Birabhadra Raju.

Faraizi (1838) : by Haji Saraitullah and Dadu Mian for cause of tenants.

Satavandi (Maharashtra, 1839) : by Phond Savant and Anna Sahib against British rule.

Kuka (1840) : by Bhagat Jawahar Mal or Sian Saheb in Punjab.

Gadakari (1844) : against revenue policy in Kolhapur.

Poligar (Karnool, 1846) : by Narasimha Reddy.

16. Socio-Religious Movements in 19th-20th Centuries

Socio-Religious Movements and Organisations

Year	Place	Name of the Organisation	Founder
1815	Calcutta	Atmiya Sabha	Rammohan Roy
1828	Calcutta	Brahmo Samaj	Rammohan Roy
1829	Calcutta	Dharma Sabha	Radhakant Dev
1839	Calcutta	Tattvabodhini Sabha	Debendranath Tagore
1840	Punjab	Nirankaris	Dayal Das, Darbara Singh, Rattan Chand etc.
1844	Surat	Manav Dharma Sabha	Durgaram Mancharam
1849	Bombay	Paramhansa Mandli	Dadoba Pandurang
1857	Punjab	Namdharis	Ram Singh
1861	Agra	Ṛadha Swami Satsang	Tulsi Ram
1866	Calcutta	Brahmo Samaj of India	Keshab Chandra Sen
1866	Deoband	Dar-ul-Ulum	Maulana Hussain Ahmed
1867	Bombay	Prarthna Samaj	Atmaram Pandurang
1875	Bombay	Arya Samaj	Swami Dayanand Saraswati
1875	New York (USA)	Theosophical Society	Madam H.P. Blavatsky and Col H.S. Olcott
1878	Calcutta	Sadharan Brahmo Samaj	Anand Mohan Bose
1884	Pune (Poona)	Deccan Education Society	G.G. Agarkar
1886	Aligarh	Muhammadan Educational Conference	Syed Ahmad Khan
1887	Bombay	Indian National Conference	M.G. Ranade
1887	Lahore	Deva Samaj	Shivnarayan Agnihotri
1894	Lucknow	Nadwah-ul-Ulama	Maulana Shibli Numani
1897	Belur	Ramakrishna Mission	Swami Vivekanand
1905	Bombay	Servents of Indian Society	Gopal Krishna Gokhale
1909	Pune (Poona)	Poona Seva Sadan	Mrs Ramabai Ranade and G.K. Devadhar
1911	Bombay	Social Service League	N.M. Joshi
1914	Allahabad	Seva Samiti	H.N. Kunzru

Important Socio-Religious Reformers

Swami Sahajanand (1781-1830) : His original name being Gyanashyama, founded the *Swaminarayan sect* in Gujarat, which believed in a theistic God and prescribed a moral code for its followers.

Raja Rammohan Roy (1772-1833) : Born in 1772 at Radhanagar in Burdwan district (West Bengal) founded *Atmiya Sabha* in Calcutta in 1815 to propagate monotheism and reforms in the Hindu society. The Atmiya Sabha was named *Brahmo Sabha* and finally *Brahmo Samaj* in 1828. Launched a movement for the abolition of Sati through his journal *Sabad Kaumudi* (1819).

Debendranath Tagore (1817-1905) : Took over the leadership of the Brahmo Samaj after Raja Rammohan Roy. Founded *Tattvabodhini Sabha* in 1839 and published *Tattvabodhini Patrika*, a Bengali monthly to propagate the ideas of Raja Rammohan Roy. In 1859, the Tattvabodhini Sabha was amalgamated with the Brahmo Samaj. He compiled selected passages from the Upanishads, which came to be known as *Brahma Dharma*.

Keshav Chandra Sen (1838-1884) : Keshav Chandra Sen was the leader of the Brahmo Samaj during the absence of Debendranath Tagore. He started *Bamabodhini Patrika*, a journal for women. He launched radical reforms, such as giving up of caste names, inter-caste and widow remarriages and launched movement against child marriages. These radical reforms led to to the first schism in the Brahmo Samaj. The original Brahmo Samaj came to be known as *Adi Brahmo Samaj* and the other, the *Brahmo Samaj of India* which was established by Keshav Chandra Sen in 1866. Sen formed the *Indian Reform Association* in 1870, which persuaded the British Government to enact the *Native Marriage Act of 1972* (popularly known as *Civil Marriage Act*) legalising the Brahmo marriages and fixing the minimum marriageable age for boys and girls.

Atmaram Pandurang (1823-1898) : Atmaram Pandurang founded *Prarthana Samaj* in 1867 in Bombay. M.G. Ranade joined it in 1870.

Swami Dayanand Saraswati (1824-1883) : Swami Dayanand Saraswati, originally known as *Mula Shankar* founded the *Arya Samaj* in 1875 in Bombay, wrote *Satyartha Prakash* (in Hindi) and *Veda-Bhashya Bhumika* (partly in Hindi and partly in Sanskrit).

Blavatsky (1831-91) and Olcott (1832-1907) : Madam H.P. Blavatsky, a Russian woman and Col. H.S. Olcott, an American, founded the *Theosophical Society* in New York in 1875, but shifted the headquarter of the Society to Adyar near Madras in 1882.

Swami Vivekanand (1863-1902) : Swami Vivekanand (originally *Narendranath Dutta*), founded the *Ramakrishna Mission* in 1887 as a social service league which was registered as a Trust in 1897.

Lower Caste/Caste Movements and Organisations

Movement/Organisation	Year	Place	Founder
Satya Shodhak Samaj	1873	Maharashtra	Jyotiba Phule
Aravippuram Movement	1888	Aravippuram, Kerala	Shri Narayan Guru
Shri Narayan Dharma Paripalana Yogam (S.N.D.P.) Movement	1902-03	Kerala	Shri Narayan Guru, Dr. Palpu and Kumaran Asan
The Depressed Class Mission Society	1906	Bombay	V.R. Shinde

Movement/Organisation	Year	Place	Founder
Bahujan Samaj	1910	Satara, Maharashtra	Mukundrao Patil
Justice (Party) Movement	1915-16	Madras, Tamil Nadu	C.N. Mudaliar, T.M. Nair and P. Tyagaraja Chetti
Depressed Class Welfare Institute (Bahiskrit Hitkarini Sabha)	1924	Bombay	B.R. Ambedkar
Self-Respect Movement	1925	Madras, Tamil Nadu	E.V. Ramaswami Naiker 'Periyar'
Harijan Sevak Sangh	1932	Pune	Mahatma Gandhi

17. Freedom Struggle

I. The Revolt of 1857

- The Revolt of 1857 is an important landmark in the history of India which occurred during the governer-generalship of Lord canning.
- **Causes of the Revolt :** The revolt of 1857 was a combination of political, economic, socio-religious and military causes.

  Political : Nana Sahib was refused pension, as he was the adopted son of peshwa Baji Rao II. Avadh was annexed in 1856, on charges of mal-administration Satara, Jhansi, Nagpur and Sambhalpur were annexed owing to Doctrine of Lapse.

  Economic : Heavy taxation, forcibly evictions, discriminatory tariff policy against Indian products and destruction of traditional handicrafts that hit peasants and artisans.

  Socio religious : British social reforms (abolition of sati, 1829; legalisation of widow remarriage, 1856 etc.) hurted the sentiments of orthodox and conservative People.

  Military : Discrimination with Indian soldiers.
- **Immediate cause :** The introduction of *Enfield rifles* whose cartidges were said to have a greased cover made of beef and pork sparked off the revolt.
- **The Beginning and Spread of the Revolt :** On March 29, 1857, an Indian sepoy of 34 Native Infantry, *Mangal Pandey*, killed two British officers-*Hugeson* and *Baugh*-on parade at Barrackpore (near Calcutta). The Indian soldiers present, refused to obey orders to arrest Mangal Pandey. However, he was later on arrested, put to and hanged.
- The mutiny really started at *Merrut* on 10th May 1857. The occasion was the punishment of some sepoys for their refusal to use the greased cartridges. The soldiers alongwith other groups of civilians, went on a rampage shouting *'Maro Firangi ko'*. They broke open jails, murdered Europeans, burnt their houses and marched to Delhi after sunset.
- The appearance of the marching soldiers next morning (i.e. 11th May) in Delhi was a signal to the local soldiers, who in turn revolted, seized the city and proclaimed the 82-year old *Bahadur Shah 'Zafar'*, as *Shahenshah-i-Hindustan (i.e. Emperor of India).*

Centre	Beginning Date	Ending Date	Indian Leader	British Suppressor
Delhi	11 May, 1857	20 Sep., 1857	Bahadur Shah II 'Zafar' and Bakht Khan (Commanding General)	John Nicholson
Kanpur	4 June, 1857	6 Dec., 1857	Nana Sahib and his loyal commander Tantiya Tope	Colin Campbell
Lucknow	4 June, 1857	21 Mar., 1858	Begum Hazrat Mahal	Colin Campbell
Jhansi	4 June 1857	18 June, 1858	Rani Laxmi Bai	Huge Rose
Allahabad	5 June, 1857	March, 1858	Liyaqat Ali	Colonel Neil
Jagdishpur (Bihar)	Aug., 1857	Dec., 1858	Kuer Singh and Amar Singh	William Taylor and Vincet Eyre

➢ Within a month of the capture of Delhi, the revolt spread to the different parts of India (esp. all over the North India, Central India and Western India). South remained quite and Punjab and Bengal were only marginally affected.

Note :

1. *Bahadur Shah II : was Deported to Rangoon, where he died in 1862. His sons were dead; Nana Sahib (original name – Dhundhu Pant), Begum Hazrat Mahal and Khan Bahadur Khan : Escaped to Nepal; Tantiya Tope (Original name – Ramchandra Pandurang) : was captured and executed on 15th April, 1859; Rani Laxmi Bai : Died in the battle-field; Kuer Singh : was wounded and died on 26 April, 1858.*
2. *Sir Huge Rose described Laxmi Bai as 'the best and bravest military leader of the rebel'.*
3. ***Other Important Leaders :** Khan Bahadur Khan (Bareilly), Maulavi Ahmadullah (Faizabad), Azimullah Khan (Fatehpur), Devi Singh (Mathura), Kadam Singh (Merrut) etc.*
4. *English authority re-established in India during July-Dec. 1858.*

Causes of Failure : The Revolt of 1857 was an unsuccessful but heroic effort to eliminate foreign rule. The main causes were : 1. Disunity of Indians and poor organisation 2. Lack of complete nationalism-*Scindias, Holkars, Nizam* and others actively helped the British 3. Lack of coordination between sepoys, peasants, zamindars and other classes 4. Many had different motives for participating in the revolt.

Significance : The important element in the revolt lay in Hindu-Muslim unity. People exhibited patriotic sentiment without any touch of communal feelings. It no doubt began as a mutiny of soldiers, but soon turned into a revolt against British rule in general.

Nature of the Revolt of 1857

➢ There are two main views about the nature of the Revolt of 1857 :

1. **Sepoy Mutiny :** Syed Ahmed Khan, Munshi Jeevan Lal and Durgadas Bandyopadhyaya (Contemporary Historians); Stenley (Secretary of state for India), John Lowerence, John Seeley, Malleson, R.C. Mazumdar.

2. **National Struggle/War of Independence :** Benjamin Disraely, Karl Marx, V.D. Savarkar, K.M. Pannikar, Ishwari Prasad, A.L. Shrivastva, Tarachand.

➢ **Other views :** Racial Struggle / Black-White Struggle–*Medley;* Religious Struggle / Hindu-Muslim–Christian Struggle–*Rees;* Civilisation-Barbarism Conflict / English-Indian Conflict–*T.R. Holmes;* Hindu-Muslim Conspiracy against Christian–*Outram and Taylor.*

Important Books on 1857

Book	Year	Author
The First Indian War of Independence-1857-59	1859	Karl Marx
Causes of Indian Revolt	1873	Sayed Ahmad Khan
The India War of Independence	1909	V.D. Savarkar
The Sepoy Mutiny and the rebellion of 1857	1957	R.C. Mazumdar
Civil Rebellion in Indian Mutinies	1957	S.B. Chowdhury
Rebellion, 1857 : A Symposium	1957	P.C. Joshi
1857	1957	S.N. Sen

Select Opinions on 1857

"It was wholly unpatriotic and selfish Sepoy Mutiny with no native leadership and no popular support." *John Seeley*

"The so-called First National War of Independence is neither 'First', nor 'National', nor 'a war of Independence." *R.C. Mazumdar*

"A national revolt rooted in deep mistrust."

Benjamin Disraely (Opposition Leader)

"The Revolt of 1857 was 'the First war of Independence." *V.D. Savarkar*

"What began as a fight for religion ended as a war for independence."

S.N. Sen

Impact of the Revolt of 1857

1. In August 1858, the British parliament passed an act, which put an end to the rule of the Company. The control of the British government in India was transferred to The British Crown.
2. A minister of the British government, called the Secretary of state for India was made responsible for the governance of India.
3. The British Governor-General of India was now also given the title of Viceroy, who was also the representative of the monarch.
4. Marked the end of British Imperialism and Princely States were assured against annexation. Doctrine of Lapse was withdrawn.
5. After the revolt, the British pursued the policy of *'divide and rule'*.
6. Far-reaching changes were made in the administration and increase of white soldiers in the army.
7. Total expense of the suppression was thrown on the Indian people.
8. It has been said that Julius Caesar was more powerful than Julius Caesar alive. The same may be said about the Revolt of 1857. Whatever might have been its original character, it soon became a symbol of challenge to the mighty British empire in India and remained a shining star for the rise and growth of the Indian national movement.

17. II Moderate Phase (1885-1905)

Important Organisations Before Congress

	Organisation	Place	Year	Founder(s)
1.	Landholders Society	Calcutta	1837	Dwarka Nath Tagore
2.	British India Society	London	1839	William Adam
3.	British India Association *(Result of the merger of 1 and 2)*	Calcutta	1851	Devendra Nath Tagore
4.	Madras Native Association	Madras	1852	C.Y. Mudaliar
5.	Bombay Association	Bombay	1852	Jagannath Shanker Sheth
6.	East India Association	London	1866	Dadabhai Naoroji
7.	Poona Sarvajanik Sabha	Poona	1870	S.H. Chiplunkar, G.V. Joshi, M.G. Ranade
8.	Indian Society	London	1872	Anand Mohan Bose
9.	Indian League	Calcutta	1875	Shishir Kumar Ghosh
	Indian Association	Calcutta	1876	Surendra Nath Bannerji and Anand Mohan Bose
	India National Conference	Calcutta	1883	-do-
10.	Madras Mahajan Sabha	Madras	1884	P.Rangia Naydu, V. Raghavachari, Anand Charlu, G.S. Aiyer
11.	Bombay Presidency Association	Bombay	1885	Ferozshah Mehta, K.T. Tailang, Badruddin Tyebji

Indian National Congress (I.N.C.) : Bombay, 1885, A.O. Hume

- The Indian National Union was formed in 1884 by A.O. Hume, an Englishman and a retired civil servant, in association with various national leaders who called for a conference in Pune in December 1885.
- The conference received the unanimous support of all Indian leaders, but the venue was shifted to Bombay for various reasons (esp. outbreak of cholera in Pune).
- Further, the leaders decided to rename the Indian National Union as Indian National Congress.
- The first session of the Indian National Congress was held at *Gokuldas Tejpal Sanskrit College* in Bombay under the presidentship of *W.C. Bannerji*, a veteran lawyer of Calcutta.
- It was attended by 72 delegates from all over India.
- From 1885 onwards the INC met every year and its cause spread rapidly among middle class Indians.
- With the foundation of INC in 1885, the struggle for India's independence was launched in a small, hesitant and mild but organized manner.
- The first two decade of INC are described in history as those of moderate demands and a sense of confidence in British justice and generosity. Their aim was not to be aggressive for attaining independence lest the

British should suppress this. This resulted in *Indian Council Act* in 1892 which allowed some members to be indirectly elected by Indians but keeping the official majority intact.

➢ **Moderate Leaders:**Dada Bhai Naoroji, A.O. Hume, Badruddin Tayebji, M.G. Ranade, W.C. Bannerji, Ferozshah Mehta, Surendra Nath Bannerji, C. Shankaran Naiyar, Madan Mohan Malviya, V.S. Shrinivas Shastri, Tej Bahadur Sapru, Gopal Krishna Gokhale, Anand Mohan Bose, E. Dinesh Wacha, Ras Bihari Ghosh, Mohan Lal Ghosh, P. Anand Charlu, C.Y. Chintamani, R.C. Dutt, S. Subrahmanyam Aiyer, K.T. Tailang, Madhusudan Das, Rahimtulla M. Sayani.

Select Opinions about INC

'INC represents only a microscopic minorities.'

Lord Dufferin (1884-88) **(Contemporary Viceroy)**

'The congress is tottering to its fall, and one of my great ambitions, while in India, is to assist it to a peaceful demise.'

Lord Curzon (1899-1905) **(Viceroy)**

'INC is a begging institute.' *Aurobindo Ghosh* **(Extremist Leader)**

'INC should distinguished between begging and claiming the rights.'

Bal Gangadhar Tilak **(Extremist Leader)**

'INC playing with bubbles.' *Bipin Chandra pal* **(Extremist Leader)**

17.III. Extremist Phase (1905-17)

Reasons for the Emergence of Extremists : 1. Realization that the true nature of British rule was exploitative 2. International influences and events which demolished the myth of White/European supremacy. These included-Abyssinia/Ethopia's victory over Italy (1896), Boer wars (1899-1902) in which the British faced reverse, Japan victory over Russia (1905) 3. Dissatisfaction with the achievements of Moderates 4. Reactionary policies of Curzon such as Calcutta Cooperation Act (1904), Indian Universities Act (1905) and Partition of Bengal (1905) 5. Existence of a militant school of thought and emergence of a trained leadership.

Prominent Extremist Leaders

1. **Bal Gangadhar Tilak** : 'Lokmanya' Tilak was the uncompromising leader of extremists. He was influenced by Agarkar, Ranade and Naoroji. He launched two newspapers the *Kesari* (in Marathi) and the *Maratha* (in English). He Organised *Ganpati Festival* (1893) and *Shivaji Festival* (1895). He was deported to *Mandlay Jail* (Burma) for writing seditious articles. He started *Home Rule League* in 1916. He wrote *Gita Rahasya*. Tilak asserted : *'Swarj is my Birth Right and I will have it.'*
2. **Lala Lajpat Rai** : Extremist from Punjab. Under the influence of Arya Samaj he founded National School at Lahore. He presided over the AITUC in 1920. Boycotted Simon Commission and demonstrated against it at Lahore during which he was brutally assaulted by the police and subsequently succumbed to his injuries.
3. **Bipin Chandra Pal** : Discarded orthodox Hinduism and entered Brahmo Samaj and visited England and America. He founded English

weekly *New India*. He led the Swadeshi movement. He carried gospels of Boycott, Swadeshi, National Education, Swaraj and the Passive Resistance. He founded *Vande Matram*.

4. **Sri Aurobindo Ghosh :** He Passed ICS exam with record marks in Greek and Latin. He had European upbringing. He worked for secret societies in Bengal and Maharashtra. He started Bengali daily *Jugantar*. He wrote seditious articles in Vande Matram. He was put to trial for Maniktalla (Calcutta) Bomb Conspiracy Case. He finally retired to the life of Yoga at Pondicherry.

Other Extremist Leaders : Chakravarthi Viji Raghvachariar, Aswini Kumar Dutta, Raj Narayan Bose, T. Prakasham, Chidambaram Pillai etc.

Methods of Extremists : 1.Passive Resistance i.e. non-cooperating with the British Government by boycotting government service, courts, schools and colleges.
2. Promotion of Swadeshi and boycott of foreign goods.

The Partition of Bengal (1905) and Boycott and Swadeshi Movement (1905-08)

- The Partition of Bengal came into effect on Oct. 16, 1905, through a Royal Proclamation, reducing the old province of Bengal in size by creating a new province of East Bengal, which later on became East Pakistan and present day Bangladesh.
- The government explained that it was done to stimulate growth of under-developed Eastern region of the Bengal. But, actually, the main objective was to 'Divide and Rule' the most advanced region of the country at that time. The main reason for partition of Bengal was to destroy the political influence of the educated middle class among whom the Bengali intelligentsia were the most prominent. It also set up a communal gulf between Hindus and Muslims. The INC unanimously condemned the partition of Bengal.
- The Boycott and Swadeshi movement had its genesis in the antipartition movement which was started to oppose the British decision to divide Bengal.
- With the start of the Swadeshi movement at the turn of the country, the Indian National Movement took a major leap forward.
- The INC took up the Swadeshi call in Benaras Session, 1905 presided over by G.K. Gokhle and supported the Swadeshi and Boycott Movement of Bengal. Militant nationalism spearheaded by Trio of *Lal-Bal-Pal* (Lala Lajpat Raj, Bal Gangadhar Tilak and Bipin Chandra Pal) and Aurobindo Ghosh was however, in favour of extending the movement to the rest of India and carrying it beyond the programme of just Swadeshi and Boycott of goods to full-fledged political mass struggle.
- On August 7, 1905, a resolution to boycott British goods were adopted at a meeting of the INC held in Calcutta. It was started as a purely economic measure for the development of Indian industry.
- Bonefire of foreign goods was launched on a large scale in all the major cities. *Tilak* took the movement to different parts of India esp. in Pune

and Mumbai. *Ajit singh* and *Lala Lajpat Ray* spread the Swadeshi message in Punjab and other parts of Northern India. *Syed Haidar Raza* set up the agenda in Delhi. Rawalpindi, Kangra, Jammu, Multan and Hardwar witnessed active public participation in Swadeshi Movement. *Chidambram Pillai* took the movement to Madras Presidency which was also galvanised by *Bipin Chandra pal's* extensive lecture tour.

Muslim League (1906) : In Dec., 1906, *All India Muslim League* was set up by *Nawab Salimullah* of Dacca (Dhaka) at Dacca (Dhaka). The League supported the partition of Bengal, opposed the Swadeshi movement, and demanded special safeguards for its community and a separate electorate of Muslims. This led to communal differences between Hindus and Muslims.

Calcutta session of INC (1906)-Swaraj : In Dec. 1906 at Calcutta, the INC under the leadership of *Dada Bhai Naoroji* adopted 'Swaraj' as the goal of Indian people. Naoroji in his presidential address declared that the goal of the INC was 'self government of Swaraj like that of United Kingdom'. The differences between the moderates and the extremists, esp. regarding the pace of the movement and the techniques of the struggle to be adopted, came to head in 1907 at the Surat Session of the congress where the party split with serious consequences for the Swadeshi movement.

Surat Split (1907) : The INC split into two groups—the extremists and the moderates, at the Surat session in 1907 held on the banks of the river Tapi. The extremists were led by *Tilak, Lajpat Rai* and *Bipin Chandra Pal* and the moderates were led by *Gopal Krishna Gokhle*. At the Surat session, the moderate and extremist delegates of congress met in an atmosphere surcharged with excitement and anger.

The suddenness of the Surat fiasco took the extremist leaders by surprise and they offered their cooperation to the working committee of the congress by accepting presidentship of Ras Bihari Ghose. But the moderates would not relent as they found themselves on firm ground. The government observing the opportunity launched a massive attack on the extremists by suppressing the newspaper and arresting their main leader, *Tilak*, and sending him to *Mandalay Jail* (Burma) for 6 years. The extremists were not able to organise an effective alternative party or to sustain the movement. *Aurbindo Ghosh* gave up politics and left for Pondicherry. *Bipin Chandra Pal* also left politics temporarily. *Lajpat Rai* left for Britain. After 1908, the national movement as a whole declined.

Morley-Minto Reforms (1909) : Morley-Minto Reforms were introduced in 1909 during the period when *Lord Minto* was the Viceroy of India. The reforms envisaged a separate electorate for Muslims besides other constitutional measures. The government thereby sought to create a rift within the Congress by winning the support of the moderates on the one hand, and favour of Muslims against Hindus on the other. To achieve the latter objective, the reforms introduced the system of separate electorates under which Muslims could only vote for Muslim candidates. This was done to encourage the notion that the political, economic and cultural interests of Hindus and Muslims were separate and not common. Indian political leaders were however dissatisfied by these reforms.

Home Rule Movement (1915-16) : *B.G. Tilak* founded Indian Home Rule League at Pune on 28 April, 1916. *Annie Besant*, inspired by the Irish rebellion, started Home Rule Movement in India in September, 1916. The movement spread rapidly and branches of the Home Rule League were established all over India. B.G. Tilak wholeheartedly supported this movement. He joined forces with Annie Besant and persuaded the Muslim League to support this programme.

Lucknow Pact–Congress-League Pact (1916) : An important step forward in achieving Hindu-Muslim unity was the Lucknow pact (1916). Anti-British feelings were generated among the Muslims following a war between Britain and Turkey which opened the way for the Congress and Muslim League unity. Both the Congress and the Muslim League held session at Lucknow in 1916 and concluded the famous Lucknow pact. The congress accepted the separate electorate and both organisations jointly demanded 'dominion status' for the country.

Hindu-Muslim unity alarmed the British and forced the government to announce its future policy. In 1916, a British policy was announced whereby association of Indians was in government increased and there was to be a gradual development of local self-governing institutions.

Montagu Declaration/August Declaration of 1917 : The control over the Indian government would be transferred gradually to the Indian people. This was the result of Hindu-Muslim unity exhibited in Lucknow pact.

Indian Revolutionary Organisations (India)

Organisation	Place	Year	Founder
Vyayam Mandala	Poona	1896-97	Chapekar Brothers
Mitra Mela	Nasik *(Later Poona)*	1901	Savarkar Brothers
Anushilan Samiti	Midnapur	1902	Pramath Nath Mitra
Abhinava Bharata	Poona	1904	Vikram Damodar (V.D.) Savarkar
Swadesh Bandhav Samiti	Warisal	1905	Ashwini Kumar Dutta
Anushilan Samiti	Dacca	1907	Pulin Bihari Das
Bharat Mata Society	Punjab	1907	Ajit Singh, Sufi Amba Prasad
Hindustan Republican Assoiation/Army (H.R.A.)	Kanpur	1924	Sachindra Nath Sanyal
Bharat Naujawan Sabha	Lahore	1926	Bhagat Singh
Hindustan Socialist Republican Association/ Army (H.S.R.A)	Delhi	1928	Chandrashekhar Azad

Indian Revolutionary Organisations (Abroad)

Organisation	Place	Year	Founder
India Home Rule Society (India House)	London	1904	Shyamji Krishna Verma

Organisation	Place	Year	Founder
Abhinava Bharat	London	1906	Vikram Damodar Savarkar
Indian Independence League	California (USA)	1907	Tarak Nath Das
Gadar Party	San Fransico	1913	Lala Hardayal
Indian Independence League	Berlin (Germany)	1914	Lala Hardayal and Virendra Nath Chattopadhyaya
Indian Independence League and Government	Kabul	1915	Raja Mahendra Pratap

Revolutionary Events/Cases

Name of the Event/Case	Place	Year	Accused
Murder of Rand and Amherst *(Plague Commissioners)*	Poona	1897	Chapekar Brothers, Damodar and Balkrishna.
Attempt to murder Kingsford *(a Vindictive Judge)*	Muzaffarpur	1908	Khudiram Bose and Prafulla Chaki
Manikatalla *(Calcutta)* and Alipur Bomb Conspiracy Case	Manikatalla, *(Calcutta)* Alipur	1908	Aurbindo Ghosh
Murder of Jackson *(District Magistrate)*	Nasik	1909	Anant Karkare
Murder of Curzon Wyllie	London	1909	Madan Lal Dhingra
Attempt to murder Hardinge *(Viceroy) (Delhi Bomb Case)*	Delhi	1912	Ras Bihari Bose and Basant Kumar
Kakori Train Dacoity Case *(Kakori-a station in Lucknow-Saharanpur division)*	Kakori	1925	Ram prasad Bismil and Ashafaqulla
Murder of Saunders *(A.S.P. of Lahore)*	Lahore	1928	Bhagat Singh
Assembly Bomb case	Delhi	1929	Bhagat Singh and Batukeshwar Dutta
Chittagong Armoury Dacoity	Chittagong	1930	Surya Sen
Murder of General Dwyer	London	1940	Udham singh

17. IV. The Gandhian Era (1917-47)

Mahatma Gandhi (1869-1948) : Chronological Overview

In South Africa : 1893-1914	
1893	Departure of Gandhi to South Africa.
1894	Foundation of *Natal Indian Congress*.
1899	Foundation of *Indian Ambulance Core* during Boer Wars.
1904	Foundation of *Indian Opinion* *(magazine)* and *Phoenix Farm* at Phoenix near Durban.
1906	First Civil Disobedience Movement *(Satyagraha)* against Asiatic Ordinance in Transvaal.
1907	Satyagraha against Compulsory Registration and Passes for Asians *(The Black Act)* in Transvaal.

1908	Trial and imprisonment-Johannesburg Jail *(First Jail Term).*
1910	Foundation of *Tolstoy Farm (Later Gandhi Ashrama)* near Johannesburg.
1913	Satyagraha against derecognition of non Christian marriages in Cape Town.
1914	Quits South Africa forever and returns to India, Awarded *Kaisar-i-Hind* for raising an Indian Ambulance Core during Boer wars.
In India : 1915-48	
1915	Arrived in Bombay (India) on 9 Jan, 1915; Foundation of *Satyagraha Ashrama* at Kocharab near Ahmedabad (20 May); In 1917, Ashrama shifted at the banks of Sabarmati; All India tour.
1916	Abstain from active politics (though he attended *Lucknow session* of INC held in 26-30 Dec., 1916, where *Raj Kumar Shukla*, a cultivator from Bihar, requested him to come to Champaran.)
1917	Gandhi entered active politics with *Champaran campaign* to redress grievances of the cultivators oppressed by Indigo planters of Bihar *(April 1917)*. Champaran Satyagraha was his first Civil Disobedience Movement in India.
1918	In Feb. 1918, Gandhi launched the struggle in *Ahmedabad* which involved industrial workers. Hunger strike as a weapon was used for the first time by Gandhi during Ahmedabad struggle. In March 1918, Gandhi worked for peasants of *Kheda* in Gujarat who were facing difficulties in paying the rent owing to failure of crops. Kheda Satyagraha was his first Non-Cooperation Movement.
1919	Gandhi gave a call for Satyagraha against the *Rowlatt Act* on April 6, 1919 and took the command of the nationalist movement for the first time (First all-India Political Movement), Gandhi returns Kaisar-i-Hind gold medal as a protest against *Jallianwala Bagh massacre*-April 13, 1919; *The All India Khilafat Conference* elected Gandhi as its president *(Nov. 1919, Delhi).*
1920-22	Gandhi leads the *Non-Cooperation and Khilafat Movement (Aug. 1, 1920-Feb., 1922)*, Gandhi calls off Movement *(Feb. 12, 1922)*, after the violent incident at *Chauri-Chaura* on Feb. 5, 1922. Non-Cooperation Movement was the First mass based politics under Gandhi.
1924	*Belgaum (Karnataka) session* of INC-for the first and the last time Gandhi was elected the president of the Congress.
1925-27	Gandhi retires from active politics for the first time and devotes himself to 'constructive programme' of the Congress; Gandhi resumes active politics in 1927.
1930-34	Gandhi launches the *Civil Disobedience Movement* with his *Dandi march/Salt Satyagraha* (First Phase : March 12, 1930 - March 5, 1931; *Gandhi–Irwin Pact* : March 5, 1931; Gandhi attends the *Second Round Table Conference* in London as sole representative of the Congress : Sep. 7 – Dec. 1, 1931; Second Phase : Jan. 3, 1932 – April 17, 1934)
1934-39	Gandhi retires from active politics, sets up *Sevagram (Vardha Ashram).*

1939	Gandhi resumes active politics.
1940-41	Gandhi launches *Individual Satyagraha Movement.*
1942	Call to *Quit India Movement* for which Gandhi raised the slogan, '*Do or Die*' (We shall either free India or die in the attempt), Gandhi and all Congress leaders arrested *(Aug. 9, 1942).*
1942-44	Gandhi kept in detention at the *Aga Khan Palace*, near Pune *(Aug. 9, 1942 – May, 1944)*, Gandhi lost his wife *Kasturba (Feb. 22, 1944)* and private secretary *Mahadev Desai*; this was Gandhi's last prison term.
1945	Gandhi's influence on the congress wanes perceptively after 1945.
1946	Deeply distressed by the orgy of communal violence, as a result Muslim League's Direct Action call, Gandhi travelled to *Noakhali (East Bengal–now Bangladesh)* and later on to *Calcutta* to restore communal peace.
1947	Gandhi, deeply distressed by the *Mountbatten Plan/Partition Plan (June 3, 1947)*, while staying in Calcutta to restore communal violence, observes complete silence on the dawn of India's Independence *(Aug. 15, 1947)*. Gandhi returns to Delhi *(Sep. 1947)*
1948	Gandhi was shot dead by *Nathu Ram Godse,* a member of RSS, while on his way to the evening prayer meeting at *Birla House*, New Delhi *(Jan. 30, 1948)*. He died, with 'Hey Ram' on his lips.

Note : *Gandhi has suggested the winding up of Indian National Congress after India attained independence and converting it into Lok Sevak Samaj.*

Facts about Gandhi

Date and Place of Birth : Oct. 2, 1869 and Porbandar, Gujarat.

Note : *UNO declared Oct. 2 as 'International Non-violence Day' (Antarrashtriy Ahinsa Diwas)*

Father : Karamachand Gandhi, **Mother** : Putali Bai, **Political Guru** : Gopal Krishna Gokhale, **Private Secretary** : Mahadev Desai.

Literary Influences on Gandhi : John Ruskin's *Unto This Last*, Emerson, Thoreau, Leo Tolstoy, *the Bible* and *the Gita*.

Literary Works : Hind Swaraj *(1909)*, My Experiments with Truth *(Autobiography, 1927)*–reveals events of Gandhi's life upto 1922.

As an Editor : *Indian Opinion* : 1903-15 *(in English and Gujarati, for a short period in Hindi and Tamil), Harijan* : 1919-31 *(in English, Gujarati and Hindi), Young India* : 1933-42 *(in English and Gujarati–named Navjeevan)*

Other Names : *Mahatma* (Saint)–by Rabindranath Tagore, 1917; *Malang Baba / Nanga Faqir* (Naked Saint)–by Kabailis of North-West Frontier, 1930; Indian Faqir / Traitor Faqir–by *Winston Churchill*, 1931; *Half-naked Saint* (Ardha Nanga Faqir)–by Franq Mores, 1931; *Rashtrapita* (the Father of the Naiton)–by Subhash Chandra Bose, 1944.

Main Events during the Gandhian Era

Rowlatt Act (1919) : During the viceroyalty of Lord Chelmsford, a sedition committee was appointed by the government in 1918 with Justice *Rowlatt* which made certain recommendations to curb seditious activities in India. The Rowlatt Act 1919, gave unbridled powers to the government to arrest and imprison suspects, without trial. The act caused a wave of anger among the people. Even before the act was passed, popular agitation began against it. Gandhiji decided to fight against this act and he gave a call for Satyagraha on April 6, 1919. He was arrested on April 8, 1919. This led to further intensification of the agitation in Delhi, Ahmedabad and Punjab.

Jallianwala Bagh Massacre (April 13, 1919) : The arrest of *Dr. Saifuddin Kitchlu* and *Dr. Satypal* on April 10, 1919, under the Rowlatt Act in connection with Satyagraha caused serious unrest in Punjab. A public meeting was held on April 13, 1919 in a park called *Jallianwala Bagh* in *Amritsar* where thousands of people including women and children assembled. Before the meeting could start General *O'Dyer* ordered indiscriminate heavy firing on the crowd and the people had no way out to escape. As a result hundreds of men, women and children were killed and more than 1200 people wounded. The massacre was a turning point in Indo-British relations and inspired the people to provide a more unrelenting fight for freedom.

Note : *Sardar Uddham Singh, an Indian patriot from Punjab, shot down Gen. O'Dyer in London in 1940.*

Khilafat movement (1920-22) : The Caliph (or, Khalifa) Sultan of Turkey, was looked upon by the Muslims as their religious head. During the first World War, when the safety and welfare of Turkey were threatened by the British thereby weakening the Caliph's position, Indian Muslims adopted an aggressive anti-British attitude. *The Ali Brothers–Mohammad Ali* and *Shaukat Ali*–launched an anti-British movement in 1920–the Khilafat Movement for the restoration of the Khilafat. *Maulana Abul Kalam Azad* also led the movement. It was supported by *Gandhiji* and INC which paved the way for Hindu-Muslim unity.

Non-Cooperation Movement (1920-22) : At the *Calcutta session* in Sep. 1920, the Congress resolved in favour of the Non-cooperation Movement and defined *Swaraj as its ultimate aim* (according to Gandhi). The movement envisaged : (i) Surrender of titles and honorary offices and resignation from nominated offices; (ii) Refusal to attend government darbars and official functions and boycott of British courts by the lawyers; (iii) Refusal of general public to offer themselves for military and other government jobs, and boycott of foreign goods etc. *Gandhiji*, along with the *Ali Brothers* (of Khilafat Movement fame) undertook a nationwide tour during addressing of meetings. The educational boycott was specially successful in Bengal with Punjab too, responding under the leadership of *Lala Lajpat Rai*. Apart from educational boycott, there was boycott of law courts which saw major lawyers like *Motilal Nehru, C.R. Das, C. Rajagopalachari, Saifuddin Kitchlu, Vallabh Bhai Patel, Aruna Asaf Ali,* etc. giving up their lucrative practices in their fields. The non-cooperation movement also saw picketings of shops selling foreign cloth and boycott of the foreign cloth by the followers of Gandhiji. Another dramatic event during this period was the visit of the prince of Wales. The day he landed in India (in Bombay on Nov. 17, 1921) he was greeted with empty streets and downed shutters wherever he went.

The attack on a local police station by angry peasants at *Chauri-Chaura*, in Gorakhpur district of UP, on Feb. 5, 1922, changed the whole situation. Gandhi, shocked by Chauri-Chaura incident, withdrew the Non-Cooperation Movement on Feb. 12, 1922.

Swaraj Party (1923) : Gandhi's decision to call off the agitation caused frustration among masses. His decision came in for severe criticism from his colleagues like *Motilal Nehru, C. R. Das* and *N.C. Kelkar*, who organsied the Swaraj Party. The foundations of the Swaraj party were laid on Jan. 1, 1923, as the *'Congress Khilafat-Swaraj Party'*. It proposed then an alternative programme of diverting the movement from widespread civil disobedience programme to restrictive one which would encourage its member to enter into legislative councils (established under Mont-ford Reforms of 1919) by contesting elections in order to wreck the legislature from within and to use moral pressure to compel the authority to concede to the popular demand for self government. In the election held in 1923 the Swaraj Party captured 45 of the 145 seats. In provincial elections they secured few seats but in the Central Province they secured a clear majority. In Bengal, the Swaraj Party was the largest party. They followed the policy of undiluted opposition. The Swarajists demanded the release all the political prisoners, provincial autonomy, repealing of the repressive laws imposed by the government. However, after the death of C.R. Das in 1925 they drifted towards a policy of cooperation with the government. This led to dissension and the party broke up in 1926.

Simon Commission (1927) : The activities of the Swaraj Party had induced the British government to review the working of the dyarchy system introduced by the Montague-Chelmsford Reforms of 1919 and to report as to what extent a representative government could be introduced in India. The British government appointed the Simon Commission in Nov., 1927 for the task. All members of this commission were Europeans (Whites). Indian political leaders felt insulted and decided to boycott the commission. Wherever the commission went there were cries of *'Simon Go Back'*. It was while leading a demonstration against the Simon Commission in Lahore that a fatal lathi-blow was dealt to *Lala Lajpat Rai*. It was his death *Bhagat Singh* and his comrades were seeking to avenge when they killed a white police officials, *Saunders*, in Dec. 1928.

Nehru Committee Report (1928) : The Committee was set up under the chairmanship of *Motilal Nehru* to determine the principles of the constitution before actually drafting it. The chief architects of the report were *Motilal Nehru* and *Tej Bahadur Sapru*. The recommendation evoked a lively debate concerning the goal of India–Dominion Status or Complete Independence.

14 Points of Jinnah (March 9, 1929) : Jinnah, the leader of Muslim League, did not accept the Nehru Report. Jinnah thereafter drew up a list of demands, which was called '14 points of Jinnah'.

Lahore Session (Dec., 1929) : At its annual session held in Lahore in Dec. 1929, under the presidentship of *Jawaharlal Nehru*, the Indian National Congress passed a resolution declaring *'Poorna Swaraj'* (Complete Independence) to be the goal of the national movement.

On Dec. 31, 1929, the newly adopted tricolour flag was unfurled and Jan. 26 was fixed as the Independence Day which was to be celebrated every year, pleading to the people not to submit to British rule any longer.

Dandi March/Salt Satyagraha (1930) : To achieve the goal of 'Complete Independence', *Gandhi* launched another civil disobedience movement. Alongwith 78 followers, Gandhi started his famous march from *Sabarmati Ashram* on March 12, 1930 for the small village *Dandi* (Navsari District) to break the Salt Law. Gandhi covered a distance of 240 miles in 24 days (March 12 – April 5). On reaching the seashore on April 6, he broke the Salt Law by picking up salt from the seashore. By picking a handful of salt, Gandhi inaugurated the Civil Disobedience Movement, a movement that was to remain unsurpassed in the history of Indian National Movement for the countrywide mass participation it unleashed. The movement became so powerful that is sparked off patriotism even among the Indian soldiers in the army. The Garhwal soldiers refused to fire on the people at Peshwar. Gandhiji was arrested on May 5, 1930. This was followed by another round of boycott of foreign goods and it took the shape of a nationwide Civil Disobedience Movement in which ladies also participated. Soon thereafter followed repressive measures such as mass arrests, lathi-charge, police-firing etc. About 1,00,000 people went in jail.

The First Round Table Conference (1930) : It was held in London on Nov. 12, 1930, to discuss the Simon Commission, but was totally boycotted by the Indian National Congress. The Commission had proposed self-government in the provinces and federation of British India and the princely states at the Centre. However, the representative of the Muslim League, Liberals and other parties had assembled for the discussion on the commission report. But in absence of the premier political party, the First Round Table Conference had to be adjourned to Jan. 2, 1931.

Gandhi-Irwin Pact/Delhi Pact (March 5, 1931) : Early in 1931 two moderate statesman, *Sapru* and *Jayakar*, initiated efforts to bring about rapprochement between Gandhi and the government. Six meeting with Viceroy Lord Irwin finally led to the signing of a pact between the two on March 5, 1931, whereby the congress called off the movement and agreed to join the Second Round Table Conference. Regarding Gandhi-Irwin Pact J.L. Nehru remarks, *'This is the way the worlds ends, /Not with a bang, but a whimper'*.

The Second Round Table Conference (1931) : It was held in London during the viceroyalty of *Lord Willingdon* during Sep. – Dec. 1931 and Gandhiji attended it on behalf of Indian National Congress. Nothing much was expected from the Conference for the imperialist political forces, which ultimately controlled the British Government in London, were opposed to any political or economic concession being given to India which could lead to its independence. The Conference, however, failed as Gandhiji could not agree with British Prime Minister *Ramsay Mac Donald* on his policy of communal representation and refusal of the British government on the basic Indian demand for freedom. The conference closed on Dec. 1, 1931, without any concrete result.

The Communal Award/Mac Donald Award (Aug. 16, 1932) : While Gandhi was arrested on his return from London after the Second Round Table Conference, British Prime Minister *Ramsay Mac Donald* announced his Award on communal representation in Aug. 16, 1932. Besides containing provisions for representation of Muslims, Sikhs and Europeans, it envisaged communal representation of Depressed Classes also. Gandhi was deeply grieved by this and underwent a fast in protest against this Award since it aimed to divide India on a communal basis. While many political Indians saw the fast as a diversion from the ongoing political movement, all were deeply concerned and emotionally shaken. Almost everywhere in India mass meetings took place, political leaders of different persuasions, like *Madan Mohan Malviya, B. R. Ambedkar* and *M. C. Raja* became active. In the end the succeeded in hammering out an agreement, known as the Poona Pact.

Poona Pact/Gandhi–Ambedkar Pact (Sep. 25, 1932) : As discussed, the Communal Award created immense dissatisfaction among Hindus. Gandhi who was on fast in protest staked his life to get the Award repudiated. According to the pact, the idea of separate electorate for the Depressed Classes was abandoned but seats reserved for them in the provincial legislatures were increased from 71 in the Award to 147, and in the central legislature to 18% of the total. Ultimately the fast ended with the *Poona Pact* which annulled the Award. The leaders of the various groups and parties among Hindus, and *B.R. Ambedkar* on behalf of the *harijans*, signed the pact. The Poona Pact between caste Hindus and the Depressed Classes agreed upon a joint electorate.

The Third Round Table Conference (Nov. 17–Dec. 24, 1932) : It was held in 1932 but again proved fruitless since the national leaders were in prison.

The Government of India Act, 1935 : The Simon Commission report submitted in 1930 formed the basis for the Government of India Act, 1935. The new Government of India Act received the royal assent on Aug. 4 1935. The Act continued and extended all the existing features of earlier constitutional reforms. But in addition there were certain new principle introduced. It provided for a federal type of government. Thus, the act : (i) Introduced provincial autonomy (ii) Abolished dyarchy in provinces (iii) Made ministers responsible to the legislative and federation at the centre. The Act of 1935 was condemned by nearly all sections of Indian public opinion and was unanimously rejected by the Congress. The Congress demanded itself the convening of a Constituent Assembly elected on the basis of adult franchise to frame a constitution for an independent India. Regarding the Government of India Act, 1935 J. L. Nehru remarks, *'It was a new charter of Slavery.'*

Although the Congress opposed the Act, yet it contested the elections when the constitution was introduced on April 1, 1937; and formed ministries, first in 6 provinces and then in another 2. The Muslim League was however, not happy with the Congress rule, esp. Mr. Jinnah, who described it in those words : '*Congress was drunk with power and was oppressive against Muslims*'.

Congress Ministries Resign (Dec. 22, 1939) : The Second World War broke out in Europe on Sep. 3, 1939 that brought Britain also within its fold. Without consulting the Indian leaders, the Viceroy declared India also as a belligerent country. This evoked sharp criticism from Indians and the Congress took the stand that India could not associate herself in a war said to be for democratic freedom when the very freedom was denied to her. The Congress demanded that India should be declared an independent nation. Then only would the country help Britain in the war. The Viceroy in his reply dated Oct. 17, 1939 rejected the Congress demand as impracticable and took the stand that the Government could think over the entire constitutional scheme after the war. The Congress condemned the Viceroy's reply and the Congress ministries everywhere resigned on Dec. 22, 1939. *Jinnah* was happy over this and he called upon the Indian Muslims to celebrate the resigning day of Congress ministries as *'the day of deliverance'*.

Pakistan Resolution/Lahore Resolution (March 24, 1940) : It was is 1930 that *Iqbal* suggested the union of the Frontier Province, Baluchistan, Sindh and Kashmir as Muslim state within the federations. This proved to be a creative idea which germinated during the early thirties to burst into vigorous life with the advent of the new reforms. The idealist *Chaudhry Rehmat Ali* developed this conception at Cambridge, where he inspired a group of young Muslims and invented the term '*Pakstan*' (later 'Pakistan') in 1935. His ideas seemed visionary during that time, but within 7 years they turned into a political programme by *Jinnah* with the new name as its slogan or banner. The ideology of Iqbal, the vision of Rehamat Ali, and the fears of Muslims were thus united by the practical genius of Jinnah to blind Muslim together as never before during the British period and ultimately led to the vivisection of India and creation of Pakistan. Pakistan Resolution was an important landmark in this context. The *Lahore session* of the Muslim League, held on March 24, 1940, passed *Pakistan Resolution* and rejected the Federal scheme as envisaged in the government of India Act, 1935.

August Offer/Linlithgow Offer (Aug. 8, 1940) : On Aug. 8, 1940, the Viceroy *Linlithgow* came out with certain proposals, known as *August Offer* declaring that the goal of British Government was to establish *Dominion Status* in India. It accepted that framing of a new constitution would be the responsibility of the Indians. It also laid down that full weight would be given to the views of minorities in the constitution. *Maulana Abul Kalam Azad*, President of the Congress, rejected the August Offer which aimed at bringing the Congress in the ongoing world war. The Muslim League, however welcomed the offer as it ensured that no further constitution would be adopted without the prior approval of Muslims. The League declared that the most difficult problem of India's future constitution could be solved only by the partition of India. In brief, the August Offer failed in gaining Indian's co-operation for war and, in fact, further widened the gulf between the Congress and the Britishers as well as between the Congress and the Muslim League.

Individual Civil Disobedience/Individual Satyagaraha (Oct., 1940 – Dec., 1941) : The Congress Working Committee decided to start individual civil disobedience on Oct. 17, 1940. *Vinoba Bhave* was the first Satyagrahi who was arrested on Oct. 21, followed soon by many more including *Nehru* and *Patel*. But the movement created little enthusianism and Gandhi suspended it.

The Cripps Mission (March-April 1942): In 1942, the British Government realized that it could not ignore the Indian problems any more. As a result of the World War, the situation worsened for the British with Japanese advance towards Indian borders. By March 7, 1942, Rangoon fell and Japan occupied the entire South-East Asia. The British government, with a view of getting cooperation from Indians, sent *Sir Stafford Cripps*, a member of the British cabinet to India to settle terms with Indian leaders who were forthwith released. Cripps proposed *Dominion Status* after the war but his proposal was rejected by all the political leaders. As no party agreed to accept these proposals, the Cripps Mission ended in failure. Regarding the Cripps Mission proposals Mahatma Gandhi remarks *'A post-dated cheque on a crumbling bank'*.

Quit India movement (1942) : On Aug. 8, 1942, the Congress in its meeting at *Gowaliya Tank, Bombay* passed a resolution known as 'Quit India' resolution, whereby *Gandhiji* asked the British to quit India and gave a call for *'Do or die'* (We shall either free India or die in the attempt) to his countrymen. On Aug. 9, 1942 all the prominent leaders like Gandhi, Nehru, Patel etc. were arrested but the rest most of (J.P., Lohiya, Aruna Ashaf Ali, Usha Mehta etc.) continued the revolutionary struggle. Violence spread throughout the country, several government offices were destroyed and damaged, the telegraph wires were cut and communication paralyzed. Parallel government were established in some places viz. 1. *Balia*, U.P. (by Chittu Pandeya)– first Parallel govt. 2. *Tamulak*, Midnapur Distt., Bengal (by Satis Samant) 3. *Satara*, Maharashtra (by Y. B. Chahvan and Nana Patil) – the longest (term) parallel govt. 4. *Talchar*, Orissa. The movement was, however, crushed by the government.

Gandhiji's Fast (Feb. 10 – March 7, 1943) : Gandhiji undertook a 21-day fast in jail. His condition deteriorated after 13 days and all hopes of his survival were given up. However, as a result of his moral strength and spiritual stamina, he survived and completed the 21-day fast. This was his answer to the government which had been constantly exhorting him to condemn the violence of the people in the Quit India Movement. Gandhi not only refused to condemn people resorting to violence but unequivocally held the government responsible for it.

C.R. Formula (1944) : In 1994, *Chakravarti Rajagopalachari (C.R.)* proposed to appoint a commission to demarcate the districts in North-West and East where Muslims were in majority. In such areas, a plebiscite was proposed to be held on the basis of adult suffrage to decide the issue of separation. They would be given freedom if they favoured a sovereign state. In case of acceptance of partition, agreement was to be made jointly for safeguarding defence, commerce, communications etc. Muslim League was to endorse Congress demand for independence and cooperate in the formation of provisional government. *Jinnah* objected, as he wanted Congress to accept two-nation theory and wanted only Muslims of the North-West and East of India to vote in the plebiscite. Hindu Leaders led by *V.D. Savarkar* condemned the plan.

Wavell Plan and Shimla Conference (June 14–July 14, 1945) : The war situation in Europe improved in the beginning of the year 1945. India's goodwill was, however, needed as the war against Japan was expected to last for about two years. The situation within the country was worsening day by day as a result of deteriorating economic situation and famines. The British Government was compelled to come forward with some sort of plan to satisfy the Indians. After consultations with the British Government on the Indian problem, *Lord Wavell*, the Viceroy of India, issued a statement known as *Wavell Plan*. The Plan, which chiefly concerned Viceroy's Executive Council, proposed certain changes in the structure of the council. One of the main proposals was that the Executive Council would be constituted giving a balanced representation to the main communities in it, including equal representation to Muslims and Hindus.

Soon after the Wavell Plan was issued the members of the Congress Working Committee were released from jails. A conference of 22 prominent Indian leaders called at Shimla to consider the Wavell Plan, reached no decision. What scuttled the conference was Mr. Jinnah's unflinching stand that the Muslim members approved only by the Muslim League should be included in the Executive Council. Communalism thus again became a stumbling block. For the Britishers, however, the dissension between the Congress and the Muslim League was a source of happiness.

INA Trial (Nov., 1945) : *P. K. Sehgal, Shah Nawaj Khan* and *Gurubaksh Singh Dhillon* were put on trial at the Red Fort in Nov., 1945. To elucidate, despite the best efforts of the Congress to win the legal battle the trial of INA prisoners led to their outright conviction on the charge of waging war against the King Emperor. The pressure of the Indian public opinion against this conviction however, soon mounted high. This shook the British Government and it was compelled to suspend the sentences imposed on the INA convicts. Further, disaffection spread fast among the soldiers. The chief defence advocate during the INA trial was *Bhulabhai Desai*. Other defence lawyers were *Tej Bahadur Sapru, Jawaharlal Nehru, Asaf Ali* and *Md. Ali Jinnah*.

Azad Hind Fauj *(Indian National Army –INA)*

The Japanese after defeating the British in South-East Asia, took a number of Indian soldiers as prisoners of war. In March 1942 a conference of Indians was held in Tokyo, and they formed the *Indian Independence League*. At the Bangkok conference (June 1942) *Ras Bihari Bose* was elected President of the League. INA was formed by *Mohan Singh*.

Subhas Chandra Bose had escaped to Berlin in 1941 and set up Indian League there. In July 1943, he joined the INA at Singapore. There Ras Bihari Bose handed over the leadership to him.

Provisional Government of Free India and *INA* was formed by Subhas Chandra Bose in Singapore on Oct. 21, 1943.

INA had 3 fighting brigades named after *Subhas, Gandhi* and *Nehru*. *Rani Jhansi Brigade* was an exclusive women force.

But with the defeat of Japan in 1945, the INA also died out.

Bose is said to have been killed in air crash over Taipei, Taiwan on his way to Tokyo in Aug. 18, 1945.

Royal Indian Navy (RIN)/Ratings Mutiny (Feb. 18, 1946) : On Feb., 18, 1946, Bombay Ratings of HMS Talwar struck work due to flagrant racial discrimination, unpalatable food and abuse after the arrest of B.C. Dutt who had scrawled Quit India on the ship. On Feb. 19, HMS Hindustan, in Karachi also mutinied. *VallabhBhai Patel* and *Jinnah* jointly persuaded the Ratings to surrender on Feb. 23, 1946. The Britishers for the first time seriously realized that with this awakening among the Indians and revolt in armed forces, it could not perpetuate its hold on India any more.

Cabinet Mission (March - June, 1946) : The British Prime Minister, *Lord Attlee*, made a declaration on March 15, 1946, that British Cabinet Mission would visit India to make recommendations regarding constitutional reforms to be introduced in India. The Cabinet Mission which included of *Lord Pathick Lawrence, Stafford Cripps* and *A. V. Alexander* visited India and met the representative of different political parties, but a satisfactory solution to the constitutional difficulties could not be found. The mission envisaged the establishment of a Constituent Assembly to frame the constitution as well as an interim government. The Muslim League accepted the plan on June 6, 1946, while maintaining its rights of striving for a separate Muslim state. The Congress also partially accepted the plan.

Direct Action Campaign (Aug. 16, 1946) : Provoked by the success of the Congress (in the voting for Constituent Assembly), the Muslim League launched a 'direct action' campaign on Aug. 16, 1946, which resulted in wide spread communal riots in the country.

Interim Government (Sep. 2, 1946) : On Sep. 2, 1946, an interim government was formed. Congress members led by *Pt. Jawaharlal Nehru* joined it but the Muslim League did not, on the contrary it withdrew its earlier acceptance of the Cabinet Mission Plan.

Formation of Constituent Assembly (Dec. 9, 1946) : The Constituent Assembly met on Dec. 9, 1946, and *Dr. Rajendra Prasad* was elected its President. The Muslim League did not join the Assembly.

Attlee's Announcement (Feb. 20, 1947) : On Feb. 20, 1947, British Prime Minister *Attlee* announced that the British would withdraw from India by June 30, 1948 and that Lord Mountbatten would replace Wavell.

Mountbatten Plan (June 3, 1947) : In March, 1947, *Lord Mountbatten* replaced Lord Wavell. He announced his plan on June 3, 1947. His earlier *Plan Balkan* was abandoned for this June 3, Plan. It offered a key to the political and constitutional deadlock created by the refusal of Muslim League to join the Constituent Assembly formed to frame the constitution of India. Mountbatten's formula was to divide India but retain maximum unity. The country would be partitioned but so would be Punjab and Bengal, so that the limited Pakistan that emerged would meet both the Congress and the

League's position to some extent. The League's position on Pakistan was conceded in that it would be created, but the Congress position on unity would be taken into account to make Pakistan as small as possible. He laid down detailed principles for the partition of the country and speedy transfer of political powers in the form of dominion status to the newly formed dominions of India and Pakistan. Its acceptance by the Congress and the Muslim League resulted in the birth of Pakistan.

The Indian Independence Act, 1947 : The Bill containing the provisions of the Mountbatten Plan of June 3, 1947, was introduced in the British Parliament and passed as the Indian Independence Act, 1947. The Act laid down detailed measures for the partition of India and speedy transfer of political powers to the new governments of India and Pakistan.

Integration of States : By Aug. 15, 1947, all states except *Kashmir, Junagadh* and *Hyderabad* had signed the Instrument of Accession with India. *The Maharaja of Kashmir* acceded to India in Oct., 1947 when irregular Pakistani troops invaded his state. *The Nawab of Junagadh* was a Muslim whereas most of its people were Hindus. In Feb. 1948, through a referendum the people of this state decided to join India. The Nawab of Junagadh, therefore, left for Pakistan. *The Nizam of Hyderabad* was forced to accede to the Indian Union under the pressure of internal anarchy and military action against him in Sep., 1948.

French Colonies : By the end of 1954, French colonial rule in Pondicherry, Chandranagar, Mahe, Karaikal and Yanam came to an end. These territories were integrated with India.

Portuguese Colonies : The Portuguese colonies in India were Goa, Daman, Diu, Dadra and Nagar Haveli. In 1954, Dadra and Nagar Haveli were liberated by freedom fighters. Indian troops liberated Goa, Daman and Diu from the Portuguese in 1961.

Miscellaneous

Important Dates

I. Ancient	
BC	
2500 - 1750	Indus Valley Civilization.
563-483	Buddha's life-span.
540-468	Mahavir's life-span.
327-326	Alexander's invasion of India. It opened a land route between India and Europe.
322	Accession of Chandragupta Maurya.
305	Defeat of Seleucus at the hands of Chandragupta Maurya.
273-232	Ashoka's reign.
261	Conquest of Kalinga.
145-101	Reign of Elara, the Chola king of Sri Lanka.
58	Beginning of Vikram era.

AD	
78	Beginning of Saka era.
78-101	Kanishka's reign.
319-320	Commencement of Gupta era.
380	Accession of Chandragupta II 'Vikramaditya'.
405-411	Visit of Chinese traveller Fahien.
415	Accession of Kumaragupta I
455	Accession of Skandagupta.
606-647	Harshavardhan's reign.
II. Medieval	
712	First invasion in Sindh by Arabs (Mod. Bin Qasim).
836	Accession of King Bhoja of Kannauj.
985	Accession of Rajaraja, the Chola ruler.
998	Accession of Sultan Mahmud Ghazni.
1001	First invasion of India by Mahmud Ghazni who defeated Jaipal, ruler of Punjab.
1025	Destruction of Somnath Temple by Mahmud Ghazni.
1191	First Battle of Tarain.
1192	Second Battle of Tarain.
1206	Accession of Qutubuddin Aibak to the throne of Delhi.
1210	Death of Qutubuddin Aibak.
1221	Chengiz Khan invaded India (Mongol invasion)
1236	Accession of Razia Sultana to the throne of Delhi.
1240	Death of Razia Sultana.
1296	Accession of Alauddin Khilji.
1316	Death of Alauddin Khilji.
1325	Accession of Muhammad-bin-Tughlaq.
1327	Transfer of Capital from Delhi to Devagiri (Daulatabad) in Deccan by the Muhammad-bin-Tughlaq.
1336	Foundation of Vijayanagar empire in the South.
1351	Accession of Firoz Shah Tughlaq.
1398	Timur's Invasion of India.
1469	Birth of Guru Nanak.
1494	Accession of Babur in Farghana.
1497-98	First voyage of Vasco da Gama to India (discovery of sea route to India via the Cape of Good Hope)
1526	First Battle of Panipat; Babur defeated Ibrahim Lodhi; foundation of Mughal dynasty by Babur.
1527	Battle of Khanwa—Babur defeated Rana Sanga.

1530	Death of Babur and accession of Humayun.
1539	Sher Shah Suri defeated Humayun in the battle of Chausa and became India's emperor.
1555	Humayun recaptured the throne of Delhi.
1556	Second Battle of Panipat (Akbar defeated Hemu).
1556	Battle of Talikota (Rakshasa-Tangadi).
1576	Battle of Haldighati—Rana Pratap was defeated by Akbar.
1582	Din-i-Ilahi founded by Akbar.
1600	English East India Company established.
1605	Death of Akbar and accession of Jahangir.
1606	Execution of Guru Arjun Dev, the 5th Guru of Sikhs.
1611	Jahangir marries Nurjahan.
1615	Sir Thomas Roe visits Jahangir.
1627	Birth of Shivaji and death of Jahangir.
1628	Shahjahan becomes emperor of India.
1631	Death of Mumtazmahal.
1634	The English permitted to trade in India (in Bengal)
1659	Accession of Aurangzeb, Shahjahan imprisoned.
1665	Shivaji imprisoned by Aurangzeb.
1666	Death of Shahjahan.
1675	Execution of Guru Teg Bahadur, the 9th Guru of Sikhs.
1680	Death of Shivaji.
1707	Death of Aurangzeb.
1708	Death of Guru Gobind Singh, the 10th Guru of Sikhs.
1739	Nadir Shah invades India.
III. MODERN	
1757	Battle of Plassey, establishment of British political rule in India at the hands of Lord Clive.
1761	Third Battle of Panipat.
1764	Battle of Buxar.
1765	Clive appointed Company's Governor in India.
1767-69	First Anglo–Mysore War.
1780	Birth of Maharaja Ranjit Singh.
1780-84	Second Anglo–Mysore War.
1784	Pitt's India Act.
1790-92	Third Anglo–Mysore War.
1793	The Permanent Settlement of Bengal.
1799	Fourth Anglo–Mysore War—Death of Tipu Sultan.

1802	Treaty of Bassein.
1809	Treaty of Amritsar.
1829	Practice of Sati prohibited.
1830	Raja Rammohan Roy visits England.
1833	Death of Raja Rammohan Roy at Bristol, England.
1839	Death of Maharaja Ranjit Singh.
1839-42	First Anglo–Afghan War.
1845-46	First Anglo-Sikh War.
1852	Second Anglo-Burmese War.
1853	First Railway line opened between Bombay and Thane and a Telegraph line in Calcutta.
1857	The Sepoy Mutiny or First War of Independence.
1861	Birth of Rabindranath Tagore.
1869	Birth of Mahatma Gandhi.
1885	Foundation of Indian National Congress.
1889	Birth of Jawaharlal Nehru.
1897	Birth of Subhash Chandra Bose.
1903	Tibet Expedition (Young Husband delegation).
1905	Partition of Bengal by Lord Curzon.
1906	Foundation of Muslim League by Salimullah (Nawab of Dhaka) at Dhaka.
1911	Delhi Darbar, King and Queen visit India; Delhi becomes the capital of India.
1914	World War I begins.
1916	Lucknow Pact signed by Muslim League and Congress.
1918	World War I ends.
1919	Montague-Chelmsford Reforms introduced, Jallianwala Bagh massacre at Amritsar.
1920	Khilafat Movement launched.
1927	Boycott of Simon Commission, broadcasting started in India.
1928	Death of Lala Lajpat Rai.
1929	Resolution of 'Poorna Swaraj' (complete independence) passed at Lahore Session of INC.
1930	Civil disobedience movement launched, Dandi March by Mahatma Gandhi (April 6, 1930).
1931	Gandhi-Irwin Pact.
1935	Government of India Act.
1937	Provincial Autonomy, Congress forms ministries.
1939	World War II begins (September 3).

1941	Escape of Subhash Chandra Bose from India, Death of Rabindranath Tagore.
1942	Arrival of Cripps Mission in India, Quit India movement launched (August 8).
1943-44	S.C. Bose forms Provisional Government of Free India and Indian National Army in Singapore; Bengal famine.
1945	Trial of Indian National Army at Red Fort; Shimla Conference; World War II ends.
1946	British Cabinet Mission visits India; Interim government formed at the Centre.
1947	Division of India; India & Pakistan form separate independent dominions.

Important Places

Ahichhatra : Originally *Ahikshetra* in Bareilly district of Uttar Pradesh was once the capital of Panchalas.

Aihole : In Karnataka contains chief sites of Chalukyan architecture—nearly 70 structural stone temples important in the development of Hindu architecture and sculpture.

Ajanta Caves : 66 miles north of Aurangabad in Maharashtra State. These are rock-cut Buddhist caves, 29 in number. These caves represent a record of unique painting, sculpture and architecture of the period from about the 2nd century B.C. to about 7th century A.D.

Amaravati : It is the legendary capital of Svarga. Also a historical site near modern Vijaywada, believed to have flourished under the Satavahana dynasty.

Arikamedu : It was a sea-port near Pondicherry in Chola times.

Ayodhya : A few miles from modern Faizabad, near Lucknow, was capital of the Kosala and the Solar kings of ancient India. Rama was the most prominent among them.

Badami (or Vatapi) : In Karnataka is well-known for Chalukyan sculpture found in the cave temples here. These are groups of Hindu temples dating back to 7th or 8th century and are examples of pure Dravidian architecture. Besides cave temples and rock-cut pillared halls, there is also the famous Malegitti Shivalaya temple.

Belur : In Karnataka is famous for its elaborately sculptured Cheena Kesava temple of the Hoysala period.

Bhubaneswar : In Orissa is known for ancient temples viz., Rajarani; Lingraja; Brahmesvara.

Bodh Gaya : It is situated 6 miles south of Gaya in Bihar State on the western bank of the Falgu river and connected by two metalled roads. It is famous as the place where Buddha got enlightenment. There are modern monasteries, rest houses and museum.

Chidambaram : A town 150 miles south of Chennai known as Tillai in ancient time, was once the capital of the Chola kingdom. Its temples are among the oldest in India and are gems of Dravidian architecture. It is famous as the abode of Natraja, the Dancing Shiva.

Daulatabad : Near Aurangabad in Maharashtra State is famous for rock-cut fortress of 12th century of near the tomb of the Mughal Emperor Aurangzeb.

Elephanta Caves : On the island of the same name about 6 miles from Mumbai harbour are rock-cut caves of the 7th and 8th century. The name Elephanta is due to the Portuguese, who were apparently struck by the stone elephants which were once found in the landing place.

Ellora Caves : About 15 miles north-west of Aurangabad in Maharashtra State are about 34 caves excavated in the face of a hill.

Fatehpur Sikri : 23 miles from Agra in Uttar Pradesh was the city founded by *Akbar* in 1571 but abandoned soon after. The place contains a number of places, shrines, mosques. The most notable among them is Buland Darwaza, 176 feet high and built to commemorate the conquest of Gujarat.

Halebid : In Karnataka, 10 miles from Belur, is well-known for its elaborately sculptured temples of the Hoysala period. The monuments rank among the masterpieces of Hindu art.

Hampi : In Karnataka, 9 miles from Hospet railway station, is the ruined capital of the Vijayanagar Empire.

Harappa : In Montgomery district of Punjab, now in West Pakistan, is known for excavations carried out here showing signs of Indus Valley Civilization.

Junagadh : In Gujarat State is one of the most ancient cities of India. It is situated below the Girnar Hill. The temples on the Hill are known for their architecture and paintings.

Kalibangan : In Hanumangarh district of Rajasthan where excavations brought to light the varied achievements of Indus Valley Civilisation—town planning and use of burnt bricks.

Kannauj : Capital of Harshavardhana.

Kanchipuram : Or the "Golden City", 45 miles south-west of Chennai is known for Kailashnath temple. It was the capital of successive dynasties of Hindu rulers.

Kanheri : 20 miles from Mumbai is known for its Buddhist caves dating back to the 1st century A.D.

Kanyakubja : Or modern Kannauj is an ancient city. It was the cultural centre of northern India from the seventh century to the time when the Muslims came.

Kapilvastu : A small ancient kingdom in the north of India; associated with Mahatma Buddha.

Khajuraho : In Chhattarpur in Madhya Pradesh is famous for its group of highly ornate mediaeval Hindu temples.

Kusinagar : In the district of modern Deoria, is the place where *Buddha* died.

Lothal : Ancient town, situated on the sea-plain of former Saurashtra, 450 miles south-east of Mohenjodaro. The excavation made here represent the Indus Valley Civilization.

Madurai : Popularly known as the "City of Festivals", was till the 14th century the capital of the Pandyan kingdom which had sea-borne trade with Rome and Greece. It is famous for Minakshi temple.

Mammalapuram (now *Mahabalipuram*) : Situated 53 miles from Chennai, it is known for rock-cut temples, monolithic figures and carvings of the 7th and 8th centuries A.D. The chief points of interest here are the Five Rathas or temples modelled as chariots—"Arjuna Ratha", "Draupadi Ratha", "Dharamraja Ratha" etc. Also famous for Shore temple.

Mandu : In Madhya Pradesh. It is one of the largest mediaeval city sites. It has extensive remains—fortifications and palaces—a synthesis of Hindu and Muslim styles in architecture and painting; Jama Masjid (of Mandu).

Mithila : It was the home of the three scholar sages—*Gargi, Maitreya* and *Kapila*. It was the capital town of *Raja Janak's* territory.

Mohenjodaro : In the Larkana district of Sindh (now in Pakistan) is the site of excavation revealing Indus Valley Civilization.

Nalanda : In Bihar was the seat of an ancient Buddhist University. It contains a group of Buddhist temples and monasteries.

Palitana : In Saurashtra is famous for its holly hill *Shatrunjaya*. It is the most sacred place for Shvetambara Jains.

Pandharpur : It is in Sholapur district (Maharashtra State). It stands on Bhima river and is one of the most sacred places of pilgrimage in the State.

Prabhaspatan (or **Somnath**) : In Gujarat State is the site of the famous Somnath temple which was destroyed by *Mahmud Ghazni*.

Pragjyotishpur : Was the capital of an ancient tribal kingdom in Kamarupa or modern Assam.

Rajgir : 8 miles south-west of Nalanda by road is an important place of pilgrimage for Buddhists. It was the capital of *Bimbisara* in ancient times. The *Buddha* preached at Rajgir, and so did *Mahavira*, the great preceptor of the Jains.

Sanchi : In Madhya Pradesh is famous for the largest and the most well-preserved Buddhist Stupa (108-foot in diameter and 42-foot in height).

Sarnath : Near Varanasi is the place where the *Buddha* delivered his first sermon after he became the "Englightened One". The place is known for Buddhist temples and remains.

Seringapatam : In Karnataka was the ancient capital of *Tipu Sultan*. (Now known as Seringapatnam.)

Somnathpuram : In Karnataka is known for temples of Hoysala period, Kesava temple.

Sravanbelgola : In Karnataka is famous for its Jain temples and the colossal statue of *Gomateswara (Babubali)*—65-foot high erected in A.D. 983, the tallest monolithic in the world.

Srirangam : An island on the Cauvery river two miles north of Tiruchirapalli. It contains one of the largest temples in south India of the Vijayanagar period.

Sringeri : In Karnataka is a place of pilgrimage on the banks of Tung river where the great philosopher *Sankara* founded one of the principal *maths* (monasteries).

Tamralipti : A flourishing sea port in ancient India.

Tanjore : Was the capital of Cholas. It is situated in the delta of the Cauvery in Tamil Nadu. Also known for Brihadeeswara temple.

Taxila : Ancient capital of Gandhara and one of the most renowned cities of ancient north-west India.

Tirupati : In Andhra Pradesh State, situated about 100 miles to the north-west of Chennai is one of the holiest places in South India. This hill temple of Sri Venkateswara is an example of early Dravidian architecture and is one of the finest in the south.

Ujjain : Known to be the seat of king *Vikrama*, is situated on the bank of Sipra river in Madhya Pradesh. It is one of the seven sacred cities also known as *Avanti*. The Oriental Museum here has some valuable manuscripts and pieces of sculpture. Mahakaleshwar temple here is known as a pilgrimage centre.

Vaishali : In the district of Vaishali in Bihar was the capital of famous Vajji kingdom in ancient times.

Vatapi : *See* **Badami.**

Vikramasila : Was a great Tantrik University established by the Pala King *Dharampala* in A.D. 810. It was a hotbed of moral corruption, sorcery and idolatry. In AD 1198, the soldiers of Ikhtiar Khilji destroyed the structure to the ground and killed all the monks in the university.

Association of Places

Place	Associated with	Place	Associated with
Bardoli	Sardar Patel	Pondicherry	Aurobindo Ghosh
Belur	Rama Krishna Paramhans	Porbandar	Mahatma Gandhi
Chittor	Rana Pratap	Rajghat	Mahatma Gandhi
Fatehpur Sikri	Akbar, the Great	Sabarmati	Mahatma Gandhi
Jallianwala Bagh	Massacre of Indians by the British on April 13, 1919	Seringapatnam	Tipu Sultan
Haldighati	Rana Pratap	Shanti Van	Jawahar Lal Nehru
Kapilvastu	Mahatma Buddha	Shantiniketan	Rabindranath Tagore
Lumbini	Mahatma Buddha	Talwandi	Guru Nanak
Macedonia	Alexander, the Great	Ujjain	Mahavira
Mecca	Prophet Mohammed	Vrindaban (U.P.)	Lord Krishna

Important Foreign Travellers/Envoys

Megasthenes (302-298 BC) : An ambassador of Selecus Nikator, who visited the court of *Chandragupta Maurya*. He wrote an interesting book *'Indica'* inwhich he gave a vivid account of Chandragupta Maurya's reign.

Fa-Hien (405-411 AD) : He came to India during the reign of *Chandragupta II Vikramaditya*. The object of his visit was to see the holy places of Buddhism and to collect Buddhist books and relics. He was the first Chinese pilgrim to visit India.

Hiuen-Tsang (630-645 AD) : He visited India during the reign of *Harshavardhana.*

I-tsing (671-695 AD) : A Chinese traveller, he visited India in connection with Buddhism. His work Biographies of Eminent Monks, provides us useful information about the social, religious and cultural life of the people of this country.

Al-Masudi (957 AD) : An Arab traveller, he has given an extensive account of Idnia in his work 'Muruj-ul-Zahab'.

Al-beruni (1024-1030 AD) : His real name was *Abu Rehan Mahamud* and he came to India along with *Mahmud of Ghazni* during one of his Indian raids. He travelled all over India and wrote a book *'Tahqiq-i-Hind'*. The book dealts with the social, religious and political conditions in India.

Marco Polo (1292-1294 AD) : A Venetian traveller, he visited South India in 1294 A.D. *(during the reign of Pandyan ruler of Madurai, Madverman Kulshekhara : 1272–1311)*. His work 'The Book of Sir Marco Polo' gives an invaluable account of the economic history of India.

Ibn Batuta (1333-1347 AD) : A Morrish traveller, he visited India during the reign of *Muhammad-bin-Tughlaq*. His book *'Rehla'* (the Travelogue) throws a lot of light on the reign of Muhammad-bin-Tughlaq and the geographical, economic and social conditions in India.

Shihabuddin al-Umari (1348 AD) : He came from Damascus. He gives a vivid account of India in his book, *'Masalik albsar fi-mamalik al-amsar'*.

Nicolo Conti (1420-1421 AD) : A Venetian traveller, he gives a comprehensive account of the Hindu kingdom of Vijayanagar.

Abdur Razzaq (1443-1444 AD) : He was a Persian traveller, who came to India and stayed at the court of the Zamorin at Calicut. He has given a vivid account of the Vijayanagar empire, especially of the city. He describes the wealth and luxurious life of the king and the nobles.

Athanasius Nikitin (1470-1474 AD) : He was a Russian merchant, who visited South India in 1470. He describes the condition of the Bahmani kingdom under *Muhammad III* (1463-82).

Duarte Barbosa (1500-1516 AD) : He was a Portuguese traveller. He has given a valuable narrative of the government and the people of the Vijayanagar empire.

Dominigo Paes (1520-1522 AD) : He was Portuguese traveller, who visisted the court of *Krishnadeva Raya* of the Vijayanagar Empire.

Fernao Nuniz (1535-1537 AD) : A Portuguese merchant, who visited the Vijayanagar empire. He wrote the history of the empire from its earliest times of the closing years of *Achyutdeva Raya's* reign.

John Hughen Von Linschotten (1583 AD) : He was a Dutch traveller, who has given a valuable account of the social and economic life of South India.

William Hawkins (1608-1611 AD) : He was an English ambassador of the British King James I to the court of Jahangir (1609).

Sir Thomas Roe (1615-1619 AD) : He was an ambassador of James I, King of England, at the court of Jahangir, the Mughal emperor.

Franciso Palsaert (1620-1627 AD) : He was a Dutch traveller, who stayed at Agra and gave a vivid account of the flourishing trade at Surat, Ahmedabad, Broach, Cambay, Lahore, Multan etc.

Peter Mundy (1630-34 AD) : He was an Italian traveller to the Mughal empire in the reign of *Shahjahan*. He gives valuable information about the living standard of the common people in the Mughal Empire.

John Albert de Mandesto (1638 AD) : He was German traveller, who reached Surat in 1638.

Jeen Baptiste Tavernier (1638-1663 AD) : He was a French traveller, who visited India six times. His account covers the reign of *Shahjahan* and *Aurangzeb*.

Nicolao Manucci (1653-1708 AD) : He was an Italian traveller, who got service at the court of *Dara Shikoh*.

Francois Bernier (1656-1717 AD) : He was French physician and philosopher. Danishamand Khan, a noble of *Aurangzeb*, was his patron.

Jean de Thevenot (1666 AD) : He was French traveller, who has given a good account of cities like Ahmedabad, Cambay, Aurangabad and Golconda.

John Fryer (1672-1681 AD) : He was an English traveller, who has given a vivid account of Surat and Bombay.

Gemelli Careri (1695 AD) : He was an Italian traveller who landed at Daman. His remarks on the Mughal emperor's military organisation and administration are important.

Abbreviated or Alternative Names

Abbreviated/Alternative Name	Original Name
Andhra Kesari	T. Prakasam
Anna	C.N. Annadurai
Badshah Khan	Abdul Ghaffar Khan
Bapu, Mahatma Gandhi	Mohan Das Karam Chand Gandhi
Beacon of Light of Asia	Subhash Chandra Bose
Chacha	Jawahar Lal Nehru
C.R.	C. Rajagopalachari
Deenbandhu	C.F. Andrews
Deshbandhu	C.R. Das
Enlightened One, The	Mahatma Buddha

Abbreviated/Alternative Name	Original Name
Father of Indian Unrest	Bal Gangadhar Tilak
Father of the Local Self-government	Lord Ripon
Father of the Nation (India)	Mahatma Gandhi
Frontier Gandhi	Abdul Ghaffar Khan
Grand Old Man of India	Dadabhai Naoroji
Gurudev	Rabindranath Tagore
Indian Bismarck	Sardar Vallabhbhai Patel
Indian Einstein	Nagarjuna
Indian Napoleon	Samudragupta
J.P./Loknayak	Jayaprakash Narayan
Lal, Bal, Pal	Lala Lajpat Rai, Bal Gangadhar Tilak and Bipin Chandra Pal
Liberator of the Indian Press	Sir Charles Metcalfe
Lion of Punjab (Sher-i-Punjab)	Lala Lajpat Rai
Lokmanya	Bal Gangadhar Tilak
Mahamana	Pt. Mandan Mohan Malaviya
Martin Luther of India	Dayanand Saraswati
Man of Iron/Iron Man of India	Sardar Patel
Netaji	Subhas Chandra Bose
Nightingale of India	Sarojini Naidu
Parrot of India (Tuti-e-Hindustan)	Amir Khusrau
Patriot of Patriots	Subhash Chandra Bose
Punjab Kesari	Lala Lajpat Rai
Scourge of God	Chengiz Khan
Strong Man of India	Sardar Patel

Important Sayings

'Back to Vedas.' — *Dayanand Saraswati*

'Dharma Chakra Pravartana.' — *Mahatma Buddha*

'Dilli Chalo!' — *Subhash Chandra Bose's battle cry of Azad Hind Fauj*

'Do or Die.' — *Mahatma Gandhi* *(while launching Quit India movement in 1942)*

'Give me blood and I will give you freedom.' — *Subhas Chandra Bose* *(in his address to soldiers of Azad Hind Fauj)*

'My ultimate aim is to wipe every tear from every eye.' — *Jawahar Lal Nehru*

'Swaraj is my birthright and I will have it.' — *Bal Gangadhar Tilak*

'Every blow that is hurled on my back will be a nail in the coffin of the British Empire'. — *Lala Lajpat Rai*

'The Congress is tottering to its fall and one of my greatest ambitions while in India is to assist it to a peaceful demise'. — *Lord Curzon*

Important Battles

Name of the	Year	Battle between	Won by	Significance
Battle of Hydaspes	326 BC	Alexander and Porus	Alexander	Fought on the bank of the Jehlum, which is called 'Hydaspes' in Greek;openedrelations between India and the West.
Kalinga War	260 BC	Ashoka and King of Kalinga	Ashoka	Vast destruction and bloodshed changed the attitude of Ashoka and the embraced Buddhism.
First Battle of Tarain or Thaneswar	1191 AD	Prithviraj Chauhan and Mohd Ghori	Prithiviraj Chauhan	
Second Battle of Tarain	1192 AD	– do –	Mohd. Ghori	Establishment of an Islamic empire in India
First Battle of Panipat	1526 AD	Ibrahim Lodhi and Babur	Babur	Onset of the Mughal empire in India.
Battle of Khanwa	1527 AD	Babur and Rana Sanga	Babur	
Battle of Chausa	1539 AD	Sher Shah and Humayun	Sher Shah	Sher Shah became emperor of India.
Second Battle of Panipat	1556 AD	Akbar and Hemu	Akbar	Ended Afghan rule, strengthened mughal rule
Battle of Talikota	1565 AD	Combined force of 4 Muslim rulers of DeccanandRamraja of Vijayanagar	Muslim forces	Destroyed Hindu kingdomoftheDeccan; sealed the fortunes of Vijayanagar empire.
Battle of Haldighati	1576 AD	Rana Pratap and Akbar	Akbar	Rana Pratap fought gallantly and took refuge in a remote fortress.
Battle of Samugarh	1659 AD	Aurangzeb and Imperial forces led by Dara	Aurangzeb	Aurangzeb captured the Mughal throne.
Battle of Plassey	1757 AD	Sirajuddaula and English forces under Clive	English forces	Fought at Plassey. The English became masters of Bengal; foundation of British rule.

Name of the	Year	Battle between	Won by	Significance
Third Battle of Panipat	1761 AD	AhmedShahAbdali and Marathas	Ahmed Shah Abdali	Gave a setback to Marathas in the north; sealed destiny of Mughal empire and made British entry easier.
Battle of Buxar	1764 AD	Joint forces of Muslim and English forces	English forces	Led to English occupation of India.
Third Mysore War	1790 - 1792 AD	English forces and Tipu Sultan	English forces	Tipu Sultan had to sign treaty of the Seringa-pattam.
Fourth Mysore War	1799 AD	English forces and Tipu Sultan	English forces	Fought at Malavali and brought the Mohammedandynasty of Mysore to end.
Second Sikh War	1848 - 1849 AD	English forces and Sikhs	English forces	Sikh kingdom came under the British.

Reforms/Acts

Nomenclature of the Reforms/Acts	Year	During the term of	Significance
Prohibition of Sati & Female infanticide	1829	Lord William Bentick	Supported by Raja Rammohun Roy.
Doctrine of Lapse	1848	Lord Dalhousie	Adoption of sons by rulers in the absence of their natural heirs was banned.
Indian Councils Act	1861	Lord Canning	Envisaged association of Indians with the administration at higher level.
Ilbert Bill	1883	Lord Ripon	To bring Indian and European magistracy on equal footing.
Indian Councils Act	1892	Lord Lansdown	Membership of central legislative councils was enlarged.
Morely-Minto Reforms	1909	Lord Minto II	Separate electroates to widen the gulf between Hindus & Muslims.
Dyarchy	1919	L. Chelmsford	Meaning dual system of Govt.
Jallianwala Bagh Massacre	1919	L. Chelmsford	Massacre at Jallianwala Bagh in Amritsar by General Dyer
Rowlatt Act	1919	L. Chelmsford	Extraordinary powers were given to suppress the freedom struggle with General Dyer as the Commandant.

Nomenclature of the Reforms/Acts	Year	During the term of	Significance
Simon commission	1928	Lord Irwin	To report working of the reforms; recommended dyarchy in provinces; India to be constituted as a federation and Indianization of armed forces.
Gandhi-Irwin Pact	1931	Lord Irwin	Congress called off the agitation and agreed to participate in the Second Round Table Conference.
Communal Award	1932	Lord Willingdon	Envisaged communal representation for depressed classes besides Hindus, Muslims and Sikhs.
Separate electrorates	1932	Lord Willingdon	(*See* Communal Award)
Government of India Act	1935	Lord Willingdon	Provided for a federal type of constitution.
Cripps Mission	1942	Lord Linlithgow	Proposed Dominion status for India after the Second World War.
INA Trial	1945	Lord Wavell	INA prisoners of war were trialed at Red Fort, Delhi and Bhulabhai Desai defended them.
Wavell Plan	1945	Lord Wavell	Envisaged constitution of executive council in such a way as to give representation to all major communities in India.
Cabinet Mission Plan	1946	Lord Wavell	Envisaged establishment of Constituent Assembly to frame the Constitution.
Mountbatten Plan	1947	L. Mountbatten	Partition Plan
IndianIndependence Act	1947	L. Mountbatten	India partitioned and attained independence.

Educational Committees/Commissions

Viceroy	Committee/ Commission	Year	Chairman	Objectives
Lord Ripon (1880-1884)	Hunter Commission	1882	William Hunter	To study the development in education.
Lord Curzon (1899-1905)	University Commission	1902	Thomas Raleigh	To study the Universities and introduce reforms.
Lord Chelmsford (1916-1921)	Calcutta University Commission	1917	Michael Sadler	To study the condition of University.

Viceroy	Committee/ Commission	Year	Chairman	Objectives
Lord Reading (1921-1926)	Indian Disbandment Committee	1923	Lord Itchcap	To discuss the Central Committee of Education
Lord Wavell (1943-1947)	Sargeant Plan	1944	John Sargeant	To raise the standard of Education like Britain.
Famine Commissions				
Lord Lytton (1876-1880)	Famine Commission	1880	Richard Strachey	To give relief of faminestricken.
Lord Elgin (1894-1899)	Famine Commission	1897	James Lyall	To give suggestion on earlier reports
Lord Curzon (1899-1905)	Famine Commission	1900	Anthony McDonnell	To give the suggestion on famine report
Lord Wavell (1943-1947)	Famine Inspection Commission	1943-44	John Woodhood	To investigate in the events of Bengal Famine.
Economic Committees/Commissions				
Lord Lansdown (1888-1894)	Harshell Committee	1893	Hershell	To give suggestion regarding currency.
Lord Lansdown (1888-1894)	Opium Commission	1893	----	To investigate about the effect of opium on health.
Lord Elgin (1894-1899)	Henry Fowler Commission	1898	H. Fowler	To give suggestions on currency.
Lord Curzon (1899-1905)	Irrigation Commission	1901	Sir Wolvin Scott Monkinj	Toplanfortheexpenditure on Irrigation
Lord Hardinge (1910-1916)	Maclagon Committee	1914-15	Maclagon	To advise for cooperative finances
Lord Irwin (1926-1931)	Linlithgow Commission	1928	----	To study the problem in agriculture. (Report by Linlithgow)
Lord Irwin (1926-1931)	Whitelay Commission	1929	J.H. Whitelay	To study the condition of labour in Industries and gardens.
Lord Wellingdon (1931-1936)	Indian Measurement Committee	1935	Lary Hamand	To arrange for inclusion of labour in Federal Assembly.
Lord Linlithgow (1936-1943)	National Planning Committee	1938	Jawaharlal Nehru	To prepare economic plan.

Viceroy	Committee/ Commission	Year	Chairman	Objectives
Administrative Committees/Commissions				
Lord Dufferin (1884-1886)	Etkinson Commission	1886	Charles Etkinson	To involve more Indians in Civil Service
Lord Curzon (1899-1905)	Fraser Commission	1902	Fraser	To investigate the working of police
Lord Hardinge (1910-1916)	Royal Commission on Civil Service	1912	Lord Islington	To give 25% high posts to Indian
Lord Reading (1921-1926)	Royal Commission	1924	Lord Lee	To remove defects of Civil Service
Lord Reading (1921-1926)	Sandhurst Committee	1926	Andrews Skeen	To suggest Indianization of Indian army
Lord Irwin (1926-1931)	Butler Committee	1927	Hercourt Butler	To Examine nature of crown relation with native States

Important Congress Session

Year	Place	Importance
1885	Bombay	At Gokuldas Tejpal Sanskrit College, 72 delegates
1886	Calcutta	436 delegates
1887	Madras	Tayabji became first Muslim President.
1888	Allahabad	George Yule became first English President
1889	Bombay	Congress represented all areas of British India.
1890	Calcutta	Decision taken to organise a session of Congress in London.
1895	Poona	Demand for a representative body only for educated class
1898	Madras	Social reform was set as the main goal.
1907	Surat	Congress split.
1908	Madras	Constitution for the Congress.
1916	Lucknow	Congress merger. Pact with Muslim League, Gandhi attended.
1917	Calcutta	Annie Besant became 1st women President.
1920	Nagpur	Gandhian programme was adopted. Change in congress constitution.
1921	Ahmedabad	Hasrat Mohani demanded for complete independence.
1922	Gaya	Formation of Swaraj Party.
1924	Belgaum	Gandhi became President.
1925	Kanpur	Sarojini Naidu became 1st Indian women President.
1927	Madras	Nehru and S. C. Bose moved resolution for independence and it was passed for the 1st time.

Year	Place	Importance
1928	Calcutta	First All India Youth Congress.
1929	Lahore	'Poorna Swaraj' (Complete Independence) resolution and pledge for Independence day on 26 January 1930.
1931	Karachi	Resolution for Fundamental Rights and National Economic Policy.
1934	Bombay	Formation of Congress Socialist Party.
1936	Lucknow	Support for socialism through democracy.
1937	Faizpur	Demand for Constituent Assembly.
1938	Haripura	Purna Swaraj was to cover also princely states.
1939	Tripuri	S. C. Bose resigned due to difference with Gandhi, after resignation Rajendra Prasad became of INC President.

Governor-General and Viceroys

Governors of Bengal (1757-74)

Robert Clive : Governor of Bengal during 1757-60 and again during 1765-67 and established Dual Government in Bengal from 1765-72.

Vanisttart (1760-65) : The Battle of Buxar (1764).

Cartier (1769-72) : Bengal Famine (1770).

Warren Hastings (1772-74) : Abolished Dual Government (1772).

Governor-Generals of Bengal (1774-1833)

Warren Hastings (1774-85) : Became Governor-General in 1774 through the Regulating Act, 1773; Wrote introduction to the first English translation of the 'Gita' by Charles Wilkins; Founded the Asiatic Society of Bengal with William Jones in 1784.

Revenue Reforms : Auctioned the right to collect land revenue to the highest bidder; Divided Bengal into districts and appointed collectors and other revenue officials.

Judicial Reforms : Started Diwani and Faujdari adalats at the district level and Sadar diwani and Nizamat adalats (appellate courts) at Calcutta; Redefined Hindu and Muslim laws; A translation of the code in Sanskrit appeared in 1776 under the title of "Code of Gentoo laws".

Wars : Rohilla War (1774); 1st Anglo-Maratha War (1776-82); 2nd Anglo-Mysore War (1780-84).

Lord Cornwallis (1786-93) : First person to codify laws in 1793. The code separated the revenue administration from the administration of justice; Created post of district judge; Introduced Permanent Settlement in Bengal (1793); Cornwallis is called 'the father of civil service in India'.

Wars : 3rd Anglo-Mysore War (defeat of Tipu and the Treaty of Seringapatanam, 1792)

Sir John Shore (1793-98) : Introduced the 1st Charter Act (1793).

Wars : Battle of Kharda between Nizam and the Marathas (1795)

Lord Wellesley (1798-1805) : Started Subsidiary Alliance system to achieve British paramountcy in India, Nizam Ali (Nizam of Hyderabad) was the first Indian native ruler to accept the system of subsidiary Alliance (1798); Madras Presidency was formed during his tenure.

Wars : 4th Anglo-Mysore War (1799)—defeat and the death of Tipu Sultan; 2nd Anglo -Maratha War (1803-05)–defeat of the Scindia, the Bhonsle and the Holkar; Treaty of Bassein (1802).

George Barlow (1805-1807) : Vellore Mutiny (1806)

Lord Minto I (1807-1813) : Concluded Treaty of Amritsar with Ranjit Singh (1809); Charter Act of 1813 was passed.

Lord Hastings (1813-1823) : Adopted the policy of intervention and war.

Wars : Anglo-Nepalese War (1813-23); 3rd Anglo-Maratha War (1817-18). Hastings forced humiliating treaties on Peshwa and the Scindia; Introduced the Ryotwari settlement in Madras by Thomas Munro, the Governor.

Lord Amherst (1823-28) : *Wars* : 1st Burmese War (1824-26); Acquisition of territories in Malay Penisula; Capture of Bharatpur (1826).

Lord W. Bentick (1828-33) : Most liberal and enlightened Governor-General of India; Regarded as 'the Father of Modern Western Education in India'; Abolished Sati and other cruel rites (1829); Annexation of Mysore (1831). Concluded a treaty of perpetual friendship with Ranjit Singh (1831); Passed the Charter Act of 1833, which provided that no Indian subject of Company was to be debarred from holding an office on account of his religion, place of birth, descent and colour.

Governor Generals of india (1833-58)

Lord W. Bentick (1833-35) : Macaulay's minutes on education were accepted declaring that English should be the official language of India; Abolished provincial courts of appeal and circuit set up by Cornwallis, appointment of commissioners of revenue and circuit.

Wars : Annexed Coorg (1834), Central Cachar (1834) on the plea of misgovernment.

Sir Charles Metcalfe (1834-1836) : Passed the famous Press Law, which liberated the press in India.

Lord Auckland (1836-42) : 1st Anglo–Afghan War (1836-42)—great blow to the prestige of the British in India.

Lord Ellenborough (1842-44) : Brought an end to the Afghan War; Annexation of Sindh (1843); War with Gwalior (1843); Abolished slavery (1843).

Lord Hardings I (1844-48) : 1st Anglo-Sikh war (1845-46) and the Treaty of Lahore, 1846 (marked the end of Sikh sovereignty in India); Gave preference to English educated in employment.

Lord Dalhousie (1848-56) : Abolished Titles and Pensions, Widow Remarriage Act (1856).

Wars : Introduced Doctrine of Lapse (Captured Satara (1848), Jaitpur and Sambhalpur (1849), Baghat (1850), Udaipur (1852), Jhansi (1853) and Nagpur (1854); Fought 2nd Anglo-Sikh War (1848-49) and annexed the whole of the Punjab; 2nd Anglo–Burmese War (1852) and annexation of Lower Burma or Pegu; Annexation of Berar in 1853; Annexation of Avadh in 1856 on charges of mal-administration.

Administrative Reforms : Introduced the system of Centralized control in the newly acquired territories known as Non-Regulation system; Raised Gurkha regiments.

Educational Reforms : Recommended the Thomsonian system of Vernacular education for whole of the Northwestern Provinces (1853); Wood's Educational Despatch of 1854 and opening of Anglo-Vernacular Schools and Government Colleges; An Engineering College was established at Roorkee.

Public Works : Started the first railway line in 1853 (connecting Bombay with Thana); Started electric telegraph service. Laid the basis of the modern postal system (1854); A separate public works department was set up for the first time; Started work on the Grand Trunk Rod and developed the harbours of Karachi, Bombay and Calcutta.

Lord Canning (1856-58) : The last Governor General of India; Revolt of 1857; Passed the Act of 1858, which ended the rule of the East India Company. Withdrew Doctrine of Lapse.

Governer Generals and Viceroys (1858-1947)

Lord Canning (1858-62) : The Indian Councils Act of 1861 was passed, which proved to be a landmark in the constitutional history of India; The Indian Penal Code of Criminal Procedure (1859) was passed; The Indian High Court Act (1861) was enacted; Income Tax was introduced for the first time in 1858; The Universities of Calcutta, Bombay and Madras founded in 1857; The Indigo riots in Bengal (1860).

Lord Elgin I (1862-63) : Wahabi Movement (Pan-Islamic Movement)

Sir John Lawrence (1864-69) : Telegraphic communication was opened with Europe; High Courts were established at Calcutta, Bombay and Madras in 1865; Expanded canal works and railways; Bhutan War (1865); Advocated State-managed railways; Created the Indian Forests Department and reorganized the native judicial service.

Lord Mayo (1869-72) : Introduced financial decentralization in India, Established Mayo College at Ajmer for the princes; Organised the Satistical Survey of India, Established the Department of Agriculture and Commerce, He was the only Viceroy to be murdered in office by a convict in Andamans in 1872, Introduction of State Railways.

Lord Northbrook (1872-76) : Kuka Movement of Punjab took rebellious turn during his period.

Lord Lytton (1876-80) : Most infamous Governor-General, Pursued free trade and abolished duties on 29 British manufactured goods which accelerated drain of wealth of India, Arranged the Grand Darbar in Delhi (in 1877) when the country was suffering from a severe famine; Passed the Royal Title Act (1876) and Queen Victoriya was declared as the Kaisar-i-Hind; Arms Act (1878) made mandatory for Indians to acquire license for arms; Passed the infamous Vernacular Press Act (1878); Proposed the plan of Statutory Civil Service in 1878-79 and lowered the maximum age limit from 21 to 19 years, the 2nd Afghan war proved a failure.

Lord Ripon (1880-84) : Repeal of the Vernacular Press Act, 1882; The First Factory Act, 1881 to improve labour condition, Resolution of Local Self Government in 1882, Resolution on Land Revenue Policy; Appointed Hunter Commission (for education reforms) in 1882; The Ilbert Bill controversy erupted during his time (1883).

Lord Dufferin (1884-88) : 3rd Burmese War (Annexation of upper and lower Burma in 1885, Establishment of Indian National Congress in 1885.

Lord Lansdowne (1888-94) : The Factory Act of 1891; Categorization of Civil Services into imperial, provincial and subordinate; Indian Council Act of 1892 (introduced elections which was indirect); Appointment of the Durand Commission to define the line between British India and Afghanistan (1893).

Lord Elgin II (1894-99) : The Munda uprising (Birsa Munda) of 1899, Convention delimiting the frontier between China and India was ratified, Great famine of 1896-97, Lyall Commission appointed after famine (1897), Assassination of two British officials–Rand and Amherst–by Chapekar Brothers in 1897.

Lord Curzon (1899-1905) : Appointed a Police Commission in 1902 under Andrew Frazer; Set up the Universities Commission and accordingly the Indian Universities Act of 1904 was passed; Set up the Department of Commerce and Industry; Calcutta Corporation Act (1899); Passed the Indian Coinage and Paper Currency Act (in 1899) and put India on a gold standard; Partition of Bengal took place in 1905 (It was cardinal blunder of Curzon); The idea to build Victoria Memorial (Calcutta) was conceived by Lord Curzon. The foundation stone of memorial was laid in 1906 and it was opened in 1921.

Lord Minto II (1905-10) : Swadeshi Movement (1905-08); Foundation of the Muslim League, 1906; Surat session and split in the Congress (1907), Newspapers Act, 1908; Morley-Minto Reforms, 1909.

Lord Hardinge (1910-16) : Annulment of the partition of Bengal (1911), Transfer of capital from Calcutta to Delhi (1911); Delhi Darbar and Coronation of King George V and Queen Mary (1911); Establishment of Hindu Mahasabha by Madan Mohan Malviya (1915).

Lord Chelmsford (1916-21) : Home Rule Movement launched by Tilak and Annie Besant (1916); Lucknow Pact between Congress and Muslim League (1916); Arrival of Gandhi in India (1915); Champaran Satyagraha (1917); Montague's August Declaration (1917); Kheda Satyagraha and Satyagraha at Ahmedabad (1918); Government of India Act (1919), Repressive Rowlatt Act (1919); Jalianwala Bagh Massacre (April 13, 1919), appointment of Hunter Commission to probe Jalianwala Bagh Massacre (Oct. 19, 1919), Khilafat Movement (1920-22); Non-Cooperation Movement (1920-22).

Lord Reading (1921-26) : Criminal Law Amendment Act and abolition of cotton excise; Repeal of Press Act of 1910 and Rowlatt Act of 1919; Violent Moplah rebellion in Kerala (1921); Foundation of CPI (1921); Chauri Chaura incident (1922); Foundation of Swaraj Party (1923); Kakori Train Dacoity (1925); Foundation of RSS (1925); Murder of Swami Shardhanand (1926).

Lord Irwin (1926-31) : Simon Commission announced in 1927; Butler Commission (1927); Nehru Report (1928); 14 points of Jinnah (1929); Lahore session of Cognress and 'Poorna Swaraj' declaration (1929); Civil Disobedience Movement (1930); Dandi March (1930); Ist Round Table Conference (1930); Gandhi-Irwin Pact (1931).

Lord Willingdon (1931-36) : IInd Round Table Conference (1931); Civil Disobedience Movement (1932); Announcement of MacDonald's Communal Award (1932); IIIrd Round Table Conference; Foundation of Congress Socialist Party — CSP (1934); Government of India Act (1935); Burma separated from India (1935), All India Kisan Sabha (1936).

Lord Linlithgow (1936-43) : General Election (1936-37); Congress ministries in 1937 and Resignation of Congress ministries in 1939; 'Deliverance Day' by Muslim Legue in 1939; Foundation of forward Block by S.C. Bose (1939); Lahore Resolution (1940); August Offer (1940); Cripps Mission (1942); Quit India Movement (1942).

Lord Wavell (1943-1947) : C. R. Formula 1944; Wavell Plan and Shimla Conference in 1945; End of IInd World War in 1945; INA Trials in 1945; Naval mutiny in 1946; Cabinet Mission, 1946 and acceptance of its proposals by Congress; Direct Action Day by the Muslim League on 16th August, 1946.

Lord Mountbatten (Mar-Aug 1947) : Announced the 3 June, 1947 Plan; Introduction of Indian Independence Bill in the house of Commons; Appointment of 2 boundary commissions under Sir Cryil Radicliffe.

Governor Generals of Free India (1947-50)

Lord Mountbatten (1947-48) : The first Governor General of free India; Kashmir acceded to India (Oct., 1947); Murder of Gandhi (Jan. 30, 1948).

C. Rajagopalachari (June 1948 – Jan. 25, 1950) : The last Governor General of free India; The only Indian Governor-General.

★★★

WORLD HISTORY 2

Ancient World : Down to 500 AD

Bronze Age Civilizations

Sl. No.	Name of the Civilization	Modern Area	River Valley
1.	Mesopotamian Civilization (4000 BC - 6th Cen. BC)	Iraq	Tigris and Euphrates
2.	Egyptian Civilization (3400 BC—1000 BC)	Egypt	Nile
3.	Harappan Civilization (2500 BC—1750 BC)	India and Pakistan	Indus
4.	Chinese Civilization (1765 BC—250 BC)	China	Hwang-Ho

Mesopotamian Civilization : The Oldest Civilization of the World

- *Mesopotamia* means 'land between the rivers'. Mesopotamia is the land between the *Tigris* and *Euphrates* rivers.
- Mesopotamia comprises four regions : Sumer (Southernmost region), Babylonia and Akkad (middle region) and Assyria (Northernmost region).
- *Hammurabi* (C.2100 BC), the greatest Baylonian ruler, united the whole of what is now called Iraq into a single Kingdom. Hammurabi gave his people a code of laws. His code covered every aspect of life. His code was based on the law of 'eye for eye' and 'tooth for tooth' i.e., the law of 'tit for tat'.
- Hittites, who came from Asia Minor (now Turkey) and destroyed the Babylonian kingdom, were the first to make regular use of horses for war chariots and to make iron implements.
- The potter's wheel was perhaps first used in Mesopotamia.
- The Mesopotamians also seem to have been the first to make glass ware.
- The Sumerians were the first to evolve a proper system of writing. This system is called *cuneiform*. The cuneiform script was deciphered by *Henry Rawlinson.*
- The Mesopotamian system of counting is known as *sexagesimal* because the Mesopotamian people counted by sixties as we count by tens (decimal system). Their sexagesimal system is no longer in use but we still use it as the basis of division of time into minutes and seconds and of a circle into 360 degrees.
- In geometry, the Mesopotamians had discovered what was later called the Pythagoras' theorem.
- In astronomy, the Mesopotamians made astonishing progress. They could calculate the length of the day and the night. They divided the

whole day into 24 hours. They divided the sky into 12 parts, each assigned a name. This has come down to us as the 12 signs of *zodiac* or *rashis* as we call them in India. Another remarkable achievement of the Mesopotamians was the invention of a lunar calender, based on the moon.

Egyptian civilization

➢ Egypt is called the 'Gift of the Nile'.

➢ Historians divide the history of Egypt into three periods : the *Old Kingdom*, the *Middle Kingdom* and the *New Kingdom.*

➢ The Old Kingdom is also called the 'Age of the Pyramids'.

➢ The Egyptian king was called the *pharaoh.*

➢ The Egyptians were the worshipper of the nature and the sun was their most important god.

➢ The Egyptians believed that after death both the body and the soul live while other people believed that only the soul lives and body perishes. So Egyptians took great care in preserving the body of the dead. The body was embalmed in spices and then wrapped in strips of fine linen. Such a preserved body is called a *mummy*. The mummy was put in a wooden box and buried.

➢ The *Pyramids* and the *Sphinx* are the two specimens of Egyptian architectural excellence.

➢ The *Pyramids* were the tombs of kings and they contained the mummies of these monarchs. The most imposing of all is *the Great Pyramid* at Gizeh in *cairo,* built by the king *Cheops (Khufu)* of the old kingdom. The Great Pyramid is one of seven wonders of the ancient world.

➢ The *Sphinx* is a mythological animal with the body of a lion and the head of a man. Each Sphinx was carved out of a single solid stone.

➢ The Egyptian script, known as *hieroglyhic,* was deciphered by *champollion.*

➢ The Egyptians developed a decimal system of numeration.

➢ The crowning achievement of the Egyptians was the solar calender.

Harappan civilization

The Harappan Civilization extended over a bigger area than any of the contemporary civilization.

Note : *For Details, See 'Indus Civilization'.*

Chinese civilization

➢ The earliest Chinese civilization is the *Shang* civilization.

➢ The Shang dynasty was overthrown by the *Chou* dynasty.

➢ The Chinese script is a pictographic script. It is remarkable that the Chinese script has changed very little since the earliest times.

➢ The Chinese calender — Solar-lunar calender, was a combination of solar and lunar calender. The Chinese were the first to calculate the length of the year as 365 1/4 days.

- In 3rd century BC, the *Chin* dynasty became important. To keep out invaders from the north, he began construction of a wall known as the *Great Wall.*
- The *Han* dynasty followed the Chin dynasty in 202 BC and the Han emperors ruled China for almost 400 years.
- The political practices of the Han rulers were greatly influenced by the teachings of *Confucius.* During Han rule, to qualify for appointment, the youngmen had to pass through an elaborate system of examination before they were chosen. Such 'scholar-officials' came to be known as *mandarins.* The Chinese was the first civilization in history to have a system of selecting public officials on the basis of education and competitive examination.
- Under the Hans, silk was a principal item of export.
- Two main roads were built across the Great Wall to carry on trade with the West.
- The two major religions of ancient China are Taoism (based on the teachings of *Lao-tse* : b. 604 BC) and Confucianism (based on the teachings of *Confucius*: 551 BC—479 BC). Confucius was a contemporary of Mahavira and Buddha.
- Buddhism was brought into China by Indian during the Han rule.
- The Great Wall is a mightly monument to the building skill of ancient China. This wall, built of stone and earth to a height of 6 metres and extending over 2400 km.
- The Chinese script was standardized by the Chin ruler. The Chinese script spread to other countries also. It influenced the Japanese, Korean and Vietnamese scripts.
- In the 1st century AD, paper was invented in China. The invention of paper and its importance in spreading knowledge within the outside China makes it one of the great contribution of China to the world.
- Some of the first historical works in the world were written in China. Each dynasty compiled its own history. The pattern of these histories was set by *Ssuma Chien* (1st or 2nd cent. BC), and is commonly remembered as the 'Herodotus of China'.
- The water clock, abacus, umbrella were invented by Chinese.
- In the 2nd cent. AD, Chinese invented a seismograph.

Iranian civilization

- In the middle of the 6th century BC, a powerful empire — *Achaemenid empire* — arose in Iran (Persia). The founder of this empire was *Cyrus* with his capital at Pasaragadae.
- He was succeeded by *Darius I* (522 BC — 486 BC). The empire reached its greatest extent under him and covered entire Iran, Mesopotamia, Syria, Egypt, Asia minor and north-western India. He built a new capital at Persepolis.
- Darius I and his successors were involved in wars with the Greek states. They were defeated by Greeks. *Alexander* dealt the empire a final blow during the reign of *Darius III.*

- In the 3rd century AD, a new and powerful empire — Sassanid empire — arose in Iran. This empire which was founded by *Ardashir* in 226 AD held sway in Iran up to the middle of the 7th century AD.
- The Arabs, who emerged as a strong power after the rise of Islam, conquered Iran in 651 AD.
- The Achaemenids had introduced the use of money — coins of gold and silver — on a large scale throughout the empire.
- Iran in ancient times produced a number of famous sailors and explorers. One of them, *Scylax*, undertook a voyage from the mouth of Indus to Egypt on orders of Darius.
- The main religion of the ancient Iranians was Zoroastrianism. This religion was founded by *Zarathustra* or *Zoroaster* (628 BC — 551 BC) as the Greeks called him in 7th century BC. The teachings of Zarathustra are recorded in the *Zend Avesta*, the holy book of Parsis. Zarathustra said that the world consists of two forces, good and evil. The god, *Ahura Mazda* represents the forces of good, and *Ahirman*, the forces of evil. The sun and the fire came to be worshipped as visible symbols of Ahura Mazda, who represents light. Both Judaism and Christianity indebted to Zoroastrianism.
- During the Achaemenid empire the official language was *Aramaic*. The Sassanids revived old *Persian* and made it the official language of their empire. But then a new script called *Pahlavi* had also developed. The best known ancient literature of Iran is the Zend Avesta, which contains the work of Zarathustra.

Greek civilization

- The early Greeks (or Hellens), like the Aryans in India, lived in tribes, each composed of a number of families under a leader. A group of tribes had a king.
- The main occupations are agriculture and herding.
- The early Greeks had many gods whom they imagined to be like human beings, though more powerful and immortal. *Zeus* was the god of the sky and hence caused thunder. *Poseidon,* god of the sea, raised stroms that sank ships.
- *Appollo,* the sun god, could reveal the future. *Athena,* was the goddess of victory and patroness of the arts. *Dionysus* was the god of wine and there were many others. The Greeks thought their gods lived on *Mount Olympus.*
- Around 800 BC, groups of Greek villages began joining into larger units to form city-states. At the highest point in a city-state, an *acropolis* or citadel was built for defence and city spread out around the acropolis. Such cities were Sparta, Athens, Macedonia, Corinth, Thebes and others. Sparta and Athens were two most important city-states.
- The Spartans' main concern was with militarism and war so much so that the word 'spartan' is often used to mean militaristic.
- Spartans were fine soldiers, but they contributed little else to Greek culture.

- The city-state of Athens developed along lines quite different from Sparta. The territories it ruled had been occupied gradually and peacefully and militarism had not developed. Athens had excellent harbours and mineral deposits. Athenians built a prosperous trade and culture. *Pericles* (469 BC — 429 BC) was the most important ruler of Athens.
- *The Battle of Marathon (490 BC) :* The Greek defeated the Iranian (Persian) king Darius I at Marathon near Athens.
- The *Peloponnesian war*, between Sparta and Athens from 431 BC to 404 BC, ended in tragedy for Athens.
- *Philip* of Macedonia conquered most of states in the years following Athens' defeat.
- Then his son, *Alexander,* set out at the age of 20 — to conquer the world.
- During the 13 years (336 BC — 323 BC), he compelled all Greece to accept his leadership and conquered the Achaemenid empire. This brought him to borders of India where he defeated king *Porus* on the Jhelum in 326 BC. He sailed down the Indus and then returned to Mesopotamia where he died of fever in 323 BC at the age of 32.
- Alexander's conquests brought many important changes to the world. Trade between Europe and Asia was developed. Many new cities were founded.
- In the 2nd century BC, the Roman empire started expanding eastward. As a result of Roman attacks, almost the entire territory of the Greeks and their empire became a part of the Roman empire.

Contributions of Greek Civilization

- The glory of Greece that the world has never forgotten was largely the glory of Athens at the time of Pericles.
- The *Olympic games* were first held in 776 BC by the Greeks in honour of God Zeus at Mouut Olympus (Olympia) in Greece, hence the name, and they continued till 394 AD. From 394 AD these games started degenerating and by 580 AD they altogether vanished. They were banned by the Roman Emperor *Theodosius* as Pagan manifestations.

  It was the French Baron, *Pierre de Coubertin,* who (nearly over 1500 years after the last ancient Olympics) revived these games in 1894 and the modern series of the Olympic games started in 1896 at Athens and since then they are being held every fourth year.
- *Homer's* 'Iliad' and 'Odyssey' are among the best epics of the world. The *Iliad* is the story of seize and destruction of the city of Troy, as the western coast of Asia Minor. The *Odyssey* describes the adventures and home coming, from Troy, of a Greek hero, Odysseus.
- The founder of Greek tragedy was *Aeschylus,* author of 'Promethus Bound'. *Sophocles* is considered the greatest of Greek tragedians. His famous plays are 'Oedipus Rex', 'Antigone' and 'Electra'.

  Aristophanes, is considered the master of Greek comedy.

- Greece produced some of the world's earliest great historians e.g. *Herodotus* (known as 'the father of History'), *Thucydides, Plutarch* etc.
- The most famous philosophers of Greece were *Socrates, Plato* (disciple of Socrates and author of 'Republic'), and *Aristotle* (disciple of Plato). Aristotle was both philosopher and scientist. He made important contribution to philosophy, medicine, biology and astronomy. He believed in the principle of the Golden Mean, that is, neither extreme luxary nor self-denial.
- The Greek made many contributions to mathematics, especially to geometry as is seen in the work of *Euclid* and *Pythagoras*.
- In medicine, *Hippocrates* laid the foundation of modern medicine. He is the known as the 'father of medicine'.
- The most important astronomers were: *Aristarchus, Ptolemy, Hipparchus, Eratosthenes* etc. Ptolemy's belief that the earth was the centre of the universe was accepted as truth untill the 16th century. Eratosthenes prepared a fairly accurate map of the globe and was the first to suggest that one could reach India from Europe by sailing west.
- The temple of Athena, the Parthenon, is the best example of Greek architecture. Myron and Phidias are two best-known sculptors of ancient Greece. It was Phidias whom Pericles appointed to supervise the construction of the Acropolis in Athens.

Roman civilization

- The centre of the Roman civilization was Italy, the peninsula that projects into the Mediterranean sea in the west of Greece. The river Tiber on which the city of Rome is located runs through the central part of the peninsula.
- The city of Rome was founded about 1000 BC by *Romulus,* in the district of Latium. The language of the ancient Romans, *Latin,* gets its name from Latium.
- The early Romans had a king, an assembly and a senate.
- Towards the end of the 6th century BC the king was overthrown and a republic was established. Under the Republic the Romans conquered other parts of the peninsula, and by 265 BC controlled all of Italy. The political system of the Roman republic consisted of two consuls, the senate & the assembly.
- The Romans were involved in a series of wars with carthage, a city on the north coast of Africa. The danger of Carthaginian occupation of Sicily led the Romans to attack Carthage. The wars that followed, known as the *Punic Wars,* lasted from 264 BC to 146 BC. The Carthaginians were defeated in this war.
- By the beginning of the 1st century BC the Roman had conquered Greece and Asia Minor and established a protectorate over Egypt.
- Rivalry for power grew between two generals, *Pompey* & *Julius Caesar.* War between them followed and Pompey was murdered by his enemies

in Egypt. Caesar remained in Egypt for some time, attracted by the captivating beauty of the Egyptian queen *Cleopatra.* On his return to Rome, in 46 BC, he made himself dictator. However, on the charge that Caesar intended to become king, he was assassinated in 44 BC, in a senate meeting.

➢ After the assassination of Caesar, power passed into the hands of *Mark Antony* and *Lapidus*, Caesar's friends and *Octavian,* Caesar's grand-nephew. The leaders of the conspiracy, *Brutus* and *Cassius,* fled and organised a large army, but they were captured and slain.

➢ In 37 BC, *Octavian* became the most powerful man in the Roman empire. He ruled for 44 years under the titles of *Augustus Imperator,* meaning 'holy victorious-general.' He also called himself *Princeps,* 'first citizen of the state'.

The period of Roman history beginning with his rule up to 284 AD is called 'the Principate'. His rule and the period following it were peaceful and are known in history as *Pax Romana,* which means 'Roman Peace'.

➢ In 284 AD, *Diocletian* became ruler. From this time on, Roman civilization declined more rapidly. One of Dioclectian's successor, *Constantine,* built a new capital called Constantinopole, on the site of ancient Byzantium, in 330 AD. Not long after, the Roman empire was divided into two empires — Western & Eastern. The Western part soon broke into many pieces. But Eastern part, called as Byzantine empire, continued for a thousand years more.

➢ The final blow to the Roman empire at the hands of northern invaders they were German tribes. By 476 AD,the once powerful Roman empire was no more.

➢ The Roman worshipped as many gods & goddesses as the Greeks. *Jupiter* sent rain for the corps; *Mars* helped them in war; *Mercury* carried their messages; *Neptune,* the god of sea; *Vesta* guarded the home; *Juno* protected their women.

Contributions of Roman Civilization

➢ Roman law and principles of governance are Rome's greatest contribution to the world.

➢ So complete was Rome's system of road linking all parts of empire that people could say 'All roads lead to Rome'.

➢ The Roman developed their own alphabet and the *Latin* language became the language of all educated people in western Europe. Latin words are still widely used in science, and Latin is the basis of several European languages — esp. French, Spanish & Italian.

➢ *Lucretius, Cicero, Marcus Aurelius & Seneca* were the famous Roman philosophers.

➢ *Horace* ('Odes') & *Virgil* ('Aeneid') were the famous Roman poets.

➢ *Tacitus* ('Annals' & 'Histories') was the most famous Roman historian and *Pliny, the elder,* was the another famous Roman historian.

➢ The Romans were the inventors of concrete and could firmly cement bricks and stones together. They also introduced two architectural improvements — the arch and cupolas or domes.

➢ Fights between gladiators or between a gladiator and a wild animal, was a popular Roman amusement. Special arenas or amphitheatres were built for these contests. The ruins of the Colosseum, one of the greatest of arenas, can be seen in Rome.

Seven Wonders of Ancient World
1. Hanging garden of Babylon
2. Pyramids of Egypt
3. The Pharaoh at Alexandria
4. Statue of Zeus at Olympia
5. Colossus at Rhodes-912 ft. statue of Helos, the sun god, stands at one side of the harbour
6. Temple of Diana at Epheus (Rome)
7. Mausoleum of Mausolus (Ruler of Halicarnassus)

MEDIEVAL WORLD : (500 AD — 1500 AD)

Medieval Europe

➢ The Eastern Roman empire or Byzantine empire was a vast empire and its capital *Constantinople* was the largest city of that time.

➢ The Byzantines built beautiful churches. The most famous of these is the *church of St. Sophia* in Constantinople. This church was built during the reign of Byzantine emperor *Justinian* in the 6th century AD.

➢ The Ottoman Turks conquered the Byzantine territories in 1453.

Feudalism

➢ The word 'feudal' comes from *feud* which originally meant a fief or land held on condition or service. In a feudal society, land was the source of power.

➢ Feudalism originated in the 8th & 9th centuries.

➢ First of all in western Europe the feudal system developed

➢ The main division in feudal society was between '*feudal lords*', who either got a share of the peasants' produce or had peasants to work on their lands without any payment, and *'Peasants'*, who worked on the land.

Feudal Hierarchy :

1. *Feudal Lords* : a. Kings b. Dukes & Earls c. Barons d. Knights.
2. *Peasants* : three categories of peasants — freeholders, villeins & serfs.

In feudal hierarchy, the king stood at the top and peasant stood at the bottom.

➢ The economic life under the feudal system was predominantly rural. The unit of land, which was like a village-farm, was called '*manor*'.

Crusades : 1095 AD — 1291 AD

➢ Crusades means the military expeditions, under the banner of the cross, organised in western christendom primarily to recover the *Holy Places of Palestine* from Muslim occupation.

- Four Crusades were fought by the European Christian to liberate *Jerusalem* from Seljuq Turks (Muslims) who did not permit Christian pilgrims to enter the holy land.
- The *Ist Crusade (1095-99)* was launched after the provoking preachings of Pope Urban II. Jerusalem was captured and the Crusader states of the Kingdom of Jerusalem, the country of Edessa, Antioch and Tripoli were created.
- The fall of Edessa (1144) inspired the unsuccessful *IInd Crusade (1147-48).*
- The capture of Jerusalem by Saladin in 1187 led the inconclusive *IIIrd Crusade (1189-92),* led by Philip II Augustus of France, Frederich I Barbarossa of Germany, and Richard I (the 'Lion Heart') of England.
- The *IVth Crusade (1202-91)* was diverted from its original objective, Egypt, and sacked Constantinople (1204). This Crusade failed to recover lost ground and Acre, the last foothold of West is Palestine, was lost in 1291.

Arab civilization

- In the 7th century, a new religion, Islam, arose in Arabia, which led to the establishment of a big empire.
- *Muhammad,* the Prophet of Islam, was born in Mecca in 571 AD.
- When he was 40, he had 'visions of truth' and became a prophet.
- Muhammad's visions completely convinced him that *Allah* was the only god.
- He forbade the worship of idols and made many enemies. Ultimately, he had to leave Mecca and take refuge in Medina. This event took place in 622 AD and is known as the year of *Hijira,* or migration, and from it Muslims date their era (*Hijira Samvat*).
- The *Quran,* the holy book of Islam, is divided into a number of suras, or chapters, and contains the teachings of Muhammad. Besides the Quran, the life of a Muslim is guided by the *Sunna,* the practices of Muhammad, and the *Hadees,* the sayings of the Muhammad.
- Muhammad was not only a religious leader but also a political leader.
- After his death (632 AD), his successors, were known as *Caliphs,* or *Khalifas* who held both religious and political authority.
- Nearly all Arabia had accepted the new religion and become a unified state before the death of Prophet Muhammad in 632 AD.
- From Arabia, Islam spread very fast to many other parts of the world. Within a hundred years, the Khalifas and their generals, had conquered Iran, Syria, Egypt, Central Asia, North Africa and Spain. The Arab empire was the largest that world had so far seen.
- The first three Khalifas ruled from the city of *Medina*. Then the capital was shifted *Kufah.*
- By 660 AD, when the *Omayyad* dynasty took over the reins of government, the principal city was *Damascus.*
- About 750, the Omayyad were overthrown by *Abbasids,* who made

Baghdad their capital. *Harun Rashid,* famous in many legends, was an Abbasid ruler.

- The Abbasids ruled for about 300 years, till the *Seljuq Turks* took Baghdad and ended the Arab rule. During the next four centuries, the Turks dominated the Islamic world.
- In the 15th century, most of these territories came under the domination of the *Ottoman Turks*. It was the Ottoman Turks who took *Constantinople* and ended the Eastern Roman empire in 1453.

Contributions of Arab Civilization

- The establishment of a vast empire facilitated the coming together of intellectual and scientific traditions of various civilizations, particularly Greek, Iranian & Indian. The Arabs made all knowledge their own and developed in further.
- *Al Razi (Rhazes),* an Arab scientist discovered the true nature of small pox, and *Ibn Sina (Avicenna)* discovered that tuberculosis is infectious.
- In Mathematics, the Arab learned the Indian numerals *(Hindsah)* and spread their use far and wide, so that in the West they are to this day called Arabic numerals.
- Some of the famous literary work of the Arab civilization are the 'Rubaiyat' by *Omar Khayyam,* 'Shahnama' by *Firdausi* and the 'Arabian Nights', a collection of 1001 stories.
- The Arabs developed their own decorative designs. Their buildings had bulblike domes, small minarets, horse-shoe arches and twisted columns.
- The Arabs also developed a decorative style of writing called *Calligraphy* and made book-illumination an art.
- Arab carpets, leather work, beautiful swords, silks, inlays, metal-work, and enamelled glassware were prized everywhere.

Medieval China

- From the early 7th century, China was ruled by the *Tang* dynasty.
- The rule of Tang dynasty (618 AD — 906 AD) was followed by the *Sung* dynasty for about 300 years.
- After this, for about 100 years China was ruled by the *Mongols*.
- The rule of the Mongols in China was followed by that of *Ming* dynasty which continued for about 300 years.
- In 1644, China was conquered by the *Manchus* who continued to rule until 1911 AD.

Contributions of Medieval China

- To prevent drain on the country's wealth the Sung rulers started the use of paper-money.
- The invention of gun-powder was made in China in the 10th century about 400 years before the knowledge reached the Western World.
- The Chinese made iron-chain suspension bridges as early as the 10th century.

- The Chinese devised the first method of printing in 10th century. The importance of this invention for the spread of knowledge was as great as the invention of paper.

Medieval Japan

- Japan consists of hundreds of small islands of which four are major islands — Hokkaido, Honshu, Kyushu & Shikoku.
- Almost the entire country was unified into a single state by around the 7th century AD.
- In the 8th century *Edo* (modern *Kyoto*) became the capital and continued to be the seat of the emperors of Japan for over 1000 years. The real power, however, was in the hands of an aristocratic family.
- Towards the end of the 12th century, a new political institution *Shogun* came into being. The Shogun or the 'General' became the commander of Japan's army and ruled Japan, while the emperor remained at his capital at Edo (Kyoto).
- Until 1867, the Shoguns were the real rulers of Japan. *Tokugawa Leyasu* was the founder of last Shogun dynasty.
- In 1867, the last Shogun of Tokugawa dynasty was overthrown and the power was restored to the emperor. Now Japan launched herself on the road of industrial development, modernization and expansion.
- *Samurai* or the warriors were similar to the Knights of Western Europe.
- The most unique contribution of medieval Japan to literature was a form of poetry called *Haiku*. Haiku poems are short poems of only 17 syllables.
- The important contribution of medieval Japan to art was *Ikebana* or the art of flower arrangement, which is being imitated throughout the world.

Seven Wonders of Medieval World
1. Collosseum of Rome
2. Great Wall of China
3. Porcelain Tower of Nanking
4. Stonehenge of England
5. Mosque at St. Sophia (Constantinople)
6. Catacombs of Alexandria
7. Leaning Tower of Pisa.

- *Buddhism* reached Japan early in the 6th century from China through Korea and during the course of centuries it became widespread. In certain periods it even eclipsed *Shintoism*, the old religion of Japan.
- Gradually, the Japanese developed their own distinct schools of Buddhism, the most famous of which is *Zen Buddhism*. The word *Zen* is derived from 'Dhyana'.

MODERN WORLD : (1500 AD Onwards)

Renaissance

- The 16th century is commonly designated as the 'Age of Renaissance', also called the 'Revival of learning'.
- It is said to have started from the capture of Constantinople (now Istanbul) by the Turks in 1453 and the dispersal of the scholars throughout Europe, who sought asylum in Italy.

➢ *Italy* practically became the home of the Renaissance-and fundamental to the Renaissance was the revival of classical learning, art and architecture and the concept of the dignity of the man, which characterized *Humanism.* It resulted in the emancipation of the mind of man from the shackles of effete dogmatism, and in the creation of fresh intellectual atmosphere and ideals of life.

➢ Great writers of the Italian Renaissance included *Dante, Petrarch, Boccaccio & Machiavelli.* Great painters of Italian Renaissance included *Leonardo da Vinci* (Famous Paintings:' The Last Supper'& 'Monalisa'), *Michelangelo*('The Last Judgement' & 'The Fall of Man') & *Raphel* ('Madona'). Great astronomers of Italian Renaissance included *Bruno & Galileo.*

➢ The movement spread to other countries of Europe also, especially to France & Germany; and at last it reached the shores of England, where it manifested itself in the poems of *Chaucer* & *Spenser,* the plays of *Shakespeare,* the essays of *Francis Bacon* & utopianism of *Thomas More,* and particularly in the courts of such rulers as Elizabeth I of England.

➢ The Renaissance movement was enormously, helped by the invention of the printing press (in 1454 by *Gutenberg* of Germany; 'Gutenberg Bible' 1456 – the first printed book); with the help of which old and classical books were multiplied leading to a great increase in knowledge and in the spirit of enquiry and experiment.

Great Litterateurs of Renaissance

Italian	*Dante* ('Divine Comedy'), *Petrarch* (founder of Humanism & known as the 'father of Humanism), *Boccacio* ('Decameron'), *Machiavelli* ('The prince').
Spanish	*Cervantes* ('Don Quixote').
Portuguese	*Cameos* ('The Lusiad').
Dutch	*Erasmus* ('In the praise of Folly').
French	*Rebelais* ('Pantagruel' & 'Gargantua'), *Montaigne* ('Essais').
German	*Thomas Kempis* ('The Imitation of Christ').
English	*Chaucer* ('Canterbury Tales'), *Spenser* ('The Faerie Queen'), *Bacon* ('The Advancement of Learning'), *Shakespeare* ('Romeo & Juliet','The Merchant of Venice','As You Like It','Julieus Caesar', 'Hamlet', Macbeth), *Thomas More* ('Utopia').

Reformation

➢ The Reformation was another movement that the 16th century witnessed.

➢ It was started by *Martin Luther* in *Wittenburg,* Germany in 1517 by publicly protesting against the sale of letters of *Indulgence.*

(Indulgence : the letters which remitted punishments of the sinners who bought them and which began to be considered as passports to heaven.)

➢ It was a revolt against the control of conscience by the priests.

- Thanks to the inborn spirit of revolt against the Catholic Church, Henry VIII of England could take the bold step of breaking away from the papacy i.e., authority of the Pope on the issue of his first divorce in 1534. Henry VIII declared himself the head of the church when the Pope would not give him permission to divorce his wife, Catherine.
- With the breaking away from the Roman Catholic Church by such leaders as *Luther* of Germany and *Calvin* of Switzerland, Western Europe was split between Catholic & Protestant countries, a situation which developed enmities of the fiercest nature.
- The movement, which began within the Catholic Church to combat the effects of the Protestant Reformation, was known as *Counter-Reformation Movement.*

Geographical Discoveries

- A great development which marked the beginning of the modern age in Europe was a series of geographical discoveries.
- Helped by some remarkable inventions viz. the Compass and Astrolabe, daring sailors sailed from distant lands.
- They were financed by rulers and merchants.
- The main motivation behind these adventures was the lure of profits that trade with the East would bring.
- During 1288-93, *Marco Polo* (1256-1326), Venetian traveller, travelled from Venice to China and Japan. He was the 'first European to visit China'. From his travelogue the Europeans learned about the all round prosperity of the East.
- The first great steps in the exploration of the earth were taken by the sailors under the patronage of Portuguese and Spanish rulers.
- *Prince Henry* (1394-1460), the Navigator of Portugal, encouraged sailors by making maps based on trips to the African coast.
- In 1487, *Bartholomew Diaz,* reached the point which the Portuguese named *Cape of Good Hope* (the southern-most point of Africa).
- *Vasco da Gama* followed this route and sailed on round the cape and reached Calicut in India in 1498.
- Italian sailor *Columbus'* trip was financed by Spain from where he sailed in 1492. When he had reached land, he thought he had reached India; so he called the islands, the 'Indies'; but it was America.
- The land discovered by Columbus was soon to be called the 'Americas' after the name of a later Italian explorer, *Amerigo Vespucci.*
- *Magellan,* a Portuguese sailor, went beyond the lands that had stopped Columbus. He sailed went around the tip of South America, which is named after him—the straits of Magellan. He called the new ocean

Colonialism : *Colony* means the country or territory settled by migrants from another country. Thus, the policy of having colonies and keeping them dependent is called Colonialism.

Imperialism : The policy of extending a state's rule over other territories, and of incorporating such colonized into an empire is called Imperialism.

that he entered, 'The Pacific' because it seemed more quiet than the Atlantic. Magellan reached what is now called the Phillippine Island where he died. Magellan was the first to sail round the world.

- Other countries—England, France & Holland—also sent out their ships to join the race for explorations. *Francis Drake* of England sailed round the world in 1577.
- These voyages laid the foundations for the almost complete geographical knowledge of the world.

Geographical Discoveries

Discovery	year	Discoverer (Nationality)	Sponsered by
Cape of Good Hope	1487	Bartholomew Diaz (Portuguese)	Portugal
America	1492	Christopher Columbus (Geneo, Italian)	Spain
Newfoundland	1497	John Cabot (Italian)	England
Sea-route of India via Cape of Good Hope	1498	Vasco da Gama (Portuguese)	Portugal
Brazil	1500	Pedro Alvarez Cabral (Portuguese)	Portugal
Strait of Magellan	1520	Magellan (Portuguese)	Spain
Island of Tasmania & New Zealand	1642	Tasman (Dutch)	Holland
Sandwich Island / Hawaiian Island	1770	Captain James Cook (British)	England
North pole	1909	Robert Peary (American)	USA
South Pole	1911	Amundsen (Norwegian)	Norway

Glorious Revolution : 1688, England

- *James II* was a Roman Catholic. His tactless attempt to secure freedom of worship for Catholics united the Whigs and Tories of the Anglican Church against him.
- People tolerated the rule of James II, because they thought that he would be succeeded by his daughter Mary who was a Protestant. But a son was born to James II. The knowledge that James' policies might be continued by a son to be brought up as a Catholic turned against him many Tories, hitherto loyal to him.
- So a few leading men—Whigs as well as Tories—dispatched an invitation to *William* of Orange, ruler of Holland, to succeed to the English throne and save England form Catholic tyranny.
- William accepted the invitation and came to England for his purpose.
- James II, throwing the great seal into the Thames, fled to France.
- This event is known as *Glorious* or *Bloodless Revolution* in England.
- **Effects :** (1) The despotic rule of the *Stuarts* ended; the supremacy of Parliament was established. (2) The system of requiring estimate

and accounts for supplies and, of specific appropriations—which is nucleus of modern budgetary system—now became fixed. (3) *The Bill of Right (1689) :* It settled down the problem of succession; it also laid the provision that no Roman Catholic can wear the Crown. As *William III* and his wife *Mary II* (daughter of James II and a Protestant by faith), the joint monarchs accepted the Bill of Rights.

Magna Carta (or The Great Charter), 1215 : It was the Charter of liberties which king *John II* of England was forced to sign in 1215 at Runnymede. It meant to put a check upon the arbitrary powers of king. The most important principle that it laid down was that English man should be governed by definite laws and not by the whims or the will of a despotic ruler. Magna Carta was said to be the 'Foundation-stone of rights and liberties of the English people'.

Habeas Corpus Act, 1679 : This act during the reign of *Charles II* of England provided that no one was to be imprisoned without a writ or warrant stating the charge against him. It also gave facilities to a prisoner for obtaining either speedy trial or release on bail. The Act safeguarded the personal liberties of the people against arbitrary imprisonment by King's orders.

Industrial Revolution

- The process of change that transformed Britain first and then other countries from agricultural to industrial economics.
- The Industrial Revolution began about 1750 when the agricultural revolution was well under way. Inventions were made in the textile industry by such men as *James Hargreaves* (Spinning Jenny, 1764), *Richard Arkwright* (Water Frame, 1769), *Samuel Crompton* (Mule, 1779), and *Emmund Cartwright* (Power Loom, 1785), which made the production of cloth much faster and the yarn produced of better quality.

Capitalism : Economic system in which a country's trade and industry are organised and controlled by the owners of capital, the chief elements being competition, profit, supply and demand.

- These new machines required factories to house them, at first near rivers for water power and then, when the steam engine was invented (by *James Watt* in 1769), near coalfields.
- England, an agriculutral country was now turned into a manufacturing country. The production increased manifold. Things were available at cheaper rates. Improved methods of communication followed.
- The economic progress and industrialisation of England influenced the social & cultural life of the people. It had far-reaching affects on the political history of England.
- By 1850 the Industrial Revolution had penetrated into Belgium, France, Germany, Switzerland and USA. By 1900 it had extended to Sweden, Italy, Russia, Japan & Argentina. Presently it is penetrating into China, India and Africa.

American Revolution or American War of Independence : 1775-83

- The American Revolution is the name given to the struggle by which

13 colonies of England in North America declared their independence from England and fought a war to make it a reality.

- By the middle of the 18th century, differences in thought and interests had developed between the colonies one the one hand and the mother country (England) on the other.
- Attempts to collect new taxes such as the *Stamps Act (1765)* and *Tax on tea (1767)* angered the colonists who maintained that the British government was imposing *'taxation without representation'* and that only the colonial representative assemblies could rightfully tax the Americans.
- *Boston Tea Party (1773) :* The tax on tea led to trouble. In 1773, several colonies refused to unload the tea coming in English·ships. In Boston, when the governor ordered a ship to be unloaded, a group of citizens dressed as American Indians, boarded the ship and dumped the crates of tea into the water. This incident is known as the 'Boston Tea Party'.
- The American Revolution started in 1775 and lasted until 1781.
- On July 4, 1776, the *Declaration of Independence* was issued. Its author was *Thomas Jafferson.* The Declaration started that all men are created equal; that they have a natural and inalienable right to life, liberty and pursuit of happiness; and that they are justified in revolting when these rights are violated by any government.
- The colonies won the war against England. The American Revolution made possible the establishment of a new nation, the United States of America (U.S.A.).
- In 1783 England acknowledged American independence in the *treaty of Paris* and *George Washington* was elected the first President of USA.

French Revolution : 1789-93

- The French Revolution was a great event in the history not only of France & Europe but of mankind as a whole. It gave to humanity new ideas of *'Liberty, Equality* & *Fraternity'*.
- The French Revolution is the name given to the struggle which swept away the Old Regime in France and brought about fundamental changes in the socio-political set-up.
- This political upheaval began in 1789. King *Louis XIV* and his successors had brought divine-right absolutism to the peak. The French king, in the 18th century, had unlimited powers. Opponents were put in prison without trial.
- French society consisted of *three estates* or classes. The first (clergy) and second (nobility) estates were privileged in many ways. Members of third estate—commoners (middle class, workers & peasants) were the 'under dogs'. They made 90% of the population. Almost the entire tax burden fell on third estate. But the privileged classes were exempted from these taxes.
- These undemocratic features of French society were sharply criticised by able writers and thinkers like *Montesquieu (1689-1775), Voltaire (1694-1778)* and *Rousseau (1712-1778).*

- The *immediate cause* of the French Revolution was the bankrupt condition of the French treasury brought about in part by the extravagant expenditure and inefficiency of *Louis XV & Louis XVI.*
- The French Revolution started with the *fall of Bastille Fort.* The mobs in Paris attacked the Bastille on July 14, 1789, killed its governor and freed the prisoners. This ancient fortress, where political prisoners were kept, was the symbol of tyranny in France. Its capture aroused the whole nation. Peasants in the provinces plundered and burnt several castles.
- *'Liberty, Equality and Fraternity'* became the watchword.
- Government in France broke down, as royal officials fled and the people stopped paying taxes. The National Assembly governed France from 1789-1791. It drafted a constitution which created a limited monarchy. Its preamble was the famous Declaration of the Rights of Man. All feudal rights were abolished. Local government was reorganised. The old provinces were replaced by 83 departments. Church lands were confiscated and sold to peasants. Special Church privileges were abolished. The first Republic was proclaimed on sep. 21, 1792. King *Louis XVI* and his queen *Marie Antoinette* were beheaded on the guillotine on Jan. 21, 1793 and oct. 16, 1793 respectively on charges of treason. Napolean, after some time, emerged as the strong man of France.
- The French Revolution was an event of fundamental importance not only for France but for whole of Europe and ultimately for the whole world. In France, the Revolution established the political supremacy of the middle class in the towns and transferred the bulk of landed property to the peasantry in the countryside. For Europe and the world, it represented an ideal of popular sovereignty and equality before the law.

Unification of Italy : 1848-70

- One of the major features of the history of Europe in 19th century was the struggle for the national unification and independence. Italy & Germany were the two important nations which emerged as united, independent states in the 19th century.
- In the early 19th century, Italy was divided into a number of states in which the Kingdom of *Sardinia* was the most powerful.
- The struggle for Italian independence and unification was organised by the two famous revolutionaries — *Mazzini* & *Garibaldi*. The movement led by them is known as the 'Young Italy' movement.
- After the revolution of 1848, *Count Cavour,* the Prime Minister of Sardinia, took the initiative of uniting Italy under the leadership of Sardinia.
- By the year of 1861, the entire states (except Rome) had been united and then *Victor Emmanuel II,* the king of Sardinia took the title of 'King of Italy'.
- Rome was still outside the kingdom of Italy. It was ruled by the Pope. Italian soldiers liberated the city of Rome in 1870, and in 1871, Rome became the capital of united Italy.

Unification of Germany : 1848-71

➢ Like Italy, Germany was also divided into a number of states. At the end of the Napoleonic wars (1792-1815) there were 38 independent states in Germany in which *Prussia* was the most powerful.

➢ In 1815, the German states along with Austria were organised into a Germanic confederation.

➢ In 1848 revolts occurred in every German state and the rulers were forced to grant democratic constitutions. To unite Germany and to frame a constitution for the united Germany, a constituent assembly met in Frankfurt.

➢ The *Frankfurt Assembly* proposed the unification of Germany as a constitutional monarchy under the king of Prussia who would become the emperor of Germany. However, the king of Prussia declined the offer. Repression soon followed.

➢ With the failure of the revolution of 1848 to unify Germany, one phase in the struggle for unification came to an end.

➢ Now Germany was to be unified not into a democratic country by the efforts of revolutionaries but by the rulers into militaristic empire. The leader of this policy was *Bismarck* who belonged to a Prussian aristocratic family. He wanted to achieve the unification of Germany under the leadership of the Prussian monarchy.

➢ Bismarck described his policy of unification as one of *'blood and iron'*. The policy of blood and iron meant a policy of war.

➢ He defeated Austria and dissolved the Germanic confederation. Thus Austria was separated from other German states. In place of old confederation, he united 22 states of Germany into *North German Confederation* in 1866.

➢ The unification of Germany was completed as a result of Prussia — France War (1870) in which the French emperor Louis Bonaparte was defeated and captured. This war enabled Bismarck to absorb the remaining German states into a united Germany.

➢ The formal ceremony at which William I, the king of Prussia, took the title of German Emperor was not held on the German soil. It took place at Versailles in France, in the palace of the French kings.

➢ After unification, Germany emerged as a very strong power in Europe.

First World War : July 28, 1914 — Nov. 11, 1918

Causes : The causes of First World War are as under—

1. Militarism : This means the dangerous and burdensome mechanism of great standing armies and large navies along with an espionage system.
2. Narrow Nationalism or Competitive Patriotism : The love of one's country demanded the hatred of the other. Love of Germany demanded the hatred of France and vice-versa.
3. Economic Imperialism : It led to international rivalries. Every country tried to capture markets in every nook and corner of the world. This led to bitterness and heart-burning.

4. Anglo-German Rivalry & The charter of William II : Anglo-German rivalry proved to be the main cause of World War I. Germany had become a great industrial country and wanted to have more markets for trade. Germany was jealous of the colonial and naval greatness of England. William II, emperor of Germany was very ambitious and wanted to gain influence in Turkey by linking Berlin with Baghdad by a railway line. This gave rise to a great rivalry between England and Germany.

   William II was arrogant, haughty and ambitious. He wanted Germany to be the strongest power in the world. He believed in the policy of 'world power or downfall'.

5. Lack of International Organisation : There was lack of International Organisation to control international relations.

Immediate Cause : The immediate cause of the war was the murder of Archduke *Ferdinand* who was the heir to the Austrian throne. He and his wife *Sophie* were killed at Serajevo, the capital of Bosnia, an annexed territory of Austria, by a Serbian. The Austrians held Government of Serbia responsible for the murder and ultimately attacked Serbia. There was strong rivalry already between Austria-Hungary and Serbia in the Balkans.

Course of War : To begin with, Austria was in favour of local war but as time passed, the situation became more grave. Other countries jumped into the fray. Germany, Austria-Hungary Turkey & Bulgaria were on one side; they were called *Central Powers.* On the other side were England, France, Serbia, Belgium, Japan and Russia; they were called the *Allied Powers.* The Allied powers joined by Italy in 1915 and USA in 1917. The war started on July 28, 1914 and ended on Nov. 11, 1918.

Peace Settlement (1919-20) : The Central Powers were completely defeated by the Allied Powers and an Armistice was

WWI : Central Powers Vs Allied Powers

Central Powers :

Germany, Austria-Hungary, Turkey *(entered Nov. 1914),* Bulgaria *(entered Oct. 1915)* etc.

The Allies or Entente Powers :

Great Britain / England / United Kingdom (UK), France, Serbia, Belgium, Japan, Russia / USSR *(left Dec. 1917),* Italy *(entered in April 26, 1915),* Romania *(entered Aug. 1916),* USA *(entered April 6, 1917)* etc.

Woodrow Wilson's 14 Points

In an address to the Congress in Jan., 1918, American President Woodrow Wilson outlined the basis of a peace settlement. His famous Fourteen Points for lasting peace in the world are : (1) There was to be no more secret diplomacy; (2) freedom of the seas; (3) removal of economic barriers of international trade; (4) reduction of armaments; (5) impartial adjustment of all colonial claims on the basis of the interests of the subject population; (6) national self-determination; (7) establishment of a league of Nations for the purpose of affording mutual guarantees of political independence and territorial integrity of great and small states alike.

The remaining points dealt with the formation of new boundaries and new states on the basis of nationality and demanded that Germany must evacuate all lands she had forcibly occupied.

signed on Nov. 11, 1918, followed by a Peace Conference at Paris. The defeated countries were not represented at the Peace Conference. Though the number of countries represented at the Peace Conference was 27, the terms of the peace treaties were really decided by three countries —USA, Britain and France. The three persons who played the determining role in framing the terms of the treaties were Woodrow Wilson (President of USA), Lloyed George (Prime Minister of Britain) and George Clemenceau (Prime Minister of France). After prolonged discussion, the *Treaty of Versailles* (Versailles — a city of France) was signed between the Allies and allies & Germany on June 28, 1919. This Treaty rearranged the boundaries of Europe, and many new states — Poland, Czechoslovakiya, Yugoslavia, Estonia, Lithuania, etc. were formed. William II, the German Emperor, abdicated and took asylum in the Netherland (Holland). The treaty also contained provisions for disarming Germany, the strength of her army was to be limited to 1,00,000 troops. Germany was to pay £ 6,50,00,000 as war-reparations for damage done to the Allies during the war. The Treaty of Versailles was followed by the *Treaty of St. Germaine (1919)*, the *Treaty of Neuilly (1919)*, the *Treaty of Trianon (1920)* and the *Treaty of Severes (1920)*.

The peace settlement of 1919-20 has been severely criticised. The terms of the Treaty of Versailles were harsh and humiliating for Germany. The peace settlement was based on the principle : 'To the victors belong the spoils and Allies are the victors'. Meanwhile the many suggestions were made from time to time for the creation of an international organisation which could check wars in the future. At the instance of *Woodrow Wilson*, the President of America, the *League of Nations* officially came into existence of Jan. 10, 1920. Its headquarter was fixed at Geneva in Switzerland.

Socialism

Political and Economic Theory that land, transport, the chief industries, natural resources e.g. coal, water, power etc., should be owned and managed by the state, and wealth equally distributed.

In 1848, *Karl Marx* and *Engels* laid down the principles of scientific socialism in *'Communist Manifesto'*, and Marxism became the theoretical basis for most socialist thought.

Socialism was split in Russia between the reformist *Mensheviks* and revolutionary *Bolsheviks* that led to the term *Socialism* and *Communism* as they are now generally understood.

Russian Revolution : 1917

- The Russian Revolution of 1917 was one of the most significant events of 20th century. It established the ideology of Marxism. It was a great revolution after French revolution which was not limited to Russia but affected several countries of the world.
- The great revolution in Russia took place in two stages. The first stage of Russian Revolution began in March 1917 with the overthrow of the *Czar Nicholas II*. The second stage in Nov. of the same year led to the establishment of the world's first communist state by Bolsheviks under Lenin.
- The basic causes of the revolution were deep-seated. The government was autocratic. The Czar was the source of all authority and his powers were vigorously exercised by corrupt and inefficient bureaucracy. The general standard of living of the people was tragically low. There was

little social freedom. All Russians were forced to support the orthodox church.

- ➢ The immediate cause of the event was however the suffering and confusion caused by Russian disastrous defeats during world war I. Her armies lacked arms and ammunition. Prices soared high and the economy was in shambles.
- ➢ Russian Revolution began with *March Revolution* (*February Revolution*, according to old Russian Calender). Disorders broke out in Petrograd (now Leningrad), the Russian capital, in March 1917. *Czar Nicholas II* was forced to abdicate. (He and his family were later killed by the revolutionaries).
- ➢ A provisional government composed of liberal and democratic elements (Mensheviks group) under the successive premiership of *Prince Lvov* and then *Aleksandr Kerensky* lost ground to the radical wing (Bolsheviks group) of the Social Democratic Labour Party.
- ➢ The Bolsheviks, led by *Lenin*, seized Power in Petrograd on Nov. 7, 1917—*Novemeber Revolution* (*October Revolution*, according to the old Russian calender). The Kerensky Government was overthrown and authority was vested in a council of Commissars (Ministers) with Lenin as Premier.
- ➢ The new Government immediately decreed the abolition of private land ownership and set up a dictatorship of the Proletariat—actually of the communist Party, as the Bolsheviks came to called.
- ➢ The Bolsheviks extended their authority over a large part of European Russia, but elsewhere they faced the resistance of the anti-Bolshevik Parties. The resulting civil war lasted till 1920 and was complicated by foreign intervention. The communists were ultimately in undisputed control of the country.
- ➢ In the period between 1917 and 1920, the Communists took drastic action against internal enemies, or counter-revolutionaries, as they were called. Former landlords, capitalists, Czarist officers, etc. were arrested, exiled or executed, the Czar and his family were killed.
- ➢ In 1923, the *Union of Soviet Socialist Republics (U.S.S.R.)* came into being. Its constitution declared the establishment of a 'republic of workers and peasants'. Ownership of the means of production, including land, factories, mines, banks and railroads, was vested in the state. The state which is known officially as the Union of Soviet Socialist Republics (U. S. S. R.), also commonly referred to as the Soviet Russia, or just Russia.
- ➢ Lenin died in 1924 and was succeeded by *Stalin (1924-53)*.

Note : *In 1991, Communist Party rule in Soviet Union collapsed following the failure of an anti-Gorbachov coup by Communist hardliners. The constituent republics asserted their independence and the Soviet Union was officially dissolved on Dec. 25, 1991. In the same month the Commonwealth of Independent States (C. I. S.), a looser organisation with responsibility for economic & military co-operation, was formed by Russia, Ukraine & Belarus. Nine other former Soviet republics joined later. Now CIS is a community of 12 independent states. Three former Soviet republics (Baltic States) — Estonia, Latvia & Lithuania*

— are fully independent states. It is notable that Soviet Union was a federal state consisting of 15 seperate republics.

Chinese Revolution :
1911 (Republican Revolution); 1949 (Communist Revolution)

➢ In Oct., 1911, a revolution under the leadership of *Sun Yat-sen* ousted the Manchu or Ch'ing Dynasty and a republic was set up.

➢ However, first President San Yat-sen resigned in 1912, in favour of strongman *Yuan Shik-Kai (1912-16)*.

➢ The period 1916-18, known as the *Warlord Era,* was one of great chaos, as a number of generals seized control of different provinces.

➢ A party known as the *Kuomintang (KMT)* or Nationalists (formed by Sun Yat Sen in 1912) was trying to govern China and control the generals who were busy fighting each other. The KMT leaders were Sun Yat sen and after his death in 1925, General *Chiang Kai-shek.*

➢ The Chinese Communist Party (CCP) was founded in 1921, and at first it cooperated with the KMT in its struggle against the warlords.

➢ As the KMT gradually established control over more and more of China, it felt strong enough to do without the help of the communists, and it tried to destroy them.

➢ The communists, under their leader *Mao Tse-tunge (Mao Zedong),* reacted vigorously, and after escaping from surrounding KMT forces, embarked on the 6000 mile *Long March (Oct. 1934-Oct. 35)* to form a new power base in northern China.

➢ Civil war dragged on, complicated by Japanese interference with culminated in a full-scale invasion in 1937.

➢ When the Second World War ended with defeat for Japan and their withdrawal from China, the KMT and the CCP continued to fight it out.

➢ Chiang Kai-shek had help from the USA, but in 1949 it was Mao Tse-tunge and the communists who finally triumphed.

➢ Chiang Kai shek and his supporters fled to island of Taiwan (Formosa).

➢ Mao Tse-tunge quickly established control over the whole of China, and he remained leader until his death in 1976.

Turkish Revolution : 1923

➢ Turkey was called *'Sickman of Europe'*.

➢ The disintegration of Ottoman empire began in the 19th century and was completed after Turkey's defeat in the First World War.

➢ The Allies wanted to establish their domination over Turkey itself and to give away parts of Turkey to Greece and Italy.

➢ The treatment meted out to Turkey by the Allies had led to a mass upsurge in India directed against Britain. This upsurge is known as the *Khilafat Movement*.

➢ The nationalist movement in Turkey was organised to prevent the domination of the country by the Allied Powers and the annexation of parts of Turkey agreed to the terms dictated by the Allied Powers.

➢ However, even before the treaty was signed by the Sultan, a national government had been established under the leadership of *Mustafa Kemal Pasha* with its headquarter in Ankara.

- Following the treaty with the Sultan, Turkey had been invaded by Greece.
- The turks under Kemal's leadership were able to repel the invasion and the Allies were forced to repudiate the earlier treaty. The Allied troops were withdrawn from Turkish territory and the areas which were to be annexed by European countries remained in Turkey. Thus, Turkey was able to win her complete independence.
- The success of the Turks in winning the complete independence of their country was followed by a programme to modernize Turkey and to end the influence of backward-looking feudal elements.
- Turkey was proclaimed a republic in Oct. 29, 1923 and Kemal became the first President of Turkey. He ruled the new republic for 15 years (1923-38). The Turkish Sultan had carried the title of Caliph (Khalifa); the new government abolished the institution of Caliph (Khalifa) in 1924. Education was taken out of the hands of the religious leaders. Religion was separated from the State.
- Mustafa Kemal Pasha is known as the 'founder of modern Turkey' and 'Ataturk' (the father of the Turks).

Economic Depression of the World : 1929-34

- In Economic terms, a decline in trade and general prosperity is called *Depression*.
- The Great Depression of 1929-34 was worldwide, starting with an agricultural recession followed by financial panic and collapse, known as the *Wall Street Crash (Oct., 1929)*, in the USA.
- The effects on the USA were catastrophic : by 1933 almost 14 million people were out of work and American President *Hoover's* efforts failed to make any impression on crisis.

  Nobody was surprised when the Republicans lost the presidential election of Nov., 1932. The new Democrat President, *Franklin D. Roosevelt,* introduced policies known as the *New Deal* to try and put the country on the road to recovery.
- The Great Depression is turn affected financial institutions and money markets in other parts of the world and caused a run on the pound in the UK. The result was a decline in internal consumption and exports in industrialized countries, factory closures and massive unemployment.

Fascism in Italy

- The unification of Italy was only completed in 1870, however, the new state suffered from economic and political weaknesses.
- The First World War (1914-18) was a great strain on her economy, and there was bitter disappointment at her treatment by the Versailles settlement.
- Between 1919 and 1922 there were five different governments, all of which were incapable of taking the decisive action that the situation demanded.

> **Fascism**
>
> The ideology and political system of Benito Mussolini, which encouraged militarism and extreme nationalism, organizing Italy along right-wing hierarchical authoritarian lines fundamentally opposed to democracy and liberalism. The term is also applied to any ideology or movement inspired by such principles, e.g., German National Socialism.

- In 1919 *Benito Mussolini* founded the Italian Fascist Party, which won 35 seats in the 1921 elections.
- At the same time there seemed to be a real danger of a left-wing revolution; in an atmosphere of strikes and riots, the fascists staged a 'March on Rome' which culminated in *King Victor Emmanuel* inviting Mussolini to form a government (Oct., 1922); he remained in power until July 1943.
- Gradually Mussolini took on the powers of a dictator and attempted to control the entire way of life of the Italian people.
- At first it seemed as though his authoritarian regime might bring lasting benefits to Italy, and he won popularity with his adventurous and successful foreign policy.

  Later he made the fatal mistake of entering the Second World War on the side of Germany (June, 1940) even though he knew Italy could not afford involvement in another war.
- After the Italians suffered defeats by the British, who captured her African possessions and occupied Sicily, they turned against Mussolini. He was deposed and arrested (July, 1943), but was rescued by the German (Sep., 1943) and set up as ruler in northern Italy, backed by German troops.
- In April, 1945, as British and American troops advanced northwards through Italy towards Milan. Mussolini tried to escape to Switzerland but was captured and shot dead by his Italian enemies (known as partisans).

Nazism in Germany

- As Germany moved towards defeat in 1918, public opinion turned against the government, and in Oct., the Kaiser, in a desperate bid to hang on to power, appointed *Prince Max* as Chancellor. He was known to be in favour of more democratic form of government in which parliament had more power.
- But it was too late; in Nov. revolution broke out, the Kaiser escaped to Holland and abdicated, and Prince Max resigned. *Friedrich Ebert*, leader of the left-wing Social Democrat Party, became head of the government.
- In Jan., 1919, a general election was held, the first complete democratic one ever to take place in Germany. The Social Democrats emerged as the largest single party and Ebert became first President of the Republic. They had some Marxist ideas but believed that the way to achieve socialism was through parliamentary democracy.
- The new government was by no means popular with all German : even before the elections the communist had attempted to seize power in the *Spartacist Rising (Jan., 1919)*.
- In 1920 right-wing enemies of the republic occupied Berlin (the *Kapp*

Putsch). The government managed to survive these threats and several later ones, including *Hitler's Munich Beer Hall Putsch (1923)*.

➢ By the end of 1919 a new constitution had been agreed by the National Assembly (Parliament), which was meeting at Weimer because Berlin was still torn by political unrest. This Weimer constitution, gave its name to the *Weimar Republic* and lasted until 1933, when it was destroyed by Hitler. The Great Depression, beginning with the Wall Street Crash in Oct., 1929, had disastrous effects on Germany, producing massive 6·5 million unemployed. The Government was unable to cope with the situation and by the end of 1932 the Weimer Republic seemed on the verge of collapse.

➢ Meanwhile *Adolf Hitler* and his *National Socialists (Nazis)* had been carrying out a great propaganda compaign blaming the government for all the ills of Germany, and setting out Nazi solutions to the problems.

➢ In Jan., 1933, President *Hindenberg* appointed Hitler as Chancellor, and soon afterwards Hitler saw to it that democracy ceased to exist; the Weimar Republic was at an end, and from then until April 1945, Hitler was the dictator of Germany. Only defeat in the Second World War and the death of Hitler (April 30, 1945) freed the German people from the Nazi tyranny.

Militarism in Japan

➢ During the 20 years after Mussolini's March on Rome (1922), many other countries, faced with severe economic problems, followed the examples of Italy and Germany and turned to fascism or right-wing nationalism.

➢ In Japan the democratically elected government, increasingly embarrassed by economic, financial and political problems, fell under the influence of the army in the early 1930s.

➢ The military soon involved Japan in war with China, and later took the country into the Second World War with its attack on *Pearl Harbor (1941)*.

➢ After a brilliant start, the Japanese eventually suffered defeat and devastation when the two atomic bombs were dropped.

➢ After the Second World War, Japan returned to democracy and made a remarkable recovery, soon becoming one of the world's most powerful states economically.

SECOND WORLD WAR : Sep. 1, 1939 — Sep. 2, 1945

Causes : The causes of Second World War as under —

1. **The Treaty of Versailles (1919) :** The treaty of Versailles had in itself the germs of the Second World War. The Germany was very badly treated. She was forced to sign the treaty at the point of a bayonet, in a spirit of revenge. To tear away the treaty of Versailles, Hitler joined hands with Mussolini of Italy.

2. **Nationalist Movements of Germany & Italy :** The rise of the national movement in Germany & Italy added fuel to the fire. Although Hitler tried to assure the world that he meant peace, he could not conceal his ambition for long. He embarked on a career of aggression which ultimately led to war. The same was the case with Mussolini who had established his dictatorship in Italy in 1922.

3. **Conflict of Ideology between Dictatorship & Democracy :** Countries like Germany, Italy & Japan represented the ideology of dictatorship while Great Britain, France & USA represented the ideology of democracy. Mussolini described the conflict between the two ideology thus : 'The struggle between the two worlds can permit no compromise. Either we or they'.
4. **Inefficiency of League of Nations :** Unfortunately, when hostility was growing between the two camps there was no effective international organisation which could bring the leaders of the two camps on a common platform and bring about a reconciliation between them. The League of Nations was practically dead.
5. **Colonial & Commercial Rivalry :** The colonial and commercial rivalry between England and France on one side, and Germany and Italy on the other brought them in conflict with each other.
6. **Aggressiveness of Berlin-Rome-Tokyo Axis :** Hitler had became very aggressive. He annexed the Saar Valley, occupied Rhineland and Austria, captured Chechoslovakia etc. Mussolini attacked Abyssinia (Ethiopia) Japan attacked China. This aggressive mood of the Fascist Powers got its fullest expression when they formed an Axis providing for mutal aid in the international sphere.

➢ **Immediate Cause :** The immediate cause of the war was the refuse of Poland to surender. Germany gave an ultimatum to Poland regarding : (i) surrender the port of Dazing, (ii) the right of establishing a rail link between Germany and East Prussia through the Polish corridor. These two demands were rejected by Poland. So Germany invaded Poland on Sep. 1, 1939. Britain and France as they were under treaty obligations to aid Poland, declared war against Germany on Sep. 3, 1939.

Course of War : On one side were Germany, Italy and Japan, called the *Axis Powers* (or *Central Powers*), and on the other were Great Britain, Francee, USSR, USA, China etc. called the *Allied Powers* (or *Allies*).

Germany had to face defeat once again. Hitler, Goebbels & Himmler committed suicide (April 30, 1945) and their successors surrendered unconditionally on May 7, 1945. After the fall of Germany, USA and UK concentrated their focus against Japan. On Aug. 6, 1945, an atom bomb, '*Little Boy*', was dropped on the city of Hiroshima. Japan was asked to surrender and when she refused another atom bomb, '*Fat Man*', was dropped on Aug. 9, 1945, on the city of Nagasaki. It is estimated that more than one lakh persons were killed and leaving thousands more slowly dying of radiation poisoning. On Aug. 14, 1945, Japan conveyed its acceptance of the Allied demand to surrender but the actual surrender took place on Sep. 2, 1945. With the Japanese surrender, the Second World War came to an end.

Effects of WW II : (i) After about 15 months of preparatory work, the peace treaties were given a final shape by the 21 participating countries and they were signed on Feb. 10, 1947, in Paris by the representatives of the five enemy states and the Allied Powers. As regards Germany she was occupied by the Big Four. After its fall in May, 1945, it was divided into four zones, each of which was administered separated by one of the occupying powers. Berlin came under joint occupation. Ultimately out of one Germany came two countries — West Germany and East Germany. Italy was also deprived of her colonies. As regards Japan, a peace treaty was signed with her at San Francisco in 1951. (ii) The United Nation Organisation (UNO) was established in Oct. 24, 1945. (iii) The USA and USSR emerged as the two most powerful nations in the world. (iv) The emergence of Russia (USSR) gave rise to the desire for freedom in colonies under European control in Asia. (v) The British empire thus rapidly lost its leadership as more and more colonies won independence. (vi) France also lost much of their past glory. (vii) Nearly all the East European countries embraced communism and communist rule was established in the Chinese mainland also.

WW II : Axis Vs Allies

The Axis Powers or Central Powers :

Germany, Italy *(entered June 1940)*, Japan *(entered Dec. 1941)* etc.

The Allies or Entente Powers :

Great Britain, France, USSR *(entered June 1941)*, USA *(entered Dec. 8, 1941)*, China *(entered Dec. 1941)* etc.

Important Axis Leaders of WW II : Adolf Hitler (Nazi dictator of Germany), Benito Mussolini (Prime Minister of Italy) and Hirohito (Emperor of Japan) & his Prime Ministers Hidehi Tojo & Fumimaro Konoe.

Important Allied Leaders of WW II : Franklin D. Roosevelt — upto April 12, 1945 & Harry Truman — after April 12, 1945 (Presidents of USA), Winston Churchill (Prime Minister of Britain), Joseph Stalin (Premier of USSR), Paul Reynaud & Charles De Gaulle (Prime Ministers of France) and Chiang Kai-shek (Head of the Nationalist Government of China).

Miscellaneous

Important Dates

B. C.	
776	First Olympiad in Greece.
753	Rome founded.
490	Battle of Marathon; the Greeks defeated the Iranians / Persians.
327-26	Invasion of India by *Alexander*, Battle of Hydaspes.
221	*Chin-Hung* Ti 'Univesral Emperor' in China, Great Wall of China completed.
55	Invasion of Britain by *Julius Caesar*, the Great Roman General.
44	Assassination of *Julius Caesar* by *Brutus*.
4	Birth of *Jesus Christ*.
A. D.	
29	Crucifixion of *Jesus Christ*.
43	Roman conquest of Britain.
570	Birth of Prophet *Muhammad* at Mecca.
622	Migration of *Muhammad* from Mecca to Medina (*'Hijira'*), Beginning of Hijira Era (Muhammadan calender) on July 15.
800	Charlemagne crowned Roman Emperor at St. Peter's.
871	Accession of *Alfred the Great* to the throne of Britain.
901	Death of king *Alfred the Great*.

1066	Battle of Hastings; Norman invasion of England. *William the Conqueror*, Duke of Normandy, defeated the English king *Harold II* at Hastings.
1215	Magna Carta or the Great Charter signed by king *John II* at Runnymede in England on June 15.
1280	Gunpowder invented by *Roger Bacon*.
1338	The Hundred Years War broke out; it lasted upto 1453.
1431	*Joan of Arc*, a brave French peasant girl, obtained victory over the English at Orleans. She was burnt alive at the stakes.
1443	The Black death i. e., plague broke out in England.
1453	The capture of Constantinople (the home of classical learning) by the Ottoman Turks compelled the Greek scholars to flee to Italy and other West European countries, where they spread the knowledge of Greek philosophy and literature. This was the beginning of Renaissance in Europe.
1486	*Bartholomew Diaz* rounded the Cape of Good Hope.
1492	*Columbus* sailed on his first expedition to the West Indies which later led to the discovery of America (the New World).
1498	*Vasco da Gama*, a Portuguese, discovered the seat-route to India via the Cape of Good Hope.
1517	Beginning of Reformation.
1529-36	Reformation in England under *Henry VIII*.
1564	Birth of *Shakespeare*.
1571	Battle of Lepanto; Turks defeated by the Christian League.
1577	*Drake*, the famous English Admiral, started his voyage round the world for the first time and plundered Spanish ships and ports in South America.
1588	Admiral *Drake* defeated the Spanish 'Armada'; England became the 'Mistress of the Seas'.
1600	Establishment of the British East India Company in India (31st Dec.)
1605	Gunpowder plot in England to blow up the English Parliament.
1616	*Shakespeare* passes away.
1649	Trial and execution of *Charles I*, beginning of Commonwealth.
1649-60	The Commonwealth and the Protectorate in England.
1660	Restoration of Monarchy in England.
1665	The Great Plague in London.
1679	Habeas Corpus Act.
1688	The Glorious or Bloodless Revolution in England. Despotic rule of the Stuarts ended, and the Parliamentary rule began. Establishment of parliamentary supremacy and abolition of the Divine Rights of Kings.
1704	Battle of Blenheim; Marlborough and Eugene inflicted a crushing defeat on the French army.
1707	Union of England and Scotland.
1763	Treaty of Paris; It ended the Seven Years' War (1756-63); weakened France, made England a great colonial power.

1776	Declaration of American Independence and formation of a Federal Republic of 13 states called the United States of America (July 4).
1783	Treaty of Versailles; England recognised the independence of the United States of America.
1789	*George Washington* elected First President of USA. Beginning of French Revolution : Fall of the Bastille Fort (July 14).
1798	Battle of the Nile; The English under Nelson gained victory over the French.
1805	Battle of Trafalgar; Death of Nelson.
	Battle of Austerliz — *Napolean Bonaparte* routed a combined army of the Russians and the Austrians.
1815	Battle of Waterloo — *Napolean* was defeated and exiled to St. Helena.
	Congress of Vienna, it aimed at rearranging the map of Europe; The Vienna settlement proved unsatisfactory, because it disregarded national claims.
1821	Death of *Napolean* at St. Helena (May 5).
1827	Battle of Navatino; the allied fleets of England, Russia and France destroyed the Turkish fleet; This victory practically secured the independence of Greece.
1832	Reforms Bill passed; French captured Antwerp.
1833	Emancipation Act of 1833; It abolished slavery in the British dominions.
1837	Accession of *Queen Victoria* to the throne of England.
1839	Introduction of Penny Postage system in England by Sir Rowland Hill; Aden annexed by England.
1854	The Crimean War began; Russia attacked Turkey; England and France came to the rescue of Turkey.
1861	American Civil War started. *Abraham Lincon* elected 16th President of USA.
1863	Slavery abolished in America.
1869	Suez Canal opened for traffic.
1885	General Gordon captured and slain at Khartoum.
1899	Beginning of the Boer War.
1904	Outbreak of the Russo-Japanese War.
1905	Battle of the sea of Japan; Japan inflicted a crushing naval defeat on Russia; a wave of nationalism spread in Asia.
1911	Chinese Republican Revolution; *Amundsen* reached South Pole (Dec. 14).
1914	Outbreak of World War I (July 28).
1916	Battle of Jutland (Naval Battle). The British Grand Fleet under Admiral Jellico defeated the German Fleet under Admiral Scheer.
1917	March / Feb. Revolution in Russia : the Czar abdicated and later assassinated; reformist Mensheviks came into power *(Prince Lvov, Kerensky)*.
	Nov./Oct. Revolution in Russia : Revolutionary Bolsheviks came into power (*Lenin*).

1918	End of World War I (Nov. 11).
1919	The Paris Conference; the Treaty of Versailles.
1920	Foundation of the League of Nations (Jan. 10).
1921	The Irish Free State established with the status of a Dominion like Canada (Dec. 6).
1923	Turkish Republic proclaimed with *Kemal Ataturk* as its First President.
1924	*Lenin* died, and power passed into the hands of *Stalin* in Russia.
1925	Treaty of Locarno (between Great Britain, France, Germany, Italy and Belgium).
1928	Kellogg Pact (signed in Paris by the principal powers of the world for the prevention of war; it had no effect).
1933	*Hitler* became the Chancellor of Germany.
1935	War between Italy and Abyssinia (Ethiopia); Italy annexed Abyssinia (Ethiopia); Plebiscite in Saar.
1939	Germany invaded Poland : Outbreak of World War II (Sep. 1).
1940	Fall of France after German invasion (June 5); Italy entered World War II (June 11).
1941	*Hitler* invades Russia (June 22); Framing of the Atlantic Charter (Aug. 14); Japan attacked Pearl Harbour (Hawaii Islands) (Dec. 7); USA entered World War II (Dec. 8); China entered World War II (Dec. 10) Air raids by Japan on Rangoon (Dec. 22).
1942	Capture of Singapore by Japanese forces (Feb. 15); Battle of Coral Sea, Japanese fleet suffered heavy losses at the hands of the American fleet (May 3); Battle of Stalingrad (Sep. 19).
1943	Defeat of Germany at Stalingrad (Feb. 8); Battle of the Bismarck Sea, America defeated Japan in a naval battle (March 4); Invasion of Italy by the Allies, Armistice between Italy & the Allies (Sep. 3).
1944	Allied forces landed in Normandy under the supreme command of *General Ike (Eisenhower)*; (D—Day) (June 6); Liberation of Paris (Aug. 25).
1945	Execution of *Mussolini* (Apr. 22); Unconditional surrender of Germany to the Allies (May 7); USA dropped atom bomb on Hiroshima & Nagasaki of Japan (Aug, 6 & Aug. 9); Actual surrender of Japan (Sep. 2); World War II ended (Sep. 2); Foundation of UNO (Oct. 24).

Association of Places

Place	Associated with
Corsica	Napoleon Bonaparte
Hiroshima	Dropping of first atom bomb
Jerusalem	Jesus Christ
Macedonia	Alexander, the Great
Mecca	Prophet Muhammad

Place	Associated with
Medina	Prophet Muhammad
Pearl Harbour	Japan's attack during World War II
St. Helena	Napolean Bonaparte
Trafalgar	Nelson
Waterloo	Napoleon Bonaparte

Abbreviated or Alternative Names

Abbreviated or Alternative Name	Original Name
Apostle of Free Trade	Richard Cobden
Bangabandhu	Sheikh Mujibur Rahman
Bard of Avon	Shakespeare
Desert Fox	Gen. Rommel
Father of English Poetry	Geoffery Chaucer
Fuehrer	Adolf Hitler
G. B. S.	George Bernard Shaw
Grand Old Man of Britain	Gladstone
Great Commoner	Pitt, the Younger
Ike	D. Eisenhower
Iron Duke, The	Duke of Wellington
King Maker	Earl of Warwick
Lady of the Lamp	Florence Nightingle
Li-Kwan	Pearl Buck
Little Corporal	Napoleon
Maiden Queen	Elizabeth I
Maid of Orleans	John of Arc
Man of Blood and Iron	Bismarck
Man of Destiny	Napoleon
Mark Twain	Samuel Clemens
Scourge of God	Chengiz Khan
Uncle Ho	Ho Chi Minh
Voltaire	Francois Marie Arouet de
Wizard of the North	Sir Walter Scott

Important Battles

Name of the Battle	Year	Countries involved
Battle of Marathon	490 BC	Athenians and Persians. King *Darius* of Persia defeated.
Battle of Thermoplaye	480 BC	Spartans led by *Leonidas* and Persians led by *Xerexes*. Greeks defeated.

Name of the Battle	Year	Countries involved
Battle of Salamis	480 BC	Athenian fleet and Persian fleet in Bay of Salamis; Persian fleet defeated.
Battle of Platae	479 BC	Greek and Persians forces; Persian forces defeated.
Battle of Mycale	479 BC	Greek and Persian fleets; Persian fleet defeated.
Spartan War I (Peloponesian War)	459 BC	Sparta and Athens, lasted for 30 years.
Spartan War II	431 BC-421 BC	Sparta and Athens; Spartans victorious.
Battle of Arabia	331 BC	Greek and Persian forces; Greeks victorious.
Battle of Magnesia	190 BC	Syrian and Roman forces; Syrian forces defeated (north-west Lydia).
Battle of Pharasalus	48 AD	*Caesar* defeated *Pompey*.
Battle of Hastings	1066	*William*, the Duke of Normandy defeated *Harold*, the King of England. England came under the control of Normans.
Hundred-Year War	1338-1453	Fought between France and England. The cause of the war was the succession question to the throne of France which was claimed by *Edward III* of England. The war was resumed by *Henry V* and was brought to an end by the heroism of *Joan of Arc* — 'A country girl who overthrew the power of England'. Joan of Arc was burnt alive at the stakes in 1431.
War of the Roses	1455-1485	Civil War in England; The cause of the war was a struggle for the throne of England between the two royal houses of Lancaster and York.
Anglo-Spanish War (Spanish Armada War)	1588	Spanish and English fleets fought in the English Channel; The English fleet under *Lord Howard* defeated of the Spanish Armada.
Battle of Gibraltar Way	1607	The Dutch defeated the Spanish and Portuguese.
Thirty-Year War	1618-1648	Started as religious-cum-political war between the Lutherans and Catholics in Germany and developed into an international war.
Civil War in England	1642-1649	Between Cavaliers (King Charles I suppoters) and forces of Parliament led by *Oliver Cromwell*, King Charles I executed.
Battle of Blenheim	1704	England and Austria headed by *Marlborough* defeated france and Russia.

Name of the Battle	Year	Countries involved
War of Austrian Succession	1740-1748	Queen of Austria, *Maria Theresa* (daughter of Charles VII) was challenged by *King Frederick II* of Prussia. England supported the queen and Frederick II was helped by France. Ended with a Treaty which recognised the Queen's right to the throne after the death of King Frederick.
Seven-Year War (Anglo-French War III)	1756-1763	Britain and France against Austria and Prussia; the British alliance won.
Battle of the Nile	1798	British and French fleets, Britain victorious.
Battle of Trafelgar	1805	British fleet defeated fleets of France and Spain. British fleets were commanded by Admiral *Nelson*, who was killed during the battle.
Battle of Austerliz	1805	Britain, Austria, Russia and Prussia on one side and France on the other. *Napoleon* (France) defeated Austria and Russia.
Battle of Borodino	1812	Between France and Russia. *Napolean* invaded Russia at Borodino, and nearly defeated the Russians. However on reaching Moscow, his army suffered heavy losses and was forced to retreat. Napolean's ill-fated attack on Russia marked the beginning of the downfall of the French Empire.
Battle of Leipzig	1813	Germany and combined forces of Austria, Prussia and Russia, defeated *Napolean*.
Battle of Waterloo	1815	British forces led by Duke of Wellington *(Sir Arthur Wellesly)* defeated French forces led by *Napolean*. Napolean was captured and exiled to St. Helena where he died in 1821.
First Opium War	1840	China and Britain; Chinese yielded opium. It was a trade war.
Crimean War	1854-1856	The combined forces of the British, French and Turks defeated Russia.
American Civil War	1861-1865	Northern states of America under *Abraham Lincon* defeated the Southern states and established a Federal state and abolished the slavery.
Sino-Japanese War	1894-1895	Japan defeated China and occupied Formosa and Korea.
Battle of Omdurman	1898	The British and Egyptian forces defeated the forces of Khalifa (Mehdists).
Boer War	1899-1901	The revolt of Transvaal Boers was suppressed by the British forces. Boers belonged to Dutch Protestant stock who opposed Britishers because of abolition of slavery by Britain.

Name of the Battle	Year	Countries involved
Russo-Japanese War (Battle of Port Arthur & Battle of Yalu)	1904-1905	Russia and Japan in the sea of Japan. Russia defeated; It led the wave of the idea of Asian Resurgence.
Balkan War I	1912	Turkey and Balkan countries (Montenegro, Serbia, Bulgaria and Greece), Turkey defeated.
Balkan War II	1913	Invasion of Serbia and Greece by Bulgaria. Bulgaria was defeated by combined forces of Serbia, Greece, Rumania, Montengro who stripped Turkey of most of its European territories.
World War I	1914-1918	Central Powers (Germany and its allies) against the Allied Powers (Britain and its allies); Central Power were defeated. Famous Battles : 1. First battle of Marne (1914) — France defeated Germany. 2. Battle of Jutland (1916)— Naval battle between England and Germany. England defeated Germany. 3. Battle of Verdun (1916) — Fought between France & Germany. 4. Second battle of Marne (1918) — France defeated Germany. *(See details on page 156)*.
World War II	1939-1945	Axis Powers (Germany and its allies) against the Allied Powers (Britain and its allies); Axis Powers were defeated. Famous Battle : Battle of El Alamein (1942) — The Allies victory during the World War II and retreat of General Rommel's forces. *(See details on page 163)*.

★★★

GEOGRAPHY

3

Universe

- The universe is commonly defined as the totality of everything that exists, including all physical matter and energy, the planets, stars, galaxies and the contents of intergalactic space.
- The study of universe is known as Cosmology.

  Cosmology = cosmos *(universe)* + logos *(science)*
- The universe has no limit.

Galaxy

- A galaxy is a vast system of billions of stars, which also contains a large number of gas clouds (mainly of hydrogen gas) and dust, isolated in space from similar systems.
- There are about 100 billion galaxies (10^{11} galaxies) in the universe, and each galaxy has, on an average, 100 billion stars (10^{11} stars). So, the total number of stars in the universe is 10^{22} stars.
- The Milky Way Galaxy is the home of the Earth and our Solar System. It is spiral in shape.
- Milky Way Galaxy was formed 5 billion years after the Big Bang.
- Latest known galaxy is the Dwarf Galaxy.
- According to the modern thought, universe can be classified into two parts namely—(a) Atmosphere and (b) Space.
- Origin of the universe is explained by the Big Bang Theory, formulated and proposed by the Belgian astronomer and cosmologist Georges Lemaitre.
- Andromeda is our nearest galaxy.

The Big Bang Theory

- All the matter in the universe was originally a concentrated lump called primeval atom.
- Big Bang was an explosion that occurred 15 billion years ago, leading to the formation of galaxies of stars and other heavenly bodies.
- Since then, all the galaxies have been flying away from one another causing expansion of the universe.

Star

- Clumps of dust and gas in a nebula come together due to gravity and form stars.
- Stars are made of hot burning gases.
- They emit light of their own and are very large and very hot.
- Light takes about 4.3 years to reach us from the next nearest star *proxima centauri.*

The Solar System

- The solar system consists of the sun, the eight planets and their satellites (or moons), and thousands of other smaller heavenly bodies such as asteroids, comets and meteors.

- The sun is at the centre of the solar system and all these bodies are revolving around it.
- The gravitational pull of the sun keeps all the planets and other objects revolving round it. Thus, the motion of all the members of the solar system is governed mainly by the gravitational force of the sun.
- Planets revolve around the sun in elliptical orbit.

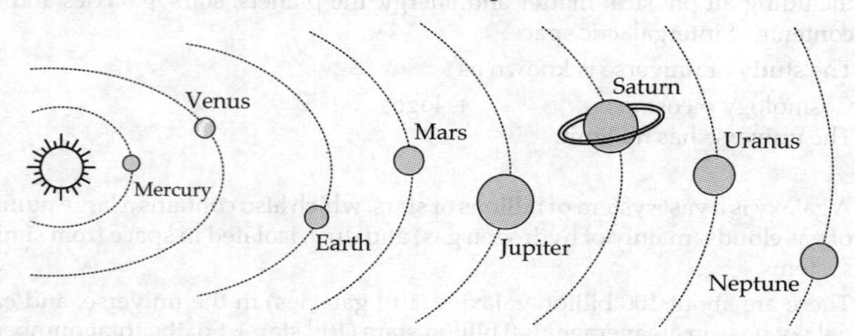

- In the solar system the planet nearest to the sun is Mercury and the planet farthest from the sun is Neptune (not Pluto).
- The size of solar system has been estimated to at about 10^5 A.U.
- The solar system is dominated by the sun which accounts for almost 99.9% of the matter in the whole solar system.
- The sun is also the source of all the energy in the solar system.
- Pluto is a dwarf planet.
- Mercury, Venus, Earth, Mars are called terrestrial planets and Jupiter Saturn, Uranus and Neptune are called gaseous planets.

Members of the Solar System

The Sun

- The Sun is at the centre of the Solar System.
- Its size is thirteen lakh times as that of the Earth.
- It is the nearest star to the Earth.
- It is an ultimate source of energy for life on Earth.
- Its diameter is 14 lakh kms.
- It is composed of 71%Hydrogen, 26.5% Helium and 2.5% other elements.
- Hydrogen and Helium are the main gases present in the Sun.
- Within the Sun, hydrogen is converted to Helium due to nuclear fusion releasing a tremendous amount of heat and light.
- It has a surface temperature of about 6000^0 C.
- The temperature at the centre is around $15,000,000^0$ C.
- Shining surface of the sun is called photosphere, it appears like a disc, radiates energy and acts as a source of energy.
- The outer layer of sun's atmosphere made up of thin hot gases, is called Corona. Corona is visible only during a total eclipse of the sun (or with a special solar telescope called Coronagraph).

- The planet travels with the sun through millions of stars in our galaxy at a speed of about 70,000 km per hour.
- The Sun is about 150 million kms away from the Earth.
- Light (at the speed of 300,000 km per second) takes about 8.5 minutes to reach the Earth from the Sun.

The Planets

- These are opaque bodies which continuously revolve around and are lighted by the Sun.
- There are eight planets in the Solar system.
- A ninth planet has been recently discovered by NASA named as Carla.
- The sequence of planets according to their distance from the Sun is Mercury, Venus, Earth, Mars, Jupiter, Saturn, Uranus, Neptune.
- The sequence of planets according to their size (in descending order i.e. from big to small) is Jupiter, Saturn, Uranus, Neptune, Earth, Venus, Mars, Mercury.
- Jupiter is the biggest and mercury is the smallest planets of our solar system.

Classification of Planets

- The eight planets have been divided into two groups. All the planets of a particular group have some common features. 'Terrestrial planets' or 'Rocky planets and' 'Jovian planets' or 'Gaseous planets' (Gas giants) are the two groups of planets.
- The four planets nearest to the Sun – Mercury, Venus, Earth and Mars are called terestrial planets, because their structure is similar to the earth.
- Other four planets — Jupiter, Saturn, Uranus and Neptune are called Jovian planets.
- Planets are classified into the following two groups inner and outer planets. These are separated by asteroid belt. :

Inner Planets	Outer Planets
They include Mercury, Venus, Earth, Mars.	They include Jupiter, Saturn, Uranus Neptune etc.
They are nearer to the sun.	They are far away from the sun.
They are made up of dense metallic minerals.	They are made up of hot gases, mainly hydrogen and helium.
They move faster and have a shorter period of revolution.	They move rather slowly and have a longer period of revolution.
They have thin, rocky crust.	They are all gaseous bodies.
They have a mantle rich in iron and magnesium.	Made of gases.
They have a core of molten metals.	They have ring systems around them.
They have thin atmosphere.	
They have very few natural satellites (or moons) or no satellites.	They have a large number of natural satellites (or moons).

Some Notable Facts About Various Planets and Satellites

Mercury

- Mercury is the closest planet to the Sun.
- It is extremely hot planet.
- The planet has no water on it.
- Mercury planet has no gases like CO_2, N_2, H_2 and O_2 which can act as building blocks of life.
- Mercury planet has no protective blanket like Ozone around it to prevent us from harmful radiations.

Venus

- Venus is the second planet in distance from the Sun. This planet is nearest to the Earth and is also the brightest planet.
- Venus is known as the "Evening Star" as well as "Morning Star".
- Venus is surrounded by a thick cloud cover, hence known as the "Veiled Planet" ('veil' means unclear / cover).
- Venus is like the Earth in size and mass, and hence also known as the "Earth's twin". It also rotates clockwise like Uranus.
- Venus is the hottest planet (even hotter than Mercury) of our Solar System, due to its veil of cloud.
- Venus has no water on it. There is no sufficient oxygen on the Venus.

The Earth

- Earth is the largest of the inner planets.
- The Earth is 23½° tilted on its axis and thus makes 66½° angle.
- It takes 23 hours 56 minutes and 4.091 seconds to rotate on its axis.
- It takes 365 days, 5 hours and 48 minutes to revolve around the Sun.
- Earth is known as the "watery planet" or the "blue planet" due to the presence of huge amount of water on it.
- Earth is the only known planet which provides sustenance or life on it. It has a large quantity of oxygen which supports life.
- The earth has all the essential elements like carbon (in the form of CO_2), hydrogen (H_2), nitrogen (N_2) and oxygen (O_2) which act as building blocks for the origin of life.
- The earth is neither too hot nor too cold. It has 'Goldilock Zone'.
- 'Goldilock Zone' is the habitable zone of solar system where all conditions are available for life to sustain.
- The earth has a lot of water in the form of lakes, rivers and oceans for the growth and survival of life.
- The earth has enough oxygen gas in its atmosphere for the survival of living beings through breathing.

- The earth has a protective blanket of ozone layer high up in its atmospehre to save life from the harmful ultraviolet radiations coming from the sun.

The Moon

- The Moon is the only satellite of the earth.
- It has a diameter of 3475 km. and its circumference is 10864 km. while its orbit is elliptical.
- The maximum distance (apogee) of the moon from the earth is 4,06,000 km. and the minimum distance (perigee) is 3,64,000 km.
- It takes 27 days, 7 hours and 43 minutes to rotate on its axis (this period of about 27½ days is called the *sideral month*) and approximately the same period of time it takes to revolve around the earth. The moon's period of revolution with reference to the sun is about 29.53 days (29 days, 12 hours, 44 minutes and 2.8 seconds). This period is called a *synodic month*.
- Only 59 per cent of the total surface of the moon is visible from the earth.
- The bright part of the moon is full of mountains whereas the dark patches are low lying plains.
- 'Sea of tranquility', made of the plain of dust particles, is on the rear side of the moon, which always remains dark.
- The highest mountain on the moon is *liebuity mountain,* which is 10,660 meter high.
- The moon has no atmosphere, no twilight and no sound.
- The temperature during daytime is about 100°C and during night it drops down to about –180°C.
- The light from the moon takes 1.3 seconds to reach the earth.
- The size of the Moon is one-fourth (1/4th) the size of the Earth.
- Gravitational pull of Moon is one-sixth (1/6th) that of the Earth.
- Mainly silicon, iron, magnesium etc. elements are found on the Moon's surface.
- The study of the Moon is called "Selenology".
- Moon is also known as the fossil planet.

Mars

- Iron-rich red soil and pink sky of Mars give it the name, "Red Planet".
- Phobes and Demos are two satellites of Mars.

Jupiter

- Jupiter is the largest planet of the Solar System.
- Jupiter is also known as winter planet as its average temperature is very low (–148^0 C).
- Gannymeda, satellite of Jupiter is the largest satellite in the Solar System.

Saturn

- Saturn is the second largest planet in the Solar System.
- Saturn has bright concentric rings which are made up of ice and ice-covered dust particles which revolve around it.

- ➢ Titan is the largest satellite of Saturn.

Uranus

- ➢ Uranus is about four times the size of the Earth. This planet appears greenish in colour because of methane gas present in its atmosphere.
- ➢ Uranus was discovered in 1781 by Sir William Hersiel.
- ➢ Uranus is the 7th planet from the Sun.
- ➢ Uranus is the first planet to have been discovered by the use of a telescope. Uranus is the third biggest planet of the Solar System.
- ➢ Uranus is extremely cold, having surface temperature–190°C and is surrounded by 13 rings namely zeta (ζ) / R1986U2, 6, 5, 4, alpha (α), beta (β), eta (ε), gamma (γ), delta ( ), lambda (λ), epsilon (∈), nu (ν) and mu ( ).
- ➢ Uranus rotates from east to west on its axis, which is opposite to other planets except Venus.
- ➢ The axis of Uranus has large inclination so that it appears to be lying down, hence it bears the name "A Planet on its Side".

Neptune

- ➢ Neptune is the 8th planet of the Solar System.
- ➢ The temperature on the surface of Neptune remains low.
- ➢ Neptune is very similar to Uranus and can be considered as its twin.
- ➢ Neptune is surrounded by methane rings of sub zero temperature.

Pluto is not a Planet now

- ➢ On the basis of the new definition of planet given by the IAU (International Astronomical Union), the world's top institution on space science research, leading astronomers participating in IAU's meet at Prague (Czech Republic) on August 24, 2006, declared that Pluto would no logner remain a planet.
- ➢ Under the IAU's new guidelines, the number of planets in the Solar System has thus been reduced from nine to eight. Its merits mentioning here that, prior to this decision, Pluto had been holding the planetary status since its discovery in 1930 by Clyde Tombaugh.
- ➢ Now, with the omission of Pluto from the Solar System, its membership has been restricted to the eight "classical" planets, namely Mercury, Venus, Earth, Mars, Jupiter, Saturn, Uranus and Neptune.

Pluto Gets a Numerical Denomination

Weeks after it was demoted to a sub—planetary status, Pluto was given a new name to reflect its new status as a dwarf planet in September 2006. The former 9th planet was assigned the asteroid number 134340 by the Minor Planet Centre (MPC), the official organisation responsible for collecting data about asteroids and comets in our Solar System.

Pluto's companion satellites, Charon (Pluto's largest moon), Nix and Hydra are considered part of the same system and will not be assigned separate asteroid numbers. Instead, they will now be called 134340 I, II and III respectively.

- ➢ Before loosing its planetary status on 24th August, 2006 Pluto was the outermost planet of the Solar System.

Some Facts and Figures about the Planets

Name of planet	Distance from the Sun	Time taken for one revolution around Sun	Time taken to turn once on its axis	Diameter of planet	Mass of planet compared to earth taken as 1	No. of satellites (or moons)
Mercury	58×10^6 km	88 days	58.6 days	4,878 km	0.055	None
Venus	108×10^6 km	224.7 days	243 days	12,100 km	0.8	None
Earth	150×10^6 km	365.26 days	23.9 hours (23 hours 56 min 04 sec.)	12,760 km	1	1
Mars	228×10^6 km	687 days	24.6 hours	6,780 km	0.1	2
Jupiter	778×10^6 km	11.9 years	9.9 hours	1,42,800 km	318	63
Saturn	1427×10^6 km	29.5 years	10 hours	1,20,000 km	95	21
Uranus	2870×10^6 km	84 years	16.2 hours	50,800 km	15	15
Neptune	4504×10^6 km	164.8 years	18.5 hours	48,600 km	17	8

Asteroids (or Planetoids)

- Asteroids are the also known as minor planets.
- They are objects that revolve around the Sun.
- They are mostly found between the orbits of Mars and Jupiter. They are a belt of debris which failed to assemble into planets and keeps on revolving around the Sun. This has come to be called as 'asteroid belt'.
- More than 5000 asteroids have been identified.
- Asteroids may be spherical, elongated or irregular in shape.
- All asteroids rotate on their axis, every 5 to 20 hours. Certain asteroids may have satellites.
- Trojan asteroids are found in two clouds moving in the orbit of Jupiter, one moving ahead of it and the other moving behind it.
- Scientists believe that these asteroids occupy a place where a planet could have existed but was prevented from its formation by the disruptive gravitational force of the nearby giant planet, Jupiter.

Meteors and Meteorites

- Meteors and Meteorites are also called shooting stars.
- Meteors are fragments of rocks coming towards the earth, formed due to the collision of asteroids with one another.
- Meteors are usually small, and due to the heat produced by air resistance, burn up before they reach the Earth's surface.
- When meteors are large and do not burn up completely, they land on the Earth's surface and are known as Meteorites.
- All meteorites are believed to originate in the asteroid belt, where a sudden collision may send them towards the Earth and the Earth's gravity attracts them towards its surface.

Comets

- Visitors of the Solar System.
- Comets (the name derived from the Latin words *stella cometa* meaning "hairy star") are among the most spectacular and unpredictable bodies in the Solar System.
- Comets move around the Sun in regular orbits, but their orbits are elongated ellipses that it takes them hundreds and, sometimes. even thousands of years to complete one revolution around the Sun.
- Comets are made up of frozen gases which hold together rocky and metallic materials.
- A comet becomes visible only when it travels close to the Sun.
- Its ice melts and the gas and dust is swept back into a tail.
- The tail always points away from the Sun. So when it is travelling away from the Sun it is led by its tail.

Features of a Comet

- A comet is characterised by a long luminous tail, which emits light.
- But this is visible only when the comet's orbit passes close to the Sun.
- When the comet travels close to the Sun, the ice melts to a head of gas called a Coma.
- The Sun's radiation sweeps this into a gas tail.
- Dust particles are also swept back to form a dust tail.

Stars

- Stars are heavenly bodies made up of hot burning gases, thus shining by their own light.
- Stars seem to be fixed with respect to each other. In fact they are in rapid motion but they are at such great distance that relative changes in position become noticeable only over the centuries.
- According to NASA Proxima Centauri is the closest star to the Earth after the Sun. It is about 4.24 light years away.
- Pole star (or Polaris), Sirius, Vega, Capella, Alpha centauri, Beta centauri, Proxima centauri, Spica, Regulus, Pleiades, Aldebaran, Arcturus, Betelgeuse, and of course the Sun are some of the important examples of the stars.

Facts about Stars

- There are billions and billions of stars in the sky but only about 2000 stars can be seen with the naked eye on a clear moonless night.
- There are 10^{22} stars in the Universe.
- About 8000 stars are visible from the Earth with naked eye. Out of this, 4000 stars are visible in the Northern Hemisphere and 4000 in the Southern Hemisphere.
- In either hemisphere, only 2000 stars are visible at any given time.
- The other 2000 are located in the day-time sky and the brightness of the Sun renders them invisible.

Constellations

- To enable astronomers to identify roughly the position of the stars, the sky has been divided into units. These units are known as Constellations.
- These constellations were named in the honour of mythological characters.
- At present 88 constellations are recognized.

Some well known constellations

- Some well known constellations, with their Indian names are given below :

Constellations	Indian names	Constellations	Indian names
Ursa Major (Great Bear)	Saptarishi	Cancer*	Kark
Ursa Minor (Little Bear)	Dhruva Matsya	Leo*	Simha
Orion (Hunter)	Mriga	Virgo*	Kanya
Draco (Dragon)	Kaleya	Libra*	Tula
Scorpio*	Vrishchika	Sagittarius*	Dhanu
Aries*	Mesh	Capricorn*	Makar
Taurus*	Vrish	Aquarius*	Kumbh
Gemini*	Mithun	Pisces*	Meen

*12 Zodiac signs

Galaxy

- A large group of stars, dust and light gases, bound together by their own gravity, is called a galaxy.
- There are 10^{11} galaxies in the universe.
- We live on the outer edge of a spiral type of galaxy called the Milky Way, which is about 100,000 light years in diameter and is rotating slowly.

Earth's Galaxy : The Milky Way

- The Milky Way is a large spiral-shaped galaxy.
- It spans about 100,000 light-years across and is about 10,000 light-years thick at the centre.
- It is called the Milky Way because it appears as a soft glowing light of billions of stars. These stars are so far that they can be seen only in constellation, not separately..
- Galileo discovered that this band of light was produced by countless individual stars which a naked eye cannot see.
- It takes about 250 million years to complete one revolution.

Light year

- Large distances in outer space are measured in light years.
- A light year is the distance light travels in one year at the speed of 299,792,458 metres per second or roughly 300,000 km per second (3×10^5 km/s or 3×10^8 m/s)
- One light year is equal to 9,461,000,000,000 km (9.461×10^{12} km).
- No star, apart from the Sun, is close enough to Earth to appear as anything but a point of light.

Andromeda : Earth's closest Galactic neighbour

- Andromeda is a spiral galaxy and also our closest neighbour.
- It appears as a fuzzy patch of light and contains millions of stars.
- It is the farthest object that can be seen with the naked eye.
- Along with the Milky Way, it belongs to a group of galaxies known as the Local Group, which in turn is a part of Virgo Cluster of groups.
- Like stars, galaxies are grouped into clusters. Some clusters contain thousands of galaxies.
- About 30 galaxies, along with the Milky Way and the Andromeda are grouped together in one cluster called the Local Group.
- Clusters may group together into upper clusters.
- Super clusters are also spread randomly throughout the universe.

Nebulae

- Nebulae are huge interstellar clouds of gas and dust that appear as faint, misty patches of light scattered all over the sky.
- They appear either as bright luminous clouds or as dark patches against a brighter background.
- A nebula depends for its luminosity upon the presence of stars that have either arisen from it or are contained in it.
- If the stars are extremely hot, the hydrogen in the nebula is ionized and emits a certain amount of light of its own.
- If a star is less hot, the nebula shines only by reflection.
- If there are no suitable stars, the nebula does not shine and remains dark and can be detected only because it blots out the light of the stars beyond.

The Earth–Shape and Size

Shape of the Earth

- Pythagoras (572-500 B.C.), a Greek philosopher and mathematician, was among the first to suggest that the Earth was shaped like a globe.

The Earth is not flat

- If the Earth were a flat disc, then the rising Sun would have been seen at all places at the same time. But this does not happen. Places in the east see the rising Sun earlier.
- When a ship approaches land, its funnel or mast is seen first and then the hull. If the Earth had been flat, the whole ship would have been seen at the same time.

The Earth is a sphere

- The Earth is rarely oriented in the same position during successive eclipses but it always casts a circular shadow, thus proving that the Earth is a sphere. A sphere is the only solid body that will always cast a circular shadow.
- At the North Pole, the Pole Star can always be observed at 90 degrees in the sky, since the star lies in the line with the axis of the Earth.

- As one travels southwards, the angle of Pole Star decreases.
- At the Equator the angle becomes zero degree.
- This observation proves that the path of travel is an arc of a circle.
- The Sun, Moon and all the heavenly bodies appear to be spherical when viewed from different positions. It seems logical to conclude that the Earth is no exception.
- The photographs of the Earth taken from the space prove beyond any doubt that the Earth is a sphere.

The Earth as an Oblate Spheroid

- Refined measurements of the Earth have proved that the true form of the Earth resembles a sphere that has been compressed at the poles and made to **bulge** at the Equator. This form is known as an oblate spheroid.

The various factors which make the earth suitable for life to evolve and survive are

- The earth has all the essential elements like carbon (in the form of CO_2), hydrogen (H_2), nitrogen (N_2) and oxygen (O_2) which act as building blocks for the origin of life.
- The earth is neither too hot nor too cold. It has the right temperature range for carrying out the life-sustaining chemical reactions.
- The earth has a lot of water in the form of lakes, rivers and oceans for the growth and survival of life.
- The earth has enough oxygen gas in its atmosphere for the survival of living beings through breathing.
- The earth has a protective blanket of ozone layer high up in its atmosphere to save life from harmful ultraviolet radiations coming from the sun.

Statistical Data of The Earth

The Earth is the fifth largest planet in the Solar System.

Age	4,550 million years
Mass	5.976×10^{24} kg.
Volume	1.083×10^{24} litres
Mean Density	5.518 kg/litre
Total surface area	510,065,700 sq.km.
Total Land area	148, 647,000 sq.km.
Total Water area	361,150,000 sq.km.
Average Density	5.52 (corresponding to the density of water)
Diameter	
Equatorial diameter	12,756 km
Equatorial radius	6,377 km
Polar diameter	12,714 km
Polar radius	6,371 km (IUGG)

Circumference	
Equatorial circumference	40,077 km
Polar circumference	40,009 km
Highest land point (Mt. Everest)	8,848 m.
Lowest land point (Dead Sea)	397 m.
Greatest ocean depth (Mariana Trench)	11,033 m.
Maximum distance from the Sun (At Aphelion)	152 million km. (approx.)
Minimum distance from the Sun (At Perihelion)	147 million km. (approx.)

➢ 29.2% of the total surface area of Earth is covered by continents (land), while 70.8% is covered by oceans (water).

➢ The total water area of the earth including the oceans, lakes, rivers, ice sheets and the water in the atmosphere is called hydrosphere and it covers about 71% of the earth's surface.

Composition of Whole Earth	
1. Iron	35%
2. Oxygen	30%
3. Silicon	15%
4. Magnesium	13%
5. Nickel	2.4%
6. Sulphur	1.9%
7. Calcium	1.1%
8. Aluminium	1.1%
9. Others	0.5%
Total	100%

Continents of The World

Asia, Africa, North America, South America, Europe, Australia and Antarctica are the seven continents.

Facts about Asia

Latitude	:	10° S and 80° N
Longitude	:	25° E and 170° W
Area	:	44,579,000 sq. km. (approx 30% of the world)
Population	:	4,299 million (est. 2013)
Oceans and Seas	:	Arctic Ocean, Pacific Ocean, Indian Ocean, Red Sea, Gulf of Aden, Persian Gulf, Gulf of Oman, Arabian Sea, Bay of Bengal, China Sea, Yellow Sea of Okhotsk, Bering Sea.
Highest and Lowest Points	:	Everest (8,848 metres) and Dead Sea (–396.8 m) respectively.
Straits	:	Strait of Malacca, Bering Strait.
Lakes	:	Caspian Sea, Aral Sea, Lake Baikal, Lake Balkhash.
Islands	:	Kurile, Sakhalin, Honshu, Hokkaido, Taiwan, Borneo, Sumatra, Java, Celebes, New Guinea, Philippines, Sri Lanka, Bahrain, Cyprus.
Mountains	:	Pamir Knot, Himalayas, Karakoram, Kunlun, Tien Shan, Altai, Hindu Kush, Elbruz, Pontic, Sulaiman, Zagros, Taurus, Urals, Yablonovoi, Stanovoi.
Plateaus	:	Anatolia Plateau, Plateau of Iran, Plateau of Arabia, Plateau of Tibet, Tarim Basin, Plateau of Mongolia, Plateau of Yunnan, Decan Plateau.

Peninsulas : Kamchatka Peninsula, Peninsula of Korea, Peninsula of Indo-China, Malay Peninsula, Indian Peninsula, Arabian Peninsula.

Deserts : Arabian Desert, Thar Desert, Gobi Desert.

Rivers : Eupharates, Tigris, Indus, Ganga, Brahmaputra, Hwang–Ho, Yang-tse, Si-kiang, Amur, Lena Yenisei, Ob, Irrawady, Salween, Mekong.

Important cities : Aden, Karachi, New Delhi, Mumbai, Kolkata, Colombo, Yangon (former Rangoon), Kuala Lumpur, Bangkok, Ho Chi Minh City (former Saigon), Singapore, Manila, Guangzhou (former Canton), Hong Kong, Shanghai, Tokyo.

Facts about Africa

Latitude : 35° S and 37° N

Longitude : 50° E and 17° W

Population : 1,033 million (est. 2013)

Area : 30,065,000 sq. km (approx.) 20.3% of the world).

Oceans and Seas : Indian Ocean, Red Sea, Atlantic Ocean, Gulf of Guinea, Mediterranean Sea.

Highest and Lowest Points : Kilimanjaro (5,895 m.) and Lake Assai (–156.1 m.) respectively.

Straits : Strait of Bab-el-Mandeb, Straits of Gibraltar.

Lakes : Victoria, Tanganyka, Malawi, Chad, Rudolf, Albert.

Islands : Madagascar, Cape Verde Islands, The Comoros, Mauritius, Seychelles.

Mountains : Atlas, Drakensberg, Kilimanjaro.

Plateaus : Plateau of Africa – the entire continent is a plateau.

Deserts : Sahara, Kalahari, Namib.

Facts about North America

North America, northern continent of Western Hemisphere, comprising U.S.A., Canada, Central America and the Caribbean, on west high chain of mountains, lower range in east and central plains. Climate varies considerably owing to wide range of latitude and altitude.

Latitude : 7° N and 84° N

Longitude : 20° W and 180° W

Area : 24,235,280 sq. km (approx. 16.3% of the world)

Population : 529 million (est. 2013).

Major Deserts : Chihuahuan, Colorado, Mujave, Sonoran.

Major Lakes : Lake Superior (largest sweet water lake in the world), Huron, Michigan, Great Slave, Great Bear, Erie, Ontario, etc.

Major Rivers : Mississippi, Missourie, St. Lawrence, Mackenzie, Colorado, Hudson, Potomac, Ohio etc.

Oceans and Seas	:	Atlantic Ocean, Pacific Ocean, Arctic Ocean, Gulf of Mexico, Caribbean Sea, Gulf of California, Gulf of Alaska, Bering Sea, Hudson Bay.
Highest and Lowest Points	:	Mckinley (6,194 m.) and Death Valley (–85.9 m.) respectively.
Straits	:	Bering Strait.
Islands	:	Greenland, Baffin, Victoria, Newfoundland, Cuba, Jamaica, Haiti.
Mountains	:	Rockies, Appalachain, Brooks, Kuskolkwim, Alaska Range, Cascade Range, Coastal Range, Sierra Nevada, Sierra Madre etc.
Plateaus	:	Columbia Plateau, Colorado Plateau, Mexican Plateau, Canadian Shield.
Agriculture	:	Temperate and tropical products, cereals, tobacco, sugarbeet, potatoes etc.
Minerals	:	Coal, petroleum, iron, manganese etc.
Industries	:	Ship building, occupied formerly by Red Indians; now mainly by Whites with many Blacks in the south.
Important cities	:	New York, Washington D.C., Boston, Chicago, Dallas, Detroit, San Francisco, Los Angeles, Seattle, Montreal, Toronto, Vancouver, Mexico City, Havana, Kingston, Ottawa etc.
Climate	:	Extending to within 10° of latitude of both the equator and the North Pole, North America has every climatic zone, from tropical rain forest and Savanna on the lowlands of Central America to areas of permanent ice cap, besides Sub-arctic and Tundra climates and arid as well as semi-arid zones.

Facts about South America

Latitude	:	12° N and 55° N
Longitude	:	35° W and 81° W
Area	:	17,820,770 sq. km (approx 12% of the world).
Population	:	386 million (est. 2013)
Ocean and Seas	:	Atlantic Ocean, Pacific Ocean, Caribbean Sea.
Highest and Lowest Points	:	Aconcagua (6,960 m.) and Valdes Penin (–39.9 m.) respectively.
Straits	:	Straits of Magellan
Lakes	:	Lake Maracaibo, Lake Titicaca
Islands	:	Galapagos, Falkland, Tierra del Fuego
Mountains	:	Andes
Plateaus	:	Plateau of Bolivia, Plateau of Equador.
Deserts	:	Atacama, Pantagonia
Rivers	:	Amazon, Orinoco, Paraguay, Parana, Uruguay

Important cities : Buenos Aires, Rio de Janeiro, Montivideo, Quito, Santiago, La Paz, Lima, Bogota, Valparaiso, Sao Paulo, Belem, Caracas, Manaus.

Facts about Europe

Latitude : 35° N and 73° N

Longitude : 25° W and 65° E

Area : 10,530,750 sq. km (approx.) (7.1%); greatest length north to south 3,860 km; breadth east to west 5,300 km.

Population : 733 million (est. 2013)

Oceans and Seas : Atlantic Ocean, Arctic Ocean, Mediterranean Sea, Caspian Sea, Black Sea, White Sea, North Sea, Norwegian Sea, Baltic Sea, Gulf of Bothnia, Gulf of Finland, Bay of Biscay, Aegean Sea, Adriatic Sea.

Highest and Lowest Points : Mt. Elbrus (5,642 m.) and Caspian Sea (–28.0 m.) respectively.

Straits : Straits of Gibraltar

Lakes : Lake Ladoga, Onega, Peipus, Vanern, Vaitern.

Islands : British Isles, Iceland, Sardinia, Sicily, Crete.

Mountains : Alps, Pyrenes, Appenines, Dinaric Alps, Carpathians, Transylvanian Mts., Balkans, Caucasus, Urals.

Plateaus : Plateau of Bohemia, Plateau of Spain, Central Massif.

Rivers : Volga, Danube, Rhine, Po, Dnieper, Don, Vistula, Elbe, Oder, Seine, Loire, Garrone, Douro, Tagus. Ural.

Important cities : London, Paris, Madrid, Antwerp, Amsterdam, Bonn, Copenhagen, Oslo, Stockholm, Moscow, Frankfurt, Berlin, Warsaw, Venice, Athens, Budapest, Belgrade, Munich, Rome, Prague, Vienna etc.

Facts about Australia

Australia is an island continent and a British Dominion.

Latitude : 12° S and 38°S

Longitude : 114° E and 154° E

Area : 7,830,682 sq. km (5.3%).

Population : 32 million (est. 2009)

Oceans : Pacific Ocean, Indian Ocean.

Seas : Tasman Sea, Timor Sea, Arafura Sea, Gulf of Carpentaria, Coral Sea, Great Australian Bight.

Highest Point : Puncak Jaya (4884 m) in island of New Guinea [Kosciuszko (2,228 m.) in Australian main land], Mt. Wilhelm (4509 m.) in Papua New Guinea.

Lowest Point : Lake Eyre (–15.8 m.)

Straits : Bass Strait

Lakes : Lake Eyre

Islands	:	Tasmania
Mountains	:	Great Dividing Range
Plateaus	:	Western Plateau.
Deserts	:	Gibson Desert, Great Sandy Desert, Great Victoria Desert, Simpson Desert.
Important cities	:	Sydney, Melbourne, Adelaide, Perth, Darwin, Canberra, Brisbane, Hobart.

Oceania

➢ Australia with New Zealand, Tasmania, New Guinea and the Pacific Islands (Micronesian, Melanesian and Polynesian Islands) is called Australasia by some geographers while some others call it "Oceania", which includes proximate islands (Caribbean countries etc.).

Oceans on The Earth

➢ There are four oceans. In order of their size, they are : Pacific Ocean, Atlantic Ocean, Indian Ocean and Arctic Ocean.

Pacific Ocean

➢ The explorer Ferdinand Magellan, who circumnavigated the Earth, named the ocean "Pacific" meaning calm or peaceful.

➢ The Pacific Ocean (Area : 166,240,000 sq. km.) is the largest ocean of the world.

➢ It is the deepest ocean with an average depth of 4,200 m.

➢ The Mariana Trench is the world's deepest trench with a depth of 11,033 metres (36,201 feet).

➢ Most of the islands of this ocean are of volcanic or coral origin.

Atlantic Ocean

➢ The Atlantic Ocean (Area : 86,560,000 sq. km.) is the second largest ocean in the world

➢ Its name is derived from Atlas, a Titan (giant) in Greek mythology.

➢ The Atlantic Ocean has the longest coastline.

➢ The Atlantic Ocean is the busiest ocean for trade and commerce since its shipping routes connect the two most industrialized regions, namely Western Europe and N.E. United States of America.

➢ The Atlantic Ocean was formed millions of years ago when a rift opened up in the Gondwanaland and the continents of South America and Africa separated. The separation continues even today and the Atlantic Ocean is still widening.

➢ The continental islands of Newfoundland and British Isles are the major ones.

➢ Volcanic islands are fewer and they include those of Cuba, Jamaica and Puerto Rico. Iceland is the largest island of volcanic origin.

Indian Ocean

➢ The Indian Ocean (Area : 73,430,000 sq. km.) is the only ocean named after a country.

➢ The Indian Ocean is deeper than the Atlantic Ocean.

➢ It contains numerous continental islands, Madagascar and Sri Lanka are being the largest ones.

➢ Some of the islands of volcanic origin are those of Mauritius, Andaman and Nicobar, Seychelles, Maldives and Lakshadweep are of coral origin.

South Indian Ocean

➢ Warm currents : 1. South Equatorial 2. Mozambique 3. Madagascar 4. Agulhas.

➢ Cool Currents : 1. Antarctic drift 2. West Australian currents.

Arctic Ocean

➢ The Arctic Ocean (Area : 13,230,000 sq. km.) is the smallest of all the oceans.

➢ It lies within the Arctic Circle, hence the name Arctic Ocean.

➢ The North Pole lies in the middle of the Arctic Ocean.

➢ Most of the parts of Arctic Ocean remains frozen with thick ice for most of the days every year.

➢ It is the shallowest of all oceans, with an average depth of 1,500 m.

➢ It has the least salinity of all the oceans. It has a salinity of 20 unit per thousand.

Ocean Currents

➢ The flow of a large amount of water in a definite direction with a great intensity is known as Ocean Current.

➢ Ocean Currents are of two types-Hot and Cold.

Hot Currents

➢ The currents flowing from tropical zones of lower latitudes to higher temperate and sub polar zones are known as hot water currents.

Cold Currents

➢ The currents flowing from higher latitudes to lower latitudes are known as cold water currents.

➢ The only exception to the conduction of ocean currents is found in the Indian Ocean. The flow of currents changes here with a change in the direction of the Monsoon Winds. The hot currents flow towards cooler oceans and the cold currents flow towards the warmer oceans.

Biosphere

➢ The part of the Earth where life exists is called the Biosphere ('bios' means 'life').

➢ The Earth is the only planet of the solar system that supports life. Life is possible because of its unique lithosphere, hydrosphere and atmosphere.

Lithosphere

➢ The uppermost layer of the Earth's crust which is capable of supporting life is called Lithosphere.

➢ The Lithosphere (or land) covers two-sevenths or 29.22% (14,90,41,182 sq. km.) of the total surface area of the earth.

Hydrosphere

- Hydrosphere (or sea) covers five-sevenths or more accurately 70.78% (36,10,59,226 sq. km.) of the total surface area of the earth.
- Water is freely available in the gaseous, liquid and solid state.
- It is necessary for carrying out chemical reactions within the bodies of the living organisms.
- Water also dissolves and transports nutrients from the soil to the plants.
- It is used by plants for making food.

Latitude and Longitude

Any location on Earth is described by two numbers--its *latitude* and its *longitude.*

Latitude

On a globe of the Earth, lines of latitude are circles of different size. The longest is the equator, whose latitude is zero, while at the poles--at latitudes 90° north and 90° south (or -90°) the circles shrink to a point.

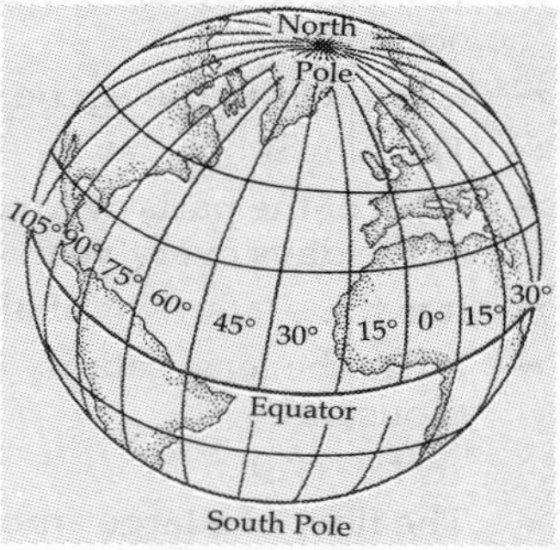

Longitude

On the globe, lines of constant longitude ("meridians") extend from pole to pole.

Every meridian must cross the equator. Since the equator is a circle, we can divide it--like any circle--into 360 degrees, and the longitude of a point is then the marked value of that division where its meridian meets the equator.

For historical reasons, the longitude (meridian) passing the old Royal Astronomical Observatory in *Greenwich, England,* is the one chosen as *zero longitude.* Located at the eastern edge of London, the British capital, the observatory is now a public museum and a *brass band* stretching across its yard marks the *"prime meridian."*

A line of longitude is also called a meridian, derived from the Latin, from meri, a variation of "medius" *which denotes* "middle", *and diem, meaning* "day." *The word once meant "noon", and times of the day before noon were known as* "ante meridian", *while times after it were* "post meridian." *Today's abbreviations* a.m. and p.m. *come from these terms, and the Sun at noon was said to be* "passing meridian". *All points on the same line of longitude experienced noon (and any other hour) at the same time and were therefore said to be on the same* "meridian line".

Local Time (LT) and Time Zones

Two important concepts, related to latitude and (especially) longitude are Local time (LT) and Universal time (UT)

Longitudes are measured from zero to 180° east and 180° west (or -180°), and both 180-degree longitudes share the same line, in the middle of the Pacific Ocean.

As the Earth rotates around its axis, at any moment one line of longitude--"the noon meridian"--faces the Sun, and at that moment, it will be noon everywhere on it. After 24 hours the Earth has undergone a full rotation with respect to the Sun, and the same meridian again faces noon. Thus each hour the Earth rotates by 360/24 = 15 degrees.

The Date Line and Universal Time (UT)

Longitude determines only the hour of the day--not the date, which is determined separately. The international date line has been established--most of it following the 180th meridian--where by common agreement, whenever we cross it the date advances one day (going west) or goes back one day (going east).

That line passes the *Bering Strait* between Alaska and Siberia, which thus have different dates, but for most of its course it runs in mid-ocean and does not inconvenience any local time keeping.

Astronomers, astronauts and people dealing with satellite data may need a time schedule which is the same everywhere, not tied to a locality or time zone. The *Greenwich mean time,* the astronomical time at Greenwich (averaged over the year) is generally used here. It is sometimes called Universal Time (UT).

Heat Zones of The Earth

Torrid Zone

- This is also referred to as Tropical zone. The Tropics is a region on the Earth surrounding Eqauator by the Tropic of Cancer in the northern hemisphere at 23°26′16″ N (approx) and the Tropic of Capricorn in the sourthern hemisphere at 23°26′16″ S (approx). The Tropics include all the areas on the Earth where the sun reaches a point directly overhed at least once in a year.
- This area receives maximum heat and is called the Torrid (hot) Zone.

Frigid Zone

- Near the polar regions, the rays of the Sun are very slanting and so it is very cold.
- The region/area between the Arctic Circle and the North Pole in the Northern Hemisphere is called the Frigid Zone.
- There are similar regions in the Southern Hemisphere between the Antarctic Circle and the South Pole, also called the Frigid Zone (frigid means cold).

Rotation of the Earth

- The Earth spins (rotates), west to east on its axis once in 24 hours approximately.
- The Earth's axis is not vertical. It makes an angle of 23°30′ with the vertical or 66°30′ with the plane of the Earth's orbit.
- The Earth's axis always remains pointed in the same direction (towards the Pole Star) as the Earth moves around the Sun. The tilt of the Earth's axis is known as the inclination of the Earth's axis.

Effect of the Tilted Axis on Day and Night

- Rotation of the Earth on its tilted axis causes days and nights to be of different length in different parts of the Earth.

- Since the Earth's axis is tilted in the same direction, the orientation of the Earth's axis to the Sun's rays is constantly changing as the Earth moves around the Sun. This results in a continuous change in the length of days and nights throughout the year.

Perihelion

- The position of the earth or any other planet in its orbit when it is at its nearest point to the sun.
- The earth reaches its perihelion about 3rd January at a distance of about 147 million kilometer near one extremity of the major axis of the earth's elliptical orbit, the axis being called Apsides line.

Aphelion

- The position of the earth or any other planet in its orbit when it is at its distant point from the sun.
- The earth reaches its aphelion on 4th July when the earth is at a distance of 152 million kilometer near the other extremity of the major axis.

Solstice

- Solstice is one of the two dates in the year on which the sun reaches greatest altitude north or south of the equator and is directly overhead along one of the lines of the tropics.

Summer Solstice

- On June 21, the earth is so located in its orbit that the sun is overhead on the Tropic of Cancer (23½°N).
- On this date the northern hemisphere is tipped towards the sun having the *longest day,* while the southern hemisphere is tipped away from the sun having the *shortest day.*

Winter Solstice

- On December 22, the earth is in an equivalent position on the opposite points in its orbit, so the southern hemisphere is tipped towards the sun and the northern hemisphere away from it.
- The sun is overhead on the Tropic of Capricorn (23½°S), resulting in the *shortest day* in the northern hemisphere.

Equinoxes

- Two days in a year when day and night are equal throughout the world are equinoxes.
- Falling midway between the dates of solstices, on these dates, the earth's axis lies at 90° to the line joining the centres of the earth and the sun and neither the northern nor the southern hemisphere is inclined towards the sun.
- The *'vernal equinox'* occurs on March 21 and it is also called the spring equinox in the northern hemisphere.
- The *'autumnal equinox'* occurs on September 23.

Midnight Sun

- This phenomenon is observed in the Arctic and Antarctic zones around mid-summer, when the sun does not sink below the horizon throughout 24 hours of the day and therefore, may be seen at midnight.

➢ This is the direct consequence of the inclination of the axis of the earth to the plane of the orbit.

➢ Norway is the place of midnight sun where the sun is continuously visible between May and July.

➢ In the southern hemisphere, the phenomenon is seen in the Antarctica continent.

Eclipses

➢ An Eclipse occurs when the sun, moon and earth are in a straight line.

➢ A *'solar eclispe'* occurs between sunrise and sunset on new moon when the moon passes directly in front of the sun so that its shadow lies on the earth. In other words, the moon lies between the sun and the earth.

➢ The *'lunar eclipse'* takes place when the earth comes in between the sun and the moon so that the shadow of the earth is cast on the moon.

➢ A lunar eclipse takes place on a full moon.

➢ Generally a total of seven eclipses, including solar and lunar eclipses, take place every year.

Atmosphere

➢ The envelope of air that completely surrounds the earth is known as atmosphere.

➢ The atmosphere extends to about 1000 km from the surface of the earth. But 99% of the total mass of the atmosphere is found within 32 km.

➢ This is because the atmosphere is held by the gravitational pull of the earth.

Composition of the Atmoshpere

(i) Nitrogen-78% (ii) Oxygen-21% (iii) Argon-0.93% (iv) Carbondioxide-0.03% (v) Neon-0.0018% (vi) Helium-0.0005% (vii) Ozone-0.0006% (viii) Hydrogen-0.00005%.

➢ Carbon dioxide is present in small quantity in the atmosphere.

➢ It is an important constituent of air because it has the ability to absorb heat and thus keep the atmosphere warm, thereby, balancing the heat of the earth.

➢ Water vapour is the most significant component of the atmosphere as far as its effect on weather is concerned although its quantity varies considerably from practically none (0) to up to about 4% by volume.

➢ Water vapour is the source of all clouds and precipitation (rain, hail storm etc.). Water vapour, like carbon dioxide, has the ability to absorb heat energy. It also regulates the hydrological cycle.

➢ Dust intercepts and reflect incoming insolation.

➢ The polluted particles present in the air not only absorb larger amount of insolation but also greatly absorb the terrestrial radiation.

➢ Dust in the atmosphere contributes to the red and orange colour of sunrise and sunset.

Layers of the Atmosphere

There are five distinct layers of the atmosphere–(a) Troposphere (b) Stratosphere (c) Mesosphere (d) Thermosphere and (e) Exosphere.

Troposphere

- This is the first layer of the atmosphere. It extends to a height of 18 km at the equator and 8 km at the poles.
- In this layer temperature decreases with height. This is due to the fact that the density of air decreases with height and so the heat absorbed is less. It contains more than 90% of gases in the atmosphere.
- Since most of the water vapour form clouds in this layer, all weather changes occur in the troposphere ("*tropo*" means 'change').
- The height at which the temperature stops decreasing is called tropopause. Here the temperature may be as low as -58^0 C.

Stratosphere

- This the second layer of the atmosphere. It extends from the tropopause to about 50 km.
- Temperature increases due to the absorption of the ultraviolet radiation of the Sun by **ozone** present in this layer. The temperature slowly increases to 4^{0}C.
- This layer is free from clouds and associated weather phenomena. Hence, it provides ideal flying conditions for large jet planes.
- At about 50 km the temperature begins to fall again. This marks the end of the stratosphere. The end of the stratosphere is called the stratopause.

Mesosphere

- Above the stratosphere lies the mesosphere.
- The mesosphere extends to a height of 80 km.
- Here the temperature decreases again, falling as low as -90^{0}C.
- The end of this layer is known as the mesopause.

Thermosphere

- The thermosphere lies above the mesosphere.
- This layer extends to a height of about 640 km.
- In this layer temperature rises dramatically, reaching upto 1480^{0}C.
- This increase in temperature is due to the fact that the gas molecules in this layer absorb the X-rays and ultraviolet radiation of the Sun.
- This results in the break up of the gas molecules into positively and negatively charged particles or ions. Thus, this layer is also known as the ionosphere.
- The electrically charged gas molecules of the thermosphere reflect radio waves from the Earth back into space. Thus, this layer also helps in long distance communications.
- The thermosphere also protects us from meteors and obsolete satellites, because its high temperature burns up nearly all the debris coming towards the Earth.

Exosphere

- This layer lies above the thermosphere.
- The exosphere extends beyond the thermosphere upto 960 km.
- It gradually merges with interplanetary space.

- The temperatures in this layer range from about 300°C to 1650°C.
- This layer contains only traces of gases like oxygen, nitrogen, argon and helium because the lack of gravity allows the gas molecules to escape easily into space.

How the Sun Creates Energy

- Hydrogen and helium are the predominant gases that constitute the Sun. The proportion of hydrogen to helium is 3 : 1.
- The core of the Sun acts like a gigantic nuclear reactor and converts huge quantity of hydrogen into helium. In this process of **nuclear fusion**, the Sun releases tremendous amount of energy in all directions.
- The Sun radiates energy (both heat and light) in all directions.
- Because of its small size in relation to the Sun, the Earth intercepts only a small part of the Sun's radiant energy.
- Solar radiations are the primary source of heat and light to the Earth.

Insolation

- The incoming solar radiation (energy intercepted by the Earth) is known as insolation and it is received in the form of short waves.

Terrestrial Radiation

- The Sun's energy absorbed by the Earth's surface when radiated out into space is called terrestrial radiation.

Weather and Climate

- Weather is the description of the atmospheric conditions of a particular place at a particular time for a short period of time.
- Climate is the composite or integrated picture of the weather conditions over a long period of time.
- Climatic data is based on calculated averages of data recorded over a period of 35 years. The classical period is 30 years, as defined by WMO.

Atmospheric Pressure

- Atmospheric pressure is the pressure at any point on the surface of the Earth due to the weight of the column of air above that point.

Measurement and Units of Atmospheric Pressure

- The mercury barometer is the standard instrument for measuring atmospheric pressure.
- Pressure is expressed in centimeters or inches **of** mercury, a true measure of the height of the mercury column.
- Standard sea level pressure is 76 cm or 29.92 inches on this scale.
- Another pressure unit used by meteorologists in drawing weather charts is millibars (mb).
- One bar is divided into 1000 millibars.
- Millibars are now known as hectopascals.

Pressure Measuring Instruments

1. Mercurial Barometer (or Fortin's Barometer)
2. Aneroid Barometer
3. Altimeter or Altitude Barometer
4. Barograph (automatic recording Aneroid Barometer)
5. Microbarometer
6. Microbarovariograph

- One atmospheric pressure (76 cm of mercury) = 760 mm of Hg. = 1013.25 milli bars (mb).

Winds

- Wind is the movement of air caused by the uneven heating of the Earth by the Sun.
- Sometimes wind blows gently, refreshing us. At other times, it blows strongly creating storms that cause widespread damages.
- We need measurements of two quantities : direction and speed, to give a description of the wind.

Trade Winds

- They blow from the Sub-tropical High Pressure Belt to the Equatorial Low Pressure Belt in the tropics between 30^0 North and 30^0 South latitudes.
- They blow as the N.E. Trades in the Northern Hemisphere and as the S.E. Trades in the Southern Hemisphere.
- The name "Trade" is derived from a nautical expression " to blow tread" meaning to bl ow along a regular path or "tread."

Wind Measurement Instruments

Windvane or Weather-cock measures the wind-direction.

Anemometer measures the wind velocity.

Westerlies

- They blow from the Sub-tropical high Pressure Belt to the Sub-polar low Pressure Belt in the temperate latitudes between 30^0 and 60^0, on either side of the Equator.
- They are more constant and stronger in the Southern Hemisphere because there are no large landmasses to interrupt them.
- In places they become so strong that these winds are known as the Roaring Forties or the Brave West Winds and the Furious Fifties.
- The belts of the Westerlies move north and south following the Sun's movement. These are known as Westerlies because they blow out of the west.

Polar Winds

- They blow from the Polar High Pressure Belt to the Sub-polar Low Pressure Belt between latitudes 60^0 and the poles on both sides of the Equator.
- These winds blow from the east to form the Polar Easterlies.
- They are more regular in the Southern Hemisphere.
- Polar winds are extremely cold and dry.

Climatic Winds or Periodic Winds

- These winds change their direction along with change in time or change in climate. Land and sea breezes and the Monsoon winds are typical examples of periodic winds.

Monsoon Winds

- Monsoon winds are seasonal winds characterised by a complete reversal in their direction from one season to another.
- They blow from the sea to the land in summer.
- They blow from the land to the sea in winter.

Intermal Structure of The Earth

The Earth's Crust

- The outermost solid cover or shell of the earth is known as the earth's crust.
- The thickness of the crust is about 30 km.
- It is thicker in the region of the continents and thinner in the region of the ocean floors.
- The density of the rocks in the earth's crust ranges from 2.7 to 3 g/c.c (grams per cubic centimeter).
- The upper part of the crust consists of silica and aluminium in greater proportions. That is why, it is called 'Sial'.
- Whereas the lower part of the crust is called 'Sima' because the proportion of silica and magnesium is higher in this part.

Mantle

- This layer lies below the crust.
- Its thickness is about 2900 km and the density of substances in the mantle ranges from 3.0 to 4.7.

Core

- The earth's core lies below the mantle. Its thickness may be about 3471 km.
- Its radius is 6371 km., according to IUGG.
- It is divided into two parts – the outer core and the inner core. The outer core is probably in a liquid state and the inner core in a solid state.
- The core mainly consists of iron with some amount of nickel and sulphur (NIFE).
- After the mantle, the earth's density goes on increasing rapidly towards its centre and finally is more than 13.
- The temperature of the central part of the earth may be about 5000^0C.
- The study of the earth's interior helps us to understand the original rocks in the earth's crust and their later transformation.

Rocks

- The solid parts of the earth's crust are called rocks. Most of the rocks are made up of two or more minerals.
- In the same type of rocks, the proportions of minerals may be different in different areas.
- Rocks may not always necessarily be hard.
- Minerals are obtained from rocks.
- Rocks are classified in three main types depending on the process of their formation : (a) Igneous, (b) Sedimentary, (c) Metamorphic.

Igneous rocks

- Hot lava pours out at the time of volcanic eruptions and cools down later on, forming rocks.
- The molten materials known as magma, sometimes cool down beneath the earth's crust, again forming rocks.

- Both these types of rocks are known as Igneous rocks.
- When the earth's surface first became solid after it cooled down from its hot liquid state, the original rocks of the earth's crust were formed. They are the Primary Igneous rocks, which are usually not found today.
- Igneous rocks are generally harder and granular.
- There are no layers in Igneous rocks.
- Fossils are not found in Igneous rocks.
- The formation of Igneous rocks takes place beneath and above the surface of the earth.
- Rocks formed by the cooling of molten matter beneath the earth's surface are called intrusive igneous rocks. 'Granite' and 'Gabbro' are the main examples of these rocks.
- The intrusive rocks are thus crystalline rocks.
- Sometimes, the molten matter oozes out through cracks in the earth's crust and spreads on the surface, forming extrusive igneous rocks.
- Gabbro, Obsidian, Basalt etc. are examples of extrusive igneous rocks.
- A very large area of the Deccan Plateau consists of basalt rocks.
- These rocks contain silica from 40 to 80%, others are felspar, magnesium and iron etc.
- Other examples of Igneous rocks are–Granite, Pumic stone, Basalt and Gabbro.

Igneous rocks	Metamorphic rocks
Granite	Gneiss
Gabbro	Sarpentine

Sedimentary rocks

- They are formed by the deposition, sedimentation and lethification of sediments over a long period of time.
- As layers over layers get deposited, over a period of time, unified sedimentary rocks are formed on account of the tremendous pressure exerted by the layers above.
- Sometimes the remains of plants, dead animals etc. are found in the deposited material. Such fossil containing sedimentary rocks are useful for studying life on earth.
- Sandstone, limestone, shale are some examples of sedimentary rocks.

Sedimentary rocks	Metamorphic rocks
Limestone	Marble
Sandstone	Quartzite
Shale / clay	Slate, Phyllite, Schist
Coal	Diamond

- Limestone is white as well as black.
- Sandstone is dull white, pink, bright red or sometimes black.

Metmaorphic rocks

- The nature of igneous and sedimentary rocks changes due to the effects of tremendous heat or pressure, and new, transformed rocks, called metamorphic rocks, are formed.
- Minerals in the rocks get restructured on account of heat and pressure. This brings about a change in the original formation of the rocks.

Some examples of metamorphic rocks formed from igneous and sedimentary rocks :

Type of rock	Original rock	Metamorphic rock
Igneous	granite	gneiss
Igneous	basalt	homblend
Sedimentary	limestone	marble
Sedimentary	coal	graphite coal
Sedimentary	sandstone	quartzite
Sedimentary	shale/clay	slate, mica schist

Earthquakes and Volcanoes

Earthquakes

- The sudden tremors or shaking of the earth's crust is called an earthquake. When a part of the earth's surface moves backward and forward or up and down, the earth's surface 'quakes', and these are called the 'earthquake'.
- The earth's crust is made up of different parts of various sizes. They are called plates.
- Most of the earthquakes in the world are caused by the movements of the plates.
- 'Seismology' the special branch of Geology, It deals with the study of earthquake.
- 'Richter scale' and 'Mercalli scale' are the instruments to measure/record the magnitude and the intensity of an earthquake respectively.

Seismic Waves

- The place where the seismic waves originate beneath the earth's surface is called the focus of the earthquake.
- The epicenter is that point on the ground surface which is closest to the focus.
- Seismic waves are recorded on the seismograph. Seismic waves are mainly of three types–(i) Primary waves (ii) Secondary waves and (iii) Surface or Long waves.

The earthquake zones in India

- The Indian plate is moving from south to north. That is why there are earthquakes in the Himalayan region.
- Earthquakes occur in Assam, Arunachal Pradesh, Nagaland, Tripura, Manipur, Mizoram, Andaman and Nicobar Islands, Jammu and Kashmir, the north-western region of Uttar Pradesh, the northern region of Bihar etc.
- During the last few years, there have been several earthquakes of varying intensities in Maharashtra and Gujarat.

Volcanic Activity

- Magma or molten rock is formed beneath the ground surface due to various reasons.

- This molten rock ruptures the ground and pours out. Sometimes, it cools down beneath the ground surface instead of pouring out.
- All these activities are called volcanic activities.
- Volcanic activities have been taking place since times immemorial.
- There are three types of Volcanoes :

  (i) Active Volcanoes (ii) Dormant Volcanoes (iii) Extinct Volcanoes.

Volcanic eruptions

- The pouring out of the magma or molten rock through ground surface is called a volcanic eruption.
- At the time of eruption, the magma, steam, fragments of rock, dust and gaseous substances are ejected with great force from under the ground surface through a pipe like passage.
- The opening of this pipe on the earth's surface is known as the vent which forms a crater.
- The lava which is thrown into the sky during an eruption, falls to the ground in the form of solid fragments. Dark clouds gather in the sky and it begins to rain heavily.
- The volcanic ash and dust mixes with the rainwater giving rise to hot mud flows.

Types of Volcanic Eruptions

- Volcanic eruptions are classified into two types depending on the manner of ejection of the magma :

  (i) Central eruption, (ii) Fissure eruption.

Central eruption

- This type of eruption is sometimes very explosive, because lava, steam, gas, dust, smoke, stone fragments are ejected from a narrow pipe from under the ground with greater intensity. This type of eruption gives rise to conical or dome-shaped hills.

  Some examples of volcanic mountains formed due to central eruption are Mt. Kilimanjaro in Africa, the Fujiyama in Japan and the Vesuvius and Mount Etna in Italy.
- It is basically poured acidic lava.

Fissure eruption

- A very long fissure (cracks) develops in the ground surface and so, the molten rock, rock fragments, steam and gases within, pour out slowly.
- These eruptions take place at a very slow speed. Since this lava is more fluid, it spreads over longer distances.
- The lava cools down on the ground over a period of time, increasing the thickness of the surface in that area. Basalt plateaus are formed due to these eruptions.
- Basalt plateaus are also found in Brazil in South America and Saudi Arabia in West Asia and Deccan plateau in India.
- In Maharashtra, the fertile black regur soil has been formed from basalt rocks. It is also called black cotton soil.

Various Landforms

Mainly there are three types of landforms—Mountains, Plateaus, Plains.

Mountains

The height of mountains are over 600 m and have conical peaks. On the basis of origin there are four types of mountains : Block Mountains, Residual Mountains, Accumulated Mountains and Fold Mountains.

Block Mountains

- The middle part of such mountains is lower and the parts on both the sides are higher.The middle lower portion is called as Rift valley. The longest rift valley is the valley of the Jordan river.
- Black Forest (Germany), Vindhyachal and Satpura (India), Salt Range (Pakistan) are some examples of block mountains.

Residual Mountains

- Such mountains are formed as a result of weathering. Examples—Aravalli, Nilgiri, Parasnath, Hills of Rajmahal (India), Siera (Spain).

Accumulated Mountains

- These are formed due to accumulation of sand, soil, rocks, lava etc. on the Earth's Crust., e.g. Sand Dunes.

Fold Mountains

- These are formed because of the folds in the rocks due to internal motions of the earth. These are wavelike mountains which have numerous peaks and lows, e.g. Himalayas, Ural, Alps, Rockies, Andes etc.

Plateaus

- Plateaus are extensive upland areas characterised by flat and rough top surface and steep walls which rise above the neighbouring ground surface at least for 300 m.
- Generally the height of plateau ranges from 300 to 500 feet.

Intermountainous Plateaus : Plateaus formed between mountain, Example-Tibetan Plateau.

Mountainstep Plateaus : The flat region between a plain and the base of a mountain.

Continental Plateaus : These are formed when the Lacolith inside the Earth comes to the surface due to weathering. e.g. the Southern Plateau

Bank Plateaus : These are the plateaus on the banks of the oceans.

Some plateaus having more than average height	
Tibetan Plateau	16000 ft
Bolivian Plateau	11800 ft
Columbian Plateau	7800 ft

Domelike Plateaus : These are formed due to the movement of man and animals on the surface. e.g. Ramgarh Plateau.

Plains

Plains can be defined as flat areas with low height (below 500 ft.)

Weathered Plains : The plains formed due to weathering by rivers, glaciers, winds etc.

Loess Plains : These are formed by the soil and sands brought by winds.

Karst Plains : Plains formed due to the weathering of limestone.

Erosional Plains : Plains near the river banks formed by river erosion.

Glacial Plains : Marshy plains formed due to the deposition of ice.

Desert Plains : These are formed as a result of the flow of rivers.

Deposition Plains : Large plains are formed due to the silt brought by the rivers. Such plains are plains of Ganga, Sutlej, Mississipi, Hwang Ho.

Forests

They are of the following types :

(a) Tropical Evergreen Rain Forests : Such forests are found in the equatorial and the tropical regions with more than 200 cms annual rainfall. The leaves of trees in such forests are very wide. Ex– Red wood, palm etc.

(b) Tropical Semi Deciduous Forests : Such forests recieve rainfall less than 150 cms. Saagwan, saal, bamboo etc. are found in such forests.

(c) Temperate mixed Forests : Such forests are a mixture of trees and shrubs. Corks, Oak etc. are the major trees of these forests.

(d) Coniferous Forests or Taiga : These are evergreen forests. The trees, in these forests, have straight trunk, conical shape with relatively short branches and small needlelike leaves. Example–Pine, Fir etc.

(e) Tundra Forests : Such forests are covered with snow. Only Mosses, a few sladges and Lichens grow here in the summers. This type of vegetation is chiefly confined to the northern hemisphere (e.g. in Eurasia, North Americal and Greenland Coast).

(f) Mountainous Forests : Vegetation varies according to altitude.

Pastures (or Grasslands)

➢ They can be divided into two types :

(i) Tropical Pastures and (ii) Temperate Pastures

Tropical Pastures : They have different names in different countries. Savanna in Africa, Campos in Brazil, Lanos in Venezuela and Columbia.

Temperate Pastures : They are known by the following names-Praries in USA and Canada, Pampas in Argentina, Veld in South Africa, Rangelands or Downs in Australia and Newzealand, Steppes in Eurasia (Ukraine, Russia).

Land forms created by the river system

V-shaped valley

➢ A river flows with a greater velocity in the mountainous region and big, pointed fragments of rock also flow with a great speed along with the water.

➢ The river bed is scoured and downcutting starts, ultimately giving rise to a deep valley with steep sides. This valley is called a v-shaped valley.

➢ These valleys are found in mountainous regions.

➢ A deep and narrow valley with steep sides is called a gorge.

➢ The gorge of the river Ulhas in Thane district in Maharashtra and the gorge of the river Narmada at Bhedaghat near Jabalpur in Madhya Pradesh are well known.

➢ There are many gorges in the Himalayas.

Waterfall

➢ If there are both hard (resistant) and soft (less resistant) rocks in the course of the river, the less resistant rock is eroded faster.

➢ The resistant rock does not erode so easily. That is why, the river falls with a great speed from a cliff-like part of hard rock. This is called a waterfall.

➢ The Niagara Falls on the Niagara river is in North America.

Potholes

➢ In areas where the river bed consists of hard rock, the stones carried along with the river water due to the whirling impact of water.

➢ That is why holes of various shapes are formed in the rocky river bed. Such holes are called potholes.

➢ Many patholes are observed in the river bed of the Kukadi, Krishna, Godavari etc. in Maharashtra.

Meanders and ox-bow lakes

➢ Meanders are formed by lateral erosion. As the erosion increases over a period of time, the meanders in the river again starts flowing in a straight line.

➢ The loop previously formed then separates from the main course of the river. Water accumulates in this separated part.

➢ As this loop resembles on ox-bow it is called ox-bow lake. It formed due to impounding of water in the abandoned meander loop.

Fan-shaped plains

➢ In the region near the source of a river the tributaries joining the main river deposit materials carried by them on the banks of the main river.

➢ This deposition creates fan-like plains. They are called fan-shaped plains or alluvial fans.

Flood plains

➢ When, during the floods, the river-water overflows its banks and spreads in the surrounding areas, the silt carried by the water gets deposited in those areas. This creates flat plains on both the banks of the river. Plains created by this depositional work done during floods are called flood plains.

➢ The Gangetic Plain is a flood plain.

Natural levees

➢ When a river is over flooded, its water crosses its banks. At that time, the speed of the water is reduced, and the pebbles and stones carried by the river get deposited near the banks.

➢ On account of frequent floods, the area where these sediments are deposited near the bank of the river rises higher than the flood plain.

➢ This high wall is called a natural levee or natural embankment.

➢ Such levees are found on the banks of the Mississippi, the Huang-ho etc., Southern bank of river Ganga.

Delta

➢ Delta was coined by Herodotus (the 'Father of History') after the Greek letter delta (Δ) because of the deltoid shape at the mouth of the Nile.

➢ A delta is a land form that is formed at the mouth of a river where that river flows into an ocean, sea, estuary, lake, reservoir, flat arid area or another river.

➢ Deltas are formed from the deposition of the sediment carried by the river as the flow leaves the mouth of the river. Over long periods of lime, this deposition builds the characteristic geographic pattern of a river delta.

Delta-region

➢ A river meets a sea or a lake. The silt carried by the river is deposited on the bed near its mouth.

➢ The area near the mouth of the river gets gradually filled up by this deposition and gets raised causing an obstruction for the river to flow in a single channel. It, therefore, splits into two branches and meets the sea.

➢ Over a period of time, there is deposition also at the mouth of these branches. In this manner, the main course of the river gets split into a network of small channels. These sub-channels are called distributaries.

➢ A triangular region of innumerable such distributaries is formed near the mouth of the river. This region is called the delta region.

➢ There are delta regions near the vent (opening) of the rivers Godavari, Ganga, Nile, Mississippi etc. Deltas are very fertile.

➢ The largest delta of the world is 'Sunderbans Delta' (350 km.).

Land forms created by the actions of river

Erosion	Erosion Deposition	Deposition
V-shaped valley	Meanders	Fan-shaped plains
Gorge	Ox-bow	Flood Plains
Potholes	Lakes	Delta
Waterfall		Natural Levees

Glacier

➢ A mass of ice sliding down the slope from a snow-clad region is called a glacier. On an average a glacier moves 1 to 15 metres a day.

➢ While a glacier is moving, the friction of the ice at the bottom slows down the movement of the bottom layers.

➢ There are two main types of glaciers : (i) Continental Glacier and (ii) Alpine Glacier.

Continental Glacier

➢ An extensive sheet of ice spreading across a vast region sometimes begins to move due to the pressure of the ice.

➢ This moving sheet of ice is called a continental glacier.

➢ Such glaciers are seen in Antarctica and Greenland.

Alpine or mountain glacier

➢ There are snow-field in the mountainous regions of the Himalayas, the Alps, the Andes, the Rocky mountains etc.

➢ The ice accumulating in these areas starts sliding down the slopes.

- This mass of ice sliding down from the mountains is called a mountain glacier or an alpine glacier.

Iceberg

- Blocks of ice break off from the continental glaciers and float away into the sea.
- A block of ice floating in the sea is called an iceberg. These icebergs are huge in size.
- The density of ice being slightly less than that of water, a very little portion of an iceberg is seen above the water and the rest of it is submerged under water.

Land forms of glaciation

- Various land forms are created on account of the transportation, erosion and depositional work of a glacier. Let us consider the major land forms thus created.

Cirque

- When the snow from the mountain peaks slides, it gets deposited in a hollow, if there is one on any side of the peak.
- The accumulated snow starts sliding down the slope. This causes friction at the floor and at the sides of the hollow, thus enlarging it further. This is called a cirque.
- The back wall of a cirque is like a high cliff and the floor is concave and huge in size. The total shape resembles an armchair.
- When a glacier melts completely, water accumulates in the cirque and forms a lake which is known as tarn.

Fiord

- Where the lower end of the trough is drowned by the sea it forms a deep steep-side inlet called 'Fiord' as on the Norwegian and South Chilean Coasts.

U-shaped valley

- When a glacier is flowing through a valley in a mountainous region, the sides of the valley get eroded. Ice causes friction on the sides of the valley.
- As the erosion of the sides is greater than that of the floor, a valley is formed with vertical sides and a wide floor. This valley is called a U-shaped valley.

Hanging valley

- In the mountainous region, many tributaries join the main glacier.
- The quantity of ice in a tributary is comparatively smaller. Hence, it causes less friction.
- The valley of a tributary is at a higher level than a valley of the main glacier, the valley of the tributary appears to be hanging. That is why, such a valley is called a hanging valley.

Moraine

- The material transported and deposited by a glacier is known as moraine.

- Moraines are made up of pieces of rocks that are shattered by frost action and are brought down the valley.

Moraines are of the following types

(1) lateral moraine, (2) medial moraine (3) terminal moraine and (4) ground moraines.

- After a glacier has melted, different land forms of deposition are seen.
- The oval-shaped hills of lesser height are called drumlins.
- Zig-zag hills, with many steep slopes, made up of long stretches of sand and gravel are called eskers.

Land forms created by the action of wind

Mushroom rock

- The wind blowing in desert regions erodes the rock near the ground surface to a great extent. At the same time, the upper part of the rock gets eroded to a lesser extent.
- As this is a continuous process, the foot of the rock becomes narrow.
- The top portion of the rock then looks like an umbrella. This land form is called a mushroom rock.

Sand dunes

- Sand gets transported from one place to another along with the wind.
- At a spot where the wind meets an obstruction or where the speed of the wind reduces, dunes are formed out of the sand which gets deposited.
- The side of the dune facing the wind has a gentle slope and the opposite side has a steep slope.
- Because of the slow speed of the wind, the sand on the gentle slope gets carried to the top and comes down the steep slope on the other side. Sand dunes gradually move forward in this manner.

Barkhan

- The fine sand particles carried by the wind get deposited when the speed of the wind is reduced forming crescent shaped dunes. Such hills are called barkhans.

Loess

- Loess is a soil finer than sand.
- Loess is a silt transported by the wind from the desert regions and deposited much further way.
- Loess transported from the desert regions of Central Asia has been deposited in layers in China. The plain they form is known as the Loess plain.

Groundwater

- Some water from the rainfall received on the earth's surface seeps through the ground.
- This water trickles down until it reaches an impervious rock.
- Water accumulated under the ground surface in this manner, is called ground water.

- ➢ Some rocks on the earth's surface are porous and some have cracks or joints. Water seeps in through these pores or joints.
- ➢ Groundwater gushes out in the form of springs.

Land forms created by the actions of groundwater

Sink holes

- ➢ Water on the ground surface seeps through limestone. Some portion of the limestone dissolves in that water. If this process takes place continuously, it makes holes in these rocks.
- ➢ As this process continues over a number of years, these holes get enlarged. These holes are called sink holes.

Caves

- ➢ In limestone region, water goes very deep through sink holes.
- ➢ If there is a layer of impervious and hard rock underneath, water flows horizontally on the impervious rock instead of going deeper.
- ➢ Hence, soft rocks get eroded and a cave is formed.

Stalactites and stalagmites

- ➢ Inside the cave created by groundwater under the ground surface in a limestone region, water is always seeping through the roof. This water contains calcium carbonate.
- ➢ As the seeping water evaporates, some of the calcium carbonate, it contains, is deposited on the cave's roof. This deposition continues to grow very slowly. Hence a column is seen growing from the roof towards the floor. It is called a stalactite.
- ➢ The water dripping on the floor of the cave also evaporates leaving behind calcium carbonate which accumulates over a period of time.
- ➢ A column then starts growing from the floor to the roof. This column which grows upwards is called a stalagmite.
- ➢ Stalactites and stalagmites are observed in the Parner Taluka of Ahmadnagar district, in Bastar District in Chhattisgarh and also in the Karst region of former Yugoslavia now Serbia and Montenegro.

Land forms created by the actions of sea waves

Sea Cliff

- ➢ The base of the rocks on the coast get eroded because of the impact of the ocean waves and notches develop in these rocks.
- ➢ The crest of the rock overhangs the notch. These notches in the rocks gradually extend landwards over a period of time. Then the crest falls and a steep cliff, which has receded away from the sea is formed.

Sea cave

- ➢ Rocks on the coast have many cracks. They become wider and wider with the impact of the waves, creating small caves. They are called sea caves.
- ➢ Such sea cliffs and sea caves are observed at Shrivandhan, Ratnagiri, Malvan, Vengurle etc.

Beach

- ➢ The fine sand and other material that flows along with the waves get deposited in a direction parallel to the sea coast.

- This deposition of sand is called a beach.
- There are extensive beaches in the coastal regions of the states of Maharashtra, Goa, Kerala, Tamil Nadu, Odisha and West Bengal in India and in other countries like Bangladesh and Canada.

Sand bar

- A deposition of sand which results in a long, narrow embankment in the sea near the coast is called a sand bar.

Lagoon

- A shallow lake is formed between the sand and the sea coast. It is called a lagoon. Such a lake is called Kayal in Kerala.

The Indian Subcontinent : Position, Extent and Physical Features

Location of the Sub Continent

- Mainland of the Indian subcontinent, comprising India, Pakistan, Bangladesh, Nepal and Bhutan extends between $8^0 4'$N and $37^0 6'$N latitudes and between $68^0 7'$E and $97^0 25'$E longitudes.
- If the sixth country of this subcontinent Sri Lanka, is included, then it starts from 6^0N latitude.
- The Tropic of Cancer (23½° N) passes through the middle of India.

Size and Extent of Subcontinent

- Total area of the Indian subcontinent is 44.9 lakh sq. km i.e. India 32,87,263 sq. km, Pakistan 7,96,095 sq. km, Bangladesh 1,48,393 sq. km., Nepal 1,47,181 sq km., Bhutan 46,500 sq. km. and Sri Lanka 65,610 sq. km. From North to South this subcontinent stretches over 3,200 km and from east to west it is 3,000 km. $82^0 30'$ E meridian helps in calculating the Indian Standard Time (IST) which is 5 hours 30 minutes ahead of the Greenwich Mean Time (GMT).
- This very meridian ($82½^0$ E) dictates time in Sri Lanka and Nepal also.

Political Divisions of India

- India is divided into 28 States and 7 Union Territories.

Position and Extent of India and its Locational Advantage

- India forms part of the large continental land mass of Eurasia.
- It is located on one of the peninsulas of Southern Asia. The country extends from Kashmir in north to Kanyakumari in the south.
- The Arabian sea and the Bay of Bengal are situated on western and eastern side of peninsular India respectively.
- The latitudinal extent of the country is from $8^0 4'$ North to $37^0 6'$ North.
- The Tropic of Cancer (23½° N) which passes through the middle of the country measures from 68^0 7′ E to $97^0 25'$E. The location of the country is in the northern and the eastern hemispheres.
- The importance of location of India is that it is located on the world's major sea routes.
- Due to its location, India has maritime contacts with south-west Asia and Africa on the west and south-east Asia in the east. Its location has given India an advantage of the route of the Suez Canal for trade with North America and Europe.

Size of India (in terms of area and population)

- India is the seventh largest country (in terms of area) in the world.
- The area of India is about 3.28 million sq. km.
- The area of India is nearly equal to the area of the continent of Europe excluding Russia.
- India is eight times as large as Japan. India ranks as the second largest country in terms of population (next to China only).
- No continent of the world except Asia has a largest population than that of India.
- **India contains about one-sixth of the total population of the world.**

Physical Divisions of the Indian Subcontinent

- A chain of high mountains radiate out from the Pamir Knot which lies just in the north of India
- In these mountains the Hindukush, the Sulaiman and the Kirthar in the east and the Himalayas in the west separate the Indian subcontinent from rest of Asia.
- Indian subcontinent can be divided into following physical divisions :
  - The Great Mountain Wall of the North
  - The Great Northern Plains
  - The Great Peninsular Plateau
  - The Coastal Plains
  - The Great Indian Desert
  - The Island Groups.

The Great Mountain wall of the North

- The Himalayas, the highest mountain wall of the world, are situated on the northern boundary of India like an arc.
- From west to east the Himalayas are 2500 km long. The average breadth of the Himalayas is between 250 km to 400 km.
- Mount Everest, the highest peak in the word, lies in these mountains in Nepal.

Division of the Himalayas

- The Himalayas consist of three parallel mountain ranges : (i) The Greater Himalayas (ii) The Lesser Himalayas and (iii) The Outer Himalayas.

The Greater Himalayas (or Himadri)

- This is the loftiest of the three ranges of Himalayas. Mount Everest lies in this range.
- These snow-covered mountains give birth to many glaciers.
- The Ganga originates from this glacier.

Location	Important Passes
Jammu & Kashmir	Burzi-La, Joji-La
H.P.	Bara La, Cha-La, Shipki-La
U.P.	Niti-La, Lipu-Lekh-La
Sikkim	Jelep-La, Nathu-La
Arunachal Pradesh	Bomdi-La

The Lesser Himalayas (or the Himachal Himalayas)

➢ South of the Greater Himalayas, the range also lies parallel to it from west to east. This ranges 60 to 80 km wide and its average height ranges between 3500 to 4500 metres.

➢ Tourist centres like Shimla, Mussorie and Nainital are situated in this range.

The Outer Himalayas (or Shiwaliks)

➢ This is the southernmost and the third parallel range of the Himalayas with an average height of 900 to 1200 metres.

➢ Its breadth is only 10 to 50 km. Shivalik range is broader in the west.

Heights of Major Mountain Peaks in India

Peaks	Elevation● (in mts.)	Peaks	Elevation● (in mts.)
Godwin Austin (K2)	8611*	Masherbrum (East)	7821*
Kanchenjunga	8598	Nanda Devi	7817
Nanga Parvat	8126*	Masherbrum (West)	7806*
Gasherbrum	8068*	Rakoposhi	7788*
Broad Peak	8047*	Kamet	7756
Dastegil	7885*	Saser Kangdi	7672

● Above mean sea level in metres.
* Situated in Pak occupied Kashmir (PoK)

The Great Northern plains

➢ The northern plains are divided into three sub-divisions. These are the Punjab and Haryana plains. The Ganga plains and the Brahamaputra valley.

➢ The Ganga plains form the largest lowland drained by the Ganga and its tributaries.

➢ The Yamuna is the most important tributary of the Ganga.

➢ The Ghaghara, the Gandak, the Kosi and the Tista are other tributaries of the Ganga.

➢ The Sone and the Damodar are tributaries of the Ganga while the Chambal and the Betwa are tributaries of the Yamuna from the peninsular plateau.

➢ The Ganga plain has an extremely gentle slope. Parts of the plain are subject to floods in the rainy season. In the lower course, the Ganga divides itself into tributaries to form a large delta along with the Brahmaputra.

➢ The Punjab and Haryana plains represent a part of the Indus basin.

➢ A low watershed separates these plains from the Ganga plains.

The Great Pensinsular Plateau

➢ Anamudi or Anaimudi (2695 m) is the highest peak of the peninsula.

➢ The Deccan plateau includes the area to the south of the Vindhyas.

- The western edge of the plateau rises steeply from the Arabian Sea to form the Western Ghats (which includes the Shahyadri).
- The Deccan plateau slopes gently towards the east. The surface of the plateau is dissected into a rolling upland by a number of rivers.
- The elevation ranges from 300 to 900 metres.
- The eastern edge of the plateau is known as the Eastern Ghats.
- The north-western region of the Deccan plateau is covered by nearly horizontal sheets of lava. This region is called 'Deccan trap region.' The Deccan plateau is drained by many long east flowing rivers. These rivers originate in the Western Ghats, flow towards the east and enter the Bay of Bengal.
- The Godavari, the Mahanadi, the Krishna and the Cauvery are the major rivers that have built deltas along the coast.
- The Narmada and the Tapti rivers are west flowing.
- Both the rivers enter the Arabian Sea along the Gujarat coast.
- These rivers do not have deltas.

Major Plateaus : Marwar Upland, Central Highland, Bundelkhand, Malwa Plateau, Baghelkhand, Chhotanagpur Plateau (Hazaribagh Plateau, Ranchi Plateau and Raj Mahal Hills), Meghalaya Plateau, Deccan Plateau, Maharashtra Plateau, Karnataka Plateau, Telengana Plateau, Chhatisgarh Plain.

The Coastal Plains

- Narrow strips of flat land on eastern and western coasts are known as the East Coastal Plain and the West Coastal Plain respectively.

The West Coastal Plain

- This plain which lies between the Arabian Sea and the Western Ghats spreads from Gujarat in the north to Kanyakumari in the south.
- It is broader in the north and narrower in the south. This uneven plain has been dissected by many fast flowing rivers.
- Its northen part from Gujarat to Goa is called Konkan, while southern part from Goa to Kanyakumari is known as Malabar. Several lagoons (salt water lakes separated from the main sea by sand bars and spits) are found on the coastal plain.
- Important ports developed on its coast from north to south are : Kandla, Mumbai, New Jawahar Port Mumbai, Marmagao, Mangalore and Cochin.

The East Coastal Plain

- This broader coastal plain spreads along the Bay of Bengal from Odisha in the north to Kaynakumari in the south.
- Its northern part is known as Northern Circar plains and the southern part is called Coromandal Coast. Rivers like Mahanadi, Godavari, Krishna and Cauvery form deltas on this plain.
- This coast is famous for rice cultivation.
- A large number of lagoons are also found here.
- Chilka and Pulicat lakes are fine examples of lagoons on our east coast.

The Great Indian Desert

- It lies to the west of the Aravali range.
- It extends over major part of Rajasthan and Sindh in Pakistan.
- This desert does not get much rain as the Aravali range run parallel to the south-western monsoon winds.
- It is in the rain shadow area of the Bay of Bengal current.
- Lake Sambhar is found here.

The Island Groups

- Lakshadweep is a group of 36 coral islands in the Arabian Sea.
- It is located 300 km to the west of the coast of Kerala.
- Andaman and Nicobar islands are a group of about 324 islands.
- Most of these islands are uninhabited.
- Andaman and Nicobar islands are separated by the Ten Degree Channel because 10^0N latitude passes through this place.

Climatic Diversity in the Indian Subcontinent

- Due to the vastness of the country and a variety of relief features there are regional variations in the climate of India.
- The interior of the country, specially in the north, has a continental type of climate.
- The coastal areas have a more equable climate. In mountainous areas, altitude determines the climate. There is a great deal of variation in the amount of annual rainfall.
- In June, the highest temperature in Rajasthan may go up to 55^0C.
- But, in Drass and Kargil the night temperature in January may go down to -45^0C to -50^0C.
- Mawsynram or Cherrapunji in Meghalaya has an annual rainfall of 2500 cm.
- But, in the Thar Desert the annual rainfall is less than 13 cm.
- Along the Malabar Coast (Kerala) the annual range of temperature is about 3^0C.
- But, it is 20^0C in Hissar, Ambala and other parts of the interior.

Soil Resources of the Indian Sub-continent

Soil

- Soil forms the upper layer of the earth's crust capable of supporting life.
- It is made up of loose rock materials and humus.
- The soil forming processes are mainly influenced by the parent rock, climate, vegetation and animal life.

Importance of Soil Resources

- Soil is an extremely important resource, especially in agricultural countries like India, Pakistan and Bangladesh.
- Most food items, like rice, wheat, pulses, fruits and vegetables and much of our clothing are derived from the soil directly or indirectly.

- Soil also gives us firewood, timber, rubber, fibers, etc. Food like milk, meat and eggs are obtained indirectly from the soil. Flowers, grass, plants and trees are also grown out of soil.

Soil Erosion and its types

- Removal of top layer of soil when it is exposed to wind and rain, is easily blown or washed away. This condition is known as soil erosion.
- Basically, soil cover is removed by two powerful agents – (i) Running water, (ii) Wind.

Types of Soil found in India

- Indian Council of Agricultural Research (ICAR) divides Indian soils into eight groups : (a) Alluvial soil (b) Black soil (c) Red soil (d) Laterites and Lateritic soil (e) Arid and Desert soil (f) Saline and Alkaline soil (g) Forest soil (h) Peaty and other organic soil. However, Indian soils are generally divided into four broad types : (1) Alluvial soils (2) Regur soils (3) Red soils and (4) Laterite soils.

Alluvial Soils

- This is the most important and widespread category. It covers 40% of the land area. In fact the entire Northern Plains are made up of these soils.
- They have been brought down and deposited by three great Himalayan rivers- Sutlej, Ganga and Brahmaputra and their tributaries.
- Through a narrow corridor in Rajasthan they extend to the plains of Gujarat.
- They are common in Eastern coastal plains and in the deltas of Mahanadi, Godavari, Krishna and Cauveri.
- Crops Grown : Suitable for Kharif & Rabi Crops like cereals, Cottons, Oilseeds and sugarcane. The lower Ganga-Brahmaputra Valley is useful for jute cultivation.

Regur or Black Soils

- These soils are of volcanic origin. These soils are black in colour and are also known as black soils.
- Since, they are ideal for growing cotton, they are also called black cotton soils, in addition to their normal nomenclature of Regur soils.
- These soils are most typical of the Deccan trap (Basalt) region spread over north-west Deccan plateau and are made up of lava flows.
- They cover the plateaus of Maharashtra, Saurashtra, Malwa and southern Madhya Pradesh and extend eastward in the south along the Godavari and Krishna Valleys.
- Crops Grown : Cotton, Jowar, Wheat, Sugarcane, Linseed, Gram, Fruit & Vegetable.

Red Soils

- Formed by weathering of crystalline and metamorphic mixture of clay and sand.
- These soils are developed on old crystalline Igneous rocks under moderate to heavy rainfall conditions.

- They are red in colour because of their high Iron-oxide (FeO) content.
- They are deficient in phosphoric acid, organic matter and nitrogenous material.
- Red soils cover the eastern part of the peninsular region comprising Chhotanagpur plateau, Odisha (Orissa), eastern Chhattisgarh, Telangana, the Nilgiris and Tamil Nadu plateau.
- They extend northwards in the west along the Konkan coast of Maharashtra.
- Crops Grown : Wheat, Rice, Millets, Pulses.

Laterite Soils

- The Laterite soils are formed due to weathering of lateritic rocks in hightemperatures and heavy rainfall with alternate dry and wet period.
- They are found along the edge of plateau in the east covering small parts of Tamil Nadu, Odisha and a small part of Chhotanagpur in the north and Meghalaya in the north-east.
- Laterite soils are red in colour with a high content of iron-oxides; poor in Nitrogen and Lime.
- Crops Grown : Unsuitable for agriculture due to high content of acidity and inability to retain moisture.

Arid & Desert Soil

- Region : NW India. Covers entire area of the west Aravalis in Rajsthan and parts of Haryana, Punjab & Gujarat.
- Characteristics : Rich in Phosphates and Calcium but deficient in Nitrogen and humus.
- Corps Grown : Fertile if irrigated e.g. Ganga Nagar area of Rajasthan (Wheat basket of Rajasthan).

Agriculture In India

- About 65-70% of the total population of the country is dependent on agriculture.
- Role of agriculture is paramount in the economy of India.
- About two-third of our population derives its livelihood from agriculture.
- It provides food to the second biggest population and the biggest population of cattle in the world.
- Our agro-based industries are fully dependent on raw material provided by agriculture.
- Agriculture with its allied activities accounts for 45% of our national income.

Types of Agriculture in India

Subsistence Farming

- In this type of agriculture, farmers work hard to grow enough food to survive only.
- In this type of farming the produce is consumed mainly by farmer and his family.

- There remains no surplus to sell in the market.

Mixed Farming

- The combination of agriculture and pastoral farming is called mixed farming.
- In this type of farming, cultivation of crops and rearing of animals are done together on the same farm.

Shifting Cultivation

- This is a primitive form of agriculture, in which a plot of land is cultivated for a few years and then is deserted.
- This slash and burn method of farming is carried on in jungles of north-eastern part of India.
- A plot of land is cleared for cultivation. As the yield decreases after two or three years, the plot is abandoned and a fresh clearing is made.

Extensive Farming

- This is a system of farming in which the cultivator uses a limited amount of labour and capital on relatively large area.
- This type of agriculture is practised in countries where population size is small and land is enough.
- Here, per acre yield is low but overall production is in surplus due to less population.
- Agriculture is done with the help of machines.

Intensive Farming

- This is a system of farming in which the cultivator uses large amount of labour and capital on a relatively small area.
- In countries where the size of population is big but land is less, this type of farming is done.
- Annually two or three crops are grown due to the demand of food for the large size of population.
- Agriculture is done with the help of manual labour.

Plantation Agriculture

- In this type of agriculture, trees or bushes are planted on huge estates.
- A single crop like rubber, sugarcane, coffee, tea or banana is grown.
- These crops are major items of export.

Problems of Indian Agriculture

- The low productivity of our agriculture is mainly due to the difficulties faced by our peasants.
- Indian agriculture is chiefly of subsistence type where a large manual labour is employed to work on farms to grow just enough food for the needs of the family and very little is left for marketing.
- A major part of the Indian soil has been impoverished because it has been under plough for the last 4000 or 5000 years.
- Deforestation, overgrazing and heavy rainfall have led to soil erosion.
- Divisions of land have led to fragmentation.

- The size of land holding is very small and uneconomic.
- The farmers are poor, illiterate and ignorant.
- They use primitive tools and out-dated method.
- They lack financial credit and investment.
- Good seeds, fertilizers and improved technology are not available to them.
- They lack irrigation facilities and are still on the mercy of nature.
- Most of the farmers have no security against crop failure or loss caused by nature.
- Generally farmers are uneducated and have no scientific approaches.

Different Crop Seasons in India

- There are three crop seasons in India :
  (i) Rabi (ii) Kharif and (iii) Zayad.

Rabi

- This season starts after the rainy season.
- Sowing begins in September-October and harvesting takes place in February-March.
- Rabi season is cooler and drier than the Kharif season.
- Wheat, barley, pulses and some oil seeds are grown in the Rabi season.

Kharif

- The Kharif season begins with the onset of the monsoons in June-July.
- The crop grows in the rainy season and harvesting takes place after the retreat of monsoon in September-October. Rice, maize, millets, groundnuts, cotton and jute are grown in the Kharif season.

Zayad

- This is the summer season for growing crops which remain till April, May and June.
- Products are mainly vegetables and fruits.

Green Revolution

- The increase in agriculture productivity of cereals that has taken place since the 1960s mainly as a result of introduction of high yielding varieties of wheat and rice and use of fertilizers, machines and irrigation etc., is known as green revolution.
- Green revolution has made us self-sufficient in food production.
- This has not only saved our much precious foreign exchange but has also made us self-reliant.
- But green revolution has proved more beneficial to rich farmers only, because it involves a lot of investment.

Land use Patern of India

- The total geographical area of India is 32.88 crore hectares.
- Of this, data is available for only 92.5% land area. Though land is put to different uses, but cultivation of land is its most important use.

Uses of Land

Uses of land	% put to use of land
Cultivated land	43.41
Forested area	22.57
Wasteland (arid, rocky and sandy areas)	6.29
Cultivable waste	4.41
Fallow land	10.85
Pastures and meadows	3.45
Area under non-agricultural use	6.29

Water Resources and Their Utilization in India

➢ Water resources of India can be divided into two parts : (i) Surface Water Resources and (ii) Underground Water Resources.

Surface Water Resources

➢ According to the estimate, India receives an average of 109 cm of rainfall annually.

➢ This rainfall amounts to 37,000 million cubic metre. Out of this, 12,500 million cubic metres evaporates and another 7,900 million cubic metres is absorbed by land. Only 16,600 million cubic metres water is available in our rivers.

➢ Out of this, only 6,600 million cubic metres of water can be used for irrigation.

Underground Water Resources

➢ Out of total rainfall, only 7900 million cubic metres of water percolates inside/beneath the earth.

➢ Out of this, only 4300 million cubic metres of water is able to reach the upper layer of the soil.

➢ This water is more important for agricultural production.

➢ Rest 3600 million cubic metres reaches the impervious rocks which can be used by digging wells or tubewells. Out of this only 2250 million cubic metres of water is economically viable.

Sources of Irrigation in india

There are various sources of irrigation which are :

(a)	Wells & Tubewells	46% of total irrigation
(b)	Canals	39% of total irrigation
(c)	Tanks	8% of total irrigation
(d)	Other Sources	7% of total irrigation (Dongs, Kuhls, Springs etc.)

Power Resources of India

India uses a large amount of fossil fuels as a source of energy alongwith a number of renewable sources of energy, viz., hydroelectric power, thermal power, petroleum, nuclear or atomic power, solar energy, wind energy, tidal energy, bio-gas etc.

Multipurpose Projects of India

Multipurpose river valley projects, once referred by Jawaharlal Nehru as 'Temples of Modern India', present an integrating system of controlling floods, generation of hydroelectricity, irrigation, development of fishery and tourists spots, boating, navigation, and draining away extra water. These projects aim at all round development of river valleys.

Multipurpose River Valley Projects

Project/River	Purposes	Name of Power Houses
Bhakhra-Nangal Project On river Sutlej 518 m long, 226 m high, highest dam in Asia.	1. Irrigation, 2. Hydroelectricity generation, 3. Soil conservation	1. Bhakhra, 2. Ganguwal, 3. Nangal, 4. Kotla
Damodar Valley Project On river Damodar, located in West Bengal and Jharkhand	1. Irrigation, 2. Generation of Hydro and Thermal power, 3. Navigation, 4. Flood control (Damodar has turned from a "Valley of Sorrow" "Valley of Plenty")	1. Maithon, 2. Tilaia, 3. Panchet Hill, 4. Bokaro, 5. Durgapur, 6. Chandrapura
Hirakud Project On Mahanadi river in Odisha; 4800 m long.	1. Irrigation, 2. Production of Hydel power, 3. Navigation for over 480 km.	1. Hirakud, 2. Chiplima
Tungabhadra Project At Malappuram on the river Tungabhadra, it is 2441 m long and 49.3 m high; in Andhra Pradesh and Karnataka.	1. Irrigation, 2. Generation of Hydro electricity	1. At Malappuram, 2. At Hampi, 3. On left side of Malappuram
Rihand Project On river Rihand	Hydroelectricity production.	Pimpri

Transport In India

- The present transport system of the country comprises several modes of transport including rail, road, coastal shipping, air transport etc.

Road Transport

- The share of road in total traffic has been growing from 13.8% of freight traffic and 15.4% of passenger traffic in 1950-51 to an estimated 61% of freight traffic and 85% of passenger traffic by the end of 2003-04.
- The Tenth Plan (2002-07) outlay for the Central Sector Roads Programme Rs. 59,700 crore.
- Indian road network of 41 lakh km. is the one of the largest in the world and consists of—

Expressways/ National Highways	70,934 km.	Major District Roads, Rural and other roads	38,84,136 km.
State Highways	1,54,522 km.	Total length 41 lakh km. (approx.)	

National Highways

- ➢ They are constructed and maintained by the central government.
- ➢ The National Highways has 71,772 km. length comprising only 2% of the total length of roads, carries about 40% of the total traffic of India.
- ➢ The central government has taken up in a phased manner during 2005–2012 an expanded programme of 4/6 lanning of 12,109 kms. of National Highways (NH) under the National Highways Development Programme (NHDP) On Build, Operate and Transfer (BOT) basis.
- ➢ A 'Special Accelerated Road Development Programme for North-East (SARDPNE)' has been taken up. The two phased (Phase-A and Phase-B) programme includes improving 6418 km of roads (including 2319 km. of roads under Arunachal Package). The Phase-A is likely to be completed during 2010–17. Phase-B involves two-laning of 3723 km. of roads.

Some Important National Highways

- ➢ According to the 2001 census, there are 219 National Highways in the country. Some of them are :

N.H. 1	Delhi – Ambala – Amritsar – Indo-Pak Border (546 km)
N.H. 2	Delhi – Agra – Kanpur – Varanasi - Kolkata (1490 km)
N.H. 3	Agra – Gwaliar – Indore – Nasik – Mumbai (1161 km)
N.H. 4	Junction with N.H. 3 near Thane – Belgaum – Bangalore – Ranipet – Chennai (1235 km)
N.H. 7	Varanasi – Jabalpur – Nagpur – Hyderabad – Bangalore – Madurai – Kanyakumari (2369 km).
N.H. 8	Delhi- Jaipur – Ahmedabad– Vadodara – Mumbai (1428 km)
N.H. 9	Pune - Solapur – Hyderabad – Vijayawada (791 km)
N.H. 15	Pathankot – Amritsar – Bhatinda – Ganganagar – Bikaner – Jaisalmer – Kandla (1526 km).
N.H. 22	Ambala – Kalka – Shimla – Rampur – Indo – Tibet (China) Border near Shipki La (459 km)
N.H. 24	Delhi – Bareilly – Lucknow (438 km)
N.H. 39	Numaligarh- Imphal – Palel – Indo – Myanmar Border (436 km)
N.H. 44	Shillong – Passi Badarpur – Agartala (495 km)
N.H. 47	Salem – Coimbatore – Trichur Ernakulam Thiruvanantha-puram – Kanyakumari (640 km)
N.H. 48	Bangalore – Hasan – Mangalore (328 km)
N.H. 49	Kochi – Madurai – Dhanushkodi (440 km)
N.H. 55	Siliguri – Darjeeling (77 km)
N.H. 80	Makamah – Farakka (310 km.)
N.H. 102	Chapra – Muzaffarpur (80 km.)
N.H. 205	Ananthpur – Chennai (442 km.)

➢ The longest National highway in India is NH-7; which has a length of 128 kms in Uttar Pradesh, 504 kms in Madhya Pradesh, 232 kms in Maharashtra, 753 kms in Andhra Pradesh, 125 kms in Karnataka, 627 kms in Tamil Nadu i.e. total 2369 kms.

State Highways

➢ They are constructed and maintained by the state government. The length of roads in some states is :

State	Metalled Roads	Unpaved Roads	Total
Bihar	32998 km.	55354 km.	88352 km.
Madhya Pradesh	88620 km.	111517 km.	200137 km.
Maharashtra	271684 km.	90209 km.	361703 km.
Odisha / Orissa	86929 km.	175774 km.	26703 km.
Uttar Pradesh	148303 km.	107164 km.	255467 km.

➢ Maharashtra has the maximum length of roads.

➢ Maharashtra also has the maximum length of metalled roads.

➢ Odisha / Orissa has the maximum length of unpaved roads.

➢ West Bengal has the maximum road density.

➢ Roads on the borders are constructed and maintained by the Border Roads Organisation (BRO).

➢ BRO was established in May 1960.

➢ BRO is a premier construction agency roads airfields, bridges, buildings, hospitals and schools.

➢ The BRO, through 'Project Dantak' is constructing and maintaining a large road infrastructure and executing other prestigious projects in Bhutan.

➢ The BRO is doing highly commendable jobs of cosntruction and maitenance in Myanmar and Afghanistan too.

Rail Transport

➢ The Indian Railways have been a great integrating force for more than 160 years.

➢ From a very modest beginning in 1853, Indian Railways have grown into a vast network of 7,031 stations spread over a route-length of 63,221 km. with a fleet of 7,817 locomotives, 5,321 passenger service vehicles 4,904 other coaching vehicles and 2,28,170 wagons as on 31 March, 2004.

➢ Indian Railway network is the largest in Asia and second largest in the World.

➢ The first rail in India started in 1853 between Mumbai and Thane (34 kms).

➢ Indian Railway Board was established in March 1905.

➢ Indian Railway was nationalised in 1950.

➢ There are three types of rail lines in India :
(i) Broad Gauge (ii) Meter Gauge and (iii) Narrow Gauge.

- The network runs multigauge operations extending over 63,974 route kilometres.

Gauge	Route (km.)	% contribution
1. Broad Gauge (1.676 mts)	54,257	84.81
2. Meter Gauge (1.000 mts)	7,180	11.22
3. Narrow Gauge (0.762 and 0.610 mts)	2,537	3.97
Total (as on 31st March 2010)	63,974	100.00

- The management and governance of the Indian railways is in the hands of the Railway Board.
- Railways have been divided into 17 zones.
- Recently a new zone Kolkata Metro Zone (17th zone) has been established on 29 December, 2010.

Divisional Organization of the Zonal Railways

Zone	Headquarters	Divisions
Zones that started functioning on 1st April, 2003		
East Coast Railway	Bhubaneshwar	Khurda Road, Waltair and Sambalpur divisions of SER
South Western Railway	Hubli	Bangalore and Mysore divisions of, SR reorganizedHublidivisionofSCR,including Hospet-Toraagal, (Earlier costituted to have Gutakal division of SCR as well.)
West Central Railway	Jabalpur	Jabalpur and Bhopal divisions of CR, reorganized Kota division of WR
North Central Railway	Allahabad	Reorganized divisions : Allahabad of NR, Jhansi of CR, and new Agra division
South East Central Railway	Bilaspur	Nagpur division and reorganized Bilaspur division of SER, new Raipur division
Zones that were created on 10th October, 2002		
North Western Railway	Jaipur	Jodhpur division and reorganized Bikaner division of NR, reorganized Jaipur and Ajmer division of WR
East Central Railway	Hajipur	Sonepur and Smastipur divisions of NER, Danapur, Mughalsarai and Dhanbad divisions of ER, (was earlier constituted to have Katihar division of NFR as well.)
Old Zones as they are after April, 2003		
Western Railway	Mumbai	Bhavnagar and Mumbai divisions, reorganized Ratlam, Rajkot and Vadodara divisions, new Ahmedabad division
Eastern Railway	Kolkata	Howrah, Malda, Sealdah and Asansol divisions

Zone	Headquarters	Divisions
Central Railway	Mumbai	Bhusawal and Nagpur divisions, reorganized Mumbai CST and Solapur divisions, new Pune divisions (including Pune Kolhapur)
Southern Railway	Chennai	Chennai, Palghat, Thiruvananthapuram, Tiruchirapalli and Madurai divisions
Northern Railway	New Delhi	Ferozpur, Ambala, Lucknow and Moradabad divisions, reorganized Delhi division
North Eastern Railway	Gorakhpur	Lucknow and Varanasi divisions, reorganized Izzatnagar division
South Central Railway	Secunderabad	Reorganized Secunderabad, Hyderabad, Guntakal (including Bellary-Guntakal (MG) and Bellary-Rayadurg) and Vijayawada divisions, new Guntur and Nanded divisions.
South Eastern Railway	Kolkata	Kharagpur division, reorganized Adra and Chakradharpur divisions, new Ranchi division
North-East Frontier Railway	Guwahati	Katihar, Lumding, Tinsukia divisions, reorganized Alipurduar division, new Rangiya division

Air Transport

- Airways in India started in 1911.
- Indian National Airways Company was started in 1933.
- All the airway companies were nationalised in 1953 and were put under two corporations namely — Indian Airlines and Air India.
- Indian Airlines provides its services to the internal parts of India along with neighbouring countries of Nepal, Bangladesh, Pakistan, Afghanistan, Sri Lanka, Myanmar and Maldives.
- Air India provides its services to the foreign locations.
- Vayudoot was established in 1981 for domestic services, but was later merged in Indian Airlines.

Merger of Air India and Indian Airlines

Indian Airlines operates to 54 domestic stations alongwith its subsidiary Airlines 'Alliance Air'. Besides it also operates to 18 international stations.

The Indian Airlines has a fleet of 75 aircraft. 41 aircraft were expected to be added in its fleet by April 2010.

On the 1st March, 2007 the Union Cabinet approved the proposal to merge Indian Airlines and Air India.

Accordingly, a new company, viz. National Aviation Company of India Limited (NACL) has been incorporated on 30th March, 2007 with its Headquarters at Mumbai.

The brand name of the new airlines will be Air India (or Indian) and its logo will be Maharaja.

Major International Airports of India

Name of Airport	Place
Chhatrapati Shivaji Int. Airport (Santa Cruz Airport)	Mumbai
Subhash Chandra Bose Airport (DumDum Airport)	Kolkata
Indira Gandhi International Airport	Delhi
Anna (Meenambkam) International Airport	Chennai
Trivendram International Airport	Thiruvananthpuram
Guru Ramdasji (Rajasansi) International Airport	Amritsar
B. R. Ambedkar International Airport	Nagpur
Kampagowada (Bengaluru) International Airport	Bengaluru
Devi Ahilyabai Holkar International Airport	Indore (M.P.)
Calicut International Airport	Kozhikode (Kerala)
Veer Savarkar International Airport	Port Blair
Rajeev Gandhi International Airport	Hyderabad
Lokpriya Gopinath Bordoloi International Airport	Guwahati
Loknayak Jai Prakash Narayan Inter. Airport	Patna
Goa International Airport	Goa
Sardar Vallabh bhai Patel International Airport	Ahmedabad
Mangaluru International Airport	Mangalore
Aranmula International Airport	Pathanamthitta
Raja Bhoj International Airport	Bhopal
Lal Bahadur Shastri International Airport	Varanasi
Choudhary Charan Singh International Airport	Lucknow

Water Transport

- The Central Water Tribunal was established in 1887.
- Its headquarter is in Kolkata.
- The waterways of the country have been divided into Internal waterways and Oceanic waterways.

Internal Waterway

- This transport is through rivers, canals and lakes.
- India has got about 14,544 km. of navigable waterways which comprise rivers, canals, backwaters, creeks etc.
- About 44 million tonnes of Cargo is being moved annually by Inland Water Transport (IWT).
- The waterway from Haldia to Allahabad was made a National Water way in 1986.
- The Inland Waterways Authority of India (IWAI) came into existence on 27 October, 1986 for development and regulation of inland waterways in the country.

Oceanic Waterway

- The peninsular bank is very important for this purpose.
- There are 13 large and 200 small ports on the major bank of 5600 kms.

➢ Large ports are maintained by the central government whereas small ports are included in the concurrent list and are managed by the state government.

➢ At the beginning of the Tenth Plan, the capacity of major ports was about 344 MT. It is proposed to be increased to 470 MT by the end of the Tenth Plan.

Major Ports of India

Name	State/UT	River/Strait/Ocean
Kolkata	West Bengal	Hoogly River
Mumbai	Maharashtra	Arabian Sea
Chennai	Tamil Nadu	Bay of Bengal
Kochhi	Kerala	Arabian Sea
Vishakhapatnam	Andhra Pradesh	Bay of Bengal
Paradip	Odisha (Orissa)	Bay of Bengal
New Tuticorin	Tamil Nadu	Bay of Bengal
Marmagao	Goa	Arabian Sea
Kandla	Gujarat	Arabian Sea
New Mangalore	Karnataka	Arabian Sea
Nhavasheva (JawaharLal Nehru Port)	Maharasthra	Arabian Sea
Ennore	Tamil Nadu	Bay of Bengal
Port Blair	Andman and Nicobar	Bay of Bengal

➢ Largest port of India is Jawaharlal Nehru Port in Mumbai.

➢ The largest natural port is in Vishakhapatnam.

➢ Kandla in Gujarat is a tidal port. It has been made into a free trade zone.

India Facts and Figures

Capitals of Different States of India (Table on the next page)

★ The state and union territory capitals are sorted according to the administrative, legislative and judicial capitals.

★ The administrative capital is where the executive government offices are located.

★ The legislative capital is where the state assembly convenes.

★ The judicial capital is the location of the state or territorial High Courts of India.

★ The date mentioned in the table refers to when the city became the capital of the state or territory.

★ In the following table *S* and *W* refers to the summer and winter sessions respectively. *B* refers to the budget session of the legislature.

★ The administrative capital is considered to be the *main* capital of the state.

★ The former capital refers to a city which was the capital from admission into the Indian Union.

★ An absence of a legislative capital means that it is administered by the Central government.

States and Their Capitals

State / UT	Administrative Capital	Legislative Capital	Judicial Capital	Since
Andaman and Nicobar Islands	Port Blair	—	Kolkata	1956
Arunachal Pradesh	Itanagar	Itanagar	Guwahati	1972
Andhra Pradesh	Hyderabad	Hyderabad	Hyderabad	1956
Assam	Dispur	Dispur	Guwahati	1972
Former Capital : Shillong (1874-1972)				
Bihar	Patna	Patna	Patna	1936
Chhatisgarh	Raipur	Raipur	Bilaspur	2000
Chandigarh	Chandigarh	—	Chandigarh	1966
Dadra and Nagar Haveli	Silvasa	—	Mumbai	1961
Daman and Diu	Daman	—	Mumbai	1987
NCT-Delhi	Delhi	Delhi	Delhi	1956
Goa	Panaji	Porvorim	Mumbai	1961
Gujarat	Gandhinagar	Gandhinagar	Ahmedabad	1970
Former Capital : Ahmedabad (1960-1970)				
Haryana	Chandigarh	Chandigarh	Chandigarh	1966
Himachal Pradesh	Shimla	Shimla	Shimla	1948
Jammu and Kashmir	* Srinagar (S) * Jammu (W)	* Srinagar (S) * Jammu (W)	Srinagar	1948
Jharkhand	Ranchi	Ranchi	Ranchi	2000
Karnataka	Bangalore	Bangalore	Bangalore	1956
Kerala	Thiruvananthapuram	T'puram	Ernakulam	1956
Former Capital : Kochhi (1949-1956)				
Lakshadweep	Kavaratti	—	Ernakulam	1956
Madhya Pradesh	Bhopal	Bhopal	Jabalpur	1956
Maharashtra	Mumbai	*Mumbai (S+B) *Nagpur (W)	Mumbai	1818 1960
Manipur	Imphal	Imphal	Imphal	2013
Meghalaya	Shillong	Shillong	Shillong	2013
Mizoram	Aizawl	Aizawl	Guwahati	1972
Nagaland	Kohima	Kohima	Guwahati	1963
Odisha (Orissa)	Bhubaneshwar	Bhubaneshwar	Cuttack	1948
Former Capital : Cuttack (1936-1948)				
Puducherry	Pondicherry	Pondicherry	Chennai	1954

State / UT	Administrative Capital	Legislative Capital	Judicial Capital	Since
Punjab	Chandigarh	Chandigarh	Chandigarh	1966
Former Capital : Lahore (1936-1947) & Shimla (1947-1966)				
Rajasthan	Jaipur	Jaipur	Jodhpur	1948
Sikkim	Gangtok	Gangtok	Gangtok	1975
Tamil Nadu	Chennai	Chennai	Chennai	1956
Tripura	Agartala	Agartala	Agartala	2013
Uttarakhand	Dehradun	Dehradun	Nainital	2000
Uttar Pradesh	Lucknow	Lucknow	Allahabad	1937
West Bengal	Kolkata	Kolkata	Kolkata	1905

Population of India States and UTs (Census 2011)

India			1,210,569,573
Uttar Pradesh	199,812,341	Jammu and Kashmir	12,541,302
Maharashtra	112,374,333	Uttarakhand	10,086,292
Bihar	104,099,452	Himachal Pradesh	6,864,602
West Bengal	91,276,115	Tripura	3,673,917
Andhra Pradesh	84,580,777	Meghalaya	2,966,889
Madhya Pradesh	72,626,809	Manipur	2,570,390
Tamil Nadu	72,147,030	Nagaland	1,978,502
Rajasthan	68,548,437	Goa	1,458,545
Karnataka	61,095,297	Arunachal Pradesh	1,383,727
Gujarat	60,439,692	Puducherry	1,247,953
Odisha	41,974,218	Mizoram	1,097,206
Kerala	33,406,061	Chandigarh	1,055,450
Jharkhand	32,988,134	Sikkim	610,577
Assam	31,205,576	Andaman & Nicobar lslands	380,581
Punjab	27,743,338	Dadra and Nagar Haveli	343,709
Chhattisgarh	25,545,198	Daman and Diu	243,247
Haryana	25,351,462	Lkshadweep	64,473
Delhi*	16,787,941	* *Provisional data (census 2011)*	

Union Territories : Facts and Figures (Census 2011)

UT	Capital	Area in sq.km.	Population
Puducherry	Pondicherry	490	12,47,953
Chandigarh	Chandigarh	114	10,55,450
Andaman & Nicobar	Port Blair	8,249	3,80,581
Dadra & Nagar Haveli	Silvassa	491	3,43,709
Daman & Diu	Daman	111	2,43,247
Lakshadweep	Kavaratti	30	64,473

***National Capital Territory / Region (Census 2011)**

State	Capital	Area	Population
Delhi	Delhi	1,483 sq. km.	1,67,87,941

Top 10 Most Populous Countries (Projected as of July 1, 2013)

Sl.	Country	Population	Sl.	Country	Population
1.	China	1,34,95,85,838	6.	Pakistan	19,32,38,868
2.	India	1,22,08,00,359	7.	Nigeria	17,45,07,539
3.	U.S.A.	31,66,68,567	8.	Bangladesh	16,36,54,860
4.	Indonesia	25,11,60,124	9.	Russia	14,25,00,482
5.	Brazil	20,10,09,622	10.	Japan	12,72,53,075

Source : *U.S. Census Bureau, Internation Data Base*

Wildlife Sanctuaries and National Parks in India

	Name	Location	Important Species
1.	Bandipur National Park	Mysore, Karnataka	Elepahant, Tiger, Bear, Sambhar, Panther
2.	Balpakram Sanctuary	Garo Hills, Meghalya	Tiger, Elephant, Bison
3.	Chandraprabha Sanctuary	Varanasi, UP	Asiatic Lion, Tiger, Panther, Indian Gazelle, Sloth bear
4.	Corbett National Park	Nainital, Uttarakhand	Elephant, Tiger, Sloth bear, Nilgai, Panther, Sambhar
5.	Dachigam Sanctuary	Jammu and Kashmir	Kashmir stag (Hangul)
6.	Dudhwa National Park	Lakhimpur Kheri, UP	Tiger, Panther, Sambhar, Nilgai
7.	Ghana Bird Sanctuary	Bharatpur, Rajasthan	Siberian Crane, Spoonbill, Heron teal, Stork
8.	Gir National Park	Junagarh, Gujarat	Asiatic Lion, Panther, Sambhar, Nilgai, Crocodile, Rhinoceros
9.	Hazaribagh National Park	Hazaribagh, Jharkhand	Tiger, Leopard, Sambher, Chital
10.	Jaldapara Sanctuary	West Bengal	Tiger, Leopard, Sambher, Chital
11.	Kanha National Park	Mandla and Balaghat, MP	Tiger, Panther, Antelope, Barking Deer, Nilgai
12.	Kaziranga National Park	Assam	Great Indian one horned rhinoceros, Wild Buffalo, Sambhar, Tiger

Name	Location	Important Species
13. Manas	Barpeta, Assam	Tiger, Elephant, Panther, Wild Buffalo, One horned rhinoceros
14. Mudumalai Sanctuary	Nilgiri Hills, Tamil Nadu	Elephant, Dear, Pigs
15. Namdapha National Park	Tirap district, Arunachal Pradesh	Tiger and Elephant
16. Palamau	Daltonganj, Jharkhand	Tiger, Elephant, Panther, Leopard
17. Parkal	Warangal, AP	Tiger, Panther, Chital, Nilgai
18. Periyar	Idukki, Kerala	Elephant,Tiger, Panther, Wild boar, Gaur, Sambhar
19. Ranganthitoo Bird Sanctuary	Karnataka	Birds
20. Shivpuri National Park	Shivpuri, MP	Tiger, Birds
21. Sunderbans	West Bengal	Tiger, Wild boar, Crocodile, Deer
22. Vedanthangal Bird Sanctury	Tamil Nadu	Birds
23. Wild Ass Sanctuary	Little Rann of Kutch, Gujarat	Wild Ass, Wolf, Nilgai, Chinkara

Important Irrigation and Power Projects

Name of the Project	Location	State	Purpose
Nagarjuna Sagar Multipurpose Project	River Krishna	Andhra Pradesh	Irrigation, Hydroelectricity
Pochampad Project	River Godawari	Andhra Pradesh	Irrigation
Lower Sileru Project	River Sileru (Godawari)	Andhra Pradesh	Hydro-electricity
Kakarpara Project	River Tapi	Gujarat	Irrigation
Kothagudam Project	Singareni coalfields	Andhra Pradesh	Thermal power
Kosi Project	River Kosi	Bihar	Flood control, Irrigation
Gandak Project	River Gandak	Uttar Pradesh, Bihar	Irrigation, Hydroelectricity

Name of the Project	Location	State	Purpose
Dhuvaran Power Station	Kheda District	Gujarat	Thermal Power
Sabarigiri (Pamba-Kakki) Project	River Pamba-Kakki	Kerala	Hydoelectricity
Idduki Projact	Rivers Periyar Cherutheni Idukki	Kerala	Hydrelectricity
Chambal Project	River Chambal	Rajasthan, Madhya Pradesh	Irrigation, Hydroeleccity
Tawa Project	River Tawa (Narmada)	Madhya Pradesh	Irrigation
Korba Project	Near Korba Coalfields	Chhattisgarh	Thermal Power
Satpura Power	Patharkada Station	MP Coalfield	Thermal Power
Koyna Project	River Koyna	Maharashtra	Hydroelectricity
Nagpur Power Station	Koradi, Near Nagpur City	Maharashtra	Thermal Power
Tungabhadra	River Tungabhadra Multipurpose Project	Karnataka Andhra Pradesh	Irrigation, Hydroelectricity
Upper Krishna Project	River Krishna	Karnataka	Irrigation
Sharavati Project	River Sharavati	Karnataka (near Jog falls)	Hydroelectricity
Hirakud Multipurpose Project	River Mahanadi	Odisha	Irrigation, Hydroelectricity
Mahanadi Delta Project	River Mahanadi	Odisha	Irrigation
Talcher Power Station	Near Talcher	Odisha	Thermal power
Bhakra-Nangal Multiperpose Project	River Sutlej	HP, Punjab Haryana	Irrigation, Hydroelectricity
Rajasthan Canal Project	River Sutlej in Punjab	Rajasthan Headworks in Punjab	Irrigation
Kundah Project	River Kundah	Tamil Nadu	Hydroelectricity
Neyveli Power Station	Neyveli	Tamil Nadu	Hydroelectricity
Ramganga Multipurpose Project	Chuisot stream (near Kalagarh)	Uttarakhand	Irrigation, Hydroelectricity
Matatilla Multipurpose Project	River Betwa	Uttar Pradesh, Madhya Pradesh	Irrigation, Hydroelectricity
Rihand scheme	River Rihand	Uttar Pradesh	Hydroelectricity

Name of the Project	Location	State	Purpose
Obra Power Station	Obra	Uttar Pradesh	Thermal power
Damodar Valley Project	River Damodar	Jharkhand shared with West Bengal	Flood control Hydroelectricity
Ukai Project	River Tapi	Gujarat	Irrigation
Mahi Project	River Mahi	Gujarat	Irrigation
Ghataprabha Project	River Ghataprabha	Andhra Pradesh and Karnataka	Irrigation
Bhima Project	River Bhima	Maharashtra	Irrigation
Sardar Sarowar Project	River Narmada	Gujarat and Madhya Pradesh	Irrigation and Hydoelectricity
Bana Sagar Project	River Sone	Chhattisgarh, MP, UP and Jharkhand	Irrigation
Dul Hasti Project	River Chenab	Jammu and Kashmir	Hydroeletricity
Salal Project	River Chenab	Jammu and Kashmir	Hydroelectricity
Thein Dam Project	River Ravi	Punjab	Irrigation, Hydroelectricity
Malaprabha Project	River Malaprabha	Karnataka	Irrigation
Jaykwadi Project	River Godawari	Maharasthra	Irrigation
Beas Project	River Beas	Punjab and Haryana	Hyroelectricity
Sharda Shayak	River Ghaghra	Uttar Pradesh	Irrigation
Mayurakshi Project	River Mayurakshi	West Bengal	Irrigation, Hydroelectricity
Rana Pratap Sagar	River Chambal	Rajasthan	Hydroelectricity
Suratgarh Super Thermal Project	Suratgarh	Rajasthan	Thermal Power
Mettur	River Cauvery	Tamil Nadu	Hydroelectricity
Pallivasal	River Mundirapujha	Kerala	Hydroelectricity
Papanasam Project	River Tambiraparani	Tamil Nadu	Hydroelectricity
Loktak Project	Lake Loktak	Manipur	Hydroelectricity
Tehri Project	River Bhilangana (Ganga)	Uttarakhand	Hydroelectricity
Farakka Project	Ganga	West Bengal	Irrigation

Indian Satellites : At a Glance

Satellite	Launch Date	Wt (Kg.)	Launching Station	Launch Vehicle	Purpose
Aryabhatta	19Apr, 1975	360	R.R.L.S., USSR	ICR	Scientific (S)
Bhaskar-1	07 Jun, 1979	442	R.R.L.S., USSR	ICR	Earth Scanning (S)
Rohini RS-1	10 Aug, 1979	35	R.L.C., Sriharikota	SLV-3	Earth Scanning
Rohini RS-2	18 Jul, 1980	35	R.L.C., Sriharikota	SLV-3	Earth Scanning
Rohini RSD-1	31 May, 1981	38	R.L.C., Sriharikota	SLV-3	Scientific
Apple	19 Jun, 1981	670	E.R.L.S., Kourou	Ariane-1	Commun.(S)
Bhaskar-2	20 Nov, 1981	436	R.R.L.S., USSR	ICR	Earth Scanning (S)
INSAT-1A	10 Apr, 1982	1160	A.R.L.S., USA	Delta 3910	Multipurpose (S)
Rohini RSD-2	17 Apr, 1983	41.5	R.L.C., Sriharikota	SLV-3	Scientific (S)
INSAT-1B	30 Aug, 1983	1193	K.S.C., USA	Shuttle (PAM-D)	Multipurpose (S)
SROSS-1	24 Mar, 1987	150	R.L.C., Sriharikota	ASLV-D1	R. Sensing
IRS-1A	17 Mar, 1988	980	R.S.S., Baikanour	Vostok	R. Sensing (S)
SROSS-2	13 Jul, 1988	150	R.L.C., Sriharikota	ASLV-D2	R. Sensing
INSAT-1C	21 Jul, 1988	–	E.R.L.S., Kourou	Ariane-3	Multipurpose
INSAT-1D	12 Jun, 1990	650	K.S.C., USA	Delta 4925	Multipurpose
IRS-1B	29 Aug, 1991	985	R.S.S., Baikanour	Vostok	R. Sensing (S)
SROSS C-1	20 May, 1992	106	R.L.C., Sriharikota	ASLV-D3	R. Sensing (S)
INSAT-2A	10 Jul, 1992	1416	E.R.L.S., Kourou	Ariane	R. Sensing(S)
INSAT-2B	23 Jul, 1993	1906	E.R.L.S., Kourou	Ariane	Multipurpose (S)
IRS-1E	20 Sep, 1993	850	R.L.C., Sriharikota	PSLV-D1	R. Sensing
SROSS C-2	04 May, 1994	113	R.L.C., Sriharikota	ASLV-D4	R. Sensing(S)
IRS-P2	15 Oct, 1994	870	R.L.C., Sriharikota	PSLV-D2	R. Sensing(S)
INSAT-2C	7 Dec, 1995	2050	E.R.L.S., Kourou	Ariane	Multipurpose (S)
IRS-1C	29 Dec, 1995	1250	B.L.S., Kazakhstan	Molniya	R. Sensing(S)
IRS-P3	21 Mar, 1996	930	R.L.C., Sriharikota	PSLV-D3	R. Sensing(S)
INSAT-2D	04 June, 1997	2070	E.R.L.S., Kourou	Ariane-4	Multipurpose (S)

Satellite	Launch Date	Wt (Kg.)	Launching Station	Launch Vehicle	Purpose
IRS-1D	29 Sep, 1997	1200	R.L.C., Sriharikota	PSLV-C1	R. Sensing (S)
INSAT-2E	03 Apr, 1999	2550	E.R.L.S., Kourou	Ariane 42P	Multipurpose (S)
IRS-P4	26 May, 1999	—	R.L.C., Sriharikota	PSLV-C2	R. Sensing(S)
INSAT-3B	22 Mar, 2000	2070	E.R.L.S., Kourou	Ariane-5G	—
GSAT-1	18 Apr, 2001	1540	S.H.A.R., Andhra Pradesh	GSLV-D1	C C
TES	22 Oct, 2001	1109	S.H.A.R., Andhra Pradesh	PSLV - C3	Techno. Ex (S)
INSAT-3C	24 Jan, 2002	—	E.R.L.S., Kourou	Ariane-4	Comm.(S)
METSAT*	12 Sep, 2002	1060	S.H.A.R., Andhra Pradesh	PSLV - C4	Mete. (S)
INSAT-3A	10 Apr, 2003	2958	A.L.S.C., Kourou	Ariane-5G	Comm.. Met. and Tele. (S)
GSAT-2	08 May, 2003	1800	Sriharikota, Andhra Pradesh	GSLV-2	Comm. (S)
INSAT-3E	28 Sep, 2003	2795	Kourou	Ariane-5G	Comm. (S)
RESOURCE SAT-1	17 Oct, 2003	1360	Sriharikota, Andhra Pradesh	PSLV-C5	R. Sensing (S)
EDUSAT	20 Sep, 2004	1950	Sriharikota, Andhra Pradesh	GSLV-F01	Education (S)
CARTO SAT-1	05 May, 2005	1560	S. S.C.,Sriharikota, Andhra Pradesh	PSLV-C6	Mapping Satellite (S)
HAMSAT	05 May, 2005	—	S.S.C., Sriharikota, Andhra Pradesh	PSLV-C6	Radio Comm. (S)
INSAT- 4A	22 Dec, 2005	3080	Kourou	Ariane	Comm.(S)
INSAT- 4C	10 Jul, 2006	2168	S.S.C., Sriharikota	GSLV-F02	Comm.
INSAT-4B	12 Mar, 2007	3025	Arianespace's Ariane	5-ECA	DTH and Comm. (S)
INSAT-4CR	02 Sep, 2007	2130	S.S.C., Sriharikota, Andhra Pradesh	GSLV-F04	Comm.(S)
CARTOSAT-2A	28 April, 2008	690	S.H.A.R., Andhra Pradesh	PSLV-C9	R. Sensing (S)
IMS-1 (TWsat)[1]	28 April, 2008	83	S.H.A.R., Andhra Pradesh	PSLV-C9	Micro Satellite Imaging
Chandrayaan-1[2]	22 Oct., 2008	1380	S.D.S.C., S.H.A.R.	PSLV-C11	R. Sensing (S)
RISAT-2[3]	20 April, 2009	300	S.D.S.C., S.H.A.R.	PSLV-C12	R. I. Satellite

Satellite	Launch Date	Wt (Kg.)	Launching Station	Launch Vehicle	Purpose
ANUSAT	20 April, 2009	40	S.D.S.C., S.H.A.R.	PSLV-C12	Research microsatellite
Oceansat-2[4]	23 Sep., 2009	960	S.H.A.R., Andhra Pradesh	PSLV-C14	R. Sensing (S)
GSAT-4	15 April, 2010	2180	S.D.S.C., S.H.A.R., Andhra Pradesh	GSLV-D3	Commun.(S)
CARTOSAT-2B	12 July, 2010	694	S.H.A.R., Andhra Pradesh	PSLV-C15	R. Sensing (S)
GSAT-5P[5]	25 Dec., 2010	2310	S.D.S.C., S.H.A.R., Andhra Pradesh	GSLV-F06	C-band Comm.
RESOURCESAT-2[6]	20 April, 2011	1206	S.H.A.R., Andhra Pradesh	PSLV-C16	R. Sensing (S)
GSAT-8/INSAT-4G	21 May, 2011	3093	Kourou	Ariane-5	Comm.(S)
GSAT-12	15 July, 2011	1410	S.H.A.R., Andhra Pradesh	PSLV-C17	Comm.(S)
Megha-Tropiques[7]	12 Oct., 2011	1000	S.D.S.C., S.H.A.R. Andhra Pradesh	PSLV-C18	Tracking weather
RISAT-1[8]	26 April, 2012	1858	S.D.S.C., S.H.A.R., Andhra Pradesh	PSLV-C19	R. Sensing (S)
GSAT-10[9]	29 Sept., 2012	3400	Kourou	Ariane-5	Comm.(S)
INSAT–3D[10]	26 July, 2013	2026	Kourou	Ariane–5	Mete. (S)
GSAT–7	30 Aug., 2013	—	Kourou	Ariane–5	Geost. (S)
Mangalyaan	05 Nov., 2013	1350	S.D.S.C., S.H.A.R., Andhra Pradesh	PSLV–C25	Mars mission (S)
GSAT–14	05 Jan., 2014	1982	Shriharikota Andhra Pradesh	GSLV-D5	Comm.(S)

Abbreviations used in the above table :

R.R.L.S. : *Russian Rocket Launching Station, Cosmodrome*
R.I.S. : *Radar Imaging Satellite*
R.L.C. : *Rocket Launching Centre, Sriharikota Range, A.P.*
E.R.L.S. : *European Rocket Launching Station, Kourou, French Guiana*
A.R.L.S. : *American Rocket Launching Station, Cape Canaveral, USA*
K.S.C. : *Kennedy Space Centre, Cape Canaveral, USA*
R.S.S. : *Russian Space Station, Baikanour, USSR*
S.H.A.R. : *Sriharikota High Altitude Range, Andhra Pradesh (A.P.)*
S.S.C. : *Satish Dhawan Space Centre, Sriharikota, A.P.*
A.L.S.C. : *Ariane Launching Space Centre, South America*
★ *(named after Kalpana Chawla)*

Note : (CC) — *Commercial Communication;* (S) — *Successful;* (Comm.) — *Communication;* (Techno. Ex.) — *Technology Experiments;* (Mete.) — *Meteorological*

1. Third World Satellite (TWSAT) : Launched as co-passenger with CARTOSAT-2A for low cost micro satellite imaging.
2. Unmanned lunar probe, that carried 11 scientific instruments built in India, USA, UK, Germany, Sweden and Bulgaria.
3. Co-passenger with ANUSAT
4. IRS-P4 : Gathers data for oceanographic, coastal and atmospheric applications. Continues mission of Oceansat-1.
5. INSAT-4D : Indian communication satellite, failed to reach orbit due to GSLV-F06 failure.
6. PSLV-C16 placed three satellites with a total payload mass of 1404 kg - RESOURCESAT-2 weighing 1206 kg, the Indo-Russian YOUTHSAT weighing 92 kg and Singapore's X-SAT weighing 106 kg – into an 822 km polar Sun Synchronous Orbit (SSO).
7. PSLV-C18 is configured to carry four satellites in which, one satellite, developed by India and France will track the weather, two were developed by educational institutions, and the fourth is from Luxembourg.
8. First indigenous all-weather Radar Imaging Satellite.
9. India's advanced communication satellite.
10. Advanced meteorological satellite, enhancing India's capability in Weather Forcasting and Disaster warning areas.
11. The successful use of indigenous cryogenic engine in the GSLV-D5 puts India among a league, five other nations—the US, Russia, France, Japan and China, that passess the technology that is considered the ultimate frontier in rocket science.

General Introduction to Asia

- The word 'Asia' is derived from the word 'Asu' (of Hibru language), which literally means 'the rising sun'.
- Asia is the largest of all the seven continents of the world.
- With 44.6 million sq. km. area, it covers about one-third of the land surface of the world.
- With 4,299 million people, it contains about 60% of the world population and emerges as the most populous continent of the world.
- This vast continent comprises the greatest diversity in terms of physical features, climate, vegetation, wildlife and people.
- It has the highest mountain peak on the Earth, Mount Everest (8848 m) and the lowest point, the Dead Sea (396.8 m below sea level).
- It has the coldest place. Vostok, Antarctica has winter temperature of -89.2°C. Jacobabad in Sindh is the hottest place on the Earth.
- Mawsynram, Cherrapunji (India) has the world's highest average rainfall of 2600 cm. Simultaneously, it has desert areas of central asia.
- Asia has the world's deepest fresh water lake, i.e. Baikal Lake (Russia) which is 1741 meters deep.
- It has the largest delta 'Sunderbans', the most fertile river valleys (Ganga, Indus, Brahmaputra, Yangtze Kiang and Hwang Ho etc.) and the extensive barren lands of Baluchistan.
- It has rich and varied wildlife which is peculiar to this continent.

Bangladesh

Bangladesh is our eastern neighbouring country.

Location : It is bordered on the north, west and east by India and on the south by the Bay of Bengal.

Latitude : Bangladesh lies between latitudes 21^0N and $26^030'$N. The Tropic of Cancer passes through the middle of it.

Longitude : It lies between longitudes 88^0E and $92^030'$E.

Physical Division of Bangladesh : Nearly whole of Bangladesh lies in the largest delta of the world.

- It is a vast flat alluvial plain. It is a land of big rivers, lakes, swamps and marshes.
- A large part of Bangladesh is flooded every year during rainy season.
- It has an area of 1,47,570 sq. km.
- The Jamuna (Brahmaputra), Padma (Ganga) and Meghna are the important rivers.
- A small hilly area in the south-east forms the Chittagong Hill tract.

Climate

- It has hot and humid climate.
- Rainfall varies from 250 to 40 cm. It has distinct dry and rainy season.
- In early summer, Bangladesh experiences cyclone storms.

Natural Vegetation

- In the fringes of delta Mangrove forests are found.
- Sundari and bamboo trees are found in these Sunderbans.

Agriculture

- Because of fertile alluvial soil and abundant water supply, rice is the main crop of Bangladesh as it covers 85% of the cultivated area.
- Jute the main cash crop.
- Tea plantations are found in some areas in the north.
- Sugarcane, cotton and tobacco are also grown.

Animal Rearing

- Most of the animals reared in Bangladesh work as beasts of burden.
- Bangladesh has become a leading supplier of animal hides and skins.

Fishing

- Large number of rivers and nearness to the sea make fishing an important activity in Bangladesh.

Language–Bangla, Currency–Taka, Religion–Islam

Minerals

- Bangladesh is not rich in mineral resources.
- Coal, natural gas and oil are mined in a small quantity.

Industries

- The important industries of Bangladesh include jute and cotton textiles, cement, fertilizers, sugar, paper, glass etc.

Population, Language and Religion

- The population of Bangladesh is about 137,636,000 (2005).
- The density of population here is 763 persons per sq. km.
- Bengali is the official language of Bangladesh.
- Most of the people follow Islam.
- Dhaka, Chittagong, Khulna and Narayanganj are some of the important cities of Bangladesh.

Countries with Their Capital & Currency

Country	Capital	Currency
Afghanistan	Kabul	Afghani
Algeria	Algiers	Dinar
Angola	Luanda	Kwanza
Argentina	Buenos Aires	Argentino Sentavos
Australia	Canberra	Australian Dollar
Austria	Vienna	Shilling
Azerbijan	Baku	Manat
Bahrain	Manama	Bahrain Dinar
Bangladesh	Dhaka	Taka
Belgium	Brussels	Euro
Belarus	Minsk	Belaros Rubbe
Bhutan	Thimphu	Nugultram
Brazil	Brasilia	Real (BRC)
Brunei	Bander Seri Begawan	Brunei Dollar or Ringhit
Bulgaria	Sofia	Lev
Cambodia	Phnom Penh	Rial
Chanada	Ottawa	Dollar
China, Peoples Republic	Beijing	Yuan
Cuba	Havana	Peso
Cyprus	Nicosia	Cyprus Pound
Denmark	Copenhagen	Danish Krone
Egypt	Cairo	Pound
Ethiopia	Adis Ababa	Birr
Fiji	Suva	Dollar
Finland	Helsinki	Euro
France	Paris	Euro
Germany	Berlin	Euro
Ghana	Accra	Cedi
Greece	Athens	Euro

Country	Capital	Currency
Guatemala	Guatemala City	Quetzal
Hong Kong	Victoria	Dollar
Hungary	Budapest	Florint
Iceland	Reykjavik	Krona
India	New Delhi	Rupee
Indonesia	Jakarta	Rupiah
Iran	Teheran	Rial
Iraq	Baghdad	Iraqui Dinar
Ireland	Dublin	Euro
Israel	Jerusalem	New Shekel
Italy	Rome	Euro
Jamaica	Kingston	Dollar
Japan	Tokyo	Yen
Jordan	Amman	Dinar
Kazakhistan	Almati	Ruble
Kirghizistan	Bishkek	Ruble
Korea (North)	Pyongyang	Won
Korea (South)	Seoul	Won
Kuwait	Kuwait	Dinar
Laos	Vientiane	New Kiplao
Lebanon	Beirut	Pound
Libya	Tripoli	Dinar
Luxembourg	Luxembourg Ville	Euro
Macau	Macau	Pataka
Malaysia	Kuala Lumpur	Ringrit
Maldives, Republic of	Male	Rufia
Mauritius	Port Luis	Rupee
Mexico	Mexico City	New Peso
Mongolia	Ulan Bator	Tugrik
Myanmar	Naypyidaw	Kyat
Mozambique	Maputo	Metical
Nauru	Yaren	Dollar
Nepal	Kathmandu	Rupee
Netherlands	Amsterdam	Euro
New Zealand	Wellington	Dollar
Nigeria	Abuja	Naira

Country	Capital	Currency
Norway	Oslo	Kroner
Oman	Muscat	Rial
Pakistan	Islamabad	Rupee
Panama	Panama City	Balboa
Philippines	Manila	Peso
Poland	Warsao	Zloty
Portugel	Lisbon	Euro
Qatar	Doha	Riyal
Romania	Bucharest	Lau
Russia	Moscow	Rouble
Saudi Arabia	Riyadh	Riyal
Senegal	Dakar	CFA Franc
Serbia and Montenegro	Belgrade	Dinar
South Africa	Cape Town	Rand
Spain	Madrid	Euro
Singapore	Singapore	Dollar
Sri Lanka	Colombo	Rupee
Syria	Damascus	Pound
Syprus	Nicosia	Pound
Taiwan	Taipei	New Taiwan Dollar
Thailand	Bangkok	Baht
Trinidad & Tobago	Port of Spain	Dollar
Tunisia	Tunis	Dinar
Turkey	Ankara	Lira
United Arab Emirates	Abu Dhabi	Dirham
Uganda	Kampala	Shilling
Ukraine	Kiev	Karbovanets
U.K.	London	Pound Sterling
U.S.A.	Washington D.C.	U.S. Dollar
Venezuela	Caracas	Bolivar
Vietnam	Ho Chi Minh City (Hanoi)	Dong
Yemen	Sena'a	Riyal
Zaire	Kinshasa	Zaire
Zambia	Lusaka	Kwacha
Zimbabwe	Harare	Dollar

River Side Cities

Town	River	Town	River
Kabul	Kabul	Canton	Si-Kiang
Allahabad	Confluence of Ganga, Jamuna, Saraswati	Basra (Iraq)	Tigris and Euphrates
Nasik	Godawari	Cairo (Egypt)	Nile
Kolkata	Hooghly	Ankara (Turkey)	Kizil
Cuttack	Mahanadi	Baghdad (Iraq)	Tigris
Patna	Ganga	Berlin (Germany)	Spree
Chittagong	Maiyani	Khartoum (Sudan)	Nile
Lucknow	Gomati	Belgrade	Dunube
Jamshedpur	Subarnarekha	Cologne (Germany)	Rhine
Haridwar	Ganga	Lisbon (Portugal)	Tangus
Delhi	Jamuna	Glasgow (Scotland)	Clyde
Kanpur	Ganga	Paris (France)	Seine
Surat	Tapti	Hamburg (Germany)	Elbe
Srinagar	Jhelum	Budapest (Hungary)	Danube
Ferozepur	Sutlej	Rome (Italy)	Tiber
Ludhiana	Sutlej	Warsaw (Poland)	Vistula
Karachi (Pak)	Indus	Bristol (U.K.)	Avon
Lahore (Pak)	Ravi	London (U.K.)	Thames
Vijayawada	Krishna	New Castle (U.K.)	Tyre
Varanasi	Ganga	New York	Hudson
Yangon (Myanmar)	Irawady	Philadelphia	Delaware
Akyab (Myanmar)	Irawady	New Orleans	Mississippi
Shanghai	Yang-tse-Kiang	Montreal (Canada)	Ottawa
Nanking	Yang-tse-Kiang	Quebec (Canada)	St. Lawrence
Chungking	Yang-tse-Kiang		

Wonders of The World

Seven Wonders of the Ancient World	Seven Wonders of the Medieval World
1. Hanging Garden of Babylon	1. Great Wall of China
2. Temple of Diana at Ephesus *(Rome)*	2. Porcelain Tower of Nanking *(China)*
3. Statue of Jupiter at Olympia	3. Colosseum of Rome *(Italy)*
4. Pyramids of Egypt	4. Stone henge of England
5. Mausoleum of Mausolus *(Ruler of Halicarnasus)*	5. Leaning Tower of Pisa *(Italy)*
6. Light house of Alexandria	6. Catacombs of Alexandria
7. Colossus at Rhodes *(912 ft. high Statue of Helos, the Sun God)*	7. Mosque at St. Sophia *(Constantinople)*

New Seven Wonders of the World

As declared on July 7, 2007 by New Seven Wonders Foundation of Switzerland, at a grand ceremony organised in 'Stadia da Lutz, Benefica stadium in Lisbon (Portugal).

1. The Taj Mahal *(Agra, India)*
2. The Great Wall of China *(China)*
3. The Pink Ruins of Petra *(Jordan)*
4. The Statue of Christ the Redeemer in Rio de Janerio *(Brazil)*
5. Incan Ruins of Machu Pichu *(Peru)*
6. The ancient Mayan City of Chichen Itza *(Mexico)*
7. The Colosseum of Rome *(Italy)*

Other Wonders of the World

1. The Sphinx, near Gizeh *(Ghiza)* in Egypt
2. The Catacombs at Rome
3. The Circus Maximus at Rome
4. Angkor Vat temple in Combodia
5. The Alhambra at Granada in S. Spain
6. Shew Dragon Pagoda or the Golden Pagoda at Yangon in Myanmar
7. Mosque at St. Sophia *(Constantinople)*

Countries and their main Produces/ Industries

Afghanistan	Dry and fresh fruits, carpets, wool
Australia	Wood, dairy products, wheat, meat, lead, zinc
Austria	Machinery, textiles, leather goods
Brazil	Coffee
Belgium	Glass, textiles
Chile	Copper Nitrate
Canada	Wheat, newsprint, machinery
China	Silk, tea, rice
Congo	Copper, uranium, cobalt, ivory
Cuba	Sugar, tobacco, cigar
Denmark	Textiles, paper
France	Textile, wine, silk
Germany	Machinery, chemical, iron and steel equipments
Ghana	Coco, gold, coffee
India	Jute, textiles, sugar, spices, tobacco, tea, cement, mica
Indonesia	Sugar, spices, rubber, rice, cinchona, petroleum
Iran	Petroleum, carpets, dry fruits
Iraq	Dates, petroleum
Italy	Mercury, textiles
Japan	Machinery, textiles, toys, silk, automobiles
Kenya	Coffee, tea, meat, sisal, hides and skins, cement, soda ash
Kuwait	Petroleum
Malaysia	Rubber, tin

Netherlands	Machinery, aircraft, electricals
Saudi Arabia	Oil, date
Spain	Lead
Sweden	Matches, timber
Switzerland	Watches, chemicals, electricals
Taiwan	Camphor, rice
UK	Textiles, medicines, machinery, cars
USA	Petroleum, wheat, machinery, coal, automobiles, iron
Russia	Petroleum, wheat, chemicals, heavy machinery
Vietnam	Tin, rice, rubber, teak

Towns Associated with some important industries

Town	**Industry**
Ahmedabad (Gujarat)	Cotton Textiles
Agra (U.P.)	Leather, marble
Baku (Russia)	Petroleum
Bangaluru (Karnataka)	Aircraft and telephones
Bhilai (Chhattisgarh)	Steel Plant
Bangkok (Thailand)	Ship-building, teak and wood
Bhagalpur (Bihar)	Silk
Mumbai (Maharashtra)	Film industries
Buenos Aires (Argentina)	Dairy products, meat
Cadiz (Portugal)	Cork
Kolkata (W. Bengal)	Jute, paper, leather works
Chittaranjan (W. Bengal)	Locomotives
Cochin (Kerala)	Ship-building
Chicago (USA)	Agricultural equipments, automobiles
Dhaka (Bangladesh)	Jute
Dalmianagar (Bihar)	Cement
Darjeeling (W. Bengal)	Tea
Delhi (India)	Textiles, chemicals, Small Scale Industries
Detroit (USA)	Motor car
Dhariwal (Punjab)	Woolen goods
Digboi (Assam)	Oil refinery
Ferozabad (U.P.)	Bangles, Glass refinery
Guntur (Andhra Pradesh)	Tobacco
Havana (Cuba)	Sugar, tobacco, cigars
Jamshedpur (Jharkhand)	Steel

Town	Industry
Jharia ((Jharkhand)	Coal mines
Khetri (Rajasthan)	Copper mines
Johannesberg (South Africa)	Gold mines
Kolar (Karnataka)	Gold fields
Los Angeles (USA)	Film Production
Ludhiana (Punjab)	Hosiery
Lyons (France)	Silk Industry
Chennai (Tamil Nadu)	Leather, Integral Coach Factory
Moradabad (U.P.)	Brassware, cutlery
Nagpur (Maharashtra)	Oranges, Cotton mills
Nepanagar (M.P.)	Newsprint
Pittsburgh (USA)	Iron and steel, coal, petroleum
Perambur (Tamil Nadu)	Integral Coach Factory
Raniganj (W.B.)	Coal mines
Sialkot (Pakistan)	Sports goods
Sindri (Jharkhand)	Fertilizers and chemicals
Sheffield (UK)	Cutlery
Titagarh (W. Bengal)	Paper and Jute
Venice (Italy)	Ship-building
Varanasi (U.P.)	Silk, Brocade Industry

Famous Sites (India)

Site	Location
Ajanta	Maharashtra
Akabar's Tomb	Agra (U.P.)
Amarnath Cave	Kashmir
Ambar Palace	Jaipur (Rajasthan)
Anand Bhawan	Allahabad (UP)
Bhakra Dam	Punjab
Birla Planetorium	Kolkata (West Bengal)
Island Palace	Udaipur (Rajasthan)
Jagannath Temple	Puri (Odisha)
Jai Stambh (Tower of Victory)	Chittorgarh (Rajasthan)
Jama Masjid	Delhi
Black Pagoda	Konark (Odisha)
Brihadeeshwara Temple	Tanjavur
Brindaban Gardens	Mysore (Karnataka)
Buland Darwaza	Fatehpur Sikri (U.P.)

Site	Location
Char Minar	Hyderabad (Andhra Pradesh)
Chilka Lake	Near Bhubaneswar (Orissa)
Dal Lake	Srinagar (J & K)
Dilwara Temples	Mt. Abu (Rajasthan)
Elephanta Caves	Mumbai (Maharashtra)
Ellora Caves	Aurangabad (Maharashtra)
Gateway of India	Mumbai (Maharashtra)
Golden Temple	Amritsar (Punjab)
Gol Gumbaz	Bizapur (Karnataka)
Hanging Gardens	Mumbai
Hawa Mahal	Jaipur (Rajasthan)
Howrah Bridge	Kolkata (W. Bengal)
Mt. Girnar (Jain Temple)	Junagadh (Gujarat)
Nataraja Temple	Chennai (Tamil Nadu)
Nishat Bagh	Srinagar (J & K)
Padmanabha Temple	Thiruvananthapuram (Kerala)
Palitana	Junagadh (Gujarat)
Panch Mahal	Fatehpur Sikri (U.P.)
Pichola Lake	Udaipur (Rajasthan)
Prince of Wales Museum	Mumbai (Maharashtra)
Qutub Minar	Delhi
Raj Ghat	Delhi
Rashtrapati Bhawan	Delhi
Red Fort	Delhi
Jantar Mantar	New Delhi
Kailash Temple	Ellora (Maharashtra)
Kanya Kumari	Tamil Nadu
Kirti Stambha (Tower of fame)	Chittorgarh (Rajasthan)
Lal Bagh Garden	Bangaluru (Karnataka)
Lingaraj Temple	Bhubaneshwar (Odisha)
Mahakaleshwar	Ujjain (M.P.)
Maheshmukh (Trimurti) Temple	Elephanta Cave (Maharashtra)
Malabar Hills	Mumbai (Maharashtra)
Man Mandir Palace	Gwalior Fort (M.P.)
Marble Rocks	Jabalpur (M.P.)
Marina Beach	Chennai (T.N.)
Minakshi Temple	Madurai (T.N.)
Sidi Sayyid Masjid	Ahmedabad (Gujarat)

Site	Location
Shalimar Bagh	Srinagar (J & K)
Shahi Chashma	Srinagar (J & K)
Shanti Van	Delhi
Statue of Gomateshwara	Shravanabelagola, Hasan (Karnataka)
Sun Temple (Black Pagoda)	Konark (Odisha)
Taj Mahal	Agra (Uttar Pradesh)
Tower of Silence	Mumbai (Maharashtra)
Victoria Memorial	Kolkata (W. Bengal)
Victoria Garden	Mumbai (Maharashtra)
Vijay Ghat	Delhi

Famous Sites (World)

Site	Location
Al-Aqusa Mosque	Jerusalem (Israel)
Big Ben	London (U.K.)
Bradenberg Gate	Berlin (Germany)
Broadway	New York (U.S.A.)
Brown House	Berlin (Germany)
Buckingham Palace	London (U.K.)
Colossium	Rome (Italy)
Downing Street	London (U.K.)
Eiffel Tower	Paris (France)
Fleet Street	London (U.K.)
Harley Street	London (U.K.)
Hyde Park	London (U.K.)
India House	London (U.K.)
Kaaba	Mecca (Saudi Arabia)
Kremlin	Moscow (Russia)
Leaning Tower	Pisa (Rome)
Louvre	Paris (France)
Merdeka Palace	Jakarta (Indonesia)
Oval	London (U.K.)
Pentagon	Washington (U.S.A.)
Potala	Nanking (China)
Pyramid	Egypt
Red Square	Moscow (Russia)
Scotland Yard	London (U.K.)
Shwe Dragon Pagoda	Yangon (Myanmar)

Site	Location
Sphinx	Egypt
Statue of Liberty	New York (U.S.A.)
Vatican	Rome (Italy)
Wailing Wall	Jerusalem (Israel)
Wall Street	New York (U.S.A.)
Westminster Abbey	London (U.K.)
White Hall	London (U.K.)
White House	Washington (U.S.A.)

Changed Names of Cities, States and Countries

Old Name	New Name	Old Name	New Name
Abyssinia	Ethiopia	Ceylon	Sri Lanka
Angora	Ankara	Christina	Oslo
Aurangabad	Sambhaji Nagar	Cochin	Kochi
Banaras	Varanasi	Constantinople	Istanbul
Bangalore	Bangaluru	Dacca	Dhaka
Baroda	Vadodara	Dahomey	Benin
Batavia	Djakarta	Dutch East Indies	Indonesia
Basutoland	Lesotho	Dutch Guiana	Surinam
Bechuanaland	Botswana	Ellice Islands	Tuvalu
Bhatinda	Bathinda	Formosa	Taiwan
Bombay	Mumbai	Gauhati	Guwahati
British Guiana	Guyana	Gold Coast	Ghana
Burma	Myanmar	Holland	The Netherlands
Calcutta	Kolkata	Ivory Coast	Cote D'Ivoire
Calicut	Kozhikode	Jubbulpore	Jabalpur
Cape Canaveral	Cape Kennedy	Jullundur	Jalandhar
Cawnpore	Kanpur	Leopoldville	Kinshasa
Central Provinces	Madhya Pradesh	Madagascar	Malagasy
Madras	Chennai	Malaya	Malaysia
Manchukuo	Manchuria	Mesopotamia	Iraq
New Hebrides	Vanuatu	Nippon	Japan
Northern Rhodesia	Zambia	Nyasaland	Malawi
Ooty	Udhagamandalam	Orissa	Odisha
Panjim	Panaji	Peking	Beijing
Petrograd	Leningrad	Persia	Iran
Palghat	Palakkad	Pondicherry	Puducherry
Poona	Pune	Pretoria	Tshwane

Old Name	New Name	Old Name	New Name
Quilon	Kollam	Rangoon	Yangon
Rhodesia	Zimbabwe	Saigon	Ho Chi Minh City
Salisbury	Harare	Sandwich Islands	Hawaiian Islands
Siam	Thailand	Simla	Shimla
South West Africa	Namibia	Spanish Guinea	Equatorial Guinea
Stalingrad	Volgograd	Tanganyika and Zanzibar	Tanzania
Trichur	Thrissur	Trivandrum	Thiruvananthapuram
United Provinces	Uttar Pradesh	Upper Volta	Burkina Faso
Uttaranchal	Uttarakhand	Vizagapattam	Visakhapatnam
Zaire	Republic of Congo	Tanjore	Thanjavur

Continent's Earth Area

Continent	% of Earth Area	Continent	% of Earth Area
1. Asia	29.5	2. Africa	20.4
3. North America	16.3	4. South America	11.8
5. Europe	7.1	6. Australia	5.3
7. Antarctica	9.6		

Continent's Highest & Lowest Points

	Continent	Highest Point	Lowest Point
1.	Asia	Mt. Everest (8848 m)	Dead Sea (-396.8 m)
2.	Africa	Mt. Kilimanjaro (5895 m)	Lake Assal (–156.1 m)
3.	North America	Mt. Mckinley (6194 m)	Death Valley (-85.9 m)
4.	South America	Aconcagua (6960 m)	Valdis Penin (-39.9 m)
5.	Europe	Elbrus (5663m)	Caspian Sea (-28.0 m)
6.	Australia	Koscisko (2228 m)	Lake Eyre (-15.8 m)
7.	Antarctica	Vinson Massif (4897 m)	Bentlay Trench (–2555 m)

Highest Mountain Peaks (World)

	Name	Height (in metres)	Range
1.	Mount Everest	8848	Himalayas
2.	K2 (Godwin Austen)	8611	Karakoram
3.	Kanchenjunga	8598	Himalayas
4.	Lhotse	8511	Himalayas
5.	Makalu I	8481	Himalayas
6.	Dhaulagiri I	8167	Himalayas
7.	Manaslu I	8156	Himalayas
8.	Cho Uyo	8153	Himalayas
9.	Nanga Parvat	8126	Himalayas
10.	AnnapuranaI	8091	Himalayas

Three Deepest Oceans

Name	Greatest depth (in metres)	Greatest depth location
1. Pacific Ocean	11,033	Mariana Trench
2. Atlantic Ocean	9,460	Puerto Rico Trench
3. Indian Ocean	7,542	Java Trench

Geographical Epithets (Sobriquets)

Blue Mountains	Nilgiri Hills, India
City of Sky Scrapers	New York, USA
City of Seven Hills	Rome, Italy
City of Dreaming Spires	Oxford, England
City of Golden Gate	San Francisco, USA
Cockpit of Europe	Belgium
China's Sorrow	Hwang Ho
Dark Continent	Africa
Eternal City	Rome
Forbidden City	Lhasa, Tibet
Gate of Tears	Bab-el-Mandeb, Jerusalem
Granite City	Aberdeen, Scotland
Herring Pond	Atlantic Ocean
Hermit Kingdom	Korea
Island Continent	Australia
Island of Cloves	Madagascar
Island of Pearls	Bahrain
Key to the Mediterranean	Gibraltar
Land of Golden Fleece	Australia
Land of Mid Night Sun	Norway
Land of Rising Sun	Japan
Land of White Elephant	Thailand
Never Never Land	Prairies of N. Australia
Pearl of Antilles	Cuba
Pillars of Hercules	Strait of Gibraltar
Pearl of the Pacific	Guyayaquil Port of Ecuador
Pink City	Jaipur, India
Queen of the Adriatic	Venice, Italy
Sugar Bowl of the World	Cuba
Venice of the East	Cochin, India
Venice of the North	Stockholm
Windy city	Chicago, USA
Yellow River	Hwango Ho

Some Important Boundary Lines

Durand Line	between Pakistan and Afghanistan
Hindenberg Line	between Germany & Poland
49th Parallel	between USA & Canada
Mac Mahon Line	between India & Tibet/China
Maginot Line	between France & Germany
38th Parallel	between North & South Korea
Oder Neisse Line	between Germany and Poland
Radcliffe Line	between India & Pakistan
17th Parallel	between India & Pakistan (as claimed by Pakistan)

Some Important Tribes and their Homeland (World)

Eskimos : Greenland, North Canada, Alaska, N. Siberia	Lapps : N. Finland, Scandinavian country
Koryaks : N. Siberia, Eurassian Tunda, N.E. Asia	Chukchi : N.E. Asia, U.S.S.R., North Siberia
Aleuts : Alaska	Bedouin : Sahara and Middle East
Bushman : Kalahari	Bindibu or Aborigins : Australia
Turregs : Sahara	Gobi Mongols : Gobi
India Tribes : Amazon basin	Orang Asli : Malaysia
Pygmies : Congo basin, Zaire	Masai : East & Central Africa
Hausa : North Nigeria	Aeta : Phillipines
Ainus : Japan	Tapiro : Papua New Guinea
Maoris : New Zealand	Fulani : Western Africa
Hotten tots : Hot tropical Africa	Zulus : South Africa
Ibans : Equatorial rain forest region of South-East Asia	Kirghiz : Asiatic steppes
Kalmuk : Central Asia	Kazakhs : Kazakhistan
Buryak : Central Asia	Red Indian : N. America
Yoakuts : Siberia	Samoyeds : Siberia
Berbers : N. Africa	Guicas : Amazon forest area
Kareus or Meos : Myanmar	Semangs : East Sumatra

Glossary of geographical terms

Ablation : Loss of ice in the body of a glacier through melting etc.

Abrasion : Erosion of rocks by water, wind or ice (glacier).

Absolute humidity : Amount of water vapour present in a unit volume of air; usually expressed as grammes per cubic metre.

Advection : Transfer of heat through horizontal movement of air.

Aeolian : Relating to or caused by wind. Example, aeolian landforms.

Alluvium: The fine debris transported and deposited by a river. Landforms formed by deposition of such material are called alluvial landforms, for example, alluvial plains. Soils formed through river deposition are called alluvial soils.

Altimeter : A type of aneroid barometer for measuring height, used mainly in aeroplanes.

Anemometer : An instrument used for measuring wind velocity.

Anticline : The arch or crest of a fold in the rocks. Its opposite is a syncline, the bottom of a fold.

Antipodes : Two points diametrically opposite on the surface of earth.

Aphelion : The position of the earth in its orbit when it is at its greatest distance from the sun. At its nearest distance from the sun the earth is said to be in *perihelion*.

Apogee : The position of the moon or any other heavenly body, when it is at its greatest distance from the earth. At its shortest dis-tance from the earth the moon is said to be in *perigee*.

Asteroids or planetoids : Minor planets revolving around the sun between the orbits of Mars and Jupiter.

Atmosphere : The envelope of air surrounding the earth. The most abundant among its constituents are nitrogen and oxygen.

Atoll : A ring or horseshoe-shaped coral reef.

Attrition : Mutual wearing down of rock particles during transportation by wind, water or ice.

Aurora Australis and Aurora Borealies : The light phenomena seen in the sky at night in the higher latitudes of the southern and northern hemisphere respectively. Aurora comprises an electrical discharge and is usually accompanied by a magnetic storm.

Avalanche : A large mass of snow and ice at high altitude, sliding downslope on a mountain. Usually a large amount of rock material is also involved in an avalanche.

Azonal soil : Soil which has not been subjected sufficiently to soil forming processes and thus has changed little from the parent material. Such soils do not have a mature profile.

Barometer : Instrument used for measuring pressure. A self-recording barometer giving a continuous record of pressure conditions in the form of a line graph is called a barograph and the graph thus provided is called a barogram.

Barysphere, Bathysphere or Centrosphere : Inner portion of the earth below the lithosphere or outer crust.

Base level : The lowest level to which a river can deepen its valley. It is the level of the surface of the water body, a lake or sea, in which the stream finally falls.

Beach : A gently sloping strip of land along the coast. This lies between the high and low tide levels and is formed by depositional action of waves.

Bearing : The horizontal angle between the direction of an object and the meridian through the observer, measured in degrees (zero to 360) clockwise from the north.

Beufort scale : A scale identifying wind strength. The lowest point on the scale is zero which refers to calm conditions and the highest is 12 referring to a hurricane.

Biogeography : Study of geographical distribution of plants and animals.

Biosphere : That portion of the earth and its environment occupied by various forms of life.

Blizzard : A storm of powdery snow in the polar regions.

Bog : An area of soft, wet, spongy ground consisting mainly of decayed or decaying moss and other vegetable matter.

Bora : A cold and often dry wind experienced along the eastern coast of the Adriatic Sea.

Bore : A high tidal wave causing backflow of water in river.

Caatinga : Thorn-forest of Brazil.

Canyon : A narrow, deep, steep-sided river valley cut in the soft rocks.

Cape : A headland, a more or less pointed piece of land jutting out into the sea.

Cardinal points : The four main directions of the compass.

Cartography : The art of drawing maps and charts.

Celestial equator : The imaginary circle formed by the intersection of a plane through the centre of the earth perpendicular to its axis and the celestial sphere.

Celestial sphere : A sphere of infinite radius having its centre at some point in the solar system, for example, at the centre of the earth, on to which all members of the solar system may be projected.

Chaparral : The low, dense scrub, characteristic of Mediterranean type of climatic regions.

Chronometer : An accurate time-keeping instrument.

Climate : The average weather conditions of region throughout the seasons.

Climatology : The science studying climates and their influence on other components of the environment.

Clinometer : An instrument used for determining the difference in elevation between two points.

Cloud : A mass of tiny water droplets or ice crystals formed by condensation of water vapour in the atmosphere.

Condensation : The process by which a substance changes from vapour to liquid.

Condensation nuclei : Microscopic particles having an affinity for water. These serve as the nuclei for the formation of raindrops. The presence of these particles in the atmosphere is necessary for condensation to occur.

Coniferous : Cone-bearing plants with needle-shaped leaves.

Connate water : Water entrapped in the interstices of rocks during their formation; also called fossil water.

Convection : The uplift of air as a result of surface heating or instability due to other reasons. Generally this term refers to vertical movement of gases in contrast to advection.

Convection currents : Due to instability in air some vertical motions in the atmosphere are set up which are more or less in the form of currents.

Coral : A kind of rock formed of polyps forming reefs in the oceans.

Colour of the sky : Seems blue because of the selective scattering of light in the atmosphere by gases and dust particles.

Deciduous forest : Consists of trees that shed their leaves in the dry season.

Downs : Grasslands of Australia.

Denudation : Wearing away of rocks by various agencies like wind, water and ice (glaciers).

Eclipse : Partial or full obscuring of the moon when the earth comes between the sun and the moon is called lunar eclipse. It occurs usually on the day of the full moon.

A partial or complete obscuring of the sun because of the presence of the moon between the sun and the earth is called the solar eclipse and it occurs on the day of the new moon, that is, on the day the moon is not visible.

Ecliptic : The apparent track of the sun throughout the year as a result of the motion of the earth around it. The plane of the ecliptic is the plane passing through this path and is coincident with the plane of the earth's orbit.

Ecology : Studies of organisms in relation to their environment.

Edaphic : Relating to soil.

Eluviation : Removal of material in solution or suspension from the upper horizons of the soils to the lower.

Epicentre : Point on the surface of the earth vertically above the seismic focus or deep focus, that is, the point where an earthquake originates.

Estuary : Mouth of a river where tidal effects are evident and where fresh water and sea water mix. The term also refers to river valleys which have been flooded by sea due to coastal subsidence.

Eustatic movement : A large scale rise or fall of sea level.

Evapotranspiration : The term signifies total loss of water (moisture) from soil in the form of water vapour, including that lost by evaporation from open water bodies, the surface of rocks and also that lost by transpiration from growing plants.

Fathometer : Instrument used for measuring the depth of the ocean.

Fauna : The animal life of a region or a geological period.

Fiord : A glacial valley or part there of now under the sea.

Flood-Plain : A plain bordering a river and formed by river deposition.

Flora : The plant life of a region or geological period.

Fluvial : Belonging or relating to a river.

Fog : A dense mass or small water drops or smoke or dust particles in the lower layers of the atmosphere.

Geosyncline : A large depression or trough in the earth's crust, that is a syncline on a large scale.

Geyser : A thermal spring which throws up a jet of hot water and steam intermittently.

Glacier : A moving mass of ice.

Gorge : A narrow and deep valley of a river.

Great circle : A circle on the earth's suface whose plane passes through its centre and thus bisects it into two hemispheres.

Great circle route : A route between any two points on the earth's surface which follows the great circle between them.

Gulf : A large, deep bay.

Habitat : Natural environment of a plant or animal.

Halophyte : A plant which grows naturally in saline environment.

Hemisphere : One half of the earth's surface, formed when a plane passing through its centre bisects it.

Hinterland : Area from which a port gets most of its exports.

Horse latitudes : Subtropical belt of high pressure over the oceans.

Humidity : State of the atmosphere with respect to the water vapour it contains.

Humus : Decomposed and partly decomposed organic matter in the soil.

Hydrology : The study of the water content on the earth.

Hyetograph : A self-recording rain-gauge.

Hygrometer : Instrument used for measuring humidity in the atmosphere.

Hygrophyte : Plant growing in wetlands.

Iceberg : A mass of land ice which has been broken off or carved from the end of a glacier and is afloat in the sea.

Illuviation : Deposition, in the lower soil horizon, of material romoved by eluviation from the upper horizons of the soil.

Insolation : Energy radiated from the sun received by the earth.

International date line : The line approximating to 180° East or West longitude, where the date changes by one day as it is crossed. The date is one day earlier east of this line.

Intertropical convergence zone or inter-tropical front : Zone of low atmospheric pressure near the equator where the northeast and southeast trade winds converge.

Intrazonal soil : Soil which has been influenced in its development, less by climate and vegtation than by factors like parent material and drainage.

Isopleth : Line drawn on the map along which the value of a particular phenomenon or product is uniform.

Isonomal : Isopleth of anomaly.

Isorithm : Any line representing continuous value on maps.

Isobars : Lines of equal pressure.

Isobaths : Lines of equal depth in sea.

Isobronts : Lines joining places experienceing a thunderstorm at the same time.

Isochrones : Lines joining places located at equal travel time from a common centre.

Isogonals : Lines joining places with same magnetic declination.

Isohalines : Isopleths of salinity.

Isohels : Isopleths of equal amount of sunshine.

Isohyet : Isopleth of rainfall.

Isohypse or contour lines : Isopleths of elevation above sea level.

Isonif : Isopleth of amount of snow.

Isophene : Isopleth of seasonal phenomena, for example, flowering dates of plants.

Isopotential : Surface to which artesian water can rise.

Isorymes : Lines of equal frost.

Isoseismals : Lines of equal seismic activity.

Isotherms : Isopleths of temperature.

Isthmus : A narrow strip of land joining two land masses, viz.–the isthmus of Panama joining North and South America.

Karst region or Karstland : Limestone region in which most of the drainage is underground, the surface being dry and barren.

Katabatic wind : Local wind caused by the flow of air down mountain slopes and valleys.

Lagoon : Part of sea partially cut off from it by deposits of sand or coral reefs, viz. Chilika Lake in Odisha.

Lapse rate : The rate of change of temperature in atmosphere with height; it is said to be positive when temperature decreases with height, as it normally does, and negative when temperature increases with height, as in temperature inversion.

Latitude : The angular distance of a point on the earth's surface north or south of the equator, as measured from the centre of the earth. Latitudinal lines are also called parallels of latitude.

Leaching : The process by which soluble substances are washed out of the upper layers of the soils into lower layers by percolating rainwater.

Leeward : The side or direction sheltered from the wind.

Light year : Distance travelled by light in one year, the speed being 1,86,000 miles per second. The unit is used for measuring the distance of stars from the earth.

Lithosphere : The solid crust of the earth.

Loess : A deposit of fine silt or dust generally held to have been transported to its present situation by wind.

Longitude : The angular distance measured along the equator, between the meridian through a given point and a standard or prime meridian.

Lunar month : The interval of time in which the moon makes one complete revolution around the earth-about 29.5 days.

Magnetic storms : Large, irregular variations or disturbances in the earth's magnetic field.

Meridian : A line of longitude, or half of one of the great circles that pass through the poles and cut the equator at right angles.

Mesophyte : A plant that requires a moderate amount of moisture. Most common trees and shrubs are mesophytes.

Mestizo : Offspring of a European and an American Indian-the term is used mostly in South America.

Meteors : Small pieces in the atmosphere appearing as shooting stars.

Midnight sun : A phenomenon observed in high latitudes around midsummer when the sun does not sink below the horizon throughout the 24 hours of a day and night cycle and may thus be visible even at midnight.

Monsoon : A type of wind system in which there is complete reversal or almost so, of prevailing wind direction from season to season.

Moraine : The debris or fragments of rock material brought down with the movement of glacier.

Mulatto : The offspring of a white and a black person, commonly used in America.

Nivation : Erosion due to action of snow.

Nomadism : The practice, among certain primitive people, of frequently changing their habitation. These people keep moving residence in search of food and fresh pasture for animals. People following this mode of life are called nomads.

Oasis : Area in the desert where water is available.

Ocean Current : Movement of the surface water of the ocean.

Opisometer : Instrument used for measuring distances on a map.

Orbit : Path of a heavenly body through space in relation to some selected point.

Orographic rain : Rain caused by mountains standing in the path of moisture-laden winds.

Outwash Plain : Alluvial plain formed by streams originating from the melting ice of a glacier.

Pampas : The mid-latitude grasslands of South America.

Pastoralism : Practice of breeding and rearing cattle. Some pastoral communities may be nomadic in their habits.

Pedology : The science of the study of soils.

Pelagic : Belonging to the open sea.

Peninsula : A stretch of land almost surrounded by water.

Perigee : The point in the orbit of moon or a planet or in the apparent orbit of the sun, nearest to the earth.

Perihelion : The position of the earth in its orbit or any other heavely body, nearest to the sun.

Permafrost : Ground that is permanently frozen.

Petrology : The study of the composition, structure and history of rocks forming the crust of the earth.

Phenology : Science dealing with the effects of seasonal changes upon animal and plant life.

Phytogeography : The study of the distribution of plants, on the earth, in relation to environment.

Piedmont : Belonging to or related to the foot of a mountain.

Planetary winds : The general distribution of winds throughout the lower atmosphere which is determined by differences in insolation and would be set up similarly on any rotating planet possessing an atmosphere.

Planimeter : Instrument for measuring irregular plane areas on maps.

Plateau : Extensive level or near level area of elevated land.

Prairies : Mid-latitude grasslands of North America.

Precipitation : Falling water (in liquid or solid form, as the case may be) from the atmosphere to the earth.

Pressure gradient : Rate at which pressure declines horizontally on the earth's surface.

Psychrometer : Instrument used for measuring humidity of the atmosphere.

Radiation : Process by which a body emits radiant energy, viz.– in the form of heat.

Rain shadow : Area having relatively lower average rainfall because it is sheltered from the prevailing rain-bearing winds by a range of mountains or hills.

Reef : Ridge of rocks lying near the surface of the sea, which may be visible at low tide, but usually covered by water.

Reg : A stony desert. A sandy desert is called an erg.

Rhumb line of loxodrome : Line on the earth's surface which cuts all meridians at the same angle.

Saprophyte : A plant which lives on decaying organic matter. Most such plants are fungi.

Satellite : A relatively small body revolving around a planet.

Savanna : An area of tropical grassland with scattered trees.

Seismic focus or deep focus : Point below the earth's surface where an earthquake originates.

Seismograph : Instrument used for measuring and recording earthquake shocks.

Seismology : Science of the study of earthquakes.

Selvas : Dense equatorial forests of the Amazon basin in South America.

Sericulture : The culture of silkworms for production of raw silk.

Sidereal day : The period of time during which a star describes a complete circle in its apparent journey around the pole star, representing the period of one rotation of the earth on its axis and equal to 23 hours 56 minutes 4 seconds. It is thus about 4 minutes shorter than the mean solar day.

Sleet : Precipitation consisting of a mixture of snow and rain.

Smog : Fog heavily laden with smoke.

Snow-line : Lower limit of perpetual snow. The snow above this line does not melt completely even in summer.

Soil erosion : The wearing away and loss of soil mainly by the action of wind and water.

Solar constant : Intensity of the sun's radiation in space at the mean distance of the earth from the sun.

Solar day : The average period taken by the earth in making one rotation on its axis in relation to the sun-24 hours.

Solstice : The time during summer or winter when the sun is vertically above the point which represents its farthest distance north or south of the equator-the two tropics.

Steppe : Mid-latitude grasslands of Eurasia.

Strait : Narrow stretch of sea connecting two extensive areas of sea.

Syncline : Trough or inverted arch of a fold in rock strata.

Sublimation : Change of state of water from solid to vapour directly or vice versa.

Taiga : Coniferous forestland of Siberia.

Temperature inversion : Condition when the temperature is found to be increasing instead of decreasing with height.

Theodolite : Instrument used for measuring angular distances in the vertical plane (elevation) and the horizontal plane (azimuth).

Thermograph:Self-recordingthermometer-aninstrumentformeasuring temperature.

Tidal range : Average difference in water level between hight and low tide at one place.

Topographic map : Map on sufficiently large scale to show the detailed surface features of an area.

Trans-humance : Practice among pastoral communities to move with their animals seasonally between two regions of different climate.

Tributary : Smaller river which joins a larger river.

Tropics : The Tropic of Cancer and the Tropic of Capricorn located at degrees N and S, respectively, are the northward and southward limits up to which the sun's vertical rays can reach.

Tropical Zone : The area bounded by the two tropics is called the tropical zone.

Tropophyte : A plant which acts as hygrophyte in one season and xerophyte in the other.

Tsunami : A large sea wave caused by an earthquake originating on the sea bed.

Van Allen's Radiation Belts : Named after the physicist who discovered them, these are two bands of the outermost layer of the atmosphere (magnetosphere), at heights of 3000 km and 16000 km above the earth's surface. Here the ionized particles trapped by the earth's magnetic field from the solar radiation, concentrate.

Viticulture : The culture of grape vine.

Volcano : Vent in the earth's crust caused by magma forcing its way to the surface through which molten or solid rock flow from the interior of the earth.

Watershed : Elevated boundary line separating headstreams which are tributaries to different river systems or basins.

Weather : Condition of the atmosphere at certain time or over a certain period of time as described by meteorological phenomena including temperature, atmospheric pressure and humidity.

Weathering : Decay and disintegration of rocks of the earth's crust by exposure to the atmosphere; it is one of the main processes of denudation.

Willy-willy : Tropical cyclone in the Pacific near the east coast of Australia.

Wind vane : Instrument used to indicate the direction of the wind.

Xerophyte : Plant which is adapted, to living in a region where little moisture (or dry climatic condition) is available.

Yazoo river : Tributary which is prevented from joining the main river because the latter has built up high natural levees; it thus runs parallel to the main stream for a considerable distance before joining it downstream.

Zenith : Point in the celestial sphere vertically above one's head.

Zodiac : Zone of the heavens in which lie the paths of the sun, the moon and the chief planets.

Zonal soil : A soil which owes its well developed characteristics largely to the influence of climate and vegetation. They are characterised by well-developed soil profiles.

Zoogeography : Study of the distribution of animals and successio- nal development on the earth's surface.

Zoophyte : An animal which resembles a plant, viz.-a coral polyp, a sponge.

★★★

INDIAN POLITY AND CONSTITUTION 4

Constitution : Constitution is the foundational law of a country which ordains the fundamental principles on which the government (or the governance) of that country is based. It lays down the framework and principal functions of various organs of the government as well as the modalities of interaction between the government and its citizens. With the exception of the United Kingdom (U.K.), almost all democratic countries possess a written constitution. India also possesses an elaborate written constitution which was enacted by a constituent assembly specifically set up for the purpose.

Our Constitution : Our present constitution— the first Constitution of India framed and given to themselves by the people of India was adopted by the Constituent Assembly on 26 November, 1949. It came into full operation with effect from 26 January, 1950. The Constitution as originally adopted had 22 parts, 395 articles and 8 schedules. Its present text is as amended from time to time.

1. Evolution of Indian Constitution

Although the systems of ancient India do have their reflections in the Constitution of India, the direct sources of the Constitution lie in the administrative and legislative developments of the British period. A concise and chronological description of the Acts, documents and events that culminated in the framing of the world's largest written Constitution is given here.

Administrative & Legislative Reforms Before 1857

Regulating Act of 1773

- This Act was based on the report of a committee headed by the British Prime Minister Lord North.
- Governance of the East India Company was put under British parliamentary control.
- The Governor of Bengal was nominated as Governor General for all the three Presidencies of Calcutta, Bombay and Madras. Warren Hastings was the first such Governor General.
- A Supreme Court was established in Calcutta (now Kolkata).
- Governor General was empowered to make rules, regulations and ordinances with the consent of the Supreme Court.

Pitts India Act of 1784

- It was enacted to improve upon the provisions of Regulating Act of 1773 to bring about better discipline in the Company's system of administration.
- A 6-member Board of Controllers was set up which was headed by a minister of the British Government. All political responsibilities were given to this board.
- Trade and commerce related issues were under the purview of the Court of Directors of the company.

- Provinces had to follow the instructions of the Central Government, and Governor General was empowered to dismiss the failing provincial government.

Charter Act of 1793

- Main provisions of the previous Acts were consolidated in this Act.
- Provided for the payment of salaries of the members of the Board of Controllers from Indian revenue.
- Courts were given the power to interpret rules and regulations.

Charter Act of 1813

- Trade monopoly of the East India Company came to an end.
- Powers of the three Councils of Madras, Bombay and Calcutta were enlarged, they were also subjected to greater control of the British Parliament.
- The Christian Missionaries were allowed to spread their religion in India.
- Local autonomous bodies were empowered to levy taxes.

Charter Act of 1833

- The Governor General and his Council were given vast powers. This Council could legislate for the whole of India subject to the approval of the Board of Controllers.
- The Council got full powers regarding revenue, and a single budget for the country was prepared by the Governor General.
- The East India Company was reduced to an administrative and political entity and several Lords and Ministers were nominated as ex-officio members of the Board of Controllers.
- For the first time the Governor-General's Government was known as the 'Government of India' and his Council as the 'Indian Council'.

Charter Act of 1853

- This was the last of the Charter Acts and it made important changes in the system of Indian legislation.
- This Act followed a report of the then Governor General Dalhousie for improving the administration of the company.
- A separate Governor for Bengal was to be appointed.
- Legislative and administrative functions of the Council were separately identified.
- Recruitment of the Company's employees was to be done through competitive exams.
- British Parliament was empowered to put Company's governance of India to an end at any suitable time.

Administrative & Legislative Reforms After 1857

Government of India Act, 1858

- British Crown decided to assume sovereignty over India from the East India Company in an apparent consequence of the Revolt of 1857, described as an armed sepoy mutiny by the British historians and remembered as the First War of Independence by the Indians.

- The first statute for the governance of India, under the direct rule of the British Government, was the Government of India Act, 1858.
- It provided for absolute (British) imperial control over India without any popular participation in the administration of the country.
- The powers of the crown were to be exercised by the Secretary of State for India, assisted by a council of fifteen members, known as the Council of India.
- The country was divided into provinces headed by a Governor or Lieutenant-Governor aided by his Executive Council.
- The Provincial Governments had to function under the superintendence, direction and control of the Governor-General in all matters.
- All the authority for the governance of India was vested in the Governor-General in Council who was responsible to the Secretary of State.
- The Secretary of State was ultimately responsible to the British Parliament.

Indian Councils Act, 1861

- This is an important landmark in the constitutional history of India. By this Act, the powers of the crown were to be exercised by the Secretary of State for India, assisted by a council of fifteen members (known as the Council of India). The Secretary of State, who was responsible to the British Parliament, governed India through the Governor General, assisted by an Executive council.
- This Act enabled the Governor General to associate representatives of the Indian people with the work of legislation by nominating them to his expanded council.
- This Act provided that the Governor General's Executive Council should include certain additional non-official members also while transacting legislative business as a Legislative Council. But this Legislative Council was neither representative nor deliberative in any sense.
- It decentralised the legislative powers of the Governor General's Council and vested them in the Governments of Bombay and Madras.

Indian Councils Act, 1892

- The non-official members of the Indian Legislative Council were to be nominated by the Bengal Chamber of Commerce and the Provincial Legislative Councils while the non-official members of the Provincial Councils were to be nominated by certain local bodies such as universities, district boards, municipalities, *zamindars* etc.
- The Councils were to have the power of discussing the Budget and addressing questions to the Executive.

Morley-Minto Reforms and the Indian Councils Act, 1909

- Reforms recommended by the then Secretary of States for India (Lord Morley) and the Viceroy (Lord Minto) were implemented by the Indian Councils Act, 1909.
- The maximum number of additional members of the Indian Legislative Council (Governor-General's Council) was raised from 16 (under the Act of 1892) to 60 (excluding the Executive Councillors).
- The size of Provincial Legislative Councils was enlarged by including elected non-official members so that the official majority was gone.

- An element of election was also introduced in the Legislative Council at the centre also but here the official majority there was maintained.
- The Legislative Councils were empowered to move resolutions on the Budget, and on any matter of public interest, except certain specified subjects, such as the Armed forces, Foreign Affairs and the Indian States.
- It provided, for the first time, for separate representation of the Muslim community and thus sowed the seeds of separatism.

The Government of India Act, 1915

- This act was passed to consolidate the provisions of the preceding Government of India Acts.

Montague-Chelmsford Report and the Government of India Act, 1919

- The then Secretary of State for India Mr. E.S. Montagu and the Governor General Lord Chelmsford formulated proposals for the Government of India Act, 1919.
- Responsible Government in the Provinces was to be introduced, without impairing the responsibility of the Governor (through the Governor General), for the administration of the Province, by resorting to device known as 'Dyarchy' or dual government.
- The subjects of administration were to be divided into two categories Central and Provincial.
- Central subjects were those which were exclusively kept under the control of the Central Government.
- The provincial subjects were sub-divided into 'transferred' and 'reserved' subjects.
- The 'transferred subjects' were to be administered by the Governor with the aid of Ministers responsible to the Legislative Council in which the proportion of elected members was raised to 70 percent.
- The 'reserved subjects' were to be administered by the Governor and his Executive Council with no responsibility to the Legislature.
- The previous Central control over the provinces in administrative, legislative and financial matters was relaxed. Sources of revenue were divided into two categories so that the provinces could run the administration with the revenue raised by the provinces themselves.
- The provincial budget was separated from the central budget.
- The provincial legislature was empowered to present its own budget and levy its own taxes relating to the provincial sources of revenue.
- The Central Legislature, retained power to legislate for the whole country on any subject.
- The control of the Governor General over provincial legislation was retained by providing that a Provincial Bill, even though assented to by the Governor, would become law only when assented to also by the Governor General.
- The Governor was empowered to reserve a Bill for the consideration of the Governor General if it was related to some specified matters.
- The Governor General in Council continued to remain responsible only to the British Parliament through the Secretary of State for India.

- The Indian Legislature was made more representative and, for the first time 'bi-cameral'.
- The Upper House was named the **Council of State.** This was composed of 60 members of whom 34 were elected.
- The Lower House was named the Legislative Assembly. This was composed of about 144 members of whom 104 were elected.
- The electorates were arranged on a communal and sectional basis, developing the Morley-Minto device further.
- The Governor General's overriding powers in respect of Central legislation were retained as follows :

  (a) His prior sanction was required to introduce Bills relating to certain matters; (b) he had the power to veto or reserve for consideration of the Crown any Bill passed by the Indian Legislature; (c) he had the converse power of certifying Bill or any grant refused by the Legislature; (d) he could make Ordinances, in case of emergency.

Simon Commission

- This commission, headed by Sir John Simon, constituted in 1927 to inquire into the working of the Act of 1919, placed its report in 1930. The report was examined by the British Parliament and the Government of India Bill was drafted accordingly.

The Government of India Act, 1935

- The Act of 1935 prescribed a federation, taking the Provinces and the Indian States (native states) as units.
- It was optional for the Indian States to join the Federation, and since they never joined, the Federation never came into being.
- The Act divided legislative powers between the Centre and Provinces.
- The executive authority of a Province was also exercised by a Governor on behalf of the Crown and not as a subordinate of the Governor General.
- The Governor was required to act with the advice of Ministers responsible to the Legislature.
- In certain matters, the Governor was required to act 'in his discretion' without ministerial advice and under the control and directions of the Governor General, and, through him, of the Secretary of State.
- The executive authority of the Centre was vested in the Governor General (on behalf of the Crown).
- Counsellors or Council of Ministers responsible to the Legislature was not appointed although such provisions existed in the Act of 1935.
- The Central Legislature was bi-cameral, consisting of the Federal Assembly and the Council of State.
- In six provinces, the legislature was bi-cameral, comprising a Legislative Assembly and a Legislative Council. In other provinces, the Legislature was uni-cameral.
- Apart from the Governor General's power of veto, a Bill passed by the Central Legislature was also subject to veto by the Crown.

➢ The Governor General could prevent discussion in the Legislature and suspend the proceedings on any Bill if he was satisfied that it would affect the discharge of his special responsibilities.

➢ The Governor General had independent powers of legislation, concurrently with those of the Legislature.

➢ On some subjects no bill or amendment could be introduced in the Legislature without the Governor-General's previous sanction.

➢ A three-fold division in the Act of 1935— There was a Federal List over which the Federal Legislature had exclusive powers of legislation. There was a Provincial List of matters over which the Provincial Legislature had exclusive jurisdiction. There was a Concurrent List also over which both the Federal and Provincial Legislature had competence.

➢ The Governor-General was empowered to authorise either the Federal or the Provincial Legislature to enact a law with respect to any matter which was not enumerated in the above noted Legislative Lists.

➢ Dominion Status, which was promised by the Simon Commission in 1929, was not conferred by the Government of India Act, 1935.

Cripps Mission

➢ In March 1942, Sir Stafford Cripps, a member of the British cabinet came with a draft declaration on the proposals of the British Government.

➢ These proposals were to be adopted at the end of the Second World War provided the Congress and the Muslim League could accept them.

➢ According to the proposals

★ The Constitution of India was to be framed by an elected Constituent Assembly by the Indian people.

★ The Constitution should give India Dominion Status.

★ There should be one Indian Union comprising all the Provinces and Indian States;

★ Any Province (or Indian State) not accepting the Constitution would be free to retain its constitutional position existing at that time and with such non-acceding Provinces the British Government could enter into separate Constitutional arrangements.

Cabinet Mission Plan

➢ In March 1946, Lord Attlee sent a Cabinet Mission to India consisting of three Cabinet Ministers, namely Lord Pethick Lawrence, Sir Stafford Cripps and Mr. A.V. Alexander.

➢ The object of the Mission was to help India achieve its independence as early as possible, and to set up a Constituent Assembly.

➢ The Cabinet Mission rejected the claim for a separate Constituent Assembly and a separate State for the Muslim.

➢ According to Cabinet Mission Plan there was to be a Union of India, comprising both British India and the States, and having jurisdiction over the subjects of Foreign Affairs, Defence and Communication. All residuary powers were to be vested in the Provinces and the States.

➢ The Union was to have an Executive and a Legislature consisting of representatives of the Provinces and the States.

- Any decision involving a major communal issue in the legislature was to require a majority support of representatives of each of the two major communities present and voting as well as a majority of all the members present and voting.
- The provinces could form groups with executives and legislatures, and each group could be competent to determine the provincial subjects.

The Mountbatten Plan

- The plan for transfer of power to the Indians and partition of the country was laid down in the Mountbatten Plan.
- It was given a formal shape by a statement made by the British Government on 3rd June, 1947.

The Indian Independence Act, 1947 of the British Parliament

- In pursuance of this Act, the Government of India Act, 1935, was amended by the Adaptation Orders, both in India and Pakistan, for setting up an interim Constituent Assembly to draw up the future Constitution of the country.
- From the 15th August, 1947 India ceased to be a Dependency, and the suzerainty of the British Crown over the Indian States and the treaty relations with Tribal Areas lapsed from that date.
- The office of the Secretary of State for India was abolished.
- The Governor-General and the Governors lost extraordinary powers of legislations to compete with the Legislature.
- The Central Legislature of India, composed of the Legislative Assembly and the Council of States, ceased to exist on August 14, 1947.
- The Constituent Assembly itself was to function also as the Central Legislature with complete sovereignty.

2. Constituent Assembly and Making of the Constitution

- The Cabinet Mission envisaged the establishment of a Constituent Assembly to frame a Constitution for the country. Members of the Constituent Assembly were elected by the Provincial Legislative Assemblies.
- Each Province and each Indian State were allotted seats in proportion of its population, roughly in the ratio of one to a million. The seats so ascertained were distributed among the main communities in each Province. The main communities recognised were Sikh, Muslim and General.

Important Committees of the Constituent Assembly and their Chairman

S.	Name of the Committee	Chairman
1.	Committee on the Rules of Procedure	Dr. Rajendra Prasad
2.	Steering Committee	
3.	Finance and Staff Committee	
4.	Ad hoc Committee on the National Flag	
5.	Union Constitution Committee	Pt. Jawaharlal Nehru
6.	Union Powers Committee	
7.	State Committee	

S.	Name of the Committee	Chairman
8.	Advisory Committee on Fundamental Rights, Minorities and Tribal and Excluded Areas	Sardar Vallabhbhai Patel
9.	Drafting Committee	Dr. B.R. Ambedkar
10.	Credential Committee	Alladi Krishnaswami Ayyar
11.	House Committee	B.Pattabhi Sitaramayya
12.	Order of Business Committee	K. M. Munshi
13.	Committee on the Functions of the Constituent Assembly	G.V. Mavalankar
14.	Minorities Sub-Committee	H.C. Mookherjee
15.	Fundamental Rights Sub-committee	J. B. Kripalani
16.	North-East Frontier Tribal Areas and Assam Excluded & Partially Excluded Areas Sub-Committee	Gpinath Bardoloi
17.	Excluded and Partially Excluded Areas (other than those in Assam) Sub-Committee	A. V. Thakkar

➢ The total number of members of the Constituent Assembly was 385, of whom 93 were representatives from the Indian States and 292 from the Provinces (British India).

➢ After the partition of India number of members of the Constituent Assembly came to 299, of whom 284 were actually present on the 26th November, 1949 and signed on the finally approved Constitution of India. The Constituent Assembly, which had been elected for undivided India, held its first meeting on December 9,1946, and reassembled on August 14, 1947, as the sovereign Constituent Assembly for the dominion of India.

➢ It took two years, eleven months and eighteen days for the Constituent Assembly to finalise the Constitution.

➢ Objective Resolution was moved in the first session of the Constituent Assembly (on 13 December, 1946) by Pandit Jawaharlal Nehru which was adopted after considerable deliberation and debate in the Assembly on 22 January, 1947. The following objectives were embodied in the resolution :

★ To foster unity of the Nation and to ensure its economic and political security, to have a written Constitution, and to proclaim India as a Sovereign Democratic Republic.

★ To have a federal form of Government with the distribution of powers between the centre and states.

★ To guarantee and secure justice, equality, freedom of thought, expression, belief, faith, worship, vocation, association and action to all the people of India.

★ To provide adequate safeguards for minorities, backward and tribal areas and depressed and other backward classes.

- ★ To maintain the integrity of the territory of the republic and its sovereign rights on land, sea and air according to justice and the law of civilised nations.
- ★ To attain rightful and honoured place in the world and make its full and willing contribution to the promotion of the world peace and the welfare of mankind.

➢ The principles of the Constitution were outlined by various committees of the Assembly, and there was a general discussion on the reports of these Committees. The Assembly appointed the Drafting Committee with Dr. B.R. Ambedkar as the Chairman on August 29, 1947.

➢ The Drafting Committee, headed by Dr. B.R.Ambedkar, submitted a Draft constitution of India to the President of the assembly on 21 February 1948.

➢ The members of Drafting Committee were N. Gopalaswamy Ayyangar, Alladi Krishnaswamy Ayyar, K.M. Munshi, Mohd. Saadullah, B.L. Mitter (later replaced by N. Madhava Rao), Dr. D.P. Khaitan (replaced on death by T.T. Krishnamachari).

➢ The third and final reading of the draft was completed on November 26, 1949. On this date, the signature of the President of the Assembly was appended to it and the Constitution was declared as passed.

➢ The provisions relating to citizenship, elections and provisional Parliament etc. were implemented with immediate effect, that is, from the 26th November, 1949. The rest of the provisions of the constitution came into force on January 26, 1950 and this date is referred to in the Constitution as the *date of its commencement*.

3. Different Sources of the Indian Constitution

Although the skeleton of the constitution was derived from the Government of India Act 1935, many provisions were imported from other constitutions of the world. Some of them are listed below along with the Government of India Act, 1935 :

Government of India Act, 1935 : This Act formed the basis or 'blueprint' of the consititution of India with the features of Federal system, office of Governor, emergency powers etc. Besides, the Constitution of India has borrowed from the—

Constitution of Britain : Law making procedures, Rule of law, Single citizenship, Bi-cameral Parliamentary system, office of CAG.

Constitution of USA : Independence of judiciary, judicial review, fundamental rights , removal of Supreme Court and High Court judges, Preamble and functions of President and Vice-president.

Constitution of Canada : Federation with strong Centre, to provide residuary powers to the Centre, Supreme Court's advisory jurisdiction.

Constitution of Ireland : Directive Principles of State policy, method of presidential elections, and the nomination of members to Rajya Sabha by the President.

Weimar Constitution of Germany : Provisions concerning the suspension of fundamental rights during emergency.

Constitution of Australia : Idea of the Concurrent List, Trade and Commerce provisions.

Constitution of South Africa : Amendment with 2/3rd majority in Parliament and election of the Members of Rajya Sabha on the basis of proportional representation.

Constitution of France : Republican System, Principles of Liberty, Equality and Fraternity.

Constitution of former USSR : Fundamental Duties, Ideals of justice in Preamble.

4. Important Articles of the Constitution

	Articles	Subject
Part I	Art. 1-4	The Union and its territory.
Part II	Art. 5-11	Citizenship
Part III	**Fundamental Rights**	
Art. 12	Definition	
Art. 13	Laws inconsistent with or in derogation of the fundamental rights	
Right to Equality		
Art. 14	Equality before law	
Art. 15	Prohibition of discrimination on grounds of religion, race, caste, sex or place of birth	
Art. 16	Equality of opportunity in matters of public employment	
Art. 17	Abolition of untouchability	
Art. 18	Abolition of titles	
Right to Freedom		
Art. 19	Protection of certain rights regarding freedom of speech, etc.	
Art. 20	Protection in respect of conviction for offences	
Art. 21	Protection of life and personal liberty	
21A.	Right to education	
Art. 22	Protection against arrest and detention in certain cases	
Right against Exploitation		
Art. 23	Prohibition of traffic in human beings and forced labour	
Art. 24	Prohibition of employment of children in factories, etc.	
Right to Freedom of Religion		
Art. 25	Freedom of conscience and free profession, practice and propagation of religion	
Art. 26	Freedom to manage religious affairs	
Art. 27	Freedom as to payment of taxes for promotion of any particular religion	
Art. 28	Freedom as to attendance at religious instruction or religious worship in certain educational institutions	
Cultural and Educational Rights		
Art. 29	Protection of interests of minorities	
Art. 30	Right of minorities to establish and administer educational institutions	

Saving of certain Laws

Art. 31A Saving of laws providing for acquisition of estates, etc.

Art. 31B Validation of certain Acts and Regulations

Art. 31C Saving of laws giving effect to certain directive principles

Right to Constitutional Remedies

Art. 32 Remedies for enforcement of rights conferred by this Part

Art. 33 Power of Parliament to modify the rights conferred by this Part in their application to Forces, etc.

Art. 34 Restriction on rights conferred by this Part while martial law is in force in any area

Art. 35 Legislation to give effect to the provisions of this Part

Part IV Directive Principles of State Policy

Art. 36 Definition

Art. 37 Application of the principles contained in this Part

Art. 38 State to secure a social order for the promotion of welfare of the people

Art. 39 Certain principles of policy to be followed by the State

Art. 39A Equal justice and free legal aid

Art. 40 Organisation of village panchayats

Art. 41 Right to work, to education and to public assistance in certain cases

Art. 42 Provision for just and humane conditions of work and maternity relief

Art. 43 Living wage, etc. for workers

Art. 43A Participation of workers in management of industries

Art. 43B The State shall endeavour to promote voluntary formation, autonomous functioning, democratic control and professional management of co-operative societies.

Art. 44 Uniform civil code for the citizens

Art. 45 Provision for early childhood care and education to children below the age of six years

Art. 46 Promotion of educational and economic interest of Scheduled Castes, Scheduled Tribes and other weaker sections

Art. 47 Duty of the State to raise the level of nutrition and the standard of living and to improve public health

Art. 48 Organisation of agriculture and animal husbandry

Art. 48A Protection and improvement of environment and safeguarding of forests and wild life

Art. 49 Protection of monuments and places and objects of national importance

Art. 50 Separation of judiciary from executive

Art. 51 Promotion of international peace and security

Part IVA Art. 51A Fundamental Duties

Part V The Union

Chapter–I : The Executive

Art. 52 The President of India
Art. 53 Executive power of the Union
Art. 54 Election of President
Art. 61 Procedure for impeachment of the President
Art. 63 The Vice-President of India
Art. 64 The Vice-President to be *ex-officio* Chairman of the Council of States
Art. 65 The Vice-President to act as President or to discharge his functions during casual vacancies in the office, or during the absence of President
Art. 66 Election of Vice-President
Art. 72 Power of President to grant pardons, etc. and to suspend, remit or commute sentences in certain cases
Art. 74 Council of Ministers to aid and advise President
Art. 76 Attorney-General for India

Chapter–II : Parliament

Art. 79 Constitution of Parliament
Art. 80 Composition of the Council of States (Rajya Sabha)
Art. 81 Composition of the House of the People (Lok Sabha)
Art. 83 Duration of Houses of Parliament
Art. 84 Qualification for membership of Parliament
Art. 85 Sessions of Parliament, prorogation and dissolution
Art. 86 Right of President to address and send messages to Houses
Art. 87 Special address by the President
Art. 88 Rights of Ministers and Attorney General as respects Houses
Art. 89 The Chairman and Deputy Chairman of the Council of States
Art. 90 Vacation and resignation of, and removal from, the office of Deputy Chairman
Art. 93 The Speaker and Deputy Speaker of the House of the People
Art. 94 Vacation and resignation of, and removal from, the offices of Speaker and Deputy Speaker
Art. 95 Power of the Deputy Speaker or other person to perform the duties of the office of, or to act as, Speaker
Art. 98 Secretariat of Parliament
Art. 99 Oath or affirmation by members
Art. 100 Voting in Houses, power of Houses to act notwithstanding vacancies and quorum
Art. 105 Powers, privileges, etc. of the Houses of Parliament and of the members and committees thereof
Art. 106 Salaries and allowances of members
Art. 107 Provisions as to introduction and passing of Bills
Art. 108 Joint sitting of both Houses in certain cases
Art. 109 Special procedure in respect of Money Bills
Art. 110 Definition of "Money Bills"
Art. 111 Assent to Bills

Art. 112 Annual financial statement (Budget)
Art. 113 Procedure in Parliament with respect to estimates
Art. 114 Appropriation Bills
Art. 115 Supplementary, additional or excess grants
Art. 116 Votes on account, votes of credit and exceptional grants
Art. 117 Special provisions as to financial Bills
Art. 118 Rules of procedure
Art. 119 Regulation by law of procedure in Parliament in relation to financial business
Art. 120 Language to be used in Parliament
Art. 121 Restriction on discussion in Parliament
Art. 122 Courts not to inquire into proceedings of Parliament

Chapter–III : Legislative Powers of the President

Art. 123 Power of President to promulgate Ordinances during recess of Parliament

Chapter–IV : The Union Judiciary

Art. 124 Establishment and Constitution of Supreme Court
Art. 125 Salaries, etc. of Judges
Art. 126 Appointment of acting Chief Justice
Art. 127 Appointment of *ad hoc* Judges
Art. 128 Attendence of retired Judge at sittings of the Supreme Court
Art. 129 Supreme Court to be a Court of record
Art. 130 Seat of Supreme Court
Art. 131 Original jurisdiction of Supreme Court
Art. 132 Appellate jurisdiction of Supreme Court in appeals from High Court in certain cases
Art. 133 Appellate jurisdiction of Supreme Court in appeals from High Court in regard to civil matters
Art. 134 Appellate jurisdicition of Supreme Court in regard to criminal matters
Art. 134A Certificate for appeal to the Supreme Court
Art. 135 Jurisdiction and powers of the Federal Court under existing law to be exercisable by the Supreme Court
Art. 136 Special leave to appeal by the Supreme Court
Art. 137 Review of judgements or orders by the Supreme Court
Art. 138 Enlargement of the jurisdiction of the Supreme Court

Lokpal

- ★ A Lokpal is a proposed 'Ombudsman' in India. It has jurisdiction over all members of Parliament (MPs), the Prime Minister (with certain exceptions), ministers and all Civil servants etc. in cases of corruption. Lokpal is empowered to sanction prosecution.
- ★ The amended 'Lokpal and Lokayukta Bill 2011' was passed on Rajya Sabha and Lok Sabha on 17th and 18th December, 2013 respectively. Samajwadi Party opposed the Bill.
- ★ The selection of the Lokpal will be held by a committee comprising the P.M., the Lok Sabha Speaker, the Leader of the opposition in Lok Sabha and the Chief Justice of India etc.
- ★ Lokpal is to have Chairperson and maximum 8 members, 50% of them judicial members and at least 50% members to be from SC/ST/women/minorities.

Art. 141	Law declared by Supreme Court to be binding on all Courts
Art. 143	Power of President to consult Supreme Court
Art. 144	Civil and judicial authorities to act in aid of the Supreme Court
Chapter–V : Comptroller and Auditor-General of India	
Art. 148	Comptroller and Auditor-General of India
Art. 149	Duties and powers of the Comptroller and Auditor-General
Part VI	**The States**
Art. 152-237	The Government at the State level : The Executive, The State Legislature, The High Courts and Subordinate Courts
Part VIII	Art. 239-241 The Union Territories
Part IX	Art. 243 to 243-O The Panchayats
Part IXA	Art. 243-P to 243-ZG The Municipalities
Part IXB	Art. 243-ZH to 243-ZT The Co-operative Societies
Part X	Art. 244-244A The Scheduled and Tribal Areas
Part XI	Art. 245-263 Relations between The Union and the States
Part XII	Art. 264-300 Finance, property, contracts and suits; Distribution of revenue between Union and States; Finance Commission; Borrowing, Property, Contracts, Rights, Liabilities, Obligations and Suits
Art. 300A	Right to Property
Part XIII	Art. 301-307 Trade, commerce and intercourse within India
Part XIV	**Services Under The Union and The States**
Art. 309	Recruitment and conditions of service of persons serving the Union or a State
Art. 310	Tenure of office of persons serving the Union or a State
Art. 311	Dismissal, removal or reduction in rank of persons employed in civil capacities under the Union or a State
Art. 312	All-India Services
Art. 315	Public Service Commissions for the Union and for the States
Art. 316	Appointment and term of office of members
Art. 317	Removal and suspension of a member of a Public Service Commission
Art. 318	Power to make regulations as to conditions of service of members and staff of the Commission
Art. 320	Functions of Public Service Commissions
Art. 321	Power to extend functions of Public Service Commissions
Art. 323	Reports of Public Service Commissions
Part XIVA	Art. 323A-323B Tribunals
Part XV	**Elections**
Art. 324	Superintendence, direction and control of elections to be vested in an Election Commission
Art. 325	No person to be ineligible for inclusion in, or to claim to be included in a special, electoral roll on grounds of religion, race, caste or sex
Art. 326	Elections to the House of the People and to the Legislative Assemblies of States to be on the basis of adult suffrage

Art. 327	Power of Parliament to make provision with respect to elections to legislatures
Art. 328	Power of Legislature of a State to make provision with respect to elections to such Legislature
Art. 329	Bar to interference by Courts in electoral matters
Part XVI	Art .330–342 Special provisions for certain classes
Part XVII	Art. 343-351 Official languages
Part XVIII	Art. 352–360 Emergency Provisions
Part XIX	**Miscellaneous**
Art. 361A	Protection of publication of proceedings of Parliament and State Legislatures
Art. 363	Bar to interference by courts in disputes arising out of certain treaties, agreements, etc.
Art. 363A	Recognition granted to Rulers of Indian States to cease and privy purses to be abolished
Art. 364	Special provisions as to major ports and aerodromes
Art. 365	Effect of failure to comply with, or to give effect to, directions given by the Union
Part XX	Art. 368 Amendment of the Constitution
Part XXI	Art. 369-392 Temporary, Transitional and Special Provisions—Special status of States
Part XXII	Art. 393-395 Short Title, Commencement, Authoritative text in Hindi and Repeals

Schedules of the Indian Constitution

The Constitution of India at the time of its adoption had only eight Schedules to which four more were added during the succeeding sixty-five years.

1st Schedule	28 States and 7 Union Territories with Territorial demarcations
2nd Schedule	
Part 'A'	Salary and emoluments of the President and Governors of the States
Part 'B'	Omitted
Part 'C'	Salary and emoluments of the Speaker / Deputy Speaker or Chairman / Vice Chairman of the Lok Sabha, Rajya Sabha and State Legislative Assemblies or Councils.
Part 'D'	Salary and emoluments of the judge of the Supreme Court and High Courts
Part 'E'	Salary and emoluments of the Comptroller and Auditor General of India
3rd Schedule	Forms of oath and affirmations of members of legislatures, ministers and judges.
4th Schedule	Allocation of seats to States and Union Territories in the Rajya Sabha.
5th Schedule	Administration and control of Scheduled Areas and STs.
6th Schedule	Administration of Tribal Areas of North-Eastern States

7th Schedule	Distribution of power between the Union and the State Government. (Union List, State List and Concurrent List)
8th Schedule	Description of 22 languages recognised by the Constitution.
9th Schedule	Validation of certain Acts and Regulations
10th Schedule	Provisions as to disqualification on ground of defection (Anti-defection Law introduced by the 52nd Constitutional Amendment Act.). This Schedule followed latest developments by 91st amendment to the constitution in 2003.
11th Schedule	Powers, authority and responsibilities of Panchayats, 29 subjects over which the Panchayats have jurisdiction (refer to the 73rd Constitutional Amendment Act).
12th Schedule	Powers, authority and responsiblities of Municipalities, 18 subjects over which the Municipalities have jurisdiction (refer to the 74th Constitutional Amendment Act).

5. Some important Amendments of the Constitution

1st Constitutional Amendment Act, 1951 : This amendment added Article, 15(4) and Article, 19(6) and brought changes in the right to private property in pursuance with the decision of Supreme Court concerning fundamental rights. Ninth schedule to the Constitution was also added by it.

7th Constitutional Amendment Act, 1956 : Through this amendment the implementation of State Reorganisation Act, was made possible. The categorisation of States into Part A, Part B and Part C ceased henceforth. Part C states were redesignated as Union Territories. The seats in the Rajya Sabha and in the Union and State Legislatures were reallocated. It also effected changes regarding appointment of additional and acting judges, High Courts and their jurisdictions etc.

10th Constitutional Amendment Act, 1961 : Incorporated Dadra and Nagar Haveli as Union Territory.

12th Constitutional Amendment Act, 1962 : Inclusion of territories of Goa, Daman and Diu into the Indian Union.

13th Constitutional Amendment Act, 1962 : Insertion of Art. 371 A to make special provisions for the administration of the State of Nagaland.

14th Constitutional Amendment Act, 1962 : Pondicherry, Karaikal, Mahe and Yenam, the former French territories, were specified in the Constitution as the Union Territory of Pondicherry (now Puducherry). Enabled the UTs of Himachal Pradesh, Manipur, Tripura, Goa, Daman and Diu and Pondicherry to have Legislatures and Council of Ministers.

15th Constitutional Amendment Act, 1963 : It raised the age of retirement of a High Court Judge from 60 to 62. Extended the jurisdiction of a High Court to issue writs under Art. 226 to a Government or authority situated outside its territorial jurisdiction where the cause of action arises within such jurisdiction.

16th Constitutional Amendment Act, 1963 : Changes were effected in Art. 19 to enable the Parliament to make laws providing reasonable restrictions on the freedom of expression in the larger interests of sovereignty and integrity of India. Amendments were made in the form of oath contained in the third Schedule with emphasis on upholding the sovereignty and integrity of India.

19th Constitutional Amendment Act, 1966 : Art. 324 was amended to clarify the duties of the Election Commission. It deprived the Election Commission of the power to appoint election tribunals for deciding election disputes of members of Parliament and State Legislatures.

21st Constitutional Amendment Act, 1967 : Sindhi language was included as 15th regional language in the Eighth Schedule.

24th Constitutional Amendment Act, 1971 : It was a retaliatory act of the Parliament to neutralise the effect of the judgement in Golak Nath Case. It affirmed the parliament's power to amend any part of the Constitution, including Fundamental Rights by amending Arts. 368 and 13. It made obligatory for the President to give assent to Amendment Bills, when they are presented to him/her.

25th Constitutional Amendment Act, 1971 (came into force on 20.04.1972): It restricted the jurisdiction of the Courts over acquisition laws with regard to adequacy of Compensation. This amendment came primarily in the wake of Bank Nationalisation case and the word 'amount' was substituted in place of 'compensation' in Article 31.

It also provided that no law passed by the State to give effect to Directive Principles specified under clauses (b) and (c) of Art. 39 can be declared void on the ground that it was inconsistent with Fundamental Rights conferred by Arts. 14, 19 and 31.

26th Constitutional Amendment Act, 1971 : This amendment withdrew the recognition to the rulers of Princely States and their privy purses were abolished.

30th Constitutional Amendment Act, 1972 (w.e.f. 27.02.1973): It provided that only such appeals can be brought to the Supreme Court which involve a substantial question of law. The valuation aspect of Rs. 20,000 for appeals in civil cases to the Supreme Court was abolished.

31st Constitutional Amendment Act, 1973 : By this amendment, the seats of the Lok Sabha was increased from 525 to 545 but reduced the representation of UTs in Lok Sabha from 25 to 20.

35th Constitutional Amendment Act, 1974 (w.e.f. 01.03.1975) : Accorded status of Associate State to Sikkim by ending its protectorate kingdom status which was a novel concept introduced in the Constitution.

36th Constitutional Amendment Act, 1975 : Made Sikkim a full fledged State of the Union of India.

38th Constitutional Amendment Act, 1975 : Clarified that declaration of emergency by the President and promulgation of Ordinance by the President or Governor cannot be challenged in any Court on any ground.

39th Constitutional Amendment Act, 1975 : The disputes or questions regarding elections of President, Vice-President, Prime Minister and Speaker of Lok Sabha were taken out of the purview of judicial review of the Supreme Court or High Courts.

42nd Constitutional Amendment Act, 1976 (Mini Constitution) : The 42nd Amendment made fundamental changes in the contitutional structure and it incorporated the words 'SOCIALIST', 'SECULAR' and 'INTEGRITY' in the Preamble. Fundamental Duties were added in Part IVA. Directive Principles were given precedence over Fundamental Rights and any law made to this effect by the Parliament was kept beyond the scope of judicial review by the Court. It made the power of Parliament supreme so far as amendment to the Constitution was concerned. It authorised the Supreme Court to transfer certain cases from one High Court to another and redefined the writ jurisdiction of the High Courts. It provided for Administrative Tribunals for speedy justice. It empowered the Centre to deploy armed forces in any State to deal with the grave law and order situation. It authorised the President to make Proclamation of Emergency for any part of the country or to whole of India. It made it obligatory for the President to act on the advice of the Council of Ministers. Tenure of the Lok Sabha and the State Assemblies was increased by one year.

43rd Constitutional Amendment Act, 1977 (w.e.f. 13.04.1978) : The 43rd Amendment omitted many articles inserted by 42nd Amendment. It restored the jurisdicition of the Supreme Court and the High Courts, which had been curtailed under the 42nd Amendment.

44th Constitutional Amendment Act, 1978 (w.e.f June–September, 1979): The amendment was brought by the Janata Party Government which repealed some of the changes effected by 42nd Amendment, omitted a few and provided alterations. Right to property was taken away from the list of Fundamental Rights and placed in a new Art. 300A as an ordinary legal right. Constitutionality of the Proclamation of Emergency by the President could be questioned in a court on the ground of malafide (42nd Amendment had made it immune from judicial review). It brought the revocation of a Proclamation under Parliamentary control. In Article 352 regarding National Emergency, the words ' internal disturbance' were substituted by the words 'armed rebellion'. It authorised the President to refer back the advice to the Council of Ministers for reconsideration, but made it binding for the President to act on the reconsidered advice. The power of the Courts to decide disputes regarding election of Prime Minister and Speaker was restored. Constitutional protection on publication of proceedings of Parliament and State Legislatures was provided.

52nd Constitutional Amendment Act, 1985 : This amendment was brought about during Rajiv Gandhi regime with a view to put an end to political defections. It added Tenth Schedule to the Constitution containing the modes for disqualification in case of defection from the Parliament or State Legislature.

55th Constitutional Amendment Act, 1986 (w.e.f. 20.02.1987) : The formation of Arunachal Pradesh took place with special powers given to the Governor. It also provided for a 30-member State Assembly.

56th Constitutional Amendment Act, 1987 : Goa was made a full fledged State with a State Assembly but Daman and Diu stayed as UT.

57th Constitutional Amendment Act, 1987 : It provided for reservation of seats for Scheduled Tribes of Nagaland, Meghalaya, Mizoram and Arunachal Pradesh in Lok Sabha. Seats were also reserved for the Scheduled Tribes of Nagaland and Meghalaya in the State Assemblies of Nagaland and Meghalaya.

58th Constitutional Amendment Act, 1987 : An authoritative text of the Constitution in Hindi was provided to the people of India by the President.

59th Constitutional Amendment Act, 1988 : It amended Art. 356 to provide that the declaration of Emergency may remain in operation upto 3 years and also authorised the Government to proclaim emergency in Punjab on ground of 'internal disturbance'. The amendment made in Art. 352 thus provided that the emergency with respect to Punjab shall operate only in that State.

61st Constitutional Amendment Act, 1988 (w.e.f. 28.03.1989) : It brought about an amendment to Article 326 for the reduction of voting age from 21 to 18 years .

62nd Constitutional Amendment Act, 1989 : It increased the period of reservation of seats provided to the Scheduled Castes and Scheduled Tribes for another 10 years i.e. upto 2000 A.D. The reservation for Anglo-Indians through nomination in case of their inadequate representation, was also extended upto 2000 A.D.

65th Constitutional Amendment Act, 1990 (w.e.f. 12.03.1992) : A National Commission for Scheduled Castes and Scheduled Tribes with wide powers was provided to take care of the cause of SCs/STs.

66th Constitutional Amendment Act, 1990 : This amendment provided for the inclusion of 55 new land reform Acts passed by the States into the Ninth Schedule.

69th Constitutional Amendment Act, 1991 (w.e.f. 01.02.1992) : Arts. 239-AA and 239-AB were inserted in the Constitution to provide a National Capital Territory designation to Union Territory of Delhi with a legislative Assembly and Council of Ministers.

70th Constitutional Amendment Act, 1992 : Altered Art. 54 and 368 to include members of legislative assemblies of Union Territories of Delhi and Pondicherry in the electoral college for the election of the President.

71st Constitutional Amendment Act, 1992 : It included Manipuri, Konkani and Nepalese languages in the 8th Schedule.

73rd Constitutional Amendment Act, 1992 (w.e.f. 24.04.1993) : The institution of Panchayati Raj received Constitutional guarantee, status and legitimacy . XIth Schedule was added to deal with it. It also inserted part IX, containing Arts, 243, 243A to 243O.

74th Constitutional Amendment Act, 1992 (w.e.f. 01.06.1993) : Provided for constitutional sanctity to Municipalities by inserting Part IX-A, containing Arts. 243P to 243ZG and the XIIth Schedule which deals with the items concerning Municipalities.

77th Constitutional Amendment Act, 1995 : By this amendment a new clause 4A was added to Art. 16 which authorised the State to make provisions for Scheduled Castes and Scheduled Tribes with regard to promotions in Government jobs.

78th Constitutional Amendment Act, 1995 : This amended the Ninth Schedule of the Constitution to insert 27 Land Reform Acts of various States. After this the total number of Acts included in the Ninth Schedule went upto 284.

79th Constitutional Amendment Act, 1999 : Amended Art. 334 to extend the reservation of seats for SCs / STs and Anglo-Indians in the Lok Sabha and in the State Legislative Assemblies upto 60 years from the commencement of the Constitution (i.e., till 2010).

80th Constitutional Amendment Act, 2000 : Amended Art. 269 and substituted a new Article for Art. 270 and abolished Art. 272 of the Constitution. This was based on the recommendation of the Tenth Finance Commission. This amendment was deemed to have come into operation from 1st April 1996. The Amendment widened the scope of the Central taxes and duties on the consignment of goods levied by the Government of India and distributed among States.

81st Constitutional Amendment Act, 2000 : Amended Art. 16(1) of the Constitution and added a new clause (4-B) after clause (4-A) to Art. 16(1) of the Constitution. The new clause (4-B) ends the 50% ceiling on reservation for Scheduled Caste and Scheduled Tribes and other Backward Classes in backlog vacancies.

82nd Constitutional Amendment Act, 2000 : This amendment restored the relaxation in qualifying marks and standards of evaluation in both job reservation and promotions to Scheduled Castes and Scheduled Tribes which was set aside by a Supreme Court's judgement in 1996.

84th Constitutional Amendment Act, 2001 (w.e.f. 21.02.2002) : This amendment provided that till the publication of the relevent figures of the first census after 2026 the ascertainment of the population of a State for following purposes shall be made on the basis of the census shown against each of them :

- Election of the President under Art. 55 — 1971 census.
- Allotment of seats to each State in Lok Sabha — 1971 census.
- Division of State into territorial Lok Sabha constituencies — 1991 census.
- Composition of Legislative Assemblies under Art. 170 — 1991 census.
- Reservation of seats for SC / ST in the Lok Sabha under Art. 330 — 1991 census

85th Constitutional Amendment Act, 2001 : It amended clause (4-A) of Art. 16 and substituted the words "in matters of promotion, with consequential seniority, to any class" for the words "in matter of promotion to any class".

The amendment provided for 'consequential seniority' to the SCs / STs for promotion in government service.

86th Constitutional Amendment Act, 2002 : Added a new Art. 21A after. Art. 21 which makes the right of education for children of the age of 6 to

14 years a Fundamental Right. Substitutes Article 45 to direct the State to endeavour to provide early childhood care and education for all children until they complete the age of six years. Added a new Fundamental Duty to Part IV (Art. 51A) of the Constitution.

87th Constitutional Amendment Act, 2003 (w.e.f. 19.02.2004) : Provided that the allocation of seats in the Lok Sabha and division of each State into territorial Constituencies will be done on the basis of population as ascertained by the '2001 census' and not by '1991' census.

88th Constitutional Amendment Act, 2003 (w.e.f. 15.01.2004) : This amendment inserted a new Article 268A after Article 268 which empowered the Union of India to levy 'service tax'.

This tax shall be collected and appropriated by the Union and States in the manner as formulated by Parliament.

89th Constitutional Amendment Act, 2003 : Provided for the establishment of a separate National Commission for Scheduled Tribes by bifurcating the existing National Commission for Scheduled Castes and Scheduled Tribes. The commission shall consist of a Chairman, Vice-Chairman and three other members. They shall be appointed by the President of India.

90th Constitutional Amendment Act, 2003 : This amendment was necessitated due to creation of Bodoland Territorial Areas District within the State of Assam by agreement reached between the Centre and Bodo representatives for solving Bodoland problem. It stated that the representation of Scheduled Tribes and non-Scheduled Tribes in the Constitution of the Bodoland Territorial Areas District shall be maintained. It meant that the representation of the above categories shall remain the same as existed prior to the creation of Bodoland Territorial Areas District.

91st Constitutional Amendment Act, 2003 (w.e.f. 01.01.2004) : This amendment limits the size of Ministries at the Centre and in States. According to new Clause (1-A) the total number of Ministers, including the Prime Minister in the Union Council of Ministers or Chief Minister in the State Lagislative Assemblies shall not exceed 15 per cent of the total members of the Lok Sabha in the Centre or Vidhan Sabha in the states. The new Clause (1-B) of Article 75 provides that a member of either House of Parliament belonging to any political party who is disqualified for being member of that house on the ground of defection shall also be disqualified to be appointed as a minister under Clause (1) of Art. 75 and 164 until he is again elected. However, the number of Ministers, including the Chief Minister in a State shall not be less than 12 (in smaller States like Sikkim, Mizoram and Goa).

92nd Constitutional Amendment Act, 2003 (w.e.f. 07.01.2004): It amended the Eighth Schedule of the Constitution and has inserted 4 new languages in it, namely—Bodo, Dogri, Maithili and Santhali. After this amendment the total number of constitutionally recognised official languages has become 22.

93rd Constitutional Amendment Act, 2005 (w.e.f. 20.01.2006) : Provided reservation in admissions in private unaided educational institutions for students belonging to scheduled castes/tribes and other backward classes.

94th Constitutional Amendment Act, 2006 : Excluded Bihar from the provision to Clause (1) of Art. 164 of the constitution which provides that there shall be a minister in charge of tribal welfare who may in addition be in charge of the welfare of the Scheduled Castes and backward classes in Bihar, Madhya Pradesh and Orissa (now Odisha). It extends the provisions of clause(1) of Art. 164 to the newly formed States of Chhattisgarh and Jharkhand.

95th Constitutional Amendment Act, 2009 : Extended the reservation of seats for SCs and STs in the Lok Sabha and State assemblies by another 10 years (beyond January 25, 2010). The time period of 60 years under Art. 334 of the consititution was to lapse on January 25, 2010. Through this amendment in Art. 334 the words 'sixty years' has been substituted by 'seventy years'.

6. Some Special Features of the Indian Constitution

- The Constitution of India is the lengthiest and the most comprehensive of all the written Constitutions of the world.
- Originally the Constitution consisted of 395 Articles divided into 22 parts and 8 Schedules.
- Now it consists of about 442 Articles divided into 22 parts and 12 Schedules.
- Unlike the federal Constitutions of the USA and Australia the Indian Constitution lays down provisions relating to the Governmental machinery not only in the Centre but also in the States.
- The Indian Constitution provides for matters of administrative detail.
- The Constitution contains detailed provisions relating to Centre-State relations including the emergency provisions.
- Special status has been given to Jammu & Kashmir and some other states such as Nagaland, Mizoram, Assam, Gujarat etc.
- Under the Constitution the people of India are the ultimate sovereign.
- The Constitution of India establishes a parliamentary form of Government both at the Centre and in the States.
- The Indian Constitution, though written, is sufficiently flexible.
- The Constitution declares certain Fundamental Rights of the individual.
- It is a unique feature of the Indian Constitution that it makes the citizens' duties a part of the basic law of the land.
- One of the most important and unique features of the Indian Constitution is the provisions of Directive Principles of State Policy to secure a truly welfare State.
- The Indian Constitution, distributes the legislative subjects on which the Parliament and State Legislature can enact laws under three lists viz. Union List, State List and Concurrent List.
- The Indian Constitution unlike other federal Constitutions provides for a single unified judiciary with the Supreme Court at the apex, the High Courts in the middle and the Subordinate Courts at the bottom.

- There are provisions in the Constitution to ensure independence of judiciary.
- The Constitution of India has adopted a balance between the American system of Judicial Supremacy and the British principle of Parliamentary Supremacy.
- The most remarkable feature of the Indian Constitution is that being a federal Constitution it acquires a unitary character during the time of emergency.
- Under the Indian Constitution every adult above 18 years of age has been given the right to elect representatives for the legislature without prescribing any qualification based either on sex, property, education or the like.
- A distinctive feature of the Indian Constitution is that it provides for the establishment of a Secular State. Regardless of their religious beliefs, all Indian citizens enjoy equal rights.
- The State cannot discriminate against anyone on the ground of religion or caste, nor can it compel anybody to pay taxes for the support of any particular religion.
- The Indian Constitution has special reservation of seats for the Scheduled Castes and Tribes in public appointments and in educational institutions and in the Union and State Legislatures.
- An outstanding feature of the Constitution is Panchayati Raj. The idea for organising village Panchayats was provided in the Constitution under Article 40 of Part IV which received Constitutional legitimacy through the 73rd Amendment to the Indian Constitution.

7. Federal and Unitary Features of the Indian Union

- India is different from the United States of America because in United States the federation is based on an agreement between different States, and the States have the right to secede from the Union.
- The Indian Constitution has the features both of a federal and unitary forms of Government.

Federal features

- ★ Distribution of powers between Union and the States has been made as per the three lists.
- ★ The Union Government as well as the State Governments have to function strictly in accordance with the Constitution. They can neither alter the distribution of powers nor override the dictates of the Constitution.
- ★ Indian Constitution is entirely written. An amendment to it must be passed by the Parliament and if an amendment affects the federal structure it must be ratified by at least half the State Legislatures.
- ★ Like other federal states our country also has an independent Judiciary as an essential feature.

Unitary features of the Indian Constitution

- ★ In a federation, people enjoy dual citizenship, that of the Centre and of the State to which they belong . But the Indian Constitution provides every Indian with single citizenship.

- ★ The most important subjects are included in the Union List which has been allocated to the centre.
- ★ The centre can legislate on the subjects in the concurrent list.
- ★ Residuary powers belong to the Centre.
- ★ Single Constitutional Framework has been provided for the Centre as well as for the State.
- ★ The proclamation of National emergency can immediately turn the federal system of India into a Unitary one.
- ★ In a federation, each State should get equal representation irrespective of its size or population. But in the Rajya Sabha in India, States are represented on the basis of population. Besides, the President has the power to nominate twelve members to the Rajya Sabha.
- ★ The Governors of the States are appointed by the President and they continue to hold office only during his pleasure.
- ★ The Indian Constitution provides for single judiciary, a single system of civil and criminal law and command All India Services.
- ★ The authority of the Comptroller and Auditor General and the Chief Election Commissioner uniformly prevails over the Union as well as States.

8. The Preamble

- ➢ The Preamble to the Constitution states the object which the Constitution seeks to establish and promote, and also aids the legal interpretation of the Constitution where the language is found ambiguous.
- ➢ The ideals embodied in the Objectives Resolution is faithfully reflected in the Preamble to the Constitution, which, as amended in 1976, summaries the aims and objects of the Constitution.
- ➢ Text of the Preamble : "We, the People of India having solemnly resolved to constitute India into a Sovereign Socialist Secular Democratic Republic and to secure to all citizens Justice, social, economic and political; Liberty of thought, expression, belief, faith and worship Equality of status and of opportunity; and to promote among them all Fraternity assuring the dignity of the individual and the unity and integrity of the Nation in our Constituent Assembly on this twenty sixth day of November, 1949, do hereby adopt, enact and give to ourselves this constitution."
- ➢ The Preamble specifies the source of authority, i.e. people of India, the system of Government, the objectives to be attained by the political system and the date of adoptation and enactment of the Constitution.
- ➢ Though, the Preamble is not enforceable in a court of law, it provides a key to the understanding and interpretation of the Constitution.
- ➢ In case of doubt, the Supreme Court has referred to the Preamble to elucidate vague aspects of the Constitution.
- ➢ In the Berubari case, the Supreme Court held that the Preamble was not part of the Constitution, but later, in the Keshavananda Bharti case, it declared that it was part of the Constitution.

9. Lapse of Paramountcy

➢ When the Indian Independence Act 1947, was passed, it declared the lapse of suzerainty (paramountcy) of the crown, in sec. 7(i)(b) of the Act.

➢ As from the appointed day–the suzerainty of His Majesty over the Indian States lapses, and with it, all treaties and agreements in force at the date of the passing of this Act between His Majesty and the rulers of Indian States, all functions exercisable by His Majesty at the date with respect to Indian States, all obligations of His Majesty existing at that date towards Indian States or the rulers thereof, and all powers, rights, authority, or jurisdiction exercisable by His Majesty at that date in or in relation to Indian States by treaty, grant, usage, sufferance or otherwise ....

➢ Of the states situated within the geographical boundaries of the Dominion of India, all (numbering 552) save Hyderabad, Kashmir, Bahawalpur, Junagarh and the N.W.F. (North West Frontier) states (Chitral, Phulra, Dir, Swat and Amb) had acceded to the Dominion of India by the 15th August, 1947, i.e. before the 'appointed day' itself.

10. Integration and Merger of Indian States

➢ The main objective of shaping the Indian States into sizeable or viable administrative units was sought to be achieved by a three-fold process of integration (known as the 'Patel Scheme' after Sardar Vallabhbhai Patel, Minister-in-charge of Home Affairs)—

1. 216 states were merged into respective Provinces, geographically contiguous (connected) to them.
   ★ These merged states were included in the territories of the states in Part B in the First Schedule of the constitution.
   ★ The process of merger started with the merger of Orissa and Chhattisgarh States with the then Province of Orissa on January 1, 1948.
2. 61 states were converted into Centrally administered areas and included in Part C of the First Schedule of the Constitution.
3. The third form of integration was the consolidation of groups of states into new viable units, known as Union of States.
   ★ As many as 275 states were integrated into 5 Unions — Madhya Bharat, Patiala and East Punjab States Union, Rajasthan, Saurashtra and Travancore–Cochin. These were included in the States in Part B of the First Schedule.
   ★ The other three States included in Part B were—Hyderabad, Jammu and Kashmir and Mysore.
   ★ Jammu and Kashmir acceded to India on October 26, 1947, and so it was included as a state in Part B, but the Government of India agreed to take the accession subject to confirmation by the people of the state, and a constituent. Assembly subsequently confirmed it, in November, 1956.
   ★ Hyderabad did not formally accede to India, but the Nizam issued a Proclamation recognising the necessity of entering

into a constitutional relationship with the Union of India and accepting the Constitution of India subject to ratification by the Constituent Assembly of the State, and the Constituent Assembly of that state ratified this.

➢ It is noteworthy here that the Rajpramukhs of the five Unions as well as the Rulers of Hyderabad, Mysore, Jammu and Kashmir all adopted the Constitution of India, by Proclamations.

➢ The process of integration culminated in the Constitution (7th Amendment) Act, 1956, which abolished Part B states as a class and included all the states in Part A and B in one list.

➢ The special provisions in the constitution relating to Part B states were, consequently omitted. The Indian States thus lost their identity and become on uniform political organisation embodied in the Constitution of India.

11. The Union and its Territories

➢ Article 1 lays-down that India, i.e. Bharat, shall be a Union of States. The Territory of India shall consist of (i) the Territories of the States, (ii) the Union Territonies and (iii) any Territories that may be acquired.

➢ Article 1 of the Constitution describes India as a Union of States not as a federation of states. Union of India is not the result of an agreement, nor has any State the right to secede from it.

➢ The Federation is called a Union of States, because it is indestructible.

➢ The Union Territories are not included in the "Union of States". Whereas the expression "Territory of India" includes the States, the Union Territories and such other territories as may be acquired by India.

➢ The States and their territories are specified in the First Schedule to the Constitution. The Constitution empowers the Parliament for the admission or establishment of new States.

➢ Article 2 provides that Parliament may by law admit new States into the Union of India or establish new States on such terms and conditions as it deems fit.

➢ The Parliament has admitted the French settlements of Pondicherry, Karaikal, Mahe and Yenam, the Portuguese settlements of Goa, Diu and Daman and Sikkim, etc. into India after independence.

➢ Article 3 of the Constitution empowers the Parliament to form a new State by altering boundaries of existing States.

12. Reorganization of States

➢ A Bill seeking to create a new State or alter boundaries of existing States can be introduced in either House of the Parliament, only on the recommendation of the President.

➢ President refers the State Reorganization Bill to the State Legislature concerned for its opinion, fixing a time limit.

➢ Parliament is not bound to accept or act upon the views of the State Legislature on a state Reorganization Bill. The State Reorganization Bill requires simple majority in both Houses of the Parliament.

➢ It is not necessary to obtain the views of legislatures of Union territories before a bill affecting their boundaries or names is introduced.

- ➢ The States Reorganization Act, 1956 reorganised the boundaries of different States to establish a new State of Kerala and merge the former States of Madhya Bharat, Pepsu, Saurashtra, Travancore, Cochin, Ajmer, Bhopal, Coorg, Kutch and Vindhya Pradesh in other adjoining States and thus 14 states and 6 Union Territories were established in India.
- ➢ The Bombay Reorganization Act, 1960, divided the State of Bombay to establish two States of Gujarat and Maharashtra.
- ➢ In 1962 Nagaland was created as a separate State.
- ➢ In 1966, Punjab was divided into Punjab and Haryana.
- ➢ Union Territory of Himachal Pradesh was made the State of Himachal Pradesh by an Act of 1970.
- ➢ States of Manipur, Tripura, Meghalaya and Union Territories of Mizoram and Arunachal Pradesh were established in 1971. Later Mizoram and Arunachal Pradesh achieved statehood in 1986.
- ➢ Sikkim was made part of India by 36th Amendment of the Constitution.
- ➢ In 1987 Goa was made a separate State of the Union.
- ➢ Chhattisgarh came into existence on 1st November, 2000.
- ➢ Uttaranchal (now Uttarakhand) came into existence on 8th November, 2000.
- ➢ The State of Jharkhand, which was established on 15th November 2000 is the newest (28th) State of India.
- ➢ The Union Government (on 30 July, 2013) gave a go ahead to create 'Telangana' (the proposed 29th State) bifurcating Andhra Pradesh.
- ➢ Telangana came into being on the 2nd June 2014.

13. Citizenship

- ➢ The Constitution of India provides for a single and uniform citizenship for whole of India.
- ➢ Citizenship of India was granted to every person who domiciled in the territory of India at the commencement of the constitution and who was born in the territory of India or —
  - ★ Either of whose parents was born in the territory of India or
  - ★ Who had been ordinarily residing in the territory of India for not less than five years immediately preceding commencement of the Constitution.
- ➢ Indian citizens have the following rights under the Constitution which aliens do not possess:
  - ★ Some of the Fundamental Rights enumerated in part III of the Constitution. e. g. Articles 15, 16, 19, 29, 30.
  - ★ Only citizens are eligible for offices of the President, Vice-President, Judge of the Supreme Court or a High Court, Attorney General, Governor of a State, Member of a legislature etc.
  - ★ Only citizens have the right to vote.
- ➢ Enemy aliens are not entitled to the benefit of the procedural provisions in clauses (1)-(2) of Article 22 relating to arrest and detention.
- ➢ The Citizenship Act, 1955, provides for the acquisition of Indian citizenship in the following ways :

- ★ Generally, every person born in India on or after January 1950, shall be a citizen of India if either of his parents was a citizen of India at the time of his birth.
- ★ A person who was outside India on or after 26 January; 1950, shall be a citizen of India by descent, if his father was a citizen of India at the time of that person's birth.
- ★ A person can apply for and get registered as a citizen of India by the competent authority if he satisfies the conditions laid down.
- ★ A person residing in India for more than 7 years and having adequate knowledge of a constitutionally recognised Indian language can seek citizenship by naturalisation, provided he is not a citizen of a country where Indian citizens are prevented from becoming citizens by naturalisation.
- ★ If any new territory becomes a part of India, the persons of the territory become citizens of India.

➢ Citizenship of India may be lost by :

- ★ Renunciation of citizenship.
- ★ Termination of citizenship, if a citizen of India voluntarily aquires the citizenship of another country.
- ★ Deprivation of citizenship by the Government of India

14. Fundamental Rights

➢ Six Fundamental Rights have been provided by the Constitution :

1. Right to equality	2. Right to liberty
3. Right against exploitation	4. Right to freedom of religion
5. Cultural and educational rights	6. Right to constitutional remedy

➢ Article 14 of the constitution provides that the State shall not deny any person equality before the law or equal protection of the laws within the territory of India.

➢ Exceptions to the provision of equality before law, allowed by the Indian Constitution are :

★ The President or the Governor of a State is not answerable to any Court for the exercise and performance of the powers and duties of his office. ★ No criminal proceeding can be instituted or continued against the President or a Governor in any Court during his term of office. ★ No civil proceeding in which relief is claimed against the President or the Governor of a State can be instituted during his term of office in any Court in respect of any act done by him in his personal capacity, without a prior notice of two months. ★ The above immunities do not bar Impeachment proceeding against the President and Suits or other appropriate proceeding against the Government of India or the Government of a State. ★ Exceptions acknowledged by the comity of nations in every civilized country, in favour of foreign Sovereigns and ambassadors. ★ The guarantee of 'equal protection' is a guarantee of equal treatment of persons in 'equal circumstances', permitting differentiation in different circumstances.

- Article 15 of the Constitution states that : The State shall not discriminate against any citizen on grounds only of religion, race, caste, sex, place of birth or any of them.
  - ★ No citizen shall, on grounds only of religion, race, caste, sex, place of birth or any of them be subjected to any disability, liability restriction or condition with regard to access to shops, public restaurants, hotels and places of public entertainment or the use of wells, tanks, bathing ghats, roads and places of public resort maintained wholly or partly out of State funds or dedicated to the use of general public.
  - ★ Nothing in this article shall prevent the State from making any special provisions for women, children or any socially and educationally backward classes.
- Article 16 guarantees Equality of opportunity in matters of public employment. It says that :
  - ★ There shall be equality of opportunity for all citizens in matters relating to employment or appointment to any office under the State.
  - ★ No citizen shall, on grounds only of religion, race, caste, sex, descent, place of birth or any of them, be ineligible for any employment under the State.

The Mandal Commission Case

A nine-Judge Bench of the Supreme Court has laid down in *Indra Sawhney's* case (popularly known as the Mandal Commission Case) regarding reservation in Government employment, that :

★ Under Article 16(4) provisions can be made in favour of the backward classes in the matter of employment by Executive orders also. ★ Backward class of citizens is not defined in the Constitution. A caste may also constitute a class. ★ The backwardness contemplated by Art. 16(4) is mainly social. It need not be both social and educational. ★ Income or the extent of property can be taken as a measure of social advancement and on that basis the 'creamy layer' of a given caste can be excluded. ★ The reservations contemplated in Art. 16(4) should not exceed 50%. ★ Reservation of posts under Art. 16(4) is confined to initial appointment only and cannot extend to providing reservation in promotion.

Note : *Mandal Commission was set up in 1979 under the Chairmanship of B.N. Madal, M.P. (Former Chief Minister of Bihar).*

- The 77th Amendment has provided to continue reservation in promotion for the S.C. and S.T.
- Identification of backward classes is subject to judicial review.
- Article 17 ensures Abolition of Untouchability. The word 'untouchability' has not been defined either in the Constitution or in the relevant Act of Parliament. It has been assumed that the word has a well known connotation.
- Article 18 ensures Abolition of titles. It prevents the State from conferring any title.
- This ban is only against the State and not against other public institutions, such as Universities.
- The State is not debarred from awarding military or academic distinctions, even though they may be used as titles.

- The State is not prevented from conferring any distinction or award which cannot be used as a title. *Bharat Ratna* or *Padma Vibhushan* cannot be used by the recipient as a title and therefore does not come within the Constitutional prohibition.
- Article 19 **provides the six freedoms of :**
  ★ Speech and expression; ★ Assemble peacefully and without arms; ★ Form associations or unions; ★ Move freely throughout the territory of India; ★ Reside and settle in any part of the territory of India; and ★ Practise any profession, or to carry on any occupation, trade or business.
- State can impose restrictions on the freedom of speech in the interest of the sovereignty and integrity of India, the security of the State, friendly relations with foreign States, public order, decency or morality, or in relation to contempt of Court, defamation or incitement to an offence.
- Restrictions can be imposed on the right to form associations in the interests of the sovereignty and integrity of India or public order or morality. Restrictions can also be imposed on freedom of movement and reside and settle in the interests of the general public or for the protection of the interests of any Scheduled Tribe.
- State can prescribe the professional or technical qualifications necessary for practising any profession or carrying on any occupation, trade or business. State can exclude any citizen from a business or industry run by the Government or a body of Government.
- There is no specific provision in the Constitution guaranteeing the freedom of the press because freedom of the press is included in the wider freedom of 'expression' which is guaranteed by freedom of expression under Art. 19.
- Article 20 guarantees certain protection in respect of conviction for offences. It prohibits :
  ★ Restrospective criminal legislation, commonly known as ex post facto legislation. ★ Double jeopardy or punishment for the same offence more than once. ★ Compulsion to give self-incriminating evidence.
- Article 21 (A) makes the right of education for children of the age of 6 to 14 years a fundamental right . {Ref. : 86th Amendment Act, 2002}
- Article 21 of Constitution provides that no person shall be deprived of his life or personal liberty except according to the procedure established by law.
- Under the 'Due Process' Clause of the American Constitution, the Court has assumed the power of declaring unconstitutional any law which deprives a person of his liberty without reasonableness and fairness.
- In England courts have no power to invalidate a law made by Parliament.
- In the case of Gopalan Supreme Court held that our Constitution had embodied the English concept.
- In Maneka's case the Supreme Court held that a law made by the State which seeks to deprive a person of his personal liberty must prescribe a procedure for such deprivation which must not be arbitrary, unfair or unreasonable. It follows that such law shall be invalid if it violates the principle of natural justice.

- Article 22 provides that no person who is arrested shall be detained in custody without being informed of the grounds for such arrest.
- No arrested person can be denied the right to consult, and to be defended by a legal practitioner of his choice.
- Every person who is arrested and detained in custody is to be produced before the nearest magistrate within a period of twenty-four hours of arrest excluding the time necessary for the journey from the place of arrest to the court of the magistrate and no such person can be detained in custody beyond that period without the authority of a magistrate.
- The above safeguard is not available to an enemy alien and a person arrested or detained under a law providing for preventive detention.
- The Constitution authorises the Legislature to make laws for preventive detention for the security of State, the maintenance of public order, or the maintenance of supplies and services essential to the community, or for reasons connected with Defence and Foreign Affairs {Ref.: Art. 22}
- Article 23 provides Right against Exploitation in following respects :
- Traffic in human beings and begar and other similar forms of forced labour are prohibited.
- The State can impose compulsory service for public purposes, and in imposing such service the State can not make any discrimination on grounds only of religion, race, caste or class or any of them.
- Special provision for the protection of children is made in Art. 24 which provides that no child below the age of fourteen years can be employed to work in any factory or mine or engaged in any other hazardous employment.
- Article 25-28 provides Right to Freedom of Religion.
- Article 25 provides freedom of conscience and free profession, practice and propagation of religion subject to public order, morality and health.
- Under Art. 25 State can regulate religious activities and provide for social reforms and throw open Hindu religious institutions of public character to all sections of Hindus.
- Article 26 guarantees following rights to all religious groups subject to public order, morality and health :

  ★ Establish and maintain institution for religious and charitable purposes; ★ Manage its own affairs in matters of religion; ★ Own and acquire movable and immovable property; ★ Administer such property in accordance with law.
- The State can not compel any citizen to pay any taxes for the promotion or maintenance of any particular religion or religious institution {Ref. : Art. 27}
- No religious instruction can be provided in any educational institution wholly maintained out of State funds {Ref. : Art. 28}
- Where a religious community is in the minority, the Constitution enables it to preserve its culture and religious interests by providing that the

State shall not impose upon it any culture other than the community's own culture {Ref.: Art. 29(1)}

- Such community shall have the right to establish and administer educational institutions of its choice and the State shall not, in granting aid to educational institutions, discriminate against such an educational institution maintained by a minority community on the ground that it is under the management of a religious community {Ref. : Art. 30}.
- Full compensation has to be paid if the State seeks to acquire the property of a minority educational institution {Ref.: Art. 30 (1A)].
- The Fundamental Rights are guaranteed by the Constitution not only against the action of the Executive but also against that of the Legislature.
- Right to constitutional remedy, which was termed "soul of the constitution" by Dr. B.R. Ambedkar, has been guaranteed by Art. 32 of the Constitution.

The Writs

- For enforcement of fundamental rights, the judiciary has been armed with the power to issue the writs.
- The power to issue these writs for the enforcement of the Fundamental Rights is given by the Constitution to the Supreme Court {Ref. : Art. 32} and High Courts {Ref. : Art. 226}.
- Supreme Court has the power to issue writs only for the purpose of enforcement of the Fundamental Rights whereas under Art. 226 a High Court can issue writs for the purpose of enforcement of Fundamental Rights and/or for the redress of any other injury or illegality.
- Supreme Court can issue a writ against any person or Government within the territory of India, while High Court can issue a writ against a person, Government or other authority only if they are located within the territorial jurisdiction of the High Court.
- A writ of Habeas Corpus calls upon the person who has detained another to produce the latter before the court, in order to let the court know on what ground he has been confined and to set him free if there is no legal justification for the imprisonment. The words 'habeas corpus' literally mean 'to have a body'. This writ may be addressed to an official or a private person, who has another person in his custody.
- Mandamus literally means a command. It commands the person to whom it is addressed to perform some public or quasi- public legal duty which he has refused to perform and the performance of which cannot be enforced by any other adequate legal remedy. Mandamus can not be granted against the President, or the Governor of a state, for the exercise and performance of the powers and duties of his office.
- The writ of prohibition is a writ issued by the Supreme Court or a High Court to an inferior court forbiding the latter to continue proceeding therein in excess if its jurisdiction or to usurp a jurisdiction with which it is not legally vested.
- While mandamus is available not only against judicial authorities but

also against administrative authorities, prohibition and certiorari are issued only against judicial or quasi-judicial authorities.

- Though prohibition and certiorari are both issued against Courts or Tribunals exercising judicial or quasi-judicial powers, certiorari is issued to quash order or decision of the Court or Tribunal while prohibition is issued to prohibit the Court or Tribunal from making the ultra vires order or decision. Prohibition is available during the pendency of the proceedings and before the order is made, certiorari can be issued only after the order has been made.
- Quo warranto is a proceeding whereby the court enquires into the legality of the claim which a party asserts to a public office, and to oust him from its enjoyment if the claim is not well founded.
- The conditions necessary for the issue of a writ of quo warranto are as follows :

  ★ The office must be public and it must be created by a statute or by the constitution itself. ★ The office must be a substantive one and not merely the function or employment of a servant at the will and during the pleasure of another. ★ There has been a contravention of the Constitution or a statute or statutory instrument, in appointing such person to that office.
- The limitations on the enforcement of the fundamental rights are as follows :

  Parliament has the power to modify the application of the Fundamental Rights to the members of the Armed Forces, Police Forces or intelligence orgnisations so as to ensure proper discharge of their duties and maintenance of discipline amongst them {Ref.: Art. 33}.

  ★ When martial law is in force, Parliament may indemnify any person in the service of the Union or a State for any act done by him {Ref.: Art. 34}.

  ★ Certain fundamental rights guaranteed by the Constitution may remain suspended, while a Proclamation of Emergency is made by the President under Art. 352.

Right to Information

- Right to information has been granted to every citizen of India under Right to information Act, 2005 which came into force on 12th October, 2005.
- It is not a Fundamental Right but it entails a clause for penalty in case of delay in giving information to the applicant.
- Information Commission has been set- up at central and state levels to oversee implementation of the Act.

15. Directive Principles of State Policy

The Directive Principles are contained in Part IV of the Constitution. They aim at providing the social and economic base of a genuine democracy.

Important Directive Principles

Broadly speaking, there are three types of Directive Principles aimed at providing social and economic justice and ushering in a welfare state.

1. **Socio-Economic Principles :** They require the State :
   (a) to provide adequate means of livelihood to all citizens; (b) to prevent concentration of wealth and means of production and ensure equitable distribution of wealth and material resources; (c) to secure equal pay for equal work of men as well as women; (d) to ensure a decent standard of living and leisure for all workers; (e) to provide necessary opportunities and facilities to children and youth to prevent their exploitation; and (f) to make efforts to secure the right to work, education and public assistance in case of unemployment, sickness, old age etc.
2. **Gandhian Principles :** These are the embodiment of the Gandhian programme for reconstruction. These include :
   (a) the establishment of village panchayats to function as units of self government; (b) the promotion of educational and economic interests of weaker sections of society; (c) the promotion of cottage industries; (d) the prohibition of intoxicating drugs and drinks; and (e) prevention of the slaughter of cows, calves and other milch cattle etc.
3. **Liberal Principles :** The principles are based on liberal thinking and emphasise the need for;
   (a) a uniform civil code for the country; (b) free and compulsory education for all children up to the age of 14 years; (c) separation of the judiciary and executive; (d) organisation of agriculture and animal husbandry along scientific lines; (e) securing the participation of workers in the management of industries; (f) safeguarding the forests and wildlife of the country; and (g) protecting monuments and places of artistic or historical importance.

The real significance of the directive principles lies in the fact that they intend to provide social and economic democracy in the country without which political democracy is a farce.

Difference Between Fundamental Rights and Directive Principles

➢ Fundamental rights constitute limitations upon State action, while the Directive Principles are instruments of instruction to the Government.

➢ The directives require to be implemented by legislation while fundamental rights are already provided in the Constitution.

➢ The Directives are not enforceable in the Courts and do not create any Justiciable rights in favour of the individuals, while the Fundamental Rights are enforceable by the Courts {Ref.: Arts. 32, 37, 226(1)}

➢ In case of any conflict between fundamental rights and directive principles the former should prevail in the Courts.

➢ 42nd Amendment Act ensured that though the directives themselves are not directly enforceable it would be totally immune from unconstitutionality on the ground of contravention of the fundamental rights conferred by Arts. 14 and 19.

➢ This attempt to confer a primacy upon the directives against the fundamental rights was foiled by the decision of the Supreme Court in Minerva Mills Case to the effect that a law would be protected by Art. 31C only if it has been made to implement the directive in Art. 39(b)-(c) and not any of the other Directives included in Part IV.

Directives Provided outside Part IV of the Constitution

➢ State and every local authority within the state to provide adequate facilities for instruction in the mother-tongue at the primary stage of education to children belonging to linguistic minority groups. {Ref. :Art 350 A}

➢ Union to promote spread of Hindi language and to develop it as a medium of expression of all the elements of the composite culture of India. {Ref.: Art. 351.}

➢ The claims of the members of the Scheduled Castes and the Scheduled Tribes shall be taken into consideration, consistently with the maintenance of efficiency of administration, in the making of appointments to services and posts in connection with the affairs of the union or a state. {Ref.: Art. 335}

➢ Though the Directives contained in Arts. 335, 350A and 351 are not included in Part IV, Courts have given similar attention to them meaning that all parts of the Constitution should be read together.

16. Fundamental Duties

➢ The Fundamental Duties are eleven in number, incorporated in Art. 51A [Part IVA], which has been incorporated by the 42nd Amendment Act, 1976.

➢ Under this Article, it is the duty of every citizen of India:

1. *to abide by the Constitution and respect its ideals and institutions, the National Flag and the National Anthem;*
2. *to cherish and follow the noble ideals which inspired our National Struggle for freedom;*
3. *to uphold and protect the sovereignty, unity and integrity of India;*
4. *to defend the country;*
5. *to promote harmony and the spirit of common brotherhood amongst all the people of India;*
6. *to value and preserve the rich heritage of our composite culture;*
7. *to protect and improve the natural environment;*
8. *to develop the scientific temper and spirit of inquiry;*
9. *to safeguard public property;*
10. *to strive towards excellence in all spheres of individual and collective activity.*
11. *to provide opportunities for education to his child or ward as the case may be between the age of six and fourteen years.*

Note : *The 11th Fundamental Duty was added by the 86th Constitutional Amendment Act, 2002.*

➢ There is no provision in the Constitution for direct enforcement of any of the Fundamental Duties nor for any sanction to prevent their violation.

17. Procedure for Amending the Constitution

- The alteration of certain provisions of the Constitution are not considered amendment of the constitution. Such provisions can be altered by the Parliament by a simple majority.
- Other provisions of the Constitution can be changed only by the process of 'amendment' prescribed in Art. 368.
- In the case of provisions which affect the federal structure, a ratification by the Legislatures of at least half of the states, is required before the Bill is presented to the President for his assent. Such provisions are :

  ★ The manner of election of the President {Ref: Arts. 54,55} ★ Extent of the executive power of the Union and the States {Ref: Arts. 73, 162}; ★ The Supreme Court and the High Courts {Art. 241, Chap. IV of part V, Chap. V of part VI}; ★ Distribution of legislative power between the Union and the States [Chap.I of Part XI]; ★ Any of the Lists in the 7th Schedule; ★ Representation of the States in Parliament {Arts. 80-81, 4th Schedule}; ★ Provisions of Art. 368 itself,
- There is no separate Constituent body provided for by our Constitution for the amending process.
- An amendment of the Constitution can be initiated only by the introduction of a Bill for the purpose in either House of Parliament.
- The Amendment Bill should be passed by each House by a special majority i.e., more than 50% of the total membership of that House and by a majority of not less than two-thirds of the members of that House present and voting.
- Constitution stands amended in accordance with the terms of the Amendment Bill after President's assent is accorded to it.

The blend of rigidity and flexibility in the procedure for amendment

- The procedure for amendment is 'rigid' in so far as it requires a special majority and a special procedure.
- There is no separate body for amending the Constitution, as exists in some other countries (e.g., a Constitutional convention)
- The State Legislatures cannot initiate any Bill or proposal for amendment of the Constitution.
- Subject to the provisions of Art. 368, Constitution Amendment Bills are to be passed by the Parliament in the same way as Ordinary Bills.
- The procedure for joint session is not applicable to Bills for amendment of the Constitution.
- The previous sanction of the President is not required for introducing any Bill for amendment of the Constitution.
- The requirement relating to ratification by which the state Legislatures is more liberal than the corresponding provisions in the American constitution. The latter requires ratification by three fourths of the states.
- The amendment of Art. 368 in 1971 has made it obligatory for the President to give his assent to a Bill for amendment of the Constitution,

when it is presented to him after its passage by the Legislature {Ref.: 24th Amendment 1971}.

Whether Fundamental Rights are Amendable

- Until the case of Golak Nath, Supreme Court held that no part of our Constitution was unamendable.
- In Golak Nath's case(1967) a majority of six judges, in a special bench of eleven, overruled the previous decisions and held that if any of such rights is to be amended, a new Constituent Assembly must be convened for making a new Constitution or radically changing it.
- Constitution (24th Amendment) Act, 1971, held that an amendment of the Constitution passed in accordance with Art. 368, will not be law within the meaning of Art. 13 and the validity of a Constitution Amendment Act shall not be questioned on the ground that it takes away or affects a fundamental right {Ref.: Art. 368(3)}
- Validity of the 24th Constitution Amendment Act itself was challenged in the case of Keshavananda Bharati.
- In the case of Keshvananda Bharati the Supreme court overruled its own decision given in the case of Golak Nath and held that the Parliament could amend any provision of the constitution including fundamental rights in accordance with.

The Doctrine of Basic Features

- The Supreme court held in the case of Keshavananda Bharati that there are certain basic features of the Constitution of India, which cannot be altered by an amendment under Art. 368.
- Article 31C, introduced by 25th Amendment Act provided that if any law seeks to implement the directive principles contained in Art. 39(b)-(c) i.e. *regarding socialistic control and distribution of the material resources of the country,* such law shall not be void on the ground of contravention of Art. 14 or 19. The Supreme Court later held that Art. 368 did not empower the Parliament to take away judicial review, in the name of 'amending' the Constitution.
- The 42nd Amendment 1976 inserted two clauses in Art. 368 to the effect that Constitution Amendment Act "shall be called in Question in any court on any ground". These clauses were nullified by the Supreme Court in the Minerva Mills case.
- There are three implications of the decision in Keshavananda Bharati's case.

  ★ *Any part of the Constitution may be amended as per the procedure laid down in Art. 368.* ★ *No referendum or reference to Constituent Assembly is required to amend any provision of the Constitution.* ★ *Basic features of the Constitution can not be amended.*
- There is no limited list of basic features. In so many decisions the Supreme Court has declared different things a basic features. Prominent among them are the following :

  ★ Supremacy of the Constitution. ★ Rule of law. ★ The principle of separation of powers. ★ The objectives specified in the Preamble to the Constitution.

- Judicial review; Art. 32.
- Federalism.

★ Secularism. ★ The Sovereign, Democratic, Republican structure.
- Freedom and dignity of the individual.
- Unity and integrity of the Nation.
- The Principle of equality, not every feature of equality, but the quintessence of equal justice.
- The ' essence' of fundamental rights in Part III.
- The concept of social and economic justice to build a Welfare State.
- The balance between fundamental rights and directive principles.
- The Parliamentary system of Government.
- The principle of free and fair elections.
- Limitations upon the amending power conferred by Art. 368.
- Independence of the Judiciary.
- Effective access to justice.
- Powers of the Supreme Court under Arts. 32,136,141,142.

18. Executive of the Union

The President

- President is the head of the Union Executive.
- The President of India is indirectly elected by an electoral college, in accordance with the system of proportional representation by means of the single transferable vote.
- The electoral college for the President consists of :

★ The elected members of both Houses of Parliament; ★ The elected members of the Legislative Assemblies of the states; and ★ The elected members of the Legislative Assemblies of Union Territories of Delhi and Pondicherry (now Puduchery) {Ref.:Art. 54}.
- In the President's election vote value of an

$$\text{MLA} = \frac{\text{Total population of the state}}{\text{Total number of elected members of state}} \div 1000$$

- In the President's election vote value of an

$$\text{MP} = \frac{\text{The sum of vote value of elected members of all the Legislative Assemblies}}{\text{The sum of elected members of both the houses of Parliament}}$$

- **Indirect election of the President is supported on two grounds :**

★ Direct election by a large electorate of people would be very costly.

★ Real power is vested in the Ministry, so , it would be anomalous to elect the President directly without giving him real powers.

Qualifications for election as President are :

★ Be a citizen of India; ★ Have completed the age of thirty-five years; ★ Be qualified for election as a member of the House of the People; and

★ Must not hold any office of profit under the Government of India or the Government of any State or under any local or other authority subject to the Control of any of the said Governments {Art. 58}

➢ A sitting President or Vice- President of the Union or the Governor of any state or a Minister either for the Union or for any state is not disqualified for election as President {Ref.:Art 58}

➢ The President's term of office is five years from the date on which he enters upon his office.

➢ President can submit resignation in writing under his hand addressed to the Vice-President of India.

➢ The only ground for impeachment of President specified in Art 61(1) is 'violation' of the Constitution.

➢ An impeachment is a quasi-judicial procedure in Parliament.

➢ Either House may prefer the charge of violation of the Constitution by the President provided that :

★ A resolution containing the proposal is moved after a 14 days' notice in writing signed by not less than 1/4 of the total number of members of that House; and

★ The resolution is then passed by a majority of not less than 2/3 of the total membership of the House.

★ Charge preferred by one House is investigated by the other House.

➢ The President has a right to appear and to be represented at such investigation.

➢ If a resolution is passed by not less than 2/3 of the total membership of the investigating House declaring that the charge had sustained, the President shall be removed from office {Ref.: Art. 61}.

➢ The President shall not be a member of either House of Parliament or of a House of the Legislature of any State.

➢ If a member of either House of Parliament or a House of the Legislature of any State is elected President, he shall be deemed to have vacated his seat in that House.

➢ A vacancy in the office of the President can be caused in any of the following ways :

★ On the expiry of his term of five years. ★ By his death. ★ By his resignation. ★ On his removal by impeachment. ★Otherwise, e. g. on the setting aside of his election as President.

➢ An election to the office of the President must be completed before the expiration of the term.

➢ The outgoing President continues to hold office, notwithstanding that his term has expired, until his successor enters upon the office {Ref.: Art 56 (1) (c)}. There is no scope for the Vice-President getting a chance to act as President in this case.

➢ If vacancy arises other than by expiry of the term an election to fill the vacancy must be held within six months from the date of occurrence of the vacancy.

➢ If a mid-term vacancy arises in the office of the President, Vice-President acts as President until a new President is elected.

Presidents of India

S.	Name	Tenure
1.	Dr. Rajendra Prasad (1884-1963)	26 Jan., 1950–13 May, 1962
2.	Dr. S. Radhakrishnan (1888-1975)	13 May, 1962–13 May, 1967
3.	Dr. Zakir Hussain (1897-1969)	13 May, 1967–3 May, 1969
4.	Sri V. V. Giri (1894-1980)	24 Aug., 1969–24 Aug., 1974
5.	Dr. Fakhruddin Ali Ahmed (1905-1977)	24 Aug., 1974–11 Feb., 1977
6.	Sri N. Sanjeeva Reddy (1913-1996)	25 July, 1977–25 July, 1982
7.	Giani Zail Singh (1916-1994)	25 July, 1982–25 July, 1987
8.	Sri R. Venkataraman (1910-2009)	25 July, 1987–25 July, 1992
9.	Dr. Shankar Dayal Sharma (1918-1999)	25 July, 1992–25 July, 1997
10.	Sri K. R. Narayanan (1920-2005)	25 July, 1997–25 July, 2002
11.	Dr. A.P.J. Abdul Kalam(b. 1931)	25 July, 2002–25 July, 2007
12.	Smt. Pratibha Devi Singh Patil (b. 1934)	25 July, 2007 –25 July, 2012
13.	Sri Pranab Mukherjee	25 July, 2012– —

Powers of President

Administrative power

Oath and Resignation

Post	Oath	Resignation
President	Chief Justice of SC	Vice President
V. President	President	President
Governor	Chief Justice of High Court	President
ChiefJustice of India	President	President
P. Minister	President	President
Speaker, Lok Sabha	no oath	Deputy Speaker

➢ The President is the formal head of the administration. All executive actions of the Union are expressed to be taken in the name of the President. {Ref. : Art. 77}

➢ All officers of the Union are the President's subordinates and he or she has a right to be informed of the affairs of the Union {Art. 78,53(1)}.

➢ The President shall have the power to appoint and remove high dignitories including :

★ The Prime Minister of India
★ Other Ministers of the Union
★ The Attorney-General for India
★ The Comptroller and Auditor General of India✦
★ The Judges of the Supreme Court✦
★ The Judges of the High Courts of the states✦
★ The Governors of states✦
★ The Chief Election Commissioner✦

✦ *can be removed from office through special constituional provisions (by impeachment)*

Military power

➢ The Supreme command of the Defence Forces is vested in the President of India, but the Parliament can regulate or control the exercise of such powers {Ref : Art. 53(2)}.

- Certain acts cannot be done by the President without approaching Parliament for sanction, e.g. acts which involved the expenditure of money {Ref. : Art. 114(3)}, such as the raising, training and maintenance of the Defence Forces.

Diplomatic power :

- The President is empowered to negotiate treaties and agreements with other countries on the advice of his Ministers , subject to ratification by Parliament.
- President of India represents India in International affairs, appoints Indian representatives to other countries and receives diplomatic representatives of other States.

Legislative power :

- President has the power to summon or prorogue the Houses of Parliament and to dissolve the Lok Sabha. {Ref. : Art. 85}
- He also has the power to summon a joint sitting of both Houses of Parliament in case of a deadlock between them {Ref: Art. 108}.
- The President addresses both Houses of Parliament assembled together, at the first session after each general election to the Lok Sabha and at the commencement of the first session of each year.
- The President has the right to address either Houses or their joint sitting, at any time and to require the attendance of members for this purpose [Art. 86(1)]
- In the Rajya Sabha 12 members are nominated by the President from persons having special knowledge or practical experience of literature, science, art and social service {Ref : Art. 80(1)}.
- The President is empowered to nominate not more than two Anglo-Indian members to the Lok Sabha, if that community is not adequately represented in that House {Ref. : Art. 331}.
- Previous sanction or recommendation of the President is required for introducing legislation on following matters :

  ★ A Bill for the formation of new states or the alteration of boundaries, of existing states {Ref. : Art. 3}. ★ A Bill providing for any of the matters specified in art 31A (1) ★ A money Bill {Ref.: Art. 117(1)}. ★ A Bill involving expenditure from the Consolidated Fund of India {Ref.: Art. 117(3)}. ★ A Bill affecting taxation in which States are interested. ★ State Bills imposing restrictions upon the freedom of trade {Ref.:Art. 304}.
- A Bill becomes an Act of the Indian Parliament only after it receives the assent of the President.
- When a Bill is presented to the President for assent :
  - ★ He may declare his assent to the Bill; or
  - ★ He may withhold his assent to the Bill; or
  - ★ He may, in the case of Bills other than Money Bills return the Bill for reconsideration of the Houses, with or without a message suggesting amendments. If the Bill is passed again by both Houses of Parliament with or without amendment and again presented to the President it would be obligatory upon him to declare his assent to it {Ref.: Art. 111}.

- The veto power of the Indian President is a combination of the absolute, suspensive and pocket vetos.
- President of India has the power of disallowance or return for reconsideration of a Bill of the state legislature, which are reserved for his consideration by the Governor of the State {Ref.: Art. 201}. A Money Bill so reserved, can not be returned by the President.
- It is not obligatory upon the President to give his assent even to the Bills reconsidered by the state legislature {Ref.: Art. 201}.
- The President can legislate by Ordinances at a time when it is not possible to have a Parliamentary enactment on the subject, immediately {Ref.: Art. 123}.

Pardoning Power :

- President as well as the Governors possess power to grant pardon {Ref.: Arts. 72,161}
- Pardon rescinds (abrogates or revokes) both the sentence and the conviction and absolve the offender from all punishment and disqualifications.
- Commutation merely substitutes one form of punishment for another of a lighter character.
- Remission reduces the amount of sentence without changing its character.
- Respite means awarding a lesser sentence instead of the penalty prescribed in view of pregnancy of a woman offender etc.
- Reprieve means a stay of execution of a sentence, e.g. pending a proceeding for pardon or commutation.

Comparison Between Pardoning Powers of the President and a Governor

- President has the power to grant pardon, reprieve, respite, suspension, remission or commutation, in respect of punishment or sentence by court-martial. Governor has no such power.
- President's powers extend up to the executive power of the union. Governor's powers extend up to the executive power of the state.
- Governor has no power to pardon in case of sentence of death, but he can suspend, remit or commute a sentence of death. Only President can pardon a death sentence.

Emergency power :

- The President has extraordinary powers to deal with a situation of emergency.

Miscellaneous powers :

- The President has the Constitutional authority to make rules and regulations relating to various matters.
- He/she has the power to give instruction to a Governor to promulgate an Ordinance if a Bill containing the same provisions requires previous sanction of the President.
- President has the power to refer any question of Public importance for the opinion of the Supreme Court.
- President has the power to appoint certain commissions for the purpose of reporting on specific matters, such as, Commissions to report on the

administration of Scheduled Areas and welfare of Scheduled Tribes and backward classes; the Finance Commission; Commission on Official Language; an Inter-State Council.

- ➢ President has some special powers relating to Union Territories or territories which are directly administered by the Union.
- ➢ The President shall have certain special powers in respect of the administration of Scheduled Area and Tribes, and Tribal Area in Assam.
- ➢ The President has certain special powers and responsibilities regarding the administration of the Scheduled Caste.

The Vice-President

- ➢ Vice-President is indirectly elected by means of single transferable vote.
- ➢ State Legislatures do not take part in the election of Vice-President.
- ➢ The electoral college for Vice-President consists of the members of both Houses of Parliament {Ref.:Art. 66(1)}.
- ➢ **To be elected as Vice-President of India a person must be :**
  ★ A citizen of India. ★ Over 35 years of Age. ★ Must not hold an office of profit save that of President, Vice-President, Governor or Minister for the Union or a state {Ref.: Art. 66}. ★ Qualified for election as a member of the Rajya Sabha.
- ➢ In case a member of the Legislature is elected Vice-President, he shall be deemed to have vacated his seat in the House to which he belongs.
- ➢ Term of the office of Vice-President is five years from the date on which he enters upon his office. Office of Vice- President may terminate earlier than the fixed term either by resignation or by removal.
- ➢ A formal impeachment is not required for Vice-President's removal.
- ➢ Vice-President can be removed by a resolution of the Rajya Sabha passed by a majority of its members and agreed to by the Lok Sabha {Ref. : Art 67}.
- ➢ A sitting Vice-President is eligible for re-election. Dr. S. Radhakrishnan was elected as the Vice-President of India for a second term in 1957.
- ➢ No functions are attached to the office of the Vice-President. The normal function of the Vice-President is to act as the ex-officio Chairman of the Rajya Sabha.
- ➢ If any vacancy occurs in the office of the President ,Vice- President acts as President until a new President is elected and enters upon his office {Ref.:Art. 65(1)}.
- ➢ For the first time during the 15-day visit of Dr. Rajendra Prasad to the Soviet Union in June 1960, the then Vice-President, Dr. S. Radhakrishnan acted as the President owing to the 'inability' of the President to discharge his duties.
- ➢ The power to determine when the President is unable to discharge his duties or when he should resume his duties is understood to belong to the President himself.
- ➢ If the offices of both the President and the Vice-President fall vacant by reason of death, resignation, removal etc. the Chief Justice of India or in his absence the senior most Judge of the Supreme Court acts as President.

➢ For the first time in 1969 when the President Dr. Zakir Hussian died and the Vice-President Shri V. V. Giri resigned, the Chief Justice Md. Hidayatullah acted as President.

➢ When the Vice-President acts as President, he gets the emoluments of the President; otherwise, he gets the salary of the Chairman of the Rajya Sabha. When the Vice-President acts as President, the Deputy Chairman of the Rajya Sabha acts as its Chairman [Art. 91].

➢ Determination of doubts and disputes relating to the election of a President or Vice-President is described in Art. 71. Main provisions are as follows :

★ Such disputes are decided by the Supreme Court whose jurisdiction is exclusive and final. ★ No such dispute can be raised on the ground of any vacancy in the electoral college. ★ If the election of the President or the Vice-President is declared void by the Supreme Court, acts done by him prior to the date of such decision of the Supreme Court is not invalidated. ★ Matters other than the decision of such disputes are regulated by law made by Parliament.

The Prime Minister and The Union Council Of Ministers

➢ In a parliamentary system of Government, the Prime Minister occupies a unique position as the most powerful functionary who controls both the Parliament and the Executive.

➢ Prime Minister is appointed by the President. Other ministers are appointed and / or dismissed by the President on the advice of the Prime Minister.

➢ Prime Minister, must be the leader of the party in majority in the Lok Sabha or a person who can win the confidence of the majority in that House.

➢ As the head of the Council of Ministers, the Prime Minister (PM) is the head of the Government. Also, he / she is the leader of his / her party or / and of a coalition of parties in Parliament and usually the Leader of the Popular House.

➢ The PM enjoys large powers of patronage. All the ministers are appointed at his / her recommendation and stand dismissed at his / her demand.

➢ The PM allots work among the ministers. Also, he / she can change their portfolios at will.

➢ The PM is the channel of communication between the Council of Ministers and the President.

➢ Ministers get the salaries and allowances etc. as payable to members of parliament. In addition they get a sumptuary allowance at a varying scale and a residence, free of rent. Cabinet Ministers attend meeting of the Cabinet.

➢ Ministers of State are not members of the Cabinet and they can attend a Cabinet Meeting only if invited to attend any particular meeting.

➢ A Deputy Minister assists the Minister in discharge of his duties and takes no part in Cabinet meetings.

➢ There is no bar to the appointment of a non- MP as Minister, but he cannot continue as Minister for more than 6 months unless he secures a seat in either House of Parliament.

- Though the ministers are collectively responsible to the legislature, they are individually responsible to the President.
- A Minister can take part in the proceedings of both Lok Sabha and Rajya Sabha, but he / she can vote only if he / she is a member of that House.

The Attorney-General for India

- The Attorney-General is the first Law Officer of the Government of India, who gives advice on legal matters and performs other duties of a legal character as assigned to him by the President.
- The Attorney-General for India is appointed by the President and holds office during the pleasure of the President. He must have the same qualifications as are required to be a judge of the Supreme Court.
- He discharges the functions conferred on him by the Constitution or any other law {Ref.: Art. 76}.
- The Attorney-General for India is not a member of the Cabinet. But he has the right to speak in the Houses of Parliament or in any Committee thereof, but he has no right to vote {Ref.: Art 88}.
- He is entitled to the privileges of a member of Parliament [Art. 105(4)]. In the performance of his official duties, the Attorney-General has the right of audience in all Courts in the territory of India.
- He is not a whole-time counsel for the Government nor a Government servant.

The Comptroller & Auditor General of India

- The CAG controls the entire financial system of the Union as well as the States {Ref.: Art. 148 }.
- Though appointed by the President, the Comptroller and Auditor-General can be removed only on an address from both Houses of Parliament on the ground of proved misbehaviour or incapacity.
- His salary and conditions of service are laid down by Parliament and can not be varied to his disadvantage during his term of office.
- The term of office of the Comptroller and Auditor-General (CAG) is 6 years from the date on which he assumes office.
- CAG vacates office on attaining the age of 65 years even without completing the 6-year term. He can resign by writing under his hand, addressed to the President of India. He can be removed by impeachment {Ref.: Arts. 148(1); 124(4)}.
- His salary is equal to that of a Judge of the Supreme Court.
- Other conditions of his service are similar to an I. A. S. of the rank of Secretary to the Government of India.
- He is disqualified for any further Government office after retirement.
- The salaries, etc. of the Comptroller and Auditor-General and his staff and the administrative expenses of his office are charged upon the Consolidated Fund of India and thus non-votable {Ref.: Art. 148 (6)}.
- The main duties of the Comptroller and Auditor General are :

  ★ To audit and report on all expenditure from the Consolidated Fund of India and of each state and each Union Territory having a Legislative Assembly as to whether such expenditure has been in accordance with the law. ★ To audit and report on all expenditure from the Contingency

Funds and Public Accounts of the Union and of the states. ★ To audit and report on all trading manufacturing profit and loss accounts etc. kept by any department of the Union or a state. ★ To see that rules and procedures in that behalf are designed to secure an effective check on the assessment, collection and proper allocation of revenue. ★ To audit and report on the receipts and expenditure of all bodies and authorities substantially financed from the Union or State revenues, Government companies; and other corporations or bodies, if so required by the laws relating to such corporations or bodies.

19. The Parliament of India

➢ The Parliament of India consists of the President, the Lok Sabha and the Rajya Sabha. {Ref.: Art. 79}.

➢ The President is a part of the Legislature, even though he or she does not sit in Parliament.

➢ The main functions of Parliament are :
★ Providing the cabinet. ★ Control of the Cabinet. ★ Criticism of the Cabinet and of individual Minister. ★ Parliament secures the information authoritatively. ★ Legislation i. e. making laws {Ref.: Arts. 107; 108; 245}
★ Financial control.

➢ Bill passed by the House of Parliament cannot become law without the President's assent.

Rajya Sabha and Lok Sabha

➢ The Rajya Sabha is composed of not more than 250 members of whom 12 are nominated by the President and 238 are representatives of the states and the Union Territories elected by the method of indirect election {Ref.: Art 80}.

➢ The 12 nominated members are chosen by the President from amongst persons specialised in science, art, literature and social service.

➢ Representatives of each State are elected by the elected members of the Legislative Assembly of the state in accordance with the system of proportional representation by means of the single transferable vote.

➢ Prescribed composition of the Lok Sabha is :
★ Not more than 530 representatives of the States; ★ Not more than 20 representatives of Union Territories. ★ Not more than 2 members of the Anglo-Indian community, nominated by the President.

➢ The representatives of the States are directly elected by the people of the States on the basis of adult suffrage.

➢ Every citizen who is not less than 18 years of age and is not otherwise disqualified is entitled to vote at such election {Ref.: Art. 326}.

➢ There is no reservation for any minority community other than the Scheduled Castes and the Scheduled Tribes {Ref.: Arts. 330,341, 342}.

➢ The Council of State is not subject to dissolution. It is a permanent body. 1/3 of its members retire on the expiration of every second year.

➢ The normal term of the Lok Sabha is 5 years, but it may be dissolved earlier by the President.

➢ The normal term of Lok Sabha can be extended by an Act passed by Parliament itself during Emergency.

- ➢ The extension cannot be made for a period exceeding one year at a time.
- ➢ Such extension cannot continue beyond a period of six months after the proclamation of Emergency ceases to operate.
- ➢ Parliament must meet at least twice a year and not more than six months shall elapse between two sessions of Parliament.
- ➢ A session is the period of time between the first meeting of Parliament and prorogation of Parliament.
- ➢ The period between prorogation of Parliament and its re-assembly in a new session is called recess. Within a session, there are a number of daily sittings separated by adjournments which postpone the further consideration of a business for a specified time.

  The sitting of a House can be terminated by dissolution, prorogation or adjournment :

  ★ While the powers of dissolution and prorogation are exercised by the President on the advice of the Council of Ministers. The power to adjourn the daily sittings of Lok Sabha and Rajya Sabha belongs to the Speaker and the Chairman, respectively.

  ★ A dissolution brings Lok Sabha to an end so that there must be a fresh election while prorogation merely terminates a session. Adjournment does not put an end to the session of Parliament but merely postpones the further transaction of business for a specified time, hours, days or weeks.

  ★ On dissolution of the Lok Sabha all matters pending before the House lapse. If these matters have to be pursued, they must be re-introduced in the next House after fresh election.

  ★ But a Bill pending in the Rajya Sabha which has not yet been passed by the Lok Sabha shall not lapse on dissolution.

  ★ A dissolution does not affect a joint sitting of the two Houses, if the President has notified his intention to hold a joint sitting before the dissolution {Ref.: Art. 108(5)}.

- ➢ Adjournment has no such effect on pending business.

  Qualifications for becoming a member of Parliament are :

  ★ Must be a citizen of India. ★ Must not be less than 25 years of age in the case of Lok Sabha and 30 years in the case of Rajya Sabha. ★ Additional qualifications may be prescribed by Parliament by law {Ref.: Art. 84}.

  A person can be disqualified for being a member of either House of Parliament, if :

  ★ He holds any office of profit under the Government of India or the Government of any State; ★ He is of unsound mind and stands so declared by a competent Court; ★ He is not a citizen of India or has voluntarily acquired citizenship of a foreign State or is under acknowledgment or allegiance or adherence to a foreign power; ★ He is so disqualified by or under any law made by Parliament {Ref.:Art. 102}. ★ In a dispute regarding qualification the President's decision in accordance with the opinion of the Election Commission, is final {Ref.:

Art. 103}. ★ The House can declare a seat vacant if the member absents himself from all meetings of the House for a period of 60 days without permission of the house.

Speaker and Deputy Speaker of The Lok Sabha

➢ Speaker presides over the Lok Sabha.

➢ The Speaker or the Deputy Speaker, normally holds office during the life of the House, but his office may terminate earlier in any of the following ways:

★ By his ceasing to be a member of the House.

★ By resignation in writing, addressed to the Deputy Speaker, and *vice versa*.

★ By *removal* from office by a resolution, passed by a majority of all the then members of the House {Ref.: Art. 94}.

➢ A resolution to remove the speaker can not be moved unless at least 14 days notice has been given of the intention to move the resolution.

➢ While a resolution for his removal is under consideration, the Speaker can not preside but he can speak in, take part in the proceedings of the House and vote except in the case of equality of votes {Ref.: Art. 96}.

➢ At other meetings of the House the Speaker can not vote in the first instance, but can exercise a casting vote in case of equality of votes.

➢ The Speaker has the final power to maintain order within the Lok Sabha and to interpret its Rules of Procedures.

➢ In the absence of a quorum the Speaker adjourns the House or suspends the meeting until there is a quorum.

➢ The Speaker's conduct in regulating the procedure or maintaining order in the House can not be questioned in a Court {Ref.: Art. 122}.

➢ The Speaker presides over a joint sitting of the two Houses of Parliament {Ref.: Art. 118(4)}.

➢ When a Money Bill is transmitted from the Lok Sabha to the Rajya Sabha the Speaker may certify that it is a Money Bill {Ref.: Art. 110(4)}.

➢ The decision of the Speaker on whether a Bill is Money Bill is final.

➢ While the office of Speaker is vacant or the Speaker is absent from a sitting of the House, the Deputy Speaker presides, except when a resolution for his *own* removal is under consideration.

Chairman and Deputy Chairman of the Rajya Sabha

➢ Vice-President of India is *ex-officio* Chairman of the Rajya Sabha and functions as the Presiding Officer of that House so long as he does not officiate as the President.

➢ When the Chairman acts as the President of India, the duties of the Chairman are performed by the Deputy Chairman.

➢ The Chairman may be removed from his office only if he is removed from the office of the Vice-President.

➢ The powers of Chairman in the Rajya Sabha are similar to those of the Speaker in the Lok Sabha except that the Speaker has certain special powers like certifying a Money Bill, or presiding over a joint sitting of the two Houses.

Privileges of Parliament

➢ The privileges of each House can be divided into two groups :
- ★ Those which are enjoyed by the members individually.
- ★ Those which belong to each House of Parliament, as a collective body.

➢ The privileges enjoyed by the members individually are :
- ★ *Freedom from Arrest* exempts a member from arrest during the continuance of a meeting of the House or Committee thereof of which he is a member and during a period of 40 days before and after such meeting or sitting.
  - ♦ This immunity is confined to arrest in civil cases and not in criminal cases or under the law of Preventive Detention.
  - ♦ A member cannot be summoned, without the leave of the House to give evidence as a witness while Parliament is in session.
- ★ There is *Freedom of Speech* within the walls of each House.
  - ♦ The limitation on freedom of speech is that no discussion can take place in Parliament with respect to the conduct of any judge of the Supreme Court or of a High Court in the discharge of his duties except upon a motion for removal of the judge {Ref.: Art. 121}.

➢ The privileges of the House *collectively* are :
- ★ The right to publish debates and proceedings and to restrain publication by others.
- ★ The right to exclude others.
- ★ The right to regulate internal affairs of the House.
- ★ The right to publish Parliamentary misbehaviour.
- ★ The right to punish members and outsiders for breach of its privileges.

The Legislative Procedures in Parliament

➢ The different stages in the legislative procedure in Parliament relating to Bills *other than Money Bills* are as follows :

1. *Introduction* of a Bill in either House of Parliament 2. *Motions after introduction* 3. *Report by Select Committee* 4. *Passing of the Bill* in the House where it was introduced 5. *Passage in the other House* 6. *President's Assent*

Money Bills and Financial Bills

➢ A Bill is called Money Bill if it contains only provisions dealing with all or any of the following matters :

★ The imposition, abolition, remission, alteration or regulation of any tax. ★ The regulation of the borrowing of money by the Government. ★ The custody of or the withdrawal of moneys from the Consolidated Fund of India. ★ The appropriation of moneys out of the Consolidated Fund of India. ★ The declaring of any expenditure to be expenditure charged on the Consolidated fund of India. ★ The receipt of money on account of the Consolidated Fund of India or the public account of India or the custody or issue of such money or the audit of the accounts of the Union or of a State.

➢ The procedure for passing of Money Bills in Parliament is :

➢ A Money Bill can not be introduced in the Rajya Sabha.

★ After a Money Bill has been passed by the Lok Sabha, it is transmitted to the Rajya Sabha (with the Speaker's certificate that it is a Money Bill). ★ The Rajya Sabha can neither reject a Money Bill nor amend it. It must, within a period of fourteen days from the date of receipt of the Bill, return the Bill to the Lok Sabha with its recommendations. Lok Sabha may accept or reject all or any of the recommendations of the Rajya Sabha. ★ It is upto the Lok Sabha to accept or reject the recommendations of the Rajya Sabha. If the Lok Sabha accepts any of the recommendations the Money Bill is deemed to have been passed by both Houses with the amendment recommended by the Rajya Sabha and accepted by the Lok Sabha. ★ If a Money Bill is not returned by the Rajya Sabha within fourteen days, it shall be deemed to have been passed by both Houses in the form in which it was passed by the Lok Sabha {Ref.: Art. 109}.

➢ Only those Financial Bills are Money Bills which bear the certificate of the Speaker as such.

➢ Financial Bills which do not receive the Speaker's certificate are of two classes (Art. 117) :

(a) A Bill which contains any of the matters specified in Art. 110 but does not consist *solely* of those matters. It can be introduced in Lok Sabha only on the recommendation of President. Rajya Sabha can amend or reject such Bills.

(b) Any Ordinary Bill which contains provisions involving expenditure from the Consolidated Fund {Ref.: Art. 117(3)}.

Joint Sittings

➢ The President can summon Lok Sabha and Rajya Sabha for a joint sitting in case of disagreement between the two Houses in following ways :

If, after a Bill has been passed by one House and transmitted to the other House—

★ the Bill is rejected by the other House;

★ the Houses have finally disagreed about the amendments to be made in the Bill; or

★ more than six months have elapsed from the date of the reception of the Bill by the other House without the Bill being passed by it.

➢ The Speaker presides the joint sitting. In the absence of the Speaker, Deputy Speaker or Chairman of Rajya Sabha or Deputy Chairman of Rajya Sabha or a person chosen by the MPs may preside {Art. 118(4)} in the same order.

Financial legislation in Parliament

➢ At the beginning of every financial year, on behalf of the President of India, a statement of the estimated receipts and expenditure of the Government of India for that year is laid before both the Houses of Parliament.

➢ This is known as the "annual financial statement' (i.e., the 'Budget') [Ref. Art. 112]

➢ It also states the ways and means of meeting the estimated expenditure.

➢ The Annual Financial Statement or the Budget contains :

★ Estimates of expenditure. ★ Ways and means to raise the revenue. ★ An analysis of the actual receipts and expenditures of the closing year and the causes of any surplus or deficit in relation to such year. ★ An explanation of the economic policy and spending programme of the Government in the coming year and the prospects of revenue. ★ Estimates relating to expenditure charged upon the Consolidated Fund of India are not put to vote of Parliament but each House can discuss any of these estimates. ★ Estimates of other expenditure are submitted in the form of demands for grants to the Lok Sabha and it has the power to assent, or to refuse to assent to any demand.

➢ No demand for a grant can be made except on the recommendation of the President. [Ref. Art. 113]

➢ The scrutiny of budget proposals is done by the Parliament's Committee on Estimates in order to :

★ Report to the House about the effect on economy, improvements in organisation, administrative reform etc. ★ Suggest alternative policies. ★ Examine whether the money is well laid out. ★ Suggest the form in which estimates are to be presented to Parliament. ★ The report of the Estimates Committee is not debated in the House.

➢ The Comptroller and Auditor General is the guardian of the public purse and it is his function to see that not a paisa is spent without the authority of Parliament.

★ The report of the Comptroller and Auditor General laid before the Parliament, is examined by the Public Accounts Committee.

★ Public Accounts Committee is a committee of the Lok Sabha (having 15 members from that House), but seven members of the Rajya Sabha are also associated with this Committee, in order to strengthen it.

➢ Public Accounts Committee examines that :

★ The money disbursed was legally available and used for the right purpose.

★ The expenditure conforms to the authority which governs it.

★ Every re-appropriation has been made in accordance with the rules framed by competent authority.

Representation of States and Union Territories in the Rajya Sabha

State	No.	State / UT	No.
Uttar Pradesh	31	Haryana	5
Maharashtra	19	Jammu & Kashmir	4
Tamil Nadu	18	Himachal Pradesh	3
Andhra Pradesh (Telangana 7 + Seemandhra 11, Proposed)	18	Uttarakhand	3
Bihar	16	Goa	1
West Bengal	16	Manipur	1

State	No.	State / UT	No.
Karnataka	12	Nagaland	1
Gujarat	11	Sikkim	1
Madhya Pradesh	11	Tripura	1
Rajasthan	10	Arunachal Pradesh	1
Odisha (Orissa)	10	Mizoram	1
Kerala	9	Meghalaya	1
Assam	7	**Union Territories**	
Punjab	7	Delhi	3
Jharkhand	6	Puducherry	1
Chhattisgarh	5		

Representation of States and Union Territories in the Lok Sabha

State	No.	State / UT	No.
Uttar Pradesh	80	Uttarakhand	5
Maharashtra	48	Himachal Pradesh	4
Andhra Pradesh (Telangana 17 + Seemandhra 25)	42	Tripura	2
West Bengal	42	Manipur	2
Bihar	40	Meghalaya	2
Tamil Nadu	39	Goa	2
Madhya Pradesh	29	Arunachal Pradesh	2
Karnataka	28	Nagaland	1
Gujarat	26	Sikkim	1
Rajasthan	25	Mizoram	1
Odisha (Orissa)	21	**Union Territories**	
Kerala	20	Delhi	7
Jharkhand	14	Puducherry	1
Assam	14	Chandigarh	1
Punjab	13	Lakshadweep	1
Chhattisgarh	11	Dadra & Nagar Haveli	1
Haryana	10	Daman & Diu	1
Jammu & Kashmir	6	Andaman & Nicobar	1

Parliamentary Terms

Question Hour : The day's business normally begins with the Question Hour during which questions asked by the members are answered by the Ministers. The different types of question are :

(i) Starred Question is one for which an oral answer is required to be given by the Minister on the floor of the House. Supplementary decides if a question should be answered orally or otherwise. One member can ask only one starred question in a day.

(ii) Unstarred Question is one for which the Minister lays on the table a written answer. A 10-day notice has to be given to ask such questions and no supplementary questions can be asked with regard to such questions.

(iii) Short Notice Question is one for which can be asked by members on matters of public importance of an urgent nature. It is for the Speaker to decide whether the matter is of urgent nature or not. The member has also to State reasons for asking the question while serving notice.

Zero Hour : This period follows the Question Hour and it generally begins at noon. Usually the time used by the members to raise various issues for discussion.

Cut Motion : A motion that seeks reduction in the amount of a demand presented by the Government is known as a cut motion. Such motion are admitted at the Speaker's discretion. It is a device through which members (generally of the Opposition) can draw the attention of the Government to a specific grievance or problem. There are three types of cut motions :

(i) Disapproval of policy cut which is to express disapproval of the policy underlying a particular demand, says that 'the amount of the demand be reduced by Rs. 1.

(ii) Economy cut asks for a reduction of the amount of the demand by a specific amount. The aim is to affect economy in the expenditure.

(iii) Token cut : Is a device to ventilate specific grievances within the sphere of the Government's responsibility. The grievance has to be specified. Usually the motion in the form, "the amount of the demand be reduced by Rs. 100.

Adjournment Motion : It is a motion to adjourn the proceedings of the House so as to take up for discussion some matter of urgent public importance. Any member can move the motion and, if more than fifty members support the demand, the Speaker grants permission for the motion. The notice for such a motion has to be given before the commencement of the sitting on the day.

Calling Attention Motion : A member may, with prior permission of the Speaker, call the attention of a Minister to any matter of urgent public interest or ask for time to make a Statement.

Privilege Motion : It is a motion moved by a member if he feels that a Minister has committed a breach of privilege of the House or of any one or more of its members by withholding facts of a case or by giving a distorted version of acts.

Point of Order : A member may raise a point of order if the proceedings of the House do not follow the normal rules. The presiding officer decides whether the point of order raised by the member should be allowed.

Vote on Account : As there is usually a gap between the presentation of the Budget and its approval, the vote on account enables the Government to draw some amount from the Consolidated Fund of India to meet the expenses in the intervening period.

Guillotine : On the last of the allotted days at the appointed time the Speaker puts every question necessary to dispose of all the outstanding matters in connection with demands for grants. This is known as guillotine. The guillotine concludes the discussion on demands for grants.

Quorum : It is the minimum number of members whose presence is essential to transact the business of the House. Article 100 provides that the quorum of either House shall be one-tenth of the total number of members of the House.

No-Confidence Motion : According to the Constitution, the Council of Ministers stays in office only so long as it enjoys the confidence of the Lok Sabha; once the confidence is withdrawn the Government is bound to resign. The rules of parliamentary procedure accordingly provide for moving a motion to ascertain this confidence. The motion is generally known as the "no-confidence motion".

Censure Motion : A censure motion differs from a no-confidence motion in that the latter does not specify any ground on which it is based, while the former has to mention the charges against the Government for which it is being moved. A censure motion can be moved against the Council of Ministers or against an individual Minister for failing to act or for some policy. Reasons for the censure must be precisely enumerated. The Speaker decides whether or not the motion is in order, and no leave of the House is required for moving it.

Lame-duck Session : Session held when a new parliament has been elected but the old Parliament meets for the last time before it is dissolved. The lame-ducks are the members of the parliament who have not got re-elected.

Shadow Cabinet : A Parliament practice prevalent in the UK where senior members of the Opposition cover the areas of responsibility of the actual cabinet. They will form the cabinet if their party is elected to the government.

Leader of the Opposition

- Government has given statutory recognition to the leaders of the Opposition in the Lok Sabha and Rajya Sabha.
- Necessary legislation to this effect was passed by parliament in 1977 and the Rules framed thereunder were brought into effect on November 1, 1977.
- For the first time Y.B. Chavan of the Congress (I) was given the official status of Leader of the Opposition in the Lok Sabha with the rank of a Cabinet Minister.

The Funds

- All money received by or on behalf of the Government of India is credited to either the Consolidated Fund of India, or the Public account of India.
- The consolidated Fund of India consists of :

  ★ All revenues received by the Government of India ★ All loans raised by the Government of India. ★ All money received by Government in repayment of loans {Ref.: Art 266(1)}. ★ All other public money received by or on behalf of the Government of India is credited to the Public Accounts of India.

- Art. 267 of the Constitution empowers Parliament and the Legislature of a state to create a 'Contingency Fund' for India or for a State, as the case may be for meeting *unforeseen expenditure*.

Extents of the Powers of Rajya Sabha

- A money Bill can not be introduced in Rajya Sabha.
- The Rajya Sabha has no power to reject or amend a Money Bill.
- The Speaker of the Lok Sabha has sole and final power of deciding whether a Bill is a Money Bill.
- Though the Rajya Sabha can discuss, it cannot vote for the public expenditure and demands for grants are not submitted for the vote of the Rajya Sabha.
- The Council of Ministers is responsible to the Lok Sabha and not to the Rajya Sabha {Ref.: Art. 75(3)}.
- Rajya Sabha suffers by reason of its numerical minority, in case of a joint session to resolve a deadlock between the two Houses [Art. 108(4)].
- Parliament can legislate on a State subject only if Rajya Sabha resolves for this by a 2/3 majority. [Ref. : Art. 249]
- New All-India services can be created only after Rajya Sabha resolves for this with a 2/3 majority. [Ref. : Art. 312]

20. Executive of the States

The Governor

- The Governor of a state is appointed by the President and holds his office at the pleasure of the President.
- Qualifications for the post of Governor are :
  ★ Should be a citizen of India. ★ Should be over 35 years of age. ★ Must not hold other office of profit and should not be a Member of the Legislature of the Union or of any State {Ref. : Art. 158}.
- If a Member of a Legislature is appointed Governor, he ceases to be a Member immediately upon such appointment .
- The normal term of a Governor's office is five years, but it may be terminated earlier by :
  - ★ Dismissal by the President {Ref. : Art. 156 (1)};
  - ★ Resignation {Art. 156(2)}.
- There is no bar to a person being appointed Governor more than once.

Why an appointed Governor

- Because it would save the country from the evil consequences of still another election , run on personal issues.
- If the Governor is elected by direct vote, then he might consider himself superior to the Chief Minister, leading to *friction* between the two.
- The expenses involved and the elaborate machinery of election would not match the powers of Governor.
- A second rate man of the party may get elected as Governor.
- Through an appointed Governor the Union Government can maintain its control over the states.
- The method of election may encourage separatist tendencies.

Powers of Governor

The Governor has no diplomatic or military powers like the President, but he has *executive, legislative* and *judicial powers* analogous to those of the President.

Executive : Governor has the power to appoint Council of Ministers, Advocate General and the members of the State Public Service Commission.

- The Ministers as well as Advocate General hold office during the pleasure of the Governor but the Members of the State Public Service Commission can be removed only by the President on the report of the Supreme Court and in some cases on the happening of certain disqualifications {Ref.: Art. 317}.
- The Governor has no power to appoint Judges of the State High Court but he is entitled to be consulted by the President in the matter {Ref.: Art. 217(1)}.
- Like the President the Governor has the power to nominate members of the Anglo-Indian community to the Legislative Assembly of his State.
- To the Legislative Council, the Governor can nominate persons having special knowledge or practical experience of literature, science, art, co-operative movement and social service {Ref.: Art. 171(5)}.
  - ★ 'Co-operative movement' is not included in the corresponding list for Rajya Sabha.

Legislative : Governor is a part of the State Legislature and he has the right of addressing and sending messages, and of summoning, proroguing and dissolving the State Assembly.

Judicial : The Governor has the power to grant pardons, reprieves, respites, or remission etc. of punishments {Ref.: Art. 161}.

Emergency :The Governor has no emergency powers to counter external aggression or armed rebellion.

- He has the power to report to the President if Government of the State cannot be carried on in accordance with the Constitution {Ref.:Art. 356}.

Chief Minister and The State Council of Ministers

- Chief Minister is the head of the State Council of Ministers.
- The Chief Minister is appointed by the Governor.
- The other Ministers are appointed by the Governor on the advice of Chief Minister.
- Any person may be appointed a Minister but he must become member of the legislature within six months of such appointment.
- The Council of Ministers is collectively responsible to the Legislative Assembly of the state but individually responsible to the Governor.
- The relation between the Governor and his Ministers is similar to that between the President and his Ministers.

Discretionary functions of the Governor

- The functions which are specially required by the Constitution to be exercised by the Governor in his discretion are :
  - ★ The Governor of Assam can determine the amount payable by

the State of Assam to the District Council, as royalty accruing from licences for minerals. ★ Where a Governor is appointed administrator of an adjoining Union Territory, he can function as such administrator independently of his Council of Ministers. ★ The President may direct that the Governor of Maharashtra or Gujarat shall have a special responsibility for taking steps for the development of Vidarbha and Saurashtra. ★ The Governor of Nagaland has similar special responsibility with respect to law and order in that State. ★ Governor of Manipur has special responsibility to secure the proper functioning of the Committee of the Legislative Assembly consisting of the members elected from the Hill Areas of that State. ★ Governor of Sikkim has special responsibility for peace and equitable arrangement for ensuring the social and economic advancement. ★ The Governor has the power to dismiss an individual Minister at any time. ★ Governor can dismiss a Council of Ministers or the Chief Minister, *only* when the Council of Ministers has lost confidence of the Legislative Assembly and the Governor does not think fit to dissolve the Assembly.

The Advocate General

➢ Each state has an Advocate-General, an official corresponding to the Attorney-General of India and having similar functions for the State.

➢ He is appointed by the Governor of the state and holds office during the pleasure of the Governor.

➢ Only a person who is qualified to be a judge of a High Court can be appointed Advocate-General. He receives such remuneration as the Governor may determine.

➢ He has the right to speak and to take part in the proceedings of, but no right to vote in, the Houses of the Legislature of the state {Ref. : Art. 177}.

The State Legislature

➢ Some states have bi-cameral Legislature (having two Houses). The Seven States having two Houses are Andhra Pradesh, Telangana, Bihar, Karnataka, Maharashtra, Uttar Pradesh and Jammu & Kashmir.

➢ In the remaining States, the Legislature is uni-cameral and has the Legislative Assembly only.

The Strength of Legislative Councils

State	Total Seats
Andhra Pradesh	50
Telangana	40
Bihar	75
Jammu & Kashmir	36
Karnataka	75
Maharashtra	78
Uttar Pradesh	99

➢ For creation or abolition of Legislative Council, the Legislative Assembly of the State should pass a resolution by a special majority followed by an Act of Parliament {Ref. : Art. 169}.

➢ The size of the Legislative Council may vary, but its membership should not be more than 1/3 of the membership of the Legislative Assembly but not less than 40.

➢ Legislative Council is a partly nominated and partly elected body.

- Election to the Legislative Council is indirect and in accordance with proportional representation by single transferable vote.
- 5/6 of the total number of members of the Council is indirectly elected and 1/6 is nominated by the Governor.
- 1/3 of the total members of the Council is elected by *local bodies* such as municipalities, district boards.
- 1/12 is elected by *graduates* of three years' standing residing in the State.
- 1/12 is elected by *teachers* of secondary schools or higher educational institutions.
- 1/3 is elected by members of the Legislative Assembly from amongst persons who are not members of the Assembly.
- The remainder is nominated by the Governor from persons specialised in literature, science, art, co-operative movement and social service.
- The Court cannot question the *bona fides* or propriety of the Governor's nomination in any case.
- The Legislative Assembly of each State is directly elected on the basis of adult suffrage from territorial constituencies.
- The Number of members of the Assembly can not be more than 500 nor less than 60.
- The Assembly in Mizoram and Goa have only 40 members each. While the Assembly in Sikkim has only 32 members.
- Governor can nominate one member of the Anglo-Indian community in the Assembly {Ref.: Art. 333}.
- The duration of the Legislative Assembly is five years. It may be dissolved sooner than five years, by the Governor.
- The term of five years may be extended by the Parliament in case of a Proclamation of Emergency by the President for not more than one year at a time {Ref.: Art. 172(1).}
- Legislative Council (Vidhan Parishad) is a permanent body like the Council of State (Rajya Sabha).
- The Legislative Council is not dissolved. One-third of the members of Legislative Council retire on the expiry of every second year {Ref.: Art. 172(2)}.
- A Legislative Assembly has its Speaker and Deputy Speaker and a Legislative Council has its Chairman and Deputy Chairman, and the provisions relating to them are analogous to those relating to the corresponding officers of the Union Parliament.
- Qualifications for membership of State Legislature are :
  - ★ Should be a citizen of India;
  - ★ For Legislative Assembly, not less than twenty-five years of age and for Legislative Council not less than thirty years of age;
  - ★ Should possess other qualifications prescribed in that behalf by or under any law made by Parliament {Ref.: Art. 173}.

The Strength of Legislative Assembly in States/U.Ts

State/U.T.	Strength	State/U.T.	Strength
Uttar Pradesh	403	Haryana	90
West Bengal	294	Jharkhand	81
Maharashtra	288	Jammu-Kashmir	76
Bihar	243	Uttarakhand	70
Tamil Nadu	234	Delhi (NCT)	70
Madhya Pradesh	230	Himachal Pradesh	68
Karnataka	224	Arunachal Pradesh	60
Rajasthan	200	Manipur	60
Gujarat	182	Meghalaya	60
Andhra Pradesh	175	Nagaland	60
Orissa	147	Tripura	60
Kerala	140	Goa	40
Assam	126	Mizoram	40
Telangana	119	Sikkim	32
Punjab	117	Puducherry	30
Chhattisgarh	90		

Comparison of Legislative Procedures between a Bi-cameral State Legislature and the Parliament

- For Money Bills, the position is the same.
- For other Bills the only power of the Council is to interpose a *delay* of 3 months. In case of disagreement, the Bill is second time referred to the Legislative Council and this time the Council has no power to withhold the Bill for more than a month {Ref.: Art. 197(2)(b)}.

Governor's Power of veto

- When a Bill is presented before the Governor after its approval by the Houses of the Legislature, the Governor can :
  - Declare his *assent* to the Bill, in that case it would become law at once.
  - Declare that he withholds his assent to the Bill, such a Bill fails to become a law.
  - Declare that he withholds his assent to the Bill (other than a Money Bill) and the Bill is returned with a message.
  - Reserve a Bill for the consideration of the President. Such reserving is compulsory where the law in question would derogate the powers of the High Court.

Power of Governor to Promulgate Ordinances

- The Governor can promulgate Ordinance only when the Legislature, or both Houses there of, are not in session.
- It must be exercised with the aid and advice of the Council of Ministers.
- The Ordinance must be laid before the State Legislature when it reassembles.

- An Ordinance ceases to have effect after 6 weeks from the date of re-assembly, unless disapproved earlier by that Legislature.
- The Governor himself is competent to withdraw the Ordinance at any time.
- The scope of the Ordinance-promulgating power of the Governor is confined to the subjects in Lists II and III of the Seventh Schedule.
- Governor cannot promulgate Ordinances without instructions from the President if :
  - ★ A Bill containing the same provisions would require previous sanction of the President.
  - ★ Bill is required to be reserved for consideration of the President.

Privileges of State Legislature

- Privileges of State Legislature are similar to those of Union Parliament.
- Each House of the State Legislature can punish for breach of its privileges or for contempt.
- Each House is the sole judge of the question whether any of its privileges has been infringed. Court has no jurisdiction to interfere with the decision of the House on this point.
- No House of the Legislature can create any new privilege for itself. Court can determine whether the House possesses a particular privilege.

21. Special Position of Jammu & Kashmir

- The jurisdiction of the Parliament in relation to Jammu & Kashmir is confined to the Union List, and the Concurrent List.
- Residuary power belongs to the Legislature of Jammu & Kashmir.
- Proclamation of Emergency under Art. 352 on the ground of internal disturbance has no effect in the State of Jammu & Kashmir, without the concurrence of the Government of the State.
- No decision affecting the disposition of the State can be made by the Government of India, without the consent of the Government of the State.
- The Union has no power to suspend the Constitution of the State on the ground of failure to comply with the directions given by the Union under Art. 365.
- Arts. 356-357 relating to suspension of constitutional machinery have been extended to Jammu & Kashmir by the Amendment Order of 1964. But "failure" would mean failure of the constitutional machinery of Jammu & Kashmir.
- The Union has no power to make a Proclamation of Financial Emergency with respect to the State of Jammu & Kashmir under Art. 360.
- Directive Principles of States Policy *do not* apply to the State of Jammu & Kashmir.
- Jammu & Kashmir has its own Constitution made by a separate Constituent Assembly and promulgated in 1957.
- The Constitution of Jammu & Kashmir (accepting the provisions relating to the relationship of the State with the Union of India), can be amended

by an Act of the Legislative Assembly of the State, passed by not less than 2/3 majority.

➢ No alteration of the area or boundaries of Jammu & Kashmir can be made by Parliament without the consent of the Legislature of the State.

➢ The jurisdictions of the Comptroller and Auditor-General, the Election Commission, and the Special Leave jurisdiction of the Supreme Court have been extended to Jammu & Kashmir.

22. Panchayats

➢ Part IX of the Constitution envisages a three tier system of Panchayats:
  - ★ Panchayat at the village level;
  - ★ The District Panchayat at the district level;
  - ★ The Intermediate Panchayat in States where the population is above 20 lakhs.

➢ All the seats in a Panchayat is filled by direct election.

➢ The electorate is named 'Gram Sabha'.

➢ The Chairperson of each Panchayat is elected according to the law passed by a State.

➢ Seats are reserved in Panchayat for Scheduled Castes, and Scheduled Tribes in proportion to their population [Art. 243D].

➢ Out of the reserved seats, 1/3 is reserved for women belonging to Scheduled Castes and Scheduled Tribes. 1/3 of the total seats to be filled by direct election in every Panchayat is reserved for women.

➢ A State can make similar reservation for Chairpersons in the Panchayats.

➢ Every Panchayat can continue for 5 years from the date of its first meeting. It can be dissolved earlier in accordance with State law.

➢ A Panchayat reconstituted after premature dissolution, continues only for the remainder of the period. But if the remainder of the period is less than 6 months it is not necessary to hold elections.

➢ All persons above 21 years of age and qualified to be a member of the State Legislature are qualified as a member of a Panchayat [Art. 243F].

➢ Panchayats can be entrusted to prepare and implement plans for economic development and social justice.

➢ A State can authorise a Panchayat to levy, collect and appropriate taxes, duties, tolls etc.

➢ After the 73rd amendmend of the Constitution (25 April, 1993), every 5 years the States appoint a Finance Commission to review the financial position of the Panchayats and make recommendations.

➢ State Election Commission consisting of a State Election Commissioner is appointed by the Governor for superintendence, direction and control of elections to Panchayats [Art. 243K].

➢ The Community Development Programme was launched on Oct. 2, 1952.

➢ The Democratic Decentralisation was implemented for the first time in 1958 in some areas of Andhra Pradesh on experimental basis.

➢ The Panchayati Raj was introduced for the first time on Oct. 2, 1959 in Nagur District of Rajasthan by the Prime Minister Jawahar Lal Nehru.

➢ Rajasthan is the first state in India, where Panchayati Raj was implemented in the whole state.

23. Municipalities

➢ PART IXA gives a constitutional foundation to the local self government units in urban area.

➢ Most provisions for municipalities are similar to those contained in PART IX, e.g. Structure, Reservation of Seats, Functions, Sources of Income etc.

➢ *Nagar Panchayat,* is for an area being transformed from a rural area to an urban area.

➢ *Municipal Council* is for a smaller urban area.

➢ *Municipal Corporation* is for a larger urban area. The municipal corporation is the topmost urban local government.

➢ The members of a municipality are generally elected by direct election.

➢ The Legislature of a State can provide for representation in municipalities of :

★ Persons having special knowledge or experience in municipal administration. ★ Members of Lok Sabha, State Assembly, Rajya Sabha and Legislative Council. ★ The Chairpersons of Ward Committees.

Note : *If the population is 3 lacs or more Ward Committees are constituted.*

➢ Two Committees constituted for preparing development plan are :

★ A District Planning Committee at the district level

★ A Metropolitan Planning Committee at the metropolis level

24. The Supreme Court

➢ Every Judge of the Supreme Court after consulting the Chief Justice of the Supreme Court, is appointed by the President of India.

➢ In appointment of the Chief Justice of India, President can consult such Judges of the Supreme Court and the High Court as he thinks appropriate.

➢ A person is qualified for appointment as a judge of the Supreme Court, if he is :

★ A citizen of India

★ Has been a High Court Judge for at least 5 years

★ Has been an Advocate of a High Court, or two or more courts in succession for at least 10 years {Ref.: Art. 124(3)}.

➢ No minimum age or fixed period of office is prescribed for appointment as a Judge of the Supreme Court.

➢ A Judge of Supreme Court ceases to be so, on :

★ Attaining the age of 65 years; ★ Resigning in writing addressed to the President; ★ On being removed by the President. ★ The only grounds for such removal are proved misbehaviour and incapacity {Ref.: Art. 124(4)}.

- Procedure for removal or impeachment of a Supreme Court Judge :
  - ★ A motion addressed to the President signed by at least 100 members of the Lok Sabha or 50 members of the Rajya Sabha is delivered to the Speaker or the Chairman.
  - ★ The motion is investigated by a Committee of 3 (2 Judges of the Supreme Court and a distinguished Jurist).
  - ★ If the Committee finds the Judge guilty, report of Committee is considered in the House where the Motion is pending.
  - ★ If the motion is passed in each House by majority of the total membership of the House and by a majority of not less than two-thirds of the members present and voting the address is presented to the President.
- The Judge is removed after the President gives his order for removal on such address.
- The procedure for impeachment is the same for Judges of the Supreme Court and the High Courts.
- After retirement a Judge of the Supreme Court can not plead or act in any Court or before any authority within the territory of India {Ref.: Art. 124(7)}.
- Jurisdiction of the Supreme Court is three-fold :

  1. Original; 2. Appellate; and 3. Advisory.
- Disputes between different States of the Union or between Union and any state is within exclusive Original jurisdiction of the Supreme Court {Ref.: Art. 131}
- The jurisdiction of the Supreme Court to entertain an application under Art. 32 for the issue of writs for the enforcement of Fundamental Rights is treated as an 'original' jurisdiction of the Supreme Court though called Writ Jurisdiction
- The Supreme Court is the highest court of appeal from all courts in the territory of India.
- Supreme Court is the highest authority for interpretation of the Constitution.
- Supreme Court may hear appeals by granting special leave against any kind of judgement or order made by any court or tribunal (except a military tribunal).
- Under advisory jurisdiction, Supreme Court can give its *opinion* on any matter of law or fact of public importance referred to it by the President. {Ref.: Art. 143}.

25. The High Court

- The High Court is the head of the Judiciary in the State.
- Every Judge of a High Court is appointed by the President.
- In making appointment as a High Court Judge, President can consult the Chief Justice of India, the Governor of the State and also the Chief Justice of that High Court.
- A Judge of the High Court can hold office until the age of 62 years.
- A High Court Judge can leave his office :
  - ★ By resignation in writing addressed to the President.

- ★ By being appointed a Judge of the Supreme Court or being transferred to any other High Court by the President.
- ★ By removal by the President.
- ★ The mode of removal of a Judge of the High Court is same as that of a Judge of the Supreme Court.

➢ The qualifications for being a Judge of the High Court are :
★ Be a citizen of India. ★ Not above 62 years of age. ★ Must have held for at least 10 years a judicial office in territory of India or experience of at least 10 years as advocate of a High Court, or of two or more such courts in succession in India.

➢ Salaries and allowances of the High Court Judges are charged on the Consolidated Fund of the State [Art. 202(3) (d)].

➢ After retirement a permanent Judge of High Court can not plead or act in a Court or before any authority in India, except the Supreme Court and a High Court in which he has not worked.

The High Courts : Seats and Jurisdiction

Name	Established	Territorial Jurisdiction	Seat
Allahabad	1866	Uttar Pradesh	Allahabad (Bench at Lucknow)
Andhra Pradesh	1954	Andhra Pradesh	Hyderabad
Bombay	1862	Maharastra, Dadar & Nagar Haveli. Goa, Daman & Diu.	Bombay (Benches at Nagpur, Panji, Aurangabad)
Calcutta	1862	West Bengal, Andman & Nicobar Islands.	Kolkata (Bench at Port Blair)
Delhi	1966	Delhi	Delhi
Guwahati	1948	Assam, Nagaland, Mizoram and Arunachal Pradesh	Guwahati (Benches at Kohima, Aizawl and Itanagar)
Gujarat	1960	Gujarat	Ahmedabad
Himachal Pradesh	1966	Himachal Pradesh	Shimla
Jammu and Kashmir	1928	Jammu & Kashmir	Srinagar & Jammu
Karnataka	1884	Karnataka	Bengaluru (Bench–Dharwad and Gulbarga)
Kerala	1958	Kerala & Lakshadweep	Ernakulam
Madhya Pradesh	1956	Madhya Pradesh	Jabalpur (Bench–Indore, Gwalior)
Madras	1862	Tamil Nadu & Puducherry	Chennai (Bench–Madurai)
Orissa	1948	Odisha	Cuttack
Patna	1916	Bihar	Patna

Name	Established	Territorial Jurisdiction	Seat
Punjab & Haryana	1975	Punjab, Haryana, Chandigarh	Chandigarh
Rajasthan	1949	Rajasthan	Jodhpur (Bench–Jaipur)
Sikkim	1975	Sikkim	Gangtok
Chhattisgarh	2000	Chhattisgarh	Bilaspur
Uttarakhand	2000	Uttarakhand	Nainital
Jharkhand	2000	Jharkhand	Ranchi
Manipur	2013	Manipur	Imphal
Meghalaya	2013	Meghalaya	Shillong
Tripura	2013	Tripura	Agartala

26. Inter-State Council

- Inter-State Council was constituted in April, 1990 under Art. 263.
- Inter-State Council consists of Prime Minister, 6 Union Cabinet Ministers, the Chief Ministers of all the States and administrators of all UTs.
- The Sarkaria Commission recommended the constitution of a permanent Inter-State Council for co-ordination among States and with the Union. (Justice R.S. Sarkaria died in 2007.)
- Inter-state Council is chaired by the Prime Minister and it meets thrice a year.

27. Finance Commission

- The Constitution provides for the establishment of a Finance Commission (Art. 270, 273, 275 and 280) by the President. The first Finance Commission was constituted in 1951.

Finance Commissioners of India

Sl.	Constituted	Chairman	Report Implementation Year
1.	1951	K. C. Niyogi	1952–1957
2.	1956	K. Santhanam	1957–1962
3.	1960	A. K. Chanda	1962–1966
4.	1964	Dr. P. V. Rajamannar	1966–1969
5.	1968	Mahavir Tyagi	1969–1974
6.	1972	Brahmanand Reddy	1974–1979
7.	1977	J. M. Schelet	1979–1984
8.	1983	Y. B. Chavan	1989–1995
9.	1987	N. K. P. Salve	1989–1995
10.	1992	K. C. Pant	1995–2000
11.	1998	A. M. Khusro	2000–2005
12.	1 Nov., 2002	C. Rangarajan	2005–2010
13.	Nov., 2007	Dr. Vijay L. Kelkar	2010–2015
14.	2 Jan. 2013	Y.V. Reddy	2015–2020

- ➢ The Finance Commission consists of a Chairman and four other members.
- ➢ According to the qualifications prescribed by the Parliament, the chairman is selected among persons who have had experience in public affairs, while the members are selected among persons who :
  - ★ are or have been or are qualified to be appointed judges of the High Court; or
  - ★ have special knowledge of the finance and accounts of government; or
  - ★ have had wide experience in financial matters and in administration; or
  - ★ have special knowledge of economics.
- ➢ The members of the commission hold office for such period as may be specified by the President in his orders and are eligible for reappointment.
- ➢ The main functions or *duties* of the Finance Commission are :
  - ★ To recommend to the President the basis for distribution of the net proceeds of taxes between the centre and states.
  - ★ To recommend the principles which should govern the grants in-aid to be given to states out of the consolidated Fund of India.
  - ★ To tender advice to the President on any other matter referred to the Commission in the interest of sound finance.
  - ★ To suggest amounts to be paid to the states of Assam, Bihar, Odisha and West Bengal in lieu of the assignment of system of export duty on Jute products.
- ➢ The commission submits its recommendations to the President which are generally accepted by the Central Government. The recommendations of the Commission are applicable for a period of five years.

28. Planning Commission

- ➢ Planning Commission is not mentioned in the Constitution.
- ➢ Planning Commission is an economic advisory body set up by a resolution of the Union Cabinet in 1950.
- ➢ At present, the Planning Commission consists of the Chairman, four Ministers as part time members and seven full-time members.
- ➢ Prime Minister is the Chairman of Planning Commission.
- ➢ *Main functions* of the Planning Commission are :
  - ★ To prepare an integrated Five Year Plan for the most effective and balanced utilisation of the country's resources for economic and social development.
  - ★ To act as an advisory body to the Union Government and State Governments.

29. National Development Council (NDC)

- ➢ The National Development Council was formed in 1952, to associate the States in the formulation of the Plans.
- ➢ All members of the Union Cabinet, Chief Ministers of States, the Administrators of the Union Territories and member of the Planning Commission are members of the NDC.

- *Functions* of the NDC are :
  - ★ Review working of national plan.
  - ★ Recommend measures to meet targets of national plan.
- It is an extra constitutional and extra legal body.

30. National Integration Council

- National Integration Council was set-up in 1986, to deal with welfare measures for the minorities on an All-India basis.
- It includes Union Ministers, Chief Ministers of State, representatives of National and Regional political parties, labour, women, public figures and media representatives. NDC is a non-constitutional body.

31. Inter-State Relations

- Art. 131 provides for the judicial determination of disputes between states by vesting the Supreme Court with exclusive jurisdiction in the matter, while Art. 262 provides for the adjudication of one class of such disputes by an extra judicial tribunal.
- Art. 263 provides for the prevention of inter State disputes by investigation and recommendation by an administrative body.
- Under Art. 262 Parliament has constituted the Inter-State Water Disputes Tribunal for adjudication of disputes between States for the waters of any inter-State river or river valley.
- Inter-State river water disputes are excluded from the jurisdiction of all Courts including the Supreme Court.
- An Inter-State Council has been constituted for co-ordinating in Inter-State disputes {Ref. : Art. 263 (a)}.
- Six Zonal Councils have been established to discuss and advise on matters of common interest. These are :
  - ★ The Central Zone : Uttar Pradesh, Madhya Pradesh, Uttarakhand and Chhattisgarh.
  - ★ The Northern Zone : Haryana, Himachal Pradesh, Punjab, Rajasthan, Jammu & Kashmir, and the Union Territories of Delhi & Chandigarh.
  - ★ The Western Zone : Gujrat, Maharashtra, Goa and the Union Territories of Dadra & Nagar Haveli and Daman & Diu.
  - ★ The Southern Zone : Andhra Pradesh, Karnataka, Tamil Nadu, Kerala, and the Union Territory of Puducherry.
  - ★ The Eastern Zone : Bihar, Jharkhand, West Bengal and Odisha.
  - ★ The North - Eastern Council : Arunachal Pradesh, Assam, Manipur, Mizoram, Tripura, Meghalaya, Nagaland and Sikkim.
- Each Zonal Council consists of the Chief Minister and two other Ministers of each of the States in the Zone and the Administrator in the case of a Union Territory.
- The Union Home Minister has been nominated to be the common chairman of all the Zonal Councils.

32. Emergency Provisions

- President can make proclamation of emergency under Art. 352 in case of war, external aggression or armed rebellion or threat thereof only on recommendation of the Cabinet.

- ➢ Every such proclamation must be laid before Parliament and it ceases to be in operation unless it is approved by resolutions of both Houses of Parliament with special majority within *one month* from the date of its issue.
- ➢ The proclamation gets a fresh lease of 6 months from the date it is approved by both Houses of Parliament.
- ➢ After the 44th amendment, proclamation of emergency under Art. 352 can be made in respect of whole of India or only a part thereof.
- ➢ During proclamation of emergency the Union can give directions to any State regarding exercise of the executive power {Ref.: Art. 353(a)}.
- ➢ During emergency Parliament can extend the normal life of the Lok Sabha for one year at a time, and not exceeding 6 months after the proclamation has ceased to operate.
- ➢ Normal life of Lok Sabha was extended only once in 1976.
- ➢ During emergency, Parliament can legislate regarding State subjects.
- ➢ During Emergency the President can modify the provisions of the Constitution relating to the allocation of financial resources [Art. 268–279] between the Union and the States by his own Order. Such Order is subject to approval by Parliament [Art. 354] and has no effect beyond the financial year in which the Proclamation itself ceases to operate.
- ➢ *Effects of emergency on Fundamental Rights* :
  - ★ Art. 358 provides that the rights provided by Art. 19, would be non-existent against the State during emergency.
  - ★ Under Art. 359, the *right to move the Courts* for the enforcement of the rights can be suspended, by Order of the President.
  - ★ Articles 20 and 21 cannot be suspended during emergency.
- ➢ The first proclamation of emergency under Art. 352 was made by the President on October 26, 1962 in view of Chinese aggression in the NEFA.
- ➢ For the first time on June 25, 1975 proclamation of emergency under Art. 352 was made on the ground of "*internal* disturbance".
- ➢ A proclamation of emergency for failure of constitutional machinery can be made by the President when the Constitutional Government of State cannot be carried on for any reasons {Ref. : Art. 356}.
- ➢ During Emergency under Art. 352, the Centre does not get power to suspend the State Government.
- ➢ In case of failure of the Constitutional machinery, the State Legislature is suspended and the executive authority of the state is assumed by the President in whole or in part. This is popularly called the 'President's rule'.
- ➢ Under a proclamation of emergency under Art. 352, Parliament can legislate in respect of state subjects only by itself; but under a proclamation under Art. 356 of the other kind, it can delegate its power to legislature for the State, —to the President or any other authority specified by him.
- ➢ Proclamation of emergency for failure of constitutional machinery, can be extended by Parliament upto three years {Art. 356(4), Provision 1}.

33. Public Service Commissions

- ➢ Constitution provides a Public Service Commission for the Union, a Public Service Commission for each State or a Joint Public Service Commission for a group of States.
- ➢ A Joint Public Service Commission can be created by Parliament in pursuance of a resolution passed by the State Legislatures concerned.
- ➢ The Union Public Service Commission can serve the needs of a State, if so requested by the Governor of that State and approved by the President {Ref.: Art. 315}.
- ➢ The appointment, determination of number of members of the Commission and their conditions of service is done by :
  - ★ The President in the case of the Union or a Joint Commission, and
  - ★ The Governor of the State in the case of a State Commission.
- ➢ Conditions of service of a member of the Public Service Commission can not be varied to his disadvantage after his appointment [Art. 318].
- ➢ Half of the members of a Commission should be persons who have held office under the Government of India or of a State for at least 10 years {Art. 316}.
- ➢ The *term of service* of a member of a Commission is 6 years from the date of his entering upon office, or until the age of retirement, which ever is earlier.
- ➢ Age of retirement for a member of UPSC is 65 years.
- ➢ Age of retirement for a member of PSC of a State or a Joint Commission is 62 years.
- ➢ Services of a member of a Public Service Commission can be terminated by:
  - ★ *Resignation* in writing addressed to the President (to the Governor in the case of a State Commission).
  - ★ *Removal* by the President.
- ➢ President can remove a member if he is :
  - ★ adjudged insolvent; or
  - ★ engages himself in paid employment outside the duties of his office; or
  - ★ is infirm in mind or body; or
  - ★ found guilty of misbehaviour by the Supreme Court.
- ➢ Even in the case of a State Commission, only the President can remove a member, while Governor has only the power to pass an interim order of suspension.
- ➢ The expenses of the Commission are charged on the Consolidated Fund of India or of the State (as the case may be) {Ref.: Art. 322}.
- ➢ Disabilities imposed upon the Chairman and members of the Commission for future employment under the Government are :
  - ★ The Chairman of the UPSC is ineligible for further employment either under the Government of India or under the Government of a State.
  - ★ The Chairman of a State Public Service Commission is eligible for appointment as the Chairman or member of the Union Public

Service Commission or as the Chairman of any other State Public Service Commission, but not for any other employment either under the Government of India or under the Government of a State.

➢ A member of a State Public Service Commission is eligible for appointment as the Chairman of a State Public Service Commission and Chairman or member of UPSC, but not for any other employment either under the Government of India or under the Government of a State.

➢ The Public Service Commissions are *advisory bodies*. Government can accept its recommendation or depart from it.

➢ Functions of Public Service Commission :

★ To conduct examination for appointments to the services of the Union and States.

★ To advise on any matter so referred to them and on any other matter which the President or the Governor of a state may refer to the appropriate Commission [Art. 320]

★ To exercise such additional functions as may be provided for by an act of Parliament or of the Legislature of a State.

34. Election

➢ The general election is held on the basis of adult suffrage.

➢ Every person who is a citizen of India and not less than 18 years of age is entitled to vote at the election, provided he is not disqualified by law.

➢ Election to Parliament or the Legislature of a State can be called in question only by an election petition in the High Court, with appeal to the Supreme Court [Art. 329].

➢ The exclusive forum for adjudicating disputes relating to the election of the President and Vice-president is the Supreme Court [Art. 71].

Election Commission

➢ In order to supervise the entire procedure and machinery for election and for some other ancillary matters, the Constitution provides for this independent body [Art. 324].

➢ The Election Commission is independent of executive control to ensure a fair election.

➢ The Election Commission consists of a Chief Election Commissioner and two other Election Commissioners .

➢ President can determine the number of Election Commissioners [Art. 324(2)].

Chief Election Commissioner (CEC)

➢ The President appoints the Chief Election Commissioner who has a tenure of 6 years, or up to the age of 65 years, whichever is earlier.

➢ The CEC enjoys the same status and receives the same salary and perks as available to judges of the Supreme Court.

➢ The Chief Election Commissioner can be removed from his office only in a manner and on the grounds prescribed for removal of judge of the Supreme Court.

➢ Other Election Commissioners can be removed by the President on the recommendation of the Chief Election Commissioner.

- The Election Commission has the power of superintendence, direction and conduct of all elections to Parliament and the State Legislatures and of elections to the offices of the President and Vice-President {Ref.: Art. 324(1)}.
- Regional Commissioners can be appointed by the President in consultation with the Election Commission for assisting the Election Commission {Ref.: Art. 324(4).

Chief Election Commissioner of India

Sl.	Name	Tenure
1.	Sukumar Sen	21 March, 1950–19 Dec., 1958
2.	K. V. K. Sundaram	20 Dec., 1958–30 Sept., 1967
3.	S. P. Sen Verma	01 Oct., 1967–30 Sept., 1972
4.	Dr. Nagendra Singh	01 Oct., 1972–06 Feb., 1973
5.	T. Swaminathan	07 Feb., 1973–17 June, 1977
6.	S. L. Shakdhar	18 June, 1977–17 June, 1982
7.	R. K. Trivedi	18 June, 1982–31 Dec., 1985
8.	R. V. S. Peri Shastri	01 Jan., 1986–25 Nov., 1990
9.	Smt. V. S. Rama Davi	26 Nov., 1990–11 Dec., 1990
10.	T. N. Seshan	12 Dec., 1990–11 Dec., 1996
11.	M. S. Gill	12 Dec., 1996–13 June, 2001
12.	J. M. Lyngdoh	14 June, 2001–07 Feb., 2004
13.	T. S. Krishna Murthy	08 Feb., 2004–15 May, 2005
14.	B. B. Tandon	16 May, 2005–07 Feb., 2006
15.	N. Gopalaswami	08 Feb., 2006–19 April, 2009
16.	Naveen Chawla	20 April, 2009–29 July, 2010
17.	S. Y. Quraishi	30 July, 2010–10 June, 2012
18.	V. S. Sampath	11 June, 2012– —

- The main functions of the Election Commission are :
  1. The preparation of electoral rolls before each general election and registration of all eligible voters.
  2. The delimitation of constituencies.
  3. The recognition of various political parties and allotment of election symbol to these parties.
  4. The preparation of a code of conduct for the political parties.
  5. The tendering of advice to the President regarding disqualification of the members of the parliaments etc.
  6. The appointment of election officers to look into disputes concerning election arrangements.
  7. The preparation of roster for central broadcasts and telecasts by various political parties.
  8. Keep voters lists up-to-date at all times.
  9. To issue identity cards to the voters.

35. Delimitation Commission of India

- ➢ Delimitation Commission or Boundary Commission of India is a Commission established by Government of India under the provisions of the Delimitation Commission Act.
- ➢ The main task of the Commission is to redraw the boundaries of the various assembly and Lok Sabha Constituencies based on a recent census (Art. 82).
- ➢ The representation from each state is not changed during this exercise. However, the number of SC and ST seats in a state are changed in accordance with the census.
- ➢ The Commission in India is a high power body whose order have the force of law and cannot be called in question before any court.
- ➢ These orders come into force on a date to be specified by the President of India in this behalf. The copies of its orders are laid before the House of the People and the state Legislative Assembly concerned, but no modifications are permissible there in by them.
- ➢ In India, such Delimitation Commissions have been constituted 4 times– in 1952, 1963, 1973 and in 2002.
- ➢ The recent Delimitation Commission was set up on 12 July 2002 (after 2001 census) with Justice Kuldip Singh (retd. Judge of Supreme Court of India) as its Chairperson.
- ➢ The recommendation of this commission was approved by the then President Pratibha Patil on 19 February 2008.
- ➢ The Constitution of India was specifically amended in 2002 (84th Amendment Act, 2001, which amended the provisions 170 (3) of Art. 82) not to have delimitation of constituencies till the first census after 2026.
- ➢ The recent delimitation has been done on the basis of census 2001.
- ➢ Election Commissioners of all the States and Union Territories, alongwith the Chief Election Commissioner (CEC) of India are the members of the Delimitation Commission.

No. of Reserved seats after delimitation

Category	Present seats	Seats after new delimitation
SC	79	85
ST	41	48
Unreserved	423	410
Total Seats in Lok Sabha	543	543

N.B. : Assam, Manipur, Arunachal Pradesth, Nagaland and Jharkhand are such states which could not be covered by the Delimitation Commission 2002.

36. The Official Languages

- ➢ The Official language of the Union is Hindi in Devanagri script [Art. 343]. English was to continue to be used as principal official language of the Union side-by-side with Hindi till 1965.
- ➢ The first Official Language Commission was appointed in 1955 under Shri B.G. Kher as Chairman and it recommended that a rigid date line for change over of language should not be prescribed. This recommendation was accepted.

Language of the State/Link Language :

- Article 345 seeks to tackle the issue of the official language for each state and the language for intra-State official transactions.
- The Legislature of a State can adopt any one or more languages used in the State or Hindi for the official purposes of that State. There is also a provision for the recognition of any other language for the official purpose of a State or any part thereof, upon a substantial popular demand for it being made to the President {Ref. : Art. 347}.

Language of the SC and HCs and authoritative text of laws :

- Until Parliament by law provides otherwise, English is the language of authoritative text of—

  ★ All proceedings in the Supreme Court and in every High Court. ★ All Bills or amendments thereto moved in either House of Parliament or the State Legislature. ★ All Acts passed by Parliament or the Legislature of a State. ★ All Ordinances promulgated by the President or the Governor of a State. ★ All orders rules, regulations and by-laws issued under Constitution or under any law made by Parliament or the legislature of a State.
- A State Legislature can prescribe the use of any language other than English for Bills and Acts passed by itself or Subordinate Legislation made thereunder.
- The languages included in the 8th Schedule of the Constitution are: Assamese, Bengali, Gujrati, Hindi, Kannada, Kashmiri, Konkani, Malyalam, Manipuri, Marathi, Nepalese, Oriya, Punjabi, Sanskrit, Sindhi, Tamil, Telugu, Urdu, Maithili, Santhali, Dogri and Bodo.
- Sindhi was inserted by the Constitution (21st Amendment) Act, 1967.
- Konkani, Manipuri and Nepali were inserted by the Constitution (71st Amendment) Act, 1992.
- Maithili, Dogri, Bodo and Santhali were inserted by the Constitution (92nd Amendment) Act, 2003.
- The only privileges gained by the languages included in the 8th Schedule are
  - ★ To have a member in the Official Language Commission.
  - ★ To be considered for contribution towards the development of Hindi language.

37. National Symbols

National Flag

- The National flag is a horizontal tricolour of deep saffron *(Kesaria)* at the top, white in the middle and dark green at the bottom in equal proportion. The ratio of width of the flag to its length is two to three. In the centre of the white band is a navy-blue wheel which represents the *chakra*. Its design is that of the wheel which appears on the abacus of the Sarnath Lion Capital of Ashoka. Its diameter approximates to the width of the white band and it has 24 spokes. The design of the National Flag was adopted by the Constituent Assembly of India on 22 July 1947.
- Apart from non-statutory instructions issued by the Government from time to time, display of the National Flag is governed by the provisions of the Emblems and names (Prevention of Improper Use) Act, 1950

(No.12 of 1950) and the Prevention of Insults to National Honour Act, 1971 (No. 69 of 1971).

- The Flag Code of India, 2002, took effect from 26 January 2002 which brings together all such laws, conventions, practices and instructions for the guidance and benefit of all concerned.
- In an important judgement in January, 2004 the Supreme Court (under the chairmanship of the Chief Justice B. N. Khare) pronounce that unfurling (hoisting) of National Flag is a fundamental right under Article 19 (1) (A).

Note : For the first time the National Flag of India was hoisted in the mid-night of 14th August, 1947.

State Emblem

- The state emblem is an adaptation from the Sarnath Lion Capital of Ashoka. In the original, there are four lions, standing back to back, mounted on an abacus with a frieze carrying sculptures in high relief of an elephant, a galloping horse, a bull and a lion separated by intervening wheels over a bell-shaped lotus. Carved out of a single block of polished sandstone, the Capital is crowned by the Wheel of the Law *(Dharma Chakra)*.
- In the state emblem, adopted by the Government of India on 26th January 1950 only three lions are visible, the fourth being hidden from view. The wheel appears in relief in the centre of the abacus with a bull on right and a horse on left and the outlines of other wheels on extreme right and left. The bell-shaped lotus has been omitted. The words Satyameva Jayate from Mundaka Upanishad, meaning 'Turth Alone' Triumphs, are inscribed below the abacus in Devanagari script.
- The use of the state emblem of India, as the official seal of the Government of India, is regulated by the State of India (Prohibition of Improper Use) Act, 2005.

National Anthem

- The song *Jana-gana-mana,* composed originally in Bengali by Rabindranath Tagore, was adopted in its Hindi version by the Constituent Assembly as the National Anthem of India on 24 January, 1950. It was first sung on 27 December, 1911 at the Kolkata Session (Chairman-Pt.Vishan Narayan Dutt) of the Indian National Congress. The complete song consists of five stanzas.
- Rabindranath Tagore had published it in *'Tatvabodhini'* in 1912 with the title' Bharat Bhagya Vidhata' and translated it into English in 1919 with the title 'Morning song of India'. The credit of composing the present tune (Music) of our national anthem goes to Captain Ram Singh Thakur (an I N A sepoy)
- Playing time of the full version of the national anthem is approximately 52 seconds. A short version of the first and last lines of the stanza (Playing time approximately 20 seconds) is also played on certain occasions.

National Song

- The song *'Vande Mataram',* composed in Sanskrit by Bankimchandra Chatterji, was a source of inspiration to the people in their struggle for freedom. It has an equal status with *Jana-gana-mana.* The first political occasion when it was sung at the 1896 session (Chairman-Rahimtulla Sayani) of Indian National Congress.

- The song was published in the novel 'Anandmath', authored by Bankimchandra Chatterji and was adopted as the National Song on 26 January ,1950.
- Playing time of this song one (1) minute and five (5) seconds (65 seconds). No body can be forced is to sing the National Song.

Note : *Session of Parliament begins with 'Jana-gana-mana'and concludes with 'Vande Mataram.'*

National Calendar

- The National Calendar based on the Saka Era, Chaitra as its first month and a normal year of 365 days was adopted from 22nd March 1957 along with the Gregorian calendar for the following official purposes: (i) Gazette of India, (ii) news broadcast by All India Radio, (iii) calendars issued by the Government of India and (iv) Government communications addressed to the members of the public.
- Dates of the National Calendar have a permanent correspondence with dates of the Gregorian calendar, 1 Chaitra falling on 22 March normally and on 21 March in leap year.

National Animal : The magnificent tiger, *Panthera tigris.*

National Bird : The Indian peacock, *Pavo cristatus.*

National Flower : Lotus (Nelumbo Nucipera Gaertn).

National Tree : The Banyan Tree *(Ficus benghalensis).*

National Fruit : Mango *(Manigifera indica).*

National Aquatic Animal : The mammal Ganges River Dolphin (Platanista gangetica).

38. Glossary of Constitutional Terms

Act of God, is a direct, violent, sudden and irresistible act of nature, which could not be by any reasonable care have been foreseen or resisted.

Act of Parliament, means a bill passed by the two Houses of Parliament and assented to by President and in the absence of an express provision to the contrary, operative from the date of notification in the Gazette.

Act of State, means the act of sovereign power of a country or its agent (if acting intra-vires). By its very nature such an act cannot be questioned by any Court of Law.

Address of President, is the prepared speech delivered by the President of India to both Houses of Parliament assembled together at the commencement of the first Session after each general election to Lok Sabha and at the commencement of the first Session of each year informing Parliament of the causes of its summons which is later laid before and discussed on a formal Motion of Thanks in each House of Parliament or an address by the President of India to either House of Parliament of both Houses, assembled together on any other occasion.

Adjournment Motion, if Speaker gives his consent after satisfying himself that the matter to be raised is definitely urgent and of public importance and holds that the matter prepared to be discussed is in order, he shall call the member concerned who small rise in his place and ask for leave to move the adjournment of the House. If objection to leave being granted is taken, the Speaker shall request those members who are in favour of leave being granted to rise in their places, and if not less than fifty members rise accordingly, the Speaker shall intimate that leave is granted, if not, he shall inform the House that the members have not to leave the House,

Adjournment of House, in Lok Sabha the Speaker determines when sitting of House is to adjourn *sine die* or to a particular day or to an hour or part of same day while in Rajya Sabha it is the Chairman who determines.

Admonition, is a judicial or ecclesiastic censure or reprimand.

Advocate-General, the Attorney-General and after him, the advocate-General of a State have precedence over other advocates.

Affirmation, is a solemn declaration without oath.

Amendment, is a device to alter a motion moved or question under discussion in the legislature, includes omission, substitution, addition and insertion of certain words, figures or marks to the clause of a bill, a resolution or a motion or to an amendment made thereof.

– Is a structural improvement.

Anglo-Indian, is of a British birth but living or having lived long in India.

Appeal, is the judicial examination of the decision by a higher court of the decision of an inferior court.

Appropriation Bill, is the act of devoting or reserving for special or distinct purpose or of destining to a particular end; anything set aside especially money for a specific use.

Arrest, is the restraining of the liberty of a man's person in order to compel obedience to the order of a court of justice, or to prevent the commission of a crime, or to ensure that a person charged or suspected of a crime may be forthcoming to answer it.

– Is when one is taken into custody and restrained from his liberty.

Assent to Bill, is ratification, sovereign's formal acquiescence in a measure passed by legislature.

Attorney-General, is the Chief Law Officer of a country, legal adviser to the Chief Executive.

Backward Classes, the list of OBCs are prepared by the Central Government and are revised after the expiry of every 10 years.

– Are the classes slow in development.

Ballot, is a small ball ticket or paper used in secret voting.

Begar, is a labour or service exacted by court or a person in power without giving remuneration.

Bill, is a draft of a law proposed to a lawmaking body.

–Is the draft or form of an Act presented to a legislature but not enacted.

Breach of privilege, disregard of any of the privileges, rights and immunities either of the members of Parliament individually or of either House of Parliament in its collective capacity or of its committees, also includes action which obstruct the House in the performance in its functions and thereby lower its dignity and authority such as disobedience of its legitimate order or libel upon itself, or its member or officers which are called contempt of the House.

Budget, refers to the statement of the estimated receipts and expenditure of the Government of India known as annual financial statement; it is caused to be laid before both House of Parliament by the President in respect of every financial year on such day as he may direct.

Bulletin, is an official notice of a public transaction or matter of public importance.

Business to the House, is the relative order of the items of business in the House of a legislature to be taken up on a particular day.

Cabinet, is a private and confidential assembly of the most considerable minister of State of concert measures for the administration of public affairs.

Censure Motion, is a motion moved against the government censuring its policy in some direction or an individual minister or minister of the Government.

Certiorari, is a writ of High Court to an inferior court to call up the records of a case therein depending that conscionable justice may be therein administered.

–Is issued by the superior Court to inferior judicial or quasi-judicial body, grounds for invoking are excess of jurisdiction, violation of natural justice, fraud and terms on the face of the record. Conditions for issuing this writ are: (i) a body of persons having legal authority, (ii) to determine questions altering rights of subjects, (iii) having the duty to act judicially, (iv) act in excess of their legal authority, (v) issued on constitutional grounds also.

Chief whip, is the chief of the whips of different political parties in Parliament (generally the Minister of Parliamentary Affairs).

Citizen, is a member of a State or nation, especially one with a republican form of government, who owes allegianes to it by birth or naturalisation and is entitled to full civil rights.

Closure, is the Parliamentary Procedure by which debate is closed and the measure under discussion brought up for an immediate vote.

– is the procedure in deliberative assemblies whereby debate is closed.

Coalition, usually takes place in multi-party system in which no single party is able to command support of a working majority.

Comptroller and Auditor-General, is the officer who is responsible for the auditing of all public accounts.

Concurrent List, is a list of subjects appended to a federal Constitution in respect of which the federal legislature and the State of regional legislatures have power to make laws, federal law prevailing in case of conflict.

Consolidated fund, is a repository of public money which now comprises the produce of customs, excise, stamps and several other taxes, and some small receipts from the royal hereditary revenue surrendered to its public use.

Constituent Assembly, is a legislative body charged with task of framing or revising a Constitution, set up for India after it became independent in 1947 for the purpose of framing its Constitution.

Constitution, is the system of fundamental laws and principles of a government written or unwritten.

–is the basic law defining and delimiting the principal organs of Government and their jurisdiction as well as the basic rights of men and citizens.

Contempt of court, is a disobedience to or disregard of the rules, orders, process, or dignity of a court, which has power to punish for such offence by committal.

Contingency fund, is placed at the disposal of the executive to meet the unforeseen expenditure.

Court, is a place where justice is judicially administered.

Debate, is a Parliamentary discussion.

Defection, is abandonment of loyalty, duty, principle etc.,

Delegated legislation, is rules and regulations with the effect of law made by the executive under statutory sanction by Parliament.

Deprivation, is a loss of dismissal from office.

– refers to property taken under the power of eminent domain.

Deputy Speaker, is the Officer of the House of a legislature who takes the Chair during the absence of the Speaker and performs his duties in relation to all proceedings in the House.

Directive Principles of State Policy, lay down guidelines which can be implemented only by passing legislation.

Discrimination, is a difference in treatment of two or more persons or subject.

– is an act of depriving an individual or a group of equality of opportunity.

Dissolution, is the civil death of Parliament.

Doctrine of severability, is a rule of interpretation; it means that where some particular provision of statute offends against a constitutional limitation, but that provision is severable from the rest of the statute, only the offending provision will be declared void by the court and not the entire statute.

Double jeopardy, is subjection of an accused person to repeated trial for the same alleged offence.

Due process of law, is the law in conformity with due process a concept adopted by the American Constitution; the process of law which hears before it condemns; judiciary can declare a law bad, if it is not in accordance with due process even though the legislation may be within the competence of the legislature concerned.

Election, is act of selecting one or more form a greater number for an office.

Election Commission, is a constitutional body created for the purpose of holding elections to Parliament, State Legislatures and Offices of President and Vice-President.

Electoral college, is an intermediary body chosen by electors to choose the representatives in an indirect election.

Electoral roll, is known as voter's list in common parlance; is the basic document on which the whole electoral process is founded.

Equal protection, all individuals and classes will be equally subjected to the ordinary law administered by the law courts.

Equality, is the state of being equal in political, economic and social rights.

Existing law, is the law in force at the passage of an Act.

Expulsion, is the unseating of members for offences committed against the House or for grave misdemeanours.

Extradition, is the surrender by a foreign State of a person accused of a crime to the State where it was committed.

Financial memorandum, is a memorandum required to accompany all bills involving expenditure.

Fundamental duties, are certain obligations on the part of a citizen which he or she owes towards the State so that the individual may not overlook his duties to the community while exercising his fundamental right or commit wanton destruction of public property or life.

Fundamental rights, is protected and guaranteed by the written Constitution of a State.

Gazette, is the official newspaper of the Government.

– Is known as the Gazette of India or the Official Gazette of a State.

Government, is a established system of political administration by which State is governed.

Habeas corpus, commands a Judge of the inferior court to produce the body of the defendant with a statement of the cause of his detention, to do and to receive whatever the higher court shall decree.

Hung Parliament, is a Parliament wherein no party has won a working majority.

Impeachment, a person found guilty may be removed from his office.

Joint sitting, is a joint sitting of both Houses of a bicameral legislature for setting a disagreement between them.

Judgment, order or sentence given by a judge or law court.

Judicial review, is the power of the court to review statutes or administrative acts and determine their constitutionality. The examination of federal and State legislature statutes and the acts of executive officials by the Courts to determine their validity according to written Constitutions.

Judiciary, is the body of officers who administer the law.

Law, all the rules of conduct established and enforced by the authority.

Legislative relations, in case of conflict the union law prevails.

Legislature, is the body of persons in a State authorised to make, alter and repeal law. It may consist of one or two Houses with similar or different powers.

Liberty, is something which results from a permission given to or something enjoyed under sufferance by a particular person or body or persons as opposed to enjoyment by all and sundry.

Locus standi, means a place for standing, right to be heard.

Maiden speech, is one's first or earliest speech especially in Parliament.

Martial law, is arbitrary in its decisions and is not built on any settled principles.

Migration, means coming to India with the intention of residing here permanently.

Minority, is racial, religious or political groups smaller than and differing from larger, controlling group of which it is a party.

Money Bill, is a bill which contains only provisions dealing with the imposition, repeal, remission, alteration or regulation of taxes etc.

Motion, is a proposal made in the House of a legislature to elicit its decision on a subject.

Oath, is a ritualistic declaration, based on an appeal to God or some revered person or object that one will speak the truth, keep a promise, remain faithful etc.

Office of profit, is an employment with fees and emoluments attached to it; where pay or salary is attached to an office, it immediately and indisputably makes the office and "office of profit".

Official gazette, means the Gazette of India or the Official Gazette of a State.

Ordinance, is a State paper operative as a fundamental law, yet not describable as either a Constitution or a statute.

Personal liberty, consists in the power of locomotion, of changing situation or moving one's person to whatever place one's own inclination may direct, without imprisonment or restraint unless by due course of law.

Petition, is a solemn, earnest supplication or request to a superior or to a person or group in authority.

Pith and substance, is a doctrine relating to the interpretation of statutes, evolved by the Privy Council, to solve the problem of two competing legislatures.

Preamble, is an introduction, especially one to a constitutional statute etc., stating its reason and purpose.

President, is Chief executive of a Republic.

Presumption of constitutionality, is an assumption made failing proof of the contrary that an enactment is in accordance with the Constitution. The presumption is always in favour of the constitutionality of an enactment and the burden is upon him who attacks it to show that there has been a clear transgression of the constitutional principles.

Privilege, is an exceptional right or advantage.

Privy purse, was the sum fixed by the Government of India for covering the expenses of each of the rulers of former Indian States and their families in consideration of their agreement of merger in the Indian Union.

Probationer, is one who is on probation or trial.

Procedure established by law, is the procedure prescribed by the law of the State. It does not mean the due process of law.

Prohibition, is a remedy provided by the Common Law against the encroachment of jurisdiction.

Proportional representation, is a method of representation designed to secure the election of candidates in proportion to the numerical strength of each section of political opinion thus accurately reflecting the political feeling of the country in Parliament.

Question hour, is the time fixed for asking and answering oral questions in a sitting in a legislature; it is fixed under the rules of the House or standing orders.

Qua warranto, is a writ ordering a person to show by what right he exercises an office, franchise or privilege.

Quorum, is a minimum number required to be present at an assembly before it can validly proceed to transact business.

Reasonable restriction, is restrictions imposed by State on the enjoyment of the fundamental rights.

Religion, is the specific system of belief, worship, conduct involving a Code of ethics and philosophy.

Repugnancy, is contradictory of each other, set of clauses in statutes, will, etc,.

Res judicata, is final judgment already decided between the same parties or their privies on the same questions by a legally constituted court having jurisdiction is conclusive between the parties, and the issue cannot be raised again.

Rule, is an established guide or regulation for action, conduct.

Rule of law, is absolute supremely or predominance of regular law as opposed to the influence of arbitrary power's equality before the law or the equal subjection of all classes to the ordinary law court; Constitution is the result of the ordinary law of the land.

Session, connotes the sitting together of the legislative body for the transaction of business.

Shadow cabinet, is a body of opposition leaders meeting from time to time and ready to take office.

State, comprises people, territory, government through which its policies are implemented and sovereignty having authority to make final legal decisions and having physical power to enforce them.

State Act, is an Act passed by Legislature of a State established or continued by the Constitution.

Statute, is synonymous with Act of Parliament.

Subordinate legislation, is a making of statutory instruments or orders by a body subordinate to the legislature in exercise of the power within specific limits conferred by the legislature, also covers statutory instruments themselves.

Swear, is to make a solemn declaration or affirmation with an appeal to God or to someone or something held sacred for confirmation.

Untouchability, is social disabilities historically imposed on certain classes of people by reason of their birth in certain castes.

Vote, is a decision by one or more persons on a proposal, resolution expressed by ticket, ballot, or voice.

Vote on account, is estimate of an advance payment to enable Government Departments to carry on their work from beginning of financial year till the passing of Appropriation Act.

Walk out, is a strike, an informal or unauthorised strike, an action of leaving a meeting or organisation as an expression of disapproval; continued absence from the meetings of an organisation as an expression of disapproval.

Zero hour, is a time set for the beginning of an attack or other military operation; any crucial or decisive moment.

– Is usually noisy interregnum between the Question Hour and the beginning of the rest of day's business in a legislature; members raise often without notice various matters during this period.

★★★

5 INDIAN ECONOMY

- Since 2007-08, USA and European countries have been facing severe economic crisis, considered to be worst-ever economic crisis since the great depression of the 1930s. Slowdown of these economies caused some troubles for Indian economy initially, as it faced the problem of stagnation of demand especially, export demand. Realty and other sectors of the economy were also affected.
- This resulted in a slowdown of Indian economy and growth of GDP decelerated from an average of 8.8% between 2002-03 and 2007-08 to only 6.7% in 2008-09
- Later, Indian economy showed signs of recovery and achieved 8.6% and 9.3% growth in 2009-10 and 2010-11 respectively. But growth rate once again slided down to only 6.2% in 2011-12 and 5.0% in 2012-13.

1. Characteristics of Indian Economy

Indian Economy became the fourth largest economy of the world as per the latest report of World Bank. However, Indian Economy is still lagging behind in many spheres. In India, in 2011-12, 58.2% of total working populace was engaged in agriculture and allied activities. In 2008, its contribution to national income was 17.5%. This is an indicator of backwardness of the economy. In UK and USA, only 1 and 4% of the working population is engaged in agriculture; in France, the population is about 7%; and in Australia, this is about 6%. It is only in backward and less developed countries that the working population engaged in agriculture is quite high.

After independence, the basic economic structure of the country has become more powerful. In quantitative terms there has been substantial development. The annual growth rate, however was 8.0% during 2008-09.

Main characteristics and various aspects of Indian Economy are :

(i) Agrarian Economy : Even after six-decades of independence, 58.2% of the work force of India is still agriculturist and its contribution to Gross Domestic Product (GDP) in 2011-12 is 14.1%.

(ii) Mixed Economy : Indian Economy is a unique blend of public and private sector, i.e. a mixed economy. In its entire plan period, the government has invested 45% capital in public sector. However major sources and resources of production are still in the hands of private sector (approximately 80%). After liberalisation, Indian Economy is going ahead as a capitalist economy or market economy.

(iii) Developing Economy : The following facts show that Indian Economy is a developing economy :

(a) National income of India is very low on international standards and per capita income ($ 1180 in 2009) is much low in India as compared to other developed countries.

(b) India currently has 260 million people or 26.1% population living below *Poverty Line.*

(c) Level of unemployment is very high. Unemployment in India is mainly structural in nature because the productive capacity is inadequate to create sufficient number of jobs. There is an acute problem of disguised unemployment in the rural areas. *A person is considered employed if he/she works for 273 days of a year for eight hours every day.*

(d) Savings are low in India due to low national income and high consumption expenditure. The low savings results in shortage of capital formation. Capital is an important factor of production.

Note : *There has been lack of capital and resources during the recent years, but here it is gratifying to note that Gross Domestic Saving of India in 2008 had reached a high level of 38.0% and Gross capital formation was 39.7%.*

(e) India is the second most populated country of the world. During 1991-2001, population increased by 21.34%. With this high growth rate of population about 1.7 crore new persons are being added to Indian population every year. According to 2001 census, the total Indian population stands at a high level of 102.7 crore which is 16.7% of the world's total population. To maintain 16.7% of world population India holds only 2.42% of total land area of the world.

(f) India lacks in large industrialisation based on modern and advanced technology, which fails to accelerate the pace of development in the economy.

Important facts relating to characteristics of Indian Economy

➢ *Primary sector* of Indian Economy is agriculture and the related sectors. The contribution of agriculture sector in GDP in 2008-09 was 18.9%.

➢ *Secondary sector* of Indian Economy is related to industry, manufacturing, electricity etc. Its contribution to GDP is approximately 23.8%.

➢ *Tertiary sector* of Indian Economy is related to business, transport, communication and services. Its contribution (the share of services) in GDP is approximately 57.3% in 2008-09.

➢ The contribution of public sector in the gross production is less than 20%.

➢ The best indicator of economic development of any country is per capita income.

➢ During 2000–01 and 2004–05, NNP growth rate accelerated to 6.4% and per capita NNP grow at the rate of 4.7% per annum (at 1999-00 prices). During 2004–05 and 2009–10 further acceleration found in the NNP growth rate to 8.4% and that of per capita income to 6.85% (at 2004–05 prices).

The following factors are important in Economic Development of a developing country :

(1) Natural resources, (2) Capital gain, (3) Skilled labour force, (4) Surplus sale of agriculture, (5) Justified social organisation, (6) Political freedom, (7) Freedom from corruption, (8) Technological knowledge and general education

2. Agriculture and Land Development

➢ Agriculture is the mainstay of the Indian Economy.

➢ The share of agricultural sector's capital formation in GDP declined from 1.92% in the early 1990s to 1.28% in early 2000s. This has improved to 2.12% in 2006–07.

➢ Agriculture and allied sectors contribute nearly 18% of national income (GNI of India), while about 60% of the population is dependent on agriculture for their livelihood.

➢ The agricultural output, depends on monsoon as nearly 60% of area sown in is dependent on rainfall.

➢ Land utilisation data is available for 92.9% of total geographical area of 3,287.3 lakh hectares.

➢ Agriculture accounts only for about 10.6% of the total export earnings in 2009–10.

Share of Agricultural Sector in Total Gross Domestic Product

(At 1999-00 prices, in percentage terms)

Year	Agriculture*
1950-51	56.5
1970-71	45.9
1990-91	34.0
2007-08	17.8
2008–09 (Q) (2004–05 Prices)	15.7
2009–10 (R) (2004–05 Prices)	14.6

* *Agriculture includes agriculture, forestry and fishing.*

(Source : Economic Survey 2007-08, Statistical Abstract of India 2008. CSO, National Accounts Statistics, 2010, (2004–05 prices)).

➢ Figures provided by the Central Statistical Organisation reveal that between 1950-51 to 1960-61, the share of agriculture in GDP has been in the range of 55 to 52%. The share of agriculture indicated a sharp decline and reached a level of 14.6% in 2009-10.

➢ Importance of agriculture in the national economy is indicated by many facts, e.g.– agriculture is the main support for India's transport systems, secure bulk of their business from the movement of agricultural goods. Internal trade is mostly in agricultural products.

➢ Agricultural growth has direct impact on poverty eradication. It is also an important factor in containing inflation raising agricultural wages and employment generation.

➢ But, since 2002–03, Indian agricultural sector is almost going through a crisis—huge food grains surplus wiped out, large imports of wheat being planned and farmers' suicides more frequent all over the country.

➢ Besides, the allied sectors like horticulture, animal husbandry, dairy and fisheries have an important role in improving the over all economic conditions and nutrition of the rural masses.

- To maintain the ecological balance, there is need for sustainable and balanced development of both agriculture and the allied sectors.
- The *Tenth Plan* asserts emphatically that the agricultural sector acts as a bulwork in maintaining food security and, in the process, national security as well.
- Agricultural growth rate achieved in 9th Plan was 2.1%, while the target for the 10th Plan (2002-07) was 4% and for 11th plan (2007–12) is also 4%.
- Commercial crops are those crops which are produced for trade purpose and not for self consumption by the farmers. It includes - Oilseeds crops, Sugar crops, Fibre crops, Narcotic crops, Beverage crops.
- To encourage the agricultural products, the government announces to minimum support price for important agricultural crops.
- The function of Agriculture Cost and Price Commission (ACPC) is to decide the minimum support prices on behalf of the government.
- Minimum Support Price (MSP) announced by the government is that price at which government is ready to purchase the crop from the farmers directly, if crop price falls below the MSP.
- For providing facilities relating to storage of agriculture products, "National Co-operative Development and Warehousing Board" was established in 1956 and "Central Warehousing Corporation" was established in 1957. Thereafter in states also the State Warehousing Corporation were established.
- The programme of High Yielding Variety Seeds was combined with a guiding project I.A.D.P. and a target was set to extend this system of development in entire country.
- The credit of green revolution in India is given to the Agriculture Scientist Dr. Norman Borlaug. However, the contribution of Dr. M.S. Swaminathan is not less. But, its termed name is the contribution of American scinentific Dr. William Gande.
- Due to horrible famine during 1965-66 and 1966-67, the government implemented the new agriculture policy of high yielding seeds so as to increase agriculture production.
- India is the largest milk producing country in the world.
- There is significant increase in the milk production to the level of 108.5 million tonnes in the year 2008-09 as compared to 53.9 million tonnes in 1990–91.
- Speedy increase in the field of milk production is called White Revolution.
- To increase the pace of White Revolution, the Operation Flood was started.
- In milk production of the country the share of Buffalo, Cow and Goat is 50%, 46% and 45% respectively.
- The Father of Operation Flood was Dr. Verghese Kurien.
- The *Operation Flood* was the largest integrated dairy development programme of the world. It was started by National Dairy Development Board in 1970.

- ➢ The increase in oil seeds production was due to "Yellow Revolution".
- ➢ The progress in increase of fish production was called "Blue Revolution".
- ➢ Assam is the biggest tea producer in the country.
- ➢ India ranks sixth in world coffee production and contributes only 4% of world coffee production.
- ➢ Cuba is known as the *Sugar Bowl of the world.* Here, sugar is made of Beetroot.
- ➢ India holds first position in the world in the production of sugar-cane and sugar.
- ➢ The importance of agriculture in the industrial sector is not only for supply of raw material, but it provides foodgrains for the people working in that sector and market for industrial products.

Agricultural Production

- ➢ Indian agriculture still depends upon monsoon.
- ➢ Agricultural production can be divided into two parts – Foodgrains and Non-foodgrains, in which the share of foodgrains is two-third and non-foodgrains is one-third.

Pattern of Government Outlay on Agriculture in the Plans

Five Year Plans	Total Plan Outlay	Outlay on Agriculture and Irrigation	Per cent of total outlay
First Plan (1951-56)	1,960	600	31
Second Plan (1956-61)	4,600	950	20
Third Plan (1961-66)	8,600	1,750	21
Fourth Plan (1969-74)	15,780	3,670	23
Fifth Plan (1974-79)	39,430	8,740	22
Sixth Plan (1980-85)	1,09,290	26,130	24
Seventh Plan (1985-90)	2,18,730	48,100	22
Eighth Plan (1992-97)	4,85,460	1,02,730	21
Ninth Plan (1997-2002)	8,59,200	1,76,217	20.5
Tenth Plan (2002-07)	15,25,639	3,05,055	20
Eleventh Plan (2007-12)	36,44,718	6,74,105	18.5

Note : 1. *Agricultural sector is composed of agriculture and allied activities rural development, special area programmes and irrigation and flood controls.*

2. *Tenth and Eleventh Plan figures are at 2006-07 prices.*

Source : *Various Five-Year Plan Documents (Courtsey : Indian Economy)*

- ➢ The percentage of plan outlay on agriculture and allied sectors to total plan outlay varied between 31% and 14.9% from the First Plan to Tenth Plan.
- ➢ Actual outlay on the agricultural sector ranged between 18 and 24% of the total Plan outlay (except during the First Plan, it was as high as 31%).

> **Foodgrains Production**
>
> This was at a record high of 259.32 million tonnes in 2011-12 in India.

- During Eleventh Plan (2007–12) the plan outlay on agriculture has declined to only 18.5%.
- During the first decade of planning (1951-61) when the First and Second Five Year Plans were implemented, the annual rate of growth in agriculture was 3.3%.
- During the next two decades of planning in 1961-81, despite spectacular progress achieved under the new agricultural strategy and IADP and HYVP, the overall progress in agriculture was dismal; the annual average rate of growth declined to 2.2% and 1.7% respectively, mainly because of bad weather and poor monsoon conditions.
- The growth rate in the 1980's was highly respectable (3.9%).
- *The Tenth Plan* had fixed a target rate of growth of 4% in agriculture to achieve 8% rate of growth in GDP.
- During *the Eleventh Plan* also, the Planning Commission has fixed the target of 4% rate of growth in agriculture.
- The Tenth Plan was the first plan which did not fix targets of crop production.
- Actual production of rice ranged between 82 and 93 million tonnes in between 1997 and 2007.
- The production of wheat which stood at 11 million tonnes in 1960-61 rose to 76 million tonnes in 1999-2000, but declined to 72 million tonnes in 2003-04.
- Actual production of wheat ranged between 69 and 75 million tonnes in between 1997-2007.
- Even now the production of pulses fluctuates between 13 and 15 million tonnes per year.
- Green revolution did not cover barley, ragi and minor-millets.
- The Green revolution was confined only to High Yielding Varieties (HYV) mainly rice, wheat, maize and jowar.
- National Agriculture Insurance Scheme was implemented in Oct. 1999.
- On 28th July 2000, the Central government fixed target for rate of growth in agriculture sector at more than 4% by 2005 under the National Agriculture Policy.

Land Reforms Programmes in India include

- Elimination of intermediaries
- Tenancy Reforms
- Determination of ceiling of holdings per family
- Distribution of surplus land among landless people
- Consolidation of holdings (Chakbandi)

- By the end of first five year plan middlemen had been removed (except small areas).
- The following measures were made effective for the betterment of farmers :
  (i) Regulation of tax (ii) Security for the rights of farmers
  (iii) Right of land ownership for the farmers

➢ For the reorganisation of agriculture land holding mainly two measures were taken – (i) Land ceiling and (ii) Chakbandi.

➢ *Land ceiling* determines the maximum land which can be held by a farmer. Holding more than that area will be illegal.

➢ *Chakbandi* of land means to aggregate the divided and broken land.

➢ The land within area less than 1 hectare, is called *marginal land holding,* 1 to 4 hectare area is called *small land holding* and the land within area more than 4 hectare, is called *large land holding.*

➢ Chakbandi was implemented first time in India in the year 1920 in Baroda.

➢ The irrigation potential in India in 2000-01 was 9.47 crore hectare.

➢ Green Revolution was started in the Third Five Year Plan.

➢ The most positive effect of Green Revolution was on wheat. There was 500% increase in crop production.

➢ *Unorganised sources* of agriculture finance are money-lenders, money-dealers, relatives, businessmen, landlords and commission agents.

➢ *Organised sources* of agriculture finance are Co-operative Committees, Co-operative Banks, Commercial Banks, Regional Rural Banks, the Government etc.

➢ Co-operative Credit Organisation started first time in 1904.

➢ Primary Co-operative Committees provide credit for short period.

➢ State Co-operative Agriculture and Rural Development Banks provide credit for long period.

➢ Land Development Bank provides long-term loans.

➢ Land Development Bank was established in the year 1919 in the form of Land Mortgage Bank.

➢ National Bank for Agriculture and Rural Development (NABARD) is the apex institution of Rural Credit. It was established on 12th July, 1982 by the merger of Agriculture Credit department and reconstruction of Agriculture and Development Corporation of the Reserve Bank of India. Its establishment is based on the recommendations of Shivraman Committee.

➢ Authorised share capital of NABARD was Rupees 500 crore. However, after an amendment its authorized share increased upto 5000 crore with effect from 1st February, 2001.

➢ Food stocks are maintained by the central government for 3 purposes :
(i) Maintaining prescribed buffer stock norms for food security,
(ii) Monthly supply through Public Distribution System (PDS),
(iii) Market intervention to stabilise open market prices.

➢ Buffer stock on January 1, 2002 was a 58 million tonnes.

➢ Two major crops of India :
(a) Kharif Crops : Sown in July and harvested in October. They include Rice, Jowar, Bajra, Maize, Cotton, Sugarcane, Soyabean, Groundnut.

(b) Rabi Crops : Sown in October and harvested in March / April. They include Wheat, Barley, Gram, Tur, Rapeseed, Mustard.

(c) Zayad Crops : Sown during March to June. It include Watermelons, Vegetables, Moong etc.

3. National Income

➢ National income is the measurement of flow of services and goods in economic system.

➢ Comparison between National income with National wealth : The national wealth is the measurement of present assets available on a given time, while the National income is the measurement of the production power of economic system in a given time period.

➢ The figures of National income are based on the financial year (i.e. from 1st April to 31st March).

➢ The base of one year is taken for calculating National income, as all the seasons come in a year.

➢ The data of estimation of India's National income are issued by Central Statistical Organisation (CSO).

Relationship among different forms of National Products

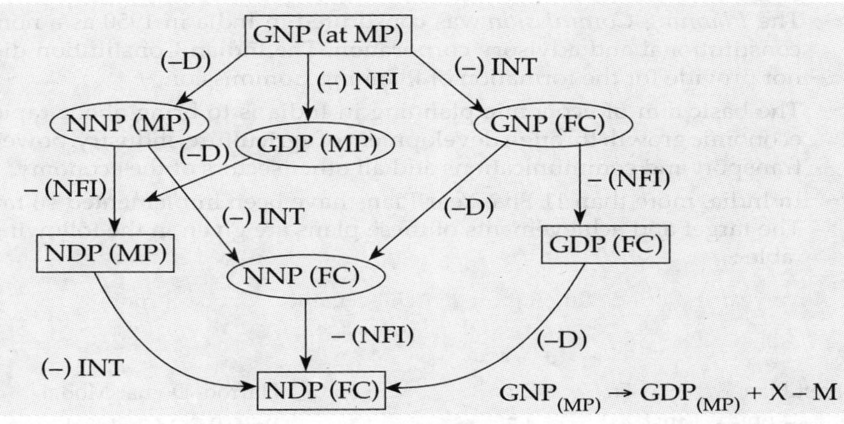

$$GNP_{(MP)} = GDP_{(MP)} + X - M$$

Where :

X = Income earned and received by nationals within the boundaries.

M = Income received by foreign nationals within the country.

NFI → Net Foreign Income.

Where :

GNP → Gross National Product
NNP → Net National Product
NDP → Net Domestic Product
GDP → Gross Domestic Product
MP → Market Price
FC → Factor Cost
D → Depreciation
INT → Indirect Net Tax

NNP at Factor Cost = NNP at market prices–Indirect Taxes + Subsidies = GNP at market prices – Indirect Taxes + Subsidies = National Incomes

4. Economic Planning

➢ Economic Planning is the process in which the limited natural resources are used skillfully so as to achieve the desired goals. The concept of Economic Planning in India, is derived from Russia (the then USSR).

➢ 'Planning' in India derives its objectives and social premises from the Directive Principles of State Policy enshrined in the Constitution.

➢ In the year 1934, the proposal relating to economic planning came for the first time in the book of Vishveshwaraiya titled "Planned Economy for India". Thereafter in 1938, the All India Congress Committee demanded for the same. In 1944 efforts were made by 8 industrialists under "Bombay Plan".

➢ Thereafter, in the same year, 'Gandhian Plan' by Mr. Mannarayan, in April, 1944 the 'People's Plan' by labour leader M.N. Roy and in January 30, 1950 the 'Sarvodaya Plan' by Mr. Jai Prakash Narayan were presented.

➢ After independence, in 1947, the committee on economic planning was constituted under the chairmanship of Jawaharlal Nehru. Thereafter, on the recommendation of this committee, Planning Commission was constituted in March, 1950 and the format of first Five Year Plan was prepared in 1951.

➢ The *Planning Commission* was constituted in India in 1950 as a non-constitutional and advisory corporation. The Indian Constitution did not provide for the formation of Planning Commission.

➢ The basic aim of economic planning in India is to bring about rapid economic growth through development of agriculture, industry, power, transport and communications and all other sectors of the economy.

➢ In India, more than 11 Five Year-Plans have been implemented so far. The target and achievements of these plans are given in the following table :

Five-year Plan	Period	Target growth rate of GDP (In % age)	Achievement (In % age)	Model
First Plan	1951-56	2.1	3.6	Harrod–Domar Model
Second Plan	1956-61	4.5	4.1	Prof. P.C. Mahalanobis
Third Plan	1961-66	5.6	2.8	Sukhmoy Chakraborty and Prof. Saddy
Fourth Plan	1969-74	5.7	3.3	Ashok Rudra and Alon S. Manney
Fifth Plan	1974-79	4.4	4.8	Alike Fourth Five-Year Plan, which is called "Investment Model of Planning Commission".
Sixth Plan	1980-85	5.2	5.7	Based on Investment Yojana, Infrastructural changing and trend to growth model

Five-year Plan	Period	Target growth rate of GDP (In % age)	Achievement (In % age)	Model
Seventh Plan	1985-90	5.0	6.0	Alike Sixth Five-Year plan prepared © Pranav Mukherjee)
Eighth Plan	1992-97	5.6	6.8	John W. Miller Model
Ninth Plan	1997-02	6.5	5.4	Created by 'Planning Commission.'
Tenth Plan	2002-07	8.0	7.2	— do —
Eleventh Plan	2007-12	9.0	—	Prepared by Prof. C Rangarajan

Source : *Planning Commission, Ninth Five Year Plan (1997-2002), Vol. I and Tenth Five Year Plan (2002-07) etc.*

- In addition to this, six yearly plans were also made. These yearly plans were made for the years 1966-67 to 1968-69, 1978-1980 and from 1990-91 to 1991-92. The plan for the year 1978-79 was continuously implemented.

First Five-Year Plan (1951-1956)

- First five year-plan was based on the "Herrod-Domar Model".
- The aim of this plan was to start process of balanced development of economy.Agriculture was on top priority in this plan.
- The First Plan emphasised, as its immediate objectives the rehabilitation of refugees, rapid agricultural development so as to achieve food self-sufficiency in the shortest possible time and control of inflation.
- This plan was successful and achieved the growth rate of 3.6%, which was more than its aim.
- During this plan there was increase of 18% in national income and 11% in per capita income.

Second Five-Year Plan (1956-1961)

- This plan was based on the P.C. Mahalanobis model.
- To establish socialist order, derived from Soviet model, the Second Plan aimed at rapid industrialisation with particular emphasis on the development of basic and heavy industries.
- In this plan, Industries and Minerals were on top priority and 20.1% of total outlay was allocated for this sector.
- Second priority was given to Transport and Communication for which 27% of total plan outlay was allocated.
- This plan was also successful and it achieved 4.1% rate of growth.
- Various important large industries like Steel Plant at Durgapur, Bhilai and Rourkela were established during this plan.

Third Five-Year Plan (1961-1966)

- The aim of this plan was to make the economy independent and to reach self active take off position. This plan is also called "Gadgil Yojana."

- This plan could not achieve its aim of 5.6% growth rate.
- In this plan, agriculture and industry both were on its priority.
- The main reason of failure of this plan was Indo-China war, Indo-Pakistan war and unprecedented drought.
- A growing trade deficit and mounting debt obligation led to more and more borrowings from the International Monetary Fund. The rupee was devalued in June 1966 to little success as it soon turned out.

Plan Holiday (From 1966-1967 to 1968–1969)

- The miserable failure of the Third Plan forced the Government to declare 'plan holiday'. Three Annual Plans were drawn in this intervening period. The economy faced another year of drought during 1966-67.
- During this period three separate plans were prepared.
- Equal priority were given to agriculture, its allied sectors and the industry sector.
- The main reason of plan holiday was Indo-Pakistan war, lack of resources and increase in price-level.

Fourth Five-Year Plan (1969-1974)

- The two main objectives of this plan were *'growth with stability'* and *'progressive achievement of self reliance'*.
- In this plan 'Establishment of socialist order' was specially aimed.
- *'Growth with justice'* and *'Garibi Hatao'* (Removal of poverty) were the main objectives of this plan.
- This plan failed to achieve its aim and it achieved only 3.3% annual rate of growth as against its aim of 5.7%.
- The shortfall during this plan was due to the adversity of climate and arrival of refugees from Bangladesh.

Fifth Five-Year Plan (1974-1979)

- The Fifth Plan draft as originally drawn up was part of a long term Perspective Plan covering a period of 10 years from 1974-75 to 1985-86.
- The two main objectives of this plan were poverty eradication and attainment of self-reliance.
- During the plan, initially, the growth rate target was fixed at 5.5.%, however, it was amended to 4.4% later on.
- Top priority was given to agriculture, next came industry and mines.
- Originally the approach paper of the Fifth Plan was prepared under C.Subramaniam in 1972, but final draft of the Plan was prepared and launched by D.P. Dhar.
- This plan was generally successful. However there was no significant decline in poverty and unemployment.
- This plan, which was started by the then ruling Janata Government was later terminated in the year 1978.

Rolling Plan (1978-1980)

- The new pattern started by Janata Government, which meant that every year performance of the plan would be assessed and a new plan based on such assessment be made for the subsequent year.

➢ The rolling plan started with an annual plan for 1978-79 and as a continuation of the terminated Fifth Plan.

Sixth Five-Year Plan (1980-1985)

➢ The Janata Government originally introduced this plan for the period 1978-83, but later a new Sixth Plan replaced it, for the period 1980-85.

➢ The basic objective of the Sixth Plan was removal of poverty. The plan aimed at achieving economic and technological self-reliance, reducing poverty, generating employment and improving the quality of life of the poorest through the Minimum Needs Programme etc.

➢ During this period the Indian economy made all round progress and most of the targets fixed by the Planning Commission were realised, though during the last year of the plan (1984-85) many parts of the country faced severe drought conditions.

➢ The target growth rate, in this plan, was fixed at 5.2% and it achieved successfully 5.7% of annual rate of growth.

➢ In this plan, important programmes like Integrated Rural Development Programme (IRDP), Minimum Needs Programme (MNP) were started.

Seventh Five-Year Plan (1985–1990)

➢ The objectives of this plan include establishment of self sufficient economy, creation of more opportunities for productive employment, slowing down the rate of population growth, to provide people with adequate nutrition and energy and environmental protection. But main aim of the plan was to increase production in all sectors and to generate opportunities for employment.

➢ There was increase in per capita income at the rate of 3.6% per annum.

➢ In this plan, for the first time private sector was given priority in comparison to public sector.

➢ In this plan, employment generating programmes like Jawahar Rozgar Yojana were started.

➢ One of the major worries during this period was widening gap between the income and expenditure of the Government, which led to mounting fiscal deficit.

Annual Plans

The Eighth Five-Year Plan (1990-95) could not take off due to the fast changing political situation at the Centre. The new government, which assumed power at the Centre in June 1991, decided that the Eight Five-Year Plan would commence on April 1, 1992 and that 1990-91 and 1991-92 should be treated as separate Annual Plans. Formulated within the framework of the Approach to the Eighth Five-Year Plan (1990-95), the basic thrust of these Annual Plans was on maximisation of employment and social transformation.

Eighth Five-Year Plan (1992–1997)

➢ The fourth version of the Eighth Plan (1992–97) was approved at a time the country was going through a severe economic crisis, a rising debt burden, ever-widening budget deficits, mounting inflation and recession in industry.

- The P.V. Narasimha Rao Government initiated the process of fiscal reforms as also economic reforms.
- In this plan the utmost priority was given to "Development of Human Resources" i.e. Employment, Education and Public Health. In addition to this, the important aim made in this plan was to strengthen the basic infrastructure by the end of the decade.
- This plan was successful and got 6.8% annual rate of growth, which was more than its target of 5.6%.
- During this period, Pradhan Mantri Rozgar Yojana (PMRY) was started in the year 1993.

Ninth Five-Year Plan (1997–2002)

- The Ninth Plan was launched in the fiftieth (50th) year of India's Independence.
- Planning Commission released the draft Ninth Plan document on March 1, 1998. The focus of the plan is "Growth with Social Justice and Equity".
- It assigned the priority to agriculture and rural development with a view to generating adequate productive employment and eradication of poverty. However, the plan failed to achieve the GDP growth target of 7% and realized only 5.35% average GDP growth.
- The recession in international economy was held responsible for the failure of ninth plan.

Tenth Five-Year Plan (2002–2007)

- In the Tenth five-year plan, it had been proposed to eradicate poverty and unemployment and to double the per capita income in next 10 years.
- The Tenth Plan has indicated that the current backlog of unemployment is around 35 million persons, i.e. 9% of the labour force.
- The Tenth Plan was expected to follow a regional approach rather than sectoral approach to bring down regional inequalities.

Some creditable achievements of the 10th Plan

- Gross domestic savings (as percent of GDP at market prices) averaged 28.2% in 10th Plan as against 23.1% in the 9th Plan.
- India's foreign exchange reserves reached a level of US $ 185 billion in February 2007.
- Though the 10th Plan could not achieve its target of 8% growth of GDP, but has taken the economy to a higher trajectory of growth rate at 7.6% as against 5.5% in the 9th Plan.
- Foreign investment flows were of the order of US $ 20.2 billion in 2005-06–US $ 7.7 billion in the form of Foreign Direct Investment (FDI) and US $ 12.5 billion in the form of Portfolio Investment (PI). In 2006–07, out of total inflows of the order of $ 29.1 billion, FDI accounted for $ 22.1 billion (i.e. 76% of total).

Eleventh Five Year Plan (2007–2012)

- The National Development Council (NDC), country's highest policy making body, endorsed the 11th Plan document on 19th December, 2007.

- It envisages an average 9% GDP growth in the first four years to end the five-year period with a growth of 10% during the terminal year 2011-12.
- Earlier 7.6% growth rate in the 10th Plan and 5.52% in the 9th Plan was achieved.
- Total Plan expenditure for the 11th Plan period (2007-12) has been proposed to the tune of Rs. 36,44,718 crore, which is more than the double of the Plan expenditure of the 10th Plan.
- Of the total Plan expenditure fixed for the 11th Plan, Centre's share would be Rs. 21,56,571 crore where as the share of the States would be to the tune of Rs. 14,88,147 crore.
- Gross Budgetary Support (GBS) for the Plan expenditure of 2007- 12 has been fixed to Rs. 14,21,711 crore, where as it was Rs. 8,10,400 crore for the 10th Plan.
- Of the GBS 74.67% will be for the Priority sectors and the rest 25.33% for non priority sectors. For the 10th Plan it was 55.20% and 44.80% respectively.
- In the 11th plan (2007–12), overall rate of growth of GDP was 8.0%. Under-achiever was the agriculture, rate of growth of which remained low at 3.3% over the plan period, as compared to the 4% target rate of growth.
- The 11th plan visualised "Faster and more inclusive growth" as its objective.
- Balance of trade deficit has reached US $ 644 billion in this plan period (2007–12), indicating at payment crisis during the terminal year of the 11th FYP. It was this payment crisis which led to sudden depreciation of rupee in 2012, when rupee plunged from ₹48.70 per US dollar in February 2012 up to ₹58 per US dollar by June 2012.
- It is noteworthy here that India's trade-deficit which was of the order of $10.69 billion in 2003–04 has shot up to $185 billion in 2011–12.
- CAD (current account deficit) has been on rise since 2006–07 and by the year 2010-11 it had reached $45.9 billion.
- Under the shadow of deceleration in our economic growth especially industrial growth, galloping inflation, depreciation of rupee and balance of payment problems, the 12th FYP has begun.

Twelfth Five Year Plan (2012 – 2017)

- The Approach Paper of the 12th Plan, approved by the NDC (National Development Council) in 2011, had set a target of 9% average-growth of GDP over the plan period (2012 – 17).
- The broad vision and aspirations of the 12th FYP (Five Year Plan) are reflected in the subtitle 'Faster, Sustainable and More Inclusive Growth'.
- The 12th Plan sets an ambitious target of one lakh MW in power-generation, where as actual realization in 11th Plan was 50,000 MW, on account of slippage in public sector power projects.
- It seems that Government is intending to withdraw from infrastructure sector in the 12th Plan and laying more emphasis on PPP (public private partnership).

- The Approach Paper of 12th FYP states that India has 1017 PPP projects accounting for ₹ 4,86,603 crores.
- India to-day is second only to China in terms of number of PPP projects and terms of investments it is second to Brazil.

Types of planning

Imperative Planning : In this type of planning the Central Planning authority decides upon every aspect of the economy and the targets set and the processes delineated to achieve them are to be strictly followed. This type of planning is mainly practised in the socialist economies.

Indicative Planning : In this type of planning the State sets broad parameters and goals for the economy. It is different from centralised planning as unlike in the latter, the State does not see Plan targets to the minutest details, but only broadly indicates the targets to be achieved. It was adopted in our country since the 8th Five-Year Plan, as practised in many developed countries.

Perspective Planning : It's a type of planning for a long period of time, usually 15-20 years. As a highly specialised task, it is operationalised through the Five Year and Annual Plans. In such form of planning, the planners formulate a perspective Plan that broadly defines the direction desired to be taken by the economy.

Rolling Plan : Under the scheme of rolling Plans, there are three different steps. First, a plan for the current year which includes the annual budget. Second, a plan for a fixed number of years, say three, four or five. It is revised every year as per the requirements of the economy. Third, a perspective plan for 10, 15 or 20 years.

Core Plan : As per this concept, the Planning Commission asks the states to submit their projected revenue estimates. On the basis of these estimates, Planning Commission determines the expenditure heads for State Annual Plans. This helps in keeping the Plan target to realistic limits and prevents diversion of funds from the priority items to the non-plan account. The concept of 'Core Plan' has emerged recently.

Planning Commission : Structure and Functions

- The Central body for making plans in India is the Planning Commission.
- Planning Commission was constituted on 15th March, 1950. The Prime Minister is the ex-officio Chairman of this Commission.
- There is no provision for (or mention of) Planning Commission in the Constitution of India.
- It was constituted in the form of an advisory and specialist institution.
- It was constituted by the Union Cabinet on the proposal of a member of Union Parliament.
- The government has changed its organisation and structure from time to time.
- Pandit Jawaharlal Nehru was the first Chairman of the Planning Commission.

- There is no fix term/ tenure of the Deputy Chairman and members of Planning Commission.
- The members are appointed by the government.
- The government can change the number of its members.
- The Deputy Chairman of the Planning Commission enjoys the status of a cabinet rank minister.
- The Commission estimates physical-capital and human resources.
- The Commission prepares plan for maximum effective and impartial use of national resources.
- The Commission makes critical analysis of each step and gives reformative suggestions.
- Final clearance to planning is given by "National Development Council". v

National Development Council

- National Development Council was constituted on 6th August, 1952.
- The Prime Minister is the ex-officio Chairman and the Secretary of Planning Commission is the ex-officio Secretary of this Council.
- Chief Ministers of all the states and the members of Planning Commission are the members of National Development Council.
- National Development Council (NDC) is an extra constitutional body.
- Its aim is to make co-operative environment for economic planning between states and Planning Commission.
- The main functions of NDC are :
  - (i) To evaluate the management of plans from time to time.
  - (ii) To analyse the policies affecting development.
  - (iii) To give suggestions to achieve the aim fixed in the plans.
  - (iv) To give final shape to the plan.

Models of economic development

Nehru-Mahalanobis Model :

- Nehru–Mahalanobis model of development emerged as the driving force of the strategy of development adopted at the time of formulation of the Second Five Year Plan and has continued right up to the eighties.
- It aimed at enlargement of opportunities for the less privileged sections of the society.
- Growth with social justice was the goal of Nehru–Mahalanobis model since it intended to foster a self–generating path of development with an assurance to the common man that poverty, unemployment, disease and ignorance would be removed so that individuals could realise their potential with the extension of social and economic opportunities.
- In the Nehru–Mahalanobis model the *State controlled the commanding heights of the economy through the public sector.*

The Gandhian Model of Growth

- 'Gandhian Plan' was brought out by Acharya S.N. Agarwala in 1944 and was re-affirmed in 1948, formed the basis of Gandhian model of growth.

- The basic objective of this model is to raise the *material as well as the cultural level* of the Indian masses so as to provide a basic standard of life.
- It aims primarily at improving the economic conditions of the villages of India and hence, it lays the greatest emphasis on the scientific development of agriculture and rapid growth of cottage and village industries.
- The Gandhian model aims at the reform of agriculture as the most important sector in economic planning in India.
- The Gandhian model's primary aim is the attainment of maximum self-sufficiency in village communities. Hence, the plan emphasises the rehabili -tation, development and expansion of cottage industries side by side with agriculture. Spinning and weaving are given the first place.
- While Nehru wanted to give prime importance to heavy industries, the Gandhian model attempts to give primacy to agriculture supported by handicrafts and cottage industries.

LPG Model of Development

- The LPG Model of development was introduced in 1991 by the then Finance Minister Dr. Manmohan Singh.
- This model was intended to charter a new strategy with emphasis on liberalisation, privatisation and globlisation (LPG).
- LPG Model of development emphasises a bigger role for the private sector.
- It envisages a much larger quantum of foreign direct investment to supplement our growth process.
- It aims at a strategy of export led growth as against import substitution practised earlier.
- It also aims at reducing the role of the State significantly and thus abandons planning fundamentalism in favour of a more liberal and market driven pattern of development.

PURA Model of Development

- The Union Cabinet on 20th Jaunary, 2004 accorded in principle approval for the execution of PURA within the gross budgetary support for bridging the rural-urban divide and achieving balanced socio-economic development.
- Though, Dr. A.P.J Abdul Kalam, ever since he became the President of India has been advocating his *Vision 2020,* and, to eradicate poverty from India, he has been emphasiging the adoption of PURA *(Providing Urban Amenities in Rural Areas);* however, it was Mahatma Gandhi who underlined the exploitation of rural society by its urban counterpart.
- The objective of PURA is to propel economic development without population transfers.
- The PURA concept is the response to the need for creating social and economic infrastructure which can create a conducive climate for investment by the private sector to invest in rural areas.

- ➢ Although PURA draws its inspiration from the Gandhian model of development which emphsises rural development as a fundamental postulate, yet in the prescription, it is neo–Gandhian is the sense, that it intends to bring rural regeneration with the avowed objective of taking modern technology and modern amenities to the rural areas.
- ➢ It does emphasize the enlargement of employment as the *sole objective* to make use of rural manpower in various development activities.
- ➢ The PURA model, however, attempts a reconciliation between employment and GDP growth objectives.
- ➢ The 11th Plan (2007–12) has provided Rs. 248 crores for implementing the PURA scheme in compact rural areas in public–private partnership (PPP) mode.

5. Unemployment

- ➢ In common parlance anybody who is not gainfully employed in any productive activity is called unemployed. However, it can be of two kinds (i) voluntary unemployed and (ii) involuntary unemployed. Here we are concerned with the second category of unemployed persons.
- ➢ Hence, unemployment can be defined as a situation when persons able and willing to work are seeking jobs at the prevailing wage level but they are unable to get the same.
- ➢ Unemployment in developing economies like India is not the result of deficiency of effective demand in the Keynesian sense, but a consequence of shortage of capital equipment or other complementary resources.
- ➢ In India unemployment is structural in nature due to lack of productive capacity and resources.

Types of Unemployment

(i) Cyclical unemployment : It is the result of depression in an economy.

(ii) Frictional unemployment : This kind of unemployment is temporary. It is the result of a situation when new industries drive out old ones and workers change over to better jobs.

(iii) Open unemployment : It refers to those who have no work to do even though they are able and willing to do work.

(iv) Seasonal unemployment : This occurs at certain period of the work when work load is comparatively less, and hence people are rendered jobless. For example, in the period between past harvest and next sowing, agricultural labourers are unemployed.

(v) Educated unemployed : This is mainly found in urban areas. Those educated persons who are unable to get work come under this category.

(vi) Under–employment (Disguised unemployment) : It results when a person contributes to production less than what he or she is capable of, for example, an engineer working as a clerk is under–employed.

(vii) Compulsory unemployment : It means the labour power which is ready to work on the current rate but does not get the work.

(viii) Seasonal unemployment : It means the unemployment of the farmers and farm labourers during non-crop seasons.

➢ During Ninth Plan, total 3.6 crore fresh unemployeds began to look for employment.

➢ The Planning Commission collects data of unemployment on the basis of 'Lakadawala Formula' effective from 11th March, 1997 and prior to this the process to collect data was on the basis of surveys of National Sample Survey Organisation (NASO).

➢ In 8th Plan, the aim was to create 1 crore employment. During Ninth Plan the additional requirement of work opportunities was approximately 5 crore 30 lakhs.

➢ In India, the data relating to unemployment are collected by National Sample Survey Organisation (NASO). This Organisation has the following concepts with regard to unemployment :

(1) General status of unemployment : In this category, generally, those unemployed for more than one year are included. As such it is a long-term unemployment.

(2) Weekly-unemployment : The persons who have not got work for even one hour in a week are included in this category.

(3) Daily unemployment : It is considered the best concept of unemployment.

➢ The main reasons for unemployment in India are slow economic development, population explosion, outdated technique, improper education system and limited effect of government planning.

Labour Force Growth and Employment Requirements during Tenth Plan

➢ Job opportunities will need to be created for 53 million persons during 1997-2002 as a consequence of labour force increase, for 58 million during 2002-07 and thereafter for 55 million during 2007-12.

➢ Out of the projected increase of employment of the order of 50 million during the Ninth Plan, 24.2 million employment opportunities - 48.2% would be created in agriculture alone.

Employment Requirements during the 11th Plan (2007–12)

➢ On account of the increasing participation of females, the total increase in labour force will be around 65 million during the 11th Plan. To this may be added the present backlog of about 35 million. Thus, the total job requirements of the 11th Plan work out be 100 million.

➢ The planners aims to provide 65 million additional employment opportunities.

➢ According to the Approach paper of the 11th plan—

★ Average daily status unemployment rate, which had increased from 6.1% in 1993–94 to 7.3% in 1999–00 increased further to 8.3% in 2004–05.

★ Among agricultural labour households, which represent the poorest groups, there was a sharp increase in unemployment from 9.3% in 1993–94 to a high level of 15.3% in 2004–05.

★ Non–agricultural employment expanded robustly at an annual rate of 4.7% during 1999–2005.

★ Employment in the organized sector actually declined by 0.38% per annum during 1994–2000.

Unemployment Rates between 1993-94 and 2004–05

➢ The results of the 61st Round of NSSO Survey Employment and Unemployment are based on a sample size which is neither large nor small by standards of previous NSSO rounds.

➢ The unemployment rate based on current daily status in 2004–05 for males was 8.0% (up from 7.2% in 1993-94) in rural areas and at 7.5% percent (up from 7.3% in 1993-94) in urban areas.

➢ The corresponding figure for females was 8.7% (up from 7.0% in 1993-94) in rural areas and 11.6% (up from 9.4% in 1993-94) in urban areas.

Employment Opportunities

➢ Instead of achieving an employment elasticity of 0.38 as projected in the Ninth Plan, the actual employment elasticity achieved during 1993-94 to 1999-2000 was 0.15.

➢ The employment projections reveal that with 6.5% GDP growth, employment will increase from a level of 397 million in 1999-2000 to 468 million in 2012 - an increase of 71 million in a period of 12 years, giving an annual average growth of 5.9 million.

Development and employment programmes at a glance

SL. No.	Programme/Plan/ Institution	Year of beginning	Objective/Description
1.	Community Development Programme (CDP)	1952	Over all development of rural area with people's participation.
2.	Intensive Agriculture Development Programme (IADP)	1960-61	To provide loan, seeds, fertilizer tools to the farmers.
3.	Intensive Agriculture Area Programme (IAAP)	1964-65	To develop the Special harvests.
4.	High Yielding Variety Programme (HYVP)	1966-67	To increase productivity of food grains by adopting latest varieties of inputs for crops.
5.	Indian Tourism Development Corporation (ITDC)	Oct. 1966	To arrange for the construction of Hotels and Guest houses at various places of the country.
6.	Green Revolution	1966-67	To increase the foodgrains, spec ially wheat production (Credit goes to Dr. M.S. Swaminathan in India and Nobel laureate Dr. Norman Borlaug in the world).

SL. No.	Programme/Plan/ Institution	Year of beginning	Objective/Description
7.	Nationalisation of 14 Banks	19 July 1969	To provide loans for agriculture, rural development and other priority sectors.
8.	Employment Guarantee Scheme of Maharashtra	1972-73	To assist the economically weaker sections of the rural society.
9.	Accelerated Rural Water Supply Programme (ARWSP)	1972-73	For providing drinking water in the villages.
10.	Small Farmer Development Agency (SFDA)	1974-75	For technical and financial assistance to small farmers.
11.	Command Area Development Programme (CADP)	1974-75	To ensure better and rapid utilisation of irrigation capacities of medium and large projects.
12.	Twenty Point Programme (TPP)	1975	Poverty eradication and raising the standard of living.
13.	National Institution of Rural Development (NIRD)	1977	Training, investigation and advisory organisation for rural development.
14.	Desert Development Programme (DDP)	1977-78	For controlling the desert expasion and maintaining environmental balance.
15.	Food for Work Programme (FWP)	1977-78	Providing foodgrains to labour for the works of development.
16.	Antyodaya Yojana	1977-78	To make the poorest families of the village economically independent (only in Rajasthan State).
17.	Training Rural Youth for Self-Employment (TRYSEM)	August 15, 1979	Programme of training rural youth for self-employment.
18.	Integrated Rural Development Programme (IRDP)	October 2, 1980	All-round development of the rural poor through a programme of asset endowment for self-employment.
19.	National Rural Employ-ment Programme (NREP)	1980	To provide profitable employment opportunities to the rural poor.
20.	Development of Women and Children in Rural Areas (DWCRA)	September 1982	To provide suitable opportunities of self-employment to the women belonging to the rural families who are living below the poverty line.
21.	Rural Landless Employment Guarantee Progra-mme (RLEGP)	August 15, 1993	For providing employment to landless farmers and labourers.
22.	Self-Employment to the Educated Unemployed Youth (SEEUY)	1983-84	To provide financial and technical assistance for self-employment.

SL. No.	Programme/Plan/ Institution	Year of beginning	Objective/Description
23.	Farmer Agriculture Service Centre's (FASC's)	1983-84	To popularise the use of improved agricultural instruments and tool kits.
24.	National Fund for Rural Development (NFRD)	February 1984	To grant 100% tax rebate to donors and also to provide financial assistance for rural development projects.
25.	Industrial Reconstruction Bank of India	March 1985	To provide financial assistance to sick and closed industrial units for their reconstruction.
26.	Comprehensive Crop Insurance Scheme	April 1, 1985	For insurance of agricultural crops.
27.	Council for Advancement of People's Actionand Rural Technology (CAPART) (H.Q.- New Delhi)	Sep. 1, 1986	To provide assistance for rural prosperity.
28.	Self-Employment Programme for the Urban Poor (SEPUP)	Sep. 1986	To provide self-employment to urban poor through provision of subsidy and bank credit.
29.	Formation of Securities and Exchange Board of India (SEBI)	April 1988	To safeguard the interest of investors in capital market and to regulate share market.
30.	Jawahar Rozgar Yojana	April 1, 1989	For providing employment to rural unemployed.
31.	Nehru Rozgar Yojana	October 1989	For providing employment to urban unemployed.
32.	Agriculture and Rural Debt Relief Scheme (ARDRS)	1990	To exempt bank loans upto Rs.10,000 of rural artisans and weavers.
33.	Scheme of Urban Micro Enterprises (SUME)	1990	To assist the urban poor people for small enterprise.
34.	Scheme of Urban Wage Employment (SUWE)	1990	To provide wages employment after arranging the basic facilities for poor people in the urban areas where population is less than one lakh.
35.	Scheme of Housing and and Shelter Upgradation (SHASU)	1990	To provide employment by means of shelter upgradation in the urban areas where population is between 1 to 20 lakh.
36.	Supply of Improved Toolkits to Rural Artisans	July 1992	To supply modern toolkits to the rural craftsmen except the weavers, tailors, embroiders and tobacco labourers who are living below the poverty line.

SL. No.	Programme/Plan/ Institution	Year of beginning	Objective/Description
37.	Employment Assurance Scheme (EAS)	October 2, 1993	To provide employment of at least 100 days in a year in villages.
38.	Members of Parliament Local Area Development Scheme (MPLADS)	December 23, 1993	To sanction Rs. 5 crore per year to every Member of Parliament for various development works in their respective areas through DM of the district.
39.	District Rural Development Agency (DRDA)	1993	To provide financial assistance for rural development.
40.	Mahila Samridhi Yojana	October 2, 1993	To encourage the rural women to deposit in Post Office Savings Account.
41.	Child Labour Eradication Scheme	August 15, 1994	To shift child labour from hazardous industries to schools.
42.	Prime Minister's Integrated Urban Poverty Eradication Programme (PMIUPEP)	November 18, 1995	To attack urban poverty in an integrated manner in 345 towns having population between 50,000 to 1 lakh.
43.	Group Life Insurance Scheme in Rural Areas	1995-96	To provide insurance facilities to rural people on low premium
44.	National Social Assistance Programme	1995	To assist people living below the poverty line.
45.	Ganga Kalyan Yojana	1997-98	To provide financial assistance to farmers for exploring and developing ground and surface water resources.
46.	Kasturba Gandhi Education Scheme	August 15, 1997	To establish girls schools in districts having low female literacy rate.
47.	Swarna Jayanti Shahari Rozgar Yojana (SJSRY)	December, 1997	To provide gainful employment to urban unemployed and under employed poor through self-employment or wage employment.
48.	Bhagya Shree Bal Kalyan Policy	Oct. 19, 1998	To uplift the girls conditions.
49.	Rajrajeshwari Mahila Kalyan Yojana (RMKY)	Oct. 19, 1998	To provide insurance protection to women.
50.	Annapurna Yojana	March 1999	To provide 10 kg. foodgrains to senior citizens (who do not get pension).

SL. No.	Programme/Plan/ Institution	Year of beginning	Objective/Description
51.	Swarna Jayanti Gram Swarozgar Yojana (SJGSY)	April 1999	For eliminating rural poverty and unemployment and promoting self-employment.
52.	Jawahar Gram Samridhi Yojana (JGSY)	April 1999	Creation of demand driven community village infrastructure.
53.	Jan Shree Bima Yojana	Aug. 10, 2000	Providing Insurance Security to people living below the poverty line.
54.	Pradhan Mantri Gramodaya Yojana	2000	To fulfill basic requirements in rural areas.
55.	Antyodaya Anna Yojana	Dec. 25, 2000	To provide food security to the poor.
56.	Ashraya Bima Yojana	June 2001	To provide compensation to labourers who have lost their employment.
57.	Pradhan Mantri Gram Sadak Yojana (PMGSY)	Dec. 25, 2000	To line all villages with Pucca Road.
58.	Khetihar Mazdoor Bima Yojana	2001-2002	Insurance of Landless Agricultural workers.
59.	Shiksha Sahyog Yojana	2001-2002	Education for Children below Poverty Line.
60.	Sampurna Gramin Rojgar Yojana	Sept. 25, 2001	Providing employment and food security to rural people.
61.	Jai Prakash Narain Rojgar Guarantee Yojana	Proposed in 2002-03 Budget	Employment Guarantee in most poor districts.
62.	Swajaldhara Yojana	2002	Started in Dec. 2002, for ensuring drinking water supply to all villages by 2004.
63.	Hariyali Pariyojana	2003	Inaugurated on January 27, 2003 by the Prime Minister. It aims at tackling the problems of irrigation and drinking water, along with boosting tree plantation programme and fisheries developments in rural areas.
64.	Social Security Pilot Scheme	Jan. 23, 2004	Scheme for labourers of unorganised sector for providing family pension, insurance and medical.
65.	Vande Matram Scheme	Feb. 9, 2004	Major initiative in public–private partnership during pregnancy check-up.

SL. No.	Programme/Plan/ Institution	Year of beginning	Objective/Description
66.	National Food for Work Programme	November 14, 2004	Inaugurated by the Prime Minister on November 14, 2004. This programme is to be implemented initially in 150 districts of the country. It aims at providing 100 days' employment in a year to all able bodied unemployed rural folk.
67.	Janani Suraksha Yojana	April 12, 2005	Takes the place of National Maternity Benefit Scheme. It will be a part of the National Rural Health Mission (NRHM).
68.	Bharat Nirman Yojana	Dec. 16, 2005	Development of Rural infrastructure including six components: Irrigation, Water supply, Housing, Road, Telephone and Eelectricity.
69.	National Rural Employment Guarantee Programme (NREGP)	Feb. 2, 2006	The provisions are the same as for food for work programme. The scheme was enforced in 200 districts of the country to begin with. To provide atleast 100 days wages employment in rural areas in a year. The scheme is 100% centrally sponsored.

Bharat Nirman Yojana

➢ The Union Government launched a new comprehensive scheme, named 'Bharat Nirman Yojana' on December 16, 2005.

➢ This scheme aims at developing rural infrastructure.

➢ The duration of implementing this scheme has been fixed for four years with an expected expenditure of Rs. 174000 crore.

➢ The major six sectors and their targets for next four years are :

★ Irrigation : To ensure irrigation for additional one crore hectare of land by 2009.

★ Roads : To link all villages of 1000 population with main roads and also to link all ST and hilly villages upto 500 population with roads.

★ Housing : Construction of 60 lakh additional houses for the poor.

★ Water supply : To ensure drinking water to all remaining 74000 villages.

★ Electrification : To supply electricity to all remaining 1,25,000 villages and to provide electricity connections to 2.3 crore houses.

★ Rural Communication : To provide telephone facility to all remaining 66,822 villages.

Mahatma Gandhi National Rural Employment Guarantee Act (MNREGA)

- ➢ The National Rural Employment Guarantee Bill was passed by Parliament on September 7, 2005. It secured Presidential assent later in 2005 itself and became an Act.
- ➢ The Act provides for at least 100 days of employment to one able bodied person in every rural household every year.
- ➢ The wages admissible are around Rs. 120 per day.
- ➢ The Act (NREGA) came into force from Feb. 2, 2006. Initially 200 districts have been selected for the enforcement of the scheme.
- ➢ Works under the NREGA generated 90 crore (nearly one billion) person days of employment in 2006-07, at a cost of about Rs. 9,000 crore.
- ➢ The Government has extended the NREGA to all 604 districts of the country, with a total budget outlay of Rs. 16,000 crore for the extended scheme for 2008-09 (April 1, 2008).

Note : *The Govt. of India, October 2, 2009 renamed the NREGA as the Mahatma Gandhi National Rural Employment Guarantee Act (MNREGA).*

Employment guarantee act, 2005

The Government, on the advice of the National Advisory Council, has passed the National Rural Employment Guarantee Act. The main features of the Act are :

1. Every household in rural India will have a right to at least 100 days of guaranteed employment every year for at least one adult member. The employment will be in the form of casual manual labour at the statutory minimum wage, and the wages shall be paid within 7 days of the week during which work was done.
2. Work should be provided within 15 days of demanding it, and the work should be located within 5 kilometer distance.
3. If work is not provided to anybody within the given time, he/she will be paid a daily unemployment allowance, which will be at least one-third of the minimum wages.
4. Workers employed on public works will be entitled to medical treatment and hospitalization in case of injury at work, along with a daily allowance of not less than half of the statutory minimum wage. In case of death or disability of a worker, an ex-gratia payment shall be made to his legal heirs as per provisions of the Workmen Compensation Act.
5. 5% of wages may be deducted as contribution to welfare schemes like health insurance, accident insurance, survivor benefits, maternity benefits and social security schemes.
6. For non-compliance with rules, strict penalties have been laid down.
7. For transparency and accountability, all accounts and records of the programme will be made available for public scrutiny.
8. The District Collector/Chief Executive Officer will be responsible for the programme at the district level.
9. The Gram Sabha will monitor the work of the Gram Panchayat by way of social audit.

Some Important Development and Employment Programmes

- During the Seventh Five-Year Plan, a scheme called 'Jawahar Rozgar Yojana' was introduced from April 1989 to solve the problem of unemployment in the rural sector. The former ongoing two main rural employment programmes National Rural Employment Programme (NREP) and Rural Landless Employment Guarantee Programme (RLEGP) were merged with Jawahar Rozgar Yojana.
- The total expenditure on Jawahar Rozgar Yojna was shared by the Centre and the State Government in the ratio of 80 : 20.
- Under the Jawahar Rozgar Yojana, 30% employment opportunities was reserved for women.
- Under the Jawahar Rozgar Yojana, it was made compulsory to spend 60% of the total expenditure on labour used in the works completed under the scheme.
- A sub-plan of Jawahar Rozgar Yojana—'Indira Awas Yojana' was made an independent scheme in itself on January 1, 1996.
- The Employment Assurance Scheme (EAS), was introduced on October 2, 1993, in selective rural areas. The aim of this scheme is to provide work in the form of unskilled physical labour to all the employment seeking men and women (of ages between 18 years to 60 years) in rural areas. The expenditure on this scheme is shared by the Centre and the States in the ratio of 80 : 20. From maximum of 2 members from one family can be benefitted under this scheme. Since January 1, 1996, the Integrated Jawahar Rozgar Yojana (IJRY) has been merged with Employment Assurance Scheme (EAS).
- The Integrated Rural Development Programme (IRDP) was started on an experimental basis in 1978-79. This programme was launched in the whole country on October 2, 1980. The basic aim of IRDP was to provide assistance to rural poor families living below the poverty line.
- The Integrated Rural Development Programme is financially assisted by the Centre and States in the ratio of 50 : 50.
- Under the Integrated Rural Development Programme, targeted group includes atleast 50% families belonging to scheduled caste and scheduled tribe. Apart from this, among the beneficiaries, 50% were females and 3% physically handicapped persons.
- Development of Women and Children in Rural Areas (DWCRA) and Training Rural Youth for Self-Employment (TRYSEM) were the sub-plans of Integrated Rural Development Programme (IRDP).
- The objective of TRYSEM was to provide training to those rural youth (ages 18-35 years) who belong to the families living below the poverty line. This programme was started on August 15, 1979.

Development of Women and Children in Rural Area Programme (DWCRA) was started in September 1982. Under this programme, a group of 10-15 women was taken, who belong to the families living below the poverty line and they were given training for starting any economic activity. Every group was given the economic assistance of Rs. 25,000.

Swarn Jayanti Shahari Rozgar Yojana

➢ The Urban Self-employment Programme and Urban Wage-Employment Programmes of the Swaran Jayanti Shahari Yojana, which substituted (in December 1997) various programmes operated earlier for poverty alleviation.

➢ SJSRY is funded on 75:25 basis between the Centre and the States.

➢ During the 3-year period (1997-98 and 1999-2000), a total of Rs. 353 crores were spent on SJSRY generating 21.8 million mandays of employment.

Swarna Jayanti Gram Swarozgar Yojana (SGSY) : The Government has introduced Swarna Jayanti Gram Swarozgar Yojana on April 1, 1999 and the previous six ongoing schemes have been merged with this scheme, they are—1. IRDP 2. TRYSEM 3. DWCRA 4. MWS 5. SITRA 6. Ganga Kalyan Yojana. The SGSY is a holistic programme covering all the aspects of self employment. The scheme is funded on 75 : 25 basis by the centre and states.

➢ The Drought-prone Area Programme was started in 1973 with the objective of developing the drought-prone area and also re-establishing the environmental balance. This programme is financially assisted by the Centre and the concerned State Governments in the ratio of 50 : 50.

➢ The Desert Development Programme was started in 1977-78 to end the ill-effects of drought in desert areas and also to stop the process of desert expansion. This programme is implemented on the basis of cent-per-cent financial assistance rendered by the Central Government.

➢ The Rural Landless Employment Guarantee Programme (RLEGP) began on August 15, 1993 and National Rural Employment Programme (NREP) on October 2, 1980. During Seventh Five-Year Plan, these programmes were *merged with* Jawahar Rozgar Yojana.

➢ Council for Advancement of Peoples Action and Rural Technology (CAPART) is an independent section of the Rural Development Department of the Government of India; which was established on September 1, 1986. For rural development works, 'CAPART' provides grants to voluntary organisations. The head office of CAPART is at New Delhi.

➢ Following programmes are being implemented by the Ministry of the Urban Development to eradicate Urban Poverty—(i) Nehru Rozgar Yojana (ii) Urban Basic Services for the Poor (iii) Programme of Environment Improvement of Urban Slums.

➢ The Nehru Rozgar Yojana began on October 1989 which was revised in March 1990. Under this Yojana following schemes were included—(i) Scheme of Urban Micro Enterprises—SUME (ii) Scheme of Urban Wage Employment—SUWE (iii) Scheme of Housing and Shelter Upgradation—SHASU.

➢ The Prime Minister's Rozgar Yojana (PMRY) was started for October 2, 1993 for the educated unemployed youth and initially was in operation in urban areas. From April 1, 1994 onwards the scheme is being implemented throughout the country. Its objective was to give employment to 10 lakhs educated unemployed urban youth by establishing 7 lakh micro enterprises during the Eighth Five Year Plan. During 1993-94, this yojana was implemented in urban areas only but since April 1, 1994 it was extended to the whole country.

★ SHGs (Self-Help Groups) are considered eligible for financing under the PMRY, effective from December 8, 2003 (terms modified on July 30, 2004) provided all members individually satisfy the eligibility criteria laid down and total membership does not exceed twenty (20). There is also a ceiling on the loan amount.

6. Trade and Commerce

➢ Indian Trade was extremely developed during ancient time.

➢ After the British East India Company was established in 1600, the trade between India and Britain was in India's favour till 1757.

➢ At that time East India Company used to purchase clothes and spices in exchange for costly metals.

➢ The British Government decided to impose heavy Duty on the clothes to destroy the structure of Industries.

➢ During the later part of 18th Century, after Industrial revolution in Britain there was heavy production of cheap items. To sell those cheap items in world market, the tradition of colonisation began.

➢ British Companies established monopoly on the sale of cotton. As a result, the Indian weaver got costly raw material and thus Indian products became costly.By 1813, Indian Handloom business was completely ruined.

➢ In the later part of 19th Century, the establishment of modern industries on the basis of power machines started. First time in India, the textile industries came into being.

➢ *First Factory of Cotton Textile* in India was established in 1818 at Ghughari near Kolkata, which failed.

➢ The Second Factory of Cotton Textile was established by a businessman Kawas Ji Nana Bhai in Mumbai in 1853.

➢ In 1855, first Jute Factory was established in Rishara (West Bengal).

➢ In 1853, after the establishment of railway in India industrial development got momentum here. Rapid expansion of Indian industries started due to development of the means of communication.

➢ Jamshedji Tata established first Steel Factory in Jamshedpur in 1907.

7. New Economic Policy

➢ New Economic Policy is related to economic reforms. Its aim is to bring about reforms in production pattern, to obtain new technology and to use full capacity expeditiously and in toto.

➢ The New Economic Policy was devised and implemented, for the first time in the year 1985 during the period of Prime Minister Rajiv Gandhi.

- The second wave of new economic reforms came in the year 1991 during the period of P.V. Narsimha Rao government.
- The main reason to start new economic policy (1991) was Gulf-War and problem of balance of payment in India.
- Three main objectives of new economic policy were – Liberalisation Privatisation, and Globalisation.
- Main sectors of new economic reform policy, 1991 were – Fiscal Policy, Monetary Policy, Value Fixation Policy, Foreign Policy, Industrial Policy, Foreign Investment Policy, Business Policy and Public Sector Policy.
- The following four main steps were taken under the Fiscal Policy, 1991:
  - (i) To control public expenditure strictly
  - (ii) To expand Tax Net
  - (iii) To observe discipline in management of funds of Central and State governments.
  - (iv) To curtail grants (subsidy)
- Under the Monetary Policy, steps were taken to control inflation.
- Measures implemented under the Industrial Reforms Policy, 1991 were:
  - (i) Delicencing of industries except the list of 18 industries.
  - (ii) M.R.T.P. norms were relaxed for disinvestment.
  - (iii) The areas reserved for public sector were opened to private sector.
- The objectives fixed for reforms in the Foreign Investment Policy, 1991 were :
  - (i) Direct foreign investment upto 50% was given automatic approval, in many industries.
  - (ii) Foreign companies, involved in export activities were allowed to invest upto 51% capital.
  - (iii) The government gave automatic approval for Technology Agreement in the industries of high priorities.
- Under the Trade Policy 1991, steps were taken to abolish the excessive protection given to many industries, for the promotion of international integration of economy.
- The measures implemented to bring efficiency and market discipline under the Public Sector Policy 1991 were as under :
  - (i) Number of reserved industries decreased to 8. Presently these are only four.
  - (ii) The work of rehabilitation of sick industries handed over to Board of Industrial Financial Reconstruction.
  - (iii) Industries were made powerful with the help of Memorandam of Understandings (MoU).
  - (iv) Voluntary Retirement Schemes started to cut down the size of work force.

Economic Reforms

➢ Economic Reforms were introduced in 1991 in India. *First Generation Reforms* were aimed at stabilisation of Indian economy and were macro level in nature. It includes liberalisation and deregulation of industry, financial sector reforms, taxation reforms etc. *Second Generation Reforms* aimed at structural changes and are micro level in nature. It will include labour reforms, land reforms, capital market reforms, expenditure reforms and power sector reforms etc.

➢ Since economic reform, poverty has been declining from 36% in 1993 to 26% by the end of 10th plan. But as far as inequality is concerned it has increased. A World Bank Report 1999-2000 confirms this rise in inequality.

➢ The New Economic Reforms Policy, by making progress from 1991 to 2005-06 has become more open, liberal and global.

➢ Disinvestment means to decrease the share of government in the industries.

➢ In 1996, Disinvestment Commission was constituted to review, give suggestions and make regulations on the issue of disinvestment.

➢ Shri G.V. Ramkrishna was the first Chairman of Disinvestment Commission.

➢ In the year 1992, National Renewal Fund was constituted for rehabilitation of displaced labourers of sick industrial units affected due to industrial modernization, technological development etc.

➢ "Navratna" is a company which is rising at world level. To encourage these companies, the government has given them complete autonomy.

➢ In the second phase of economic reforms programme, the main aim is to eradicate poverty from the country and development at the rate of 7 to 8%.

Some Important Terminology Relating to the New Economic Reforms Policy

➢ Privatisation : To increase participation of private sector in the public sector companies by capital investment or by management or both or to hand over a public sector unit to a private company is called Privatisation.

➢ Liberalisation : Liberalisation is the process by which government control is relaxed or abolished. In this process privatisation is also included.

➢ Globalisation : The process of amalgamation of an economy with world-economy is called Globalisation. It is signified by lower duties on import and export. By doing so, that sector will also get private capital and foreign technology.

➢ Disinvestment : To reduce the government share in the public sector is called disinvestment.

8. Indian Financial System

➢ Indian Financial System is a system in which People, Financial Institutions, Banks, Industrial Companies and the Government demand for fund and the same is supplied to them.

- There are two parts of Indian Financial System–first demand side and second supply side. The representative of demand side can be Individual investor, Industrial and Business Companies, Government etc. and the representative of supply side will be Banks, Insurance Companies, Mutual Fund and other Financial Institutions.
- The Indian financial system, which refers to the borrowing and lending of funds or to the demand for and supply of funds of all individuals, institutions, companies and of the Government consists of two parts, viz., the Indian money market and the Indian capital market.
- The Indian money market is the market in which short-term funds are borrowed and lent. The capital market in India, on the other hand, is the market for medium-term and long-term funds.
- The Indian financial system performs a crucial role in economic development of India through saving–investment process, also known as capital formation.
- The financial system is, commonly, classified into : (a) Industrial finance, (b) Agricultural finance, (c) Development finance and (d) Government finance.
- Devaluation means lowering the official value of the local money in terms of foreign currency or gold.
- Balance of Payments (BOP) is a systematic record of all the economic transactions between one country and the rest of the world in a given period.
- Balance of Trade (BOT) is the difference between the value of goods exported and the value of goods imported per annum. Services not included in BOT.
- BOP is divided in current account and capital account.
- EXIM Policy 2000-01 introduced Special Economic Zones Scheme (SEZ).
- 1994-95, Indian Rupee was made fully convertible on current account.
- Fiscal Policy is the policy relating to public revenue and public expenditure and allied matters.
- Usually, the Indian money market is classified into organised sector and the unorganised sector.
- The unorganised sector consists of indigenous bankers including the non-banking financial companies (NBFCs). Besides, these two, there are many sub-markets in the Indian money market.
- The organised banking system in India can be broadly divided into three categories, viz., the central bank of the country known as the Reserve Bank of India, the commercial banks and the co-operative banks which includes private sector and public sector banks and also foreign banks.
- The highest financial institution in organized sector is Reserve Bank of India and in addition to this Banks of Public Sector, Banks of Private Sector, Foreign Banks and other financial institutions are also part of organized sector.

➢ The *Reserve Bank of India* regulates and controls the money of the country.

➢ The RBI was established under the Reserve Bank of India Act, 1934 on 1st April, 1935 with a capital of Rs. 5 crore. It was nationalised on 1st January, 1949; on the recommendation of Parliamentary Committee in 1948. It is the Central Bank of India.

➢ The Reserve Bank of India is the supreme monetary and banking authority in the country and has the responsibility to control the banking system in the country. It keeps the reserves of all commerical banks and hence is known as the "Reserve Bank". Its financial year is 1st July to 30th June.

The Indian Capital Market

➢ The Indian capital market is the market for long–term capital; it refers to all the facilities and institutional arrangements for borrowing and lending "term funds" — medium term and long term funds.

➢ The Capital Market in India includes : (i) Government Securities (Gilt-edged market) (ii) Industrial Securities Market (iii) Development financial institutions like IFCI, IDBI, ICICI, SFCs, IIBI, UTI etc. (iv) Financial Intermediaries like Merchant banks.

➢ Individuals who invest directly on their own in securities are also supplier of fund to capital market. The trend in the capital market is basically affected by two important factors : (i) operations of the institutional investors in the market and (ii) the excellent results flowing in from the corporate sector.

➢ The capital market in India can be classified into :
- ★ Gilt–edged market or market for Government and semi–government securities;
- ★ Industrial securities market;
- ★ Development financial institutions; and
- ★ Non–banking financial companies.

➢ *The gilt–edged securities market* is the market for Government and semi government securities which carry fixed interest rates.

➢ *The industrial securities market* is the market for equities and debentures of companies of the corporate sector. This market is further classified into—
- (a) new issue markets for raising fresh capital in the form of shares and debentures, (commonly referred to as *primary market*) and
- (b) old issues market (or *secondary market*) for buying or selling shares and debentures of existing companies— this market is commonly referred to as the stock market or stock exchange.

➢ If shares or debentures of private corporations, primary sureties of government companies or new sureties and issue of bonds of public sector are sold or purchased in the capital market, then the market is called Primary Capital Market.

➢ Secondary Market includes transactions in the stock exchange and gilt-edged market.

- Merchant Bank, Mutual Fund, Leasing Companies, Risk Capital Companies etc. collect and invest public money into the capital market.
- Unit Trust of India (UTI) is the biggest Mutual Fund Institution of India.

Stock Exchange

- The stock exchange is the market for buying and selling of stocks, shares, securities, bonds and debentures etc. It increases the market ability of existing securities by providing simple method for public and others to buy and sell securities.
- The first organised stock exchange in India was started in Bombay (now Mumbai) when the "Native Share Brokers' Association" known as the Bombay Stock Exchange (BSE) was formed by the brokers in Bombay. BSE was Asia's oldest stock exchange.
- In 1894, the Ahmedabad stock Exchange was started to facilitate dealings in the shares of textile mills there.
- The Calcutta Stock Exchange was started in 1908 to provide a market for shares of plantations and jute mills.
- The number of stock exchanges rose from 7 in 1939 to 21 in 1945.
- Under the securities contract (Regulation) Act of 1956, the Government of India has so far recognised 23 stock exchanges. Bombay is the premier exchange in the country.
- With the setting up of National Stock Exchange, all regional stock exchanges have lost relevance.
- The BSE transformed itself into a corporate entity from being a brokers association, from the middle of August, 2005.
- As a public limited company, BSE (Bombay Stock Exchange) is obliged to dilute stock brokers stake to 49%
- To prevent excessive speculation and volatility in the stock market SEBI has introduced rolling settlements from July 2, 2001, under which settlement has to be made every day.

Some Important Share Price Index of India

- BSE SENSEX : This is the most sensitive share index of the Mumbai Stock Exchange. This is the representative index of 30 main shares. Its base year is 1978-79. BSE is the oldest stock exchange of India, founded in 1875.
- BSE 200 : This represents 200 shares of Mumbai Stock Exchange. Its base year is 1989-90.
- DOLLEX : Index of 200 BSE Dollar Value Index is called DOLLEX. Its base year is 1989-90.
- NSE-50 : From 28th July, 1998, its name is S and P CNX Nifty. National Stock Exchange has launched a new share Price Index, NSE-50 in place of NSE-100 in April 1996. NSE-50 includes 50 companies shares. This stock exchange was founded on Ferwani Committee's recommendation in 1994.

- ➢ CRISIL, set up in 1988, is a credit rating agency. It undertakes the rating fixed deposit programmes, convertible and non–convertible debentures and also credit assessment of companies.
- ➢ CRISIL 500 : is the new share Price Index introduced by Credit Rating Agency the "Credit Rating Information Services of India Limited" (CRISIL) on January 18, 1996.
- ➢ Apart from CRISIL, there is another credit rating agency called "Investment Information and Credit Rating Agency of India Limited (ICRA)." It rates debt instruments of both financial and manufacturing companies.
- ➢ The National Stock Exchange (NSE) has launched a new version of its online trading software called 'National Exchange for Automatic Trading' (NEAT).

9. Indian Fiscal System

- ➢ Fiscal System : It refers to the management of revenue and capital expenditure finances by the state. Hence, fiscal system includes budgetary activities of the government that is revenue raising, borrowing and spending activities.
- ➢ Fiscal Policy : Fiscal Policy refers to the use of taxation, public expenditure and the management of public debt in order to achieve certain specified objectives.
- ➢ Indian Fiscal System includes or refers to the management of revenue sources and expenditure of the Central and State governments, Public debt, Deficit financing, Budget, Tax structure etc.
- ➢ Sources of Revenue for Centre : The revenue of the Central Government consists of the following elements : (i) Tax revenue and (ii) Non-tax revenue. Tax revenue comes broadly from three sources— (a) taxes on income and expenditure (b) taxes on property and capital transactions (c) taxes on commodities and services. Non-tax revenue, consists of— (a) currency, coinage and mint (b) interest receipts and dividends; and other non–tax revenue.
- ➢ Sources of Revenue for State : The main sources are (a) state tax revenue (b) share in central taxes (c) income from social, commercial and economic service and profits of state-run enterprises. State tax revenue includes among others, land revenue, stamp, registration and estate duty etc.
- ➢ Expenditure of the Centre : The central government makes expenditures broadly under two heads : (i) Plan expenditure and (ii) Non-Plan expenditure.
- ➢ Under Plan expenditure comes outlay for agriculture, rural development, irrigation and flood control, energy, industry and minerals, transport, communications, Science and Technology, environment and economic services etc.
- ➢ The major non-plan expenditures are interest payments, defence, subsidies and general services.

➢ Expenditure of State: Like the Union Government, the State Governments too have two broad heads of expenditure : (a) Non–Development Expenditure; and (b) Development Expenditure.

➢ Public debt of the government of India is of two kinds–Internal and External.

➢ Internal debt : It comprises loans raised from the open market, compensation bonds, prize bonds etc. treasury bills issued to the RBI, commercial banks etc.

➢ External debt : It consists of loans taken from World Bank, IMF, ADB and individual countries like USA, Japan etc.

➢ Deficit Financing is a fiscal tool in the hands of the government to bridge the gap between revenue receipt and revenue expenditure.

Deficits

➢ In a budget statement, there is a mention of four types of deficits : (a) revenue, (b) budget, (c) fiscal, and (d) primary.

(a) Revenue Deficit refers to the excess of revenue expenditure over revenue receipts. [In fact, it reflects one crucial fact : what is the government borrowing for ? As an individual if you are borrowing to play the house rent, then you are in a situation of revenue deficit, i.e. while you are borrowing and spending, you are not creating any durable asset. This implies that there will be a repayment obligation (sometime in the future) and at the same time there is no asset creation via investment.]

Revenue Deficit = Total Revenue Expenditure – Total Revenue Receipts
= Non-plan Expenditure + Plan Expenditure – (net tax revenue + non tax revenue)

(b) Budget Deficit refers to the excess of total expenditure over total receipts. Here, total receipts include current revenue and net internal and external capital receipts of the government.

Budget Deficit = Total Expenditure – Total Receipts
= (non-plan expenditure + plan expenditure) – (Revenue Receipts + Capital Receipts)

(c) Fiscal Deficit refers to the difference between total expenditure (revenue, capital, and loans net of repayment) on one hand; and on the other hand, revenue receipts plus all those capital receipts which are not in the form of borrowings but which in the end accrue to the government.

Fiscal Deficit = Revenue Receipts *(net tax revenue + non-tax revenue)* + Capital Receipts *(only recoveries of loans and other receipts)* – Total Expenditure *(plan and non-plan)*

(d) Primary Deficit refers to fiscal deficit minus interest payments. In other words, it points to how much the government is borrowing to pay for expenses other than interest payments. Also, it underscores another key fact : how much the government is adding to future burden (in terms of repayment) on the basis of past and present policy.

Primary Deficit = Revenue Deficit – Interest Payments
Monetised Deficit = Increment in Net RBI Credit to the Central Government.

Budget

- The Budget of the Government of India, for any year, gives a complete picture of the estimated receipts and expenditures of the Government for that year on the basis of the budget figures of the two previous years.
- Every budget, for instance, gives three sets of figures : (a) actual figures for preceding year, (b) budget and revised figures for the current year, and (c) budget estimates for the following year.
- The core of the budget is called the Annual financial statement. This is the main budget document. Under article 112 of the constitution, a statement of estimated receipts and expenditure of the Govt. of India has to be laid before the parliament in respect of every financial year running from April 1 to March 31 while under article 202 of the constitution a statement of estimated receipts and expenditures of the state Governments has to be laid before the house of the state legislature concerned.
- The Annual Budget of the Central Government provides estimates of receipts and expenditures of the Government. The Budget consists of two parts viz; (i) Revenue Budget (ii) Capital Budget.
- Revenue Budget : All "current" 'receipts' such as taxation, surplus of Public enterprises, and 'expenditures' of the Government.
- Capital Budget : All "Capital" 'receipts' and 'expenditure' such as domestic and foreign loans, loan repayments, foreign aid etc.
- Finance Bill is ordinarily introduced every year to give effect to the financial proposals of the Government for the following financial year.

10. Banking in India

- The Reserve Bank of India was established on 1st April, 1935 and it was nationalized on 1st January, 1949.
- The Finance Ministry issues Currency Notes and Coins of rupee one, all other Currency Notes are issued by the Reserve Bank of India.
- The first bank of limited liability managed by Indians was Oudh Commercial Bank founded in 1881. Subsequently, Punjab National Bank was established in 1894.
- Swadeshi movement, which began in 1906, encouraged the formation of a number of commercial banks.
- The Banking Companies Act was passed in February 1949, which was subsequently amended to read as Banking Regulation Act, 1949.
- Commercial banks mobilise savings in urban areas and make them available to large and small industrial and trading units mainly for working capital requirements.
- The Indian banking system consists of commercial banks, both in public and private sector, Regional Rural Banks (RRBs) and cooperative banks.

- As on June 30, 2009, Commercial Banking system in India consisted of 171 scheduled commercial banks out of which 113 were in public sector, including 86 RRBs. The remaining 27 banks, other than RRBs, in the public sector, consisted of 19 nationalized banks, 7 banks in SBI group and IDBI Bank Limited. Public sector banks (excluding RRBs) accounted for about 76.6% of the deposits of all scheduled commercial banks.
- Commercial banks are broadly classified into nationalised or public sector banks and private sector banks, with a few foreign banks. The public sector banks account for more than 92% of the entire banking business in India-occupying a dominant position in the commercial banking. The State Bank of India and its 7 associate banks along with another 19 banks are the public sector banks.
- Oudh Commercial Bank was the first complete Commercial Bank of India.
- The Imperial Bank was established in the year 1921 by merging three main Presidency Banks.
- The largest bank-Imperial Bank was nationalised in 1955 on recommendation of Gorewala Committee and rechristened as State Bank of India.
- In 1959, 7 regional banks were nationalised and given the status of Associate Banks of State Bank of India.
- On 19th July, 1969, 14 big commercial banks with deposits worth Rs. 50 crores or more and on 15th April, 1980, six other scheduled banks were nationalised, bringing total number of nationalised banks to 27 (19 + SBI + 7 SBI Associates).
- Before the merger of New Bank of India in Punjab National Bank (in 1993) the total number of nationalised banks was 28 (8* *SBI and Associates* + 14 + 6).
  - ★ *After the merger of "State Bank of Saurashtra" and "State Bank of Indore" in the State Bank of India, the number of Associates of SBI has come to 6.*

Lead Bank Scheme

- After the nationalisation of 14 banks the Lead Bank Scheme of the RBI was adopted in 1969 for branch expansion programme of banks.
- Under the scheme, all the nationalised banks and private banks were allotted specific distracts where they were asked to take the lead in surveying the scope of banking development particularly expansion of credit facilities.

Banking Reforms

- On the recommendation of Narsimhan Committee, a number of steps taken to improve functioning of banking sector. SLR and CRR were reduced.
- Banks were given freedom to open new branches. Rapid computerisation of banks was undertaken.
- Banking "Ombudsmen Scheme" started functioning to expedite inexpensive resolution of customer's complaints.

Scheduled and Non-scheduled Banks

➢ The scheduled banks are those which are entered in the second schedule of the RBI Act, 1934. These banks have a paid-up capital and reserves of an aggregate value of not less than Rs. 5 lakhs and satisfy the RBI that their affairs are carried out in the interest of their depositors.

➢ All commercial banks (Indian and foreign), regional rural banks and state co-operative banks are scheduled banks. Non scheduled banks are those which are not included in the second schedule of the RBI Act 1934. At present there is only one such bank in the country.

Regional Rural Banks

➢ The Regional Rural Banks (RRBs), the newest form of banks, have come into existence since middle of 1970s (sponsored by individual nationalised commercial banks) with the objective of developing rural economy by providing credit and deposit facilities for agriculture and other productive activities of all kinds in rural areas.

➢ The emphasis is on providing such facilities to small and marginal farmers, agricultural labourers, rural artisans and other small entrepreneurs in rural areas.

➢ First Regional Rural Bank was established on 2nd October, 1975.

Co-operative Banks

➢ Co-operative banks are so called because they are organised under the provisions of the Co-operative Credit Societies law of the states. The major beneficiary of the Co-operative Banking is the agricultural sector in particular and the rural sector in general. The first such bank was established in 1904.

➢ The Co-operative credit institutions operating in the country are mainly of two kinds : agricultural (dominant) and non-agricultural.

➢ At the apex is the State Co-operative Bank (SCB) (co-operation being a state subject in India), at the intermediate (district) level are the Central Co-operative Banks (CCBs), and at the village level are Primary Agricultural Credit Societies (PACs); Long-term agricultural credit is provided by the Land Development Banks.

➢ In the year 1991, Narsimhan Committee was constituted to advice on the issue of reconstruction of banking system.

Development Banks

➢ Industrial Development Bank of India (IDBI), established in 1964. Main functions : Providing finance to large and medium scale industrial units.

➢ Industrial Finance Corporation of India (IFCI), established in 1948. Main functions : (a) Project finance (b) Promotional services.

➢ Industrial Credit and Investment Corporation of India Limited (ICICI), established in 1991.

Main functions : Providing term loans in Indian and foreign currencies; Underwriting of issues of shares and debentures.

➢ Small Industries Development Bank of India (SIDBI), established in 1989. Main functions : Providing assistance to small scale industries through state finance corporations, state industrial development corporations, commercial banks etc.

- ➢ Export-Import Bank of India (Exim. Bank) was established in 1982. Main functions : Coordinating the working of institutions engaged in financing export and import trade, Financing exports and imports.
- ➢ National Housing Bank (NHB) started operations in 1988.

  Main functions : Development of housing finance in the country.
- ➢ NABARD (National Bank for Agriculture and Rural Development) was established in 1982. The paid-up capital of NABARD stood at Rs. 2000 crore as on 31 March 2010.

  Main functions : to serve as an apex refinancing agency for institutions engaged in providing agricultural finance to develop credit delivery system to coordinate rural financing activities.

Insurance

- ➢ The basic concept of insurance is of spreading the loss of a few over many. Insurance industry includes two sectors-Life Insurance and General Insurance. Life Insurance in India was introduced by Britishers. A British firm in 1818 established the Oriental Life Insurance Company at Calcutta now Kolkata.
- ➢ Life Insurance Corporation (LIC) of India was established in September 1956. General Insurance Corporation (GIC) was established in November 1972.
- ➢ Indian Insurance sector has low penetration particularly in rural areas. It also has low turnover and profitability despite high premium rate. The committee on Insurance Sector Reforms was set-up in 1993 under the chairmanship of R.N. Malhotra which submitted its report in 1994.
- ➢ Since opening up, the number of particpants in the industry has gone up from 6 insurers (including Life Insurance Corporation of India, 4 public sector general insurers and General Insurance Corporation of India as the national reinsurer) in the year 2000 to 47 insurers as on March, 2010 operating in the life, non-life and reinsurance segments (including specialised insurers viz. Export Credit Guarantee Corporation and Agriculture Insurance Company of India Ltd. AICIL)
- ➢ 36 companies in the private sector are operating in the country in collaboration with established foreign insurance companies from across the globe as on 31 March, 2010.
- ➢ The Life Insurance Corporation with its Central Office in Mumbai, 8 Zonal Offices at Mumbai, Kolkata, Delhi, Chennai, Hyderabad, Kanpur, Bhopal and Patna, 109 Divisional Offices including one Salary Savings Schemes (SSS) Division at Mumbai, 2048 Branch Offices and 1004 Satellite Offices as on 31 March, 2010, spreads the message of Insurance the length and breadth of India.
- ➢ At present LIC is operating internationally through Branch Offices in Fiji, Mauritius and U.K. and through Joint Venture Companies in Bahrain, Nepal, Sri Lanka, Kenya and Saudi Arabia. Its Representative Office in Singapore was opened on 6 Nov. 2008.

11. Tax System

Tax – GDP ratio
9.9% (in 2011–12)
9.6% (in 2009–10)
11.9% (in 2007–08)

➢ A compulsory contribution given by a citizen or organisation to the Government is called Tax, which is used for meeting expenses on welfare work.

➢ Tax imposing and Tax collecting is at three levels in India – Central level, State level and Local level.

➢ The distribution of tax between Centre and State has been clearly mentioned in the provisions of Indian Constitution. For rationalising it from time to time, Finance Commission has been constituted.

➢ The tax system has been divided into two parts :

Tax by Central Government : Custom Duty, Income Tax and Corporate Tax etc.

Tax by State Government : The state government has right to collect all the taxes in this category and to spend them.

➢ There are two types of taxes : 1. Direct Taxes 2. Indirect Taxes :

★ Direct Taxes : The taxes levied by the central government on incomes and wealth are important direct taxes. The important taxes levied on incomes are—corporation tax and income tax. Taxes levied on wealth are wealth tax, gift tax etc.

★ Indirect Taxes : The main forms of indirect taxes are customs and excise duties and sales tax. The central government is empowered to levy customs and excise duties (except on alcoholic liquors and narcotics) whereas sales tax is the exclusive jurisdiction of the state governments.

➢ However, the union excise duties form the most significant part of central taxes. The major tax revenue sources for states are their shares in union excise duties and income tax, commercial taxes, land revenue, stamp duty, registration fees, state excise duties on alcohol and narcotics etc. Sales tax forms the most important component of commercial taxes.

➢ Progressive Tax : A tax that takes away a higher proportion of one's income as the income rises is known as progressive tax. Indian Income Tax is a progressive and direct tax.

➢ R. Chelliah Committee was constituted in August 1991 for suggesting reforms in Tax Structure.

➢ Chelliah Committee recommended Income Tax for agricultural income of more than Rs. 25,000 p.a. Chelliah Committee also recommended for lowering down the tax rates and reducing the tax slabs.

➢ K.L. Rekhi Committee was constituted in 1992 for suggesting uniform regulations for indirect taxation (Custom Duty and Excise Duty).

Finance Commission

➢ Finance Commission is constituted by the President under Art 280 of the constitution. Since Independence, 12 Finance Commissions have submitted their reports.

➢ 1st Finance Commission was constituted under chairmanship of K. C. Neogi while 12th Finance Commission was constituted under chairmanship of Dr. C. Rangarajan. The recommendations of 12th Finance Commission cover period 1st April, 2005 to 31st March, 2010.

- 13th Finance Commission, for the period 2010–2015, has been constituted in November, 2007 with Dr. Vijay L. Kelkar as the Chairman.

Important Taxes imposed in India

- Tax on Income and Wealth : The central government imposes different types of tax on income and wealth, viz. income tax, corporate tax, wealth tax and gift tax. Out of them income tax and corporate tax are more important from the revenue point of view.
- Personal Income Tax : Personal income tax is generally imposed on an individual combined Hindu families and total income of people of any other communities.
- In addition to tax, separate surcharges are also imposed some times.
- Agricultural income in India is free from income tax.
- Corporate Tax : Corporate Tax is imposed on Registered Companies and Corporations.
- The rate of corporate tax on all companies is equal. However, various types of rebates and exemptions have been provided.
- Custom Duties : As per the Constitutional provisions, the central government imposes import duty and export duty both. Import and Export duties are not only sources of income but with the help of it the central government regulates the foreign trade.
- Import Duties : Generally import duties are ad-velorem in India. It means import duties are imposed on the taxable item on percentage basis.
- Export Duties : Export Duties are more important, compared to Import Duties in terms of revenue and regulation of foreign trade.
- Excise Duties : Excise duties are commodity tax as it is imposed on production of an item and it has no relevance with its sale. This is the largest source of revenue for the Central Government.
- Except liquor, opium and other drugs, production of all the other items is taxable under Central Excise Duties.
- On July 15, 2010 Indian rupee got the much awaited symbol, just like other leading currencies of the world viz. Dollar, Euro, Pound Sterling and Yen.
- The new symbol is an amalgamation of Devanagari 'Ra' and the Roman 'R' without the stem. Till now the rupee was written in various abbreviated forms in different languages.
- On March 5, 2009 the Government announced a contest to create a symbol for the Rupee.
- Over 3000 entries received only 5 entries had been selected by the jury, headed by the Deputy Governor of R.B.I.
- The new symbol designed by D. Udaya Kumar, a post–graduate of IIT Bombay, was finally selected by the Union Cabinet on July 15, 2010.
- Though the symbol '₹' will not be printed or embossed on currency notes or coins, it would be included in the 'Unicode Standard' and major scripts of the world to ensure that it is easily displayed and printed in the electronic and print media.

➢ One Coin and One Rupee note belong to "Legal Tender Money" category.

➢ M_1 is known as Narrow Money.

➢ M_3 is known as Broad Money.

Types of Tax

Direct Tax	Income Tax, Property Tax, Gift Tax etc.
Indirect Tax	Sales Tax, Excise Duty, Custom Duty etc.
Taxes imposed by the Central Government.	Income Tax, Corporate Tax, Property Tax, Succession Tax, Wealth Tax, Gift Tax, Custom Duty, Tax on agricultural wealth etc.
Taxes imposed by the State Government	Land revenue tax, Agricultural income tax, Agricultural Land Revenue, State Excise Duty, Entertainment Tax, Stamp duty, Road Tax, Motor Vehicle Tax etc.

Some Financial institutions and their year of establishment

1.	Industrial Credit and Investment Corporation of India	Jan., 1955
2.	Industrial Finance Corporation of India	1948
3.	Unit Trust of India (Head Office - Mumbai)	1 Feb., 1964
4.	National Bank for Agricultural and Rural Development (NABARD)	12 July, 1982
5.	Industrial Reconstruction Bank of India	20 March, 1985
6.	Small Scale Industries Development Bank of India (SIDBI) (Head Office – Lucknow)	1990
7.	Export-Import Bank of India (EXIM Bank)	1 Jan., 1982
8.	Regional Rural Bank (RRB) (Head Office - Kolkata)	2 October, 1975
9.	Life Insurance Corporation of India (LIC) (Head Office – Mumbai)	Sep., 1956

12. Industry

➢ India started her quest for industrial development after independence in 1947.

➢ The Industrial Policy Resolution of 1948 marked the beginning of the evolution of the Indian Industrial Policy.

➢ In the Industrial Policy of 1948, the importance of both public sector and private sector was accepted. However, the responsibility of development of basic industries was handed over to Public Sector.

➢ The Industrial Policy Resolution of 1956 gave the public sector strategic role in the economy.

➢ Earmarking the pre-eminent position of the public sector, it envisaged private sector co-existing with the state and thus attempted to give the policy framework flexibility.

- ➢ The main objective of the Industrial Policy of 1956 was to develop public sector, co-operative sector and control on private monopoly.
- ➢ There were four categories of industries in the Industrial Policy of 1948 which was reduced to three in the Industrial Policy of 1956.
- ➢ In 1973, Joint Sector was constituted on the recomendations of Dutta Committee.
- ➢ The Industrial Policy of 1980 was influenced by the concept of federalism and the policy of giving concession to agriculture based industries was implemented through it.
- ➢ Various liberlised steps to be taken were declared at comprehensive level, in the Industrial Policy declared on 24th July, 1991.
- ➢ Privatisation and liberlisation are the main thrust areas in the New Industrial Policy.

New Industrial Policy, 1991

This new policy deregulates the industrial economy in a substantial manner. The Major Features of NIP, 1991 are :

- ➢ Abolition of industrial licensing : In a major move to liberalise the economy, the new indsutrial policy abolished all industrial licensing, irrespective of the level of investment, except for certain industries related to security and strategic concerns, social reasons, concerns related to safety and over-riding environmental issues, manufacture of products of hazardous nature and articles of elitist consumption.
- ➢ Entry of foreign investment and technology made easier : For the promotion of exports of Indian products in world markets, the government would encourage foreign trading companies to assist Indian exporters in export activities. Approval would be given for direct foreign investment up to 51% foreign equity in high priority industries.
- ➢ Public sector's role diluted : The new industrial policy has removed all these (the number of industries reserved for the public sector since 1956 was 17) industries from the Reserved List. Industries that continue to be reserved for the public sector are in areas where security and strategic concerns predominate. These areas are (i) arms and ammunition and allied items of defence equipment, defence aircraft and warships, (ii) atomic energy, (iii) mineral oils and minerals specified in the schedule to the atomic energy (control of production and use) order, 1953, (iv) railways.
- ➢ MRTP Act : Under the MRTP Act, all firms with assets above a certain size (Rs. 100 crore since 1985) were classified as MRTP firms. Such firms were permitted to enter selected industries only and this also on a case-by-case approval basis. The new industrial policy scrapped the threshold limit of assets in respect of 'MRTP' and dominant undertakings.
- ➢ Liberalisation of Industrial location policy : The new Industrial policy provides that in locations other than cities of more than one million population, there will be no requirement of obtaining industrial approvals from the centre, except for industries subject to compulsory

licensing. In cities with a population of more than one million, industries other than those of a non-polluting nature will be located outside 25 kms. of the periphery.

➢ Abolition of Phased Manufacturing Programmes for new projects : To force the pace of indigenisation in manufacturing, Phased Manufacturing Programmes have been in force in a number of engineering and electronic industries.

➢ Mandatory convertibility clause removed : A large part of industrial investment in India is financed by loans from banks and financial institutions. These institutions have followed a mandatory practice of including a convertibility clause in their lending operations for new projects. This has provided them an option of converting part of their loans into equity, if felt necessary by their management. This has often been interpreted as an unwarranted threat to private firms of takeover by financial institutions. This mandatory convertibility clause put forward by the financial institutions has been abolished by the new industrial policy.

➢ In the Union Budget of 1997-98, nine public sector undertakings, which performed very well were given the name of "Navratna" and were made autonomous. These "Navratnas" included :

SAIL	Steel Authority of India Limited
IOC (Sept. 1964)	Indian Oil Corporation
BPCL (Aug. 1, 1977)	Bharat Pertroleum Corporation Limited
HPCL (Est. July 15, 1974)	Hindustan Petroleum Corporation Limited
BHEL	Bharat Heavy Electricals Limited
NTPC	National Thermal Power Corporation
BEL	Bharat Electronics Limited
HAL	Hindustan Aeronautics Limited
ONGC (Est Aug. 14, 1956)	Oil and Natural Gas Corporation
Following undertakings were also included in this list later :	
GAIL (Aug. 1984)	Gas Authority of India Limited
MTNL	Mahanagar Telephone Nigam Limited
NMDC	National Mineral Development Corporation
PFC	Power Finance Corporation
PGCIL	Power Grid Corporation of India Limited
REC	Rural Electrical Corporation Limited
NALCO	National Aluminium Company
SCI	Shipping Corporation of India
CIL	Coal India Limited

Navratna Public sector enterprises have been given enhanced autonomy and delegation of powers to incur capital expenditure (without any monentary ceiling), to enter into technology joint ventures, to raise capital from domestic and international market, to establish financial joint ventures and to wholly own subsidiary.

Public Sector

- In terms of ownership public sector enterprise (PSE) comprises all undertakings that are owned by the government, or the public, whereas private sector comprises enterprises that are owned by private persons.
- **The main Objectives of Public Sector are :**
  - ★ To promote rapid economic development through creation and expansion of infrastructure;
  - ★ To generate financial resources for development;
  - ★ To promote redistribution of income and wealth;
  - ★ To create employment opportunities;
  - ★ To encourage the development of small scale and ancillary industries;
  - ★ To promote exports on the new side and import substitution on the other; and
  - ★ To promote balanced regional development.

Disinvestment and Privatisation

- There is a difference between privatisation and disinvestment. Privatisation implies a change in ownership resulting in a change in management. Disinvestment is a wider term extending from dilution for the stake of the government to the transfer of ownership (when govt. stake reduced beyond 51%).
- The Government of India constituted the Disinvestment Commission with Mr. G.V. Ramakrishna as the chairman in August 1996 to advise it on disinvestment programme of public sector enterprises. It has suggested classification of PSE in to core and non core. In core sector maximum of 49% disinvestment would be allowed while in non core disinvestment would be upto 74%. PSEs shares will given to small investors and employees to ensure wide dispersal of shares thus introduce mass ownership and workers shareholding. It has also suggested greater autonomy to PSEs.
- To minimize the financial burden on the Public Sector Enterprises the Government has started Voluntary Retirement Scheme (VRS) for the employees by giving full compensation to employees. This is called "Golden Hand Shake Scheme".
- Privatisation refers to a general process of involving the private sector in the ownership, or operation of a state owned enterprise. Thus it refers to private purchase of all or part of a company.

Small Scale Industries

Small scale and cottage industries have an important role to play in a labour surplus developing economy like India. Their importance can be explained as

(i) Employment Generation : Large scale industries are generally capital intensive. Small-scale industries, on the other hand, are generally labour intensive and have a substantially higher employment potential.

(ii) Equitable Distribution : The ownership of SSIs is more wide spread inter of both individuals as well as areas. Thus, these ensure equitable distribution of income individually and regionally.

(iii) Mobilisation of Small Savings : S.S.Is can be run with the help of small capital. Thus, they facilitate mobilisation of small savings.

(iv) Export Contribution : The share of small industries in the total export has increased over the years. It contributes 35% of total exports.

(v) Environment Friendly : As these are dispersed far away from urban centres they do not pollute urban environment.

However, Small Scale Industries are suffering from a number of problems like (i) Lack of timely, adequate and easy finance, (ii) Lack of availability of raw material, (iii) Lack of sound marketing system, (iv) Competition with large scale sector.

Sick Industries

➢ A sick unit is one which is in existence for at least five years and had found at the end of accounting year that it had fully eroded its net worth. 30,000 units fall sick every year. A weak unit is one which erode 15% or more of its net worth.

➢ Textile industry is the largest industry in the country. The share of Textile and Clothing industry in total industrial production is about 14%. It also contributes 13.14% in total merchandise exports of the country. This industry provides employment to about 350 lakh people in the country.

➢ There are about 1,100 mills (900 spinning mills and 200 composite mills) in the country with 28 million spindles and 2 lakh looms.

➢ There are 112 cotton mills in Gujarat. In Ahmedabad alone, there are 66 mills. It is known as Bostan of East. In Maharastra there are 104 mills out of which 54 alone are in Mumbai. Mumbai is called cottonopolis. In Kanpur there are 10 cotton mills and this city is called Manchester of North India.

➢ The first cycle making factory of India was established in Calcutta in 1932. India holds second place in the field of cycles production in the world. About 90 lakh cycles are produced annually in India.

➢ The share of small scale industries (SSI sector) in total exports of India is 32.3% in 2005–06

➢ Small and Cottage industries were given high priority in the Industrial Policy of 1977.

➢ District Industry Centres were established in 1977.

➢ With the aim to provide finance, *Small Industries Development Bank of India* (SIDBI) was established in 1990.

➢ Abid Husain Committee is related to reforms in small industries.

- The industries in which maximum Rs.1 crore is invested are called Small industries.
- *Industrial Finance Corporation of India* (IFCI) was established on 1st July, 1948 by a special Act of Parliament.
- The main aim of IFCI was to make available long term and mid term credit to the Industries of private and public sectors.
- *Industrial Credit and Investment Corporation of India* (ICICI) was established in 1955 under the Indian Companies Act.
- The function of ICICI is to support the establishment, development and modernization of industries in the private sector.
- Industrial Development Bank of India (IDBI) is an apex institution in the field of industrial finance.
- IDBI was established on 1st July, 1964.
- *Industrial Reconstruction Board of India* (IRBI) was established in 1971 with the aim to reconstruct the sick industrial units.
- Unit Trust of India was established in 1964.
- Unit Trust of India (UTI) collects small savings of people through sale of units and invests them into sureties.
- Life Insurance Company now *Life Insurance Corporation of India* or (LIC) was established in September 1956.
- The head office of Life Insurance Corporation of India is in Mumbai. Presently, it has 7 zonal offices and 100 regional offices.
- *General Insurance Company of India* (GIC) was established in 1972.
- Indian Industrial Investment Bank Limited was established on 17th March, 1997 by the government, under Companies Act 1956. Presently, its authorized capital is 1000 crore rupees and its head office is in Kolkata.

Industrial Growth

- The target growth of industry during the Tenth Plan (2002–07) was put at 10% consistent with an over all GDP growth 8%.
- According to the CSO's latest data, during 2006-07, (the last year of the 10th plan) the industrial goowth stood at 10.0% compared to 9.6% in the corresponding period of 2005-06.
- Manufacturing production grew by 11.3% against 9.1%, electricity generation by 7.7% against 53% and mining out put by 4.5% against 3.6% between the last two consecutive years.
- Growth of industrial sector, from a low of 2.7% in 2001-02, revived to 7.1% and 7.4% in 2002-03 and 2003-04 respectivety, and after accelerating to over 9.5% in the next two years, touched 10.0% in 2006-07.

Current Industrial Production

- The growth rate of Industrial Production, as per the Quick Estimates of Index of Industrial Production (IIP) with base year 1993-94, improved from an average of 5.0% per annum during 1997– 2002 (9th Plan) to 10.5% in 2009–10.

➢ India is the second largest manufacturer of cement in the world. *Cement industry* is one of the most advanced industries in the country.

➢ At present there are 156 large cement plants with an installed capacity of 233.94 million tonnes and more than 350 mini cement plants with an estimated capacity of 11.10 million tonnes per annum.

➢ The small scale, cottage and artisan sector account for over 75% of the leather production.

➢ More than 30% of the work force employed in this sector constitutes women.

Automobile Industry

➢ Automobile Industry was delicensed in July 1991 with the annoucement of the New Industrial Policy.

➢ The passenger car was however delicensed in 1993.

➢ At present 100% Foreign Direct Investment (FDI) is permissible under automatic route in this sector including passenger car segment.

➢ The industry also offers substantial scope of employment with 4.5 lakh direct employment and about one crore indirect employment.

Steel

➢ Iron and steel Industry took birth in India in the year 1870 when Bengal Iron Woks Company established its plant at Kulti, West Bengal.

➢ Large scale iron and steel production was started in 1907 by TISCO, established at Jamshedpur (Jharkhand).

➢ As per the data from International Iron and Steel Institute (IISI) India is the 7th largest producer of steel in the world.

➢ At present India is the 9th largest Crude Steel producing country in the world.

➢ Today, India is the largest producer of sponge iron in the world.

Small Enterprises Sector

➢ The employment provided by the sector is estimated to be over 280 lakh persons at present.

➢ In recognition of this role, the SE sector had been assigned targets of 12% annual growth in production and creation of 44 lakh additional employment opportunities in the Tenth Five-Year Plan.

Micro, Small and Medium Enterprise Development Act, 2006

➢ Small and Medium Enterprised Development Bill 2005 (which was introduced in the Parliament on May 12, 2005) has been approved by the President and thus became an Act.

➢ This new Act, named as 'Small and Medium Enterprise Development Act, 2006' has become effective from October 2, 2006.

➢ This Act makes a different category for medium level enterprises.

➢ This Act provides the first-ever legal frame work for recognition of the concept of *'enterprise'* (comprising both manufacturing and services) and integrating the three tiers of these enterprises, viz., micro, small and medium.

13. Foreign Trade

- Before independence, the foreign trade of India was being operated on the principles of colonialism. But after independence, there have been huge changes in its state and direction.
- After independence, inward looking foreign trade policies were accepted and the policy of import replacement was its base.
- Efforts were made for trade liberlisation during the decade of 1980 and the comprehensive policy of liberalisation and globalisation was made in the decade of 1990s (after the year 1991).

Volume of India's Foreign Trade

- After independence, Indian foreign trade has made cumulative progress both qualitatively and quantitatively. Though the size of foreign trade and its vlaue both have increased during post-independence era, this increase in foreign trade cannot be said satisfactory because Indian share in total foreign trade of the world has remained remarkable low.
- In 1950, the Indian share in the total world trade was 1.78%, which came down to 0.6% in 1995. According to the Economic Survey 2001-02 this share percentage of 0.6% continued in years 1997 and 1998. Since 1970, this share has remained around 0.6% which clearly indicates that India has failed to increase its share in the total world trade.
- India's total external trade (exports + imports including re–exports) in the year 2009–10 reached a level of Rs. 8,45,534 crore registering a growth of 0.57%. In US $ terms, exports reached a level of US $ 178.8 billion, registering a negative growth of –3.5% as compared to a growth of 13.6% during the previous year.

Composition of India's Foreign Trade

- Imports have been classified into Bulk imports and Non-bulk imports.
- Bulk imports are further sub-divided into Petroleum, oil and lubricants (POL) and non-POL items such as consumption goods, fertilizers and iron and steel.
- Non-bulk items comprise capital goods (which include electrical and non-electrical machinery), pearls, precious and semiprecious stones and other items.
- The structural changes in imports since 1951 show : (a) rapid growth of industrialisation necessiating increasing imports of capital goods and raw materials; (b) growing imports of raw materials on the basis of liberalisation of imports for export promotion; and (c) declining imports of food grains and consumer goods due to the country becoming self-sufficient in food grains and other consumer goods through agricultural and industrial growth.
- Exports of India are broadly classified into four categories : (i) Agriculture and allied products which include coffee, tea, oil cakes, tobacco, cashew kernels, spices, sugar, raw cotton, rice, fish and fish preparations, meat and meat preparations, vegetable oils, fruits, vegetables and pulses; (ii) Ores and minerals which include manganese ore, mica and iron ore; (iii)

Manufactured goods which include textiles and ready-made garments, jute manufactures, leather and footwear handicrafts including pearls and precious stones, chemicals, engineering goods and iron steel; and (iv) Mineral fuels and lubricants.

➢ Exports of India over the years show a clear decline in the importance of agriculture and allied products and a substantial increase in the importance of manufactured goods. This has been due to changing production structure of the economy and the overall growth of the economy.

Direction of Foreign Trade

➢ India is having maximum trade with OECD countries (mainly the USA, EU and Japan).

➢ The direction of Indian trade registered a change during recent past years. Indian trade has been partially shifted from West-Europe to East Asia and OECD countries.

➢ The high growth rate in Japan and ASEAN countries gave a high demand and favourable market to Indian exports. This has been one of the major reasons responsible for increasing Indian exports to East-Asian region of the world.

New Foreign Trade Policy (2009–2014)

➢ In the Foreign Trade policy for the year 2009–14 announced on 27 August, 2009, the Government spelt out a bold vision to double India's exports of goods and services by 2014 and to double India's percentage share of global trade by 2020 and to focus on the generation of additional employment.

➢ Stability of trade policy regime and need based support measures extended from time have yielded positive results since the inception of the Foreign Trade Policy (FTP) 2009–14.

Exim Policy 2002-07

➢ **The major highlights of Exim Policy 2002-07 are :**

(i) Removal of quantitative and packaging restrictions on agri exports.

(ii) Transport assistance for movement of agri goods.

(iii) Export thrust on items indentified in Medium Term Export Strategy.

(iv) Continuance of existing duty neutralisation schemes till the Value Added Tax (VAT) becomes fully operational.

(v) Extension of the period for fulfilling export obligations under Export Promotion Capital Goods (EPCG) Scheme from 8 to 12 years.

(vi) Exemption of banking units set up in SEZs from statutory requirements like SLR and CRR.

(vii) Easing of external commercial borrowing norms by permitting less than three years tenure loans.

(viii) Provision for repatriation of export earnings within 360 days instead of the earlier 180 days.

(ix) Retention of entire export earnings in Export Earners Foreign Currency Account (EEFA).

(x) Tax benefits on sales from domestic tariff areas to Special Economic Zones (SEZs).

(xi) Reduction of processing fees, fewer physical inspections, same day licensing in all offices of DGFT (Director Gen. of Foreign Trade).

(xii) Common classification for DGFT and customs department to eliminate classification related disputes.

(xiii) No licence requirement for relocation of overseas industrial plants in India.

(xiv) Industrial towns such as Tirpur, Panipat and Ludhiana to get Market Access Initiative (MAI) funds, priority for infrastructure development.

(xv) Allocation to states from Rs. 350 cr. Assistance to States for Infrastructure Development (ASIDE) fund linked to their export performance.

(xvi) Permission for captive power generation and duty free import of fuel for power generation, for exporters.

(xvii) Reduction in the eligibility for getting Export House status from Rs. 15 crores to Rs. 5 crores.

Balance of Payment : A statement of all transactions of a country with the rest of the world during a given period. Transactions may be related to trade, such as imports and exports of goods and services; movement of short-term and long-term investments; gifts, currency and gold. The balance of payments may be classified into current account, capital account, unilateral transfer account and gold account.

Balance of Trade : Part of the nation's balance of payments concerning imports and exports. A favourable balance of trade means that exports exceed imports in vlaue.

Invisibles : A term used to describe those items, such as financial series, included in the current Balance of Payments accounts, as distinct from physically visible Imports and Exports of goods. Invisibles include government grants to overseas countries and subscriptions to international organizations, net payment for shiping services, travel, royalties, commissions for banking and other services, transfers to or from overseas residents, Interest, Profits and Dividends received by or from overseas residents.

Foreign Exchange Reserves in India

➢ The foreign exchange reserves of the country include three important components : (i) Foreign Exchange Assets of RBI. (ii) Gold Stock of RBI (iii) SDR holdings of the Government.

Foreign Exchange Reserves in India, at the end of January 2013 was $ 295.60 billion.

➢ After 1991, Indian foreign exchange reserves have rapidly increased due to various reasons which are as follows : (i) Devlauation of Rupee. (ii) Availability of loans from international institutions. (iii) Availability of foreign exchange from NRIs under various schemes. (iv) Increased foreign investment (both direct and indirect). (v) Full convertibility of Rupee on current account.

- FEMA (Foreign Exchange Management Act) came into force in July 2000. This FEMA has replaced Foreign Exchange Regulation Act., 1973 (FERA-1973).
- Under FEMA provisions related to foreign exchange have been modified and liberalised so as to simplify foreign trade and payments. FEMA will make favourable development in foreign Money Market.

India's foreign trade

Year	Exports (Rs. crore)	Imports (Rs. crore)	Total trade (Rs. crore)	Trade deficit (Rs. crore)
1997-1998	1,30,101	1,54,176	2,84,277	-24,075
1998-1999	1,39,753	1,78,332	3,18,085	-38,579
1999-2000	1,59,561	2,15,236	3,74,797	-55,675
2000-2001	2,03,571	2,30,873	4,34,444	-27,302
2001-2002	2,09,018	2,45,200	4,54,218	-36,182
2002-2003	2,55,137	2,97,206	5,52,343	-42,069
2003-2004	2,93,367	3,59,108	6,52,475	-65,741
2004-2005	3,75,340	5,01,065	8,76,405	-1,25,725
2005-2006	4,56,418	6,60,409	11,16,827	-2,03,991
2006-2007	5,71,779	8,40,506	14,12,285	-2,68,727
2007-2008	6,55,864	10,12,312	16,68,176	-3,56,448
2008-2009	8,40,755	13,74,436	22,15,191	-5,33,681
2009-2010	8,45,534	13,63,736	22,09,270	-5,18,202

(Sources : DGCI and S, Kolkata) *(Courtesy : India 2011)*

- India's total external trade (exports plus imports including re-exports) in the year 1950-51 stood at Rs. 1214 crore. Since then, this has witnessed continuous increase with occasional downturns.
- India's share in total world trade has gone up from 1.1% in 2004–i.e. initial year of the Foreign Trade Policy (2004–09) to 1.5% in 2006.
- During 2008-09 the vlaue of India's external trade reached Rs. 22,15,191 crore.
- India's imports were highest from Asia and ASEAN (35.22%) followed by West Europe (21.17%) and America (7.78%), during 2005-06.
- During 2009–10 India's imports reached to Rs. 13,63,736 crore from Rs. 13,74,436 crore in 2008–09, registering a negative growth of 0.78% in rupee terms. In US $ terms, imports reached a level of US $ 288.37 billion in 2009–10, registering a negative growth of –5.05%.
- During 2009–10, UAE (13.4%) has been the most important country to export destination followed by USA (10.9%), China (6.5%), Hong Kong (4.4%), Singapore (4.2%), Netherlands (3.6%), U.K. (3.5%), Germany (3%), Saudi Arabia (2.2%).

- Asia and ASEAN accounted for 60.9% of India's total imports during 2009–10 followed by Europe (19.2%) and America (10.2%). Among individual countries the share of China stood highest at 10.7% followed by UAE (6.8%), Saudi Arabia (5.95%), USA (5.9%).
- During 2009–10, the share of Asia and ASEAN region comprising South Asia, East Asia, North East Asia, WANA accounted for 53.93% of India's total exports.
- Trade deficit decreased during 2009–10 to Rs. –5,18,202 crore as against Rs. –5,33,681 crore – during 2008–09. In Us $ terms also, trade deficit decreased to US $ 109.6 billion from a level of US $ 118.4 billion during 2008–09.
- The share of Europe and America in India's exports stood at 21.56% and 15.02% respectively of which EU countries (27) comprises 20.17%.

Trade Organisations

- International Monetary Fund (IMF) was established on 27th December, 1945 on the basis of decision taken in the Bretenwood Conference and it started functioning w.e.f. 1st March, 1947.
- The total member countries of IMF in 2002 were 183.
- The function of IMF is to encourage financial and economic co-operation between member countries and to extend world trade.
- International Bank for Reconstruction and Development (IBRD) was established in 1945.
- IBRD alongwith other institutions is also called World Bank. The other institutions are International Finance Corporation, International Development Agency and Multilateral Investement Guarantee Agency.
- Presently, it is helping member countries in capital investment and encouraging long-term balanced development.
- General Agreement on Tariffs and Trade (GATT), came into being on 30th October, 1947 and started functioning from 1st January, 1948.
- The principle of GATT was – equal tariffs policy, to remove quantitative ban and disposal of business dispute in a democratic way.
- On 1st January, 1995 the World Trade Organisation took over the place and position of GATT.
- The Headquarter of WTO is in Geneva and the number of its member countries in the year 2003 was 146. India is a founder member of it.
- The India–ASEAN Trade in Goods Agreement has come into effect on Jan. 1, 2010, though it was signed on August 13, 2009.
- The signing of the India–ASEAN Trade in Goods Agreement paves the way for the creation of one of the world's largest *free trade areas* (FTA)—market of almost 1.8 billion people with a combined GDP of US $ 2.75 trillion.

14. Miscellaneous Facts

- According to the World Bank, on the basis of the purchasing power parity, the economy of India is the fourth largest economy in the world.

- In the production of vegetables, India is on the second position (after China).
- India is on the first position in the production of milk.
- The highest producer of milk in India is Uttar Pradesh.
- India is the third largest producer of Tobacco. The largest producer and consumer of tobacco is China.
- Four industries which have been reserved for public sector are -Arms and Ammunition, Atomic Energy, Rail Transportation and Minerals mentioned in the scheduled list of Atomic Energy.
- The position of India is first as a producer of pulses.
- The Centre receives maximum net revenue through Excise Duty.
- First Hydel Power Plant in India was started in Darjiling.
- The Money-Order system in India was launched in 1880.
- First postal stamp was launched in India in 1852.
- Maharashtra is the 1st state which accorded the status of Industry to agriculture in 1997.
- The "Big Push Theory" has been given by R. Rodan.
- Alfred Marshal propounded the "Principle of consumer surplus".
- Central Agmark Laboratory is in Nagpur.
- First Cotton Industry of the country was established in Kolkata in 1818 and the second by Kovas Jee Nana Bhai in Mumbai in 1853.
- Sindri Fertilizer Factory, Chitaranjan Locomotives, Indian Telephone Industry, Integral Coach Factory, Penciline Factory, Indian Telephone Industry were all established during first five-year plan.
- The largest number of co-operative institutions is in India.
- Unorganised sectors are creating more employment than organised sector in India.
- The share of groundnut is the highest in the production of oil seeds.
- Three cities of India have more than 1 crore population – Mumbai, Kolkata and Delhi.
- Urbanisation is highest in Goa in India.
- Asian Development Bank was established in 1966. (Head Office – Manila)
- The social accounting method of estimating national income was developed by Richard Stone.
- TRIFED : Tribal Co-operative Marketing Development Federation of India Ltd. established by government in 1987 to benefit small tribal farmers.
- NAFED : National Agricultural Co-operative Marketing Federation of India Ltd. was established for marketing the agricultural products.
- In 1993 FERA (Foreign Exchange Regulation Act 1973) was replaced by FEMA (Foreign Exchange Management Act).
- Small Industries have been completely relaxed from licencing.

- Since 2002, price of all petroleum products are market determined. Kerosene and domestic LPG is supplied at subsidised rates to target groups.
- Foreign exchange rates are not fixed. It changes with market conditions. But for example the exchange rate as on April 4, 2013 :

1 US Dollar = 54.99 Rupees
1 Pound Sterling = 83.18 Rupees
1 Euro = 70.49 Rupees

- Average size of holding in India is continuously decreasing due to rigid population growth.
- Agriculture Income Insurance Scheme was announced in 2004 to provide insurance safeguards and economic security to farmers.
- Department of Agriculture and Co-operation formulated the Farm Income Insurance Scheme.
- Green Revolution is associated with the use of HYVS (High Yielding Variety Seeds), Chemical fertilizers and new techniques.
- Seed Crop Insurance is operational since 1999-2000.
- Seed Bank is in operation since 1999-2000. Its functions include meeting contigency requirement, development infrastructure for production and distribution of seeds.
- Types of loans provided to Indian Farmers :
  (a) Short Term Loans : Less than 15 months
  (b) Medium Term Loans : 15 months to 5 years
  (c) Long Term Loans : more than 5 years
- Loans are acquired from Institutional Sources (Banks) and Non-institutional sources (money lenders).
- Export-Import (EXIM) Bank was set up in 1982 for financing exports and imports.

Glossary of Economic and Financial Terms

Accrued interest : The interest due on a bond since the last interest payment was made. The buyer of the bond pays the market price plus accrued interest.

Acquisition : The acquiring of control of one corporation by another. In "unfriendly" takeover attempts, the potential buying company may offer a price well above current market values, new securities and other inducements to stockholders. The management of the subject company might ask for a better price or try to join up with a third company.

Active Market : This is a term used by stock exchange which specifies the particular stock or share that deals in frequent and regular transactions. It helps the buyers to obtain reasonably large amounts any time.

Administered Prices : When the prices of an item or a commodity are decided by the central power, generally the government or any other agency and not on the basis of demand and supply, such types of prices are called Administered Prices.

Ad-valorem Tax : Ad-valorem tax is a kind of indirect tax in which goods are taxed by their values. In the case of ad-valorem tax, the tax amount is calculated as the proportion of the price of the goods. Value Added Tax (VAT) is an ad-valorem tax. In other words when the tax is determined on the basis of value of a commodity, it is known as Ad-valorem tax.

Amalgamation : It means 'merger'. As and when necessity arises two or more companies are merged into a large organisation. The old firms completely lose their identity when the merger takes place.

American Depositary Receipt (ADR) : A security issued by a U.S. bank in place of the foreign shares held in trust by that bank, thereby facilitating the trading of foreign shares in U.S. markets.

Amortization : Accounting for expenses or charges as applicable rather than as paid. Includes such practices as depreciation, depletion, write-off of intangibles, prepaid expenses and deferred charges.

Annual report : The formal financial statement issued yearly by a firm, composing or corporation. The annual report shows assets, liabilities, revenues, expenses and earnings - how the company stood at the close of the business year, how it fared profit-wise during the year, as well as other information of interest to shareowners.

Appreciation : Appreciation means an increase in the value of something *e.g.* stock of raw materials or manufactured goods. It also includes an increase in the traded value of currency. It is an increase in the value of assets over a particular time period. Example : land, building, paintings etc. Appreciation is just opposite to depreciation. When the prices rise due to inflation, appreciation may occur.

Arbitrage : *A technique employed to take advantage of differences in price.* If, for example, ABC stock can be bought in New York for $10 a share and sold in London at $10.50, an arbitrageur may simultaneously purchase ABC stock here and sell the same amount in London, making a profit of $.50 a share, less expenses. Arbitrage may also involve the purchase of rights to subscribe to a security, or the purchase of a convertible security - and the sale at or about the same time of the security obtainable through exercise of the rights or of the security obtainable through conversion.

Arbitration : Where there is an industrial dispute, the Arbitration comes to the force. The judgement is given by the Arbitrator. Both the parties have to accept and honour the Arbitration. Arbitration is the settlement of labour disputes that takes place between employer and the employees.

Assets : Everything a corporation or an organisation owns or that is due to it: cash, investments, money due it, materials and inventories, which are called current assets; buildings and machinery, which are known as fixed assets; and patents and goodwill, called intangible assets.

Auction : When a commodity is sold by auction, the bids are made by the buyers. Who so ever makes the highest bid, gets the commodity which is being sold. The buyers make the bid taking into consideration the quality and quantity of the commodity.

Auction market : The system of trading securities through brokers or agents on an exchange such as the Bombay Stock Exchange. Buyers compete with other buyers while sellers compete with other sellers for the most advantageous price.

Auditor's report : Often called *the accountant's opinion,* it is the statement of the accounting firm's work and its opinion of the corporation's financial statements, especially if they conform to the normal and generally accepted practices of accountancy.

Autarchy : It means self-sufficiency and self-reliance of an economy. Autarchy is an indicator of self-sufficiency. It means that the country itself can satisfy the needs of its population without making imports from other countries.

Averages : Various ways of measuring the trend of securities prices, one of the most popular of which is the Dow Jones Industrial Average of 30 industrial stocks listed on the New York Stock Exchange. The prices of the 30 stocks are totaled and then divided by a divisor that is intended to compensate for past stock splits and stock dividends, and that is changed from time to time. As a result, point changes in the average have only the vaguest relationship to dollar-price changes in stocks included in the average.

Balance of Payment : It is the difference between country's payments and receipts from other countries during a year. In other words the balance of payment shows the relationship between the one country's total payment to all other countries and its total receipts from them. Balance of payment not only includes visible export and imports but also invisible trade like shipping, banking, insurance, tourism, royalty, payments of interest on foreign debts.

Balance of Trade : It refers to the relationship between the values of country's imports and its export, i.e. the visible balance. Balance of trade refers to the total of country's export commodities and total value of imports commodities. Thus, balance of trade includes only visible trade *i. e.* movement of goods (exports and imports of goods). Balance of trade is part of Balance of Payment statement.

Balance Sheet : Balance sheet is a statement showing the assets and liabilities of a business at certain date. Balance sheet helps in estimating the real financial situation of a firm.

Bank : Bank is a financial institution. It accepts funds on current account and savings accounts. It also lends money. The bank pays the cheques drawn by customers against current or savings bank account. The bank is a trader that deals in money and credit.

Bank Draft : Banker's draft (Demand Draft) is a negotiable claim drawn upon a bank. Drafts are as good as cash. The drafts cannot be returned unpaid. Bank Draft is safer than a cheque.

Bank Rate : It is official rate of interest charged by Reserve Bank of India on loans to other banks. It is the rate at which R.B.I. discounts first class securities including bills of exchange. Thus, it is also known as discount rate.

Bankruptcy : It is a situation in which a person is unable to discharge his debt obligations.

Basis point : One gradation on a 100 point scale representing 1%; used especially in expressing variations in the yields of bonds. Fixed income yields vary often and slightly within one percent and the basis point scale easily expresses these changes in hundredths of 1%. For example, the difference between 12.83% and 12.88% is 5 basis points.

Basket of Currency : In this system the exchange value of a country's currency is fixed in terms of some major international currencies. Indian rupee is valued against US Dollar, British Pound, Japanese Yen, French Franc and German Deutsche Mark. India opted for this system in 1975.

Bear and Bull : These terms are used in stock exchange. '*Bear*' is an individual who sells shares in a hope that the stock's price would fall. '*Bull*' is an individual who buys shares in a hope that the stock's price would rise.

Bearer bond : A bond that does not have the owner's name registered on the books of the issuer. Interest and principal, when due, are payable to the holder.

Bid and Asked : Often referred to as a quotation or quote. The bid is the highest price anyone wants to pay for a security at a given time, the asked is the lowest price anyone will take at the same time.

Bill of Exchange : It is an unconditional order in writing addressed by one person to another requiring the addressee to pay on demand or at a fixed future time a certain sum of money to the order of the specified person or to the bearer.

Birth Rate : Birth Rate (or Curde Birth Rate) is number of the births per thousand of the population during a period, usually a year. Only live births are included in the calculation of birth rate.

Black Money : It is unaccounted money which is concealed from tax authorities. All illegal economic activities are dealt with this black money. Howala market has deep roots with this black money. Black money creates parallel economy. It puts an adverse pressure on equitable distribution of wealth and income in the economy.

Block : A large holding or transaction of stock – popularly considered to be 10,000 shares or more.

Blue Chip : It is the most reliable industrial shares on a stock exchange. It is concerned with such equity shares whose purchase is extremely safe. It is a safe investment. It does not involve any risk.

Blue Collar Jobs : These Jobs are concerned with factory. Persons who are unskilled and depend upon manual jobs that require physical strain on human muscle are said to be engaged in Blue Collar Jobs. In the age of machinery, such Jobs are on the decline these days.

Blue Sky Laws : A popular name for laws various states have enacted to protect the public against securities frauds. The term (generally used in the context of U.S.A)is believed to have originated when a judge ruled that a particular stock had about the same value as a patch of blue sky.

Bond : A bond is evidence of a debt on which the issuing company usually promises to pay the bondholders a specified amount of interest for a specified length of time, and to repay the loan on the expiration date.

Book value : An accounting term. Book value of a stock is determined from a company's records, by adding all assets then deducting all debts and other liabilities, plus the liquidation price of any preferred issues. The sum arrived at is divided by the number of common shares outstanding and the result is book value per common share. Book value of the assets of a company or a security may have little relationship to market value.

Boom : The point at which price and employment are the maximum. The trade is also at its highest point and beyond this no upward movement is possible.

Bounty : It is a subsidy paid by the government to exporters. It reduces the price of exportable goods and hence act as incentive to enhance exports.

Brain-Drain : It means the drift of intellectuals of a country to another country. Scientists, doctors and technology experts generally go to other prominent countries of the world to better their lot and earn huge sums of money. This Brain-Drain deprives a country of its genius and capabilities.

Bridge loan : A loan made by a bank for a short period to make up for a temporary shortage of cash. On the part of borrower, mostly the companies, for example, a business organisation wants to install a new company with new equipments etc. While its present installed company or equipments etc. are not yet disposed off. Bridge loan covers this period between the buying the new and disposing of the old one.

Broad Banding : It means providing more flexibility to manufacturers to produce wider variety of products with same raw material mix so as to ensure optimum capacity.

Broker : An agent who handles the public's orders to buy and sell securities, commodities or other property. A commission is charged for this service

Brokers' loans : Money borrowed by brokers from banks or other brokers for a variety of uses. It may be used by specialists to help finance inventories of stock they deal in; by brokerage firms to finance the underwriting of new issues of corporate and municipal securities; to help finance a firm's own investments; and to help finance the purchase of securities for customers who prefer to use the broker's credit when they buy securities.

Budget : It is a document containing a preliminary approved plan of public revenue and public expenditure. It is a statement of the estimated receipt and expenses during a fixed period. It is a comparative table giving the accounts of the receipts to be realised and of the expenses to be incurred.

Budget Deficit : Budget deficit is the difference between the estimated public expenditure and public revenue. The government meets the deficit by way of printing new currency or by borrowing. Budget may take a shape of deficit when the public revenue falls short to public expenditure.

Buffer stocks : These are the stocks (generally of primary goods) accumulated by a government agency when supply is plentiful. These stocks are released in case of shortage of supply. In India Food Corporation of India (FCI) accumulates foodgrains as buffer stocks.

Bullion : It is gold or silver having a spesific degree of purity. Generally it is in the form of gold or silver bars.

Bull Market : It is a market where the speculators buy shares or commodities in anticipation of rising prices. This market enables the speculators to resale such shares and make a profit. The opposite is Bear Market.

Buoyancy : In the inflationary period, the increase in tax revenue is known as buoyancy. When the government fails to check inflation , it raises income tax and the corporate tax. Such a tax is called Buoyancy. It concerns with the revenue from taxation in the period of inflation.

Buyer's market : When the market is favourable to buyer's market. This situation occurs when there is a change from boom to recession i.e. demand is less than supply.

Buy side : The portion of the securities business in which institutional orders originate.

Callable : A bond issue, all or part of which may be redeemed by the issuing firm, institution or organisation under specified conditions before maturity. The term also applies to preferred shares that may be redeemed by the issuing organisation.

Call Money : It is a loan that is made for a very short period of a few days only or for a week. It carries a low rate of interest. In case of stock exchange market, the duration of the call money may be for a fortnight.

Capital : The stock of goods which are used in production and which themselves have been produced. It is one of the major factors of production, the other being land, labour and entrepreneurship .

Capitalism : The economic system based on free enterprise and private profit. Capitalism is an economic system in which all means of production are owned by private individuals. Self-profit motive is the guiding feature for all the economic activities under capitalism. Under pure capitalist system econonic conditions are regulated solely by free market forces. This system is based on 'Laissez-faire system' *i.e,* no state intervention. Sovereignty of consumer prevails in this system.

Capital Market : It is a market for long term loans. Capital market is the market which gives medium term and long term loans. It is different from money market which deals only in short term loans.

Capital stock : All shares representing ownership of a business, including preferred and common.

Capitalization : Total amount of the various securities issued by organisation or a company. Capitalization may include bonds, debentures, preferred and common stock, and surplus. Bonds and debentures are usually carried on the books of the issuing company in terms of their par or face value. Preferred and common shares may be carried in terms of par or stated value. Stated value may be an arbitrary figure decided upon by the director or may represent the amount received by the company from the sale of the securities at the time of issuance.

Cash flow : Reported net income of a corporation plus amounts charged off for depreciation, depletion, amortization, and extraordinary charges to reserves, which are bookkeeping deductions and not paid out in actual rupees and paise or dollars and cents.

Cash Reserve Ratio (CRR) : It refers to that portion of banker's total cash reserves which they are statutorily required to hold with the R.B.I. The commercial banks are required to keep a certain amount of cash reserves at the central bank i.e. RBI. This percentage amount is called CRR. It influences the commercial bank's volume of credit because variation in CRR affects the liquidity position of the banks and hence their ability to lend.

Cash sale : A transaction on the floor of the stock exchange that calls for delivery of the securities the same day. In "regular way" trade, the seller is to deliver on the third business day, except for bonds, which are the next day.

Ceiling Prices : This is the maximum limit fixed generally by government or its agency. Beyond it the prices cannot rise.

Certificate : The actual piece of paper that is evidence of ownership of stock in a company or an organisation. Watermarked paper is finely engraved with delicate etchings to discourage forgery.

Certificate of deposit (CD) : A money market instrument characterized by its set date of maturity and interest rate. There are two basic types of CDs: traditional and negotiable.Traditional bank CDs typically incur an early-withdrawal penalty, while negotiable CDs have secondary market liquidity with investors receiving more or less than the original amount depending on market conditions.

Cheap Money : It indicates a situation when bank rate and other rates of interest are low.

Cheque : Cheque is an order in writing issued by the drawer to a bank. If the customer has sufficient amount in his account, the cheque is paid by the bank. Cheques are used in place of cash money.

Clearing House : Clearing house is an institution which helps to settle the mutual indebtedness that occurs among the members of its organisation.

Closed Economy : Closed economy refers to the economy having no foreign trade (*i.e.* export and import). Such economies depend exclusively on their own internal domestic resources and have no dependence on out side world.

Collateral : Securities or other property pledged by a borrower to secure repayment of a loan.

Commercial paper : Debt instruments issued by companies to meet short-term financing needs.

Commission : The broker's basic fee for purchasing or selling securities or property as an agent.

Commission broker : An agent who executes the public's orders for the purchase or sale of securities or commodities.

Common stock : Securities that represent an ownership interest in a company. If the company has also issued preferred stock, both common and preferred have ownership rights. Common stockholders assume the greater risk, but generally exercise the greater control and may gain the greater award in the form of dividends and capital appreciation. The terms common stock and capital stock are often used interchangeably when the company has no preferred stock.

Competitive trader : A member of the exchange who trades in stocks on the floor for an account in which there is an interest. Also known as a registered trader.

Conglomerate : A company or an organisation that has diversified its operations usually by acquiring enterprises in widely varied industries.

Consolidated balance sheet : A balance sheet showing the financial condition of a corporation and its subsidiaries.

Convertible : A bond, debenture or preferred share that may be exchanged by the owner for common stock or another security, usually of the same company, in accordance with the terms of the issue.

Core Industries : Core Industries include strategic, basic and critical industries which remain generally under state control, e.g. defence, iron and steel, fertilizers etc.

Core Sector : Economy needs basic infrastructure for accelerating development. Development of infrastructure industries like cement, iron and steel, petroleum, heavy machinery etc. can only ensure the development of the economy as a whole. Such industries are core sector industries.

Corporate Tax : It is a direct tax levied on company's profit. It is calculated on profits after interest and allowance (*i.e.* capital allowance) have been deducted.

Correspondent : A securities firm, bank or other financial organization that regularly performs services for another in a place or market to which the other does not have direct access. Securities firms may have correspondents in foreign countries or on exchanges of which they are not members. Correspondents are frequently linked by private wires.

Cost Price Index (CPI) : It is used for measuring cost of living and it covers large number of commodities than Wholesale Price Index (WPI) which is used for measuring rate of inflamation.

Coupon bond : Bond with interest coupons attached. The coupons are clipped as they come due and presented by the holder for payment of interest.

Credit Control : It implies the measures employed by central bank of a country to control the volume of credit in the banks.

Credit Rating : It is the assessed credit worthiness of prospective customer.

Credit Rationing : Credit rationing takes place when the banks discriminates between the borrowers. Credit rationing empowers the bank to lend to someone and refuse to lend others. In this way credit rationing restricts lending on the part of bank.

Credit Squeeze : Monetary authorities restrict credit as and when required. This credit restriction is called credit squeeze. In other words when the credit control is very tight and restrict, this situation is known as credit squeeze.

Cumulative preferred : A stock having a provision that if one or more dividends are omitted, the omitted dividends must be paid before dividends may be paid on the company's common stock.

Current assets : Those assets of a company that are reasonably expected to be realized in cash, sold or consumed during one year. These include cash, Government bonds, receivables and money due usually within one year, as well as inventories.

Current liabilities : Money owed and payable by a company, usually within one year.

Custom Duty : It implies tax on imports. Custom duty is a duty that is imposed on the products received from exporting nations of the world. It is also called protective duty as it protects the home industries.

Cyclical Unemployment : It is that phase of unemployment which appears due to the occurance of the downward phase of the trade cycle. Such an employment is reducted or eliminated when the business cycle turns up again.

Day order : An order to buy or sell that, if not executed, expires at the end of trading day on which it was entered.

Dealer : An individual or firm in the securities business who buys and sells stocks and bonds as a principal rather than as an agent. The dealer's profit or loss is the difference between the price paid and the price received for the same security. The dealer's confirmation must disclose to the customer that the principal has been acted upon. The same individual or firm may function, at different times, either as a broker or dealer.

Death Rate : Death rate signifies the number of deaths in a year per thousand of the population. It is mostly known as *crude death rate*. Life expectancy is important determinant of death rate. A country having high life expectancy will have a high crude death rate.

Debentures : It is a document which enlists the terms or conditions of a loan. The debentures are used by corporate sector (companies). The debenture holders are to be paid a fixed annual rate of interest and they have the first claim on the assets of a company as creditors.

Debit balance : In a customer's margin account, that portion of the purchase price of stock, bonds or commodities that is covered by credit extended by the broker to the margin customer.

Decentralisation : Decentralisation means the establishment of various units of the same industry at different places. Large scale organisation or industry can not be run at one particular place or territory. In order to increase the effeciency of the industry, various units at different places are located.

Deed : It is a written contract signed under legal seal.

Deflation : Deflation is a fall in the general price level over a particular period of time. It is opposite to inflation.

Demand Draft : It is a bill of exchange payable at sight.

Depletion accounting : Natural resources, such as metals, oil, gas and timber, that conceivably can be reduced to zero over the years, present a special problem in capital management. Depletion is an accounting practice consisting of charges against earnings based upon the amount of the asset taken out of the total reserves in the period for which accounting is made. A bookkeeping entry, it does not represent any cash outlay nor are any funds earmarked for the purpose.

Depository Trust Company (DTC) : A central securities certificate depository through which members effect security deliveries between each other via computerized bookkeeping entries thereby reducing the physical movement of stock certificates.

Depreciation : It is the reduction in the value of a fixed asset due to wear and tear.

Depression : It is just opposite to "boom". It implies a state of economy when lack of demand result in heavy unemployment and stagnation in economy.

Devaluation : It is the reduction in the official rate of a currency in terms of a foreign currency. Indian rupee has been devalued thrice in 1949, 1966 and 1991.

Director : Person elected by shareholders to serve on the board of directors. The directors appoint the president, vice presidents, and all other operating officers. Directors decide, among other matters, if and when dividends shall be paid.

Direct Tax : It is a tax whose burden cannot be shifted i.e. the burden of direct tax is borne by the person on whom it is initially fixed, e.g.- personal income tax, social security tax paid by employees, death tax etc.

Discount : The amount by which a preferred stock or bond may sell below its par value. Also used as a verb to mean "takes into account" as the price of the stock has discounted the expected dividend cut.

Discretionary account : An account in which the customer gives the broker or someone else discretion to buy and sell securities or commodities, including selection, timing, amount, and price to be paid or received.

Diversification : Spreading investments among different types of securities and various companies in different fields.

Dividend : It is earnings on stocks paid to shareholders.

Dow theory : A theory of market analysis based upon the performance of the Dow Jones Industrial Average and transportation stock price averages. The theory says that the market is in a basic upward trend if one of these averages advances above a previous important high, accompanied or followed by a similar advance in the other. When both averages dip below previous important lows, this is regarded as confirmation of a downward trend. The Dow Jones is one type of market index.

Dumping : It means selling goods in international market at a price which is lower than that in domestic or home market.

Earnings report : A statement, also called an income statement, issued by a company showing its earnings or losses over a given period. The earnings report lists the income earned, expenses and the net result.

Elasticity of demand : The responsiveness of demand of a commodity to the change in its price is known as elasticity of demand.

Embargo : It means prohibition of entry of goods from certain countries into a particular country.

Engel's law : Ernest Engel, the 19th century German statistician, analysed the budget data of working families and established a relationship between the families income and expenditure. According to the Law "When a family's income increases the percentage of its income spent on food decreases."

Equity : The ownership interest of common and preferred stockholders in a company. Also refers to excess of value of securities over the debit balance in a margin account.

Exchange Rate : The rate at which central banks will exchange one country's currency for another.

Excise Tax : Tax imposed on the manufacture, sale or the consumption of various commodities, such as taxes on textiles, cloth, liquor etc.

Ex-dividend : A synonym for "without dividend." The buyer of a stock selling ex-dividend does not receive the recently declared dividend. When stocks go ex-dividend, the stock tables include the symbol "x" following the name.

Ex-rights : Without the rights. Corporations/Companies raising additional money may do so by offering their stockholders the right to subscribe to new or additional stock, usually at a discount from the prevailing market price. The buyer of a stock selling ex-rights is not entitled to the rights.

Extra : The short form of "extra dividend." A dividend in the form of stock or cash in addition to the regular or usual dividend the company has been paying.

Face value : The value of a bond that appears on the face of the bond, unless the value is otherwise specified by the issuing company. Face value is ordinarily the amount the issuing company promises to pay at maturity. Face value is not an indication of market value. Sometimes referred to as par value.

Factor cost : It is the sum total of amount paid to four main factors of production i.e. Land (rent), Labour (compensation of employees), Capital (interest), entrepreneurship (profit). It is exclusive of taxes or subsidies.

FINRA : The Financial Industry Regulatory Authority (f/k/a National Association of Securities Dealers), is the largest non-governmental regulator for all securities firms doing business in the United States. FINRA was created in July 2007 through the consolidation of NASD and the member regulation, enforcement and arbitration functions of the New York Stock Exchange.

Fiscal year : A firm's or company's or a corporation's accounting year. Due to the nature of their particular business, some companies do not use the calendar year for their bookkeeping. A typical example is the department store that finds December 31 too early a date to close its books after the Christmas rush. For that reason many stores wind up their accounting year January 31. Their fiscal year, therefore, runs from February 1 of one year through January 31 of the next. The fiscal year of other companies may run from July 1 through the following June 30. Most companies, though, operate on a calendar year basis.

Fixed charges : A company's fixed expenses, such as bond interest, which it has agreed to pay whether or not earned, and which are deducted from income before earnings on equity capital are computed.

Flat income bond : This term means that the price at which a bond is traded includes consideration for all unpaid accruals of interest. Bonds that are in default of interest or principal are traded flat. Income bonds that pay interest only to the extent earned are usually traded flat. All other bonds are usually dealt in "and interest," which means that the buyer pays to the seller the market price plus interest accrued since the last payment date.

Floating of a Currency : When the exchange value of a currency in terms of other currencies is not fixed officially, that currency is said to be floating.

Floor : The huge trading area - about the size of a football field - where stocks, bonds and options are bought and sold on the Stock Exchange.

Floor broker : A member of the stock exchange who executes orders on the floor of the Exchange to buy or sell any listed securities.

Foreign Exchange Reserves : Foreign Exchange Reserves of a country includes foreign currency assets and interest bearing bonds held by it. In India it also includes SDR and value of gold.

Formula investing : An investment technique. One formula calls for the shifting of funds from common shares to preferred shares or bonds as a selected market indicator rises above a certain predetermined point - and the return of funds to common share investments as the market average declines.

Free and open market : A market in which supply and demand are freely expressed in terms of price. Contrasts with a controlled market in which supply, demand and price may all be regulated.

Free Trade : It implies absence of any protective tariffs or trade barriers by any economy with respect to export and import.

Fundamental research : Analysis of industries and companies based on such factors as sales, assets, earnings, products or services, markets and management. As applied to the economy, fundamental research includes consideration of gross national product, interest rates, unemployment, inventories, savings, etc.

Funded debt : Usually interest-bearing bonds or debentures of a company. Could include long-term bank loans. Does not include short-term loans, preferred or common stock.

General mortgage bond : A bond that is secured by a blanket mortgage on the company's property but may be outranked by one or more other mortgages.

Gilt-edged: High-grade bond issued by a company that has demonstrated its ability to earn a comfortable profit over a period of years and pay its bondholders their interest without interruption.

Give-up : A term with many different meanings. For one, a member of the exchange on the floor may act for a second member by executing an order for him or her with a third member. The first member tells the third member that he or she is acting on behalf of the second member and "gives up" the second member's name rather than his or her own.

Good delivery : Certain basic qualifications must be met before a security sold on the Exchange may be delivered. The security must be in proper form to comply with the contract of sale and to transfer title to the purchaser.

Good 'til canceled (GTC) or open order : An order to buy or sell that remains in effect until it is either executed or canceled.

Greshan's law : "If not limited in quantity; bad money drives good money out of circulation." This statement was given by economist Sir Thomas Gresham, the economic advisor of Queen Elizabeth.

Gross Domestic Product (GDP) : It is the aggregate of total flow of goods and services produced by an economy in a year.

Gross National Product (GNP) : Gross Domestic Product plus net factor income from abroad is equal to Gross National Product.

Growth stock : Stock of a company with a record of growth in earnings at a relatively rapid rate.

Holding company : A corporation that owns the securities of another, in most cases with voting control.

Hot Money : It is a volatile money which comes easily but can also go out easily, e.g. portfolio investment.

Hypothecation : The pledging of securities as collateral - for example, to secure the debit balance in a margin account.

Income bond : Generally income bonds promise to repay principal but to pay interest only when earned. In some cases unpaid interest on an income bond may accumulate as a claim against the corporation when the bond becomes due. An income bond may also be issued in lieu of preferred stock.

Indenture : A written agreement under which bonds and debentures are issued, setting forth maturity date, interest rate and other terms.

Independent broker : Member on the floor of the Stock Exchange who executes orders for other brokers having more business at that time than they can handle themselves, or for firms who do not have their exchange member on the floor.

Index : A statistical yardstick expressed in terms of percentages of a base year or years. For instance, the BSE Composite Index of all BSE common stocks is based on 1965 as 50. An index is not an average.

Indirect Tax : Tax levied on goods purchased by the consumer (and exported by the producer) for which the tax payer's liabilities vary in proportion to the quantity of particular goods purchased or sold.

Inflation : It is a sustained increase in general price level over a particular period of time. It reduces the purchasing power of money.

Institutional investor : An organization whose primary purpose is to invest its own assets or those held in trust by it for others. Includes pension funds, investment companies, insurance companies, universities and banks.

Interest : Payments borrowers pay lenders for the use of their money. A corporation pays interest on its bonds to its bondholders.

Interim Budget : It is an addition to the general budget and is presented as a part of it through the financial year.

International Monetary Fund (IMF) : It is a multinational institution set up in 1945. It started working as an independent organisation in 1947. It seeks to maintain cooperative and orderly currency arrangements between member countries with the aim of promoting increased international trade and BOP equilibrium.

Interrogation device : A computer terminal that provides market information - last sale price, quotes, volume, etc. - on a screen or paper tape.

Investment : The use of money for the purpose of making more money, to gain income, increase capital, or both.

Investment banker : Also known as an underwriter. The middleman between the corporation issuing new securities and the public. The usual practice is for one or more investment bankers to buy outright from a corporation a new issue of stocks or bonds. The group forms a syndicate to sell the securities to individuals and institutions. Investment bankers also distribute very large blocks of stocks or bonds - perhaps held by an estate.

Investment counsel : One whose principal business consists of acting as investment advisor and rendering investment supervisory services.

I.O.U. : It means 'I owe you'. It is *non-negotiable promissory note* indicating the debt owed by one party to another.

IRA : Individual retirement account. A pension plan with tax advantages. IRAs permit investment through intermediaries like mutual funds, insurance companies and banks, or directly in stocks and bonds through stockbrokers.

Issue : Any of a company's securities, or the act of distributing such securities.

Joint Stock Company : It is a form of company in which a number of people contribute funds to finance a firm in return for 'shares' in the company.

Keogh plan : Tax-advantaged personal retirement program that can be established by a self- employed individual.

Laissez-faire : Literally it means 'to let people do as they choose'. It is an economic doctrine which emphasizes the superiority of 'free' trade and 'free' markets over state's interference in economic affairs. It is of French orgin of which British variation is 'Laissez-faire'.

Legal Tender : It is the currency (coins and bank notes) which have to be accepted in payment.

Leverage : The effect on a company when the company has bonds, preferred stock, or both outstanding. Example: If the earnings of a company with 1,000,000 common shares increases from $1,000,000 to $1,500,000, earnings per share would go up from $1 to $1.50, or an increase of 50%. But if earnings of a company that had to pay $500,000 in bond interest increased that much, earnings per common share would jump from $.50 to $1 a share, or 100%.

Liabilities : All the claims against a corporation. Liabilities include accounts, wages and salaries payable; dividends declared payable; accrued taxes payable; and fixed or long-term liabilities, such as mortgage bonds, debentures and bank loans.

Limit, limited order, or limited price order : An order to buy or sell a stated amount of a security at a specified price, or at a better price, if obtainable after the order is represented in the trading crowd.

Liquidation : The process of converting securities or other property into cash. The dissolution of a company, with cash remaining after sale of its assets and payment of all indebtedness being distributed to the shareholders.

Liquidity : The ability of the market in a particular security to absorb a reasonable amount of buying or selling at reasonable price changes. Liquidity is one of the most important characteristics of a good market.

Listed stock : The stock of a company that is traded on a securities exchange.

Load : The portion of the offering price of shares of open-end investment companies in excess of the value of the underlying assets. Covers sales commissions and all other costs of distribution. The load is usually incurred only on purchase, there being, in most cases, no charge when the shares are sold (redeemed).

Locked in : Investors are said to be locked in when they have profit on a security they own but do not sell because their profit would immediately become subject to the capital gains tax.

Manipulation : An illegal operation. Buying or selling a security for the purpose of creating false or misleading appearance of active trading or for the purpose of raising or depressing the price to induce purchase or sale by others.

Margin : The amount paid by the customer when using a broker's credit to buy or sell a security. Under Federal Reserve regulations, the initial margin requirement since 1945 has ranged from the current rate of 50% of the purchase price up to 100%.

Margin call : A demand upon a customer to put up money or securities with the broker. The call is made when a purchase is made; also if a customer's account declines below a minimum standard set by the exchange or by the firm.

Market order : An order to buy or sell a stated amount of a security at the most advantageous price obtainable after the order is represented in the trading crowd.

Market price : The last reported price at which the stock or bond sold, or the current quote.

Market value : The market value of an equity share is the price at which it is traded in the market . This price can be easily established for a company that is listed on the stock market and actively traded. (For a company that is listed on the stock market but traded very infrequently, it is difficult to obtain a reliable market quotation . For a company that is not listed on the stock market, one can merely conjecture as to what its market price would be if it were traded.)

Maturity : The date on which a loan or bond comes due and is to be paid off.

Merchant Banking : In Merchant Banking banks act as "underwriter" and do business on behalf of corporate sector . Such banking helps in larger participation of people in capital market e.g. ICICI.

Merger : Combination of two or more corporations.

MODVAT : The *modified system of value added taxation* is based on the idea of tax final products and not inputs that go into production.

Money Market : It is a market engaged in short-term lending and borrowing of money linking together the financial institutions, companies and the government.

Money market fund : A mutual fund whose investments are in high-yield money market instruments such as federal securities, CDs and commercial paper. Its intent is to make such instruments, normally purchased in large denominations by institutions, available indirectly to individuals.

Monopoly : It is a type of market structure having one seller and many buyers. There is a lack of substitute products and entry of new firms into market is not possible.

Mortgage bond : A bond secured by a mortgage on a property. The value of the property may or may not equal the value of the bonds issued against it.

MoU : The concept of *Memorandom of Understanding* (MoU) was introduced in 1988. The main objective of MoU is to reduce the quantity of control and increase the quality of accountability. The emphasis is on achieving the negotiated and agreed objectives rather than interfering in the day-to-day affairs.

Mutual Fund : It is a form of collective investment that is useful in spreading risks and optimising returns.

Nasdaq : An automated information network that provides brokers and dealers with price quotations on securities traded over-the-counter. Nasdaq is an acronym for National Association of Securities Dealers Automated Quotations.

National Income : It is equal to the total money value of goods and services produced over the given time period less capital consumption.

Negotiable : Refers to a security, the title to which is transferable by delivery.

Net asset value : Usually used in connection with investment companies to mean net asset value per share. An investment company computes its assets daily, or even twice daily, by totaling the market value of all securities owned. All liabilities are deducted, and the balance is divided by the number of shares outstanding. The resulting figure is the net asset value per share.

Net change : The change in the price of a security from the closing price on one day to the closing price the next day on which the stock is traded. The net change is ordinarily the last figure in the newspaper stock price list.

Net Domestic Product (NDP) : The money value of a nation's annual output of goods and service, less capital consumption (depreciation) experienced in producing that output.

Net National Product (NNP) : Net National Product is equal to Net Domestic Product plus Net factor income from abroad.

New York Futures Exchange (NYFE) : A subsidiary of the New York Stock Exchange devoted to the trading of futures products.

New York Stock Exchange (NYSE) : The largest organized securities market in the United States, founded in 1792. The Exchange itself does not buy, sell, own or set the prices of securities traded there. The prices are determined by public supply and demand. The Exchange is a non-profit corporation of 1,366 individual members, governed by a board of directors consisting of 10 public representatives, 10 Exchange members or allied members and a full-time chairman, executive vice chairman and president.

Noncumulative : A type of preferred stock on which unpaid dividends do not accrue. Omitted dividends are, as a rule, gone forever.

NYSE Composite Index : The composite index covering price movements of all common stocks listed on the New York Stock Exchange. It is based on the close of the market December 31, 1965, as 50 and is weighted according to the number of shares listed for each issue. The index is computed continuously and printed on the ticker tape. Point changes in the index are converted to dollars and cents so as to provide a meaningful measure of changes in the average price of listed stocks. The composite index is supplemented by separate indexes for four industry groups: industrial, transportation, utility and finance.

Octroi : It is an internal tariff system among different region of a country.

Odd Lot : An amount of stock less than the established 100-share unit.

Off-board : This term may refer to transactions over-the-counter in unlisted securities or to transactions of listed shares that are not executed on a national securities exchange.

Offer : The price at which a person is ready to sell. Opposed to bid, the price at which one is ready to buy.

Overbought : An opinion as to price levels. May refer to a security that has had a sharp rise or to the market as a whole after a period of vigorous buying which, it may be argued, has left prices "too high."

Oversold : The reverse of overbought. A single security or a market which, it is believed, has declined to an unreasonable level.

Over-the-counter : A market for securities made up of securities dealers who may or may not be members of a securities exchange. The over-the-counter market is conducted over the telephone and deals mainly with stocks of companies without sufficient shares, stockholders or earnings to warrant listing on an exchange. Over-the-counter dealers may act either as principals or as brokers for customers. The over-the-counter market is the principal market for bonds of all types.

Paper profit (loss) : An unrealized profit or loss on a security still held. Paper profits and losses become realized only when the security is sold.

Par : In the case of a common share, par means a dollar amount assigned to the share by the company's charter. Par value may also be used to compute the dollar amount of common shares on the balance sheet. In the case of preferred stocks it signifies the dollar value upon which dividends are figured. With bonds, par value is the face amount, usually $1,000.

Participating preferred : A preferred stock that is entitled to its stated dividend and to additional dividends on a specified basis upon payment of dividends on the common stock.

Passed dividend : Omission of a regular or scheduled dividend.

Penny stocks : Low-priced issues, often highly speculative, selling at less than $1 a share. Frequently used as a term of disparagement, although some penny stocks have developed into investment-caliber issues.

Per Capita Income : It implies income per person . It is obtained by dividing national income of country by its population.

Plastic Money : It refers to use of instruments like *"credit cards"* instead of cash in business transactions. It is called so because *credit cards* are made of plastic. Plastic Money also carries information about its holder in coded form which makes it theft proof. No one, but the holder is able to use the card.

Point : In the case of shares of stock, a point means $1. If ABC shares rise 3 points, each share has risen $3. In the case of bonds a point means $10, since a bond is quoted as a percentage of $1,000. A bond that rises 3 points gains 3% in $1,000, or $30 in value. An advance from 87 to 90 would mean an advance in dollar value from $870 to $900. In the case of market averages, the word point means merely that and no more.

Portfolio : Holdings of securities by an individual or institution. A portfolio may contain bonds, preferred stocks, common stocks and other securities.

Poverty Line : The poverty line has been fixed by the planning commission on the basis of an average daily intake of 2400 calories per person in rural areas and 2100 calories per capita in urban areas. In monetary terms the poverty line is commented to be Rs. 76 per month in rural and Rs. 88 in urban areas in terms of 1979- 80 prices.

Preferred stock : A class of stock with a claim on the company's earnings before payment may be made on the common stock and usually entitled to priority over common stock if the company liquidates. Usually entitled to dividends at a specified rate - when declared by the board of directors and before payment of a dividend on the common stock - depending upon the terms of the issue.

Premium : The amount by which a bond or preferred stock may sell above its par value. May refer, also, to redemption price of a bond or preferred stock if it is higher than face value.

Price-to-earnings ratio : A popular way to compare stocks selling at various price levels. The P/E ratio is the price of a share of stock divided by earnings per share for a 12-month period. For example, a stock selling for $50 a share and earning $5 a share is said to be selling at a price-to-earnings ratio of 10.

Primary distribution : Also called primary or initial public offering. The original sale of a company's securities.

Prime rate : The lowest interest rate charged by commercial banks to their most credit- worthy customers; other interest rates, such as personal, automobile, commercial and financing loans are often pegged to the prime.

Principal : The person for whom a broker executes an order, or dealers buying or selling for their own accounts. The term "principal" may also refer to a person's capital or to the face amount of a bond.

Profit-taking : Selling stock that has appreciated in value since purchase, in order to realize the profit. The term is often used to explain a downturn in the market following a period of rising prices.

Prospectus : The official selling circular that must be given to purchasers of new securities registered with the Securities and Exchange Commission. It highlights the much longer Registration Statement file with the Commission.

Proxy : Written authorization given by a shareholder to someone else to represent him or her and vote his or her shares at a shareholders meeting.

Proxy statement : Information given to stockholders in conjunction with the solicitation of proxies.

Recession : Recession cycle characterised by a modest downturn in the level of economic activity means fall up of demand.

Reflation : It is an increase in the level of *National Income and Output.* Reflation is often deliberately brought about by the authorities in order to secure full employment and to increase the rate of economic growth.

Quote : The highest bid to buy and the lowest offer to sell a security in a given market at a given time. If you ask your financial advisor for a "quote" on a stock, he or she may come back with something like "45 1/4 to 45 1/2." This means that $45.25 is the highest price any buyer wanted to pay at the time the quote was given on the floor of the exchange and that $45.50 was the lowest price that any seller would take at the same time.

Rally : A brisk rise following a decline in the general price level of the market, or in an individual stock.

Record date : The date on which you must be registered as a shareholder of a company in order to receive a declared dividend or, among other things, to vote on company affairs.

Redemption price : The price at which a bond may be redeemed before maturity, at the option of the issuing company. Redemption value also applies to the price the company must pay to call in certain types of preferred stock.

Refinancing : Same as refunding. New securities are sold by a company and the money is used to retire existing securities. The object may be to save interest costs, extend the maturity of the loan, or both.

Registered bond : A bond that is registered on the books of the issuing company in the name of the owner. It can be transferred only when endorsed by the registered owner.

Registrar : Usually a trust company or bank charged with the responsibility of keeping record of the owners of a corporation's securities and preventing the issuance of more than the authorized amount.

Regulation T : The federal regulation governing the amount of credit that may be advanced by brokers and dealers to customers for the purchase of securities.

Regulation U : The federal regulation governing the amount of credit that may be advanced by banks to customers for the purchase of listed stocks.

Rights : When a company wants to raise more funds by issuing additional securities, it may give its stockholders the opportunity, ahead of others, to buy the new securities in proportion to the number of shares each owns. The piece of paper evidencing this privilege is called a right.

Scheduled bank : It is a bank included in the second schedule of RBI. It has a minimum cash reserve of "Rs. 5 lakh".

Scale order : An order to buy (or sell) a security, that specifies the total amount to be bought (or sold) at specified price variations.

Scripophily : A term coined in the mid-1970s to describe the hobby of collecting antique bonds, stocks and other financial instruments. Values are affected by beauty of the certificate and the issuer's role in world finance and economic development.

SDRs (Special Drawing Rights) : The SDR is a reverse asset created within the framework of the International Monetary Fund in an attempt to increase international liquidity and forming a part of country's official reserves along with gold, reserve positions in the IMF and convertible foreign currencies. It is also known as "Paper Gold".

Seat : A traditional figure of speech for a membership on an exchange.

SEBI : It was set up in 1988 by the Government of India to regulate the operations in stock market of India. The SEBI stands for Securities and Exchange Board of India.

Self Reliance : Self Reliance, in short, can mean attainment of economic independence which, in turn, implies capability to sustain a higher rate of growth of economy essentially with the help of the domestic resources.

Seller's Market : It is market situation which exists for a short time period. During this period there is an excess demand for good and services at current prices which forces price up to the advantage of the seller.

Sell side : The portion of the securities business in which orders are transacted. The sell side includes retail brokers, institutional brokers and traders, and research departments. If an institutional portfolio manager changes jobs and becomes a registered representative, he or she has moved from the buy side to the sell side.

Sensex : The Stock Exchange Sensitive Index (popularly referred to as the SENSEX) reflects the weighted arithmetic average of the price relative of a group of share included in the index of sensitive shares. For example, Bombay Stock Exchange Sensitive Index is a group of 30 sensitive shares.

Serial bond : An issue that matures in part at periodic stated intervals.

Settlement : Conclusion of a securities transaction when a customer pays a broker/dealer for securities purchased or delivers securities sold and receives from the broker the proceeds of a sale.

Shares : These are the equal portions of the capital of a limited company. Shares in a company do not carry fixed rate of interest. The holders of the *ordinary shares* carry the residual risk of the business; they rank after *debenture holders* and *preference shareholders* for the payment of dividends and they are liable for losses, although this liability is limited to the value of the shares and to the limit of guarantee given by them. *Preference shares* are such shares of a company on which interest is paid before any others, and owners have prior right to repayment of capital if company is wound up.

Share Capital : Money raised by issuing of shares is called Share Capital.

Share Index : It is the statistical indicator of overall share values, based on selected group.

Short covering : Buying stock to return stock previously borrowed to make delivery on a short sale.

Short sale : A transaction by a person who believes a security will decline and sells it, though the person does not own any. Sometimes people will sell short a stock they already own in order to protect a paper profit. This is know as selling short against the box.

Sinking fund : Money regularly set aside by a company to redeem its bonds, debentures or preferred stock from time to time as specified in the indenture or charter.

Speculation : The employment of funds by a speculator. Safety of principal is a secondary factor.

Speculator : One who is willing to assume a relatively large risk in the hope of gain.

Spin off : The separation of a subsidiary or division of a corporation from its parent company by issuing shares in a new corporate entity. Shareowners in the parent company receive shares in the new company in proportion to their original holding and the total value remains approximately the same.

Split : The division of the outstanding shares of a corporation into a larger number of shares. A 3-for-1 split by a company with 1 million shares outstanding results in 3 million shares outstanding. Each holder of 100 shares before the 3-for-1 split would have 300 shares, although the proportionate equity in the company would remain the same; 100 parts of 1 million are the equivalent of 300 parts of 3 million. Ordinarily, splits must be voted by directors and approved by shareholders.

Stock exchange : An organized marketplace for securities featured by the centralization of supply and demand for the transaction of orders by member brokers for institutional and individual investors.

Stock dividend : A dividend paid in securities rather than in cash. The dividend may be additional shares of the issuing company, or in shares of another company (usually a subsidiary) held by the company.

Stockholder of record : A stockholder whose name is registered on the books of the issuing corporation.

Stop limit order : A stop order that becomes a limit order after the specified stop price has been reached.

Stop order : An order to buy at a price above or sell at a price below the current market. *Stop buy orders* are generally used to limit loss or protect unrealized profits on a short sale. *Stop sell orders* are generally used to protect unrealized profits or limit loss on a holding. A *stop order* becomes a market order when the stock sells at or beyond the specified price and, thus, may not necessarily be executed at that price.

Street name : Securities held in the name of a broker instead of a customer's name are said to be carried in "street name." This occurs when the securities have been bought on margin or when the customer wishes the security to be held by the broker.

Swapping : Selling one security and buying a similar one almost at the same time to take a loss, usually for tax purposes.

Syndicate : A group of investment bankers who together underwrite and distribute a new issue of securities or a large block of an outstanding issue.

Technical research : Analysis of the market and stocks based on supply and demand. The technician studies price movements, volume, trends and patterns, which are revealed by charting these factors, and attempts to assess the possible effect of current market action on future supply and demand for securities and individual issues.

Tender offer : A public offer to buy shares from existing stockholders of one public corporation by another public corporation under specified terms good for a certain time period. Stockholders are asked to "tender" (surrender) their holdings for stated value, usually at a premium above current market price, subject to the tendering of a minimum and maximum number of shares.

Third market : Trading of stock exchange-listed securities in the over-the-counter market by non-exchange member brokers.

Ticker : A telegraphic system that continuously provides the last sale prices and volume of securities transactions on exchanges. Information is either printed or displayed on a moving tape after each trade.

Trader : Individuals who buy and sell for their own accounts for short-term profit. Also, an employee of a broker/dealer or financial institution who specializes in handling purchases and sales of securities for the firm and/or its clients.

Transfer : This term may refer to two different operations. For one, the delivery of a stock certificate from the seller's broker to the buyer's broker and legal change of ownership, normally accomplished within a few days. For another, to record the change of ownership on the books of the corporation by the transfer agent. When the purchaser's name is recorded, dividends, notices of meetings, proxies, financial reports and all pertinent literature sent by the issuer to its securities holders are mailed directly to the new owner.

Transfer agent : A transfer agent keeps a record of the name of each registered shareowner, his or her address, the number of shares owned, and sees that certificates presented for transfer are properly canceled and new certificates issued in the name of the new owner.

Treasury stock : Stock issued by a company but later reacquired. It may be held in the company's treasury indefinitely, reissued to the public or retired. Treasury stock receives no dividends and has no vote while held by the company.

Turnover rate : The volume of shares traded in a year as a percentage of total shares listed on an exchange, outstanding for an individual issue or held in an institutional portfolio.

Unlisted stock : A security not listed on a stock exchange.

Up tick : A term used to designate a transaction made at a price higher than the preceding transaction. Also called a "plus" tick. A "zero-plus" tick is a term used for a transaction at the same price as the preceding trade but higher than the preceding different price. Conversely, a down tick, or "minus" tick, is a term used to designate a transaction made at a price lower than the preceding trade. A plus sign, or a minus sign, is displayed throughout the day next to the last price of each stock at the trading post on the floor of the New York Stock Exchange.

Variable annuity : A life insurance policy where the annuity premium (a set amount of dollars) is immediately turned into units of a portfolio of stocks. Upon retirement, the policyholder is paid according to accumulated units, the dollar value of which varies according to the performance of the stock portfolio. Its objective is to preserve, through stock investment, the purchasing value of the annuity which otherwise is subject to erosion through inflation.

VAT : It seeks to tax the value added at every stage of manufacturing and sale with a provision of refunding the amount of VAT already paid at earlier stages to avoid double taxation.

Volume : The number of shares or contracts traded in a security or an entire market during a given period. Volume is usually considered on a daily basis and a daily average is computed for longer periods.

Voting right : Common stockholders' right to vote their stock in affairs of a company. Preferred stock usually has the right to vote when preferred dividends are in default for a specified period. The right to vote may be delegated by the stockholder to another person.

Warrants : Certificates giving the holder the right to purchase securities at a stipulated price within a specified time limit or perpetually. Sometimes a warrant is offered with securities as an inducement to buy.

Working control : Theoretically, ownership of 51% of a company's voting stock is necessary to exercise control. In practice - and this is particularly true in the case of a large corporation - effective control sometimes can be exerted through ownership, individually or by a group acting in concert, of less than 50%.

Yield : Also known as return. The dividends or interest paid by a company expressed as a percentage of the current price.

Yield to maturity : The yield of a bond to maturity takes into account the price discount from or premium over the face amount. It is greater than the current yield when the bond is selling at a discount and less than the current yield when the bond is selling at a premium.

Zero coupon bond : A bond that pays no interest but is priced, at issue, at a discount from its redemption price.

Some Important Books on Economics

The Wealth of Nations	Adam Smith
Money Illusion	Irwin Fisher
Capital and growth	Hicks
General Theory of Employment, Interest and Money	J. M. Keynes
Planned Economy for India	M. Vishveshwaraiya
The Value and Capital	Hicks
The Canon (theory) of Consumer's Surplus	Marshall
Big Push Theory	A. R. Rodon
Datt & Sundharam Indian Economy	Gaurav Datt and Ashwani Mahajan

Some Noteworthy Facts

➢ Inflation, in theory, occurs when money supply grows at a higher rate than GDP in real terms.

- The existence of a large parallel economy, fluctuations in agricultural and industrial output and indirect taxation are the reasons for : *cost-push inflation.*
- Among the supply side measures to contain iflation is : *to increase the supply of products or commodities.*
- Population experts refer to the possible 'demographic bonus' that may accrue to India around 2016 A.D. They are referring to the phenomenon of : *a surge in the population in the productive age group.*
- The significant change in the new FEMA which has replaced FERA is that the emphasis from imprisonment will be shifted to : *Voluntary compliance.*
- 'Level playing field' argument industries requires : *Domestic industry to be treated at par with MNCs.*
- One of the disadvantages of the Wholesale Price Index in India is that : *it does not cover the services sector.*
- Check off system refers to the verification of membership through : *deduction of subscription from pay.*
- Direct taxation is a better form of taxation because : *it allows for taxation according to means.*
- Lender of the last resort, periodic inspection of commercial banks, issue of bank notes of all denominations are the functions of : *Reserve Bank of India.*
- Multi Fibre Agreement deals with : *Textiles.*
- Under the Medium Term Fiscal Restructuring Programme, state **governments have been permitted to borrow from international financial** institutions like the World Bank and Asian Development Bank (ADB) to : *replace their high cost debt with low cost funds.*
- Open market operation of RBI Refers to trading in securities.
- The new definition of fiscal deficit was suggested by : *Chakravarthy Committee.*
- According to the Chakravarthy Committee, one of the principal causes affecting price stability in India is : *Violent fluctuation in agricultural production.*
- The concept of Total Fertility Rate (TFR) in population means the average number of children born to a woman during her lifetime.
- Tarapore Committee recommended that before capital account was made convertible the rate of inflation should be brought down for three years within 3 – 4%.
- Tarapore Committee recommended that foreign exchange reserves should not be below the requirements of import for 6 months.
- The first bank managed by Indians was : *Oudh Bank.*
- The statement, "India has achieved national food security but has not ensured household food sercurity" means : *there is sufficient food stock but all households donot have access to it.*

- The permit for duty free trade issued by the East India Company at a price to private traders was called : *Diwani.*
- The demand for establishment of a department of agriculture in India was made by : *Manchester Cotton Supply Association.*
- The birth rate measures the number of births during a year per : *1000 of population.*
- Structural unemployment arises due to : *inadequate productive capacity.*
- 'Disguised unemployment' refers to : *more persons employed for a job which a few can accomplish.*
- The Securities and Exchange Board of India (SEBI) has imposed a restriction on money flow in equity through 'P–Notes'. The full form of 'P–Notes' is : *Participatory Notes.*
- The money which government of India spends on the development of infrastructure in country comes from the following sources — Loan from World Bank / ADB etc., Taxes collected from the people, Loan from the RBI etc.
- 'Investor Protection Fund' has been established by : *Stock Exchange*
- The full form of FII is : *Foreign Institutional Investor.*
- The Finance Ministry (on Feb. 15, 2008) has allowed companies to issue Foreign Currency Exchangeable Bonds (FCEBs) with a maturity of five years to raise funds from the overseas market by unlocking part of the holding in group companies. The investment under the scheme shall comply with Foreign Direct Investement (FDI) policy as well as the External Commercial Borrowing (ECB) policy requirements.
- The Union Goverment, on March 3, 2008, launched a conditional cash transfer scheme for the girl child. The conditions of this scheme include registration of birth of the girl, following a total immunisation schedule, school enrolment and delaying of marriage until the age of 18 years. The name of the scheme is : *Dhan Laxmi.*
- The Securities and Exchange Board of India (SEBI), on May 29, 2008 has allowed overseas sovereign wealth fund to register as foreign institutional investors (FIIs) and invest in shares and government securities.
- The Centre approved the amendment to the Prevention of Money Laundering Act (PMLA), a move aimed at bringing casinos, international credit card payment gateways such as VISA and Master Card, full fledged money changers (FFMCs) and money transfer service providers (MTSPs) such as the Western Union under the purview of Indian laws.
- The Central Government has decided on April 6, 2008 to form a strategic reserve of 5 million tonnes of foodgrains, to be consisted of 3 million tonnes of wheat and 2 million tonnes of rice.
- The National Association of Software and Service Companies (NASSCOM), the premier trade body represents : *the IT and BPO industry.*

- ➢ The biggest consumer of natural gas in the world is : *the USA.*
- ➢ The country which leads in oil-consumption in the world is : *the USA.*
- ➢ The country which leads in Internet users in the world is : *the USA.*
- ➢ World's leading gold producer country is : *South Africa*
- ➢ Entry for Normal Loss is recorded in : *Trading Account*
- ➢ In Product Life Cycle the cost per unit is generally highest in the stage of : *Introduction*
- ➢ Accounting acronym GAAP stands for : *Generally Accepted Accounting Practices*
- ➢ Limited Liability is available in the kind of business organisation called: *Company*
- ➢ Bank account is called : *Real Account*
- ➢ The form of accounting states that transactions are to be recorded in the period that they occur is : *Accrual basis of accounting*
- ➢ The most important ratio for the Sales Tax Department from the control point of view is : *Gross Profit Ratio*
- ➢ The most important ratio for the Income Tax Department from the control point of view is : *Net Profit Ratio*
- ➢ The abbreviations for debit and credit (Dr. and Cr.) come from the language : *Latin, 'debere and credere'*
- ➢ A Public Limited Company tries to maximise : *Wealth of Sharecholders*
- ➢ Anticipated losses are recorded in the books of accounts as per : *Matching of Cost and Revenue*
- ➢ Goodwill is recorded in the books of accounts only when : *It is valued*
- ➢ Depreciation Account is called : *Nominal Account*
- ➢ Monopoly is when there is single : *Seller*
- ➢ We can get the current Ratio by : *dividing current assets by current liabilities*
- ➢ The major rubber producing state in India is : *Kerala*

According to The Economic Survey 2012–13

Total government debt	51.7% of GDP
Total external debt	283.9 bn. U.S. dollar (in Spt. 2012)
Production of Coal	540 million tonnes in 2011–12 (Target for current Plan period (2012–17) is 795 million tonnes)
India's share in World exports	1.6% (Jan.–Oct. 2012)
Gross Domestic Savings	30.8% (of GDP)
Total Telephones	935.18 million (97% cell phones + 3% land lines) as of Oct. 2012 [Overall Teledensity is 77]
Project growth rate for 2013–14	6.1 to 6.7%
GDP growth rate for 2011–12 was	6.2%
Source : **The Hindu**	

★★★

6 PHYSICS

Unit : The chosen standard used for measuring a physical quantity is called unit.

Unit should be :

(i) well defined
(ii) easy to reproduce
(iii) easy to compare
(v) internationally accepted
(iv) independent of changes in physical conditions

Units are of two types–(i) Fundamental Unit; (i) Derived Unit

System of Units–Units depend on choice. Each choice of units leads to a new system (set) of units. The internationally accepted systems are (i) CGS system, (ii) MKS System (iii) FPS System (iv) SI Units.

In SI Units, there are seven fundamental units given in the following table :

Physical Quantity	SI Unit	Symbol	Physical Quantity	SI Unit	Symbol
Length	metre	*m*	Temperature	kelvin	*K*
Mass	kilogram	*kg*	Luminuous intensity	candela	*Cd*
Time	second	*s*	Amount of substance	mole	*mol*
Electric Current	ampere	*A*			

Besides these seven fundamental units, two supplementary units are also defined, viz., radian [rad] for plane angle and steradian (sr) for solid angle.

➢ All the units which are defined / expressed in terms of fundamental units are called derived units.

Some important derived units.

S. No.	Physical Quantity	cgs units	SI unit	relation
1.	Force	dyne	newton	1 newton = 10^5 dyne
2.	work	erg	joule	1 joule = 10^7 erg

Some practical units of length, mass and time

Length	Mass	Time
Light year = distance travelled by light in one year in vaccum. 1ly = 9.46×10^{15}m 1 astronomical unit (A.U.) = 1.5×10^{11} m 1 parsec = 3.26 ly = 3.08×10^{16} m 1 nautical mile or seamile = 6020 ft. 1 micron = 1 μm = 10^{-6} m 1 angstron (A°) = 10^{-15} m	1 quintol = 10^2 kg 1 metric ton = 10^3kg 1 atomic mass unit (amu) or dalton = 1.66×10^{-27} kg 1 slug = 14.59 kg 1 pound = 0.4537 kg 1 Chandrashekhar limit = 1.4 times the mass of sun = 2.8×10^{30} kg	1 solar day = 86400 sec. 1 year = 365 ½ solar days 1 lunar month = 27.3 solar days. Tropical year = It is the year in which total solar eclipse occurs. Leap year = It is the year in which the month of February is of 29 days.

Prefixes used in metric system

Prefix	Symbol	Multiplier	Prefix	Symbol	Multiplier
deci	d	10^{-1}	deca	da	10^{1}
centi	c	10^{-2}	hecto	h	10^{2}
milli	m	10^{-3}	kilo	k	10^{3}
micro		10^{-6}	mega	M	10^{6}
nano	n	10^{-9}	giga	G	10^{9}
pico	p	10^{-12}	tera	T	10^{12}
femto	f	10^{-15}	peta	P	10^{15}
atto	a	10^{-18}	exa	E	10^{18}
zepto	z	10^{-21}	zetta	Z	10^{21}
yocto	y	10^{-24}	yotta	Y	10^{24}

2. Motion

Scalar Quantities : Physical quantities which have magnitude only and no direction are called scalar quantities.

Example : Mass, speed, volume, work, time, power, energy etc.

Vector Quantities : Physical quantities which have magnitude and direction both and which obey triangle law are called vector quantities.

Example : Displacement, velocity, acceleration, force, momentum, torque etc.

Electric current, though has a direction, is a scalar quantity because it does not obey triangle law.

Moment of inertia, pressure, refractive index, stress are tensor quantities.

Distance : Distance is the length of actual path covered by a moving object in a given time interval.

Displacement : Shortest distance covered by a body in a definite direction is called displacement.

- Distance is a scalar quantity whereas displacement is a vector quantity both having the same unit (metre)
- Displacement may be positive, negative or zero whereas distance is always positive.
- In general, magnitude of displacement $\leq$ distance

Speed : Distance travelled by the moving object in unit time interval is called speed i.e. speed $= \frac{\text{Dis tan ce}}{\text{Time}}$

It is a scalar quantity and its SI unit is metre/second (m/s).

Velocity : Velocity of a moving object is defined as the displacement of the object in unit time interval i.e. velocity $= \frac{\text{Displacement}}{\text{Time}}$

It is a vector quantity and its SI unit is metre/second.

Acceleration : Acceleration of an object is defined as the rate of change of velocity of the object i.e. acceleration = $\frac{\text{Change in Velocity}}{\text{Time}}$

It is a vector quantity and its SI units is metre/second^2 (m/s^2)

If velocity decreases with time then acceleration is negative and is called retardation.

Circular Motion : It an object describes a circular path (circle) its motion is called circular motion. If the object moves with uniform speed, its motion is uniform circular motion.

Uniform circular motion is an accelerated motion because the direction of velocity changes continuously.

Angular Velocity : The angle subtended by the line joining the object from the origin of circle in unit time interval is called angular velocity.

It is generally denoted by ω and $\omega = \frac{\theta}{t}$

If T = time period = time taken by the object to complete one revolution, n = frequency = no. of revolutions in one second.

then $\boxed{nT = 1}$ & $\omega = \frac{2\pi}{T} = 2\pi n.$

➢ In one revolution, the object travels $2\pi r$ distance.

$\therefore$ Linear speed = ωr = angular speed × radius

Newton's laws of motion : Newton, the father of physics established the laws of motion in his book "principia" in 1687.

Newton's first law of motion : Every body maintains its initial state of rest or motion with uniform speed on a straight line unless an external force acts on it.

➢ First law is also called law of Galileo or law of inertia.

➢ Inertia : Inertia is the property of a body by virtue of which the body opposes change in its initial state of rest or motion with uniform speed on a straight line.

Inertia is of two types (i) Inertia of rest (ii) Inertia of motion

Some examples of Inertia :

(i) When a car or train starts suddenly, the passengers bends backward.

(ii) When a running horse stops suddenly, the rider bends forward.

(iii) When a coat/blanket is beaten by a stick, the dust particles are removed.

➢ First law gives the definition of force.

➢ Force : Force is that external cause which when acts on a body changes or tries to change the initial state of the body.

Momentum : Momentum is the property of a moving body and is defined as the product of mass and velocity of the body i.e.

momentum = mass × velocity.

It is a vector quantity. Its SI unit is kgm/s.

Newton's second law of motion : The rate of change in momentum of a body is directly proportional to the applied force on the body and takes place in the direction of force.

If F = force applied, a = acceleration produced and m = mass of body the $nF = ma$.

➢ Newton's second law gives the magnitude of force.

➢ Newton's first law is contained in the second law.

Newton's Third Law of Motion : To every action, there is an equal and opposite reaction.

Examples of third law–(i) Recoil of a gun (ii) Motion of rocket (iii) Swimming (iv) While drawing water from the well, if the string breaks up the man drawing water falls back.

Principle of conservation of linear momentum : If no external force acts on a system of bodies, the total linear momentum of the system of bodies remains constant.

As a consequence, the total momentum of bodies before and after collision remains the same.

Impulse : When a large force acts on a body for very small time, then force is called impulsive force. Impulse is defined as the product of force and time.

Impulse = force × time = change in momentum.

➢ It is a vector quantity and its direction is the direction of force. Its SI unit is newton second (Ns).

Centripetal Force : When a body travels along a circular path, its velocity changes continuously. Naturally an external force always acts on the body towards the centre of the path.

The external force required to maintain the circular motion of the body is called centripetal force.

If a body of mass m is moving on a circular path of radius R with uniform speed v, then the required centripetal force, $F = \frac{mv^2}{R}$

Centrifugal Force : In applying the Newton's laws of motion, we have to consider some forces which can not be assigned to any object in the surrounding. These forces are called pseudo force or inertial force.

Centrifugal force is such a pseudo force. It is equal and opposite to centripetal force.

➢ Cream separator, centrifugal drier work on the principle of centrifugal force.

➢ Centrifugal force should not be confused as the reaction to centripetal force because *forces of action and reaction act on different bodies.*

Moment of force : The rotational effect of a force on a body about an axis of rotation is described in terms of moment of force.

Moment of a force about an axis of rotation is measured as the product of magnitude of force and the perpendicular distance of direction of force from the axis of rotation.

i.e. Moment of force = Force × moment arm

➢ It is a vector quantity.

➢ Its SI unit is newton metre (Nm)

Centre of Gravity : The centre of gravity of a body is that point through which the entire weight of body acts. The centre of gravity of a body does not change with the change in orientation of body in space.

The weight of a body acts through centre of gravity in the downward direction. Hence a body can be brought to equilibrium by applying a force equal to its weight in the vertically upward direction through centre of gravity.

Equilibrium : If the resultant of all the forces acting on a body is zero then the body is said to be in equilibrium.

If a body is in equilibrium, it will be either at rest or in uniform motion. If it is at rest, the equilibrium is called static, otherwise dynamic.

Static equilibrium is of the following three types :

(i) Stable Equilibrium : If on slight displacement from equilibrium position, a body has tendency to regain its original position, it is said to be in stable equilibrium.

(ii) Unstable equilibrium : If on slight displacement from equilibrium position, a body moves in the direction of displacement and does not regain its original position, the equilibrium is said to unstable equilibrium. In this equilibrium, the centre of gravity of the body is at the highest position.

(iii) Neutral Equilibrium : If on slight displacement from equilibrium position a body has no tendency to come back to its original position or to move in the direction of displacement, it is said to be in neutral equilibrium. In neutral equilibrium, the centre of gravity always remains at the same height.

Conditions for stable Equilibrium : For stable equilibrium of a body, the following two conditions should be fulfilled.

(i) The centre of gravity of the body should be at the minimum height.

(ii) The vertical line passing through the centre of gravity of the body should pass through the base of the body.

3. Work, Energy and Power

Work : If a body gets displaced when a force acts on it, work is said to be done. Work is measured by the product of force and displacement of the body along the direction of force.

If a body gets displaced by S when a force F acts on it,
then the work $W = F\ S \cos\theta$
where θ = angle between force and displacement
If both force and displacement are in the same direction, then $W = FS$
Work is a scalar quantity and its SI unit is joule.

Energy : Capacity of doing work by a body is called its energy.

➢ Energy is a scalar quantity and its SI unit is joule.

➢ Energy developed in a body due to work done on it is called mechanical energy. Mechanical energy is of two types :

(i) Potential Energy (ii) Kinetic Energy

Potential Energy : The capacity of doing work developed in a body due to its position or configuration is called its potential energy.

Example : (i) energy of stretched or compressed spring (ii) energy of water collected at a height (iii) energy of spring in a watch.

PE of a body in the gravitational field of earth is mgh.

where m = mass, g = acceleration due to gravity, h = height of the body from surface of the earth.

Kinetic Energy : Energy possess by a body due to its motion is called Kinetic Energy of the body.

If a body of mass m is moving with speed v, then kinetic energy of the body is $\frac{1}{2}mv^2$

Principle of Conservation of Energy

Energy can neither be created nor can be destroyed. Only energy can be transformed from one form to another form. Whenever energy is utilized in one form, equal amount of energy is produced in other form. Hence total energy of the universe always remains the same. This is called the principle of conservation of energy.

Some Equipments used to Transform Energy

S. No.	Equipment	Energy Transformed
1.	Dynamo	Mechanical energy into electrical energy
2.	Candle	Chemical energy into light and heat energy.
3.	Microphone	Sound energy into electrical energy.
4.	Loud Speaker	Electrical energy into sound energy.
5.	Solar Cell	Solar energy into electrical energy.
6.	Tube light	Electrical energy into light energy.
7.	Electric Bulb	Electrical energy into light and heat energy.
8.	Battery	Chemical energy into electrical energy.
9.	Electric motor	Electrical energy into mechanical energy.
10.	Sitar	Mechanical energy into sound energy.

Relation between Momentum and Kinetic Energy

$$K.E = \frac{p^2}{2m} \text{ where } p = \text{momentum} = mv$$

Clearly when momentum is doubled, kinetic energy becomes four times.

Power : Rate of doing work is called power.

It an agent does W work in time t, then power of agent = $\frac{W}{t}$

SI unit of power is watt named as a respect to the scientist James Watt.

watt = joule / sec.

1 kW = 10^3 watt

1 MW = 10^6 watt

Horse power is a practical unit of power. 1 H.P. = 746 watt.

1 watt second = 1 watt × 1 second = 1 joule.

1 watt hour (Wh) = 3600 joule

1 kilowatt hour (kWh) = 3.6×10^6 joule.

W, kW, MW & H.P. are units of power.

Ws, Wh, kWh are units of work and energy.

4. Gravitation

Gravitation : Every body attracts other body by a force called force of gravitation.

Newton's law of Gravitation : The force of gravitational attraction between two point bodies is directly proportional to the product of their masses and inversely proportional to the square of the distance between them.

Consider two point bodies of masses m_1 and m_2 are placed at a distance r. The force of gravitational attraction between them, $F = G \frac{m_1 m_2}{r^2}$

Here G is constant called universal gravitational constant. The value of G is 6.67×10^{-11} Nm^2/kg^2.

Gravity : The gravitational force of earth is called gravity i.e. gravity is the force by which earth pulls a body towards its centre.

The acceleration produced in a body due to force of gravity is called acceleration due to gravity (denoted as g) and its value is 9.8 m/s^2.

➢ Acceleration due to gravity is independent of shape, size and mass of the body.

Variation in g

(i) value of g decreases with height or depth from earth's surface.

(ii) g is maximum at poles.

(iii) g is minimum at equator.

(iv) g decreases due to rotation of earth.

(v) g decreases if angular speed of earth increases and increases if angular speed of earth decreases.

➢ If angular speed of earth becomes 17 times its present value, a body on the equator becomes weightless.

Weight of a body in a lift

(i) If lift is stationary or moving with uniform speed (either upward or down ward), the apparent weight of a body is equal to its true weight.

(ii) If lift is going up with acceleration, the apparent weight of a body is more than the true weight.

(iii) If lift is going down with acceleration, the apparent weight of a body is less than the true weight.

(iv) If the cord of the lift is broken, it falls freely. In this situation the weight of a body in the lift becomes zero. This is the situation of weightlessness.

(v) While going down, if the acceleration of lift is more than acceleration due to gravity, a body in the lift goes in contact of the ceiling of lift.

Kepler's Laws of planetary motion

(i) All planets move around the sun in elliptical orbits, with the sun being at rest at one focus of the orbit.

(ii) The position vector of the planet with sun at the origin sweeps out equal area in equal time i.e. The areal velocity of planet around the sun always remains constant.

A consequence of this law is that the speed of planet increases when the planet is closer to the sun and decreases when the planet is far away from sun.

Speed of a planet is maximum when it is at perigee and minimum when it is at apogee.

(iii) The square of the period of revolution of a planet around the sun is directly proportional to the cube of mean distance of planet from the sun.

If T is period of revolution and r is the mean distance of planet from sun then $T^2 \propto r^3$.

Clearly distant planets have larger period of revolution. The time period of nearest planet Mercury is 88 days where as time period of farthest planet Pluto is 247.7 years.

Satellite : Satellites are natural or artificial bodies revolving around a planet under its gravitational attraction. Moon is a natural satellite while INSAT-IB is an artificial satellite of earth.

Orbital speed of a satellite

(i) Orbital speed of a satellite is independent of its mass. Hence satellites of different masses revolving in the orbit of same radius have same orbital speed.

(ii) Orbital speed of a satellite depends upon the radius of orbit (height of satellite from the surface of earth). Greater the radius of orbit, lesser will be the orbital speed.

➢ The orbital speed of a satellite revolving near the surface of earth is 7.9 km/sec.

Period of Revolution of a satellite : Time taken by a satellite to complete one revolution in its orbit is called its period of revolution.

i.e. period of revolution $= \dfrac{\text{circumference of orbit}}{\text{orbital speed}}$

(i) Period of revolution of a satellite depends upon the height of satellite from the surface of earth. Greater the height, more will be the period of revolution.

(ii) Period of revolution of a satellite is independent of its mass.

➢ The period of revolution of satellite revolving near the surface of earth is 1 hour 24 minute (84 minute)

Geo-Stationary Satellite : If a satellite revolves in equatorial plane in the direction of earth's rotation i.e. from west to east with a period of revolution equal to time period of rotation of earth on its own axis i.e. 24 hours, then the satellite will appear stationary relative to earth. Such a satellite is called Geo-stationary satellite. Such a satellite revolves around the earth at a height of 36000 km. The orbit of Geo-stationary satellite is called parking orbit. Arthur C. Clarck was first to predict that a communication satellite can be stationed in the geosynchronous orbit.

Escape velocity : Escape velocity is that minimum velocity with which a body should be projected from the surface of earth so as it goes out of gravitational field of earth and never return to earth.

- ➢ Escape velocity is independent of the mass, shape and size of the body and its direction of projection.
- ➢ Escape velocity is also called second cosmic velocity.
- ➢ For earth, escape velocity = 11.2 km/s.

  For moon, escape velocity = 2.4 km/s.
- ➢ Orbital velocity of a satellite $V_0 = \sqrt{gR}$ and escape velocity $V_e = \sqrt{2gR}$ where R = Radius of earth. i.e. $V_e = \sqrt{2}\, V_0$ i.e. escape velocity is $\sqrt{2}$ times the orbital velocity.

Therefore if the orbital velocity of a satellite is increased to $\sqrt{2}$ times (increased by 41%), the satellite will leave the orbit and escape.

5. Pressure

Pressure : Pressure is defined as force acting normally on unit area of the surface.

$$\text{Pressure (P)} = \frac{F}{A} = \frac{\text{Normal force on the surface}}{\text{Area of the surface}}$$

SI unit of pressure is N/m^2 also called pascal (Pa). Pressure is a scalar quantity.

Atmospheric Pressure : Atmospheric pressure is that pressure which is exerted by a mercury column of 76 cm length at 0°C at 45° latitude at the sea-level. It is equal to weight of 76 cm column of mercury of cross-sectional area 1 cm^2. Generally it is measured in bar. 1 bar = $10^5\ N/m^2$

Atmospheric pressure 1 atm = 1.01 bar = $1.01 \times 10^5\ N/m^2$ = 760 torr

One torr is the pressure exerted by a mercury column of 1 mm length.

- ➢ Atmospheric pressure decreases with altitude (height from earth's surface). This is why (i) It is difficult to cook on the mountain (ii) The fountain pen of a passenger leaks in aeroplane at height.
- ➢ Atmospheric pressure is measured by barometer. With the help of barometer, weather forecast can be made.
- ➢ Sudden fall in barometric reading is the indication of storm.
- ➢ Slow fall in barometric reading is the indication of rain.
- ➢ Slow rise in the barometric reading is the indication of clear weather.

Pressure in liquid : Force exerted on unit area of wall or base of the container by the molecules of liquid is the pressure of liquid.

The pressure exerted by liquid at depth h below the surface of liquid is given as $p = hdg$ where d is the density of liquid.

➢ Regarding pressure, the following points are worth noting :

(i) In a static liquid at same horizontal level, pressure is same at all points.

(ii) Pressure at a point in a static liquid has same value in all directions

(iii) Pressure at a point in a liquid is proportional to the depth of the point from the free surface.

(iv) Pressure at a point in a liquid is proportional to the density of the liquid.

Pascal law for pressure of liquid

(i) If gravitational attraction is negligible, in equilibrium condition, pressure is same at all points in a liquid.

(ii) If an external pressure is applied to an exclosed fluid, it is transmitted undiminished to every direction.

➢ Hydrolic lift, hydrolic press, Hydrolic brake work on Pascal law.

Effect of pressure on Melting Point and Boiling Point

(i) The M.P. of substances which expands on fusion increases with the increase in pressure; for example - wax.

(ii) The M.P. of substances which contracts on fusion decreases with the increase in temperature for example - ice.

(iii) Boiling point of all the substances increases with the increase in pressure.

6. Floatation

Buoyant Force : When a body is immersed party or wholly in a liquid, a force acts on the body by the liquid in the upward direction. This force is called Buoyant force or force of buoyancy or upthrust. It is equal to the weight of liquid displaced by the body and acts at the centre of gravity of displaced liquid. Its study was first made by Archimedes.

Archimedes Principle : When a body is immersed partly or wholly in a liquid, there is an apparent loss in the weight of the body which is equal to the weight of liquid displaced by the body.

Law of Floatation

A body floats in a liquid if

(i) density of material of body is less than or equal to the density of liquid.

(ii) If density of material of body is equal to density of liquid, the body floats fully submerged in liquid in neutral equilibrium.

(iii) When body floats in neutral equilibrium, the weight of the body is equal to the weight of displaced liquid.

(iv) The centre of gravity of the body and centre of gravity of the displaced liquid should be in one vertical line.

Centre of Buoyancy : The centre of gravity of the liquid displaced by a body is called centre of buoyancy.

Meta Centre : When a floating body is slightly tilted from equilibrium position, the centre of buoyancy shifts. The point at which the vertical line passing through the new position of centre of buoyancy meets with the initial line is called meta centre.

Conditions for stable equilibrium of Floating body

(i) The meta centre must always be higher than the centre gravity of the body.

(ii) The line joining the centre of gravity of the body and centre of flotation should be vertical.

Density : Density is defined as mass per unit volume.

$$\text{Density} = \frac{\text{mass}}{\text{volume}}. \text{ Its SI unit is } kg/m^3.$$

$$\text{Relative density} = \frac{\text{density of material}}{\text{density of water at } 4°C}$$

Since relative density is a ratio, it is unitless.

- ➢ Relative density is measured by Hydrometer.
- ➢ The density of sea water is more than that of normal water. This explains why it is easier to swim in sea water.
- ➢ When ice floats in water, its $\frac{1}{10}$ the part remain outside the water.
- ➢ If ice floating in water in a vessel melts, the level of water in the vessel does not change.
- ➢ Purity of milk is measured by lactometer.

7. Surface Tension

Cohesive Force : The force of attraction between the molecules of same substance is called cohesive force. Cohesive force is maximum in solids. This is why solids have a fixed shape. Cohesive force is negligible in case of gases.

Adhesive Force : Force of attraction between the molecules of different substances is called adhesive force. Due to adhesive force, one body sticks to other.

Surface Tension : Surface tension is the property of a liquid by virtue of which it has the tendency to have the area of its free surface minimum as if it were under tension like a stretched elastic membrane.

Surface tension of a liquid is measured by the normal force acting per unit length on either side of an imaginary line drawn on the free surface of liquid and tangential to the free surface.

So, if a force F acts on an imaginary line of length l, then surface tension, $T = F/l$.

- ➢ Work done in increasing the surface area of a liquid by unity under isothermal condition is equal to surface tension of liquid. According to this definition, unit of surface tension is joule / meter^2.

➢ Surface tension of a liquid decreases with the increase of temperature and becomes zero at critical temperature.

Capillary tube : A tube having very narrow (fine) and uniform bore is called a capillary tube.

Capillarity : If a capillary tube is dipped in a liquid, liquid ascends or descends in the capillary tube. This phenomenon is called capillarity.

➢ The height by which liquid ascends or decends in a capillary tube depends upon the radius of the tube.

The capillarity depends on the nature of liquid and solid both. The liquid which wets the wall of tube rises in the tube and the liquid which does not wet the wall of tube descends in the tube. For example, when a glass capillary tube is dipped in water, water rises in the tube and shape of water meniscus is concave, similarly when a glass capillary tube is dipped in mercury, mercury decends in the tube and shape of mercury meniscus is convex.

Illustrations of capillarity

(i) A piece of blotting paper soaks ink because the pores of the blotting paper serve as capillary tubes.

(ii) The oil in the wick of a lamp rises due to capillary action of threads in the wick.

(iii) The root hairs of plants draws water from the soil through capillary action.

(iv) To prevent loss of water due to capillary action, the soil is loosened and split into pieces by the farmers.

(v) If a capillary tube is dipped in water in an artificial satellite, water rises up to other end of tube because of its zero apparent weight, how long the tube may be.

(vi) Action of towel in soaking up water from the body is due to capillary action of cotton in the towel.

(vii) Melted wax, in a candle rises up to wick by capillary action.

➢ If a clean and dry needle is very slowly kept on the surface of water, it floats due to surface tension.

➢ The addition of detergent or soap decrease the surface tension of water and thus increases the cleaning ability.

➢ Bubbles of soap solution are big because addition of soap decreases the surface tension of water.

➢ When kerosene oil is sprinkled on water, its surface tension decreases. As a result the larva of mosquitoes floating on the surface of water die due to sinking.

➢ Warm soup is tasty because at high temperature its surface tension is low and consequently the soup spreads on all parts of the tongue.

8. Viscosity

Viscous force : The force which opposes the relative motion between different layers of liquid or gases is called viscous force.

Viscosity : Viscosity is the property of a liquid by virtue of which it opposes the relative motion between its different layers.

➢ Viscosity is the property of liquids and gases both.

➢ The viscosity of a liquid is due to cohesive force between its molecules.

➢ The viscosity of a gas is due to diffusion of its molecules from one layer to other layer.

➢ Viscosity of gases is much less than that of liquids. There is no viscosity in solids.

➢ Viscosity of an ideal fluid is zero.

➢ With rise in temperature, viscosity of liquids decreases and that for gases increases.

➢ Viscosity of a fluid is measured by its coefficient of viscosity. Its SI unit is decapoise (kg/ms) or pascal second. It is generally denoted by η.

Terminal Velocity : When a body falls in a viscous medium, its velocity first increases and finally becomes constant. This constant velocity is called Terminal velocity.

In this situation, the weight of the body is equal to the sum of viscous force and force of buoyancy i.e. the net force on the body is zero.

Terminal velocity of a spherical body falling in a viscous medium is proportional to the square of radius of the body.

Streamline Flow : If a fluid is flowing in such a way that velocity of all the fluid particles reaching a particular point is same at all time, then the flow of fluid is said to be streamline flow. Thus in streamline flow, each particle follows the same path as followed by a previous particle passing through that point.

Critical Velocity : The maximum velocity up to which fluid motion is streamline is called critical velocity. Clearly, if the velocity of flow is below critical velocity, flow is streamline and of the velocity is above the critical velocity, flow is turbulent.

If the velocity of flow is less than critical velocity, the rate of flow of fluid depends basically on viscosity of fluid. If the velocity of flow is more than critical velocity, the rate of flow depends on the density of fluid and not on viscosity. Due to this reason, on eruption of the volcano the lava coming out of it flows very swiftly although it is very dense having large viscosity.

Bernoulli's theorem : According to Bernoulli's theorem, in case of streamline flow of incompressible and non viscous fluid (ideal fluid) through a tube, total energy (sum of pressure energy, potential energy and kinetic energy) per unit volume of fluid is same at all points.

Venturimeter, a device used to measure rate of flow of fluid, works on Bernoulli's theorem.

9. Elasticity

Elasticity : Elasticity is the property of material of a body by virtue of which the body acquires its original shape and size after the removal of deforming force.

Elastic Limit : Elastic limit is the maximum value of deforming force upto which a material shows elastic property and above which the material looses its elastic property.

Stress : The restoring force per unit area set up inside the body subjected to deforming force is called stress.

Strain : The relative change in dimension or shape of a body which is subjected to stress is called strain.

It is measured by ratio of change in length to the original length (logitudional strain), change in volume to original volume (volume strain).

Hooke's law : Under elastic limit, stress is proportional to strain

i.e. stress $\propto$ strain or $\frac{\text{stress}}{\text{strain}} = E$ (constant)

E is called elastic constant or modulus of elasticity. Its value is different for different material. Its SI unit is Nm^{-2} also called pascal.

Elastic constant is of three types :

(i) Young's modulus of elasticity $Y = \frac{\text{Logitudinal stress}}{\text{Logitudinal strain}}$

(ii) Bulk modulus of elasticity $K = \frac{\text{Volume stress}}{\text{Volume Strain}}$

(iii) Rigidity modulus $(\eta) = \frac{\text{Tangential (or shear) stress}}{\text{Shear strain}}$

10. Simple Harmonic Motion

Periodic Motion : Any motion which repeats itself after regular interval of time is called periodic or harmonic motion. Motion of hands of a clock, motion of earth around the sun, motion of the needle of a sewing machine are the examples of periodic motion.

Oscillatory Motion : If a particles repeats its motion after a regular time interval about a fixed point, motion is said to be oscillatory or vibratory. i.e. oscillatory motion is a constrained periodic motion between precisely fixed limits. Motion of piston in an automobile engine, motion of balance wheel of a watch are the examples of oscillatory motion.

Time period : Time taken in one complete oscillation is called time period.

Or, Time after which motion is repeated is called time period.

Frequency = Frequency is the no. of oscillations completed by oscillating body in unit time interval. Its SI unit is Hertz.

If n = frequency, T = time period, then $nT = 1$

Simple Harmonic Motion : If a particle repeats its motion about a fixed point after a regular time interval in such a way that at any moment the acceleration of the particle is directly proportional to its displacement from the fixed point at that moment and is always directed towards the fixed point then the motion of the particle is called simple harmonic motion.

The fixed point is called mean point or equilibrium point.

Characteristics of SHM

When a particle executing SHM passes through the mean position :

(i) No force acts on the particle.

(ii) Acceleration of the particle is zero.

(iii) Velocity is maximum.

(iv) Kinetic energy is maximum.

(v) Potential energy is zero.

When a particle executing SHM is at the extreme end, then :

(i) acceleration of the particle is maximum.

(ii) Restoring force acting on particle is maximum.

(iii) Velocity of particle is zero.

(iv) Kinetic energy of particle is zero.

(v) Potential energy is maximum.

Simple Pendulum : If a point mass is suspended from a fixed support with the help of a massless and inextensible string, the arrangement is called simple pendulum. The above is an ideal definition. Practically a simple pendulum is made by suspending a small ball (called bob) from a fixed support with the help of a light string.

If the bob of a simple pendulum is slightly displaced from its mean position and then released, it starts oscillating in simple harmonic motion. Time period of oscillation of a simple pendulum is given as

$T = 2\pi\sqrt{\frac{l}{g}}$ where l is the effective length of the pendulum and g is the acceleration due to gravity.

11. Wave

➢ A wave is a disturbance which propagates energy from one place to the other without the transport of matter.

Waves are broadly of two types

(i) Mechanical Wave (ii) Non-mechanical wave

➢ Mechanical Wave : The waves which require material medium (solid, liquid or gas) for their propagation are called mechanical waves or elastic wave.

Mechanical wave are of two types

(i) Longitudinal wave : If the particles of the medium vibrate in the direction of propagation of wave, the wave is called longitudinal wave.

Waves on springs or sound waves in air are examples of longitudual waves.

(ii) Transverse Wave : If the particles of the medium vibrate perpendicular to the direction of propagation of wave, the wave is called transverse wave.

Waves on strings under tension, waves on the surface of water are examples of transverse waves.

➢ Non-mechanical waves or electromagnetic waves : The waves which do not require medium for their propagation i.e. which can propagate even through the vacuum are called non mechanical wave.

Light, heat are the examples of non-mechanical wave. In fact all the electromagnetic waves are non-mechanical.

➢ All the electromagnetic wave consists of photon.

➢ The wavelength range of electromagnetic wave is 10^{-14}m to 10^4 m.

Properties of electromagnetic waves

(i) They are neutral.
(ii) They propagate as transverse wave.
(iii) They propagate with the velocity of light.
(iv) They contains energy and momentum.
(v) Their concept was introduced by Maxwell.

Following waves are not electromagnetic

(i) Cathode rays (ii) Canal rays (iii) α rays (iv) β rays (v) Sound wave (vi) Ultrasonic wave

Some Important Electromagnetic Waves

Electro-magnetic Waves	Discoverer	Wavelength range (in meter)	Frequency range
γ–Rays	Henry Becqueral	10^{-14} to 10^{-10}	10^{20} to 10^{18}
X–Rays	W. Rontgen	10^{-10} to 10^{-8}	10^{18} to 10^{16}
Ultra-violet rays	Ritter	10^{-8} to 10^{-7}	10^{16} to 10^{14}
Visible radiation	Newton	3.9×10^{-7} to 7.8×10^{-7}	10^{14} to 10^{12}
Infra-red rays	Hershel	7.8×10^{-7} to 7.8×10^{-3}	10^{12} to 10^{10}
Short radio waves or Hertz Hertzian Waves	Heinrich	10^{-3} to 1	10^{10} tp 10^8
Long Radio Waves	Marcony	1 to 10^4	10^8 to 10^6

Note : *Electromagnetic waves of wavelength range 10^{-3} m to 10^{-2} m are called microwaves.*

Phase of vibration : Phase of vibration of a vibrating particle at any instant is the physical quantity which express the position as well as direction of motion of the particle at that instant with respect to its equilibrium (mean) position.

Amplitude : Amplitude is defined as the maximum displacement of the vibrating particle on either side from the equilibrium position.

Wavelength : Wavelength is the distance between any two nearest particle of the medium, vibrating in the same phase. It is denoted by the Greek letter lembda. (λ)

In transverse wave distance between two consecutive crests or troughs and in longitudinal wave, distance between two consecutive compressions or rarefaction is equal to wavelength.

Relation between wavelength, frequency and velocity of wave

Velocity of wave = frequency × wavelength or, $v = n\lambda$.

12. Sound Wave

➢ Sound waves are longitudinal mechanical waves.

➢ According to their frequency range, longitudinal mechanical waves are divided into the following categories :

1. Audible or Sound Waves : The longitudinal mechanical waves which lie in the frequency range 20 Hz to 20000 Hz are called audible or sound waves. These waves are sensitive to human ear. These are generated by the vibrating bodies such as tuning fork, vocal cords etc.

2. Infrasonic Waves : The longitudinal mechanical waves having frequencies less than 20 Hz are called Infrasonic. These waves are produced by sources of bigger size such as earth quakes, volcanic eruptions, ocean waves and by elephants and whales.

3. Ultrasonic Waves : The longitudinal mechanical waves having frequencies greater than 20000 Hz are called ultrasonic waves. Human ear can not detect these waves. But certain creatures like dog, cat,. bat, mosquito can detect these waves. Bat not only detect but also produce ultrasonic.

Ultrasonic waves can be produced by Galton's whistle or Hartman's generator or by the high frequency vibrations of a quartz crystal under an alternating electric field (Piezo - electric effect) or by the vibrations of a ferromagnetic rod under an alternating magnetic field (Magnetostriction)

Applications of Ultrasonic Waves

1. For sending signals.
2. For measuring the depth of sea.
3. For cleaning cloths, aeroplanes and machinery parts of clocks.
4. For removing lamp-shoot from the chimney of factories.
5. In sterilizing of a liquid.
6. In Ultrasonography.

Speed of Sound :

➢ Speed of sound is different in different mediums. In a medium, the speed of sound basically depends upon elasticity and density of medium.

➢ Speed of sound is maximum in solids and minimum in gases.

➢ When sound enters from one medium to another medium, its speed and wavelength changes but frequency remains unchanged.

➢ In a medium, the speed of sound is independent of frequency.

Effect of pressure on speed of sound: The speed of sound is independent of pressure i.e. speed remains unchanged by the increase or decrease of pressure.

Speed of sound in different mediums

Medium	Speed of sound (In m/s)
Carbondioxide	260
Air (0°C)	332
Air (20°C)	343
Steam (at 100°C)	405
Helium	965
Alcohal	1213
Hydrogen	1269
Mercury	1450
Water (20°C)	1482
Sea water	1533
Copper	3560
Iron	5130
Glass	5640
Granite	6000
Aluminium	6420

Effect of Temperature on speed of sound : The speed of sound increases with the increase of temperature of the medium. The speed of sound in air increases by 0.61 m/s when the temperature is increased by 1°C.

Effect of humidity on speed of sound: The speed of sound is more in humid air than in dry air because the density of humid air is less than the density of dry air.

Characteristics of Sound waves : Sound waves have the following three characteristics.

1. Intensity : Intensity of sound at any point in space is defined as amount of energy passing normally per unit area held around that point per unit time. SI Unit of Intensity is watt/m^2.

Intensity of sound at a point is,

(i) inversely proportional to the square of the distance of point from the source.

(ii) directly proportional to square of amplitude of vibration, square of frequency and density of the medium.

Due to intensity, a sound appears loud or faint to the ear. Actually, the sensation of a sound perceived in ear is measured by another term called loudness which depends on intensity of sound and sensitiveness of the ear. Unit of loudness is bel. A practical unit of loudness is decibel (dB) which of equal to 1/10th of bel. Another unit of loudness is phon.

2. Pitch : Pitch is that characteristic of sound which distinguishes a sharp (or shrill) sound from a grave (dull or flat) sound. Pitch depends upon frequency. Higher the frequency, higher will be the pitch and shriller will be the sound. Lower the frequency, lower will be the pitch and grave will be the sound.

3. Quality : Quality is that characteristic of sound which enables us to distinguish between sounds produced by two sources having the same intensity and pitch. The quality depends upon number, frequency and relative intensities of overtones.

Echo : The sound waves received after being reflected from a high tower or mountains is called echo.

- To hear echo, the minimum distance between the observer and reflector should be 17 m (16.6 m)
- Persistence of ear (effect of sound on ear) is 1/10 sec.
- Due to refraction, sound is heard at longer distances in nights than in day.

Resonance : If the frequency of imposed periodic force is equal to the natural frequency of a body, the body oscillates with a very large amplitude. This phenomenon is called resonance.

Interference of sound : The modification or redistribution of energy at a point due to superposition of two (or, more) sound waves of same frequency is called interference of sound.

If two waves meet at a point in same phase, intensity of sound is maximum at that point. Such type of interference is called constructive interference. Similarly, if the two waves meet at a point in opposite phase, intensity of sound at that point is minimum. Such type of interference is called destructive interference.

Diffraction of sound : Wavelength of sound is of the order of 1 m. If an obstacle of that range appears in the path of sound, sound deviates at the edge of obstacle and propagates forward. This phenomenon is called diffraction of sound.

Doppler's Effect : If there is a relative motion between source of sound and observer, the apparent frequency of sound heard by the observer is different from the actual frequency of sound emitted by the source. This phenomenon is called Doppler's effect.

When the distance between the source and observer decreases, the apparent frequency increases and vice-versa.

Mach Number : It is defined as the ratio of speed of sound source to the speed of sound in the same medium under the same condition of temperature and pressure.

- If Mach number > 1, body is called supersonic.
- If mach number > 5, body is called hypersonic.
- If mach number < 1, the body (source) is said to be moving with subsonic speed.

Shock waves : A body moving with supersonic speed in air leaves behind it a conical region of disturbance which spreads continuously. Such a disturbance is called shock wave. This wave carries huge energy and may even make cracks in window panes or even damage a building.

Bow Waves : When a motor boat in a sea travels faster than sound, then waves just like shock-waves are produced on the surface of water. These waves are called bow waves.

13. Heat

Heat is that form of energy which flows from one body to other body due to difference is temperature between the bodies. The amount of heat contained in a body depends upon the mass of the body.

- If W work is performed and heat produced is H then $\frac{W}{H} = J$ or, W = JH where J is a constant called Mechanical Equivalent of Heat. Its value is 4.186 joule/Calorie. It means if 4.186 joule of work is performed, 1 calorie of heat is consumed.

Units of Heat

C.G.S unit : calorie = It is the amount of heat required to raise the temperature of 1 g of pure water through 1°C.

International calorie : It is the amount of heat required to raise the temperature of 1 g of pure water from 14.5°C to 15.5°C.

F.P.S. unit : B.Th.U (British Thermal Unit) = It is the amount of heat required to raise the temp. of 1 pound of pure water through 1°F.

Relations between different units :

1 B.Th.U = 252 calorie
1 calorie = 4.186 joule
1 Therm = 10^5 B.Th.U.
1 pound calorie = 453.6 calorie.

Temperature : Temperature is that physical cause which decides the direction of flow of heat from one body to other body. Heat energy always flows from body at higher temperature to body at lower temperature.

Measurement of Temperature

Thermometer : The device which measures the temperature of a body is called thermometer.

Scales of temperature measurement

To measure temperature two fixed points are taken on each thermometer. One of the fixed points is the freezing point of water or ice as lower fixed point (LFP). The other fixed point is the boiling point of water or steam as upper fixed print (UFP).

The temperatures of these fixed points, the no. of fundamental interval between the two fixed points on different temperature scales is shown by the table given below :

	Celsius	Fahrenheit	Reaumur	Kelvin	Rankine
UFP	100°C	212°F	80°F	373.15K	672°Ra
↑ no. of fundamental interval ↓	↑ 100 ↓	↑ 180 ↓	↑ 80 ↓	↑ 100 ↓	↑ 180 ↓
LFP ↓	0°C ↓	32°F ↓	0°R ↓	273.15K ↓	492°Ra ↓
Absolute zero	–273.15°C	–459.6°F	–218.4°R	0K	0°Ra

Relation between Temperature on different scales

$$\frac{C-0}{100} = \frac{F-32}{180} = \frac{R-0}{80} = \frac{K-273}{100} = \frac{Ra-492}{180}$$

- Celsius was initially known as centigrade.
- While expressing temperature on kelvin scale ° (degree) is not used.
- Freezing point (F.P.) of mercury is –39°C. Hence to measure temperature below this temperature, alcohal thermometer is used. F.P. of alcohal is –115°C.

Range of different thermometers

Mercury Thermometer : from –30°C to 350°C

Constant volume gas thermometer : from –200°C to 500°C (with H_2), below – 200°C upto –268°C (with He) above 1000°C upto 1600°C (with N_2 gas and bulb of glazed porcelain)

Platinum resistance thermometer : from – 200°C to 1200°C

Thermocouple thermometer : from – 200°C to 1600°C

Total Radiation Pyrometer

When a body is at high temperature, it glows brightly and the radiation emitted by the body is directly proportional to the fourth power of absolute temperature of the body. Radiation pyrometer measures the temperature of a body by measuring the radiation emitted by the body.

This thermometer is not put in contact with the body. But it can not measure temperature below 800°C because at low temperature emission of radiation is very small and can not be detected.

Specific Heat Capacity : Specific heat capacity of a material is the amount of heat required to raise the temperature of unit mass of substance through 1°. Its SI unit is Joule / kilogram kelvin (J / kg.*k*)

➢ One calorie of heat is required to raise the temperature of 1 gram of water through 1°C. Hence specific heat capacity of water is 1 cal / gram °C.

1 calorie / gram °C = 4200 Joule / kg kelvin.

Specific Heat Capacities of different materials (J / kg K)

Water	4200
Ice	2100
Iron	460
K. Oil	210
Mercury	140
Lead	130

Thermal Expansion

When a body is heated its length, surface area and volume increase. The increase in length, area and volume with the increase in temperature are measured in terms of coefficient of linear expansion or linear expansivity (α), coefficient of superficial expansion or superficial expansivity (β) and coefficient of cubical expansion or cubical expansivity (γ).

Relation between α, β and γ.

$$\alpha : \beta : \gamma = 1 : 2 : 3 \qquad \text{or, } \beta = 2\alpha \text{ and } \gamma = 3\alpha$$

Anomalous expansion of water : Almost every liquid expands with the increase in temperature. But when temperature of water is increased from 0°C to 4°C, its volume decreases. If the temperature is increased above 4°C, its volume starts increasing. Clearly, density of water is maximum at 4°C.

Transmission of Head : The transfer of heat from one place to other place is called transmission of heat. There are three modes of heat transfer–(i) conduction, (ii) convection and (iii) radiation.

Conduction : In this process, heat is transferred from one place to other place by the successive vibrations of the particles of the medium without bodily movement of the particles of the medium. In solids, heat transfer takes place by conduction.

Convection : In this process, heat is transferred by the actual movement of particles of the movement from one place to other place. Due to movement of particles, a current of particles set up which is called convection current.

In liquids and gases, heat transfer takes place by convection.

➢ Earth's atmosphere is heated by convection.

Radiation : In this method transfer of heat takes place with the speed of light without affecting the intervening medium.

Newton's law of cooling : The rate of loss of heat by a body is directly proportional to the difference in temperature between the body and the surrounding.

Kirchhoff's law : According to Kirchhoff's law, the ratio of emissive power to absorptive power is same for all surfaces at the same temperature and is equal to emissive power of black body at that temperature.

Kirchhoff's law signifies that good absorbers are good emitter.

If a shining metal ball with some black spot on its surface is heated to a high temperature and seen in dark, the shining ball becomes dull but the black spots shines brilliantly, because black spot absorbs radiation during heating and emit in dark.

Stefan's law : The radiant energy emitted by a black body per unit area per unit time (i.e. emissive power) is directly proportional to the fourth power of its absolute temperature.

i.e. $E \propto T^4$ or, $E = \sigma T^4$

where σ is a constant called Stefan's constant.

Change of State

Any material can remain in any of its three states (solid, liquid and gas). To change the substance from one state to other state is called change of state. For this either substance is heated or heat is extracted from the substance. Change of state takes place at a fixed temp.

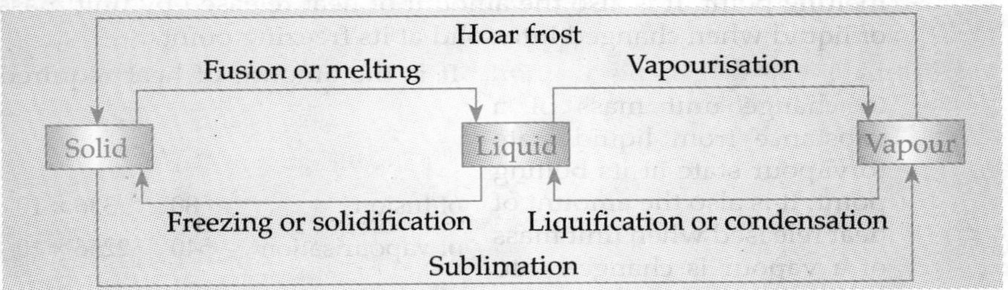

Fusion : The process by which a substance is changed from solid state to liquid state is called fusion. Fusion takes place at a fixed temperature called melting point (M.P.)

Freezing : The process by which a substance is changed from liquid state to solid state is called freezing. Freezing takes at a fixed temperature called freezing point. (F.P.) For a substance M.P. = F.P.

- M.P. of a substance changes with the change in pressure. Melting point of substances which contracts in the process of fusion (as ice) decreases with the increase in pressure. Melting point of substances which expands in the process of fusion (as wax) increases with the increase in pressure.
- With the addition of impurity (as salt in ice), melting point of a substance decreases.

Vapourisation : The process by which a substance is changed from liquid state to vapour state is called vapourisation.

Vapourisation takes place by two methods : (i) Evaporation & (ii) Boiling or Ebullition

Evaporation : The process of vapourisation which takes place only from the exposed surface of liquid and that at all temperatures is called evaporation.

Evaporation causes cooling. This is why water in a earthed pot gets cooled in summer.

Boiling : The process of vapourisation which takes place at a fixed temperature and from whole part of liquid is called boiling.

The temperature at which boiling takes place is called boiling point.

Condensation : The process by which a substance is changed from vapour state to liquid state is called condensation.

➢ Boiling point of a liquid increases with the increase in pressure.

➢ Boiling point of a liquid increases with the addition of impurity.

Latent heat or heat of transformation

The amount of heat required to change the state of unit mass of substance at constant temperature is called latent heat.

If Q heat is required to change the state of a substance of mass m at constant temperature and L is the latent heat, then $Q = mL$.

S.I. unit of latent heat is Joule / kilogram.

Any material has two types of latent heat.

(i) Latent heat of fusion : It is the amount of heat energy required to convert unit mass a substance from solid state to liquid state at its melting point. It is also the amount of heat released by unit mass of liquid when changed into solid at its freezing point.

(ii) Latent heat of vapourisation : It is the amount of heat required to change unit mass of a substance from liquid state to vapour state at its boiling point. It is also the amount of heat released when unit mass of a vapour is changed into liquid.

Latent heat of water

Latent Heat	in Cal/g	J/kg
of fusion	80	336×10^3
of vapourisation	540	2256×10^3

Sublimation : Sublimation is the process of conversion of a solid directly into vapour.

➢ Sublimation takes place when boiling point is less than melting point.

➢ Sublimation is shown by camphor or ice in vacuum.

Hoar Frost : Hoar frost is just the reverse process of sublimation i.e. it is the process of direct conversion of vapour into solid.

➢ Steam produces more severe burn than water at same temperature because internal energy of steam is more than that of water at same temperature.

Relative Humidity : Relative humidity is defined as the ratio of amount of water vapour present in a given volume of atmosphere to the amount of water vapour required to saturate the same volume at same temperature.

The ratio is multiplied by 100 to express the relative humidity in percentage.

➢ Relative humidity is measured by Hygrometer.

➢ Relative humidity increases with the increase of temperature.

Air conditioning : For healthy and favourable atmosphere of human being, the conditions are as follows

(i) Temperature : from 23°C to 25°C.

(ii) Relative humidity : from 60% to 65%.

(iii) Speed of air : from 0.75 meter / minute to 2.5 meter / minute.

Thermodynamics

First law of thermodynamics : **Heat energy given to a system is used in the following two ways :**

(i) In increasing the temperature and hence internal energy of the system.

(ii) In doing work by the system.

If ΔQ = heat energy given to the system

ΔU = Increase in the internal energy of the system.

ΔW = work done by the system

Then, $\Delta Q = \Delta U + \Delta W$ is the mathematical statement of first law of thermodynamics.

➢ First law of thermodynamics is equivalent to principle of conservation of energy.

Isothermal Process : **If the changes are taking place in a system in such a way that temperature of the system remains constant throughout the change, then the process is said to be an isothermal.**

Adiabatic Process : **If the changes are taking place in a system in such a way that there is no exchange of heat energy between the system and the surrounding, then the process is said to be an adiabatic process.**

➢ If carbon dioxide is suddenly expanded, it is changed into dry ice. This is an example of adiabatic process.

Second Law of Thermodynamics : **The first law of thermodynamics guarantees that in a thermodynamic process, energy will be conserved. But this law does not tell whether a given process in which energy is conserved will take place or not. The second law of thermodynamics gives the answer.**

Through this law can be stated in many forms, the following two forms are worth mentioning :

Kelvin's statement : **Whole of the heat can never be converted into work.**

Clausius statement : **Heat by itself can not flow from a colder body to a hotter body.**

Heat Engine : **Heat energy is a device which converts heat energy into mechanical work continuously through a cyclic process. Every heat engine basically consists of the three parts : (i) source (a hot body) (ii) sink (a cold body) and (iii) a working substance.**

Heat engine may be devided into two types :

(i) Internal Combustion Engine : **In this engine, heat is produced in the engine itself.** Example : **Otto engine or petrol engine (efficiency = 52%), Diesel engine (efficiency = 64%)**

(ii) External Cumbustion Engine : **In this engine heat is produced outside the engine. Steam engine is an example of external cumbustion engine. (efficiency = 20%)**

Refrigerator or Heat Pump : A refrigerator is an apparatus which transfers heat energy from cold to a hot body at the expanse of energy supplied by an external agent. The working substance here is called refrigerant.

In actual refrigerator, vapours of freon (CCl_2F_2) acts as refrigerant.

14. Light

Light is a form of energy which is propagated as electromagnetic waves. In the spectrum of electromagnetic waves it lies between ultra-violet and infra-red region and has wavelength between 3900 A° to 7800 A°.

- Electromagnetic waves are transverse, hence light is transverse wave.
- Wave nature of light explains rectilinear propagation, reflection, refraction, interference, diffraction and polarisation of light.
- The phenomena like photoelectric effect, compton effect are not explained on the basis of wave nature of light. These phenomena are explained on the basis of quantum theory of light as proposed by Einstein.
- In quantum theory, light is regarded as a packet or bundle of energy called photon. Photon is associated with it an energy E where $E = h\nu$.
- Clearly light behaves as wave and particle both. Thus light has dual nature.
- Speed of light was first measured by Roemer. (1678 AD).
- Speed of light is maximum in vacuum and air (3×10^8 m/s)

Refractive index : R.I. of a medium is defined as the ratio of speed of light in vacuume to the speed of light in the medium.

$$\mu = \frac{c}{v} = \frac{\text{Speed of light in vacuum}}{\text{Speed of light in the medium}}$$

- Speed of light is different in different media. Velocity of light is large in a medium which has small refractive index.

Speed of light in different mediums

Medium	Speed of light (m/s)	Medium	Speed of light (m/s)
Vacuum	3×10^8	Glass	2×10^8
Water	2.25×10^8	Terpentine oil	2.04×10^8
Rock salt	1.96×10^8	Nylon	1.96×10^8

- Light takes 8 minute 19 second (499 second) to reach from sun to earth.
- The light reflected from moon takes 1.28 second to reach earth.

Luminous bodies : Those object which emit light by themselves are called luminous bodies.

e.g.–sun, stars, electric bulb etc.

Non-luminous bodies : Those objects which do not emit light by themselves but are visible by the light falling on them emitted by self luminous bodies are called non-luminous bodies.

A material can be classified as :

(i) Transparent : The substances which allow most of the incident light to pass through them are called transparent. e.g. glass, water.

(ii) Translucent : The substances which allow a part of incident light to pass through them are called translucent bodies e.g. oiled paper.

(iii) Opaque : The substances which do not allow the incident light to pass through them are called opaque bodies. e.g., mirror, metal, wood etc.

Reflection of light : Light moving in one medium when falls at the surface of another medium, part of light returns back to the same medium. This phenomenon of returning back of light in the first medium at the interface of two media is known as reflection of light.

Laws of reflection

(i) The incident ray, reflected ray and normal to the reflecting surface at the incident point all lie in the same plane.

(ii) The angle of reflection is equal to the angle of incidence.

Reflection from plane mirror

(i) The image is virtual, laterally inverted.

(ii) The size of image is equal to that of object.

(iii) The distance of image from the mirror is equal to distance of object from the mirror.

(iv) If an object moves towards (or away from) a plane mirror with speed v, relative to the object the image moves towards (or away) with a speed $2v$.

(v) If a plane mirror is rotated by an angle θ, keeping the incident ray fixed, the reflected ray is rotated by an angle 2θ.

(vi) To see his full image in a plane mirror, a person requires a mirror of at least half of his height.

(vii) If two plane mirrors are inclined to each other at an angle θ the number of images (n) of a point object formed are determined as follows :

(a) If $\frac{360}{\theta}$ is even integer, then $n = \frac{360}{\theta} - 1$

(b) If $\frac{360}{\theta}$ is odd integer,

then $n = \frac{360}{\theta} - 1$ *for the object is symmetrically placed.* and

$n = \frac{360}{\theta}$ *for the object is not symmetrically placed.*

(c) If $\frac{360}{\theta}$ is a fraction then n is equal to integral part.

Reflection from spherical mirror

Spherical mirror are of two types (i) Concave mirror and (ii) Convex mirror

Position & nature of image formed by a spherical mirror

Position of object	Position of image	Size of image in comparison to Object	Nature of image
Concave mirror			
At infinity	At Focus	Highly diminished	Real, inverted
Between infinity and centre of curvature	Between focus and centre of curvature	Diminished	Real, inverted
At centre of curvature	At centre of curvature	Of same size	Real, inverted
Between focus and centre of curvature	Between centre of curvature and infinity	Enlarged	Real, inverted
At focus	At infinity	Highly enlarged	Real, inverted
Between focus and pole	Behind the mirror	Enlarged	Virtual, erect
Convex mirror			
At infinity	At Focus	Highly diminished	Virtual, erect
Infront of mirror	Between pole and focus	Diminished	Virtual, erect

Note : *Image formed by a convex mirror is always virtual, erect and diminished.*

Uses of Concave mirror :

(i) As a shaving glass.

(ii) As a reflector for the head lights of a vehicle, search light.

(iii) In opthalmoscope to examine eye, ear, nose by doctors.

(iv) In solar cookers.

Uses of Convex mirror :

(i) As a rear view mirror in vehicle because it provides the maximum rear field of view and image formed is always erect.

(ii) In sodium reflector lamp.

Refraction of light : When a ray of light propagating in a medium enters the other medium, it deviates from its path. This phenomenon of change in the direction of propagation of light at the boundary when it passes from one medium to other medium is called refraction of light.

When a ray of light enters from rarer medium to denser medium (as from water to glass) it deviates towards the normal drawn on the boundary of two media at the incident point. Similarly in passing from denser to rarer medium, a ray deviates away from the normal. If light is incident normally on the boundary i.e. parallel to normal, it enters the second medium undeviated.

Laws of refraction

(i) Incident ray, refracted ray and normal drawn at incident point always lie in the same plane.

(ii) Snell's law : For a given colour of light, the ratio of sine of angle of incidence to the sine of angle of refraction is a constant,

i.e. $\frac{\sin i}{\sin r} = {}^1\mu_2$ (constant)

This constant ${}^1\mu_2$ is called refractive index of second medium with respect to the first medium.

➢ Absolute refractive index of a medium is defined as the ratio of speed of light in free space (vacuum) to that in the given medium.

i.e. absolute refractive index (μ) = $\frac{\text{Speed of light in vacuum}}{\text{Speed of light in the medium}}$

➢ The refractive index of a medium is different for different colours. The refractive index of a medium decreases with the increase in wavelength of light. Hence refractive index of a medium is maximum for violet colour of light and minimum for red colour of light.

➢ The refractive index of a medium decreases with the increase in temperature. But this variation is very small.

➢ When a ray of light enters from one medium to other medium, its frequency and phase donot change but wavelength and velocity change.

Some illustrations of Refraction

(i) Bending of a linear object when it is partially dipped in a liquid inclined to the surface of the liquid.

(ii) Twinkling of stars.

(iii) Oval shape of sun in the morning and evening.

(iv) An object in a denser medium when seen from a rarer medium appears to be at a smaller distance.

This is way (a) A fish in a pond when viewed from air appears to be at a smaller depth them actual depth (b) A coin at the base of a vessel filled with water appears raised.

Critical angle : In case of propagation of light from denser to rarer medium through a plane boundary, critical angle is the angle of incidence for which angle of refraction is 90°.

Total Internal Reflection : If light is propagating from denser medium towards the rarer medium and angle of incidence is more than critical angle, then the light incident on the boundary is reflected back in the denser medium, obeying the laws of reflection. This phenomenon is called total internal reflection as total light energy is reflected, no part is absorbed or transmitted.

➢ For total internal reflection,

(i) Light must be propagating from denser to rarer medium.

(ii) Angle of incidence must exceeds the critical angle.

Illustrations of total internal reflection

(i) Sparkling of diamond

(ii) Mirage and looming.

(iii) Shining of air bubble in water.

(iv) Increase in duration of sun's visibility–The sun becomes visible even before sun rise and remains visible even after sunset due to total internal reflection of light.

(v) Shining of a smoked ball or a metal ball on which lamp soot is deposited when dipped in water.

(vi) Optical Fibre : Optical fibre consists of thousands of strands of a very fine quality glass or quartz (of refractive index 1.7), each strand coated with a layer of material of lower refractive index (1.5). In it, light is propagated along the axis of fibre through multiple total internal reflection, even though the fibre is curved, without loss of energy.

Applications :

(i) For transmitting optical signals and the two dimensional pictures.
(ii) For transmitting electrical signals by first converting them to light.
(iii) For visualising the internal sites of the body by doctors in endoscopy.

Refraction of Light Through Lens

➢ Lens is a section of transparent refractive material of two surfaces of definite geometrical shape of which one surface must be spherical. Lens is generally of two types : (i) Convex lens (ii) Concave lens.

➢ When a lens is thicker at the middle than at the edges, it is called a convex lens or a converging lens. When the lens is thicker at the edges than in the middle, it is called as concave lens or diverging lens.

➢ Some terms regarding a lens.

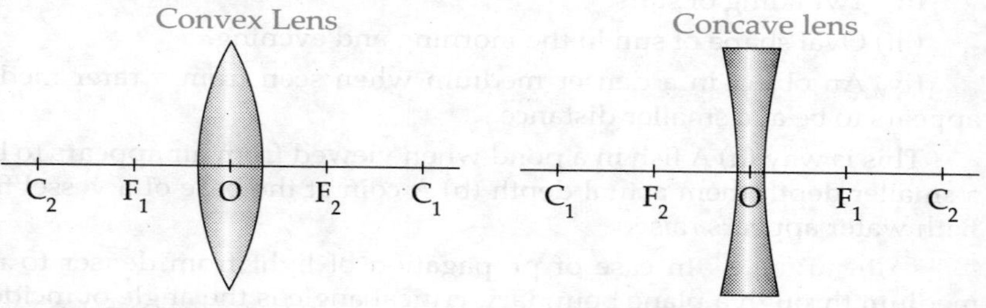

O – optical Centre

C_1C_2 – Principal axis

F_1 – First Focus

F_2 – Second Focus

Power of a lens

Power of a lens is its capacity to deviate a ray. It is measured as the reciprocal of the focal length in meters, i.e. $P = \frac{1}{f}$

SI Unit of power is dioptre (D).

➢ Power of a convex lens is positive and that of a concave lens is negative.

➢ If two lenses are placed in contact, then the power of combination is equal to the sum of powers of individual lenses.

Change in the power of a lens : If a lens is dipped in a liquid, its focal length and power both change. This change depends upon the refractive indices of lens and the liquid. If a lens of refractive index μ is dipped in a liquid of refractive index μ', then the following three situations are possible

(i) $\mu > \mu'$ i.e. lens is dipped in a liquid of smaller fractive index like a lens of glass ($\mu = 1.5$) is dipped in water ($\mu' = 1.33$), then the focal length of the lens increases and the power of the lens decreases.

(ii) $\mu = \mu'$ i.e. lens is dipped in a liquid of equal refractive index then the focal length of the lens becomes infinite i.e. its power becomes zero. The lens and the liquid behave as a single medium.

(iii) $\mu < \mu'$ i.e. lens is dipped in a liquid of higher refractive index the focal length increases i.e. power decreases as well as the nature of the lens also changes i.e. convex lens behaves as concave lens and vice-versa. For example, an air bubble trapped in water or glass appears as convex but behaves as concave lens. Similarly a convex lens of glass ($\mu = 1.5$) when dipped in carbon disulphide ($\mu' = 1.68$), it behaves as a concave lens.

Formation of images by lenses

Position of object	Position of image	Size of image	Nature of image
Convex Lens			
At infinity	At Focus	Highly diminished	Real, inverted
Beyond 2 *F*	Between *F* and 2*F*	Diminished	Real, inverted
At 2*F*	At 2*F*	Of same size	Real, inverted
Between *F* and 2*F*	Beyond 2*F*	Enlarged	Real, inverted
At *F*	At infinity	Highly enlarged	Real, inverted
Between optical centre and *F*	The same side as in the object	Enlarged	Virtual and erect
Concave Lens			
At infinity	At focus	Highly diminished	Virtual and erect
Between lens and infinity	Between lens and *F* on the same side	diminished	Virtual and erect

Dispersion of Light : When a ray of white light (or a composite light) is passed through a prism, it gets splitted into its constituent colours. This phenomenon is called dispersion of light. The coloured pattern obtained on a screen after dispersion of light is called spectrum.

- The dispersion of light is due to different deviation suffered by different colours of light. The deviation is maximum for violet colour and minimum for red colour of light. The different colours appeared in the spectrum are on the following order, violet, indigo, blue, green, yellow, orange and red. (VIBGYOR)
- The dispersion of light is due to different velocities of light of different colorus in a medium. As a result, the refractive index of a medium is different for different colours of light.

➢ The velocity of light in a medium is maximum for that colour for which refractive index is minimum. Clearly, the velocity of violet colour of light is minimum in a medium and retroactive index of that medium is maximum for violet colour. Similarly, the velocity of light in a medium is maximum for red colour and refractive index of that medium is minimum for red colour.

Rainbow : Rainbow is the coloured display in the form of an arc of a circle hanging in the sky observed during or after a little drizzle appearing on the opposite side of sun. Rainbow is formed due to dispersion of sun light by the suspended water droplets.

Rainbow is of two types : (i) Primary rainbow (ii) Secondary rainbow

➢ Primary rainbow is formed due to two refractions and one total internal reflection of light falling on the raindrops. In the primary rainbow, the red colour is on the convex side and violet on the concave side. Primary rainbow has an angular width of 2° at an average angle of elevation of 41°.

➢ Secondary rainbow is formed due to two refractions and two internal reflections of light falling on rain drops. The order of colour on the secondary rainbow is in the reverse order and has an angular width of 3.5° at an average elevation of 52.75°. Secondary rainbow is less intense than primary rainbow.

Theory of Colours : Colour is the sensation perceived by the rods in the eye due to light.

Primary Colours : The spectral colours blue, green and red are called primary colours because all the colours can be produced by mixing these in proper proportion.

Blue + Red + Green = White

Secondary Colours : The colour produced by mixing any two primary colours is called a secondary colour. There are three secondary colours yellow, magenta and cyan as

Green + Red = Yellow   Red + Blue = Magenta   Blue + Green = Cyan

When the three secondary colours are mixed, white colour is produced

Yellow + Magenta + Cyan = White

Complementary Colours : Any two colours when added produce white light, are said to be complementary colours. Clearly a secondary colour and the remaining primary colour are complementary colours. Red and cyan, blue and yellow and green and magenta are complementary of each other.

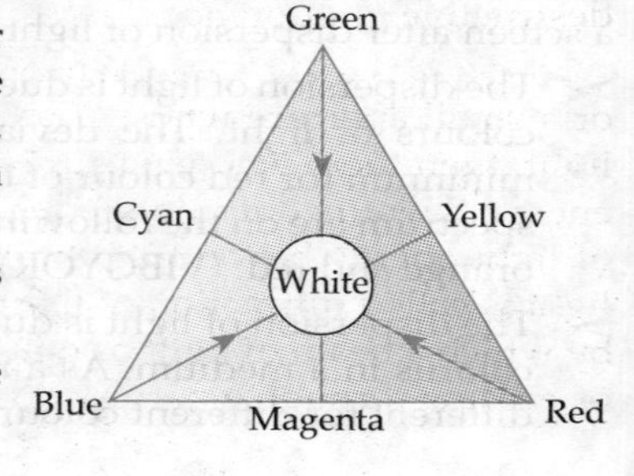

➢ The different colours and their mixtures are shown by the colour triangle.

➢ In coloured television, the three primary colours are used.

Colour of bodies : The colour of a body is the colour of light which it reflects or transmits. An object is white, if it reflects all the components of white light and it is black if it absorbs all the light incident over it. This is why a red rose appears red when viewed in white or red light but appears black when viewed in blue or green light.

➢ How a body will appear in light of different colour can be understood by the following table

Name of object	In white light	In red light	In green light	In yellow light	In blue light
White paper	White	Red	Green	Yellow	Blue
Red paper	Red	Red	Black	Black	Black
Green paper	Green	Black	Green	Black	Black
Yellow paper	Yellow	Black	Black	Yellow	Black
Blue paper	Blue	Black	Black	Black	Blue

Scattering of light : When light waves fall on small bodies such as dust particles, water particles in suspension, suspended particles in colloidal solution, they are thrown out in all directions. This phenomenon is called scattering of light.

Scattering of light is maximum in case of violet colour and minimum in case of red colour of light.

➢ Blue colour of sky is due to scattering of light.

➢ The brilliant red colour of rising and setting sun is due to scattering of light.

Interference of light : When two light waves of exactly the same frequency and a constant phase difference travel in same direction and superimpose then the resultant intensity in the region of superposition is different from the sum of intensity of individual waves. This modification in the intensity of light in the region of superposition is called interference of light. Interference is of two types

(i) Constructive interference (ii) Destructive interference

Constructive interference : At some points, where the two waves meet is same phase, resultant intensity is maximum. Such interference is called constructive interference.

Destructive interference : At some points, where the two waves meet in opposite phase, resultant intensity is minimum. Such interference is called destructive interference.

Diffraction of light : When light waves fall on a small sized obstacle or a small aperture whose dimension is comparable to the wavelength of light, then there is a departure from the rectilinear propagation and light energy flavours out into the region of geometrical shadow. The spreading of light energy beyond the limit prescribed by rectilinear propagation of light is called diffraction of light. In other words, diffraction is the process by which a beam of light or other systems of wave is spread out as a result of passing through a narrow opening or across an edge.

Polarisation of light : Polarisation is the only phenomenon which proves that light is a transverse wave. Light is an electromagnetic wave in which electric and magnetic field vectors vibrate perpendicular to each other and also perpendicular to the direction of propagation. In ordinary light, the vibrations of elecltric field vector are in every plane perpendicular to the direction of propagation of wave. Polarisation is the phenomenon of restricting the vibrations of a light in a particular direction in a plane perpendicular to the direction of propagation of wave.

➢ The visible effect of light is only due to electric field vector.

Human Eye

➢ Least distance of distinct vision is 25 cm.

Defects of human eye and the remedies :

1. Myopia or short sightedness : A person suffering from myopia can see the near objects clearly while far objects are not clear.

   Causes : (i) Elongation of eye ball along the axis.
   (ii) Shortening of focal length of eye lens.
   (iii) Over stretching of ciliary muscles beyond the elastic limit.

   Remedy : Diverging lens is used.

2. Hyperopia or hypermetropia or longsightedness : A person suffering from hypermetropia can see the distant objects clearly but not the near objects.

   Causes : (i) Shortening of eye ball along the axis.
   (ii) Increase in the focal length of eye lens.
   (iii) Stiffening of ciliary muscles.

   Remedy : A converging lens is sued.

3. Presbyopia : This defect is generally found in elderly person. Due to stiffening of ciliary muscles, eye looses much of its accommodating power. As a result distanct as well as nearby objects can not be seen.

   For its remedy two separate lens or a bifocal lens is used.

4. Astigmatism : This defect arises due to difference in the radius of curvature of cornea in the different planes. As a result rays from an object in one plane are brought to focus by eye in another plane. For its remedy cylindrical lens is used.

➢ There are two kinds of vision cells in the retina. They are called rods and cones on account of their peculiar shape. Rods decides the intensity of light where as cones distinguish colour of light.

Simple microscope : This is simply a convex lens of small focal length. The object to be enlarged is placed within the focus of lens.

Magnifying power of a simple microscope is given as

$$M = 1 + \frac{D}{f} \quad \text{where } D = 25 \text{ cm}, \ f = \text{focal length of lens.}$$

Compound microscope : It consists of two convex lenses coaxially fitted in a hollow tube. The lens facing the object is called objective and the lens towards the eye is called eye piece.

- The aperture of objective is smaller than that of eye piece.
- Both the lenses are of smaller focal lengths. This increases the magnifying power of instrument.

Telescope

Telescopes are used to view distant objects which are not visible to naked eye. Telescope can be divided as astronomical telescope, terrestrial telescope and Galilean telescope.

- Astronomical telescope consists of two convex lenses placed coaxially in a hollow tube. The lens facing the object is called objective and the lens towards the eye is called eye piece.
- The objective has large aperture so that the rays from the object can be easily collected.
- The focal length of objective is larger than that of eye piece.

15. Static Electricity

When two bodies are rubbed together, they acquire the property of attracting light objects like small bits of paper, dust particles etc. The bodies which acquire this property are said to be electrified or charged with electricity.

Charge : Charge is the basic property associated with matter due to which it produces and experiences eletrical and magnetic effects.

- Benjamin Frnkline named the two types of charges as positive and negative.
- Similar charges repel each other and opposite charges attract each other.
- Charging of bodies takes place due to transfer of electrons from one body to other body.
- A list of materials has been given below. The list is such that any of the material in the list will be positively charged when rubbed with any other material coming later in the list. The other material will naturally be negtively charged.

1.	Fur	2.	Flannel	3.	Shellac	4.	Sealing Wax
5.	Glass	6.	Paper	7.	Silk	8.	Human body
9.	Wood	10.	Metals	11.	India Rubber	12.	Resin
13.	Amber	14.	Sulphur	15.	Ebonite	16.	Gutta Percha

Surface density of charge : Surface density of charge is defined as the amount of charge per unit area on the surface of conductor.

- The surface density of charge at a point on the surface of conductor depends upon the shape of conductor and presence of other conductors or insulators near the given conductor.
- The surface density of charge at any part of the conductor is inversely proportional to the radius of curvature of the surface of that part.

  This is why surface density of charge in maximum at the pointed parts of the condcutor.

Conductor : Conductors are those materials which allow electricity (charge) to pass through themselves.

Examples : (a) Metals like silver, iron, copper (b) Earth (especially the moist part) acts like a huge conductor.

➢ Silver is the best conductor.

Insulator or Dielectric : Insulators are those materials which do not allow electricity to flow through themselves.

Examples : Wood, paper, mica, glass, ebonite.

Coulomb's law : According to Coulomb's law, the force of attraction or repulsion between two point charges at rest is directly proportional to the product of the magnitudes of the charges and inversely proportional to the square of the distance between them. This force acts on the line joining the two charges.

Electric Field : Region in space around a charge or charged body where the charge has its electrical effect is called electric field of the charge.

Electric Field Intensity : Electric field intensity at a point in an electric field is the force experienced by a unit positive charge placed at that point.

Electric Field of hollow conductor

Electric field intensity inside a charged hollow conductor is zero. Charge given to such a conductor (or conductor of any shape) remains on its surface only.

This explains why a hollow conductor acts as an electrostatic shield. It is for this reason that it is safer to sit in a car or bus during lightning.

Electric Potential : Electric potential at a point in an electric field is the work done in bringing a unit positive charge from infinity to that point.

SI unit of electric potential is volt. It is a scalar quantity.

Potential Difference : Work done in bringing a unit positive charge from one point to other point is the potential difference between the two points. Its SI unit is volt and is a scalar quantity.

Electric Capacity : Electric capacity of a conductor is defined as the charge required to increase the potential of the condcutor by unity. If potential of a conductor is increased by V when a charge Q is given to it, capacity of the conductor is $\frac{Q}{V}$. Its SI unit is farad. (F)

Electrochemical Cell : Electrochemical cell is a device which converts chemical energy into electrical energy.

Cells are basically of two types : (i) Primary cell (ii) Secodnary cell.

Primary Cell : In primary cell electrical energy is obtained from the irreversible chemical reaction taking inside the cell. After complete discharge, primary cell becomes unserviceable.

Examples : Voltaic Cell, Leclanche Cell, Daniel Cell, Dry Cell etc.

Secodnary Cell : A secodnary cell is that which has to be charged at first from an external electric source and then can be used to draw current. Such cells are rechargable.

- Production of electricity by chemical reaction was first discovered by Allexandro de volta (voltaic cell is named after him) in 1794. In voltaic cell zinc rod is used as cathode and copper rod is used as anode. These rods are placed in sulphuric acid kept in a glass vessel.
- In a Leclanche cell, carbon rod acts as anode and zinc rod acts as cathode. These rods are placed in amonium chloride kept in a glass vessel.
- The emf of Leclanche cell is 1.5 volt.
- Leclanche cell is used for intermittent works. i.e. works in which continuous electrical energy is not required like electric bell.
- In a dry cell, mixture of MnO_2, NH_4Cl and carbon is kept in a zinc vessel. A carbon rod is placed in the mixture which acts as anode. The zinc vessel itself acts as cathode. The emf of dry cell is 1.5 volt.

16. Current Electricity

Electric Current : Electric current is defined as the rate of flow of charge or charge flowing per unit time interval. Its direction is the direction of flow of positive charge. Its SI unit is ampere (A). It is a scalar quantity.

- A current of one ampere flowing through a conductor means 6.25×10^{18} electrons are entering at one end or leaving the other end of the conductor in one second.

Resistance : The opposition offered by a conductor to the flow of current through it is called resistance. It arises due to collisions of drifting electrons with the core ions. Its SI unit is ohm.

Ohm's law : If physical conditions like temperature, intensity of light etc. remains unchanged then electric current flowing through a conductor is directly proportional to the potential difference across its ends. If V is the potential difference across the ends of a conductor and I is the current through it, then according to ohm's law $V \propto I$ or, $V = RI$

where R is a constant called resistance of conductor.

Ohmic Resistance : The resistances of such condcutors which obey ohm's law are called ohmic resistance. For example resistance of manganin wire.

Non ohmic resistance : The resistances of such materials which do not obey ohm's law are called non ohmic resistance.

Example : Resistance of diode valve, resistance of triode valve.

Conductance : Reciprocal of resistance of a conductor is called its conductance i.e. conductuctance $= \dfrac{1}{\text{Resistance}}$

It is denoted by G and $\left(G = \dfrac{1}{R}\right)$

Its SI unit is ohm^{-1} (also called mho or siemen.)

- The resistance of a conductor is directly proportional to its length and inversely proportional to its cross sectional area. i.e. if l and A are respectively length and cross sectional area of a conductor and R is its resistance then $R \propto \dfrac{l}{A}$ or, $R = \rho \dfrac{l}{A}$

where ρ is a constant of material of conductor called specific resistance or resistivity. Its SI unit is ohm meter.

Specific conductance or conductivity : The reciprocal of resistivity of a conductor is called its conductivity (s). Its SI unit is mho m^{-1} or siemen/meter (sm^{-1})

Combination of Resistance : Various resistances can be combined to form a network mainly in two ways : (i) Series combination (ii) Parallel combination.

➢ In series combination, the equivalent resistance is equal to the sum of the resistances of individual conductors. ($R = R_1 + R_2 + ... R_n$)

➢ In parallel combination, the reciprocal of equivalent resistance is equal to the sum of the reciprocal of individual resistances.

$$\left(\frac{1}{2} = \frac{1}{R_1} + \frac{1}{R_2} + \ldots + \frac{1}{R_n}\right)$$

Electric Power : The rate at which electrical energy is consumed in a circuit is called electric power. Its SI unit is watt.

Kilowatt hour : It is the unit of energy and is equal to the energy consumed in the circuit at the rate of 1 kilowatt (1000 J/s) for 1 hour.

1 kilowatt hour = 3.6×10^6 joule

1 kWh is also called board of trade unit.

Ammeter : Ammeter is a device which is used to measure electric current in a circuit. It is connected in series in the circuit.

➢ The resistance of an ideal ammeter is zero.

Voltmeter : Voltmeter is a device used to measure the potential difference between two points in a circuit. It is connected in parallel to the circuit.

➢ The resistance of an ideal voltmeter is infinite.

Electric fuse : Electric fuse is a protective device used in series with an electric appliance to save it from being damaged due to high current. In general, it is a small conducting wire of alloy of copper, tin and lead having low melting point.

➢ Pure fuse is made up of tin.

Galvanometer : Galvanometer is a device used to detect and measure electric current in a circuit. It can measure current up to 10^{-6} A.

Shunt : Shunt is a wire of very small resistance. In simple words, galvanometer is an instrument for detecting and measuring small electric currents.

➢ A galvanometer can be converted into an ammeter by connecting a shunt parallel to it.

➢ A galvanometer can be converted into a voltmeter by connecting a very high resistance in its series.

Transformer : Transformer is a device which converts low voltage A.C. into high voltage A.C. and high voltage A.C. into low voltage A.C. It is based on electromagnetic induction and can be used only in case of alternating current.

A.C. Dynamo (or generator) : It is device used to convert mechanical energy into electrical energy. It works on the principle of electro-magnetic induction.

Electric motor : It is a device which converts electrical energy into mechanical energy.

Microphone : It converts sound energy into electrical energy and works on the principle of electromagnetic induction. In other words, microscope is an instrument for changing sound waves into electrical energy which may then be amplified, transmitted or recorded.

- The current generated in the power stations are alternating current having voltage 22000 volt or more. In grid substations, with the help of transformer, their voltage is increased up to 132000 volt to minimise loss of energy in long distance transmission.

17. Magnetism

- Magnetism is the property displayed by magnets and produced by the movement of electric charges, which results in objects being attracted or pushed away.
- Magnet is a piece of iron or other materials that can attract iron containing objects and that points north and south when suspended.
- A magnet is characterised by following two properties :
  - (i) Attractive property : A magnet attracts magnetic substances like iron, cobalt, nickel and some of their alloys like magnetite (Fe_3O_4)
  - (ii) Directive property : When a magnet is freely suspended, it aligns itself in the geographical north south direction.
- A magnet may be (i) Natural (ii) Artificial
- Natural magnet is oxide of iron. But due to irregular shape, weak magnetism and high brittleness, natural magnets find no use in the laboratory.
- The magnets made by artificial methods are called artificial magnets or man made magnets. They may be of different types like bar magnet, horse shoe magnet, Robinson's ball ended magnet, magnetic needle, electromagnet etc.
- The two points near the two ends of a magnet where the attracting capacity is maximum are called magnetic poles. When a magnet is freely suspended, its one pole always directs towards the north. This pole is called north pole. The other pole is called south pole.
- The imaginary line joining the two poles of a magnet is called magnetic axis of the magnet.
- Similar poles repel each other and dissimilar poles attract each other.
- When a magnetic substance is placed rear a magnet, it gets magnetised due to induction.

Magnetic Field : Region in space around a magnet where the magnet has its magnetic effect is called magnetic field of the magnet.

Intensity of magnetic field or magnetic flux density : Magnetic flux density of a point in a magnetic field is the force experienced by a north pole of unit strength placed at that point. Its SI unit is newton/ampere-meter or weber/meter^2 or tesla (T).

Magnetic lines of force : The magnetic lines of force are imaginary curves which represent a magnetic field graphically. The tangent drawn at any point on the magnetic liens of force gives the direction of magnetic field at that point.

Properties of magnetic liens of force :

(i) Magnetic lines of force are closed curves. Outside the magnet they are from north to south pole and inside the magnet they are from south to north pole.

(ii) Two lines of force near intersect each other.

(iii) If the lines of force are crowded, the field is strong.

(iv) If the liens of force are parallel and equidistant, the field is uniform.

Magnetic Substance : On the basis of magnetic behaviour, substances can be divided into three categories.

(i) Diamagnetic substance: Diamagnetic substances are such substances which when placed in a magnetic field, acquire feeble magnetism opposite to the direction of magnetic field.

Examples : Bismuth, Zinc, Copper, Silver, Gold, Diamond, Water, Mercury, Water etc.

(ii) Paramagnetic Substance : Paramagnetic substances are such substances which when placed in a magnetic field acquire a feeble magnetism in the direction of the field.

Examples : Aluminum, Platinum, Manganese, Sodium, Oxygen etc.

(iii) Ferromagnetic substance : Ferromagnetic substances are those substance, which when placed in a magnetic field, are strongly magnetised in the direction of field.

Examples : Iron, Cobalt, Nickel etc.

Domain : Atoms of ferromagnetic substance have a permanent dipole moment i.e. they behave like a very small magnet. The atoms form a large no. of effective regions called domain in which 10^{18} to 10^{21} atoms have their dipole moment aligned in the same direction. The magnetism in ferromagnetic substance, when placed in a magnetic field, is developed due to these domain by (i) the displacements of boundaries of the domains (ii) the rotation of the domains.

Curie Temperature : As temperature increases, the magnetic property of ferromagnetic substance decreases and above a certain temperature the substance changes into paramagnetic substance. This temperature is called Curie temperature.

➢ Permanent magnets are made of steel, cobalt steel, ticonal, alcomax and alnico.

➢ Electromagnets, cores of transformers, telephone diaphragms, armatures of dynamos and motors are made of soft iron, mu-metal and stalloy.

Terrestrial Magnetism : Our earth behaves as a powerful magnet whose south pole is near the geographical north pole and whose north pole is near the geographical south pole. The magnetic field of earth of a place is described in the terms of following three elements.

(i) Declination : The acute angle between magnetic meridian and geographical meridian at a place is called the angle of declination at that place.

(ii) Dip or Inclination : Dip is the angle which the resultant earth's magnetic field at a place makes with the horizontal. At poles and equator, dip is 90° and 0° respectively.

(iii) Horizontal component of earth's magnetic field : At a place it is defined as the component of earth's magnetic field along the horizontal in the magnetic meridian.

Its valve is different at different places. (approximately 0.4 gauss or 0.4×10^{-4} tesla).

18. Atomic & Nuclear Physics

Atomic Physics

➢ Atom is the smallest part of matter which takes part in chemical reactions. Atoms of the same element are similar in mass, size and characteristics. Atom consists of three fundamental particles electron, proton and neutron. All the protons and neutrons are present in the central core of atom called nucleus. Electrons revolve around the nucleus.

➢ In an atom, electrons and protons are equal in number and have equal and opposite charge. Hence atom is neutral.

Properties of Fundamental Particles

Particle	Mass (Kg)	Charge (Coulomb)	Discoverer
Proton	1.672×10^{-27}	-1.6×10^{-19}	Rutherford
Neutron	1.675×10^{-27}	0	Chadwick
Electron	9.108×10^{-31}	-1.6×10^{-19}	J.J. Thomson

Note : *Proton was discovered by Golastin and named by Rutherford.*

➢ Till today, several subatomic particles have been discovered. Some important of them are as follows.

Particle	Mass (Kg)	Charge	Discoverer	
Positron	9.108×10^{-31}	$+1.6 \times 10^{-19}$	Anderson	Antiparticle of electron
Neutrino	0	0	Pauli	
Pi-meson	274 times the mass of electron	Positive and negative both	Yakawa	unstable
Photon	0	0		Velocity equal to that of light

Cathode Rays : If the gas pressure in a discharge tube is 10^{-2} to 10^{-3} mm of Hg and a potential difference of 10^4 volt is applied between the electrode, then a beam of electrons emerges from the cathode which is called cathode rays. Hence cathode rays are beam of high energy electrons. Cathode is an electrode with a negative charge.

Properties of cathode rays :

(i) Cathode rays are invisible and travel in straight line.
(ii) These rays carry negative charge and travel from cathode to anode.
(iii) These rays emerge perpendicular to the cathode surface and are not affected by the position of anode.
(iv) Cathode rays travel with very high velocity (1/10th the velocity of light).
(v) These rays are deflected by electric and magnetic fields.
(vi) These rays can ionise gases.
(vii) These rays heat the material on which they fall.
(viii) They can produce chemical change and thus affect a photographic plate.
(ix) These rays can penetrate through thin metal foils.
(x) The source of emf used in the production of cathode rays is induction coil.
(xi) When they strike a target of heavy metals such as tungsten, they produce x-rays.
(xii) The nature of cathode rays is independent of nature of cathode and the gas in the discharge tube.

Positive or Canal rays :

If perforated cathode is used in a discharge tube, it is observed that a new type of rays are produced from anode moving towards the cathode and passed through the holes of cathode. These rays are positively charged and are called positive rays or canal rays or anode rays. These rays were discovered by Goldstein.

Properties of Canal rays :

(i) The positive rays consists of positively charged particles.
(ii) These rays travel in straight line.
(iii) These rays can exert pressure and thus possess kinetic energy.
(iv) These rays are deflected by electric and magnetic fields.
(v) These rays are capable of producing physical and chemical changes.
(vi) These rays can produce ionisation in gases.

Radioactivity

- Radioactivity is the sending out of harmful radiation or particles, caused when atomic nuclei breakup spontaneously.
- Radioactivity was discovered by Henry Becquerel, Madame Curie and Pierre Curie for which they jointly win Noble prize.
- The nucleus having protons 83 or more are unstable. They emit α, β and γ particles and become stable. The elements of such nucleus are called radioactive elements and the phenomenon of emission of α, β and γ particles is called radioactivity.
- γ rays are emitted after the emission of α and β rays.

➢ Robert Pierre and his wife Madame Curie discovered a new radioactive element radium.
➢ The rays emitted by radioactivity were first recognised by Rutherford.
➢ The end product of all natural radioactive element after emission of radioactive rays is lead.

Difference between stable and unstable nucleus

S. No.	Stable nucleus	Unstable nucleus
1.	Low atomic number	High atomic number.
2.	Low mass number	High mass number
3.	Nucleus of small size	Nucleus of bigger size
4.	$\frac{n}{p}=1$	$\frac{n}{p}>1$

Properties of α, β and γ particles

Properties	α	β	γ
Origin	Nucleus	Nucleus	Nucleus
Nature	Positively charged	Negatively charged	Neutral
Composition	He^4	$_1e^0$	Photon
Mass	6.4×10^{-31} kg	9.1×10^{-31} kg	zero
Charge	$+2e$	$-e$	zero
Chemical effect	Affects photo graphic plate	Affects photographic plate	Affects photo graphic plate
Effect of electric and magnetic field	Deflected	Deflected	No effect
Penetrating power	Minimum	In between the other two	Maximum
Ionising power	Maximum	In between the other two	Minimum
Velocity	Between 1.4×10^7 m/s to 2.2×10^7 m/s	1% to 99% of velocity of light	3×10^8 m/s

➢ With the emission an α-particle, atomic number is decreased by 2 and mass member is decreased by 4.
➢ With the emission of a β-particle atomic number is increased by one and mass number does not change.
➢ The effect on the mass number and atomic number with the emission of α, β and γ rays is decided by Group-displacement law or Soddy-Fajan Law.
➢ Radioactivity is detected by G.M. Counter.
➢ The time in which half nuclei of the element is decayed is called half life of the radioactive substance.
➢ Cloud chamber: Cloud chamber is used to detect the presence and kinetic energy of radioactive particles. It was discovered by C.R.T. Wilson.
➢ Radioactive carbon-14 is used to measure the age of fossils and plants. (Carbon dating) In this method age is decided by measuring the ratio of $_6C^{12}$ and $_6C^{14}$.

Nuclear Fission and Fusion

Nuclear Fission : The nuclear reaction in which a heavy nucleus splits into two nuclei of nearly equal mass is nuclear fission. The energy released in the nuclear fission is called nuclear energy.

➢ Nuclear fission was first demonstrated by Strassmann and O. Hahn. They found that when U^{235} nucleus is excited by the capture of a neutron, it splits into two nuclei Ba^{142} & K^{92}.

Chain Reaction : When uranium atom is bombarded with slow neutrons, fission takes place. With the fission of each uranium nucleus, on the average 3 neutrons and large energy is released. These neutrons cause further fission. Clearly a chain of fission of uranium nucleus starts which continues till whole of uranium is exhausted. This is called chain reaction.

Chain reaction is of the following two types (i) Uncontrolled chain reaction (ii) Controlled chain reaction.

Uncontrolled Chain Reaction : In each fission reaction, three more neutrons are produced. These three neutrons may cause the fission of three other U^{235} nuclei producing 9 neutrons and so on. As a result the number of neutron goes on increasing till the whole of fissionable material is consumed. This chain reaction is called uncontrolled or explosive chain reaction. This reaction proceeds very quickly and a huge amount of energy is liberated in a short time.

Atom bomb : Atom bomb is based on nuclear fission. U^{235} and Pu^{239} are used as fissionable material. This bomb was first used by USA against Japan in second world war (6th August, 1945 at Hiroshima & 9th August, 1945 at Nagashaki).

Controlled Chain Reaction : A fission chain reaction which proceeds slowly without any explosion and in which the energy released can be controlled is known as controlled reaction. Actually in this situation only one of the neutrons produced in each fission is able to cause further fission. The rate of reaction remains constant.

Nuclear Reactor or Atomic Pile : Nuclear reactor is an arrangement in which controlled nuclear fission reaction takes place.

➢ First nuclear reactor was established in Chicago University under the supervision of Prof. Fermi.

➢ There are several components of nuclear reactor which are as follows :

(i) Fissionable Fuel : U^{235} or U^{239} is used.

(ii) Moderator : Moderator decreases the energy of neutrons so that they can be further used for fission reaction. Heavy water and graphite are used as moderator.

(iii) Control rod : Rods of cadmium or boron are used to absorb the excess neutrons produced in fission of uranium nucleus so that the chain reaction continues to be controlled.

(iv) Coolant : A large amount of heat is produced during fission. Coolant absorbs that heat and prevents excessive rise in the temperature. The coolant may be water, heavy water, or a gas like He or CO_2.

Uses of nuclear reactor

(i) To produce electrical energy from the energy released during fission.

(ii) To produce different isotopes which can be used in medical, physical and agriculture science.

Fast Breeder Reactor : A nuclear reactor which can produce more missile fuel than it consumes is called a fast breeder reactor.

Nuclear Fusion : When two or more light nuclei combined together to form a heavier nucleus, tremendous energy is released. This phenomenon is called nuclear fusion. A typical example of nuclear fission is ${}_1H^2 + {}_1H^3 \rightarrow {}_2He^4 + {}_0n^1 + 17.6$ Mev.

➢ The energy released by sun and other stars is by nuclear fusion.

➢ For the nuclear fusion, a temperature of the order of 10^8 K is required.

Hydrogen bomb : Hydrogen bomb was made by American scientists in 1952. This is based on nuclear fusion. It is 1000 times more powerful than atom bomb.

Mass Energy Relation : In 1905 Einstein established a relation between mass and energy on the basis of special theory of relativity. According to this relation, mass can be converted into energy and vice versa, according to the relation $E = mc^2$ where c is the velocity of light and E is the energy equivalent of mass m.

➢ Albert Einstein was an American scientist. He was born in Germany. He was given Nobel Prize of Physics in 1921.

➢ Sun is continuously emitting energy. Earth is continuously receiving 4×10^{26} joule of energy per second from sun. As a result mass of sun is decreasing at the rate of approximately 4×10^9 kg per second. But mass of sun is so large that it is estimated that the sun will continuously supply energy for next 10^9 years.

19. Electronics

Electronics : Electronics is the branch of physics and technology concerned with the behaviour and movement of electrons.

Diode Valve : Designed by J. A. Fleming in 1904, diode valve consists of two electrodes placed inside an evacuated glass envelope. One electrode is called cathode which is made up of tungsten on which there is a thin layer of barium oxide. When heated, cathode emits electrons. These electron flow towards the other electrode called anode or plate, which is at positive potential. As a result an electric current is established in the circuit.

➢ The electrons emitted from the cathode are collected in the evaluated space around it. This collection of electrons is called space charge which is obviously negative.

➢ Diode valve acts a rectifier. Rectifier is a device which converts alternating voltage (current) into direct voltage (current).

Triode Valve : Designed by Lee de Forest in 1907, triode valve is a modified form of usual diode. It consists of a usual anode - cathode pair and one more electrode called control grid.

➢ Triode valve can be used as amplifier, oscillator, transmitter and detector.

Semi-conductor : Semi conductor are those materials whose electrical conductivity, at room temperature, lies in between that of insulator and conductor. Germenium and Silicon are two important semiconductor. In a crystal lattice of semi-conductor, some of the electrons become free from bond formation. At the sites of these electrons a deficiency of electron exists which acts as a virtual positive charge. These virtual positive charges are called holes. Semi-conductors are used in electronics industry.

Semi-conductors are of two types :

(i) Intrinsic Semi -Conductor : A semi conductor in an extremely pure form is known as intrinsic semi conductor.

(ii) Extrinsic Semi-Conductor : If a measured and small amount of chemical impurity is added to intrinsic semi-conductor, it is called extrinsic semi-conductor or doped semi conductor. As a result of doping, there is large increase in its conductivity.

➢ Extrinsic semi conductor are of two types :

(a) N type semi conductor : An extrionic semi conductor in which electrons are majority charge carrier is called N type semi conductor. Such a semi conductor is made by doping a pure semi conductor with pentavalent impurity like Arsenic, Antimony & Phosphorus.

(b) P type semi conductor : An extrinsic semi conductor in which holes are the majority charge carrier is called a P type semi conductor. Such a semi conductor is made by doping a pure semi conductor with trivalent impurity like Gallium, Indium, Boron and Aluminium.

Doping : Adding of chemical impurity to a pure semi conductor is called doping. The amount and type of impurity is closely controlled.

Donor : Pentavalent impurities are called donor.

Acceptor : Trivalent impurities are called acceptor.

➢ The electrical conductivity of a semi conductor increases with the increase in temperature.

20. Scientific Instruments

Instrument	Use
Altimeter	Measures altitudes (used in aircraft)
Ammeter	Measures strength of electric current
Anemometer	Measures force and velocity of wind and directions
Audiometer	Measures intensity of sound
Barograph	Continuous recording of atmospheric pressure
Barometer	Measures atmospheric pressure
Binoculars	To view distant objects
Bolometer	To measure heat radiation
Callipers	Measure inner and outer diameters of bodies
Calorimeter	Measures quantities of heat

Instrument	Use
Cardiogram (ECG)	Traces movements of the heart; recorded on a Cardiograph
Cathetometer	Determines heights, measurement of levels, etc., in scientific experiments
Chronometer	Determines longitude of a vessel at sea.
Colorimeter	Compares intensity of colours
Commutator	To change / reverse the direction of electric current; Also used to convert AC into DC
Cryometer	A type of thermometer used to measure very low temperatures, usually close to 0°C
Cyclotron	A charged particle accelerator which can accelerate charged particles to high energies
Dilatometer	Measures changes in volume of substances
Dyanamo	To convert mechanical energy into electrical energy
Dynamometer	Measures electrical power
Electronecephalo graph (EEC)	Records and interprets the electrical waves of the brain (brain waves) recorded on electroence-phalograms
Electrometer	Measures very small but potential difference in electric currents
Electroscope	Detects presence of an electric charge
Electromicroscope	To obtain a magnifying view of very small objects Capable of magnifying up to 20,000 times
Endoscope	To examine internal parts of the body
Fathometer	Measures depth of the ocean
Fluxmeter	Measures magnetic flux
Galvanometer	Measures electric current
Hydrometer	Measures the relative density of liquids
Hygrometer	Measures level of humidity
Hydrophone	Measures sound under water
Hygroscope	Shows the changes in atmospheric humidity
Hypsometer	To determine boiling point of liquids
Kymograph	Graphically records physiological movement. (e.g., blood pressure / heartbeat)
Lactometer	Measures the relative density of milk to determine purity
Machmeter	Determines the speed of an aircraft in terms of the speed of sound
Magnetometer	Compares magnetic movements and fields
Manometer	Measures the pressure of gases
Micrometer	Converts sound waves into electrical vibrations
Microphone	Measures distances / angles

Instrument	Use
Microscope	To obtain a magnified view of small objects
Nephetometer	Measures the scattering of light by particles suspended in a liquid
Ohmmeter	To measure electrical resistance in ohms
Ondometer	Measures the frequency of electromagnetic waves, especially in the radio-frequency band
Periscope	To view objects above sea level (used in submarines)
Photometer	Compares the luminous intensity of the source of light
Polygraph	Instrument that simultaneously records changes in physiological processes such as heartbeat, blood-pressure and respiration; used as a lie detector
Pyknometer	Determines the density and coefficient of expansion of liquids
Pyrheliometer	Measures components of solar radiation
Pyrometer	Measures very high temperature
Quadrant	Measures altitudes and angles in navigation and astronomy
Radar	To detect the direction and range of an approaching aeroplane by means of radiowaves, (Radio, Angle, Detection and Range)
Radio micrometer	Measures heat radiation
Refractometer	Measures refractive indices
Salinometer	Determines salinity of solutions
Sextant	Used by navigators to find the latitude of a place by measuring the elevation above the horizon of the sun or another star; also used to measure the height of very distant objects
Spectroscope	To observe or record spectra
Spectrometer	Spectroscope equipped with calibrated scale to measure the position of spectral lines (Measurement of refractive indices)
Spherometer	Measures curvature of spherical objects
Sphygmometer	Measures blood pressure
Stereoscope	To view two-dimensional pictures
Stethoscope	Used by doctors to hear and analyze heart and lung sounds
Stroboscope	To view rapidly moving objects
Tachometer	To determine speed, especially the rotational speed of a shaft (used in aeroplanes and motor-boats)
Tacheometer	A theodolite adapted to measure distances, elevations and bearings during survey
Tangent Galvanometer	Measures the strength of direct current

Instrument	Use
Telemeter	Records physical happenings at a distant place.
Teleprinter	Receives and sends typed messages from one place to another
Telescope	To view distant objects in space
Thermometer	Measures Temperature
Thermostat	Regulates temperature at a particular point
Tonometer	To measure the pitch of a sound
Transponder	To receive a signal and transmit a reply immediately
Udometer	Rain gauge
Ultrasonoscope	To measure and use ultrasonic sound (beyond hearing); use to make a Ecogram to detect brain tumours, heart defects and abnormal growth
Venturimeter	To measure the rate of flow of liquids
Vernier	Measures small sub-division of scale
Viscometer	Measures the viscosity of liquid
Voltmeter	To measure electric potential difference between two points
Wattmeter	To measure the power of an electric circuit
Wavemeter	To measure the wavelength of a radiowave

21. Inventions

Invention	Inventor	Country	Year
Adding machine	Pascal	France	1642
Aeroplane	Wright brothers	USA	1903
Balloon	Jacques and Joseph Montgolfier	France	1783
Ball-point pen	C. Biro	Hungary	1938
Barometer	E. Torricelli	Italy	1644
Bicycle	K. Macmillan	Scotland	1839
Bicycle Tyre	J.B. Dunlop	Scotland	1888
Calculating machine	Pascal	France	1642
Centrigrade scale	A. Celsius	France	1742
Cinematograph	Thomas Alva Edison	USA	1891
Computer	Charles Babbage	Britain	1834
Cine camera	Friese-Greene	Britain	1889
Cinema	A.L. and J.L. Lumiere	France	1895
Clock (machanical)	Hsing and Ling-Tsan	China	1725
Clock (pendulum)	C. Hugyens	Netherlands	1657
Diesel engine	Rudolf Diesel	Germany	1892
Dynamite	Alfred Nobel	Sweden	1867
Dynamo	Michael Faraday	England	1831

Invention	Inventor	Country	Year
Electric iron	H.W. Seeley	USA	1882
Electric lamp	Thomas Alva Edison	USA	1879
Electromagnet	W. Sturgeon	England	1824
Evolution (theory)	Charles Darwin	England	1858
Film (with sound)	Dr Lee de Forest	USA	1923
Fountain Pen	LE. Waterman	USA	1884
Gas lighting	William Murdoch	Scotland	1794
Gramophone	T.A. Edison	USA	1878
Jet Engine	Sir Frank Whittle	England	1937
Lift	E.G. Otis	USA	1852
Locomotive	Richard Trevithick	England	1804
Machine gun	Richard Gatling	USA	1861
Match (safety)	J.E. Lurdstrom	Sweden	1855
Microphone	David Hughes	USA	1878
Microscope	Z. Jansen	Netherlands	1590
Motor car (petrol)	Karl Benz	Germany	1885
Motorcycle	Edward Butler	England	1884
Neon-lamp	G. Claude	France	1915
Nylon	Dr W.H. Carothers	USA	1937
Photography (paper)	W.H. Fox Tablot	England	1835
Printing press	J. Gutenberg	Germany	1455
Radar	Dr A.H. Taylor and L.C. Young	USA	1922
Radium	Marie and Pierre Curie	France	1898
Radio	G. Marconi	England	1901
Rayon	American Viscose Co.	USA	1910
Razor (safety)	K.G. Gillette	USA	1895
Razor (electric)	Col. J. Schick	USA	1931
Refrigerator	J. Harrison and A. Catlin	Britain	1834
Revolver	Samuel Colt	USA	1835
Rubber (vulcanized)	Charles Goodyear	USA	1841
Rubber (waterproof)	Charles Macintosh	Scotland	1819
Safety lamp	Sir Humphrey Davy	England	1816
Safety pin	William Hurst	USA	1849
Sewing machine	B. Thimmonnier	France	1830
Scooter	G. Bradshaw	England	1919
Ship (steam)	J.C. Perier	France	1775
Ship (turbine)	Sir Charles Parsons	Britain	1894

Invention	Inventor	Country	Year
Shorthand (modem)	Sir Issac Pitman	Britain	1837
Spinning frame	Sir Richard Arkwight	England	1769
Spinning jenny	James Hargreaves	England	1764
Steam engine (piston)	Thomas Newcome	Britain	1712
Steam engine (condenser)	James Watt	Scotland	1765
Steel production	Henry Bessemer	England	1855
Stainless Steel	Harry Brearley	England	1913
Tank	Sir Ernest Swington	England	1914
Telegraph code	Samuel F.B. Morse	USA	1837
Telephone	Alexander Graham Bell	USA	1876
Telescope	Hans Lippershey	Netherlands	1608
Television	John Logie Bared	Scotland	1926
Terylene	J. Whinfield and H. Dickson	England	1941
Thermometer	Daniel Gabriel Fahrenheit	Germany	1714
Tractor	J. Froelich	USA	1892
Transistor	Bardeen, Shockley	USA & UK	1949
Typewriter	C. Sholes	USA	1868
Valve of radio	Sir J.A. Fleming	Britain	1904
Watch	A.L. Breguet	France	1791
X-ray	Wilhelm Roentgen	Germany	1895
Zip fastener	W.L. Judson	USA	1891

22. Important Discoveries in Physics

Discovery	Scientist	Year
Laws of motion	Newton	1687
Law of electrostatic attraction	Coulomb	1779
Atom	John Dalton	1808
Photography (On metal)	J. Neepse	1826
Law of Electric resistance	G.S. Ohm	1827
Law of floatation	Archemedes	1827
Electromagnetic Induction	Michael Faraday	1831
Photography (On paper)	W.Fox Talbot	1835
Dynamite	Alfred Nobel	1867
Periodic table	Mandeleev	1888
X-Rays	Roentgen	1895
Radioactivity	Henry Becquerel	1896
Electron	J.J. Thomson	1897
Radium	Madam Curie	1898
Quantum theory	Max Plank	1900
Wireless Telegram	Marconi	1901

Discovery	Scientist	Year
Diode Bulb	Sir J. S. Fleming	1904
Photo electric effect	Albert Einstein	1905
Principle of Relativity	Albert Einstein	1905
Triode Bulb	Lee de Forest	1906
Atomic Structure	Neil Bohr & Rutherford	1913
Proton	Rutherford	1919
Raman Effect	C.V. Raman	1928
Neutron	James Chadwick	1932
Nuclear Reactor	Anrico Fermi	1942
Law of electrolytic dissociation	Faraday	—
Thermionic emission	Edison	—

23. S.I. Units of Physical Quantity

Quantity	SI	Symbol
Length	meter	m
Mass	kilogram	kg
Time	second	s
Work and Energy	joule	J
Electric current	ampere	A
Temperature	kelvin	K
Intensity of flame	candela	cd
Angle	radian	rad
Solid angle	steredian	sr
Force	newton	N
Area	square meter	m^2
Volume	Cubic meter	m^3
Speed	meter per second	ms^{-1}
Angle Velocity	radian per second	rad s^{-1}
Frequency	Hertz	Hz
Moment of inertia	kilogram Square meter	kgm^2
Momentum	kilogram meter per second	Kg ms^{-1}
impulse	newton second	Ns
Angular Momentum	kilogram square meter per second	Kgm^2s^{-1}
Pressure	pascal	Pa
Power	watt	W
Surface tension	newton per meter	Nm^{-1}
Viscosity	newton second per square m.	$N.s.m^{-2}$
Thermal Conductivity	watt per meter per degree celcius	$Wm^{-1}C^{-1}$
Specific Heat capacity	joule per kilogram per Kelvin	$Jkg^{-1} K^{-1}$

Quantity	SI	Symbol
Electric charge	coulomb	C
Potential Difference	volt	V
Electric Resistance	ohm	
Electrical Capacity	farad	F
Magnetic Induction	henry	H
Magnetic Flux	weber	Wb
Luminous Flux or photometric power	lumen	lm
Intensity of illumination	lux	lx
Wave length	Angstrom	A°
Astronomical distance	light year	ly

24. Conversion of Units from One System to Another System

1 Inch	2.54 centimeter	1 grain	64.8 miligram
1 Feet	0.3 meter	1 dram	1.77 gm
1 Yard	0.91 meter	1 ounce	28.35 gm
1 Mile	1.60 kilometer	1 pound	0.4537 kilogram
1 Fathom	1.8 meter	1 dyne	10^{-5} Newton
1 Chain	20.11 meter	1 poundal	0.1383 Newton
1 Nautical mile	1.85 kilometer	1 erg	10^{-7} Joule
1 Angstrom	10^{-10} meter	1 horse power	747 Watt
1 Square inch	6.45 sq. centimeter	1 fathom	6 feet
1 Square feet	0.09 square meter	1 mile	8 furlong
1 Square yard	0.83 square meter	1 mile	5280 feet
1 Acre	10^4 sq. meter	1 nautical mile	6080 feet
1 Square mile	2.58 sq. kilometer	1 feet	12 inch
1 Cubic inch	16.38 cubic centimeter	1 yard	3 feet
1 Cubic feet	0.028 cubic meter	37^0 centigrade	98.6^0 Fahrenheit
1 Cubic yard	0.7 quebec meter	50^0 centigrade	122 Fahrenheit
1 Litre	1000 cubic centimeter	-40^0 Fahrenheit	-40^0 Centigrade
1 Pint	0.56 litre	32^0 Fahrenheit	0^0 Centigrade

★★★

7 CHEMISTRY

1. Introduction

Chemistry is the branch of science which deals with the composition of matter and also the Physical and Chemical characteristics associated with the different material objects.

A French chemist, *Lavoisier (1743–1793)* is regarded as *father of modern chemistry*.

1. Substance and its nature : Anything that occupies space, possesses mass and can be felt by any one or more of our senses is called matter.

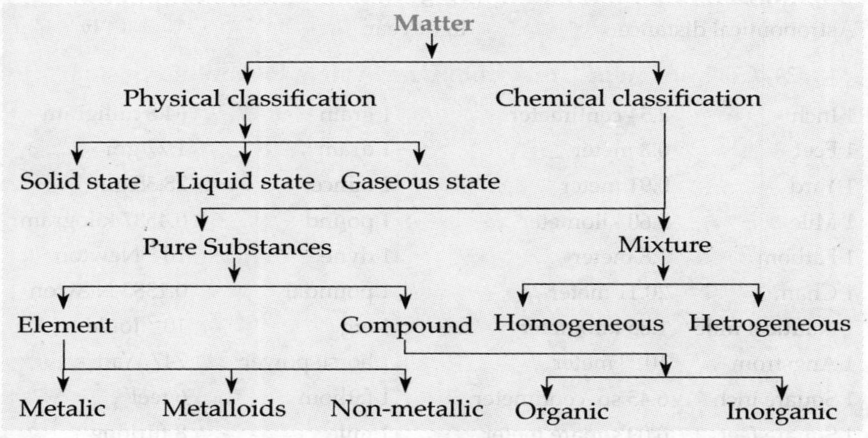

Solid State : A solid possesses definite shape and definite volume which means that it can not be compressed on applying pressure. Solids are generally hard and rigid. *Example*—metals, wood, bricks, copper etc.

Liquid State : A liquid possesses definite volume but no definite shape. This means that the liquid can take up the shape of container in which it is placed. *Example*—water, milk, oil, alcohol etc.

Gaseous State : A gas does not have either a definite volume or definite shape. It can be compressed to large extent on applying pressure and also takes the shape of the container where it is enclosed. *Examples*— Air, Oxygen, Nitrogen, Ammonia, Carbondioxide etc.

$$\text{Solid State} \underset{\text{Cool}}{\overset{\text{Heat}}{\rightleftharpoons}} \text{Liquid State} \underset{\text{Cool}}{\overset{\text{Heat}}{\rightleftharpoons}} \text{Vapour state}$$

Water exists in three different states.

$$\underset{\text{(Solid)}}{\text{Ice}} \rightleftharpoons \underset{\text{(Liquid)}}{\text{Water}} \rightleftharpoons \underset{\text{(Gas)}}{\text{Vapour}}$$

Pure substances : A single substance (or matter) which can not be separated into other kinds of matter by any physical process is called pure substance.

Pure substances have been classified as elements and compounds.

Elements : The simplest form of a pure substance which can neither be broken into nor built from simpler substances by ordinary physical and chemical methods is called element.

Elements are further classified into three types (i) Metals (ii) Non-metals and (iii) Metalloids.

Metals : Metals are solids (exception mercury which is liquid at room temperature) are normally hard. They have lustre, high *mp* and *bp* and also good conductor of electricity and heat. The conductivity of metal decreases with increase in temperature due to vibration of positive ions at their Lattice points. *Examples*—Iron, Copper, Silver, Gold, Aluminium, Zinc etc.

Non-metals : Non-metals are the elements with properties opposite to those of the metals. They are found in all states of matter. They do not possess lustre (exception–iodine). They are poor conductors of electricity (exception-graphite) and they are not malleable and ductile. *Examples*—Hydrogen, Carbon, Oxygen, Nitrogen, Sulphur, Phosphorous etc.

Metalloids : Metalloids are the elements which have common properties of both metals and non-metals. *Examples*—Arsenic, Antimony, Bismuth etc.

Compounds : Compounds are pure substances that are composed of two or more different elements in fixed proportion by mass. The properties of a compound are entirely different from those of the elements from which it is made. *Example*—Water, Sugar, Salt, chloroform, Alcohol, Ether etc.

Compounds are classified into two types

(i) Organic Compounds (ii) Inorganic Compounds,

Organic Compounds : The Compounds obtained from living sources are called organic compounds. The term organic is now applied to hydrocarbons and their derivatives. *Examples*—Carbohydrates, Proteins, Oils, Fats etc.

Inorganic Compounds : The Compounds obtained from non-living sources such as rocks and minerals are called inorganic compounds. *Examples*—Common Salt, Marble, Washing Soda etc.

Mixtures : A material obtained by mixing two or more substances in any indefinite proportion is called a mixture. The properties of the components in a mixture remain unchanged. *Example*— Milk, Sea water, Petrol, Paint, Glass, Cement, Wood etc.

There are two types of mixture—

(1) Homogeneous mixture (2) Heterogeneous mixture.

1. Homogeneous mixture : A mixture is said to be homogeneous if it has a uniform composition through out and there are no visible boundaries of separation between constituents. More over, the constituents can not be seen even by a microscope. *Examples*—Common salt dissolved in water, sugar dissolved in water, iodine dissolved in CCl_4, benzene in toluene and methyl alcohol in water.

2. Heterogeneous mixture : A mixture is said to be heterogeneous if it does not have a uniform composition throughout and has visible boundaries of separation between the various constituents. The different constituents of

the heterogeneous mixture can be seen even with naked eye. *Example*—A mixture of Sulphur & Sand, A mixture of Iron filings & Sand etc.

Separation of mixture : Some methods of separation of mixtures are given below—

1. Sublimation : In this process, a solid substance passes direct into its vapours on application of heat. The vapours when cooled, give back the original substance. This method can be used for the substances which are sublime in their separation from non-sublimate materials. *Examples* of sublimes are Naphthalene, Iodine, Ammonium Chloride etc.

2. Filtration : This is a process for quick and complete removal of suspended solid particles from a liquid, by passing the suspension through a filter paper. *Examples*—(i) removed of solid particles from the engine oil in car engine. (ii) filtration of tea from tea leaves in the preparation of tea etc.

3. Evaporation : If a solution of solid substance in a liquid is heated, the liquid gets converted into its vapours and slowly goes off completely. This process is called evaporation. *Example*—(i) Evaporation of water in summer from Ponds, wells & lakes. (ii) Preparation of common salt from sea water by evaporation of water.

4. Crystallization : This method is mostly used for separation and purification of solid substances. In this process, the impure solid or mixture is heated with suitable solvent (e.g. alcohol, water, acetone, chloroform) to its boiling point and the hot solution is filtered. The clear filtrate is cooled slowly to room temperature, when pure solid crystallizes out. This is separated by filtration and dried.

For the separation of more complex mixtures, fractional crystallization is used, in which the components of the mixtures crystallize out at different interval of time.

5. Distillation : It is a process of converting a liquid into its vapour by heating and then condensing the vapour again into the same liquid by cooling. Thus, distillation involves vaporisation and condensation both

Distillation = Vaporisation + Condensation

This method is employed to separate the liquids which have different boiling points or a liquid from non-volatile solid or solids either in solution or suspension. *Example*—A mixture of copper sulphate and water or a mixture of water (B.P 100°C) and methyl alcohol (B.P 45°C) can be separated by this method.

6. Fractional distillation : This process is similar to the distillation process except that a fractionating column is used to separate two or more volatile liquid which have different boiling points. *Example*–(i) Methyl alcohol (bp = 338 K) and acetone (bp = 329 K) can be separated by fractional distillation process. (ii) Separation of petrol, diesel oil, kerosene oil, heavy oil etc from crude petroleum. (iii) Separation of oxygen, nitrogen inert gasses and carbon dioxide from liquid air etc.

7. Chromatography : The name chromatography is derived from Latin word 'Chroma' meaning colour. The technique of chromatography is based

on the difference in the rates at which the components of a mixture are absorbed in the suitable absorbent.

There are many types of chromatography.

(a) Column (absorption) Chromatography
(b) Thin layer chromatography
(c) Paper - chromatography
(d) High pressure liquid chromatography
(e) In-exchange chromatography
(f) Gas chromatography

8. Sedimentation and Decantation : This method is used when one component is a liquid and other is an insoluble. Insoluble solid, heavier than liquid. i.e, mud and water.

If muddy water is allowed to stand undisturbed for sometime in a beaker, the particles of earth (clay and sand) settle at the bottom. This process is called sedimentation. The clear liquid at the top can be gently transferred into another beaker. This process is known as decantation.

Concept of change in state : (a) Melting Point : The temperature at which solid and the liquid forms of the substance exist at equilibrium or both forms have same vapour pressure is called melting point.

(b) Boiling point : The temperature at which the vapour pressure of the liquid is equal to atmospheric pressure is called boiling point.

Liquid	Water	Ethanol	Chloroform	Acetone
B.P.	373 K	349 K	334 K	329 K

(c) Freezing Point : The temperature at which the vapour pressure of its liquid is equal to the vapour pressure of the corresponding solid is called freezing point.

(d) Evaporation : The process of conversion of a liquid into its vapours at room temperature is called evaporation. Evaporation causes cooling. Actually, during evaporation, the molecules having higher kinetic energy escape from the surface of the liquid. Therefore, average kinetic energy of the rest of the molecules decreases. Therefore cooling takes place during evaporation because of temperature of liquid is directly proportional to average kinetic Energy. Evaporation is affected by following factors,

(i) Nature of liquid (ii) Temperature (iii) Surface area.

(e) Vapour pressure : The pressure exerted by the vapours of liquid in equilibrium with liquid at a given temperature is called vapour pressure. Vapour pressure depends upon—(i) its nature and (ii) temperature.

Higher the vapour pressure of a particular liquid lesser will be the magnitude of intermolecular forces present in molecules. Vapour pressure of a liquid increases with increase in temperature.

2. Atomic Structure

Atom : The smallest particle of an element is called an atom. An atom can take part in chemical combination and does not occur free in nature. The atom of the hydrogen is the smallest and lightest. *Example*—Na, K, Ca, H etc.

Molecule : A molecule is the smallest particle of an element or compound that can have a stable and independent existence. *Example*—O_2, N_2, Cl_2, P_4, S_8 etc.

Mole : A mole is a collection of 6.023×10^{23} particles. It means that

1 mole = 6.023×10^{23}
1 mole atom = 6.023×10^{23} atoms
1 mole molecule = 6.023×10^{23} molecules
1 mole ion = 6.023×10^{23} ions
1 mole mango = 6.023×10^{23} mangoes
1 mole Apple = 6.023×10^{23} apples

Avogadro's Number : The number 6.023×10^{23} is called Avogadro's Number.

Atomic Mass : It is the ratio of mass of one atom of the element to $\frac{1}{12}$th part of the mass of one atom of carbon–12.

$$\text{Atomic mass of an element} = \frac{\text{Mass of one atom of the element}}{\frac{1}{12} \times \text{mass of one atom of carbon-12}}$$

Actual mass of 1 atom of an element = atomic mass in amu $\times 1.66 \times 10^{-24}$ g

Molecular mass : It indicates how many times one molecule of a substance is heavier in comparison to $\frac{1}{12}$th mass of one atom of Carbon–12.

Constituents of an atom : Fundamental particles of an atom are Electron, Proton & Neutron.

Electron : (i) Electron had been discovered by J.J. Thomson.

(ii) The name of electron was given by Stoney.

(iii) Charge on an electron — relative: –1 unit; absolute: -1.6×10^{-19} coulomb or -4.8×10^{-10} e.s.u.

(iv) Mass of an electron — relative: 0.000543 amu; absolute: 9.1×10^{-28} g

(v) $\frac{\text{charge}}{\text{mass}}\left(\frac{e}{m}\right)$ ratio of electron $= -1.76 \times 10^{8} \frac{C}{g}$

(vi) An electron was obtained from Cathode rays experimental.

Proton : (i) A proton had been discovered by Goldstein

(ii) A proton was named by Rutherford.

(iii) Charge on proton — relative: + 1 unit; absolute: $+1.6 \times 10^{-19}$ C or $+4.8 \times 10^{-10}$ e.s.u.

(iv) Mass of proton — relative: 1.00763 amu; absolute: 1.673×10^{-24} g

(v) $\frac{\text{charge}}{\text{mass}}$ ratio for proton = $9.58 \times 10^4 \frac{C}{g}$

(vi) An proton was obtained from anode rays experiment.

Neutron : (i) A neutron had been discovered by James Chadwick.

(ii) Charge on neutron—zero

(iii) Mass of proton — relative: 1.00863 amu; absolute: 1.675×10^{-24} g

(iv) $\frac{\text{charge}}{\text{mass}}$ ratio for neutron = zero

(v) A neutron was obtained from radioactivity phenomenon.

$$^{9}_{4}Be + ^{4}_{2}He \xrightarrow[\alpha\text{-particle}]{} ^{12}_{6}C + ^{1}_{0}n$$

Atomic number (Z) : The number of proton or electron in an atom of the element is called atomic number. It is denoted by Z.

$Z = e = p$ where, e = no. of electrons and p = no. of protons.

Mass number (A) : The sum of number or protons and neutrons in an atom of the element is called mass number. It is denoted by A.

$A = p + n$ where, p = no. of protons and n = no. of neutrons

Let, $^{23}_{11}Na$,

In Na, $Z = 11$, $A = 23$ and,

$e = 11, p = 11$

$\therefore \quad n = A - p = 23 - 11 = 12$

Isotopes : These are atoms of the elements having the same atomic number but different mass number.

Isotopes of Carbon—$^{12}_{6}C$, $^{13}_{6}C$, $^{14}_{6}C$

Isobars : These are atoms of the elements having the same mass number but different atomic numbers. e.g.

$^{40}_{18}Ar$, $^{40}_{19}K$, $^{40}_{20}Ca$

Isotones : These are atoms of different elements having the same number of neutrons.

$^{14}_{6}C$, $^{15}_{7}N$, $^{16}_{8}O$

Isoelectronic : These are atoms/molecules/ions containing the same number of electrons.

(i) O^{2-}, F^-, Ne, Na^+, Mg^{2+} (ii) CN^-, N_2, O_2^{2+} etc.

Thomson's model of an atom : According to Thomson, an atom is treated as sphere of radius 10^{-8} cm in which positively charged particles are uninformally distributed and negatively charged electrons and embedded through them. This is also called Plum-Pudding model of an atom or water-melon model of an atom.

Rutherford's model of an atom : On the basis of scattering experiment, Rutherford proposed a model of the atom which is known as nuclear atomic model.

According to this model,

(i) An atom consists of a heavy positively charged nucleus where all protons and neutrons are present. Protons & neutrons are collectively called nucleons. Almost whole mass of the atom is contributed by these nucleons.

(ii) Radius of a nucleus = 10^{-13} cm

Radius of an atom = 10^{-8} cm

Radius of an atom = 10^5 times of the radius of the nucleons.

(iii) $$\frac{\text{volume of atom}}{\text{volume of a nucleus}} = \frac{\frac{4}{3}\pi(10^{-8})^3}{\frac{4}{3}\pi(10^{-13})^3} = \frac{10^{-24}}{10^{-39}} = 10^{15}$$

So, volume of an atom is 10^{15} times heavier than volume of a nucleus.

(iv) Electrons revolve around the nucleus in closed orbits with high speed. This model is similar to the solar system, the nucleus representing the sun and revolving electrons as planets. The electrons are therefore, generally referred as planetary electrons.

Spectrum : When white light is allowed to pass through a prism, it splits into several colours. These seven coloured band is called spectrum.

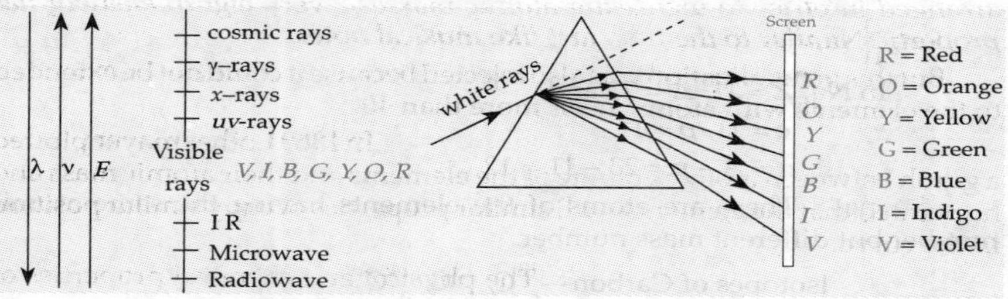

Zeeman's effect : When spectral lines obtained from atomic spectra is placed in a magnetic field, they are splitted into number of fine lines, this is called Zeeman's effect.

Stark's effect : When spectral lines obtained from atomic spectra is placed in electric field, they are splitted into number of fine lines this is called Stark's effect.

Thomson's model	Plum pudding model (watermelon model)
Rutherford's model	Nuclear theory
Bohr's model	Concept of Quantization of energy.
Planck's Quantum theory	Photon & quanta.
Sommerfeld's model	Orbital : elliptical & spherical
de-Broglie's equation	Dual nature of electron
Heisenberg's Uncertainty principle	Exact position & momentum can not be determined simultaneously
Schrodinger's wave equation	wave nature of electron.

3. Periodic classification of Elements

Father of periodic table—Mendeleev.

The arrangement of the known elements in certain groups in such a way so that the elements with similar properties are grouped together is known as classification of elements.

Genesis of periodic classification :

1. Lavoisier classified the elements into metals and non-metals.

2. Dobereinier's Triads : In 1829, Dobereiner, a German chemist arranged certain elements with similar properties in groups of three in such a way that the atomic mass of the middle element was nearly the same as the average atomic masses of the first and third elements.

Triad	Lithium	Sodium	Potassium
Atomic mass	7	23	39

$$\text{atomic mass of sodium} = \frac{39+7}{2} = \frac{46}{2} = 23$$

But only few elements could be covered under triads.

3. Newland's law of octaves : In 1866, John Newlands, An English Chemist proposed the law of octaves by stating that, *When elements are arranged in order to increasing atomic masses, every eighth element has properties similar to the first, just like musical notes.*

But this generalization was also rejected because it could not be extended to the elements with atomic mass more than 40.

4. Lother's–Mayer's atomic volume curve : In 1869 Lother mayer plotted a graph betweeen atomic volume of the elements and their atomic mass and he pointed that the elements with similar properties occupy similar position in the curve.

5. Mendeleev's periodic law : The physical and chemical properties of the elements are the periodic function of their atomic masses.

Mendeleev's arranged the elements known at that time in increasing order of atomic masses and this arrangement was periodic table.

In periodic table :

Horizontal line is called periods.
Vertical line is called group.

In Mendeleev's periodic table :

Period— 7
Group— 9 (I, II, III, IV, V, VI, VII, VIII, Zero)

6. Modern Periodic law : Modern periodic law was given by Moseley.

According to Moseley : "The physical and chemical properties of the elements are the periodic function of their atomic numbers."

In modern periodic table :

Period— 7 Group— 18

Modern periodic table are classified as :

(i) *s*–block (ii) *p*–block
(iii) *d*–block (iv) *f*–block

s–block : Alkali & Alkaline earth metals.

p–block : Chalcogen, Picogens, Halogens and inert gases.

d–block : Transition elements.

f–block : Inner transition elements.

Periodic properties :

(i) Atomic radii : The distance from the centre of the nucleus to the outermost shell containing electrons called atomic radius.

It is not possible to measure the absolute value of atomic radius of an element. However, it may be expressed in three different form covalent radii, metallic radii, Van der wall radii.

Van der wall radii > metallic radii > covalent radii.

(ii) Ionic radii : The effective distance from the centre of nucleus of the ion upto which it exerts its influence on the electron cloud is called ionic radii.

Anionic radii > atomic radii > cationic radii

(iii) Ionization Potential (I.P.) : The amount of energy required to remove an electron from isolated gaseous atom is called Ionization Potential (I.P.) or Ionization Energy (I.E.)

$$A\,(g) - e + \text{Energy required (I.P.)} \longrightarrow A^{+}\,(g)$$

(iv) Electron affinity (E_a) : The energy released during addition of an extra electron in isolated gaseous atom is called electron Affinity.

$$A\,(g) + e \longrightarrow A^{-}(g) + \text{Energy released}$$

Chlorine (Cl) has highest E_a value.

(v) Electronegativity (E_n) : The relative electron attracting tendency of its atom for a shared pair of electrons in a chemical bond is called electronegativity.

F is the most electronegative atom

$$E_n = \frac{\text{IP} + E_a}{5.6}$$

E_n value > 1.7 (ionic compound)

E_n value < 1.7 (polar covalent compound)

E_n value = 0 (nonpolar compound)

(vi) Lattice Energy : The amount of energy released during formation of one mole of ionic compound from its constituent ions is called Lattice energy.

(vii) Hydration Energy : The amount of energy released during dissolution of one mole of compound into water, is called hydration energy.

If hydration energy > Lattice energy, then compound is soluble in water and if hydration energy < Lattice energy, then compound is insoluble in water.

4. Chemical Bonding

The force that holds together the different atoms in a molecule is called chemical bond. There are many types of chemical bond.

1. Ionic bond or (Electrovalent bond) : **A bond formed by the complete transfer of one or more electrons from one atom to other atom is called ionic bond.** *Example*—

(a) Formation of NaCl :

$$Na\cdot + \cdot\ddot{\underset{..}{Cl}}: \longrightarrow Na^{+}\left[:\ddot{\underset{..}{Cl}}:\right]^{-} \longrightarrow Na^{+}\,Cl^{-}$$

Condition of ionic bond : **I. Ionization energy of metal should be low.**

II. Electron affinity of non-metal should be high.

Properties of ionic compounds :

(a) Ionic compounds have high melting point & boiling point.

(b) Ionic compounds are good conductor of electricity in molten state or in water.

(c) Ionic compounds are bad conductor of electricity in solid state.

(d) Ionic compounds are soluble in water.

(e) Ionic compounds are insoluble in non-polar covalent like Benzene, Carbon tetrachloride etc.

Covalent bond : **A bond formed between two same or different atoms by mutual contribution and sharing of electrons is called covalent bond.** Example—

(a) H_2 molecule :

$$H\cdot\cdot H \longrightarrow H - H$$

(b) Cl_2 molecule :

$$:\ddot{\underset{..}{Cl}}\cdot\ \cdot\ddot{\underset{..}{Cl}}: \longrightarrow :\ddot{\underset{..}{Cl}} - \ddot{\underset{..}{Cl}}:$$

(c) CH_4 molecule :

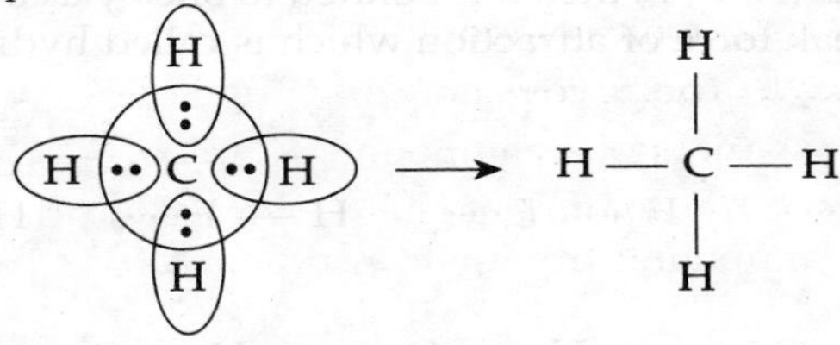

Properties of covalent compounds :

(a) Covalent compounds have high m.p. & b.p.

(b) They are generally bad conductor of electricity (exception graphite)

(c) They are generally insoluble in water.

(d) They are generally soluble in organic solvent like benzene, acetone, chloroform etc.

(e) Covalent bonds are directional.

Co-ordinate bond (or Dative bond) : **Co-ordinate bond is a special type of covalent bond in which one atom donates electrons to other atom. The** bonding between donor to acceptor atom is called co-ordinate bond. It is denoted by ⟶. *Example*—

SO_2 (Ö : : S :) ⟶ :Ö: ⟶ O = S ⟶ O

Sigma bond (σ–bond) : A bond formed by the linear overlapping of atomic orbitals is called sigma bond. Since, the extent of overlapping of atomic orbitals in σ-bond in large. Hence σ-bond is a strong bond.

Pi-bond (π-bond): A bond formed by the sidewise (or lateral overlapping of atomic orbitals is called pi-bond. since, in this case, extent of overlapping of atomic orbitals is lesser than σ-bond. So, π-bond is a weak bond.

$H \overset{}{\underset{\sigma}{—}} H$; $O \overset{\pi}{\underset{\sigma}{=}} O$; $N \overset{\pi}{\underset{\sigma}{\equiv}} N$ (π)

Bond energy : The amount of energy required to break one mole bonds of a particular type between the atoms in the gaseous state of a substance is called bond energy. The bond energy depends upon the following factors.

I. Size of atom II. Multiplicity of bonds.

Greater the size of atoms, Lesser will be bond energy.

Greater the bond multiplicity more will be bond energy.

Bond energy : Single bond < double bond < triple bond

Bond length : The average equilibrium distance between the centres of the two bonded atoms is called bond length. The bond length is influenced by the following factors—

(i) Size of atoms (ii) Multiplicity of bonds

Greater the size of atoms, greater will be bond length.

Greater the multiplicity of bonds, lesser will be bond length.

Hydrogen bond : When hydrogen atom is present between two most electronegative atoms (N, O, F) then it is bonded to one by a covalent bond and to other by a weak force of attraction which is called hydrogen bond. etc. It is denoted by …… . *Example*—

(i) $(HF)_n$

H — F ····· H — F ····· H — F ····· H — F

(ii) $(H_2O)_n$

····· H — O ····· H — O ····· H — O ·····
(each O bonded below to H)

(iii) OH, NO_2 (benzene ring) ⟶ (benzene ring with O—H ··· O←N=O)

O—Nitrophenol

There are two type of hydrogen bonding

(i) Intermolecular hydrogen bond.

(ii) Intramolecular hydrogen bond.

Intermolecular hydrogen bond arises when hydrogen bonding occurs between two or more molecules. In this case m.p. & b.p. of compound increases due to molecular association.

$$\cdots H - F \cdots \quad H - F \cdots \quad H - F \cdots$$

When hydrogen bonding occurs within a molecule then it is called intramolecular hydrogen bonding. Due to cyclisation m.p. & b.p. of the compound decreases in this case.

O—H⋯O, N, O (o-nitrophenol)

Due to intermolecular hydrogen bonding between alcohol and water. alcohol is soluble in water.

$$CH_3 - O - H \cdots O\begin{matrix} H \\ H \end{matrix}$$

Methyl alcohol   Water

5. Oxidation & Reduction

Oxidation (old concept) : Oxidation is a process which involves either of the following—

(i) addition of oxygen (ii) removal of hydrogen

(iii) addition of electro negative element or group

(iv) removal of electro positive element or group.

$2Mg + O_2 \longrightarrow 2MgO$ (oxidation of Mg)

$H_2S + Cl_2 \longrightarrow 2HCl + S$ (oxidation of H_2S)

$Fe + S \longrightarrow FeS$ (oxidation of Fe)

$2KI + H_2O_2 \longrightarrow 2KOH + I_2$ (oxidation of KI)

Reduction (old concept) : Reduction is a process which involves either of the following—

(i) addition of hydrogen (ii) removal of oxygen

(iii) addition of electro positive element or group.

(iv) removal of electronegative element or group.

$H_2 + Cl_2 \longrightarrow 2HCl$ (reduction of Cl_2)

$CuO + C \longrightarrow Cu + CO$ (reduction of CuO)

$HgCl_2 + Hg \longrightarrow Hg_2Cl_2$ (reduction of $HgCl_2$)

$2FeCl_3 + H_2 \longrightarrow 2FeCl_2 + 2HCl$ (reduction of $FeCl_3$)

Modern concept of oxidation and Reduction : According to modern concept, loss of electrons is called oxidation whereas gain of electrons is called reduction. *Example :*

$$Na \longrightarrow Na^{+} + e \quad \text{(oxidation of Na)}$$
$$Zn \longrightarrow Zn^{2+} + 2e \quad \text{(oxidation of Zn)}$$
$$Cl_2 + 2e \longrightarrow 2Cl^{-} \quad \text{(reduction of } Cl_2\text{)}$$
$$S + 2e \longrightarrow S^{2-} \quad \text{(reduction of S)}$$

Oxidising agent (O.A.) : **A substance which undergoes reduction is called oxidising agent**

$$CuO + C \longrightarrow Cu + CO$$

Oxidation – C, Reduction– CuO, Oxidising agent – CuO

Examples—O_2, O_3, H_2O_2, $KMnO_4$, $K_2Cr_2O_7$ etc.

Reducing agent (R.A.) : **A substance which undergoes oxidation is called reducing agent.**

$$H_2O + C \longrightarrow CO + H_2$$

Oxidation— C, Reduction— H_2O, Reducing agent— C

Examples— H_2, CO, H_2S, SO_2, C, $SnCl_2$ etc.

Redox Reaction : **A reaction in which both oxidation and reduction takes place simaltaneously is called redox reaction.**

Example—

$$CuO + C \longrightarrow Cu + CO$$

Oxidation – C, Reduction – CuO

Oxidation number (O.N.) : **The charge present on atom in molecule or ion is called oxidation number. It may be zero, positive or negative.**

Rules for determination of oxidation number :

(i) Oxidation number of an atom in free state is zero.

(ii) Oxidation number of alkali metals (Li, Na, K, Rb, Cs) in molecule is always +1.

(iii) Oxidation number of alkaline earth metals (Be, Mg, Ca, Sr, Ba) in a molecule is always + 2

(iv) Oxidation number of hydrogen — (+ 1) hydrogen ion; (– 1) hydride ion

(v) Oxidation number of Oxygen — (– 2) oxide; (– 1) peroxide; $-\frac{1}{2}$ superoxide

(vi) Sum of Oxidation number of atoms in a molecule is equal to zero.

(vii) Sum of oxidation number of atoms in a ion is equal to magnitude of charge with sign.

Oxidation Number of Mn in $KMnO_4$:

Let O.N. of Mn = x

$$1 + x + (-2) \times 4 = 0$$
$$1 + x - 8 = 0$$
$$x = +7$$

Oxidation Number of Cr in $K_2Cr_2O_7$:

Let O.N. of Cr = x

$$1 \times 2 + x \times 2 + (-2) \times 7 = 0$$

$$2 + 2x - 14 = 0$$

$$x = +6$$

Oxidation Number of C in $C_{12}H_{22}O_{11}$:

Let O.N. of C = x

$$x \times 12 + 1 \times 22 + (-2) \times 11 = 0$$

$$12x + 22 - 22 = 0$$

$$x = 0$$

Types of Reactions :

1. Decomposition reactions : **In these reactions, compound either of its own or upon heating decomposes to give two or more components out of which at least one is in the elemental state.**

$$2NaH\ (s) \xrightarrow{\Delta} Na\ (s) + H_2\ (g)$$

$$2H_2O\ (l) \xrightarrow{\Delta} 2H_2\ (g) + O_2\ (g)$$

2. Combination reactions: **In combination reactions, compounds are formed as a result of the chemical combination of two or more elements.**

$$H_2\ (g) + \frac{1}{2}O_2\ (g) \longrightarrow H_2O_2(l)$$

$$C\ (s) + O_2\ (g) \longrightarrow CO_2\ (g)$$

$$3Mg\ (s) + N_2\ (g) \longrightarrow Mg_3N_2\ (s)$$

3. Displacement reactions : **In these reactions, an atom / ion present in a compound gets replaced by an atom / ion of another element.**

$$FeSO_4\ (aq) + Zn\ (s) \longrightarrow Zn\ SO_4\ (aq) + Fe\ (s)$$

$$MgO\ (aq) + 2\ Na\ (s) \longrightarrow Na_2O\ (aq) + Mg\ (s)$$

4. Disproportionation reactions : **The chemical reaction in which only one substance is oxidised as well as reduced simultaneously is called disproportionation reaction.**

$$Cl_2 + 2NaOH \longrightarrow NaCl + NaOCl + H_2O$$

$$P_4 + NaOH + 2H_2O \longrightarrow 2NaH_2PO_2 + 2PH_3$$

5. Substitution reaction : **In these reactions, one or more atoms or groups present in organic molecule get substituted or replaced by suitable atoms or groups.**

$$C_2H_2Cl + KOH\ (aq) \longrightarrow C_2H_5OH + KCl$$

Ethyl chloride — Ethyl alcohol

6. Neutralisation reaction : **When an acid reacts with a base, salt and water is formed. This reaction is called neutralisation reaction.**

acid + base ⟶ salt + water

$$HCl + NaOH \longrightarrow NaCl + H_2O$$

7. Reversible reaction : A reaction in which reactants combine to form products and again products recombine to reactants is called reversible reaction.

$$N_2\ (g) + 3H_2\ (g) \rightleftharpoons 2NH_3\ (g)$$

8. Irreversible reaction : A reaction which proceeds in only one direction is called irreversible reaction.

$$CaCO_3\ (s) \xrightarrow{\Delta} CaO\ (s) + CO_2\ (g)$$

6. Acids, Bases & Salts

Acid :

An acid is a substance which

(i) is sour in taste
(ii) turns blue litmus paper into red
(iii) contains replaceable hydrogen
(iv) gives hydrogen ion (H^+) in aqueous solution (Arrhenius theorem)
(v) can donote a proton (Bronsted & Lowry concept)
(vi) can accept electron (Lewis theorem)

Uses of acid :

1. As food :
   (a) Citric acid — Lemons or oranges (Citrus fruits)
   (b) Lactic acid — sour milk
   (c) Butyric acid — Rancid butter
   (d) Tarteric acid — Grapes
   (e) Acetic acid — Vinegar
   (f) Maleic acid — Apples
   (g) Carbonic acid— Soda water aerated drinks
   (h) Stearic acid — Fats
   (i) Oxalic and — Tomato, wood sorrel.
2. Hydrochloric acid (HCl) is used in digestion
3. Nitric acid (HNO_3) is used in the purification of gold & silver.
4. Conc. H_2SO_4 and HNO_3 is used to wash iron for its galvanization.
5. Oxalic acid is used to remove rust spot.
6. Boric acid is a constituent of eye wash.
7. Formic acid is present in red ants.
8. Uric acid is present in urine of mammals

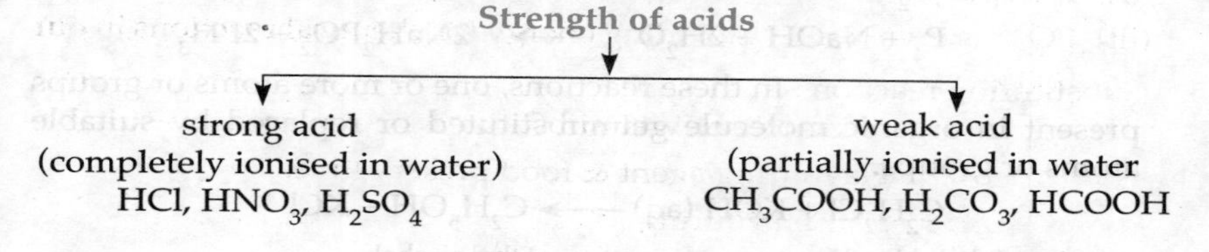

Basicity of an acid : **The number of removable hydrogen ions from an acid is called basicity of that acid.**

Mono basic acid (one removable H^+ ion) — HCl, HNO_3

Dibasic acid (two removable H^+ ion) — H_2SO_4, H_2CO_3, H_3PO_3

Tribasic acid (three removable H^+ ion) — H_3PO_4

Acidic strength (i) $HF < HCl < HBr < HI$

(ii) $CH_3COOH < H_2SO_4 < HNO_3 < HCl$

Uses of HCl :

(i) HCl present in gastric juices are responsible for the digestion.
(ii) Used as bathroom cleaner.
(iii) As a pickling agent before galvanization.
(iv) In the tanning of leather.
(v) In the dying and textile industry.
(vi) In the manufacture of gelatine from bones.

Uses of HNO_3

(i) In the manufacture of fertilizers like ammonium nitrate.
(ii) In the manufacture of explosives like TNT (Trinitro toluene), TNB (Trinitro benzene), Picric acid (Trinitro phenol) etc.
(iii) Nitro Glycerine (Dynamite)
(iv) Found in rain water (first shower)
(v) It forms nitrates in the soil.
(vi) In the manufacture of rayon.
(vii) In the manufacture of dyes & drugs.

Uses of Sulphuric acid (H_2SO_4)

(i) In lead storage battery.
(ii) In the manufacture of HCl.
(iii) In the manufacture of Alum.
(iv) In the manufacture of fertilizers, drugs, detergents & explosives.

Use of Boric acids : As an antiseptic.

Uses of Phosphoric acid :

(i) Its calcium salt makes our bones.
(ii) It forms phosphatic fertilizers.
(iii) PO_4^{-3} is involved in providing energy for chemical reactions in our body.

Uses of Ascorbic acid : Source of Vitamin C

Uses of Citric acid : Flavouring agent & food preservative.

Uses of Acetic acid : Flavouring agent & food preservative.

Uses of Tartaric acid : (i) Souring agent for pickles (ii) A component of baking powder (sodium bicarbonate + tartaric acid)

Indicator properties of an acid

Indicator	Colour changes
Blue litmus paper	turns red
Methyl orange	Form orange to pink
Phenolphthalein	Remains colourless

Bases :

A. Base is a substance which
 (i) bitter in taste
 (ii) turns red litmus paper into blue
 (iii) gives hydroxyl ions (OH^-) in aqueous solution.
 (iv) can accept proton (Bronsted & lowry concept)
 (v) can donate electrons (Lewis theory)

Indicator properties of bases

Indicator	Change of colour
Red litmus paper	turns blue
Methyl orange	from orange to yellow
Phenolphthalein	from colourless to pink

- ➢ Oxides & hydroxides of metals are bases
- ➢ Water soluble bases are called alkali e.g. NaOH, KOH, etc.
- ➢ All alkalies are bases but all bases are not alkalies because all bases are not soluble in water.

Strength of bases

Strong bases: NaOH, KOH

Weak bases: NH_4OH, $Fe(OH)_3$

Acidity of a base : The number of removable hydroxyl (OH^-) ions from a base is called acidity of a base.

Acidity of NaOH = 1
Acidity of KOH = 1
Acidity of $Ca(OH)_2$ = 2

The pH scale : pH of a solution is the negative logarithm of the concentration of hydrogen ions in mole per litre.

$$pH = -\log[H^+]$$

If pH < 7 then solution is acidic
If pH > 7 then solution is basic
If pH = 7 then solution is neutral

The pH value of some common liquids

Liquid	pH
Lemon Juice	2.5
Wine	2.8
Apple Juice	3.0
Vinegar	3.0
Urine	4.8
Coffee	5.0
Saliva	6.5
Milk	6.5
Blood	7.4
Pure water	7.0
Sea water	8.5
Toothpaste	9.0
Milk of magnesia	10.5

Salt : When an acid reacts with a base, salt and water are formed.

Acid + Base ⟶ Salt + Water
HCl + NaOH ⟶ NaCl + H_2O

Uses of some important salts :

1. Sodium Chloride : As a flavouring agent in food. In saline water for a patient of dehydration (0.9% NaCl), In the manufacture of HCl etc.
2. Sodium iodate : Iodised salt to prevent Goitre disease.
3. Sodium Carbonate : As washing soda, manufacturing of glass etc.
4. Sodium Benzoate : As a food preservative for pickles.
5. Potassium nitrate : As a fertilizer giving both K & N to the solid, In gun powder (C + S + KNO_3), In match sticks etc.

6. Calcium Chloride : Dehydrating agent used for removing moisture from gases.
7. Calcium carbonate (lime stone) : In the construction of building, In the cement industry., In the extraction of metals etc.
8. Calcium sulphate : (i) Plaster of Paris ($2\ CaSO_4 \cdot H_2O$) – For moulds & statues, in the cement industry in the form of Gypsum ($CaSO_4 \cdot 2H_2O$).
9. Calcium Phosphate : As a fertilizer (Superphosphate of lime)
10. Bleaching powder : (i) As a disinfectant (ii) As a bleaching agent (removing colours)
11. Alum (Potassium aluminium sulphate) : (i) In the purification of water. (ii) In the dyeing industry (iii) As antiseptic after shave.

The acidic and basic nature of some household substances

Acidic	Basic (Alkaline)
1. Bathroom acid	1. Milk of magnesia (Anta acids)
2. Vitamin C tablets (Ascorbic acid)	2. Toothpaste
3. Lemon juice	3. Soap solution or detergent soln.
4. Orange juice	4. Solution of washing soda.
5. Tomato juice	5. Slaked lime & white wash
6. Vinegar	
7. Fizzy drinks (Colas & Sodawater)	

7. Behaviour of Gases

1. Boyle's law : At constant temperature, the volume of a definite mass of a gas is inversely proportional to pressure.

$$V \propto \frac{1}{p} \text{ (at constant } T) \text{ or, } V = K \cdot \frac{1}{P}$$

$$pV = K \text{ (where } K \text{ is a constant)}$$

$$p_1 V_1 = p_2 V_2$$

2. Charle's law : At constant pressure, the volume of a definite mass of a gas is directly proportional to absolute temperature.

i.e. $V \propto T$ (at constant p) or, $V = K \cdot T$ or, $\frac{V}{T} = k$

$$\therefore \frac{V_1}{T_1} = \frac{V_2}{T_2}$$

3. Gay-Lussac's law : At constant volume, the pressure of given mass of a gas is directly proportional to the temp in Kelvin.

$$p \propto T \quad \text{(at constant } V) \text{ or, } p = K \cdot T$$

or, $\frac{p}{T} = K \qquad \therefore \frac{p_1}{T_1} = \frac{p_2}{T_2}$

4. Avogardo's gas law : At constant temperature and pressure the volume of a gas is directly proportional to the number of molecules.

$$V \propto n \quad \text{(at constant } T \text{ \& } p)$$

5. Ideal gas equation : $pV = nRT$ is called ideal gas equation. Where

p = Pressure, V = volume

n = number of mole T = temperature in Kelvin.

R = gas constant

$= 0.0821$ lit atm K^{-1} mol^{-1}

$= 8.314$ J K^{-1} mol^{-1}

$= 1.987$ cal K^{-1} mol^{-1}

6. S.T.P. & N.T.P. :

S.T.P. — Standard temperature and pressure.

N.T.P. — Normal temperature and pressure.

At S.T.P., for 1 mole gas

$V = 22.4$ litre = 22400 ml

$p = 1$ atm = 76 cm of Hg = 760 mm of Hg

$T = 273$ K

Diffusion of gases : The process of intermixing of gases irrespective of the density relationship and without the effect of external agency is called diffusion of gases.

In a gas, the molecules are far separated and the empty space among the molecules are very large. Therefore the molecules of one gas can move into the empty spaces or voids of the other gas and vice-versa. This leads to diffusion.

Graham's law of diffusion : Under the similar conditions of temperature and pressure, the rates of diffusion of gases are inversely proportional to the square roots of their densities.

Let r_1 and r_2 be the rates of diffusion of two gases A and B, d_1 and d_2 be their respective densities, then according to Graham's law of diffusion.

$$\frac{r_1}{r_2} = \sqrt{\frac{d_2}{d_1}} = \sqrt{\frac{M_2}{M_1}}$$

Since molecular mass = 2 × vapour density.

$$M = 2 \times d$$

Dalton's law of partial pressure : It states that– If two or more gases which do not react chemically are enclosed in a vessel, the total pressure of the gaseous mixture is equal to the sum of the partial pressure that each gases which exert pressure when enclosed separately in the same vessel at constant temperature.

Let p_1, p_2 and p_3 be the pressure of three non-reactive gases when enclosed separately. Let total pressure be p

then $p = p_1 + p_2 + p_3$

8. Electrolysis

1. Electrolytes : These are the substances which allow the electricity to pass through them in their molten states or in the form of their aqueous solution and undergo chemical decomposition. Examples— acids, bases & salts.

2. Strong electrolytes : The electrolytes which are almost completely dissociated into ions in solution are called strong electrolytes. Example—NaCl, KCl, HCl, NaOH etc.

3. Weak electrolytes : The electrolytes which do not ionise completely in solution are called weak electrolytes. *Example*—CH_3COOH, H_2CO_3, HCN, $ZnCl_2$, NH_4OH etc.

4. Electrolysis : The process of chemical decomposition of an electrolyte by passage of electric current through its molten state or its solution is called electrolysis.

5. Electrodes : In order to pass the current through an electrolytes in molten state or in aqueous solution, two rods or plates are needed to connect with the terminal of a battery. These rods or plates are called electrodes.

Anode : The electrode which is attached to positive terminal of battery is called anode. Oxidation occurs at anode.

Cathode : The electrode which is attached to negative terminal of batteries is called, Reduction occurs at cathode.

Examples— Electrolysis of molten NaCl

At anode : $Cl^- - e \longrightarrow Cl$

$Cl + Cl \longrightarrow Cl_2$

At cathode : $Na^+ + e \longrightarrow Na$

So, Cl_2 gas occurs at anode while Na at cathode.

9. Carbon and its Compounds

Carbon is non-metal having atomic number 6 and mass number 12. It is placed in group (IV) A or group 14 in periodic table

Allotropy.

The substances which have same chemical properties, but different physical properties are called allotropes and this property is called allotropy. *Example*—Allotropies of Carbon—Diamond, graphite, charcoal.

Diamond.

(i) It is the purest form of carbon.
(ii) It is the hardest natural known substance.
(iii) It is transparent, and specific gravity 3.52.
(iv) It is bad conductor of electricity and heat.
(v) It has very high refractive index 2.415.
(vi) It is chemically inert and on heating above 1500° c, transferred into graphic.
(vii) It form tetrahedral crystals and hybridisation of C–atom is sp^3.
(viii) It has high mp & density.
(ix) Black diamonds called carbonado contains traces of graphite.

Graphite (Plumbago or black lead)

(i) It is soft, greasy, dark greyish colored crystalline solid.
(ii) It is good conductor of heat and electric
(iii) Its specific gravity is 2.3
(iv) The hybridization of carbon in graphite is sp^2 and it has hexagonal layer structure

(v) It is chemically more reactive than diamond

(vi) Its layer structure is held by weak van der waal's force.

(vii) Graphite is used in making for lining and making electrodes of electric furnances, in making refractory crucibles, in making lead pencils, as a moderator in nuclear reactor as lubricant in machinery, as a reducing agent in steel manufacturing.

Forms of Amorphous carbon obtained by destructive distillation.

1.	Wood charcoal	obtained from wood
2.	Sugar charcoal	obtained from cane sugar
3.	Bone or animal charcoal	Obtained from animal bones
4.	Coke charcoal	Obtained from coal

Hydrocarbons

Compounds made of carbon and hydrogen atoms only are celled hydrocarbons. The natural source of hydrocarbons is petroleum.

Hydrocarbons are classified as :

(i) saturated hydrocarbons

(ii) unsaturated hydrocarbon

(iii) aromatic hydrocarbons.

1. Saturated hydrocarbons: The hydrocarbons in which carbon atoms and singly bonded are called saturated hydrocarbons. Saturated hydrocarbons are also called alkanes or paraffins. Alkanes are relatively unreactive under ordinary laboratory conditions. So, alkanes are also called paraffins because paraffins means little reactive.

general formula of alkane—$C_n H_{2n+2}$

Methane (CH_4) : $\begin{array}{ccccc} & & H & & \\ & & | & & \\ H & - & C & - & H \\ & & | & & \\ & & H & & \end{array}$ Ethane ($C_2 H_6$) : $\begin{array}{ccccccc} & & H & & H & & \\ & & | & & | & & \\ H & - & C & - & C & - & H \\ & & | & & | & & \\ & & H & & H & & \end{array}$

(ii) Unsaturated hydrocarbons : The hydrocarbons in which carbon atoms are either doubly or triply bonded are called unsaturated hydrocarbons. Doubly bonded (carbon carbon atoms) hydrocarbons are called alkenes. The general formula of alkene is $C_n H_{2n}$.

Ethane ($C_2 H_4$) : $\begin{array}{ccc} H & & H \\ & \diagdown\ \ \diagup & \\ & C = C & \\ & \diagup\ \ \diagdown & \\ H & & H \end{array}$ Propane ($C_3 H_6$) : $\begin{array}{ccccccc} & & H & & & & H \\ & & | & & & \diagup & \\ H & - & C & - & C & = & C \\ & & | & & | & \diagdown & \\ & & H & & H & & H \end{array}$

Triply bonded carbon : Carbon atoms containing hydrocarbons are called alkynes. The general formula of alkynes are $C_n H_{2n-2}$

(iii) Aromatic hydrocarbons : These are homocyclic compounds which contain atleast one benzene ring in which carbon atoms are linked to one another by alternate single and double bonds.

In Greek, aroma stands for sweet smell. Compounds in these classification have pleasant smell. Hence, they are called aromatic compounds.

Example : Benzene Naphthalene Anthracenc

Isomerism : Two or more compounds having same molecular formula but different physical and chemical properties are called isomers and this phenomenon is called isomerism

Polymerisation : The simple molecules which combine to form a macro molecule is called polymer. The process by which the simple molecules (monomers) are converted polymer is called polymerisation.

$$\underset{\text{ethene}}{n\,CH_2 = CH_2} \xrightarrow{\text{polymerisation}} \underset{\text{Polyethene}}{(-CH_2 - CH_2-)_n}$$

Natural occurring polymers are protein, nucleic acid, cellulose, starch etc.

Plastics : Plastics are cross linked polymers and are very tough. Lac is a natural plastic chemically plastic can be of two types.

(i) Thermoplastic (ii) Thermosetting plastics.

(i) Thermoplastic : These are the polymers which can be easily softened repeatedly when heated and hardened when cooled with little change in their properties.

Examples : Polyethylene, polystyrene, polyvinyl chloride, teflon. etc.

(ii) Thermoplastic : These are the polymers which undergo permanent change on heating. On heating they undergo extensive cross linking in moulds and become hard and infusible therefore, they can not be reused.

Examples: Bakelite, glyptal, terrylene etc.

Bakelite (Phenol-formaldehyde resins) : It is a condensation polymer and is obtained from phenol and formaldehyde in presence of either an acid or a base catalyst. It is used for making combs, fountain pens, photographs records, electrical goods etc.

Rubber : It is a polymer which is capable of returning to its original length, shape or size after being stretched or deformed. The rubber obtained from natural sources are called natural rubber and polymer prepared in laboratory which are similar to natural rubber are known as synthesize rubber.

Natural rubber

$$\underset{\text{Isoprene}}{nCH_2 = \overset{\overset{\displaystyle CH_3}{|}}{C} - CH = CH_2} \xrightarrow{\text{Polymerisation}} \underset{\text{Natural rubber}}{-\left[CH_2 - \overset{\overset{\displaystyle CH_3}{|}}{C} = CH - CH_2\right]_n-}$$

Synthetic rubber

(i) Neoprene

$$\underset{\text{Chloroprene}}{nCH_2 = CH - \overset{\overset{\displaystyle Cl}{|}}{C} = CH_2} \xrightarrow{\text{Polymerisation}} \underset{\text{Neoprene}}{-\left[CH_2 - CH = \overset{\overset{\displaystyle Cl}{|}}{C} - CH_2\right]_n-}$$

(ii) Thiokol : Thiokol is made by polymerisation of ethylene chloride and sodium polysulphide

$$Cl\,CH_2 - CH_2\,Cl + Na - S - S - Na + Cl\,CH_2 - CH_2\,Cl$$

$$\downarrow \text{Polymerisation}$$

$$-CH_2 - CH_2 - S - S - CH_2 - CH_2 -$$

Thiokol rubber

repeating unit is $- CH_2 - S - S - CH_2 -$

Thiokol is chemically resistant polymer. It is used in the manufacture of hoses and tank linings, engine gaskets and rocket fuel.

Vulcanization of rubber : Natural rubber is soft and sticky and therefore, in order to give strength and elasticity Natural rubber is vulcanized. Vulcanization is a process of treating the natural rubber with sulphur or some compound of sulphur (SF_6) under heat. Vulcanized rubber is used for manufacturing rubber bands, gloves, car, tyres etc.

Fibres : Fibres are the polymers which have quite strong intermolecular forces such as hydrogen bonding. Nylon–6,6, dacron, orlon etc are the examples of this type.

Rayon : Synthetic fibre obtained from cellulose is known as Rayon.

10. Fuels

A substance that can supply energy either alone or by reacting with another substance is known as fuel. Heat produced by fuel is measured in Calories. An ideal fuel should

(i) have high calorific value

(ii) be cheap and easily available

(iii) be easily stored & transport

(iv) be regulated and controlled

(v) have low ignition temperature

The quantity of fuel is expressed in the form of calorific value.

Calorific value is the total quantity of heat liberated by complete combustion of a unit mass of fuel in air or oxygen.

Calorific value of fuels are expressed in kcal / m^3 or British Thermal unit (B.T.U) per cubic foot.

$$1\ \text{kcal}/\text{m}^3 = 0.107\ \text{B.T.U}/\text{ft}^3$$

Fuel may be sold (e.g wood, coal etc.)

Liquid (e.g kerosene oil, petroleum, alcohol etc.) or gas (e.g water gas, producer gas, coal gas, oil gas, natural gas, gobar gas, LPG etc.) However, gaseous fuel are considered to be the best fuels.

1. Water gas (syn gas) : It is a mixture of carbon monoxide and hydrogen. It is obtained by the action of steam on a red hot coke at 1000° C.

$$C + H_2O \longrightarrow \underbrace{CO + H_2}_{\text{Water gas}} - 28\ \text{kcal}$$

It has a high calorific value (2700 kcal / m^3)

Producer gas : It is a mixture of CO and N_2. It is prepared by burning coke in limited supply of air. It is the cheapest gaseous fuel, however its calorific value is not very high because it has a large proportion of nitrogen.

Coal gas : It is a mixture of H_2, CH_4, CO and other gases like N_2, C_2H_4, O_2 etc. It is obtained by destructive distillation of coal at about 1000°C

Oil gas : It is a mixture of H_2, CH_4, C_2H_4, CO and other gases like CO_2. It is obtaineal by thermal cracking of kerosene oil. It is used in laboratories.

Gobar gas : It contains CH_4, CO and H_2. It is produced by fermentation of gobar in absence of air. It is used as a domestic fuel in villages.

Natural gas : It is a mixture of gaseous hydrocarbons viz methane 85% , ethane, propane butane etc. Liquefied petroleum mainly butane and isobutane.

Coal : On the basis of carbon % and calorific value there are four types of coal.

S.N	Nature	% of carbon	Calorific value
1.	Peat : Low grade coal produces less heat & more smoke & ash.	50 – 60%	2500 – 3500
2.	Lignite : High moisture content burns easily, low calorific value.	60 – 70%	3500 – 4500
3.	Bituminous : Black, hard, smoky, flame, domestic fuel.	75 – 80%	7500 – 8000
4.	Anthracite : Superior quality, hardest form, high calorific value.	90 – 95%	6700 – 7500

11. Metallurgy

The process of extracting metal in pure form from its ore is known as metallurgy.

Minerals : The compound of a metal found in nature is called a mineral. A mineral may be a single compound or a complex mixture.

Ores : Those minerals from which metal can be economically and easily extracted are called ores.

All ores are mineral but all minerals are not ores.

Gangue (or matrix) : The ore is generally associated with earthy impurities like sand, rocks and limestone known as gangue or matrix.

Flux : A substance added to ore to remove impurities is called flux. There are two types of flux— (i) acidic flux. (ii) basic flux.

Acidic flux is added to remove basic impurity

$$\underset{\text{acidic flux}}{SiO_2} + \underset{\text{basic impurity}}{FeO} \longrightarrow \underset{\text{Ferrous silicate}}{FeSiO_3}$$

Basic flux is added to remove acidic impurity.

$$\underset{\text{basic flux}}{CaCO_3} + \underset{\text{acidic impurity}}{SiO_2} \longrightarrow \underset{\text{Calcium silicate}}{CaSiO_3} + CO_2$$

Slag : Combination of gangue with flux in ores forms a fusible material which is called slag.

$$\text{Gangue} + \text{flux} \longrightarrow \text{slag}$$

$$SiO_2 + CaO \longrightarrow CaSiO_3$$

Concentration : The process of removal of gangue from the ore is known as concentration of ore. Concentration of ore can be carried out in the following ways depending upon the nature of the ore.

(i) Gravity separation (ii) Magnetic concentration
(ii) Froth flotation process (iv) Chemical methods

Calcination : Calcination is a process in which ore is heated, generally in the absence of air, to expel water from hydrated oxide or carbon dioxide from a carbonate at temperature below their melting point example :

$$Al_2O_3 \cdot 2H_2O \xrightarrow{\Delta} Al_2O_3 + 2H_2O$$

$$CaCO_3 \xrightarrow{\Delta} CaO + CO_2$$

Roasting : Roasting is a process in which ore is heated usually in the presence of air, at temperatures below its melting points.

$$ZnS + 2O_2 \longrightarrow ZnSO_4; \quad CuS + 2O_2 \longrightarrow CuSO_4$$

Smelting : The reduction of oxide ore with carbon at high temperature is known as smelting.

$$Fe_2O_3 + 3C \longrightarrow 2Fe + 3CO; \quad PbO + C \longrightarrow Pb + CO$$

Important metals and their ores

Metal	Ores	Chemical Formula
Sodium (Na)	Chile saltpeter	$NaNO_3$
	Trona	$Na_2CO_3, 2NaHCO_3 \cdot 3H_2O$
	Borax	$Na_2B_4O_7 \cdot 10H_2O$
	Common salt	$NaCl$
Aluminium (Al)	Bauxite	$Al_2O_3 \cdot 2H_2O$
	Corundum	Al_2O_3
	Felspar	$KAlSi_3O_8$
	Cryolite	Na_3AlF_6
	Alunite	$K_2SO_4 \cdot Al_2(SO_4)_3 \cdot 4Al(OH)_3$
	Kaolin	$3Al_2O_3 \cdot 6SiO_2 \cdot 2H_2O$
Potassium (K)	Nitre (salt peter)	KNO_3
	Carnalite	$KCl \cdot MgCl_2 \cdot 6H_2O$
Magnesium (Mg)	Magnesite	$MgCO_3$
	Dolomite	$MgCO_3 \cdot CaCO_3$
	Epsom salt	$MgSO_4 \cdot 7H_2O$
	Kieserite	$MgSO_4 \cdot H_2O$
	Carnalite	$KCl \cdot MgCl_2 \cdot 6H_2O$

Metal	Ores	Chemical Formula
Calcium (Ca)	Dolomite	$CaCO_3 \cdot MgCO_3$
	Calcite	$CaCO_3$
	Gypsum	$CaSO_4 \cdot 2\,H_2O$
	Fluorspar	CaF_2
	Asbestus	$CaSiO_3 \cdot MgSiO_3$
Strontium (Sr)	Strontianite	$SrCO_3$
	Silestine	$SrSO_4$
Copper (Cu)	Cuprite	Cu_2O
	Copper glance	Cu_2S
	Copper pyrites	$CuFeS_2$
Silver (Ag)	Ruby Silver	$3\,Ag_2\,S \cdot Sb_2S_3$
	Horn Silver	$AgCl$
Gold (Au)	Calaverite	$AuTe_2$
	Silvenites	$[(Ag, Au)\,Te_2]$
Barium (Ba)	Barytes	$BaSO_4$
Zinc (Zn)	Zinc blende	ZnS
	Zincite	ZnO
	Calamine	$ZnCO_3$
Mercury (Hg)	Cinnabar	HgS
Tin (Sn)	Casseterite	SnO_2
Lead (Pb)	Galena	PbS
Antimony (Sb)	Stibenite	Sb_2S_3
Cadmium (Cd)	Greenocite	CdS
Bismuth (Bi)	Bismuthite	Bi_2S_3
Iron (Fe)	Haemetite	Fe_2O_3
	Lemonite	$2Fe_2O_3 \cdot 3H_2O$
	Magnetite	Fe_3O_4
	Siderite	$FeCO_3$
	Iron Pyrite	FeS_2
	Copper Pyrites	$CuFeS_2$
Cobalt (Co)	Smelite	$CoAsS_2$
Nickel (Ni)	Milarite	NiS
Magnese (Mn)	Pyrolusite	MnO_2
	Magnite	$Mn_2O_3 \cdot 2H_2O$
Uranium (U)	Carnetite	$K(UO)_2 \cdot VO_4 \cdot 3H_2O$
	Pitch blende	U_3O_8

Alloys : An alloy is a metallic intimately mixed solid mixture of two or more different elements, at least one of which is metal.

Alloys are homogeneous in molten state but they may be homogeneous or heterogeneous in solid state.

Important alloys & their uses

Alloys	Compositions	Uses
Brass	Cu (70%) + Zn (30%)	In making utensils
Bronze	Cu (90%) + Sn (10%)	In making coins, bell and utensils
German Silver	Cu + Zn + Ni (60% + 20% + 20%)	In making utensils
Rolled gold	Cu (90%) + Al (10%)	In making cheap ornaments
Gun metal	Cu + Sn + Zn + Pb (88% 10% 1% 1%)	In making gun, barrels, gears & bearings
Delta metal	Cu + Zn + Fe (60% 38% 2%)	In making blades of aeroplane
Munz metal	Cu (60%) + Zn (40%)	In making coins
Dutch metal	Cu (80%) + Zn (20%)	In making Artificial ornaments
Monel metal	Cu (70%) + Ni (30%)	For base containing container
Rose metal	Bi + Pb + Sn (50% 28% 22%)	For making automatic fuse
Solder	Pb (50%) + Sn (50%)	For soldering
Magnalium	Al (95%) + Mg (5%)	For frame of Aeroplane
Duralumin	Al + Cu + Mg+ Mn (94% 3% 2% 1%)	For making utensils
Type metal	Sn + Pb + Sb (5% 80% 15%)	In printing industry
Bell metal	Cu (80%) + Sn (20%)	For casting bells, statues
Stainless steel	Fe + Cr + Ni + C (75%,15%,10%,.05%)	For making utensils and surgical cutlery
Nickel steel	Fe (95%) + Ni (5%)	For making electrical wire, automobile parts

Amalgum : An alloy in which one of the component metals is mercury, is called amalgam.

In alloys, the chemical properties of the component elements are retained but certain physical properties are improved.

Compounds of metal and non-metal and their uses :

1. Ferrous oxide (FeO) : In green glass, Ferrous salt.
2. Ferric oxide (Fe_3O_4) : In electroplating of ornaments and formation of ferric slat
3. Ferrous sulphate ($FeSO_4 \cdot 7H_2O$) : In dye industry, and Mohr's salt
4. Ferric hydroxide [($Fe(OH)_3$)] : In laboratory reagent and in making medicines.
5. Iodine (I_2) : (i) As antiseptic, (ii) In making tincture of iodine.
6. Bromine (Br_2) : (i) In dye industry (ii) As laboratory reagent
7. Chlorine (Cl_2) : In the formation of (i) Mustard gas (ii) Bleaching powder

8. Hydrochloric acid (HCl) : In the formation of aquaregia (3 HCl : 1 HNO_3) and dyes
9. Sulphuric acid (H_2SO_4) : (i) As a reagent (ii) In purification of petroleum (iii) In lead storage battery.
10. Sulphur dioxide (SO_2) : (i) As oxidants & reductants (ii) As bleaching agent
11. Hydrogen Sulphides (H_2S) : In qualitative analysis of basic radical (group separation)
12. Sulphur (S) : Antiseptics, vulcanization of rubber, gun powder, medicine.
13. Ammonia (NH_3) : As reagent in ice factory.
14. Phosphorous : (i) Red (P_4) refrigerent, in match industry etc.
    (ii) White (P_4) – Rat killing Medicine.
15. Producer gas ($CO + N_2$) : (i) In heating furnace (ii) Cheap fuel (iii) In Extraction of metal
16. Water gas ($CO + H_2$) : (i) As fuel (ii) Welding work
17. Coal gas : (i) As fuel (ii) Inert atmosphere
18. Nitrous oxide (N_2O) : Laughing gas, Surgery.
19. Carbondioxide (CO_2) : Sodawater, Fire extinguisher.
20. Carbon monoxide (CO) : In phosgene gas ($COCl_2$).
21. Graphite : As electrodes.
22. Diamond : Ornaments, Glass cutting, Rock drilling.
23. Alum [K_2SO_4 Al_2 $(SO_4)_3 \cdot 24$ H_2O] : (i) Purification of water (ii) Leather industry.
24. Aluminium sulphate [$Al_2(SO_4)_3 \cdot 18H_2O$] : In paper industry / fire extinguisher.
25. Anhydrous aluminium chloride ($AlCl_3$) : Cracking of petroleum.
26. Mercuric Chloride ($HgCl_2$) : Calomel, Insecticides (Corrosive sublimate)
27. Mercuric oxide (HgO) : Oientment, poison.
28. Mercury (Hg) : Thermometer vermillion, amalgum.
29. Zinc Sulphide (ZnS) : White pigment.
30. Zinc Sulphate (White vitriol) ($ZnSO_4 \cdot 7H_2O$) : Lithopone, Eye ointment.
31. Zinc Chloride ($ZnCl_2$) : Textile industry.
32. Zinc oxide (ZnO) : Ointment.
33. Zinc (Zn) : In battery.
34. Calcium carbide (CaC_2) : Calcium cyanide & acetylene gas.
35. Bleaching powder [Ca(OCl) Cl] : Insecticides, Bleaching actions.
36. Plaster of paris [$(CaSO_4)_2 \cdot 2H_2O$ / $CaSO_4$ ½ H_2O)] : Statue, Surgery.
37. Calcium sulphate ($CaSO_4 \cdot 2H_2O$) : Cement industry.
38. Calcium carbonate ($CaCO_3$) : Lime & toothpaste.

39. Copper sulphate ($CuSO_4 \cdot 5H_2O$) : Insecticides, Electric cells.
40. Cupric oxide (CuO) : Blue & green glass, purification of petroleum
41. Cuprous Oxide (Cu_2O) : Red glass, pesticides.
42. Copper (Cu) : Electrical wire.
43. Sodium nitrate ($NaNO_3$) : Fertilizer.
44. Sodium Sulphate (Glauber salt) ($Na_2SO_4 \cdot 10H_2O$) : Medicine, cheap glass
45. Sodium bicarbonate (Baking soda) ($NaHCO_3$) : Fire extinguisher, bakery, reagent.
46. Sodium Carbonate (Washing soda) : (i) Glass industry (ii) Paper industry (iii) Removal of permanent hardness of water (iv) washing
47. Hydrogen peroxide (H_2O_2) : Oxidants & reductants, Insecticides.
48. Heavy water (D_2O) : Nuclear reactor.
49. Liquid hydrogen : Rocket fuel.

12. Important Facts About Some Metals

- Zinc phosphide is used for killing rats.
- Wood furnitures are coated with zinc chloride to prevent termites.
- Excess of copper in human beings causes disease called Wilson.
- Galvanised iron is coated with zinc.
- Rusting of iron is a chemical change which increases the weight of iron.
- Calcium hydride is called hydrolith.
- Calcium hydride is used to prepare fire proof and waterproof clothes.
- In flash-blub, magnesium wire is kept in atmosphere of nitrogen gas.
- Titanium is called strategic metal because it is lighter than iron.
- Group 1st element are called alkali metals because its hydroxides are alkaline whereas group 2nd elements are called alkaline earth metals.
- Babbitt metal contains 89% Sn (Tin), 9% Sb (Antimony) and 2% Cu (Copper).
- Gun powder contains 75% Potassium nitrate, 10% sulphur and 15% charcoal.
- Chromium trioxide is known as chromic acid.
- Nichrome wire is used in electrical heater [(Ni, Cr, Fe)]
- Potassium carbonate (K_2CO_3) is known as pearl ash.
- Generally transition metals and their compounds are coloured.
- Zeolite is used to remove hardness of water.
- In cytochrome iron (Fe) is present.
- Selenium metal is used in photo electric cell.
- Galium metal is liquid at room temperature.
- Palladium metal is used in aeroplane.
- Radium is extracted from pitchblende.
- World famous Eiffel Tower has steel and cement base.
- Actinides are radio-active elements.

- ➢ Cadmium rod is used in nuclear reactor to slow down the speed of neutron.
- ➢ Sodium peroxide is used in submarine and also to purify closed air in hospital.
- ➢ Co (60) is used in cancer treatment.
- ➢ Onion and garlic odour due to potassium.
- ➢ Oxides of metals are alkaline.
- ➢ Silver and copper are the best conductor of electricity.
- ➢ Gold and Silver are the most malleable metal.
- ➢ Mercury and iron produces more resistance in comparison to the other during the flow of electricity.
- ➢ Lithium is the lightest and the most reductant element.
- ➢ In fireworks, crimson red colour is due to presence of strontium (Sr).
- ➢ Green colour is due to the presence of Barium in fireworks.
- ➢ Barium sulphate is used in X-ray of abdomen as barium meal.
- ➢ Barium hydroxide is known as Baryta water.
- ➢ Osmium is the heaviest metal and the Platinum is the hardest.
- ➢ Zinc oxide is known as flower of zinc. It is also known as chinese white and used as white paint.
- ➢ Silver chloride is used in photochromatic glass.
- ➢ Silver iodide is used in artificial rain.
- ➢ Silver nitrate is used as marker during election. It is kept in coloured bottle to avoid decomposition.
- ➢ Silver spoon is not used in egg food because it forms black silver sulphide.
- ➢ To harden the gold, copper is mixed. Pure gold is 24 carrat.
- ➢ Iron Pyrites (FeS_2) is known as fool's gold.
- ➢ Mercury is kept in iron pot because it doesn't form amalgum with iron.
- ➢ In tubelight there is the vapour of mercury and argon.
- ➢ Tetra-Ethyl lead is used as anti knocking compound.
- ➢ Lead-pipe is not used for drinking water because it forms poisonous lead hydroxide.
- ➢ Fuse wire is made up of lead and tin.

13. Non metal

In modern periodic table there are 24 non metals. 11 are gases, 1 is liquid (Br_2) and 12 are solid.

Electronegative elements are non metals.

Non metals are bad conductor of heat and electricity except graphite, Si & Ge are semi conductor.

Hydrogen (H_2)

The lightest gas having three isotopes

${}_1H^1$,	${}_1H^2$,	${}_1H^3$.
Protium	Deuterium	Tritium (Radioactive)

Protium is only one isotope in Periodic Table having zero neutron.

Deuterium oxide is known as heavy water and used in nuclear reactor as moderator.

Liquid hydrogen is used as rocket fuel.

Hydrogen is known as range element because it may kept in group I & group VII A.

Water (H_2O)

Hard water – Less froth with soap

Soft water – more froth with soap.

Hard water – Due to the presence of soluble impurities of bicarbonates, chlorides & sulphates of Ca & Mg.

Temporary hardness – Due to the presence of bicarbonate of calcium and magnesium.

Permanent hardness – Due to the presence of chlorides and sulphates of calcium and magnesium.

Temporary hardness is removed by boiling and by Clark's method while permanent hardness is removed by Soda ash (Na_2CO_3) process.

Permanent hardness is also removed by permutit process.

Oxygen

Important constituent of air, exists in three different isotopes.

$_8O^{16}$, $_8O^{17}$, $_8O^{18}$

Ozone (O_3) is the allotrope of Oxygen.

Ozone reduces the effect of ultraviolet rays in the atmosphere.

Nitrogen

78% by volume in atmosphere, liquid nitrogen is used for refrigeration.

Ammonia is an important compound of N_2 which is prepared by Haber's process.

Ammonia

As refrigerent, In the manufacture of HNO_3.

In fertilizer like urea, ammonium sulphate etc.

In the manufacture of Na_2CO_3 & $NaHCO_3$.

In preparation of ammonium salt.

In preparation of explosive.

In preparation of Artificial silk.

Nitrogen fixation in leguminous plants

Phosphorous

An important constituent of animals and plants. It is present in bones & DNA.

Phosphorous shows allotropy – White or yellow phosphorous, Red phosphorous, Black phosphorous etc.

White phosphorous is more reactive than red phosphorous.

Halogens

17th group elements

Uses of fluorine : In the preparation of UF_6 and SF_6 for energy production and as dielectric constant respectively.

By using HF, chloro fluoro carbon compound and polytetra fluoro ethylene can be synthesised.

Chlorofluoro carbon is known as Freon used as refrigerent and aerosol.

Non-stick utensil is made up of teflon.

Chlorine is used to prepare PVC, insecticides herbicides etc.

Bromine is used in ethylene bromide synthesis which is mixed with leaded pertrol. In the preparation of AgBr which is used in photography.

Inert gases

It belongs to 18th group of P.T.

He, Ne, Ar, Kr, Xe, Rn

Except Rn, all inert gases are present in atmosphere.

Argon is used in Arc. welding & electric bulb.

Helium is light & non-inflammable so, used in balloon, weather indicator etc.

Neon is used in discharge tube glow light.

14. Common Facts

	Catalyst	Process
1.	Fe + Mo	Synthesis of NH_3 by Haber's process.
2.	Ni	Synthesis of vanaspati Ghee (hydrogenation)
3.	Pt	Synthesis of H_2SO_4 by Contact process.
4.	NO	In the manufacture of H_2SO_4 by the Lead chamber process.
5.	Hot Al_2O_3	In the preparation of Ether from Alcohol.
6.	$CuCl_2$	Preparation of chlorine gas by Deacon process.

Some Important Explosive

- Dynamite : It was discovered Alfred Nobel in 1863. It is prepared by absorption of raw dust with Nitro-glycerine. In modern dynamite Sodium Nitrate is used in place of Nitro-glycerine.
- Tri Nitro Toluene (TNT)
- Tri Nitro Benzene (TNB)
- Tri Nitro Phenol (TNP) : It is also known as picric acid.
- R.D.X is highly explosive known as plastisizer in which Aluminium powder is mixed to increase the temperature and the speed of fire.

Some Important Facts

- Age of fossils and archeological excavation is determined by radioactive carbon (C^{14}).
- Diamond has maximum refractive index and due to total internal reflection. It has lustre.

- Chloroform in sunlight forms poisonous gas 'Phosgene' ($COCl_2$).
- To decrease the basicity of soil gypsum is used.
- In the preparation of Talcom powder theo phestal mineral is used.
- Potassium chloride is most suitable for the removal of permanent hardness of water.
- To avoid melting of ice gelatine is used.
- When dry ice is heated it is directly converted into gas.
- Saccharine is prepared from toluene.
- Cream is a type of milk in which amount of fat is increased while amount of water decrease.
- From one kilogram of honeybee 3500 calorie energy is produces.
- N_2O is known as laughing gas.
- Bones contain about 58% calcium phosphate.
- Phosphine gas is used in voyage as Holmes signal.
- Chlorine gas bleaches the colour of flower.
- Red phosphorus is used in match industry.
- Urea contains 46% nitrogen.
- In the electroplating of vessel NH_4Cl is used.
- Power alcohol is prepared from mixing pure alcohol in benzene which is used as rocket fuel.
- Artificial perfumes are prepared from Ethyl acetate.
- Urea was the first organic compound synthesised in Laboratory.
- Vinegar contains 10% acetic acid.
- Acetylene is used for light production.
- Ferric chloride is used to stop bleeding.
- Barium is responsible for green colour in fireworks.
- Cesium is used in solar cells.
- Yellow phosphorus is kept in water.
- Sea weeds contains iodine.
- During cooking maximum vitamin is lost.
- For the preparation of silver mirror, glucose is used.
- When cream is separated from milk, it's density increases.
- For artificial respiration mixture of oxygen and helium gas cylinder is used.
- In cold places, to decrease the freezing point ethylene glycol is used.
- Hydrogen peroxide is used for oil paintings.
- Sodium is kept in kerosene oil.
- The heaviest element is Osmium (Os).
- The lightest element, least dense and most reductant is lithium (Li).
- Flourine is the most oxidising agent.
- Silver is the best conductor of electricity.
- Radon is the heaviest gas.

- ➢ Polonium has the maximum number of isotopes.
- ➢ Sulphuric acid is known as oil of vitriol.
- ➢ Noble metals — Ag, Au, Pt, Ir, Hg, Pd, Rh, Ru, and Os.

15. Man made substances

1. Fertilizers : The substances added to the soil to make up the deficiency of essential elements are known as fertilizers, these are either natural or synthetic (chemical). For a chemical fertilizer, the following requirements should be met :

(i) It must be sufficiently soluble in water

(ii) It should be stable so that the element in it may be available for a longer time.

(iii) It should contain nothing injurious to plants.

Among the chemical fertilizers the two important categories are :

Phosphatic Fertilizers : All naturally occurring phosphates are orthophosphates, the most abundant of these being rock phosphate [$Ca_3(PO_4)_2$], which is mostly consumed by the fertilizer industry in the manufacture of 'superphosphate of lime', 'triple superphosphate' and 'nitrophos'— a combined phosphatic and nitrogenous fertilizer. Other phosphatic fertilizers are ammoninum dihydrogen orthophosphate and diammonium hydrogen orthophosphate, which also conteract nitrogen dificiency.

Nitrogenous Fertilizers : Plants need nitrogen for rapid growth and increase in their protein content. For this reason, nitrogenous fertilizers become more important. The chief nitrogeneous fertilizers are ammonium sulphate, calcium cyanamide, sodium nitrate, ammonium nitrate, urea, diammo-nium phosphate and ammonium phosphate.

2. Dyes : Coloured substances used for colouring textiles, foodstuffs, silk, wool, etc. are called dyes.

Different classes of dyes are given below.

(i) Nitro dyes : These are polynitro derivatives of phenol where nitro group acts as a chromophore and hydroxyl group as auxochrome. These are less important industrially because the colours are not fast.

(ii) Azo dyes : These are an important class of dyes and are characterised by the presence of azo group (—N=N—) as the chromophore. The groups like NH_2, NR_2 or —OH, etc., present in the molecule containing one or more azo gruops act as the auxochromes.

(iii) Triphenylmethane dyes : These dyes contain the paraquinoid moiety as a chromophore and —OH, —NH_2 or —NR_2 as auxochrome. These dyes are not fast to light and washing and hence are mainly used for colouring paper or typewriter ribbons, e.g. malachite green which is used for dyeing wool and silk directly and cotton after mordanting with tannin.

(iv) Mordant dyes : Those dyes which are fixed on the fibre with the help of a mordant are known as mordant dyes. For acidic dyes, basic mordants (such as hydroxides of iron, aluminium and chromium) are used, while for basic dyes, acidic mordants (like tannic acid) are used. Here the fabric is first dipped into a solution of mordant and then into the dye solution. The colour produced depends on the nature of the mordant used.

(v) Vat dyes : These are water insoluble dyes and are introduced into the fibre in its (soluble) reduced form, also known as *leuco* form (colourless). These are called vat dyes because reducing operation (using sodium hydrosulphite) was formerly carried out in wooden vats. Indigo is a vat dye and is used for dyeing cotton.

Cement : It is a complex material containing the silicates of calcium and aluminium. A paste of it in water sets into a hard rocky mass-called the setting of cement. A paste of sand, cement and water called mortar, is very conveniently used for joining bricks and plastering walls.

A mixture of stone chips (gravel) sand cement and water, known as concrete. Sets harder than ordinary mortar. It is used for flooring and making roads. Concrete with steel bars and wires called reinforced concrete (RC) forms a very strong material. It is used for constructing roofs, bridges and pillars.

Glass : Supercooled liquid is called glass. SiO_2 is it's common constituent.

(a) Soda glass or soda lime glass : It is Sodium calcium silicate (Na_2O CaO 5 SiO_2). It is the cheapest of all glasses and used for making window panes and bottles and easily attacked by chemicals.

(b) Potash glass : It contains potassium in place of sodium. it has higher softening temperature as also a greater resistance to chemicals. So used for chemical apparatus; beakers, flasks, funnels etc.

(c) Optical glass: It is used for making lenses, prisms and optical instruments like telescopes and microscopes. It contains boric oxide (B_2O_3) and silica (SiO_2)

Types : (i) Crown glass : Contains K_2O & BaO as the basic oxide

(ii) Flint glass : Contains PbO as the basic oxide.

(d) Crooks glass: for spectacles : Absorbs ultraviolet rays which are harmful for the eyes.

(e) Lead crystal and crystal glass : Lead glass sparkles used for making decorative items. It contains 24% or more of PbO called lead crystal. If it contains term than 24% lead oxide called crystal glass.

(f) Borosilicate glass : It contains less alkali (K_2O or CaO_3) and more SiO_2 than potash glass and some B_2O

(g) Coloured glass :

Colour	Substance added to the glass melt
Red	Selenium (Se) or copper (I) oxide (Cu_2O)
Green	Chromium III oxide (Cr_2O_3)
Violed	Maganese IV oxide (MnO_2)
Blue	Copper II oxide eno or cobalt II oxide (CoO)
Brown	Er on III oxide (Fe_2O_3)

It is used for making artificial jewellery, crockery and stained glass windows.

(h) Milky glass : Milky glass is prepared by adding tin oxide (SnO_2). Calcium phosphate ($Ca_3(PO_4)_2$) or cryolite (AH_33NaF) to the melt glass. All these substances are white so look milky.

(i) Glass laminates : It is made by fixing polymer sheets between layers of glass. It is used to make windows & Screens of cars, trains and aircraft specially manufactured glass laminates are used bulletproof material.

Some common man-made polymers and their uses.

Polymer	Use
Polythene	Packaging material, carry bags, bottles.
Polypropene	Bottles, Crates.
Polyvinyl chloride (PVC)	Pipes insulation
Nylon (Polyester)	Fibres, ropes
Teflon	Nonstick kitchen ware
Vinyl rubber	Rubber erasers
Polystyrene	Foam Thermocole
Poly (Styrene butadiene)	Rubber bubble gum
Bakelite	Electrical insulation buttons
Lexan	Bullet proof glass
Melamine	Crockery

Paints : Chemical, contains a pigment as a vehicle and a thinner.

White pigment : Zinc oxide, white lead and titanium dioxide. The pigment is mixed with a vehicle, which is an oil like *linseed* or *soyabean oil* or a *polymer*. A thinner is a solvent such as *turpentine oil* or *kerosene*.

Luminous paints : Glow when exposed to light. Paints are applied on a surface to protect it from corrosion and weathering or to give it an attractive look.

Soaps and Detergents : Soaps are the sodium or Potassium salts of fatty acids. They are made by the saponification of fats. Detergents are made from some petroleum products.

Antibiotic : Medicinal compounds produced by moulds and bacteria, capable of destroying or preventing the growth of bacteria in animal systems.

Antibody : Kinds of substances formed in the blood, tending to inhibit or destroy harmful bacteria, etc.

Antidote : Medicine used against a poison, or to prevent a disease from having effect.

Antigen : Substance capable of stimulating formation of antibodies.

Antimony : A brittle, crystalline, silvery white metal.

Antipyretie : A substance used to lower body temperature.

Pesticides : Many living organism destroy crops or eat away grains. They are collectively known as pests. To kill chemical used called pesticides.

Insecticides : D.D.T. aluminium phosphate gammexine.

Fungicide : Thiram, Bordeanx mixture $CaCaSO_45H_2O + (OH)_2$

Rodenticides : Aluminium phosphide.

Herbicides : Benzipram, benzadox.

Medicines : To cure diseases by biological changes in the body.

Analgesics : Painkillers are called analgesics eg, Aspirin, Paracetamol and morphine.

Antimalarial drugs : Used to treat malaria quinine derivatives eg, chlovoquine.

Destroy microorganism : Penicillin, Aminogly considers, oftoxaim, Homophonic.

Sulphadrugs: Alternatives of antibiotics, sulphanilamide, sulphadiazine, Sulpha gunamidine.

Antaoxide : Substances which remove the excess acid and raise the pH to appropriate level in scotch are called antacids. It is caused by excess of HCl in the gastric juice magnesium hydrate, magazines carbonate, magnesium truistical, aluminium phosphene are common antacids.

Epsom salt : Hydrated magnesium sulphate ($MgSO_4 \cdot 7H_2O$), used in medicines to empty bowels.

Chloroform : A sweetish, colourless liquid. It is used as a solvent and anaesthetic.

Saccharin : A white crystalline solid which is 550 times sweeter than sugar, but does not have any food value. It is used by diabetic patients.

DDT : Dichloro diphenyl tricholoro ethane, a white powder used as an insecticide.

★★★

8 BIOLOGY

1. Introduction

Biology – Branch of science in which living beings are studied.

Bios = Life & *Logos* = Study. Therefore study of life is called *biology.* The term *biology* was first coined by *Lamarck* and *Treviranus* in the year 1801. Biology has two main branch.

1. **Botany :** Study of different aspects of plants. *Theophrastus* is known as father of Botany.

2. **Zoology :** Study of various aspects of animals. *Aristotle* is called father of Zoology as well as Biology.

Important Terms of Biology :

- Anatomy : Study of internal structure of organism.
- Agrology : Soil science dealing specially with production of crop.
- Agronomy : Science of soil management and production of crop.
- Agrostology : Study of grass.
- Arthrology : Study of joints.
- Apiculture : Rearing of honey bee for honey.
- Anthropology : Study of origin, development and relationship between the culture of past and present human.
- Anthology : Study of flower and flowering plant.
- Angiology : Study of blood vascular system including arteries and veins.
- Andrology : Study of male reproductive organ.
- Bryology : Study of Bryophytes.
- Biometrics : Statical study of Biological problem.
- Biomedical engineering : Production and designing of spare part for overcoming various defects in man. e.g. artificial limbs, Iron lung, Pacemaker etc.
- Biotechnology : Technology concerned with living beings for wilful manipulation on molecular level.
- Bacteriology : Study of bacteria.
- Cytology : Study of cell.
- Cryobiology : It is the study of effect of low temperature on organisms and their preservation.
- Clone : Clones are geneticaly identical individual in a population.
- Cardiology : Study of heart.
- Demography : Study of population.
- Diffusion : Random movement of molecule / ion or gases from a region of higher concentration to lower concentration.
- Dermatology : Study of skin.

- Dendrochronology : Counting and analysing annual growth rings of tree to know its age.
- Ecology : Study of inter-relationship between living and their environment.
- Evolution : Study of origin of life, variation and formation of new species.
- Embryology : Study of fertilization of egg, formation of zygote and development of embryo.
- Eugenics : Study of factors connected with the improvement of human race.
- Euthenics : Study of environmental condition that contribute to the improvement of human beings.
- Euphenics : Treatment of defective in heredity through genetics engineering.
- Ethnology : Study of science dealing with different races of human.
- Ethology : Study of animal behaviour in their natured habitats.
- Etiology : Study of causative agent of disease.
- Entomology : Study of insects.
- Exobiology: Study of possibility of life in space.
- Floriculture : Cultivation of plant for flower.
- Food technology : Scientific processing, preservation, storage and transportation of food.
- Forensic science : Application of science for identification of various facts of civilian.
- Fishery : Catching, breeding, rearing and marketing of fishes.
- Forestry : Development and management of forest.
- Fermentation: Process of incomplete oxidation that occur in microbes and other cells in absence of oxygen, leading to the formation of ethyl alcohol.
- Genetics : Study of variation and transmission of heredity character from parents to their young ones.
- Growth : Permanent increase in weight, volume and size of an organism.
- Genetic Engineering : Manipulation of gene in order to improve the organism.
- Gynecology : Study of female reproductive organ.
- Gerontology : Study of ageing.
- Gastroenterology : Study of alimentary canal or stomach, intestine and their disease.
- Hypertonic : When two solution have differcut sdute concentration. The sol at ion which have higher concentration is called hypertonic.
- Hypotonic : In two solutions which have lower solute concentration is called hypotonic

- ➢ Homeothermic : Animals who have constant body temperature are called home thermic or warmblooded animal.
- ➢ Histology : Study of tissue organisation and their internal structure with the help of microscope.
- ➢ Hygiene : Science taking care of health.
- ➢ Hydroponics : Study of growing plant without soil in water which contain nutrient.
- ➢ Haematology : Study of blood.
- ➢ Hepatology : Study of liver.
- ➢ Ichthyology : Study of fishes.
- ➢ Immunology : Study of immun system or resistance of body to disease.
- ➢ Kalology : Study of human beauty.
- ➢ Metazoans : All multicellular animals are called metazoans.
- ➢ Monoecious : Plant which have both male and female flower
- ➢ Morphology : Study of external structure.
- ➢ Microbiology : Study of micro-organism like virus, bacteria, algae, fungi and protozoa.
- ➢ Molecular biology : Study of molecule found in the body of living organism.
- ➢ Medicine : Study of treating disease by drug.
- ➢ Mammography : Branch of science which deal test of breast cancer.
- ➢ Mycology : Study of fungi.
- ➢ Nutrients : Chemical substance taken as food which are necessary for various function, growth and heath of living.
- ➢ Neurology : Study of nervous system.
- ➢ Neonatology : Study of new born.
- ➢ Nephrology : Study of kidneys.
- ➢ Osmosis : Movement of water molecule across semipermeable membrane from the region of its higher concentration to the region of lower communication.
- ➢ Odontology : Study of teeth and gum.
- ➢ Osteology : Study of bones.
- ➢ Oncology : Study of cancer and tumours.
- ➢ Obstetrics : Science related with care of pregnant women before, during and after child birth.
- ➢ Ornithology : Study of birds.
- ➢ Ophthalmology : Study of eyes.
- ➢ Orthopaedics : Diagnosis and repair of disorder of locomotery system.
- ➢ Phytoplanlktons : Microscopic organism which passively float on the surface of water.
- ➢ Parasite : Organism which depend on other living organism for their food and shelter.

- ➢ Poikilothermic : Organism which change their body temperature according to surrounding. These are also called cold blooded animal.
- ➢ Pigment : A substance which absorb light of certain wavelength like chlorophyll found in green leaves.
- ➢ Paleontology : Study of fossils.
- ➢ Physiology : Study of function of various system of organism.
- ➢ Pathology : Study of diseases, effects, causable agents and transmission of pathogens.
- ➢ Pomology : Study of fruit and fruit yielding plant.
- ➢ Psychiatry : Treatment of mental disease.
- ➢ Psychology : Study of human mind and behavior.
- ➢ Pisciculture : Rearing of fishes.
- ➢ Phycology : Study of algae.
- ➢ Paediatrics : Branch of medicine dealing with children.
- ➢ Parasitology : Study of parasites.
- ➢ Photobiology : Effect of light on various biological processes.
- ➢ Phylogeny : Evolutionary history of organism.
- ➢ Physiotherapy : Treatment of body defects through massage and exercise.
- ➢ Radiology : Science dealing with the effect of radiation on living beings.
- ➢ Rhinology : Study of nose and olfactory organs.
- ➢ Sonography : Study of ultrasound imaging.
- ➢ Saurology : Study of lizards.
- ➢ Serology : Study of serum, interaction of antigen and antibodies in the blood.
- ➢ Sphygmology : Study of pulse and arterial pressure.
- ➢ Taxonomy : Study of classification, nomenclature and identification of organism.
- ➢ Telepathy : Communication of thoughts or ideas from one mind to another without normal use of senses. In other word this is the process of mental contact.
- ➢ Veterinary Science : Science of health care and treatment of domestic animals.

2. What is living ?

- ➢ The word living cannot be defined.
- ➢ There are certain characters by which can be distinguished from non living.
  - (i) Growth : Increase in the number of cell or mass is called growth
  - (ii) Reproduction : Living organism produce young ones of their same kind.
  - (iii) metabolism : Chemical reaction occurring inside a living cell.
  - (iv) Response of stimuli : Living have the ability to sense the condition of their surrounding and respond to these stimuli

3. Classification of Organism

- There are millions of organisms. It is impossible to study each individual separately. Classification means to categories organism into different groups. Study of an individual of a group gives us the idea of rest of the member of that group.
- *Linnaeus* divide all organism into two kingdoms - *Planate* and *Animalia* in his book "*System a Nature*". The foundation of modern classification system was laid in the line of classification system started by *Linnaeus*. Therefore *Linnaeus* is called '*Father of Taxonomy*'. Due to disputed position of organism like bacteria, virus, fungi and euglena, there is a need of reconsideration of system of classification.

Five Kingdom Classification

- Five Kingdom Classification was proposed in 1969 by *R.H. Whittaker*. The criteria of classifying organism into five kingdoms are its *complexity of cell structure, complexity of body of organism, mode of nutrition, life style and phylogenetic relationship*.

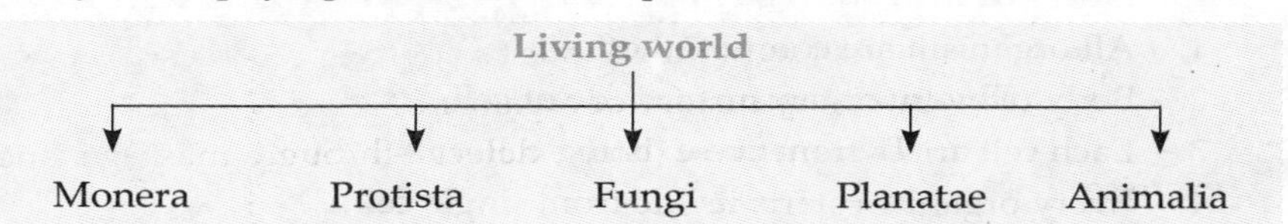

1. Monera: It includes all prokaryotic organism like bacteria, cynobacteria and archiobactera. Filamentous bacteria also come under this kingdom. All organism of this kingdom are microscopic.

2. Protista : This kingdom includes unicellular form usually found in aquatic habitats. On the basis of mode of nutrition they are autotrophic, parasitic, and saprophytic. Diatoms flagellates and protozoa come under this kingdom. *Euglena* have both heterotrophic and autotrophic mode of nutrition. So, it is placed between plant and animal.

3. Fungi : This kingdom includes non-green plants. It has saprophytic nutrition and growing on dead and decaying organic matter. The cell wall is composed of chitin. Example : *Mushroom, Mucor, Albugo* etc.

4. Planatae : This kingdom includes all plants except some algae, diatoms, fungi and member of monera and protista.

5. Animalia : Almost all animal comes under this kingdom except protozoan.

- **Binomial nomenclature :** There was the need of uniform international naming of organism. In biology every organism is given two proper names. The first name is *genus* name always started with capital letter and the second name is *species* started with small letter. For example scientific name of human is *Homo sapiens*. Homo is the name of genus, whose one species is sapiens.

Scientific Names of some Organisms

Man	*Homo sapiens*	Frog	*Rana tigrina*
Cat	*Felis domestica*	Dog	*Canis familaris*

Cow	*Bos indicus*	Housefly	*Musca domestica*
Mango	*Mangifera indica*	Rice	*Oryza sativa*
Wheat	*Triticum aestivum*	Pea	*Pisum sativum*
Gram	*Cicer arietinum*	Mustard	*Brassica campestris*

4. Study of Cell

➢ **Cell** : Cell is the basic structural and functional unit of life.

➢ The word *'cell'* was first coined by British scientist *Robert Hook* in the year 1665.

➢ The smallest cell is *Mycoplasma gallisepticum*.

➢ The longest cell is *Neuron*.

➢ The biggest cell is *egg of Ostrich*.

➢ Schilden and Schwan established cell theory in the year 1838-39.

Main features of the cell theory :

1. All organism are composed of cell.
2. Body of every organism is made of cell.
3. Each cell arises from pre-existing cell.
4. Every organism starts its life from single cell.

Cell is of two kinds

1. **Prokaryotic cell** : These are primitive cell having three basic structure of typical cell but lack nuclear membrane. Nuclear material is present in a region of cytoplasm called nucleoid. Other membrane bound organelles are absent such as mitochondria, ribosome, golgi bodies etc. Ex.- Virus, bacteria and cynobacteria are Prokaryotes.

2. **Eukaryotic cell** : These are complete cell which contain membrane bound organelles and nucleus. Unicellular and multicellular plant and animal have Eurkaryotic cell.

Difference between Prokaryotes and Eukaryotes

Prokaryotes	Eukaryotes
1. Size of cell is generally small.	1. Size of cell is generally large.
2. Nucleus absent.	2. Nucleus present.
3. It contain single chromosome which is circular in shape.	3. It contains more than one chromosome
4. Membrane bound cell organelles are absent.	4. Cell organelles present.
5. Cell division takes place by fission or budding.	5. Cell division takes place by mitosis and meiosis.

➢ **Structure of typical cell** : A cell have following structure.

1. **Cell wall** : In plant cell there is a rigid cell wall which is non living and freely permeable. It is made up of cellulose and chitin. It provide shape and rigidity to the cell.

2. Cell membrane : It is also known as *plasma membrane* which form the outer covering of animal cell. In plant cell it is found within cell wall. It is thin, elastic, living, double layer, permeable membrane. It is made up of phospholipid molecules.

Function : It regulates movement of molecules inside and outside of the cell.

3. Protoplasm : The whole fluid present inside plasma-membrane is protoplasm. The name protoplasm is given by *Purkenje* in 1839. Protoplasm is made up of various chemical substances like water, ions, salt and organic molecule. It is the living part of cell. Protoplasm is divided into two parts.

A. Cytoplasm : The fluid found outside the nuclear membrane.

B. Nucleoplasm : The fluid found inside the nuclear membrane.

4. Mitochondria : Discovered by *Altman* in the year 1886. These are cylindrical, rod shaped or spherical structure found in cytoplasm. It is surrounded by double layered membrane. Inner membrane has many fold called *cristae*. The fluid present inside mitochondria is called *matrix*, which contain many enzyme and co-enzyme.

Function : Mitochondria is the respiratory site of cellular respiration. Mitochondria synthesize energy rich compound ATP. It is also known as "Power Hosue" of the cell.

5. Golgi bodies : Discovered by scientist *Camilo Golgi*. Golgi bodies are made up of group of tubes, vesicles and vacuoles. In plant it is more in number and here it is known as dictyosomes.

Function : It work as storage, processing and packaging of material. It also involved in the synthesis of cell wall, plasma membrane and lysosomes.

6. Endoplasmic reticulum : Membranous network of tubules like structure found in cytoplasm is called *endoplasmic reticulum*. It is attached with the nucleus on one side and on other side it is joined with plasma membrane.

Function : Endoplasmic reticulum helps in the distribution of material. It forms supporting framework of cell.

7. Ribosome : Discovered by *Palade*. Small granules like structure found attached to the endoplasmic reticulum or in free state.It is made up of ribonucleic acid. (RNA)

Function : Take part in protein synthesis.

8. Lysosome : Discovered by *De Duve*. These are sac like structure bounded by single membrane and contain hydrolytic enzyme.

Function : It helps in intracellular digestion. The enzyme found in lysosome may digest the entire cell. So it is also known as suicidal bag.

9. Centrosome : Discovered by *Boveri*. It is only found in animal cell taking part in cell division. It is not bounded by membrane consist of two centriole.

Function : Help in the formation of spindle fibre during cell division.

10. Plastid : Only found in plant cell. It is of three type : (a) Chloroplast (b) Chromoplast (c) Leucoplast.

(a) Chloroplasts : These are green pigment found in green plant involve in photosynthesis. So, it is known as '*Kitchen of the cell*'. Chloroplast is bounded by two unit membrane having grana and stroma. Grana are membrane bounded sac like structure found in stacks containing chlorophyll molecule. Stroma is the matrix present inside the chloroplast which contain photosynthetic enzymes and starch grain. Granum is the site of light reaction during photosynthesis while stroma is the site of dark reaction.

Function : Chloroplast provides green colour to plant & take part in photosynthesis.

(b) Chromoplast provides various colours to the plant.

(c) Leucoplast is colourless. It stores the food in the form of starch, fat & protein.

11. Vacoule : These are fluid filled single membrane bounded, dead organelles of cell. In plant cell it is larger in size but in animal it is smaller in size.

Function : It helps in osmoregulation. It stores toxic metabolic waste.

12. Nucleus : The nucleus is a spherical, centrally located is a major structure found in the cell. In plant cell it is shifted towards periphery. It is bounded by double layered nuclear membrane having pore. Within nucleoplasm nucleolus and chromatin material is present. Nucleolus is rich in protein and RNA. Chromatin material is thin thread like structure forming network. This is made up of genetic substance DNA (deoxyribo nucleic acid) and histone protein. During cell division chromatin breaks into pieces and forms chromosome.

Function : It controls all the activity of cells. So it is also known as "control room "of cell. Chromatin transmits hereditary characters from parents to their offspring.

Difference between Plant and Animal cells

Plant cell	Animal Cell
1. Plant cells are larger in size.	1. Animal cells are generally smaller in size.
2. Cell wall present, made up of cellulose and chitin.	2. Cell wall absent.
3. Plastid present.	3. Plastid absent.
4. Centrosome absent.	4. Centrosome present.
5. Vacuoles are larger in size	5. Vacoules are smaller in size.

Chromosome

➢ Chromosome is thread like structure found in the nucleus. It becomes visible during cell division. Each chromosome is made up of two chromatids joined together at a point centromere. Bead like structure found on chromosome is called *gene*. Genes are made up of DNA (deoxyribo nucleic acid) which is the carrier of genetic information from generation to generation. In some viruses RNA is the genetic material called *rietrovirus*. In prokaryotes there is only one chromosome, like bacteria and viruses.

➢ Eukaryotic cell posses many chromosome. A particular kind of species have definite number of chromosome in their cell, which are in pair known as *diploid*. The set of unpaired chromosome is called *haploid*. Gametes have haploid set of chromosome.

Number of chromosome in different organism

Pegion	40 pairs	Dog	39 pairs	Horse	32 pairs
Chimpanzee	24 pairs	Human	23 pairs	Wheat	21 pairs
Cat	19 pairs	Frog	13 pairs	Tomato	12 pairs
Onion	8 pairs	Pea	7 pairs	Ascaris	1 pairs

➢ **Nucleic Acid :** Nucleic acid is complex organic compound found in cell. It contains special genetic instruction in coded form. Nucleic acids are of two kinds.

A. Deoxyribo nucleic Acid (DNA) : *Frederic Meischer* was the first who isolated DNA from the nucleus of pus cells. DNA is a macromolecule in which large number of nucleotides are present. Chemically a nucleotide has three components. (1) Nitrogen base (2) Sugar (3) Phosphate group.

➢ Nitrogen base are of two type—*Purines* & *Pyrimidines*. Purines contain two nitrogen base—*Adinine* and *Guanine*. Pyrimidine nitrogen base are *Thymine* and *Cytosine*. Thus there are four kinds of nucleotides present in DNA.

Watson and *Crick* give the structural model of DNA—

1. DNA molecule is consists of two polynucleotide strand, forming a *double helix*. Each strand has a backbone of sugar and phosphate. Nitrogen base is attached to the sugar.

2. Nitrogenous base of the two strands of a double helix form a pair with the help of hydrogen bonds. Adenine pairs with thymine where as guanine pairs with cytosine. Adenine and thymine are complementary to each other and cytosine is complementary to guanine. Hydrogen bonding between nitrogenous base holds the two strands together. This structure can be compared with the steps of spiral staircase.

Function : 1. It contain genetic information in coded form.
2. DNA synthesise RNA.

Note : *DNA is mainly found in nucleus. In small amount it is also found in mitochondria and chloroplast.*

Gene : Gene is hereditary unit which is made by a segment of DNA found on the chromosome.

B. Ribonucleic Acid (RNA) : RNA is single stranded nucleic acid made up of phosphate, ribose sugar and nitrogen base uracil, adinine, guanine and cytosine. It is found in nucleus as well as cytoplasm.

RNA is of three kind.

1. Messenger RNA (*m*RNA) : It brings the massage from DNA found in the nucleus to cytoplasm in the coded form.

2. Ribosomal RNA (*r*RNA) : Present in ribosome which is the site of protein synthesis.

3. Transfer RNA (*t* RNA) : It is the carrier of amino acid and transfer it to the ribosome.

Function : Synthesis of protein.

Difference between RNA and DNA

DNA	RNA
1. Sugar is deoxyribose type.	1. Sugar is ribose type.
2. It contains the base adenine, thymine and cytosine and guanine.	2. It contains uracil in place of thymine.
3. It is double stranded structure.	3. It is single stranded structure.
4. It is mainly found in nucleus.	4. It is found in both nucleus and cytoplasm.

➢ **Cell cycle :** It is the sequence of events in which cell duplicates its genetic material, synthesise the other constituents of cell and ultimately divide into two daughter cell.

➢ **Cell Division :** The process in which cell increase in their number is cell division. It is needed for growth, development and repair of body. There are mainly two kind of cell division.

A. Mitosis : Mitosis cell division occur in somatic cell which take part in growth, repair and development. In unicellular organism asexual reproduction takes place by this type of cell division.

➢ **Significance of Mitosis :** 1. After Mitosis cell division one cell divided into two daughter cell in which number of chromosome is equal to the parent cell.

2. Uncontrolled Mitosis may cause tumor or cancerous growth.

B. Meiosis : 1. Meiosis cell division occur in reproductive cell. This type of division takes place during the formation of haploid gamete. i.e. ova & sperm.

2. It is also known as *reduction division* during which each daughter cell have haploid number of chromosome.

3. Four daughter cells are produced from one meiotic cell division.

Terms related to cytology :

➢ Karyokinesis : Division of nucleus during cell division called *Karyokinesis.*

➢ Cytokineşis : Division of cytoplasm called *cytokinesis.*

➢ Diploid : Two complete set of chromosome is called *diploid,* found in somatic cell.

➢ Haploid : Single set of chromosome in cell is called *haploid* found in gametes.

➢ Crossing over : Exchange of genetic material between two non sister chromatids takes place during meiosis cell division is called *crossing over.*

➢ Homologous chromosome : A pair of chromosome having same size and shape bearing corresponding gene.

➢ Phenotype : The character of organism which can be seen directly.
➢ Genotype : Genetic constitution of organism is called genotype.
➢ Tonoplast : The membrane surrounding the vacuole.
➢ Unit membrane : The basic trilamilar structure of cell membrane.

5. Genetics

The process of transfer of hereditry character from one generation to next generation is called *Genetics. Johan Mendel* is known as *father of genetics.* Mendel experiments were based on cross breeding of two pea plant having contrasting characters for same feature i.e. tall and dwarf character of plant are for height of plant. He extended his work by two or three pair of contrasting characters called *dihybrid* and *trihybrid cross.* He concludes some result on the basis of his experiment called *Mendel's law.*

1. Law of paired unit : Mendel proposed that when two dissimilar unit factors are present in an individual only one is able to express. One that expresses itself is *dominant unit factor* while other which fails to express is *recessive unit factor.* For example tallness is dominant over dwarfness.

2. Law of dominance : Offspring of cross breed parent only show dominant characters in F_1 generation.

3. Law of segregation : In F_2 generation both the character which is governed by gene is separated.

4. Law of independent assortment : During dihybrid and tribhybrid cross two or three pair of characters are taken. These characters segregate separately without depending on other in F_2 generation.

Term related to genetics :

➢ Linkage : Linkage is an exception of Mendel law. When two different gene are present on the same chromosome their effects take place together insted of independently. This phenonmenon is known as *Linkage.* The word linkage first coined by *Morgan.*
➢ Mutation : A sudden change in the gene which is heritable from one generation to other. The term Mutation was first coined by *Hugo de Vries.*
➢ Variation : When characters are transmitted from one generation to next generation there is some change. Change in characters by recombination of gene in offspring takes place they looks different from their parents. This phenomenon is known as *Variation.*
➢ Chromosomal aberrations : Any change in chromosomal structure is known as *Chromosomal aberrations.*
➢ Cloning : It is a process of producing many identical organism from a single cell having same genetic character as his mother. Ex : *Sheep Dolly* was produced from single cell.
➢ Totipotency : It is the potential ability of a plant cell to grow into a complete plant.
➢ Pluriopotency : It is the potential ability of a cell to develop any kind of the cell of animal body.

➢ Genetically modified organism (GMO): Manipulation of gene by cutting or joining the segment of DNA to get desired varieties of organism is called *genetically modified organism.* This is also known as *genetic engineering.*

➢ Autosomes : Chromosomes found in cell which are responsible for characters other than sex are called *autosomes.*

➢ Sex Chromosome : The pair of chromosome which determine the sex of organism is called *sex-chromosome.*

Human have 23 pair of chromosome in which 22 pair are autosome and 1 pair is sex chromosome.

➢ Genome : All gene present in a haploid cell is called *genome.*

6. Sex Determination in Human

In human male sex chromosome is 'XY', where as in female sex chromosome is XX. During gamete formation in male half of the sperm contain 'X' chromosome while other half contain 'Y' Chromosome. In female all gametes contain only one type of chromosome that is 'X'. Thus when a male gamete i.e. sperm carrying 'X' chromosome fertilize an ova, the zygote develop into female. When a sperm carrying 'Y' chromosome fertilizes an egg, zygote develops into male.

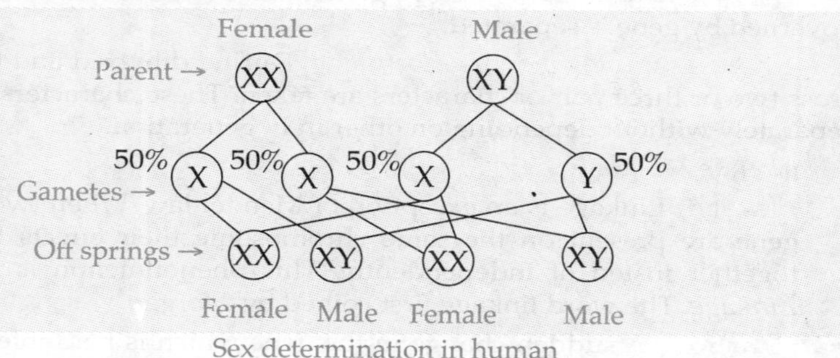

Sex determination in human

Sometime sex determination is regulated by environmental factor. In some reptiles temperature determine the sex at which the fertilized egg is incubated.

In human each cell contains 46 chromosomes. Any addition or removal in the number of sex chromosome or autosome cause genetic disorder.

1. Klinefelter Syndrome: When a male have an extra X or Y chromosome in sex chromosome then the condition will be XXY or XYY instead of XY. The individual with this syndrome have masculine development but feminine development is not completely suppressed and the individual became sterile.

In female when extra X chromosome is present instead of XX they show normal development but limited fertility. Mental retardness is also seen in this type of syndrome. Number of chromosome became 47 instead of 46.

2. Turner's Syndrome : When female has single sex chromosome (X0) their ovaries are rudimentary, lack of secondary sexual character.

3. Down's Syndrome : When an extra chromosome is added to 21st autosomal chromosomes this lead to develop Down's syndrome. In this syndrome person became Mangolism. The person is mentally retarded, eyes protruded an irregular physical structure is present.

4. Patau's Syndrome : This type of syndrome is develop by an addition of autosomal chromosome in 13th chromosome. There is a cut mark in the lip and person is mentally retarded. Discase due to change in gentical constituent of chromosome.

1. Sickle Cell Anaemia : In this disorder erythrocytes destroyed more rapidly than normal leading to anaemia. These occur due to change in 11th autosomal chromosome.

2. Phenylketonuria : It is an inborn error of metabolism which result in mental retardation cause due to change in 12th autosomal chromosomes.

3. Haemophilia : Gene responsible for this disorder is linked with sex chromosomes. This disease lead to failure of blood clotting.

4. Colour blindness : This disorder lead to failure to distinugished red & green colour. The gene responsible for this disease is situated on sex chromosomes.

Number of Chromosomes in Different Organisms :

Pigeon	80	Dog	78	Horse	64
Chimpanzee	48	Potato	48	Human	46
Rabbit	44	Wheat	42	Cat	38
Frog	26	Tomato	24	Pea	14
House-fly	12	Mosquito	6	Ascaris	2

7. Organic Evolution

More and more creation of organism by gradual changes from low categories animal to higher animal is called *organic evolution*. There are several evidence regarding organic evolution.

- Homologous organ : Organ which are seen different due to use in various function but its structure and embryonic development are similar. Ex – *Flipper of whale, feather of bat, forelimb of horse, Paw of cat,* and *hands of human.*
- Analogous organ : Organ which looks similar due to be used in similar function but their internal structure and embryonic development are different. Ex – *Feather of butterfly, bats* and *birds* all looks similar but their internal structure and origin are different.
- Vestigial organ : These are organs which appear functionless in an organism but functional in their ancestor. For example *vermiform appendix of large intestine* and *nictitating membrane of human.* Vermiform appendix is functional in herbivorous mammal even now.
- Fossils – Fossils are the remains of ancient plant or animal which provide evidences for evolution. Example–Archaeoptery.
- Archaeopteryx : It is a fossils look like bird but bear a number of features found in reptiles. So, it is a connecting link between aves and reptile.

Theories of evolution

1. **Carolus Linnaeus** (1707 – 1778) contribution to classification provide an evolutionary relationship among the organism. He was also supported an idea that no species is new. Each and every species originates from some pre-existing species.

2. **Jean Baptist Lamarck** (1744 – 1829) tried to explain the evolutionary process in his book *Philosophic zoologique.* The theory proposed by Lamark is known as *theory of inheritance of acquired characters.* According to this theory use and disuse of an organ lead to acquiring change in the features of that organ. These changes are also inherited to offspring. The favourable changes after long period of time result in evolution of new species. But Lamarckism was very strongly criticised by *August Weismann.*

3. **Charles Robert Darwin** (1809 – 1882) explain the evolutionary principle in his book *'The origin of species'*. The theory proposed by him is popularly known as *'Theory of natural selection'* or *Darwinism.* Darwin explained that despite having the enormous potential of fertility, the population of organism remains within a limit. It is due to struggle between members of same species and different species for food, space and mate. Struggle eliminates the unfit individual. The fit organism possess some variations which are favourable and they can leave the progeny to continue the favourable variation. The variation when accumalated for long time give rise to origin of new species with progress in genetics, the sources of variation were explained and Darwin's theory was modified. Now the most excepted theory of evolution is *Modern synthetic theory,* in which origin of species is based on the interaction of genetic variation and natural selection.

BOTANY

The study of different types of Trees, plants is called *Botany.*

Theophrastus is called the *father of Botany.*

1. Classification of Plantae

In the year 1883, **Eichler** has classified the Botanical world as under:-

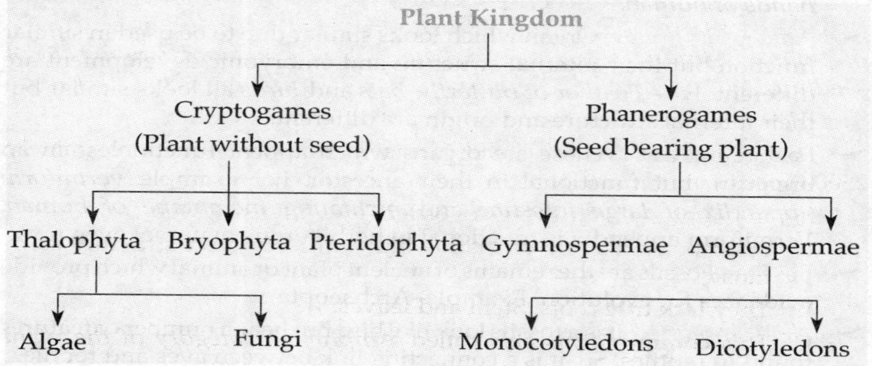

I. Cryptogamus plants

There is no flower and seed in these type of plants. These are classified into the following groups:

Thalophyta :

1. This is the largest group of the plant kingdom.
2. The body of the plants in this group is thalus like i.e., plant are not differentiated into root, stem and leaves etc.
3. There is no conducting tissue. It is divided into two groups.
   (a) Algae and (b) Fungi

(a) Algae

1. The study of algae is called *Phycology*.
2. The algae normally have *chlorophyll* and *autrotrophic* mode of nutrition.
3. Its body is thalus like. It may be *unicellular, colonial* or *filamentous.*

Useful Algae :

1. As a food : *Porphyra, Ulva, Surgassum, Laeminaria, Nostoc* etc.
2. In making Iodine : *Laeminaria, Fucus, Echlonia* etc.
3. As a manure : *Nostoc, Anabina, kelp* etc.
4. In making medicines : *Chloreloline* from *Chlorella* and *Tincher iodine* is made from *Laminaria.*
5. In research works : *Chlorella Acitabularia, Belonia* etc.

Note : *An astronaut can get protein food, water and oxygen by sowing the chlorella algae in the tank of the aircraft so chlorella is known as space algae.*

(b) Fungi

1. Study of fungi is called *Mycology.*
2. Fungi is chlorophyll less, central carrier tissue less, Thalophyte.
3. Accumulated food in fungi remains as *Glycogen.*
4. Its cell wall is made up of *chitin.* Ex. Albugo, Phytophthora Mucor etc.

Fungi may creates serious diseases in plants. Most damage is caused by rust and smut. Main Fungal diseases in plants are as :

White rust of crucifer, Loose smut of wheat, Rust of wheat, early Blight of potato, Red rot of sugarcane, Tikka diseases of ground nut, Wart disease of potato, Brown leaf spot of rice, Late blight of potato, Damping off of seedlings etc.

Bryophyta

This is the first group of land plants. In this division approximately 25000 species are included.

1. In byophyta there is lack of Xylem and phloem tissue.
2. Plant body may be of thallus like and leafy erect structure as in moss.
3. They lack true roots, Stem and leaves.
4. This community is also called *Amphibian category of the plant kingdom.*

The moss namely Sphagnum is capable of soaking water 18 times of its own weight. Therefore, gardeners use it to protect from drying while taking the plants from one place to another.

The Sphagnum moss is used as fuel.

The Sphagnum moss is also used as antiseptic.

Pteridophyta

The plants of this group are mostly found in wet shady places, forests and mountains.

1. The body of plants are differentiated into root, stem, and leaves. Stem remains as normal rhizome.
2. Reproduction occurs by spores produced inside the sporangia.
3. Gametophytic phase is short lived. The diploid zygote develops into an embryo.
4. Plants of this community have conducting tissues. But Xylem does not contain Vessels and Phloem does not contain companion cells.

   Examples : *Ferns, Azolla, Pteridium, Lycopodium* etc.

II. Phanerogamus or Floral plant

The plants in this group are well developed. All the plants in this group have flowers, fruits and seeds. The plants in this group can be classified into two sub-groups – *Gymnosperm* and *Angiosperm*.

(A) Gymnosperm

1. These plants are in the forms of trees and bushes. Plant body are differentiated into root, stem & leaves.
2. Plants are woody, perennial and tall. Plant bear naked seed.
3. Its tap roots are well developed.
4. Pollination takes place through air.

The longest plant of the Plant kingdom, *Sequoia gigentia* comes under it. Its height is 120 meters. This is also called *Red Wood of California*.

➢ The smallest plant is *Zaimia Pygmia*.

➢ Living fossils are *Cycas, Ginkgo, biloba* and *Metasequoia*.

➢ *Ginkgo biloba* is also called *Maiden hair tree*.

➢ Ovules and Antherzoids of *Cycas* is the largest in Plant kingdom.

The pollen grains of Pinus are so much in number that later it turns into Sulphur showers.

Importance of Gymnosperm

1. *As a food* – Sago is made by extracting the juice from the stems of Cycas. Therefore, Cycas is called *Sago-palm*.
2. *Wood* – The wood of Pine, Sequoia, Deodar, Spruce etc. is used for making furniture.
3. *Vapour oil* – We get Tarpin oil from the trees of Pine, Cedrus oil from Deodar tree and Cedcast oil from Juniperous wood.
4. *Tannin* - It is useful in tanning and making ink.
5. *Resin* – Resin is extracted from some conical plants which are used in making varnish, polish, paint etc.

(B) Angiosperm

1. In the plants of this sub-group seeds are found inside the fruits.
2. In there plants root, leaves, flowers, fruits and seeds are fully developed.

In the plants of this sub-group there is seed-coat in seeds. On the basis of number of cotyledons plants are divided into two categories –

1. *Monocotyledon* and (2) *Dicotyledon*

Monocotyledon plants : Those plants which have only one cotyledon in seed. Example :

Name of category	Name of main plants
1. *Liliaceae*	Garlic, Onion etc.
2. *Palmae*	Nut, Palm, Coconut, Date etc.
3. *Graminaeceae*	Wheat, Maize, Bamboo, Sugarcane, Rice, Bajra Oat etc.

Dicotyledons plants : Those plants which have two cotyledon in its seed are called dicotyledons. Example :

Name of category	Name of main plants
1. *Cruciferae*	Radish, Turnip, Mustard etc.
2. *Malvaceae*	Jute, Lady's finger
3. *Leguminaceae*	Babool, Lajwanti, Ashok, Tamarind and all the Pulse crops.
4. *Composite*	Sunflower, Marigold, Lily etc.
5. *Rutaceae*	Lemon, Orange etc.
6. *Cucurbitaceae*	Melon, Water melon, Guard, Bitter etc.
7. *Solanaceae*	Potato, Chilly, Brinjal, Belladonna, Tomato etc.
8. *Rosaceae*	Strawberry, Apple, Almond etc.

Virus

- ➢ Study of virus is virology.
- ➢ Virus was discovered by Russian scientist *Ivanovsky* in the year 1892. (During the tests of Mosaic disease on tobacco).
- ➢ In nature, there are ultra microscopic particle known as viruses. Virus are connecting a link between living & non living.
- ➢ It has both the characters of living and non living, so it is a connecting link between living & non living.

Characters of virus

1. They became active inside a living cells.
2. Nucleic acids replicate themselves and they reproduce rapidly.
3. They cause disease like bacteria & fungi.

According to parasitic nature, virus is of three types –

1. *Plant virus* – RNA is present as its nucleic acid.
2. *Animal virus* – DNA or sometimes RNA is found in it.
3. *Bacteriophage* – They depend only on bacteria. They kill the bacteria. DNA is found in them. *Example* – T-2 phage.

➢ In man virus cause disease like mumps, chicken pox, hepatitis, palio, AIDs and Herpes.

➢ **Bacteriophages :** Bacteriophages are those virus which infect the bacteria. Example —Tobacco mosaic virus.

Note : *Those viruses in which RNA substance is found as genetic material are called Retrovirus.*

Bacteria

It was discovered by Antony von Lecuwenhoek of Holland in the year 1683.

➢ *Lecuwenhoek* is called the *father of Bacteriology.*

In the year 1829 *Ehrenberg* called it bacteria.

➢ The year 1843-1892 – Robert Koch discovered the bacteria of Tuberculosis diseases.

➢ The year 1812-1892 – *Louis Pasteur* discovered the vaccine of Rabies and pasteurization of milk.

On the basis of shape, bacteria is of different types :

1. Bacillus : This is rod-like or cylindrical.
2. Round or Cocus : These are round and the smallest bacteria.
3. Comma shaped or Vibrio : Like the English sign (,), example – *Vibrio cholerae* etc.
4. Spirillum : Spring or screw shaped.

➢ Some species of *Azotobacter, Azospirillum* and *Clostridium* bacteria live freely in the soil and fix atmospheric nitrogen into the nitrogenous compound.

Anabaena and *Nostoc cynobacteria* fix atmospheric nitrogen into soil.

➢ The species of *Rhizobium* and *Bradyrhizobium* etc. bacteria live in the roots of the Leguminous plants capable of converting atmospheric nitrogen into its compound.

Note : *To preserve the milk for many days pasteurization is done. There are two methods of pasteurization –*

(a) Low temperature holding method (LTH) : ***Milk is boiled at 62.8 degree Celsius for 30 minutes.***

(b) High Temperature short time method (HTSt) : ***Milk is boiled at 71.7 degree Celsius for 15 seconds.***

➢ In leather industry separation of hair and fat from leather is done by bacteria. This is called *tanning of leather.*

➢ Pickles, syrup is kept in salt or in dense liquid of sugar so that in case of bacterial attack bacteria are plasmolysed and destroyed. Therefore, pickles etc. do not get spoiled soon and can be preserved for long time.

➢ In the Cold Storage objects are kept at low temperature (-10 degree Celsius to -18 degree Celsius).

➢ **Mycoplasma :** Smallest known prokaryotic cell causing pleuropneumonia. It is also known as PPLO

2. Plant Morphology

➢ **Morphology :** The study of forms and features of different parts of plants like roots, stems, leaves, flowers, fruits etc. is called *Morphology*.

Root

Root is the descending part of the plant which develops from *radicle*.

Root generally grows in the soil away from light.

Roots are of two types—

(i) *Tap root* and (ii) *Adventitious root*.

Modification of Tap roots are :

1. *Conical* – like Carrot
2. *Napiform* – like Turnip, beet etc.
3. *Fusiform* – like Radish.

Stem

This is the part of a plant which grows towards light.

It develops from *plumule*.

The modification of stems are as under –

Underground stem

1. *Tuber* – like Potato.
2. *Corm* – like Colocasia, Saffron etc.
3. *Bulb* – like Onion, Garlic etc.
4. *Rhizome* – like Turmeric, Ginger etc.

Leaf

It is green. Its main function is to make food through photosynthesis.

Flower

This is the reproductive part of the plant.

In the flower *Calyx, Corolla, Androecium* and *Gynoecium* are found. Out of these androecium is male sex organ and the Gynoecium is female sex organ.

➢ **Androecium :** Unit of androcium is stamen there is one or more stamens in the androecium. Pollen grains are found in anther.

➢ **Gynoecium :** Unit of gynoecium is *carpel*. There are three parts of carpel – (i) *Ovary*, (ii) *Style* and (iii) *Stigma*.

➢ **Pollination :** After maturation of Anther, the process of reaching of pollen grains to stigma is called *pollination*. Pollination is of two types – (i) *Self-pollination* (ii) *Cross-pollination*

➢ **Fertilization :** Pollen tube reaches the egg cell after entering into the ovule through a pore called *micryopyle*. After that a male nucleus fuse with egg-cell. This is called *fertilization*. Fertilized egg is called *zygote*.

In angiosperm, the fertilization is triple fusion whereas in other category of plants it is double fusion.

➢ **Parthenocarpy :** In some plants fruits are developed from ovary without fertilization. This type of fruit is called *parthenocarpy*. Normally these types of fruits are seedless. Example – Banana, Papaya, Orange, Grapes, Pine-apple etc.

Formation of fruits

Fruit is a matured or ripened ovary developed after fertilization.

Formation of fruit takes place from ovary.

Fruits are divided into three types –

1. *Simple fruits* – like Banana, Guava etc.
2. *Aggregate fruit* – Strawberry, Custard apple etc.
3. *Composite fruit* – Jackfruit, Mulbery etc.

In the development of some fruits, Calyx, Corolla and thalmus takes part. These types of fruits are called *False fruits.* Example – Apple, Jackfruit, pear etc.

Some fruits and their edible parts

Fruit	Edible part	Fruit	Edible part
Apple	Fleshy thalamus	Wheat	starchy endosperm
Pear	Fleshy thalamus	Cashew nut	Peduncle & cotyledons
Mango	Mesocarp	Lichi	Aril
Guava	Entire fruit	Gram	cotyledons & embryo
Grapes	Pericarp and Placenta	Groundnut	Cotyledons
Papaya	Mesocarp	Mulberry	entire fruit
Coconut	Endosperm	Jackfruit	Bract, Perianth and seed
Tomato	Pericarp and Placenta	Pine apple	Bract and Perianth
Banana	Mesocarp & Endocarp	Orange	Juicy hair.

3. Plant Tissue

Tissue : The group of cells of similar origin, structure and functions is called tissue.

Types of Plant Tissue

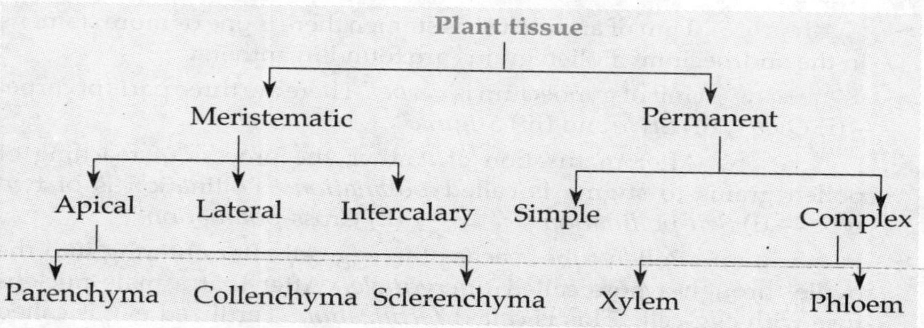

(A) Meristematic tissue : Growing regions of the plants are called *Meristem.* Meristematic tissue have capability of cell division. Daughter cells formed out. It grow and constitute the different parts of the plant. This process continues till the life-span of the plant.

Specific features of the Meristematic tissues are as follows –

(i) It is round, oval or multi-sided.

(ii) Its wall is thin and cytoplasm is homogeneous.

(iii) Cell contains dense cytoplasm and a single large nucleus.

(iv) There is lack of inter-cellular spaces between the cells.

➢ **Apical Meristems :** These tissues are found in the root and stem apex and the initial growth (specially length) of the plants take place due to these tissue.

➢ **Lateral Meristems :** Due to the division in these tissue growth in the girth of roots and stems takes place. Hence, it increases the width of the root and stem.

➢ **Intercalary Meristems :** They are located at the base of internode. In fact, this is the remains of the Apical Meristems, which is divided by the incoming of permanent tissues in the centre. Plants increase its length by the activity of this. Its importance is for those plants whose apex parts are eaten by vegetarian animals. After being eaten the apex part the plants grow with the help of intercalary meristems only. Like – grass.

(B) Permanent tissue : Permanent tissues are made of those mature tissues that have lost their capacity of division and attain a definite forms for various works. These cells can be alive or dead.

➢ **Simple tissue :** If permanent tissue is made up of similar types of cells, it is called *simple tissue.*

➢ **Complex tissue :** If permanent tissue is made up of one or more types of cells, it is called *Complex tissue.*

➢ **Xylem :** This is usually called *wood.* This is conducting tissue. Its two main functions are –

(i) Conduction of water and minerals and

(ii) To provide mechanical consistency.

The determination of age of the plant is done by counting annual rings of the xylem tissue. The method of determining the age of plant is called *Dendrochronology.*

➢ **Phloem :** This is a conducting tissue. Its main function is to conduct foods prepared by the leaves to different parts of the plant.

4. Photosynthesis

In the presence of water, light, chlorophyll and carbon dioxide, the formation of carbohydrates in plant is called *photosynthesis.*

$$6CO_2 + 12H_2O \xrightarrow[\text{Chlorophyll}]{\text{Light}} \underset{\text{Glucose}}{C_6H_{12}O_6} + \underset{\text{Water}}{6H_2O} + \underset{\text{Oxygen}}{6O_2}$$

Carbon dioxide, water, chlorophyll and sunlight are necessary for photosynthesis

➢ Terrestrial plants takes CO_2 from atmosphere whereas aquatic plants use carbon dioxide mixed in water.

➢ Water enters into the cells of the leaves through osmosis and CO_2 through diffusion from atmosphere or release during respiration.

➢ Water necessary for photosynthesis is absorbed by the roots and the oxygen produced during photosynthesis is due to photolysis of water.

- The green colour of the plants is due to the presence of chlorophyll. Chlorophyll are photoreceptor molecule, which trap the solar energy. There are different type of chlorophyll molecule like 'a', 'b', 'c', 'd' & 'e'. Chlorophyll 'a' & 'b' are most common and are found in a plant.
- There is an atom of magnesium in the centre of chlorophyll.
- Chlorophyll absorbs the violet, blue and red colours of light.

The rate of photosynthesis is maximum in red light and is minimum in violet light.

- The process of photosynthesis is a reaction of oxidation and reduction. Oxidation of water takes place forming oxygen and reduction of carbon dioxide takes place forming glucose.

The stages of process of photosynthesis

(i) Photochemical reaction or light reaction and
(ii) Dark chemical reaction

(i) Photochemical reaction : This reaction is completed in the grana part of the chlorophyll. This is also called *Hill reaction*. In this process break down of water takes place and hydrogen ion and electron is formed. For photolysis of water, energy is received from the light. At the end of this process, ATP is formed from ADP & P.

(ii) Dark chemical reaction : This reaction takes place in the stroma of chlorophyll. In this reaction reduction of carbon dioxide takes place and sugar or starch are formed. It is also known as *Calvin Benson cycle*.

5. Plant Hormones

Following five hormones are found in plants –

1. **Auxins :** Auxins was discovered by Darwin in the year 1880.
   This is the hormone which controls the growth of plants.
   Its formation takes place in the apex parts of the plants.
   Its main functions are –
   (i) It prevents the separation of the leaves.
   (ii) It destroys the straws.
   (iii) It saves the crops from falling.
2. **Gibberellins :** It was discovered by a Japanese scientist *Kurosava* in the year 1926.
   Functions :
   (i) It turns the dwarf plants into long plants. It helps in creating flowering.
   (ii) It hep in breaking the dormancy of plant.
   (iii) It motivates the seeds to be sprout.
   (iv) It increases the activity of cambium in the wooden plants.
   (v) Large sized fruits and flowers can be produced by its scattering.
3. **Cytokinins :** It was discovered by *z* in the year 1955 but it was named by Lethem.
   Functions :
   (i) It naturally works in coordination with auxins.

(ii) It help in cell division and development in the presence of auxins.

(iii) It help in breaking the dormancy of seed.

(iv) It is helpful in making RNA and protein.

4. **Abscisic Acid or ABA :** This hormone was initially discovered by Carnes and Adicote and later on by *Waring*.
Functions :
(i) This hormone is against the growth.
(ii) It keeps the seeds & bud in dormant condition.
(iii) It plays main role in separation of leaves.
(iv) It delays in flowering of long day plant.

5. **Ethylene :** This is the only hormone which is found in gaseous form.
Functions :
(i) It helps in the ripening the fruits.
(ii) It increases the number of female flowers.
(iii) It motivates the separation of leaves, flowers and fruits.

6. **Florigens :** It is formed in leaves but helps in blooming of the flowers. Therefore, it is also called *flowering hormones*.

7. **Traumatic :** This is a type of dicarboxylic acid. It is formed in injured cells by which the injury of plants is healed.

6. Plant Diseases

1. **Viral Diseases :** (i) *Mosaic disease of tobacco* – In this disease leaves get shrinked and become small. The chlorophyll of leaves get destroyed. The factor of this disease is *Tobacco Mosaic Virus* (TMV).

Control – Affected plants should be burnt.

(ii) *Bunchy top of banana* – This diseases is caused by *banana virus*. In this disease plants become dwarf and all the leaves get accumulated like a rose on the branch.

2. **Bacterial Disease :**

(i) *Wilt of Potato* : It is also known as *ring disease* because brown ring is formed on the xylem. The factor of this disease is *Pseudomonas solonacearum* bacteria. In this disease the conduction system of the plant is affected.

(ii) *Black Arm of cotton* : The factor of this disease is *Xanthomonas Bacteria*. In this disease a water body (brown) is formed on the leaves.

(iii) *Bacterial blight of Rice* : This disease is caused by *Xanthomonas oryzae bacteria*. Yellow-greenish spot is seen on both side of leaves. Vascular bundles get blocked due to bacterial growth.

(iv) *Citrus Canker* : The factor of this disease is *Xanthomonas citri* bacteria. It has originated in China. Leaves, branches, fruits all are affected by this disease.

(v) *Tundu disease of wheat* : The factors of this disease are *Corinobacterium titrici* bacteria and Enzuina Titriki Nematode. In this disease lower parts of the leaves are faded and turned.

3. **Fungal Diseases :** The diseases included in this group are caused by fungi.

Some Important Facts Regarding Botany

Facts	Example and details
Largest angiosperm tree	*Eucalyptus.*
Longest tree in the world	*Sequoia* giganteum. This is a gymnosperm. Its height is 120 meter. This is also called *Coast Red Wood of California.*
Smallest (in shape) angiosperm plant	Lemna. This is aquatic angiosperm which is found in India too.
Plant with largest leaf	Victoria Regia. This is an aquatic plant which is found in West Bengal in India.
Largest fruit	*Lodoicea.* This is also called double coconut. This is found in Kerala in India.
Smallest Pteridophyta	*Azolla.* This is an aquatic plant.
Smallest seed	*Orchid.*
Smallest flower	*Wolfia.* Its diameter is 0.1 millimeter.
Largest flower	*Reflesia arnoldii.* Its diameter is 1 meter and its weight can be 8 kilograms.
Smallest angiosperm parasite	*Arceuthobium.* is a parasite on the stems of gymnosperms.
Largest male couplet	*Cycas.* This is a gymnosperm plant.
Largest seed-egg	*Cycas.*
Alive morph	*Cycas.*
Smallest chromosomes	*In algae.*
Longest chromosomes	In *Trillium.*
The plant with the largest number of Chromosomes	Ophioglossum (*Fern*). There are 1266 chromosomes in its Diploid cell.
The plant with the least number of chromosomes	Heplapapopus *gracilis.*
The smallest gymnosperm plant	*Zamia pygmea.*
The heaviest wooden plant	*Hardwichia binata.*
The lightest wooden plant	*Ochroma lagopus-balsa.*
The smallest cell	*Mycoplasma gallisepticum.*
Fruit like a tennis ball	*Kenth.*
Fire of the forest	*Dhak.*
Coffee giving plant	*Coffea arabica.* Caffin contains in it.
Coco giving plant	*Theobroma cococa.* Theobromin and caffeine contain in it.
Caffeine	*Pepaver somniferum* morphin contains in it.

7. Ecology

- Study of inter relationship between living organisms and their environment.
- Various population of living in a definite place is called *Biotic Community*.
- Ecosystem or Ecological system word was first coined by the scientist namely *Tansley*.

  Every ecosystem is made up of two components –

  (a) Biotic component – Living part

  (b) Abiotic component – Non living part

  (a) Biotic components : It is divided into three parts –

  (1) Producer (2) Consumer (3) Decomposers

(1) Producer : Those components that make their own food. Like – green plants.

(2) Consumer : Those components that consumes the food made by plant. Consumers are of three types –

(i) *Primary consumers :* In this category those organisms are included that lives on green plants or some parts of them.

(ii) *Secondary consumers :* In this category those organisms are included that depends on the primary consumers as their food. Like – fox, wolf, peacock etc.

(iii) *Tertiary consumers :* In this category those organisms are included that depends on the secondary consumers. Like – Tiger, lion, cheetah etc.

(3) Decomposers : Mainly fungi and bacteria are included in this category. These decomposes dead producers and consumers and changes them into physical elements.

(b) Abiotic components : Abiotic components are as follows –

(i) Carbonic substance, (ii) Non-carbonic substance, (iii) Climatic factor

Example : Water, light, temperature, air, humidity, minerals etc.

- **Food Chain :** Transfer of energy from the producer through a series of organisms.

8. Nitrogen cycle

- Nitrogen fixation is a process in which free atmospheric nitrogen is converted by living organism into nitrogenous compound that can be used by plant
- **Ammonification :** Formation of ammonia from organic compound like proteins and nucleic acid by microorganism.
- **Nitrification :** A process in which ammonia is converted into nitrates and nitrates by Nitrobacteria.
- **Denitrification :** It is the process of converting fix nitrogen like nitrates, nitrites and ammonia into free nitrogen by denitrifying bacteria eg Pseudonymouna.

9. Pollution

Unwanted changes in the chemical and physical features of air, water and land (environment) that are dangerous to human and other organisms, their life conditions, industrial process and cultural achievements are called *pollution*.

The types of pollution are mainly –(i) Air pollution, (ii) Water pollution, (iii) Sound pollution, (iv) Soil pollution, (v) Nuclear pollution.

(i) Air pollution : When the pollution is in the atmosphere and the sufficient quantity of atmosphere reduces then it is called *Air pollution*.

Main air pollutants – *Carbon monoxide* (CO), Sulphur dioxide (SO_2), Hydrogen sulphide (H_2S), Hydrogen fluoride (HF), Nitrogen oxide (NO and NO_2), Hydrocarbon, Ammonia (NH_3), Smoke of tobacco, Fluorides smoke and particles of smoke, Aerosols etc.

Sulphur dioxide (SO_2), Sulphur trioxide (SO_3), Nitrogen oxide (NO) react with environmental water and creates Sulphuric acid and Nitric acid. These acids reach the earth with rain water and this is called *acid rain*.

On 3rd December, 1984 an incidence of leakage of Methyl Isocyanide gas took place in the fertilizer making Union Carbide Factory. (Bhopal)

(ii) Water pollution : Mixing of unwanted substances with water is called *water pollution*.

Sources of water pollution : The water pollution takes place mainly due to mixing up of Carbonate, sulphates of Magnesium and Potassium, Ammonia, Carbon monoxide, Carbon dioxide and Industrial remains in water. Sea-water pollution is due to mixing up of heavy metals, hydro carbon, petroleum etc. in water.

(iii) Sound pollution : The unwanted and undesirable sounds scattered in atmosphere are called *sound pollution*.

Sources of sound pollution : The source of sound pollution is loud sound or noise, in whatever ways it has produced.

(iv) Soil pollution : Distorted form of soil is called *Soil pollution*.

Sources of Soil pollution : acid rain, water from mines, excessive use of fertilizers and germicide chemicals, garbage, industrial remainins, excretion in open field etc. are the main sources of soil pollution.

(v) Nuclear pollution : This pollution is created by radioactive rays.

Following can be the sources of radioactive pollution –

(i) Pollution from the rays which are used in treatment.

(ii) Pollution created from fuels used in Atomic reactors.

(iii) Pollution created from the use of nuclear weapons.

(iv) Pollution created remaining substances coming out of Atomic power-houses.

Population, Biotic Community

➢ Population : Population is a group of individuals of same species occupying the same area at a given time.

➢ Population density : Total number of individual present in per unit area.

- ➢ Natality : Increase in the number of individuals in a given population by birth is called natality
- ➢ Mortality : Number of individuals removed from a population due to death under given environmental condition at a given time is called mortality
- ➢ Biotic potential : It refers the maximum capacity of inherent of an organism to reproduce.
- ➢ Environmental resistance : Environmental factors, which put a check on the growth of population.
- ➢ Mutalism : It is a functional association between two different species in which both the species are benefited.
- ➢ Commensalism : It is an association between individuals of two different species in which one species is benefited and other one is neither benefited nor affected.
- ➢ Population Explosion : The dramatic increase in population size over a relatively short period is called population explosion.
- ➢ Demographic transition : If the birth rate is equal to the death rate, it results in zero population growth, which is called demographic transition.
- ➢ Psychosis : It is a mild form of mental illness where the patient show prolonged emotional reaction.
- ➢ Drug abuse : When drugs are taken for a purpose other than their normal clinical use in an amount that impairs ones physical, physiological and psychological function of body is called drug abuse.

ZOOLOGY

Zoology : Scientific study of the structure, form and distribution of animals.

1. Classification of Animal Kingdom

Animals kingdom of the world is divided into two sub-kingdoms :

(i) Unicellular animal (ii) Multi-cellular animal.

Unicellular animals are kept in a single phylum Protozoa whereas multi-cellular animals are divided into 9 phylums.

Classification of animals according to *Storer* and *Usinger* –

A. Phylum Protozoa : Main features – Unicellular

(i) It's body is made of only one cell.
(ii) There is one or more nuclei in its cytoplasm.
(iii) Are both the types commensalism and parasite.
(iv) All the metabolic activity (eating, digestion, respiration, excretion, reproduction) takes place in unicellular body.
(v) Respiration and excretion take place by diffusion.

Example – *Amoeba, Euglena, Trypanosoma* etc.

B. Phylum Porifera : All animal of this group are found in marine water & bear pores in body.

(i) These are multicellular animals but cells do not make regular tissues.
(ii) Numerous pores known as *ostia* found on body wall.
(iii) Skeleton is made up of minute calcareous or silicon spicules.

Example – *Sycon, Sponge* etc.

C. Phylum Coelenterate : Main features – Coelenteron is present

(i) Animals are aquatic and diploblastic.

(ii) Around the mouth some thread-like structure are found known as tentacles, which help in holding the food.

(iii) Body radial symmetry.

(iv) Specialized cnidoblast cell are found help in catching the food.

Example – *Hydra, Jelly fish, Sea Anemone* etc.

D. Phylum Platyhelminthes : Main features – Flat worm

(i) Triploblastic and no body cavity.

(ii) Dorso-ventraly flattened animal.

(iii) Alimentary canal with single opening, anus absent.

(iv) Excretion takes place by flame cells.

(v) There is no skeleton, respiratory organ, circulatory system etc.

(vi) These are hermaphrodite animal.

Example – *Planaria, Liver fluke, Tape worm* etc.

E. Phylum Ascheleminthes : Main features – Round worm

(i) Long, cylindrical, unsegmented worm.

(ii) Bilaterally symmetrical and triploblastic.

(iii) Alimentary canal is complete in which mouth and anus both are present.

(iv) There is no circulatory & respiratory systems but nervous system is developed.

(v) Excretion takes place through *Protonephridia*.

(vi) They are unisexual.

(vii) Most form are parasitic but some are free living in soil & water.

Example – Round worm, like – *Ascaris, Thread worm, Wuchereia* etc.

Note : *(i) Enterobius (pin worm/thread worm) – It is found mainly in the anus of child. Children feel itching and often vomits. Some children urinate on the bed at night.*

(ii) Filarial disease is caused by Wuchereia bancrofti.

F. Phylum Annelida : Main features – Annulus body Bearing ring

(i) Body is long, thin, soft and metamerically segmented.

(ii) Locomotion takes place through *Setae* made up of Chitin.

(iii) Alimentary canal is well developed.

(iv) Normally respiration through skin, in some animals it takes place through *coelom*.

(v) Nervous system is normal and blood is red.

(vi) Excretion by *nephridia*.

(vii) Both unisexual and bisexual.

Example : *Earthworm, Nereis, Leech* etc.

Note : *There are four pairs of heart in earthworm.*

G. Phylum Arthropoda : Main features – Jointed leg

(i) Body is divided into three parts – Head, Thorax and Abdomen.

(ii) Body is covered with a thick chitinous exoskeleton.

(iii) Jointed leg.

(iv) Circulatory system is open type.

(v) Its body cavitys are called *haemocoel*.

(vi) *Trachea, book lungs, body surface* are respiratory parts.

(vii) These are mainly unisexual and fertilization takes place inside the body.

Example – *Cockroach, prawn, crab, bug, fly, mosquito, bees* etc.

Note : *(i) There are six feet and four wings in insects. (ii) There are 13 chamber in the Cockroach's heart. (iii) Ant is a social animal which reflects labour division. (iv) Termite is also a social animal which lives in colony.*

H. Phylum Mollusca : Main features – Soft bodies animal

(i) Body is soft divided into head and muscular foot.
(ii) Mantle is always present in it, which secretes a hard calcareous shell.
(iii) Alimentary canal is well developed.
(iv) Respiration takes place through *gills* or *ctenidia.*
(v) Blood is colourless.
(vi) Excretion takes place through kidneys.

Example – *Pila, Octopus, Loligo, Squid* etc.

Note :

Mollusca	Other name in vogue
Aplysia	Sea rabbit
Doris	Sea lemon
Octopus	Devil-fish
Sepia	Cuttle-fish

I. Phylum Echinodermata : Main features – Spiny skin

(i) All the animals in this group are marine.
(ii) Water vascular system is present.
(iii) There is Tube feet for locomotion, taking food which works as sensation organ.
(iv) Brain is not developed in nervous system.
(v) There is a special capacity of regeneration.

Example : *Star fish, Sea urchin, Sea cucumber, Brittle stars* etc.

Note : *The work of the Aristotle lantern is to chew the food. It is found in sea urchin.*

J. Phylum Chordata : Main features

(i) Notochord is present in it.
(ii) All the chordates are triploblastic, coelomate and bilaterally symmetrical.
(iii) A dorsal hollow tubular nerve cord and paired pharyngeal gill slits are other features of chordates.

According to classification there are two sub phyla in Chordata.

(a) Protochordates and (b) Vertebrata

Some main groups of phylum Chordata :

1. Pisces : Main features – Aquatic life

(i) All these are cold blooded animals.
(ii) Its heart pumps only impure blood and have two chamber.
(iii) Respiration takes place through *gills.*

Example : *Hippopotamus, Scoliodon, Torpedo.* etc.

2. Amphibia : Main features – Found both on land & water

(i) All these creatures are amphibian.

(ii) All these are cold-blooded.
(iii) Respiration takes place through gill, skin and lungs. Heart have three, chamber two auricles and one ventricle.

Example : Frog, Necturus, Toad, etc. *Icthyophis, Salamander.*

Note : *In fact the croaking of frogs is the call for sex.*

3. **Reptilia : Main features** – Crawlling animal
(i) Land vertebrate, cold-booded, terrestrial or aquatic vertebrates.
(ii) It contains two pair of limbs.
(iii) The skeleton is completely flexible.
(iv) Respiration takes place through lungs.
(v) Its eggs are covered with shell made up of Calcium carbonate.

Example : *Lizard, snake, tortoise, crocodile, turtle, sphenodon* etc.

Note : *Mesozoic era is called the era of reptiles.*
Cobra is the only snake which makes nests.
Heloderma is the only poisonous lizard.
Sea snake which is called Hydrophis is the world's most poisonous snake.

4. **Aves : Main features** – Warm blooded tetrapod vertebrates with flight adaptation.
(i) Its fore-feet modified into wings to fly.
(ii) Boat shaped body is divisible into head , neck, trunk and tail.
(iii) Its respiratory organ is lungs.
(iv) Birds have no teeth, beak help in feeding.

Example : *crow, peacock, parrot* etc.

Note : *(i) Flightless Birds – Kiwi and Emus. (ii) Largest alive bird is Ostrich. (iii) Smallest bird is Humming bird. (iv) Largest zoo in India is Alipur (Kolkata) and the largest zoo of the world is Cruiser National Park in South Africa.*

5. **Mammalia : Main features**
(i) Sweat glands and oil glands are found on skin.
(ii) All these animals are warm blooded.
(iii) Its hearts are divided into four chamber.
(iv) Tooth comes twice in these animals. (Diphyodont)
(v) There is no nucleus in its red blood cells (except in camel and lama).
(vi) Skin of mammal have hair.
(vii) External ear is present.

Mammals are divided into three sub-classes :
(i) *Prototheria* – It lays eggs. Example – *Echidna.*
(ii) *Metatheria* – It bears the immature child. Example – Kangaroo.
(iii) *Eutheria* – It bears the well developed child. Example – *Human.*

Note : *(i) In mammal the highest body temperature is of goat. (Average 39 degree Celsius). (ii) Echidna and Duck billed Platypus are the egg laying mammal.*

2. Animal Tissue

The animal tissues can be divided into following categories–(i) Epithelial Tissue, (ii) Connective Tissue, (iii) Muscular Tissue, (iv) Nervous Tissue.

(i) Epithelial Tissue : Epithelial tissue cover the external surface of the body and internal free surface of many organs. Epithelial cell arranged very close to each other. There is no blood vessels supplying nourishment to epithelial cells. They receive nourishment from underlaying connective tissue. The principle functions of epithelial tissues are covering and lining of free surface.

Example : skin, intestine, gland, hollow organ like fallopian tube, nasal passage bronchioles, trachea etc.

(ii) Connective Tissue : These tissue connect and bind different tissues or organs. It provides the structural frame work and mechanical support to body. It play role in body as defense tissue, repair fat storage etc.

Example : Adipose tissue found beneath the skin. Ligament made up of fibrous connective tissue. Cartilage, bone and blood.

Note : *Blood is only tissue which is found in the form of fluid.*

(iii) Muscular Tissue : This is also known as contractile tissue. All the muscles of the body are made up of this tissue. Muscle tissue is of three types – (a) Unstriped, (b) Striped and (c) Cardiac

(a) Unstriped : This muscle tissue is found on the walls of those parts which do not controled by will. These are called involuntary muscle, like – Alimentary canal, Rectum, Ureter, Blood vessels. Unstriped muscles control the motions of all those organs that move on their own.

(b) Striped : These muscles are found in the parts of the body that move voluntary. Normally one or both the end of these muscles turn and connect with bones as tendon.

(c) Cardiac : These muscles are found only on the walls of the heart. The contraction and expansion of the heart is due to these muscles that move throughout the life without fail.

- There are 639 muscles in the human body.
- The largest muscle of the human body is *Gluteus Maximus* (muscle of the hip).
- The smallest muscle of the human body is *Stapedius*.

(iv) Nervous Tissue : This tissue is also called sensitive tissue. The nervous systems of the organisms is made up of these tissues. This is made up of two specific cells – (a) Nerve cell or Neurons and (b) Neuroglia.

Nervous tissue controls all the voluntary & involuntary activities of the body.

3. Human Blood

- Blood is a fluid connective tissue.
- The quantity of blood in the human's body is 7% of the total weight.
- This is a dissolution of base whose pH value is 7.4
- There is an average of 5-6 litres of blood in human body.
- Female contains half litre of blood less in comparison to male.

Blood is consist of two part–

(A) Plasma and (B) Blood corpuscles.

(A) Plasma : This is the liquid part of blood. 60% of the blood is plasma. Its 90% parts is water, 7% protein, 0.9% salt and 0.1% is glucose. Remaining substances are in a very low quantity.

Function of plasma : Transportation of digested food, hormones, exeretory product etc. from the body takes place through plasma.

➢ Serum : When Fibrinogen & protein is extracted out of plasma, the remaining plasma is called *serum*.

(B) Blood corpuscles : This is the remaining 40% part of the blood. This is divided into three parts –

(i) *Red Blood Corpuscles* (RBCs)

(ii) *White Blood Corpuscles* (WBCs) and (iii) *Blood Platelets.*

(i) Red Blood Corpuscles (RBC) : Red Blood Corpuscles (RBC) of a mammal is biconcave.

➢ There is no nucleus in it. Exception – Camel and Lama.
RBC is formed in Bone marrow.
(At the embroynic stage its formation takes place in liver).

➢ Its life span is from 20 days to 120 days.

➢ Its destruction takes place in liver & spleen. Therefore, liver is called grave of RBC.

➢ It contains haemoglobin, in which *haeme* iron containing compound is found and due to this the colour of blood is red.

➢ *Globin* is a proteinous compound which is extremely capable of combining with oxygen and carbon dioxide.

➢ The iron compound found in haemoglobin, is *haematin.*

➢ The main function of RBC is to carry oxygen to all cells of the body and bring back the carbon dioxide.

➢ *Anaemia* disease is caused due the deficiency of haemoglobin.

➢ At the time of sleeping RBC reduced by 5% and people who are at the height of 4200 meters RBC increases by 30% in them.

(ii) White Blood Corpuscles (WBC) or Leucocytes : In shape and constitution this is similar to Amoeba.

➢ Its formation takes place in Bone marrow, lymph node and sometimes in liver and spleen.

➢ Its life span is from 1 to 2 days.

➢ Nucleus is present in the White Blood Corpuscles.

➢ Its main function is to protect the body from the disease.
The ratio of RBC and WBC is 600 : 1.

(iii) Blood Platelets or Thrombocytes : It is found only in the blood of human and other mammals.

➢ There is no nucleus in it.

➢ Its formation takes place in Bone marrow.

➢ Its life span is from 3 to 5 days.

➢ It dies in the Spleen.

➢ Its main function is to help in clotting of blood.

Functions of blood :

(i) To control the temperature of the body and to protect the body from diseases.

(ii) Clotting of blood.

(iii) Transportation of O_2, CO_2, digested food, conduction of hormones etc.

(iv) To help in establishing coordination among different parts.

Clotting of Blood : Three important reactions during clotting of blood.

(i) Thromboplastin + Prothrombin + Calcium = Thrombin.

(ii) Thrombin + Fibrinogen = Fibrin.

(iii) Fibrin + Blood Corpuscles = Clot.

The formation of Prothrombin and Fibrinogen of the blood plasma takes place with the help of Vitamin K. Vitamin K is helpful in making clots of blood. Normally clotting takes the time from 2 to 5 minutes.

The compulsory protein in making clots of blood is *Fibrinogen*.

Blood Group of human : Blood Group was discovered by Landsteiner in 1900. For this, he was awarded with Nobel Prize in the year 1930.

➢ The main reason behind the difference in blood of human is the glyco protein which is found in Red Blood Corpuscles called *antigen*.

Antigen are of two types – Antigen A and Antigen B.

➢ On the basis of presence of Antigen or Glyco Protein, there are four group of blood in human :

(a) That contains Antigen A – Blood Group A.
(b) That contains Antigen B – Blood Group B.
(c) That contains both the Antigens A and B - Blood Group AB.
(d) That contains neither of the Antigens - Blood Group O.

An opposite type of protein, is found in blood plasma. This is called *antibody*. This is also of two types – Antibody 'a' and Antibody 'b'.

Therefore, with the four groups of blood division of antibody is as under–

	Blood Group	Antigen (In Red Blood Corpuscles)	Antibody (In plasma)
1.	A	Only 'A'	Only 'b'
2.	B	Only 'B'	Only 'a'
3.	AB	Both 'A' and 'B'	Absent
4.	O	Absent	Both 'a' and 'b'

Blood Transfusion : Antigen 'A' and antibody 'a', Antigen 'B' and antibody 'b' cannot live together. In case of so happened these get most sticky, which spoils the blood. This is called *agglutination of blood.* Therefore, in blood transfusion adjustment of Antigen and Antibody should be done carefully so that agglutination of blood do not takes place.

Blood Group O is called Universal Donor because it does not contain any antigen.

Blood Group AB is called Universal Receptor because it does not contain any antibody.

Rh factor : In the year 1940, Landsteiner and Wiener discovered a different type of antigen in the blood. They discovered it in the *Rhesus* *monkey*; therefore, it is called *Rh-factor*. In the blood of that person it is found, their blood is called Rh-positive and in the blood of that person it is not found, is called *Rh-negative*.

At the time of blood transfusion Rh-factor is also tested. Rh+ is given to Rh^+ and Rh^- is given Rh-blood only.

If the blood of Rh+ blood group is transmitted to a person with Rh-blood group, then due to the less quantity for the first time there does not seem any bad effect but if this process is repeated then due to agglutination the person with Rh- blood group dies.

Erythroblastosis Foetalis : If the father's blood is Rh+ and the mother's blood is Rh- then the child to be born dies at the pregnancy or short span of time after the birth. (This happens in the case of second issue).

The possible blood group of the child on the basis of blood group of mother and father.

Blood group of Mother and father	Expected blood group of the child	Unexpected blood of the child
O × O	O	A, B, AB
O × A	O, A	B, AB
O × B	O, B	A, AB
O × AB	A, B	O, AB
A × A	A, O	B, AB
A × B	O, A, B, AB	None
A × AB	A, B, AB	O
B × B	B, O	A, AB
B × AB	A, B, AB	O
AB × AB	A, B, AB	O

Haemolymph : Body fluid of arthropoda is a colourless made of plasma and haemocytes. It donot contain any respiratory pigment Ex–Cockroach.

4. System of the Human Body

(a) Digestive System

The complete process of nutritioin is divided into five stages :

1. Ingestion 2. Digestion 3. Absorption
4. Assimilation 5. Defecation

1. **Ingestion :** Taking the food into the mouth is called *Ingestion.*

2. **Digestion :** Conversion of nonabsorbable food into absorbable form. The digestion of the food is started from the mouth.

- Saliva is secreted by salivary gland in mouth in which two types of enzymes are found, *ptyalin* and *maltase*. They convert starch into simple sugar and make it digestible.
- In human secretion of saliva is approximately 1.5 litre per day.
- The nature of saliva is acidic (pH 6.8).
- From the mouth the food reach into stomach through food pipe.
- No digestion takes place in food pipe.

Digestion in Stomach

- The foods lies approximately for four hours in stomach.
- After reaching the food in stomach gastric glands secretes the gastric juice. This is a light yellow acidic liquid.
- Hydrochloric acid secreted from the Oxyntic cells of the stomach kills all the bacteria coming with food and accelerates the reaction of enzymes. Hydrochloric acid makes the food acidic by which ptyalin reaction of the saliva end.
- The enzymes in the gastric juice of stomach are – Pepsin and Renin.
- Pepsin breaks down the protein into peptones.
- Renin breaks down the Caseinogen into Casein.

Digestion in Duodenum

- As soon as the food reaches the duodenum bile juice from liver combines with it. Bile juice is an alkaline and it turns the acidic medium of food into alkaline.
- Here, pancreatic juice from pancreas combines with food. It contains three types of enzymes :

(i) Trypsin : It converts the protein and peptone into polypeptides and amino acid.

(ii) Amylase : It converts the starch into soluble sugar.

(iii) Lipase : It converts the emulsified fats into glycerol and fatty acids.

Small Intestine

- Here, the process of digestion completed and absorption of digested foods start.
- From the wall of small intestine, intestinal juices secretes. The following enzymes contain :

(i) *Erepsin* : It converts the remaining protein and peptone into amino acids.

(ii) *Maltase* : It converts the maltose into glucose.

(iii) *Sucrase* : It converts the sucrose into glucose and fructose.

(iv) *Lactase* : It converts the lactose into glucose and galactose.

(v) *Lipase* : It converts the emulsified fats into glycerol and fatty acids.

Intestinal juice is alkaline in nature.

In a healthy people approximately 2 litres of intestinal juice secretes every day.

3. **Absorption :** Reaching of digested foods into blood is called absorption.

- The absorption of digested foods takes place through small intestinal villi.

4. **Assimilation :** Use of absorbed food in the body is called assimilation.

5. **Defecation :** Undigested food reaches into large intestine where bacteria turns it into *faeces,* which is excreted through anus.

Summary of Digestion

Gland juice		Enzyme	Edible substance	After reaction
1. Saliva	(i)	Ptylin	Starch	Maltose
	(ii)	Maltase	Maltose	Glucose
2. Gastric Juice	(i)	Pepsin	Protein	Peptones
	(ii)	Rennin	Casein	Calcium paracasein
3 Pancreatic juice	(i)	Trypsin	Protein	Polypeptides
	(ii)	Amylase	Starch	Sugar
	(iii)	Lipase	Fat	Fatty acid and glycerol
4. Intestinal juice	(i)	Erepsin	Protein	Amino acid
	(ii)	Maltase	Maltose	Glucose
	(iii)	Lactase	Lactose	Glucose and fructose
	(iv)	Sucrase	Sucrose	Glucose and glactose
	(v)	Lipase	Fat	Fatty acid and glycerol

The main organs participating in digestion :

Liver : This is the largest gland of the human body. Its weight is approximately 1.5 – 2 kilogram.

➢ Bile is secreted through liver only. This bile accelerate the reaction of enzymes present in the intestine.

➢ Liver convert excess of amino acid into ammonia by deamination. These ammonia are further converted into urea by ornithine cycle. Urea comes out from body through kidney.

➢ Liver converts some quantity of protein into glucose during deficiency of carbohydrate.

➢ In carbohydrates metabolism liver converts the excess of glucose found in blood into glycogen and stores it into hepatic Cell as reserve nutrients. If the necessity of glucose arises the liver convert reserve glycogen into glucose. Thus, it regulates the quantity of glucose in the blood.

➢ In case of decrease of fat in food liver converts some of the parts of the carbohydrates into fat.

➢ The production of fibrinogen protein takes place by liver which helps in clotting of blood.

➢ The production of Heparin protein takes place in liver which prohibit the clotting of blood inside the body.

➢ The dead RBC is destroyed by the liver only.

➢ The liver reserve some quantity of iron, copper and vitamin.

➢ It helps in regulating the body temperature.

➢ Liver is an important clue in investigating a person's death that has been due to poison in food.

Gall Bladder : Gall bladder is a pear shaped sac, in which the bile coming out of liver is stored.

➢ Bile comes into the duodenum from gall bladder through the bile duct.

➢ Secretion of bile into the duodenum takes place by reflex action.
➢ Bile is a yellowish-green coloured alkaline liquid, whose pH value is 7.7
➢ The quantity of water is 85% and the quantity of bile pigment is 12% in water.

The Main functions of bile are as under :

(i) It makes the medium of food alkaline so that pancreatic juice can worked.
(ii) It kills the harmful bacteria coming with food.
(iii) It emulsifies the fats.
(iv) It accelerates the bowel movement of intestine by which digestive juices in the food mix well.
(v) It is helpful in the absorption of vitamin K and other vitamins mixed in fats.

In case of obstruction in bile duct, liver cells stop taking bilirubin from blood. As a result, bilirubin spreads throughout the body. This is called *jaundice*.

Pancreas : This is the second largest gland of the human body. It acts as simultaneously endocrine and exocrine type of gland.

➢ Pancreatic juice secretes out of it in which 9.8% water and the remaining parts contain salt and enzymes. It is alkaline liquid, whose pH value is 7.5 – 8.3. It contains the enzymes which can digest all the three types of food materials (like carbohydrates, fat and protein), therefore it is called complete digestive juice.

Islets of Langerhans : This is a part of the Pancreas.

➢ It was discovered by the medical scientist Langerhans.
➢ From its β cell- insulin, from α cell-glucagons and from δ cell-somatostaintin hormones are secreted :

Insulin : It is secreted by β-Cell of islets of Langerhans which is a part of the pancreas.

➢ It was discovered by Banting and Best in the year 1921.
➢ It controls the process of making glycogen from glucose.
➢ Diabetes is caused due to the deficiency of insulin.
➢ Excessive flow of insulin causes Hypoglycemia in which one loses the reproducing capacity and vision deterioration.

Glucagon : It re-converts the glycogen into glucose.

Somatostatin : This is a polypeptide hormone which increases the duration of assimilation of food.

(b) Circulatory System

The discovery of blood circulation was done by *William Harvey* in the year 1628.

There are four parts under it –

(i) Heart (ii) Arteries (iii) Veins and (iv) Blood.

Heart : It remains safe in the *pericardial membrane*. Its weight is approximately 300 grams.

Heart of the human is made up of four chambers. In the anterior side there is a *right auricle* and a *left auricle.* In the posterior side of the heart there is a *right ventricle* and a *left ventricle* persist.

- Between the right auricle and the right ventricle there is a *tricuspid valve.*
- Between the left auricle and left ventricle there is a *bicuspid valve.*
- The blood vessels carrying the blood from the body towards the heart is called *vein.*
- In the vein there is impure blood i.e. carbon dioxide mixed blood. Its exception is pulmonary vein, which always carry pure blood.
- Pulmonary vein carries the blood from lungs to left auricle. It has pure blood.
- The blood vessels carrying the blood from the heart towards the body is called *artery.*
- In artery there is pure blood i.e. oxygen mixed blood. Its exception is pulmonary artery.
- Pulmonary artery carries the blood from right ventricle to lungs. It contains impure blood.
- In the right part of the heart, there remains impure blood i.e. carbon dioxide mixed blood and in the left part of the heart there remains pure blood i.e. oxygen mixed blood.
- The artery carrying blood to the muscles of the heart are called *coronary arteries.* Any type of hindrance in it causes heart attack.

Course of circulation : Mammals have double circulation. It mean blood have to cross two times from heart before circulating throughout the body.

- Right auricle recieve impure blood from the body which goes into right ventricle. From here the blood went into pulmonary artery which send it to the lung for purification. After purification it is collected by pulmonary vein which bring it back to heart in left auricle. From auricle it went into left ventricle. Now this purified blood is went into aorta for different organ of body.

  This circulation is done is a cardiac cycle.
- **Cardiac cycle :** Rhythmic systole (Contraction) and diastole (relaxation) of auricle and ventricle constitutes a cardiac cycle.
- **Heart beat :** Heart keeps beating rhythmically throughout the life. There is a node from which originate contraction of heart.

(i) Sino auricular node (SA node) : It is a specialised area of cardiac muscle fiber in right auricle. SA node is also known as *pace maker* as it generates each wave of cardiac impulse.

(ii) Auriculo – Ventricular node (AV node) : AV node is present close to the interatrial septum near the right AV aperture. Wave of contraction is picked up by AV node which spread through.

- Wave of excitation is picked up by AV node which spread through AV bundle of muscles fibers present on inter artrial septum as well as inter-ventricular septum.

- **Artificial pace maker :** When SA node becomes defective or damaged, the cardiac impulses do not generate. This can be cured by surgical grafting of an artificial pace maker an electric device in the chest of the patient. It stimulate the heart electrically at regular intervals.
- Systole and diastole of the heart are collectively called *heart beat.* In the normal condition the heart of the human beats 72 times and in a single beat it pumps approximately 70 ml blood.
- The blood pressure of a normal human is 120/80. (Systolic – 120 and Diastolic – 80).
- Blood pressure is measured by *sphygmomanometer.*
- *Thyroxin* and *adrenaline* are the hormones which independently controls the heart beat.
- The CO_2 present in the blood accelerates the heart beat by reducing the pH.

(c) Lymph Circulatory System

- The light yellow fluid found in the inter-cellular intervals between different tissues and cells is called *lymph.*
- Lymph is a fluid whose composition is like blood plasma, in which nutrient, oxygen and various other substances are present.
- The corpuscles found in lymph are called *lymphocytes.* In fact, these are White Blood Corpuscles (WBC).
- Lymph flows only in one direction from tissue towards heart.

Functions of lymph :

(i) The lymphocytes present in lymph helps to prevents the body from diseases by killing the harmful bacteria.

(ii) Lymph form the lymphocytes.

(iii) The node found in lymph vessels are called *lymph node* works as a filter in the human body.

(iv) Lymph helps in healing the wounds.

(v) Lymph circulates different material from tissues to veins.

(d) Excretory System

Excretion : Removal of nitrogenous substances formed during metabolism from the body of human is called *excretion.* Normally excretion means the release of nitrogenous excretory substances like urea, ammonia, uric acid etc.

The main excretory organs of human are as follows –

(i) Kidneys, (ii) Skin, (iii) Liver and (iv) Lungs.

(i) Kidneys : The main excretory organ in human and other mammals is a pair of kidneys. Its weight is 140 grams. There are two parts of it. Outer part is called *cortex* and the inner part is called *medulla.* Each kidney is made up of approximately 1,30,00000 kidney ducts which are called *nephrons.* Nephron is the structural & functional unit of the kidney. There is a cup like structure in the every nephron called *Bowman's capsule.* Glomerulus of thin blood vessels are found in the Bowman's capsule which is made up of two types of arterioles.

(i) Afferent arteriole : Which carries the blood to the glomerulus.

(ii) Efferent arteriole : By which the blood is taken out of the glomerulus.

- The process of filtration of liquids into the cavity of Bowman's capsule, is called *ultra filtration*.
- The main function of the kidneys is purification of blood plasma i.e. to excrete the unwanted nitrogenous waste substances through urination.
- The supply of blood to kidneys takes place in large quantity in comparison to other organs.
- In the kidneys average 125 ml per minute blood is filtrated i.e. 180 liters per day. Out of it 1.45 liters urine is formed daily and the remaining is absorbed back by the cells of nephron and mix into the blood.
- In the normal urine there is 95% water, 2% salt, 2.7% urea and 0.3% uric acid.
- The colour of the urine is light yellow due to the presence of *urochromes* in it. Urochrome is formed by the dissotiation of haemoglobin.
- Urine is acidic. Its pH value is 6.
- The stone formed in the kidneys is made up of calcium oxalate.

(ii) Skin : Oil gland and sweat glands found in the skin respectively secretes *sebum* and *sweat*.

(ii) Liver : Liver cells play the main role in excretion by converting more and more amino acids and ammonia of blood into urea.

(iii) Lungs : The lungs excretes two types of gaseous substances carbon dioxide and water vapour. The excretion of some substances like garlic, onion and some spices in which vapour component excreted by the lungs.

Different Animals and excretory parts

Animal	Excretory parts
1. Unicellular animal	By diffusion through general body surface
2. Animals of Porifera Phylum	By general body surface contractile vocoule
3. Coelenterates	Directly by cells.
4. Flat worm	By flame cells.
5. Animals of Annelida Phylum	By nephridia.
6. Arthropods	By Malpighian tubules.
7. Curstaceans	Antennal gland
8. Mollusca	By urinary organ.
9. Vertebrate	Mainly by kidneys

Hemodialysis : Process of removal of excess urea from the blood of patient using artificial kidney.

(e) Nervous System

Under this system thin thread like nerves are spread throughout the body. After receiving the information of environmental changes from the sensitive organs, it spreads them speedly like electrical impulses and establishes working and coordination among different organs.

Nervous System of human is divided into three parts :

(1) Central Nervous System (2) Peripheral Nervous System

(3) Autonomic Nervous System.

1. Central Nervous System – Part of the nervous system which keeps control on the whole body and on nervous system itself is called *Central Nervous System*. The Central Nervous System of human is made up of two parts - *Brain* and *Spinal Cord*.

Brain is covered by membrane called *meninges*. It is situated in a bony box called *craninum* which protect it from external injury.

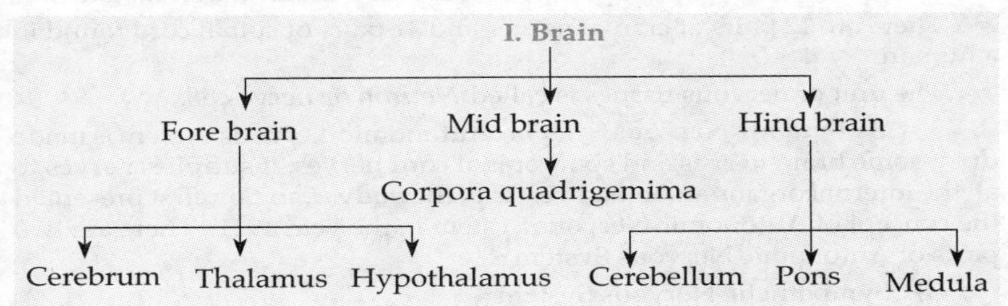

(A) Fore Brain : The weight of the brain of the human is 1350 grams.

(i) The function of the Cerebrum : This is the most developed part of the brain. This is the centre of wisdom, memory, will power, movements, knowledge and thinking. The analysis and coordination of muscular movement received from sense organs.

(ii) The function of thalamus : It is the centre of the pain, cold and heat.

(iii) The function of hypothalamus : It controls the hormonal secretion from endocrine glands. Hormones secreted from posterior pituitary gland secrete through it. This is the centre of hunger, thirst, temperature control, love, hate etc. Blood pressure, metabolism of water, sweat, anger, joy etc. are controlled by it.

(B) The function of Corpora quadrigemina : This is the centre of control on vision and hearing power.

(C) Hind Brain

(i) Function of cerebellum : It is some what at the back of head and consist of two cerebellar hemisphere like cerebrum. It is large reflex centre for coordination of muscular body movements and maintenance of posture.

(ii) Pons : It act as bridge carrying ascending and descending tracts between brain and spinal cord.

(iii) Medulla : It is posterior most part of brain and continuous into the spinal cord. It connect and communicate the brain with spinal cord. It contains the cardiac respiratory and vasomotor centres that control complex activity like heart action, respiration, coughing, sneezing etc.

➢ The brain of the human is covered in the cranium which protects it from external injury. Brain is covered by membrane called *meanings.*

➢ **Spinal cord :** The posterior region of the medulla oblongata forms the spinal cord. Its main functions are :

(a) Coordination and control of reflex actions i.e. it works as the centre of the reflex actions.

(b) It carries the wave coming out of brain.

Note : *Reflex action was first discovered by the scientist, Marshall Hall.*

2. **Peripheral Nervous System :** Peripheral Nervous System is made up of the nerves arising from brain and spinal cord. These are called cranial and spinal nerves respectively. There are sensory, motor and mixed nerve.

➢ There are 12 pairs of cranial nerves and 31 pairs of spinal cord found in a human.

➢ The unit of nervous tissues is called *Neuron* or *nerve cell.*

3. **Autonomic Nervous System :** Autonomic Nervous System is made up of some brain nerves and some spinal cord nerves. It supplies nerves to all the internal organs and blood vessel of the body. *Langley,* first presented the concept of Autonomic Nervous System in the year 1921. There are two parts of Autonomic Nervous System :

(i) Sympathetic Nervous System

(ii) Parasympathetic Nervous System.

Functions of Sympathetic Nervous System :

(i) It narrows the blood vessels in the skin.
(ii) By its action hair gets erected.
(iii) It reduces the secretion of salivary glands.
(iv) It increases the heart beat.
(v) It increase the secretion of sweat glands.
(vi) It stretches the pupil of eye ball.
(vii) It relax the muscles of urinary bladder.
(viii) It reduces the speed of contraction & relaxation of intestine.
(ix) The rate of respiration increase.
(x) It increases the blood pressure.
(xi) It increases the sugar level in the blood.
(xii) It increases the number of Red Blood Corpuscles in the blood.
(xiii) It helps in clotting of blood.
(xiv) Collective impact of this affects fear, pain and anger.

Functions of Parasympathetic Nervous System :

The functions of this system is normally the opposite of Sympathetic Nervous System. For example :

(i) It widens the lumen of blood vessels but except the coronary blood vessels.
(ii) It increases the secretion of saliva and other digestive juices.
(iii) The contraction of pupil is caused by this.
(iv) It creates contraction in the other muscles of the urinary bladder.
(v) It creates contraction and motion in intestinal walls.
(vi) The effect of this nervous system collectively creates the occasion of rest and joy.

(f) Skeletal System

The skeletal system of human is made up of two parts :

(a) Axial skeleton and

(b) Appendicular skeleton.

(a) Axial skeleton : The skeleton, which makes the main axis of the body is called *axial skeleton*. Skull, vertebral column and bones of chest comes under it. There are 80 bones in axial skeleton.

(i) Skull : There are 29 bones in it. Out of these, 8 bones jointly protect the brain of the human. The structure made up of these bones is called *forehead*. All the bones of the fore head remain joined strongly by the sutures. There are 14 bones in addition to this which form the face. Six ear ossicles and one hyoid bone.

(ii) Vertebral Column : The vertebral column of the human is made up of 33 vertebra. All the vertebra are joined by intervertebral disc. Vertebra is made flexible by these intervertebral disc. We divide the whole vertebral column into the following parts –

1.	Cervical region	7 vertebras
2.	Thoracic region	12 vertebras
3.	Lumber region	5 vertebras
4.	Sacral region	(1) 5 vertebras
5.	Caudal region	(1) 4 vertebras
	Total – 33	

➢ Its first vertebra which is called *atlas vertebra* holds the skull.

Functions of vertebral column :

(i) Holds the head.

(ii) It provides the base to the neck and body.

(iii) It helps the human in standing, walking etc.

(iv) It provides flexibility to the neck and body by which a human can move its neck and body in any direction.

(v) It provides protection to spinal cord.

(b) Appendicular skeleton : The following are the parts of it –

(i) Foot bones – Both hands and feet have 118 bones.

(ii) To hold the fore limb and hind limb on the axial skeleton in human there are two girdles.

➢ The girdle of fore limb is called *pectoral girdle* and girdle of hind limb is called *pelvic girdle*.

➢ Pectoral girdle joined with forelimb is called *humerus* and the bone from pelvic girdle join to hindlimb is called *femur*.

Functions of the skeletal system :

(i) To provide a definite shape to the body.

(ii) To provide protection to soft parts of the body.

(iii) To provide a base to the muscles for joining.

(iv) To help in respiration and nutrition.

(v) To form Red Blood Corpuscles.

➢ The total number of bones in a human's body - 206

➢ The total number of bones during childhood - 300

➢ The total number of bones of head - 29
(fore head-8, facial-14, ear-6 ,hyoid -1)

➢ The total number of bones in vertebral column, initially-33
After development - 26(5 sacral fuse into 1 and 4 caudal fuse into 1)

➢ The total number of bones of ribs 24

➢ The largest bone of the body *Femur* (bone of thigh)

➢ The smallest bone of the body *Stapes* (bone of ear)

The name and number of bones of some specific regions –

Ear bones	*Maleus*	(2)	Upper arm	*Humerus*	(2)
	Incus	(2)	Fore arm	*Radio ulna*	(2)
	Stapes	(2)	Wrist	*Carpals*	(16)
Palm	*Meta carpals*	(10)	Fingers	*Phalanges*	(28)
Thigh	*Femur*	(2)	Hind limb	*Tibia-fibula*	(4)
Knee	*Patella*	(2)	Ankle	*Tarsal*	(14)
Sole	*Meta tarsal*	(10)			

Note : *(i) The muscles and bones are join together by tendon.*
(ii) The muscle which join bone to bone is called ligaments.

(g) Endocrine System

(a) Exocrine glands : Gland which have duct are called *exocrine gland.* Secretion of enzymes pass through it. Example – *Lactic gland, Sweat gland, Mucous gland, Salivary gland* etc.

(b) Endocrine gland : These are *ductless gland.* Hormones are secreted by these gland. Hormones are sent to the different parts of the body through blood plasma. Example – *Pituitary gland, Thyroid gland, Parathyroid gland* etc.

Functions and effect of the main endocrine system of the human body and hormone secreted by them –

1. Pituitary gland : It is situated in a depression of the sphenoid bone of the fore head. This is called *sella – tunica.*

➢ Its weight is approximately 0.6 grams.

➢ This is also known as *master gland.* Pitutary gland is controlled by hypothalenus.

The functions of the hormones secreted by Pituitary gland :

(i) STH hormone (Somatotropic hormone) : It controls the growth of the body especially the growth of bones. By the excessiveness of STH *gigantism* and *acromegaly* are caused, in which height of the human grows abnormally. Lack of STH causes *dwarfism* in human.

(ii) TSH hormone (Thyroid Stimulating Hormone) : It stimulates the thyroid gland to secrete hormone.

(iii) ACTH Hormone (Adrenocorticotropic Hormone) : It controls the secretion of adrenal cortex.

(iv) GTH Hormone (Growth Hormone) : It controls the functions of gonads. This is of two types :

(a) FSH Hormone (Follicle - Stimulating Hormone) : In male it stimulates spermatogenesis in the seminiferous tubules of the testis. In female, it stimulates the Graffian follicles of the ovary to secret the hormone *Oestrogen*.

(b) LH Hormone (Luteiniging Hormone) : Interstitial cell stimulating hormone – , secretion of *testosterone* hormone takes place in male and in case of female *estrogen* hormone secreted.

(v) LTH Hormone (Lactogenic Hormone) : Its main function is to stimulate secretion of milk in breasts for infants.

(vi) ADH Hormone (Antidiuretic Hormone) : It causes increase in blood pressure. It is helpful in maintaining the water balance in the body and reduce the volume of urine.

2. **Thyroid gland** : This is situated below the larynx on both side of respiratory trachea in throat of human.

➢ The hormones secreted by it are Thyroxine and Triiodothyronine. Iodine is secretes in more quantity.

Functions of Thyroxin :

(i) It increases the speed of cellular respiration.

(ii) It is necessary for the normal growth of the body particularly for the development of bones, hair etc.

(iii) The normal functions of reproductive organs depend on the activeness of thyroid gland.

(iv) It controls the water balance of the body in coordination with the hormones of pituitary gland.

Diseases Caused by the Deficiency of Thyroxin :

(i) Cretinism : This disease affects the children. The mental and physical retardness of the child.

(ii) Myxedema : In this disease which normally attack during youth the metabolism does not take place properly which causes reduction in heart beat and blood pressure.

(iii) Hypothyroidism : This disease is caused due to a chronic deficiency of thyroxin hormone. Due to this diseases the normal reproduction is not possible. Sometimes due to this disease human becomes dumb and deaf.

(iv) Goitre : This disease is caused by the deficiency of iodine in food. In this disease the shape of the thyroid gland enlarges abnormally.

Diseases caused by the Excessiveness of Thyroxin :

Exopthalmic Goitre : In this disease eyes get bulging out of the eye socket with increased metabolic rate.

3. **Parathyroid gland** : This is situated in the right back of the thyroid gland of the throat. Two hormones are secreted by it :

(i) Parathyroid hormone : This hormone is secreted when there is a deficiency of calcium in the blood.

(ii) Calcitonin: This hormone is released when there is excess of calcium in the blood is present.

Hence, hormone secreted by parathyroid gland controls the quantity of calcium in blood.

4. Adrenal gland : There are two parts of this gland – (i) outer part is cortex and (ii) inner part is medulla.

Hormones secreted by cortex and their function –:

(i) Glucocorticoids : This controls the metabolism of carbohydrate, protein and fat.

(ii) Mineralocorticoids : Its main function is reabsorption of ion by kidney ducts and to control the quantity of other on in the body.

(iii) Sex hormone : It controls the sexual behaviour and secondary sexual characters.

Note : *(i) Cortex is essential for life. If this is extracted completely from the body, human will remain alive only for a week or two.*

(ii) In case of deformation of cortex, the process of metabolism gets disturbed; this disease is called Addison's disease.

Hormones secreted by Medulla and their function :

(i) *Epinephrine* – This is an amino acid.

(ii) *Nor epinephrine* – This is also an amino acid.

- ➢ The work of both the hormones is similar. These equally increase the relaxation and contraction of heart muscles. As a result, blood pressure increases and
- ➢ In case of sudden stop of heart beat, epinephrine is helpful in re-starting the heart beat.
- ➢ The hormone secreted by Adrenal gland is called fight flight, fright fight hormone.

5. Gonads :

(1) Ovary : The following hormones are secreted by this :

(i) Estrogen : It completes the increase of oviduct.

(ii) Progesterone : It stimulates the thickening of uterus lining during ovarien cycle.

(iii) Relaxin : During pregnancy it is found in uterus and placenta. This hormone smoothens the pubic symphysix and it widens the uterine cervix so that a child is delivered easily.

(2) Testes : The hormone secreted by it is called *testosterone*. It motivates the sexual behaviour and growth of secondary sexual characters.

(h) Respiratory System

- ➢ The most important organ of the respiratory system of human is lungs where the exchange of gases takes place.
- ➢ All those organs comes under respiratory system which help in exchange of gases are – Nasal passage, Pharynx, Larynx or Voice box, Trachea, Bronchi, Bronchioles, Lungs etc.
- ➢ **Nasal passage :** Its main function is related to sniffing. Its inner cavity is lined with mucous membrane. This secretes approximately ½ litre

of mucous everyday. This prevents the particles of sand, bacteria or other small organisms from entering into the body. It makes the air wet entering into the body and equalises it with the temperature of the body.

➢ **Pharynx :** It is situated behind the nasal cavity.

➢ **Larynx or Voice box :** The part of the respiratory way which connects the pharynx with trachea is called *Larynx* or *voice box*. Its main function is to produce sound. At the larynx entrance gate there is a thin blade-like door, which is called *epiglottis*. When any food particle is swallowed it closes the glottis, as a result food does not enter into respiration pipe.

➢ **Trachea :** It enters into the thoracic cavity. The two main branches of trachea are called *bronchi*. Right bronchi enters into the right lungs after being divided into three branches. Left bronchi enters into the left lungs after being divided into only two branches.

➢ **Lungs :** There is a pair of lungs in the thoracic cavity. Its colour is red and looks like sponge. Right lung is larger in comparison to left lung. Each lung is surrounded by a membrane which is called *pleural membrane*. There is a network of blood capillaries . Here Oxygen enters into the blood and CO_2 comes out.

The process of respiration can be divided into four parts :

1. External respiration.
2. Transportation of gases.
3. Internal respiration.
4. Cellular respiration.

1. **External respiration :** This is divided into two parts –

(a) Breathing (b) Exchange of gases.

(a) Breathing : In lungs air is taken and given out at a certain rate which is called *breathing*.

Mechanism of Breathing :

(i) Inspiration : At this stage, air from the environment enters into the lungs through the nasal passage, due to increases in the dimension of thoracic cavity a low pressure is formed in the lungs and air enters into the lungs from environment. This air continues to enter until the pressure of air inside and outside the body became equal.

(ii) Expiration : In this process air comes out of the lungs.

Constitution of air in Breathing

	Nitrogen	Oxygen	Carbon dioxide
The air inhaled	79%	21%	0.03%
The air exhaled	79%	17%	4%

Every day approximately 400 ml water is excreted through breathing.

(b) Exchange of gases : The exchange of gases takes place inside the lungs. This gaseous exchange takes place on the basis of concentration gradient through normal diffusion.

The exchange of oxygen and carbon dioxide gases takes place due to their difference in partial pressures. The direction of diffusion of both.

2. **Transportation of gases :** The process of reaching of gases (oxygen

and carbon dioxide) from lungs to the cells of body and coming back again to the lungs is called the *transportation of gases.*

➢ Transportation of oxygen takes place by haemoglobin present in blood.

➢ Transportation of carbon dioxide from cells to lung takes place by haemoglobin only to the extent of 10 to 20%.

➢ Transportation of carbon dioxide takes place through circulation of blood :

(i) By mixing with plasma : Carbon dioxide forms carbonic acid after mixing in plasma. Transportation of 7% carbon dioxide takes place in this form.

(ii) In the form of bicarbonates : 70% part of carbon dioxide in the form of bicarbonates is transported. It mixes with potassium and sodium of blood and forms potassium bicarbonate and sodium bicarbonate.

3. **Internal respiration :** Inside the body, gaseous exchange takes place between blood and tissue fluid which is called *internal respiration.*

Note : *The gaseous exchange in lungs is called external respiration.*

4. **Cellular respiration :** Glucose is oxidised by oxygen reached into the cell. This process is called *cellular respiration.*

Types of cellular respiration :

Respiration is of two type

(a) Anaerobic respiration : If the oxidation of food takes place in absence of oxygen. During this only 2 ATP molecules are produced from one molecule of glucose. Final product of anaerobic respiration in animal tissue like skeletal muscle cell is lactic acid.

In yeast and certain bacteria ethyl alcohol or ethanol is produced.

$$C_6H_{12}O_6 \rightarrow \underset{\text{(Lactic acid)}}{2C_3H_6O_3} + \text{Energy (in animal)}$$

$$C_6H_{12}O_6 \rightarrow \underset{\text{(Ethyl alcohol)}}{2C_2H_5OH} + 2CO_2 + \text{Energy (in plant)}$$

(b) Aerobic respiration : It takes place in the presence of oxygen. The complete oxidation of glucose takes place. As a result CO_2 and H_2O is formed and energy is released in huge amount.

$$C_6H_{12}O_6 + 6O_2 \rightarrow 6CO_2 + 6H_2O + 2870 \text{ KJ energy. (38 ATP)}$$

The complex process in cellular respiration is divided into two parts–

(i) Glycolysis (cytoplasm) (ii) Kreb's cycle (Mitochondria)

(i) Glycolysis : Its study was first done by *Embden Meyorh pathway.* Therefore, it is also called *EMP path*

➢ Glycolysis is present in both types of respiration, Aerobic and Anaerobic. This process takes place in cytoplasm.

➢ As a result of decomposition of one glucose atom in glycolysis two atoms of pyruvic acid is formed.

➢ To start this process 2 atoms of ATP (Adenosine Triphosphate) takes part but at the end of the process 4 atoms ATP are obtained. Therefore, as a result of glycolysis 2 atom ATP are obtained i.e. 16000 calorie (2 x 8000) energy is obtained.

- There is no need of oxygen in glycolysis. Hence, this process is similar in anaerobic respiration and aerobic respiration.
- In this, four molecules of hydrogen formed which is used in converting NAD to $2NADH_2$.

(ii) Kreb's Cycle : It was described by *Hens Krebs* in 1937.

- This is also called *Citric Acid Cycle* or *Tricarboxylic Cycle*.
- This process is completed inside the Mitochondria in the presence of specific enzymes.
- Two atoms of each ADP and ATP are formed.
- In this cycle 4 pair of hydrogen atom are released.
- The complete cycle is of 2 atom pyruvic acid, produce total 4 atoms of carbon dioxide.
- In our system maximum ATP atoms are formed during Kreb's Cycle.

Production of energy : By the oxidation of pyruvic acid one atom of ATP, five atoms of NADH and one atom of $NADH_2$ are formed. From one atom of NADH three atoms of ATP and from one atom of $NADH_2$ two atoms of ATP are obtained. Hence, from one atom of pyruvic acid 1 + (3 x 5) + (2 x 1) = 18 atoms of ATP are formed. From one atom of glucose two atoms of pyruvic acid are formed, by which 36 atoms of ATP are released. During the glycolysis, two atoms of ATP are obtained. Hence, during respiration of one atom of glucose total 2 + 36 = 38 ATP atoms are obtained.

Respiratory substances : Carbohydrate, fat and protein are the main respiratory substances. At first, oxidation of glucose takes place, then fat. After the consumption of carbohydrate and fat oxidation of protein start.

Note : *Respiration is a Catabolic Process. It also reduces the weight of the body.*

5. Nutrients

To maintain life organisms performs some basic function is called *nutrition*. Nutrition is one of the basic function of life in which intake of food, digestion, absorption, assimilation and egestion of undigested foods are included.

Nutrient : Nutrient are the substance by which an organism get energy or it is used for biosynthesis of its body.

For example carbohydrate and fat are the source of energy. Whereas proteins and minerals are the nutrient used for biosynthesis.

Carbohydrate : Carbohydrates are organic compounds in which the ratio of Carbon, Hydrogen and Oxygen is 1 : 2 : 1. Carbohydrate in the form of sugar and starch are major intake in animals and human. 50 to 75% energy is obtained by oxidation of carbohydrate. Carbohydrate containing aldehyde group is called *aldose* and with ketone group is called *ketose*. Carbohydrates are derivatives of polyhydroxy alcohols.

Classification of carbohydrate : Carbohydrates are classified into three major group.

(a) Monosaccharides : These are the simple sugar made up of single polyhydroxy or ketone unit. Most abundant monosaccharides found in nature is glucose containing six carbon atom. *Triose, tetrose, pentoses, heptoses* are the type of monosaccharides.

(b Oligosaccharides : When 2 to 10 monosaccharides join together they form oligosaccharides. They are usually crystalline in nature and sweet in test. *Maltose, sucrose, lactose* are disaccharides made up of two monosaccharides.

(c) Polysaccharides : These are the compound of sugar which are formed due to joining large number of monosaccharide. There are insoluble and tasteless. Some example of polysaccharides are *starch, glycogen, cellulose, chitin* etc.

Function of Carbohydrate

1. Carbohydrate works as fuel. During the process of respiration, glucose break into CO_2 & H_2O with the release of energy. One gram of glucose gives 4.2 kilo calories energy.
2. Nucleic acids are polymers of nucleosides and nucleotides and contain pentose sugar.
3. Lactose of milk is formed from glucose and glactose.
4. Glucose is used for the formation of fat and amino acid.
5. Carbon skeleton of monosaccharides is used in the formation of fatty acid, chitin, cellulose etc.

Source of Carbohydrate : Wheat, rice, maize, sweet potato, potato and other plant and animals are the sources of carbohydrate.

2. Protein : Protein word was first used by *J. Berzelius.* This is a complex organic compound made up of 20 type of amino acids. Approximately 15% of the human body is made up of protein. Nitrogen is present in protein in addition to C, H & O.

Twenty two types of protein is necessary for human body, out of which 12 are synthesized by body itself and remaining 10 are obtained by food are called essential amino acid.

Types of proteins :

On the basis of chemical composition

It is divided into three types.

(1) Simple Protein : It consists of only amino acid.

Example : *Albumins, Globulins, Histones* etc.

(2) Conjugated Protein : Having some another chemical compounds in addition to amino acid.

Example : *Chromoprotein, Glycoprotein* etc.

(3) Derived Protein : It is derived from the partial digestion of natural proteins or its hydrolysis.

Example : *Peptone, Peptide, Proteinase* etc.

Function of Protein :

(i) It takes part in the formation of cells, protoplasm and tissues.

(ii) These are important for physical growth. Physical growth hampers by its deficiency. Lack of proteins causes *Kwashiorkor* and *Marasmus* diseases in children.

(iii) In case of necessity these provide energy to the body.
(iv) These control the development of genetic characters.
(v) These are helpful in conduction also.

Kwashiorkor : In this disease hands and legs of children get slimmed and the stomach comes out.

Marasmus : In this disease muscles of children are loosened.

3. **Fats :** Fat is an ester of glycerol and fatty acid.

In these carbon, hydrogen and oxygen are present in different quantities, but proportionally less oxygen than carbohydrate.

Normally *fat* remains as solid at 20°C temperature, but if it is in liquid form at this temperature, this is called *oil.*

Fatty acids are of two types – Saturated and unsaturated. Unsaturated faty acids are found in fish oil and vegetable oil. Only coconut oil and palm oil are the examples of saturated oil.

9.3 kilo calorie energy is liberated from 1 gram fat.

Normally an adult person should get 20-30% of energy from fat.

Main functions of fat :

(i) It provides energy to the body.
(ii) It remains under the skin and prevents the loss of heat from the body.
(iii) It make the food material testy.
(iv) It protects different parts of the body from Injury.

Due to the lack of fat skin gets dried, weight of the body decreases and the development of the body checked.

Due to the excessiveness of fat the body gets fatty, heart disease takes place and blood pressure increases.

4. **Vitamins :** Vitamin was invented by Sir F. G. Hopkins. The term vitamin was coined by Funk.

Vitamins are organic compound required in minute quantities. No calorie is obtained from it, but it is very important in regulating chemical reactions in metabolism of the body.

On the basis of solubility, vitamins are of two types :

(i) Vitamin soluble in water : Vitamin-B and Vitamin-C.
(ii) Vitamin soluble in fat : Vitamin-A, Vitamin-D, Vitamin-E and Vitamin-K.

The diseases caused by the deficiency of vitamins and their sources

Vitamin	Chemical name	Deficiency diseases	Sources
Vitamin-A	Retinol	Colour blindness, Xerophthalmia	Milk, Egg, Cheese, Green vegetable fish liver oil
Vitamin-B_1	Thymine	Beriberi	Ground nut, Rapseed, Dried Chilli, Pulses, Liver, Egg, Vegetables etc.

Vitamin	Chemical name	Deficiency diseases	Sources
Vitamin-B_2	Riboflavin	Cracking of skin, red-dish eye, cracking of tongue	Meat, Green vegetables, Milk etc.
Vitamin-B_3	Pantothenic acid	Whitening of hair, mentally retardness	Meat, Milk, Nut, Tomato, Sugarcane etc.
Vitamin-B_5	Nicotinamide or Niacin	Pellagra or 4-D Syndrome	Meat, Ground nut, Potato, Tomato, Leafy vegetables etc.
Vitamin-B_6	Pyridoxine	Anaemia, skin disease	Liver, Meat, Grains etc.
Vitamin-B_7	Biotin	Paralysis, body pain, hair falling	Meat, Egg, Liver, Milk etc.
Vitamin-B_{12}	Cynocobalamin	Anaemia, jaundice Teroile Glutemic	Meat, Milk etc.
Folic acid	–	Anaemia, diarrhoea	Pulses, Liver, Vegetables, Eggs etc.
Vitamin-C	Ascorbic acid	Scurvy, Swelling of gums	Lemon, Orange, Tomato, Sour substances, Chilly, Sprouted grain etc.
Vitamin-D	Calciferol	Rickets (in children), Osteomalasia (in adults)	Fish liver oil, Milk, Eggs etc.
Vitamin-E	Tocopherol	Less fertility	Leafy vegetables, Milk, Butter, Sprouted wheat, Vegetable oil etc.
Vitamin-K	Phylloquinone	Non-clotting of blood	Tomato, Soybean oil Green vegetables, etc.

- Cobalt is found in Vitamin-B_{12}.
- Synthesis of vitamins cannot be done by the cells and it is fulfilled by the vitamin foods.
- However, synthesis of Vitamin-D and K takes place in our body.
- Synthesis of Vitamin-D takes place by the ultra violet rays present in the sunlight through cholesterol (Irgesterol) of skin.
- Vitamin-K is synthesized in our colon by the bacteria and from there it is absorbed.

6. Minerals : Mineral is a homogenous inorganic material needed for body. These control the metabolism of body.

Important Minerals and their functions

Minerals	Daily quantity	Main sources	Functions
Sodium (as sodium chloride)	2 – 5 gram	Normal salt, fish, meat, eggs, milk etc.	It normally found in external fluid of cell and is related to following functions : Contractions of muscles, In the transmission of nerve impulses in nerve fiber. Control of positive electrolyte balance in body etc.

Minerals	Daily quantity	Main sources	Functions
Potassium	1 gram	Approximately all edibles	It is normally found in protoplasm. It is important for following different chemical reactions in cells : Muscular contraction, nerve conduction. maintenance of positive electrolyte in body etc.
Calcium	Approx. 1.2 gram	Milk, cheese, eggs, grains, gram, fish etc.	This provides strength to bones and teeth with vitamin, Important role in blood formation, Related with muscular contruction. Help in clotting the blood etc.
Phosphorus	1.2 gram	Milk, cheese, Bajra, green leaf vegetables, etc.	This provides strength to bones and teeth, in coordination with calcium.
Iron	25 mg (boy) 35 mg (girl)	Albumen of egg, bread, Bajra, Banana, Spanich apple	Iron is important in formation of Red Blood Corpuscles and haemoglobin. This is important for tissue Oxidation.
Iodine	20 mg	Sea fish, sea food, green leaf vegetables, Iodized salt.	This is important for synthesis of thyroxin hormone secreted by Thyroid gland.
Magnesium	Very small quantity	Vegetables	For functioning of muscular system and nervous system.
Zinc	Very small quantity	Liver and fishes	For insulin functioning.
Copper	Very small quantity	Meat, fish, liver and grains.	Formation of haemoglobin and bones and as a conductor of electron.
Cobalt	Very small quantity	Meat, fish and water	For synthesis of RBC and Vitamin B_{12}.

7. **Water** : Human gets it by drinking. Water is the important component of our body. 65-75% weight of the body is water.

Main functions of water :

1. Water controls the temperature of our body by sweating and vaporizing.
2. It is the important way of excretion of the excretory substances from the body.
3. Maximum organic chemical reactions in the body perform through hydrolysis.

Balance Diet : That nutrition, in which all the important nutrients for organism are available in sufficient quantity, is called *Balance Diet*.

Balance nutrition is obtained from Balance Diet, which is given in the chart below :

Edibles	Adult male			Adult female			Children		Boy	Girl
	N	M	Hard	N	M	Hard	1-3 yrs.	4-6 yrs.	10-18 yrs.	10-16 yrs.
Grain (wheat, rice)	400 g	520 g	670 g	410 g	440 g	575 g	175 g	270 g	420 g	380 g
Pulses	40 g	50 g	60 g	40 g	45 g	50 g	35 g	35 g	45 g	45 g
Leafy vegetables	40 g	40 g	40 g	100 g	100 g	50 g	40 g	50 g	50 g	50 g
Vegetables (other)	60 g	70 g	80 g	40 g	40 g	100 g	20 g	30 g	50 g	50 g
Milk	150 g	200 g	250 g	100 g	150 g	200 g	300 g	250 g	250 g	250 g
Tuber root	50 g	60 g	80 g	50 g	50 g	60 g	10 g	20 g	30 g	30 g
Sugar	30 g	35 g	55	20 g	20 g	40 g	30 g	40 g	45 g	45 g
Fat and oil	40 g	45 g	65 g	20 g	25 g	40 g	15 g	25 g	40 g	35 g

Necessary calorie for a human being :

	Nature of work	Male	Female
1.	Light worker	2000 calorie	2100 calorie
2.	Eight hours worker	3000 calorie	2500 calorie
3.	Hard worker	3600 calorie	3000 calorie

6. Human Diseases

Diseases caused by Protozoa :

	Disease	Affected organ	Parasites	Carrier	Symptoms Mosquito
1.	Malaria	RBC & Liver	*Plasmodium*	Female Anophelies	Fever with shivering
2.	Pyorrhoea	Gums	*Entamoeba gingivelis*	—	Bleeding from gums.
3.	Sleeping sickness	Brain	*Trypanosoma*	Tse-Tse flies	Fever with severe sleep.
4.	Diarrhoea	Intestine	*Entamoeba histolytica*	—	Mucous & Diarrohea with blood.
5.	Kala-ajar	Bone marrow	*Leismania donovani*	Sand flies	High fever.

Charles Leveran discovered the Malaria Parasite, *plasmodium* in the blood of the affected person in the year 1880.

Ronald Ross (1897) confirmed the Malaria is caused by malaria parasite and told that mosquito is the carrier of it.

Diseases caused by Bacteria :

Disease	Affected organ	Name of Bacteria	Symptoms
Tetanus	Nervous system	*Clostridium Tetani*	High fever, spasm in body, Closing of jaws etc.
Cholera	Intestine	*Vibrio cholerae*	Continuous stool and vomiting.
Typhoid	Intestine	*Salmonella typhosa*	High fever, headache.
Tuberculosis	Lungs	*Mycobacterium tuberculosis*	Repeated coughing.
Diphtheria	Respiratory tube	*Corynebacterium diphtheriae*	Difficulty in respiration and suffocation.
Plague	Lungs, area between the two legs	*Pasteurella pesties*	Very high fever, muscular eruptions on the body.
Whooping cough	Respiratory system	*Hemophilis pertusis*	Continuous coughing.
Pneumonia	Lungs	*Diplococcus pneumoniae*	High fever, swelling in lungs.
Leprosy	Nervous System Skin	*Mycobacterium leprae*	Spots on body, nerves affected.
Gonorrhea	Urinary Path	*Neisseria Gonorrhoeae*	Swelling in urinary path.
Syphilis	Urinary path	*Treponema pallidum*	Wounds in urinogenial tract

Note : *In the year 1882, German scientist Robert Koch discovered the bacteria of Cholera and T.B.*

Louis Pasteur discovered the vaccine of Rabies and pasteurization of milk.

Diseases caused by Viruses

	Disease	Affected organ	Name of virus	Symptoms
1.	AIDS	Defensive system (WBC)	HIV	Immune system of body became weak.
2.	Dengue fever	Whole body particularly head, eyes and joints.	Billions of virus	Pain in eyes, muscles, head and joints
3.	Polio	Throat, backbone Nerve.	Pilio virus	Fever, body pain, backbone and intestine cells are destroyed.
4.	Influenza (flu)	Whole body	Mixo virus	Suffocation, sneezing, restlessness.
5.	Chicken pox	Whole body	Variola virus	High fever, redish eruption on body.

	Disease	Affected organ	Name of virus	Symptoms
6.	Small pox	Whole body	Varicella virus	Light fever, eruption of bile on body.
7.	Goitre	Parathyroid gland	—	Difficulty in opening the mouth with fever.
8.	Measles	Whole body	Morbeli virus	Redish eruptions on body.
9.	Trachoma	Eyes	—	Reddish eyes, pain in eyes.
10.	Hepatitis or Jaundice	Liver	—	Yellow urine, Eyes and skin become yellow.
11.	Rabies	Nervous system	Rabies virus	The patient becomes mad with sever headache & high fever.
12.	Meningitis	Brain	—	High fever.
13.	Herpes	Skin	Herpes	Swelling in skin.

Note : *AIDS – Acquired Immuno Deficiency Syndrome.*

Elisa Test : *Test of HIV Virus (AIDS)*

Diseases caused by Protozoa :

(i) Diarrhoea : The reason of this disease is the presence of internal protozoa namely *Entamoeba histolytica* which is spread through house flies. It causes wounds in the intestine. Protein digesting enzyme, trypsin is destroyed in this. This disease is mostly found in children. Disease caused by helminthes.

(ii) Filaria : This disease is caused by *Wuchereia baoncrofti.* This worm is circulated by the stings of culex mosquitoes. This disease causes swelling in legs, testes and other parts of the body. This disease is also known as *Elephantiasis.*

Diseases caused by Fungus

(i) Asthma : The spores of the fungi, namely *Aspergillus fumigatus* reaches the lungs of the human and constitutes a net like formation, thus, obstructs the function of lungs. This is a infections disease.

(ii) Athlete's foot : This disease is caused by the fungi namely *Tenia Pedes.* This is a infections disease of skin which spreads mainly due to the cracking of feet.

(iii) Scabies : This disease is caused by the fungi namely *Acarus scabies.* In this disease the skin itches and white spots found on the skin.

(iv) Baldness : This is caused by the fungi namely *Taenia capitis.* Due to this hair of the head falls.

(v) Ringworm : This disease spreads through the fungi namely *Trycophyton Lerucosum.* This is a infections disease. Round red spot found on the skin.

Some Other Diseases

1. Paralysis or Hemiplegia : In this disease within a few minutes half of the body is paralyzed. The nerves of the paralyzed part become inactive.

The reason of this disease is due to high blood pressure bursting of any nerve of brain or insufficient supply of blood to brain.

2. Allergy : Some substance like sand, smoke, chemical, clothes, cold are dangerous to some persons and there are reactions in their body, which causes various diseases. Itching, pimples, swelling in body, black spot, eczema etc. are the examples of allergy.

3. Schizophrenia : This is a mental disease which usually found in youth. The patient considers the imagination as a truth, not to the facts. These patients are lazy, emotionless etc. Electropathy is helpful in this disease.

4. Epilepsy : This disease is caused by the internal disturbance of brain. In this disease, foam coming out of the mouth and the patient falls down unconscious.

5. Diplopia : This disease is caused by the paralysis of muscles of the eyes, in which double image is formed.

6. Bronchitis : It is caused by the inflammation of tubes leading from the wind pipe to lungs.

7. Colds : This is highly infections disease and is caused by a virus which result in bad throat, headache and watery nose.

8. Colic : Severe pain in the abdomen caused by spasm of the internal organs usually the intestines.

9. Delirium : It is a serious mental disturbance occuring under the influence of poisonous drugs.

10. Hydrophobia : A disease cause by bite of a mad dog.

11. Hyper metropia (long sightedness) : One can see the object of longer distance but not the object of nearer one. It can be corected by convex lens.

12. Myopia (short sightedness) : In this disease person can see the object of nearer distance but can not see the object of longer distance. It is corrected by using concave lens.

13. Leukaemia : There is a great increase in the number of white blood corpuscles in system. Swelling of spleen takes place. Death occur within few days.

14. Migrain : An allergic disease in which there is a periodic attack of headache takes place. It is an incureble disease.

15. Obesity : Excessive fatness is called *obesity*.

16. Piles : There are a various vein in the rectum. Due to extra pressure on vein it prevent the free flow of blood creating problem. It is caused due to constipation.

17. Rheumatism : The symptiom of this disease is fever with joints pain.

Other Disease

Atherosclerosis : Deposition of cholesterol particles in the lumen of arteries which prevent the flow of blood is called atherosclerosis.

Arteriosclerosis : Due to deposition of cholesterol and calcium salt arteries became stiff and rigid. It loses the property of elasticity due to which wall of arteries may rap fun.

Uremia : Presence of excess of urea in blood is called uremia, This is caused by malfunctioning of kidney.

Glgcosuria : Presence of excess of glucose urine is known as glycosuria.

Arthritis : It is disease in which inflammation of joints takes place.

Osteoporosis : It is a age dependent disorder of bone in which low bone mass and increased fragility takes place.

Hyperglycemia : It is disorder in which the concentration of glucose in the blood is high.

Hypoglycemia : It is a condition in which the concentration of glucose in the blood is very low.

Pneumonia : Acute inflamation of alveoli of lung.

Emphysema : It is the abnormal distension of alveoli which result in the loss of elasticity. Cigarette smoke and chronic bronchitis are two main causes.

7. Miscellaneous

Medicinal Discoveries

Inventions/Discoveries	Inventor/Discoveries
Vitamin*	F. G. Hopkins, Cosimir Funk
Vitamin-A	Mc. Collum
Vitamin-B	Mc. Collum
Vitamin-C	Holst
Vitamin-D	Mc. Collum
Sulpha drugs	Dagmanck (Dogmanck)
Streptomycin	Selman Waksmann
Heart Transplantation	Christian Bernard
Homoeopathy	Hahnemann
Malaria parasite and treatment	Ronald Ross
Diarrhoea and treatment of plague	Kitajato
Sex hormone	Stenach
Open heart surgery	Waltallilehak
Contraceptive pills	Pincus
First test tube baby	Edwards and Stepto
Electrocardiograph	Iwanyaan
Antigen	Karl Landsteiner
RNA	James Watson and Arther Arg
DNA	James Watson and Crick
Insulin	Banting

* *Funk named it 'Vitamine' (in 1912)*

Inventions	Inventor
Chloroform	Harrison and Sympson
Vaccine of chicken pox	Edward Jenner
T.B. bacteria	Robert Koch
Diabetes	Banting
Penicillin	Alexander Flemming
Polio vaccine	Johan E. Salk
BCG	Guerin Calmatte
Bacteria	Luvenhauk – Leeuwenhock
Blood transfer	Karl Landsteiner

Important Informations :

Largest and heaviest mammal	Blue whale
Largest land mammal	African elephant
Largest living reptile	Sea turtle (Tortoise)
Largest living bird	Ostrich
Largest snake	Python
Largest monkey	Gorilla
Smallest bird	Humming bird
Smallest mammal	Shrew
Largest egg	Ostrich's egg.
Fastest animal	Cheetah (Panther)
Fastest flying bird	Spine tailed Swift
Egg lying mammal	Echidna and Duckbiled Platypus
Tallest mammal	Giraffe (Africa)
Busiest human organ	Heart

Some Important facts

1. The study of dreams is called Oneirology.
2. The study of the beauty of human is called Kalology.
3. At the time of creation of life there was no oxygen.
4. The strongest part in the body is the enamel of teeth.
5. The sex determination of human depends on male chromosomes not on female chromosomes.
6. The fastest nervous speed is 532 kmph.
7. The internal area of the lungs of human is 93 sq. m. which is forty times of the external area of the body.
8. The bones are as strong as concrete and as hard as granite.
9. Inside the body approximately 150 lakh cells are destroyed every second.

10. The weight of the uterus of the woman who has not given birth to a child is 50 grams and after giving birth to a child the weight becomes 100 grams.
11. The weight of the kidney is approximately 150 grams.
12. In a single inhaling, a normal adult takes 500 ml air inside the body.
13. The capacity of heart to pump the blood is 4.5 liters per minute.
14. The length of the small intestine is approximately 7 meter and its diameter is 2.5 centimeter.
15. The blood circulation inside the body takes approximately 23 seconds.
16. The antibiotic namely, penicillin is obtained from penicillium fungus.
17. Human is the most intelligent hominid of the universe.
18. Albatross is the largest sea bird, whose spread of feather is 10-12 ft.
19. There are approximately 50 lakhs hair in the body of human.
20. In the initial stage of formation of placenta, H.C.G. hormones flow at a large quantity and excreted through urine. At this time, in the testing of urine due to presence of this hormone pregnancy test is carried out.
21. The heart beat of a child is more than that of an adult.
22. A single respiration completes in 5 seconds i.e. 2 seconds of inspiration and 3 seconds of expiration.
23. Everyday blood in the body of the human carries approximately 350 liters of oxygen to the cells of the body. Out of this 97% oxygen is carried by haemoglobin and remaining 3% is circulated by blood plasma.

★★★

MISCELLANY 9

1. Firsts in India (Male)

First Governor of Bengal	*Lord Clive (1757 - 60)*
Last Governor of Bengal	*Warren Hastings (1772 - 74)*
First Governor General of Bengal	*Warren Hastings (1774 - 85)*
First Governor General of India	*Lord William Bentic (1833 - 35)*
Last Governor General and First Viceroy of India	*Lord Canning (1856-62)*
First President of Indian National Congress	*W.C. Banerjee*
First Indian Governor General of Independent India	*C. Rajgopalachari (21.06.1948 - 25.01.1950)*
First Indian to pass ICS	*Surendra Nath Banerjee*
First Indian I.C.S. Officer	*Satyendra Nath Tagore*
First Governor General of India (after independence)	*Lord Louis Mountbatten (15 Aug, 1947 - 20 June, 1948)*
First Indian Cosmonaut (to go into space)	*Sqn. Ldr. Rakesh Sharma*
First temporary President of the Constitutent Assembly	*Dr. Sachchida Nand Sinha*
First Commander-in-Chief of Free India	*General K.M. Cariappa*
First Indian Nobel Laureate	*Rabindra Nath Tagore*
First Indian Judge of the International Court of Justice	*Dr. Nagendra Singh*
First Indian to get Bharat Ratna Award	*Dr. S. Radhakrishnan*
First Field Marshal	*General S.F.J. Manekshaw*
The President of Constituent Assembly	*Dr. Rajendra Prasad*
First Indian to swim across the English Channel	*Mihir Sen*
First Indian to get Jnanpeeth Award	*G. Shankar Kurup*
First Muslim President of Indian Republic	*Dr. Zakir Hussain*
First Indian to win Palk-Strait Ocean Swimming Contest	*Baidyanath Nath*
First Speaker of Lok Sabha	*G.V. Mavlankar (1952-57)*
First person to make Printing Press popular in India	*James Hicky*
First Education Minister of Independent India	*Maulana Abul Kalam Azad*
First President of Indian Republic	*Dr. Rajendra Prasad*
First Prime Minister of Independent India	*Pt. Jawahar Lal Nehru*
First Home Minister of Independent India	*Sardar Vallabh Bhai Patel*
First Vice- President of Independent India	*Dr. S. Radhakrishnan*
First Chief of Air Staff	*Air Marshal Sir Thomas Elmhirst*
First Indian Air Chief of India	*Air Marshal S. Mukherjee*
First Chief of Army Staff	*General M. Rajendra Singh*

First Chief of Naval Staff of India	*Vice-Admiral R.D. Katari*
First large-scale Atomic Reactor of India	*Apsara (1956)*
First Person to get Paramvir Chakra	*Major Somnath Sharma*
First Atomic Submarine of India	*I.N.S. Chakra*
First Indian Scientist to get Nobel Prize	*C.V. Raman (Physics)*
First Indian Submarine	*I.N.S. Cauveri*
First Scientist of Indian origin, to get Nobel Prize in the field of Medical Science	*Dr. Hargovind Khurana*
First Aircraft Carrier Indian Ship	*I.N.S. Vikrant*
First Chinese pilgrim to visit India	*Fa - hien*
First Medium Range Missile	*Agni*
First e-business News Paper of India	*Financial Express*
First Scientist of Indian origin to win Nobel Prize in Physics	*Subrahmanium Chandrashekhar*
First Indian Missile	*Prithvi*
First Indian to win Stalin Award	*Saiffudin Kichlu*
India's first Nuclear Centre	*Tarapur*
First Indian to win Magsaysay Award	*Acharya Vinoba Bhave (1958)*
India's first Open University	*Andhra Pradesh Open University*
India's first Lok Sabha Member to be elected with a record maximum number of votes	*P.V. Narasimha Rao*
India's first minister to resign from Union Cabinet	*Shyama Prasad Mukherjee (1950)*
First British to visit India	*Hawkins*
First Asian Games organised	*Delhi (in 1951)*
India's first Election Commissioner	*Sukumar Sen*
First Muslim President of Indian National Congress	*Badruddin Tayab Ji*
First Chief Justice of India	*Justice Hiralal J. Kania*
First Person to submit the proposal of Indian Independnce in a Congress Session	*Hasrat Mohani*
India's first University	*Nalanda University*
First Indian to climb Mt. Everest without Oxy. cylinder	*Sherpa Phu Dorji*
First foreign recipient of Bharat Ratna	*Khan Abdul Gaffar Khan*
First Indian recipient of Nobel Prize in Economics	*Dr. Amartya Sen*
First Army Institute of Information Technology founded	*Hyderabad*
First Test Tube Baby of India	*Indira (Baby Harsha)*
First Indian Pilot	*J.R.D. Tata (1929)*
First Indian to reach Antarctica	*Lt. Ram Charan (1960)*
First Post- Office opened in India	*Kolkata (1727)*
First Deputy Prime Minister of India	*Sardar Vallabh Bhai Patel*

First Indian Prime Minister to resign from office	*Morarji Desai*
First Indian Prime Minister to loose an Election	*Indira Gandhi*
First President of India to die in office	*Dr. Zakir Hussain*
First Man to climb Mt. Everest twice	*Nawang Gombu*
First Indian to reach the South Pole	*Col. I.K. Bajaj*
First Indian recipient of 'Oscar Award'	*Bhanu Athaiya*
First American President to visit India	*Dwight David Eisenhower*
First British Prime Minister to visit India	*Harold Mc Millon*
First Indian author to get Anderson Award	*Ruskin Bond*
First Indian to win World Billiards Trophy	*Wilson Jones*
First Indian Space Tourist	*Santosh George*

2. Firsts in India (Female)

Indis's first Woman President	*Smt. Pratibha Patil*
India's first Woman Prime Minister	*Smt. Indira Gandhi*
India's first Woman Governor	*Sarojini Naidu*
India's first Woman ruler (on Delhi's throne)	*Razia Sultan*
India's first Woman I.P.S. officer	*Kiran Bedi*
First Woman Chief Minister of a state	*Sucheta Kripalani (U.P.)*
First Woman Union Minister	*Rajkumari Amrita Kaur*
First Woman President of INC	*Annie Besant*
First Woman Judge of the Suprime Court	*Meera Sahib Fatima Bibi*
First Woman to get Ashok Chakra	*Nirja Bhanot*
First Indian Woman Ambassador at United Nations	*Vijayalakshmi Pandit*
First Indian Woman to swim across English Channel	*Arati Saha (Gupta)*
First Indian Woman to get the Noble Prize	*Mother Teresa (1979)*
First Indian Woman to climb the Mt. Everest	*Bachendri Pal*
First Indian Woman to become 'Miss World'	*Miss Reita Faria*
First Indian Woman to climb the 'Mt. Everest' twice	*Santosh Yadav*
First Indian Woman to become 'Miss Universe'	*Sushmita Sen*
First Indian Woman to get Bharat Ratna	*Smt. Indira Gandhi*
First Woman to get Jnanpith Award	*Ashapurna Devi*
First Indian Woman to win WTA Title	*Sania Mirza*
First Indian Woman Airline Pilot	*Durga Banerjee*
First Indian Woman to win a Gold in Asian Games	*Kamaljeet Sandhu*
First Indian Woman President of I. N. Congress	*Sarojini Naidu (1925)*
First Indian Woman to win the Booker Prize	*Arundhati Roy*
First Woman Musician to get 'Bharat Ratna'	*M.S. Subbulakshmi*
First Indian Woman to go into space	*Kalpana Chawla*

3. Firsts in the world (Male & Female)

First men to climb Mt. Everest	*Sherpa Tenzing Norgay & Sir Edmund Hillary (29th May, 1953)*
First man to reach North Pole	*Robert Peary*
First man to reach South Pole	*Ronald Amundsen*
First religion of the world	*Sanatan Dharma*
First country to print books	*China*
First country to issue paper currency	*China*
First country to start Civil Services Competetion	*China*
First President of United States of America	*George Washington*
First Prime Minister of Great Britain	*Robert Walpole*
First Secretary General of United Nations	*Trigve Li*
First country to make education compulsory	*Prussia*
First country to win the World Cup Football	*Uruguay (1930)*
First country to make a constitution	*United States of America*
Pakistan's first Governor General	*Mohammed Ali Jinnah*
First summit of NAM was organised in	*Belgrade (former Yugoslavia)*
First European to visit China	*Marco Polo*
First men to fly an aeroplane	*Wright Brothers*
First person to sail around the world	*Ferdinand Magellan*
First country to send human to Moon	*United States of America*
First country to launch satellite into space	*Russia (former USSR)*
First country to host the modern Olympic games	*Greece*
First President of the Republic of China	*Dr. Sun Yat-sen*
First city to be attacked with Atom bomb	*Heroshima (Japan)*
First Radio Telescope Satellite was launched into space	*Japan*
First Russian (Soviet) Prime Minister to visit India	*V.I. Bulganin*
First University of the world	*Taxila University*
First man to set foot on the Moon	*Neil Armstrong (U.S.A.)*
First man to go into space	*Major Yuri Gagarin (USSR)*
First Space Shuttle launched	*Columbia*
First Space Ship landed on Mars	*Viking-I (July, 1976)*
First Woman Prime Minister of England	*Margaret Thacher*
First Woman Prime Minister of any muslim country	*Benazir Bhutto (Pakistan)*
First Woman Prime Minister of a country	*S. Bhandarnayake (Sri Lanka)*
First Woman cosmonaut in space	*Valentina Tereshkova (USSR)*
First Woman to climb Mt. Everest	*Junko Tabei (Japan)*

First deaf and dumb to cross the Srait of Gibralter	*Taranath Shenoy (India)*
First Woman President of UN General Assembly	*Smt. Vijayalakshmi Pandit (1953)*
First European Invader of Indian soil	*Alexander, The Great*
First Woman to reach the North Pole	*Ms. Fran*
First Woman to reach Antartica	*Caroline Michaelson*
First man to draw the map of earth	*Anexemander*
First man to compile Encyclopaedia	*Aspheosis (Athens)*
First eldest man to climb Mt. Everest	*Richard Wass*
First Asian to win Wimbledon Trophy	*Arthur Ashe (U.S.A.)*
First man to win Nobel Prize for Literature	*Rene F.A. & Sulli Pradhom (France)*
First man to win Nobel Prize for Peace	*Jin F. Dunant (Switzerland) & Frederic Peiry (France)*
First man to win Nobel Prize for Physics	*W.K. Roentgen (Germany)*
First man to win Nobel Prize for Chemistry	*J.H. Wenthoff (Howlland)*
First man to win Nobel Prize for Medicine	*A.E. Wonn Behrig (Germany)*
First man to win Nobel Prize for Economics	*Rangar Fish (Norway) & John Tinbergen (Howlland)*
First Woman President of a country	*Maria Estela Peron (Argentina)*
First Space Tourist (Male)	*Dennis Tito (U.S.A.)*
First Space Tourist (Female)	*Mrs. Anousheh Ansari (Irani American)*

Space Tourists : 1st : Dennis Tito (2001); 2nd : Mark Shuttleworth (2002); 3rd : Gregory Olsen (2003); 4th : Mrs. Anousheh Ansari (2004); 5th : Charles Simonyi (2006); 6th : Richards Gariatte (2008); 7th : Guy Laliberte (2009)

4. Superlatives : India

(Biggest, Highest, Largest, Longest, , Smallest etc.)

The longest river Bridge	*Mahatma Gandhi Setu Patna (5.575 km.)*
The largest animal Fair	*Sonepur (Bihar)*
The largest Auditorium	*Sri Shanmukhanand Hall (Mumbai)*
The largest Lake	*Wular Lake (J & K)*
The highest Dam	*Bhakhra Dam, on Sutlej river (Punjab)*
The largest Desert	*Thar (Rajasthan)*
The largest cave Temple	*Kailash Temple (Ellora, Maharashtra)*
The largest Zoo	*Zoological Garden (Kolkata)*
The largest Mosque	*Jama Masjid (Delhi)*
The highest Peak	*Godwin Austen/K–2 (8611m)*
The longest Tunnel	*Jawahar Tunnel, Banihal Pass (J & K)*
The largest Delta	*Sunderbans (W. Bengal)*
The state with maximum forest area	*Madhya Pradesh*

The longest Corridor	*Corridor of Ramnathswami Temple at Rameswaram (Tamil Nadu)*
The highest Waterfall	*Jog or Garsoppa (Karnataka)*
The longest Road	*Grand Trunk Road (Kolkata to Delhi)*
The highest Gate way	*Buland Darwaza, Fatehpur Sikri (UP)*
The longest River	*The Ganga (2640 km. long)*
The largest Museum	*Indian Museum, Kolkata*
The largest Dome	*Gol Gumbuz, Bijapur (in Karnataka)*
The tallest Statue	*Gomateswara (Karnataka)*
The largest Public Sector Bank	*State Bank of India*
The biggest canti lever Bridge	*Rabindra Setu or Howrah Bridge (Kolkata)*
The longest Canal	*Indira Gandhi Canal or Rajasthan Canal (Rajasthan)*
The longest Railway platform	*Gorakhpur (U.P.) 1355.4 m*
The longest Railway tunnel	*Pir Panjal Rly. Tunnel (J & K) 11.215 km*
The bigest Stadium	*Yuva Bharti (Salt Lake) Stadium Kolkata*
The most populous City	*Mumbai (Maharashtra)*
The largest Sea Bridge	*Anna Indira Gandhi Bridge (Tamil Nadu)*
The longest Passenger Train Route	*Dibrugarh to Kanyakumari*
The oldest Church	*St. Thomas Church at Palayar, Trichur (Kerala)*
The longest National Highway	*NH—7 (Varanasi to Kanyakumari)*
The state with longest Coast line	*Gujarat*
The highest Lake	*Devtal Lake, Gadhwal (Uttarakhand)*
The largest saline water Lake	*Chilka Lake (Odisha)*
The largest fresh water Lake	*Kolleru Lake (Andhra Pradesh)*
Largest Cave	*Amarnath (J&K)*
The longest river of southern India	*Godawari*
The longest Dam	*Hirakud Dam (Odisha)*
The highest Gallantry Award	*Param Vir Chakra*
The highest Award	*Bharat Ratna*
The largest Gurudwara	*Golden Temple, Amritsar*
The biggest Church	*Saint Cathedral at old Goa (Goa)*
The tallest TV Tower	*Fazilka (Punjab)*
The southern Indian state with Longest Coast line	*Andhra Pradesh*
The longest Sea Beach	*Marina Beach (Chennai)*
The Highest Road	*Road at Khardungla, (in Leh-Manali Sector)*
The largest Artificial Lake	*Govind Sagar (Bhakhra Nangal)*
The deepest River Valley	*Bhagirathi and Alaknanda*
The largest River without delta	*Narmada and Tapti*
The highest battle field and the longest Glacier	*Siachen Glacier*
The biggest river Island	*Majuli Bramhaputra river, (Assam)*
The largest Planetarium	*Birla Planetorium (Kolkata)*
The Highest Airport	*Leh Airport (Ladakh)*

5. Superlatives : World

(The Largest, Biggest, Smallest, Longest, Highest etc.)

Tallest Animal (on land)	*Giraffe*
Biggest Bell	*Great Bell at Moscow*
Fastest Bird	*Swift*
Largest Bird	*Ostrich*
Smallest Bird	*Humming Bird*
Longest Bridge (Railway)	*Lower Zambeji (Africa)*
Tallest Building	*Burj Khalifa, Dubai (U.A.E.)*
Tallest Office Building	*Petronas Twin Towers Kuala Lumpur (Malaysia)*
Longest Big-ship Canal	*Suez canal (linking Red Sea and Mediterranean)*
Busiest Canal (Ship)	*Baltic White Sea Canal (152 miles)*
Biggest Cinema House	*Roxy (New York)*
Highest City	*Wen Chuan (Tibet, China) 16,732 ft.*
Largest City (in population)	*Tokyo [(3,43,00,000), Est. population in 2011]*
Biggest City (in area)	*Mount Isa, Queensland, Australia (41,225 sq. km.)*
Largest Continent	*Asia*
Smallest Continent	*Australia*
Highest Country	*Tibet (The Pamirs)*
Largest Country (in population)	*China*
Largest Country (in area)	*Russia*
Largest Coral Formation	*The Great Barrier Reef (Australia)*
Largest dam	*Grand Coulee – Concrete Dam (U.S.A.)*
Longest Day	*June 21 (in Northern Hemisphere)*
Shortest Day	*Dec. 22 (in Northern Hemisphere)*
Largest Delta	*Sundarbans, India (8000 sq. miles)*
Largest Desert (world)	*Sahara, Africa (84,00,000 sq. km)*
Largest Diamond	*The Cullinan (over 1 ½ lb.)*
Biggest Dome	*Gol Gumbaz (Bizapur), (Old archi) 144 ft. diameter*
Biggest Dome (New archi)	*Astrodome, Sports*
Longest Epic	*The Mahabharata*
Largest Island	*Greenland (renamed Kalaatdlit Nunaat)*
Largest Lake (Artificial)	*Lake Mead (Bouler)*
Deepest Lake	*Baikal (Siberia); average depth 2300 feet*
Highest Lake	*Titicaca (Bolivia) 12,645 ft. above sea level*
Largest Lake (Fresh water)	*Lake Superior, U.S.A.*
Largest Lake (Salt water)	*Caspian Sea (3,71,000 sq. km.)*
Largest Mosque	*Jama Masjid, Delhi, (area 10,000 sq.ft.)*

Biggest Library	*National Kiev Library. Moscow and Library of the Congress, Washington*
Highest Mountain Peak (world)	*Everest (Nepal) 29,028 ft.*
Highest Mountain Range	*Himalayas*
Longest Mountain Range	*Andes (S. America) 5,500 miles in length*
Biggest Museum	*British Museum (London)*
Tallest Minaret (Free standing)	*Qutub Minar, Delhi 238 ft.*
Tallest minaret	*Great Hassan Mosque, Casablanca, Morocco*
Deepest And Biggest Ocean	*The Pacific*
Largest Palace	*Imperial Palace (Gugong), Beijing (China)*
Largest Park	*National Park, Greenland*
Largest Peninsula	*Arabia (32,50,000 sq. km.)*
Coldest Place or Region	*Vostok (Antarctica), Temperature –89.2°C*
Dryest Place	*Death Valley (California); rainfall 1 ½ inch*
Hottest Place (world)	*Death Valley (California, U.S.A.) (56.7°C, 134.06°F)*
Largest Planet	*Jupiter*
Brightest and Hottest Planet (also nearest to Earth)	*Venus*
Farthest Planet (from the sun)	*Neptune*
Nearest Planet (to the sun)	*Mercury*
Smallest Planet	*Mercury*
Highest Plateau	*Pamir (Tibet)*
Longest Platform (Railway)	*Gorakhpur (U.P.) India (1355.4 m)*
Largest Platform (Railway)	*Grand Central Terminal, New York (U.S.A.)*
Largest Port	*Port of New York and New Jersey (USA)*
Busiest Port	*Rotterdam (the Netherlands)*
Longest Railway	*Trans-Siberian Railway (6,000 miles long)*
Longest River	*Nile (6690 km), Amazon (6570 km)*
Longest River Dam	*Hirakud Dam (Odisha), India 15.8 miles*
Largest Sea-bird	*Albatross*
Largest Sea (inland)	*Mediterranean*
Brightest Star	*Sirius (also called Dog Star)*
Tallest Statue	*Statue of Liberty, New York (USA), 150 feet high*
Tallest Statue (bronze)	*Bronze Statue of Lrod Buddha, Tokyo (Japan)*
Longest Swimming Course	*English Channel*
Tallest Tower	*Tokyo Sky Tree (Japan) 2,080 ft*
Longest Train nonstop	*Flying Scoutsman*
Longest and Deepest Rail Tunnel	*Seikan Tunnel (Japan), (53.85 km.)*
Longest and Largest Canal Tunnel	*Le Rove Tunnel (South of France)*

Longest Tunnel (Road)	*Laerdal, Norway*
Highest Volcano	*Ojos del Salado, Andes, Argentine-Chile (6,885 m.)*
Largest Volcano	*Mauna Loa (Hawaii)*
Longest Wall	*Great Wall of China (1500 miles)*
Highest Waterfall	*Salto Angel Falls (Venezuela)*
Longest Strait	*Tartar Straits (Sakhalin Island and the Russian mainland)*
Broadest Strait	*Davis Straits (Greenland and Baffin Island, Canada)*
Narrowest Strait	*Chaliks – 45 yards (Between the Greek mainland and the island of Euboea in the Aegean Sea)*
Largest Bay	*Hudson Bay, Canada (shore line 7623 miles)*
Largest Gulf	*Gulf of Mexico, Shoreline 2100 miles*
Largest Archipelago	*Indonesia (over 3000 islands)*
Tallest Active Geyser	*Giant (geyser) Yelowstone Park U.S.A. 200 feet high*
Largest River Basin	*Amazon basin-27,20,000 sq. miles*
World's Rainiest spot	*Cherrapunji (Mawsynram), India*
Largest Gorge	*Grand Canyon, on the Colorado river, U.S.A.*
Lightest Gas	*Hydrogen*
Lightest Metal	*Lithium*
Highest Melting Point	*Tungsten, 3410^{0}C*
Hardest Substance	*Diamond*
Longest Animal	*Blue whale, (recorded length 106 feet, weight – 195 tons)*
Longest Life-span of an Animal	*190 to 200 years, (Giant tortoise)*
Largest Land Animal	*African Bush Elephant*
Fastest Animal	*Cheetah (Leopard) 70 m.p.h.*
Longest jump Animal	*Kangaroo*
Longest wing spread bird	*Albatross*
Slowest Animal	*Snail*
Domestic Dog	*Irish Wolf Hound*
Fastest Dog	*Persian grey hound (speed 43 m.p.h.)*
Longest Poisonous Snake	*King Cobra*
Biggest Flower	*Raffesia (Java)*
Largest Stadium	*Strahov Stadium in Prague, (the Czech Republic)*
Largest Church	*Basilica of St. Peter, Vatican City, Rome (Italy)*
Largest Temple	*Angkor Vat (Combodia)*
Largest Diamond Mine	*Kimbarley (S.Africa)*
Largest River in Volume	*Amazon, Brazil*
Longest Corridor	*Rameshwaram Temple's Corridor (5000 feet)*

Highest Straight Dam	*Bhakhra Dam*
Highest Capital City	*La Paz (Bolivia)*
Largest Asian desert	*Gobi, Mongolia*
Largest Democracy	*India*
Longest Thoroughfare	*Verazano-Narrows, New York City Harbour*
Largest Neck Animal	*Giraffe*
Largest Animal of the Cat Family	*Lion*
Most Intelligent Animal	*Chimpanzee*
Bird, that never makes its nest	*Cuckoo*
Wingless Bird	*Kiwi*
Reptile which changes its colours	*Chameleon*
Largest Mammal	*Whale*

6. Some Important Monuments / Structures of the World

Monuments / Structure	Country	Monuments / Structure	Country
The Leaning Tower of Pisa	Italy	Kremlin (Moscow)	Russia
Imperial Palace (Tokyo)	Japan	Parthanon (Athens)	Greece
Statue of Liberty (New York)	U.S.A.	Pyramid (Giza)	Egypt
Opera House (Sydney)	Australia	Wailing Wall	Jerusalem
Eiffel Tower (Paris)	France	Taj Mahal (Agra)	India
Great Wall (North China)	China		

7. National Emblems of some important Countries

Country	Emblem	Country	Emblem
India	Lioned Capitol	New Zealand	Kiwi
Pakistan*	Crescent & Star	Germany	Corn Flower
Bangladesh	Water Lily	Norway	Lion
Netherlands	Lion	France	Lily
U.K.	Rose	Iran	Rose
U.S.A.	Golden Rod	Spain	Eagle
Italy	White Lily	Japan	Chrysanthemum
Australia	Kangaroo	Canada	Maple Leaf, Lily

* *Jasmin and four main crops of Pakistan*

8. International Boundaries

Maginot Line	Germany & France	*Mannerhiem Line*	Russia & Finland
Mc Mahon Line	India & China	*Durand Line*	Pakistan & Afghanistan
Radcliffe Line	India & Pakistan	*38th Parallel*	North & South Korea
49th Parallel	U.S.A. & Canada	*Hindenburg Line*	Germany & Poland

9. National Animals of some Countries

	Country	Animal		Country	Animal
1.	Australia	Kangaroo	2.	New Zealand	Kiwi
3.	Canada	Eagle	4.	United Kingdom	Robin redbreast
5.	Japan	Ibis	6.	India	Tiger

10. News Agencies of some Countries

Country	Agencies
U.S.A.	Assocciated Press (AP), United Press International (UP)
U.K.	Reuters
Russia	Telegraph Agency of the Sovereign States (TASS)
Malaysia	Malaysian National News Agency (MNNA)
Italy	Agenzia Nazionale Stampa Associate (ANSA)
Israel	Associated Israel Press (AIP)
France	Agence France Presse (A.F.P.)
India	Press Trust of India (PTI), United News of India (UNI), Samachar Bharti, Univarta
China	Xin Hua
Japan	Kyodo
Indonesia	Antara
Iran	Islamic Republic News Agency (IRNA)
Germany	Deutsche Presse Agentur (D.P.A.)
Palestine	WAFA
Australia	Australian Associated Press(A.A.P.)
Russia	Novosti
Pakistan	Pakistan Press International (PPI), Associated Press of Pakistan (APP)
Egypt	Middle East News Agency (MENA)

11. Some Important Political Parties of different Countries

Country	Political Parties
U.S.A.	Republican Party, Democratic Party
Iraq	Bath Party
Israel	Labour Party, Likud Party, Hamas Party, Shas Party
France	Socialist Party, National Front, Union for French Democracy
Australia	Liberal Party, Labour Party
Bangladesh	Bangladesh Nationalist Party, Awami League, Jatiya Party
Nepal	Nepali Communist Party, Nepali Congress Party
China	Communist Party of China
Sri Lanka	United National Party, Freedom Party

Country	Political Parties
South Africa	African National Congress, National Party, Inkatha Freedom Party
U.K.	Conservative Party, Labour Party, Liberal Democratic Party,
Russia	Communist Party, Liberal Democratic Party, Russias' Choice
India	Indian National Congress, Bharatiya Janata Party, RJD, CPI, CPM, SP, BSP, LJP, TDP, AAP
Pakistan	Muslim League, Pakistan Peoples Party

12. Intelligence / Detective Agencies of the World

Detective Agencies	Country
Central External Liaison Department	China
Australian Security & Intelligence Organisation	Australia
K.G.B./G.R.U.	Russia
Bureau of State Security (B.O.S.S.)	South Africa
M.I. (Military Intelligence)-5 & 6, Special Branch, Joint Intelligence Organisation	U. K.
Inter Services Intelligence (I.S.I.)	Pakistan
Research & Analysis Wing (RAW), Intelligence Bureau (IB)	India
Central Intelligence Agencies (CIA), Federal Bureau of Investigation (FBI)	U.S.A.
MOSSAD	Israel
Mukhbarat	Egypt
Naicho	Japan
SAVAK (Sazamane Etelaat va Amniate Kechvar)	Iran
Al Mukhbarat	Iraq
D.G.S.E. (Direction General de Securite Exterieur)	France

13. Parliaments of different Countries

Country	Parliament	Country	Parliament
India	Sansad (Lok Sabha and Rajya Sabha)	Nepal	Rashtriya Panchayat
Pakistan	National Assembly	Denmark	Folketing
Britain	Parliament (House of Commons and House of Lords)	Russia	Duma and Federal Council
Germany	Bundstag (Lower House) and Bundesrat (Upper House)	China	National People's Congress
Switzerland	Federal Assembly	France	National Assembly
U.S.A.	Congress (House of Representatives and Senate)	Turkey	Grand National Assembly
Bhutan	Tshogdu	Iran	Majlis

Country	Parliament	Country	Parliament
Bangladesh	Jatiya Sansad	Afghanistan	Shora
Norway	Storting	Israel	Knesset
Spain	Cortes Generales	Maldives	Mazlis
Australia	Federal Parliament	Japan	Diet
Myanmar	Pyithu Hluttaw (People's Assembly)	Canada	Parliament

14. Some important Signs or Symbols

Pen	Symbol of Culture & Civilization
Lotus	Culture and Civilization
Red Cross	Medical Aid & Hospital
Red Flag	Revolution; also sign of danger
Black Flag	Symbol of protest
Yellow Flag	Flown on ships or vehicles carrying patients suffering from infectious diseases
Flag flown upside down	Symbol of Distress
Flag flown at half mast	Symbol of National mourning
White Flag	Symbol of Truce
Red Tringle	Sign of Family Planning
Pegion or Dove	Symbol of Peace
Red Light	Traffic sign of 'Stop', also sign of 'Danger' or 'Emergency'
Green Light	Line clear signal or traffic sign of 'Go'
A blindfolded woman holding a balanced scale	Symbol of Justice
Black strip on fore arm	Sign of mourning or protest
One skull on two bones crossing each other diagonally.	Sign of 'Danger'
Wheel (Chakra)	Symbol of progress
Olive Branch	Symbol of peace
Tricolour	National Flag of India
Union Jack	National Flag of the U.K.
Stars and Stripes	National Flag of the U.S.A.

15. Some important Official Books

Green Book	Official reports or publications of Italy & Iran
White Book	The official publications of Portugal, China & Germany
Blue Book	Any official report of the British government
Yellow Book	The report or publication of the French government

Orange Book	Official report of the government of Netherlands
White Paper	The authoritative recital of facts issued by the government stating its views on a particular matter
Grey Book	Report of the government of Belgium and Japan
Joint Paper	The joint report of two or more than two governments

16. Newspapers & their place of publication (World)

Newspaper	Place	Newspaper	Place
The Times	London	The Gardian	London
Daily Mirror	London	Daily Mail	London
La Figaro	Paris	Le Mand	Paris
Ezbestia	Moscow	Pravda	Moscow
The Island	Colombo	Khalij Times	Dubai
Eastern Sun	Singapore	Mainichi Shimbun	Tokyo
Al Ahram	Cairo	People's Daily	Beijing
Mardeka	Jakarta	La Republica	Rome
Washington Post	Washington	Daily News	New York
New York Times	New York	Financial Times	London
Star	Johanesberg	Independent	London
The Times of India	India	The Hindu	Chennei
The Sun	U.K.	Daily Telegraph	U.K.
New Statesman	U.K.	China Times	Taiwan
Red Flag	China	Toronto Star	Canada
Bangladesh Observer	Dhaka	Dawn	Karachi

17. United Nations

- The name 'United Nations' was adopted of the suggestion of the then US President F.D. Rooswelt.
- To prepare the format of the UN, a meeting of representatives of prominent countries held from 21st August to 7th October, 1944 at Dumbarton Ox building in Washington.
- The UNO was formed on the 24th October 1945.
- The *character* of the UN was signed on the 26th June, 1945 by representatives of 50 nations, though the number of founder member countries was 51 who attended the San Fransisco Conference. Later on Poland signed the Charter and become the 51st founder member.
- At present 192 countries are members of the UN. Monte Negro is the latest (192nd) member.
- The UN Charter came into force on October 24, 1945, when the Governments of China, France, the U.K., the Soviet Union and the U.S.A. and a majority of other counties had ratified it.

- The *Preamble* to the *Charter* was the work of Field Marshal Smuts.
- The Head Quarter of the UN is situated in New York (USA).
- John D Rockfeller had donated 17 acres of land in Manhutton island, on which a 39 storeyed secretariate building of the UN has been constructed.
- The main office of the UN was built in 1952, where the first meeting of the General Assembly was held in 1952.
- The UN Charter is the *Constitution* of the UN. It contains the aim and objectives of the UN and the rules and regulations for achieving these aims and purposes.
- Flag of the UN : White UN emblem (two bent olive branches open at the top, and in between them is world map) on a light blue background.
- Languages of the UN : The official languages of the UN are : (a) English (b) French (c) Chinese (d) Russian (e) Arabic and (f) Spanish. But the working Languages are English and French only.
- Major Organs of the UN : (1) General Assembly (GA) 2. Security Council (SC) (3) Economic and Social Council (ECOSOC) (4) Trusteeship Council (TC) (5) International Court of Justice (6) The Secretariat.
- International Court of Justice sits at The Hague (Netherlands), while all other organs of the UN are situated in New York (USA).
- The Security Council consists of 15 members, each of which has one representative and one vote.
- There are 5 permanent and 10 non-permanent members of the SC. The non-permanent members are elected for a 2 year term by two thirds majority of the GA.
- The five permanent members are—USA, Russia, UK, France and China.
- The proverb 'Policeman of the world' is used for the Security Council.
- Only the permanent members have the right to 'veto'.

18. World Organisations and their Headquarters

Organisation	Headquarters
GATT (General Agreement on Tariffs & Trade)	*Geneva*
Amnesty International	*London (England)*
Asian Development Bank (ADB)	*Manila (Philippines)*
ASEAN (Assosiation of South- East Asian Nations)	*Jakarta (Indonesia)*
NATO (North Atlantic Treaty Organisation)	*Brussels (Belgium)*
African Union (AU)	*Addis-Ababa (Ethopia)*
International Committee of the Red Cross (ICRC)	*Geneva (Switzerland)*
SAARC (South Asian Association for Regional Corporation)	*Kathmandu (Nepal)*
United Nations Environment Programme (UNEP)	*Nairobi (Kenya)*
INTERPOLE (International Police)	*Lyons (France)*
World Trade Organisation (WTO)(w.e.f. Jan 1, 1995)	*Geneva*
League of Arab States	*Cario (Egypt)*

COMECON	*Minsk (Belarus)*
World Council of Churches (WCC)	*Geneva*
European Energy Commission (EEC)	*Geneva*
Economic Commission of Africa (ECA)	*Addis-Ababa*
Economic Commission of West Asia (ECWA)	*Baghdad*
United Nations High Commission for Refugees (UNHCR)	*Geneva*
International Atomic Energy Agency (IAEA)	*Vienna (Austria)*
United Nations Industrial Development Organisation (UNIDO)	*Vienna (Austria)*
UNCTAD (United Nations Conference on Trade and Development)	*Geneva*
WWF (World Wildlife Fund)	*Gland (Switzerland)*
International Olympic Committee (IOC)	*Lusane*
European Common Market (ECM)	*Geneva*
CHOGM (Common wealth Heads of Governments Meet)	*London*
OPEC (Organisation of Petroleum Exporting Countries)	*Vienna*
OECD (Organisation for Economic Co-operation and Development)	*Paris*
CENTO (Central Treaty Organisation)	*Ankara (Turkey)*
Comonwealth	*London*
European Economy Community (EEC)	*Brussels*
Council of European	*Strasbourg*
European Space Research Organization (ESRO)	*Paris*
BENELUX Economic Union	*Brussels*
Economic and Social Commission for Asia and the Pacific (ESCAP)	*Bangkok (Thiland)*
Economic Commission for Europe (ECE)	*Geneva*
Economic Commission for Latin America and the Carribbean (ECLAC)	*Santiago (Chile)*
Economic and Social Commission for Western Asia (ESCWA)	*Jordan (Amman)*
ANZUS Council	*Canberra (Australia)*
United Nations Centre for Human Settlements (UNCHS)	*New York*
United Nations International Children's Emergency Fund (UNICEF)	*New York*
United Nations Fund for Population Activities (UNFPA)	*New York*
United Nations Development Programme (UNDP)	*New York*
United Nations Institute for Training and Research (UNITAR)	*New York*
United Nations Population Fund (UNFPA)	*New York*
United Natons Research Institute for Social Development (UNRISD)	*Geneva*
World Food Programme (WFP)	*Rome (Italy)*

Food and Agriculture Organisation (FAO)	*Rome (Italy)*
International Civil Aviation Organisation (ICAO)	*Montreal (Canada)*
International Fund for Agricultural Development (IFAD)	*Rome*
International Labour Organisation (ILO)	*Geneva*
International Monetary Fund (IMF)	*Washington*
International Telecommunication Union (ITU)	*Geneva*
United Nations Educational, Scientific and Cultural Organisation (UNESCO)	*Paris*
Universal Postal Union (UPU)	*Berne (Switzerland)*
World Health Organisation (WHO)	*Geneva*
World Intellectual Property Organisation (WIPO)	*Geneva*
World Meteorological Organisation (WMO)	*Geneva*
Voluntary Service Overseas (VSO)	*London*
Woman Aid International	*London*
European Free Trade Association (EFTA)	*Geneva*
Organisation of Arab Petroleum Exporting Countries	*Kuwait*
International Bank for Reconstruction and Development (IBRD) (World Bank)	*Washington*
Organisation of Economic Cooperation and Development (OECD)	*Paris*
Organisation of Islamic Conference (OIC)	*Mecca*

Secretary Generals of UNO and their Tenure

	Name	Country	Tenure
1.	Trigve Li	Norway	1946 - 1952
2.	Dag Hammarskjoeld	Sweden	1953 - 1961
3.	U - Thant	Myanmar (Burma)	1961 - 1971
4.	Kurt - Waldheim	Austria	1972 - 1982
5.	Jevier Perez de Cuellar	Peru	1982 - 1991
6.	Boutros Boutros Ghali	Egypt	1992 - 1996
7.	Kofi Annan	Ghana	1997 - 2006
8.	Ban Ki -moon	S. Korea	2007 - —

19. International Decades

1990s	Third Disarmament Decade
1990 to 1999	UN Decade of International Law
1990 to 2000	International Decade for the Eradication of Colonialism
1991 to 2000	United Nations Decade against Drug Abuse
1994 to 2004	International Decade for Indigenous people of the World
1995 to 2004	UN Decade for Human Rights Education
1997 to 2006	UN Decade for the Eradication of Poverty
2001 to 2010	Second UN Decade for the Eradication of Colonialism
2001 to 2010	International Decade for Peace and Non Violence for children

20. International Years

1987	International Year of Shelter for Homeless
1990	International Literacy Year
1992	International Space Year
1993	International Year of Indigenous Population
1994	International Year of Family
1995	International Year of Tolerance
1998	International Year of Ocean
1999	International Year of Aging (older) people
2000	International Year of Peace-Culture
2000	International Year of Gratitude
2001	International Year of Woman Empowerment
2001	International Year for Eradication of Mental Diseases (WHO)
2001	United Nation's Year for Interaction among Civilizations
2002	International Mountain Year
2002	International Year of Eco-tourism
2003	International Fresh Water Year
2004	International Rice Year
2005	International Year of Microcredit and International Year of Physics
2006	International Year of Desert and Desertification
2008	Year of Good Governance (for SAARC countries)
2010	International Year of Biodiversity
2013	International Year of Water Cooperation

21. Designated SAARC Years

1989	Year of Combating Drug Abuse and Drug Trafficking	1996	Year of Literacy
1990	Year of Girl Child	1997	Year of Participatory Governance
1991	Year of Shelter	1999	Year of Biodiversity
1992	Year of Environment	2002-03	Year of Contribution of Youth to Enviroment
1993	Year of Disabled Persons	2004	Year of TB and HIV / AIDS
1994	Year of the Youth	2005	Year of South Asian Tourism
1995	Year of Poverty Eradication	2007	Year of Green South Asia

22. International U.N. Weeks

March 21 onwards	International Week for Unity for the Struggle against Racism
October 4 to 10	World Space Week
October 24 to 30	International Desarmament Week

23. Important National & International Days

January	
Louis Braille Day	4th January
National Youth Day (Birthday of Swami Vivekanand)	12th January
Army Day	15th January
International Customs and Excise Day	25th January
Tourism Day (India)	25th January
Republic Day (India)	26th January
Martyrs' Day	30th January
Leprosy Prevention Day	30th January
Sarvodaya Day	30th January
February	
World Radio Day	13th February
Valentine Day	14th February
International Mother Tongue Day	21st February
Central Excise Tax Day	24th February
National Science Day	28th February
March	
National Safety Day (Security of Industrial Institutions)	4th March
International Women's Day	8th March
World Kidney Day	9th March
Central Industrial Security Force (CISF) Foundation day	12th March
World Consumer Day	14th March
Ordnance Manufacturing Day	18th March
World Disabled Day	20th March
World Forestry Day	21st March
World Water Day	22nd March
World Meteorological Day	23rd March
Ram Manohar Lohia's Birth Day (Anniversary)	23rd March
Bhagat Singh, Sukhdev and Rajguru's Martyrdam Day	23rd March
World TB (Tuberculosis) Day	24th March
Rural Postal Life Insurance Day	24th March
Sacrifice Day of Ganesh Shankar Vidyarthi	25th March
National Day of Bangladesh	26th March
World Theatre Day	27th March

April	
National Maritime Day	5th April
Special Protection Group (SPG) Foundation Day	7th April
World Health Day	7th April
World Homeopathy Day (Birth day of Samuel Hanimen)	10th April
World Aeronautics and Cosmology Day	14th April
Ambedkar's Birth Anniversary	14th April
World Haemophilia Day	17th April
World Heritage Day	18th April
Indian Civil Service Day	21st April
Earth Day	22nd April
World Books and Copyright Day	23rd April
Panchayat Divas	24th April
May	
International Labour Day (Worker's Day or May Day)	1st May
World Asthma Day	2nd May
World Press Freedom Day	3rd May
World Red Cross Day	4th May
World Laughter Day	1st Sunday of May
Mother's Day	2nd Sunday of May
World Migratory Birds Day	8th May
International Pthylesemia Day	8th May
National Technological Day	11th May
International Nurse Day	13th May
International Family Day	15th May
World Telecomunication Day	17th May
Anti-Terrorism Day	21st May
World Biodiversity Day	23rd May
Commonwealth Day	24th May
Death Anniversary of Jawahar Lal Nehru	27th May
World Anti-Tobacco (and No-smoking) Day	31st May
June	
World Environment Day	5th June
International Olympic Association Establishment Day	6th June
Father's Day (in many countries)	3rd Sunday of June
World Refugee Day	20th June
International Day (UN) against Drug Abuse and Illicit Trafficking	27th June

July	
Doctor's Day (Birthday of Dr. Bidhan Chandra Roy)	1st July
State Bank of India Foundation Day	1st July
World Population Day	11th July
International Nelson Mandela Day	18th July
Kargil Memorial Day	26th July
August	
World Breast Feeding Day	1st August
World Peace Day, Hiroshima Day	6th August
Quit India Day (India), Nagasaki Day	9th August
World Youth Day	12th August
Independence Day (India)	15th August
National Sports Day (Birth Day of Dhyanchand)	29th August
September	
Teacher's Day (Birth Day of S. Radhakrishnan)	5th September
World Literacy Day	8th September
World Fraternity and Apology Day	14th September
Hindi Divas (Day)	14th September
Engineer's Day (Birth Day of M. Vishweshwaraiya)	15th September
World Ozone Day	16th September
Railway Police Force (RPF) Foundation Day	20th September
Alzheimer's Day	21st September
World Deaf Day and World Heart Day	24th September
World Tourism Day	27th September
October	
International Oldmen's Day	1st October
Mahatma Gandhi's Birth Day *(International Non-violence Day)*	2nd October
Birth Day of Lal Bahadur Shastri	2nd October
World Habitat Day	3rd October
World Animal Welfare Day	4th October
World Teacher's Day	5th October
World Wild Animal Day	6th October
Indian Air Force Day	8th October
World Post Day	9th october
Birthday of Loknayak Jay Prakash Narayan	11th October
UN International Day for Natural Disaster Reduction	13th October
World Standards Day	14th October
World Food Day	16th October
World Allergy Awareness Day	16th October

World Iodine Shortage Day	21st October
United Nations (UN) Day	24th October
World Thrift Day	30th October
Death Anniversary of Indira Gandhi	31st October
November	
World Service Day	9th November
National Education Day (Birth Day of Maulana Azad)	11th November
Children's Day (Birth anniversary of Jawaharlal Nehru)	14th November
World Diabetes Day	14th November
International Day for Endurance	16th November
National Press Day	16th November
World Students Day	17th November
World Epilepsy Day	17th November
National Journalism Day	17th November
World Adult Day	18th November
World Citizen Day	19th November
Universal Children's Day	20th November
World Television Day	21st November
World Non-veg Prevention Day	25th November
World Environment Protection Day	26th November
National Law Day	26th November
December	
World AIDS Day	1st December
International Day for the Abolition of Slavery	2nd December
World Disabled Day	3rd December
Chemical Accidents Prevention Day	4th December
Navy Day	4th December
International Volunteers Day	5th December
International Civil Aviation Day	7th December
Armed Forces Flag Day	7th December
Girl Child Day (Balika Divas, India)	9th December
International Human Rights Day	10th December
World Children's Fund Day	11th December
World Asthma Day	11th December
National Energy Conservation Day	14th December
Liberation Day of Goa	19th December
Kisan Divas (Birthday of Chaudhary Charan Singh)	23rd December
X-mas Day	25th December
Central Reserve Police Force (CRPF) Foundation Day	26th December

24. India's World Heritage Sites (included in UNESCO's list)

Sl.	Site	Year of inclusion
1.	Ajanta Caves (Maharashtra)	1983
2.	Ellora Caves (Maharashtra)	1983
3.	Agra Fort (U.P.)	1983
4.	Taj Mahal (U.P.)	1983
5.	Sun Temple, Konark (Odisha)	1984
6.	Mahabalipuram Temples (TN)	1984
7.	Kaziranga National Park (Assam)	1985
8.	Manas Wildlife Sanctuary (Assam)	1985
9.	Keoladeo National Park (Rajasthan)	1985
10.	Churches and Convents of Goa	1986
11.	Khajuraho Temples (M.P)	1986
12.	Monuments at Hampi (Karnataka)	1986
13.	Fatehpur Sikri (UP)	1986
14.	Pattadakal Temples (Karnataka)	1987
15.	Elephanta Caves	1987
16.	Sundarbans National Park (W.B)	1987
17.	Chola Temples, Brihadishwara Temple, Thanjavur (1987), Brihadishwara Temple, Gangaikonda Cholapuram (2004), Airavate shwara Temple (2004)	1987–2004
18.	Nanda Devi and Valley of Flowers National Parks	1988-2005
19.	Sanchi Stupa (MP)	1989
20.	Humayun's Tomb (Delhi)	1993
21.	Qutub Minar and its Momuments (Delhi)	1993
22.	Mountain Railways *(Darjeeling Himalayan Rly.-1999, Neelgiri Mountain Rly.-2005, Kalka-Shimla Rly.-2008)*	1999–2008
23.	Mahabodhi Temple, Bodh Gaya (Bihar)	2002
24.	Rock Shelters of Bhimbetka (MP)	2003
25.	Champaner - Pavagadh Park (Gujarat)	2004
26.	Chhatrapati Shivaji Terminus (CST), Mumbai	2004
27.	Red Fort (Lal Quila) Complex, Delhi	2007
28.	Jantar Mantar of Jaipur (Rajsthan)	2010
29.	Western Ghats	2012
30.	Hill Forts of Rajasthan (6 majestic forts) *(Chittorgarh, Kumbhalgarh,Sawai Madhopur, Jhalawar, Jaipur and Jaisalmer Fort*[1] *)*	2013

[1] *First inhabited World Heritage Monument (constructed in 1156).*

25. Famous Tourist Spots of India

Site	Location	Founder
Kanheri Caves	Mumbai	Buddhists
Elephanta Caves	Mumbai	Rashtrakutas

Site	Location	Founder
Ajanta Caves	Aurangabad	Gupta Rulers
Ellora Caves	Aurangabad	Buddhists
Kandaria Mahadev	Khajurao(M.P)	Chandela Kings
Madan Palace	Jabalpur (M.P.)	Raja Madan Shah
Mrignayani Palace	Gwalior(M.P.)	Raja Man Singh Tomar
Dhar Fort	Dhar (M.P.)	Mohammad Bin Tughlaq
Golconda Fort	Hyderabad (A.P.)	Qutubshahi
Cochin Fort	Kerala	Portuguese
Vijay Stambh	Chittorgarh (Raj.)	Rana Kumbha
Qutub Minar	Delhi	Qutub-ud-din Aibak
Adhai Din Ka Jhopda	Ajmer (Raj.)	Qutub-ud-din Aibak
Hauz Khas	Delhi	Alauddin Khilji
Tughlakabad	Delhi	Ghiyasuddin Tughlaq
Firoz shah Kotla	Delhi	Firoz Shah Tughlaq
Bundi Fort	Bundi (Raj.)	Raja Nagar Singh
Pichhola Lake	Udaipur	—
Kakaria Lake	Ahmedabad	Sultan Qutub ud din
Jodhpur Fort	Jodhpur (Raj.)	Rao Jodha Ji
Fateh Sagar	Udaipur (Raj.)	Maharana Fateh Singh
Deeg Palace	Deeg (Raj.)	Raja Badan Singh
Rani Ki Badi	Bundi (Raj.)	Rani Nathvati
Chhatra Mahal	Bundi Fort	Rani Chhatrasal
Junagarh	Bikaner (Raj.)	Raja Jay Singh
Jantar-Mantar	Delhi and Jaipur	Sawai Jay Singh
Nahargarh Fort	Jaipur (Raj.)	Sawai Jay Singh
Bharatpur Fort	Bharatpur (Raj.)	Raja Surajmal Singh
Moti Masjid	Delhi Fort	Aurangzeb
Ummed Palace	Jodhpur (Raj.)	Maharaja Ummed Singh
Aram Bagh	Agra (U.P.)	Babur
Red Fort	Delhi	Shahjehan
Humayun's Tomb	Delhi	Hameeda Bano Beghum (wife of Humayun)
Shalimar Bagh (Garden)	Sri Nagar	Jehangir
St. George Fort	Chennei (T.N.)	East India Company
Sher Shah's Tomb	Sasaram (Bihar)	Son of Sher Shah
Fatehpur Sikri	Agra (U.P.)	Akbar
Old Fort (Purana Quila)	Delhi	Sher Shah Suri
Akbar's Tomb	Sikandera(U.P.)	Jehangir
Chashma - Shahi	Jammu-Kashmir	Ali Mardan Khan

Site	Location	Founder
Etamad-ud-daulah's Tomb	Agra (U.P.)	Noorjehan
Taj Mahal	Agra (U.P)	Shahjehan
Nishaat Bagh	Jammu - Kashmir	Asaf Ali
Sheesh Mahal	Agra (U.P.)	Shahjehan
Khas Mahal	Agra (U.P.)	Shahjehan
Dewan-e-Khas	Agra Fort (U.P.)	Shahjehan
Bada Imambada	Lucknow (U.P.)	Nawab Asaf-Ud-daulah
Chhota Imambada	Lucknow (U.P.)	Mohammad Ali Shah
Gol Ghar	Patna (Bihar)	British Government
Padari Ki Haveli	Patna (Bihar)	Father Capuchin
Fort William	Kolkata (W.B.)	Lord Clive
Bibi Ka Maqbara	Aurangabad (Maharashtra)	Aurangzeb
Safderjung ka Maqbara	Delhi	Shuja-ud-daulah
Belur Math	Kolkata (W.B.)	Swami Vivekanand
Anand Bhawan	Allahabad (U.P.)	Moti Lal Nehru
Laxman Jhula	Rishikesh (Uttarakhand)	—
Shanti Niketan	W. Bengal	Rabindranath Tagore
Sabarmati Ashram	Ahmedabad	Mahatma Gandhi
Prince of Wales Museum	Mumbai	George V
Gateway of India	Mumbai	British Government
President House	Delhi	British Government
Victoria Memorial	Kolkata (W.B)	—
Botanical Garden	Shivpur (W.B)	—
Sunset Point	Mount Abu (Raj.)	—
Char Minar	Hyderabad (A.P.)	Kuli Qutub Shah
Sun Temple	Konark (Orissa)	Narasingh Dev I
Jagannath Temple	Puri (Orissa)	Chola Gang Dev
Chenna KeshabTemple	Belur	Vishnu Vardhan
Laxman Temple	Chhatarpur (M.P.)	Chandela Rulers
Dilwada Jain Temple	Mount Abu (Raj.)	Vimal Shah
Vishnupad Temple	Gaya (Bihar)	Rani Ahilya Bai
Harmandir Sahib	Patna (Bihar)	Maharaja Ranjit Singh
Kali Temple	Kolkata (W.B.)	Rani Ras Moni
Laxmi Narayan Temple	Delhi	Birla Family
Khirki Masjid	Delhi	Ghiyasuddin Tughlaq
Shershahi Masjid	Patna (Bihar)	Parvez Shah
Mecca Masjid	Hyderabad (AP)	Kuli Kutub Shah
Patthar Ki Masjid	Patna (Bihar)	Parvez Shah

Site	Location	Founder
Patthar Ki Masjid	Jammu-Kashmir	Noorjehan
Jama Masjid	Agra (U.P.)	Shahjehan
Moti Masjid	Agra Fort (U.P.)	Shahjehan
Jama Masjid	Delhi	Shahjehan
Charar-e-Sarif	Sri Nagar(Kashmir)	Jainul Abedin
Hajratbal Masjid	Sri Nagar(Kashmir)	—
Nakhuda Masjid	Kolkata (W. B.)	—

26. Defence of India

➢ The defence policy of India aims at promoting and sustaining durable peace in the subcontinent and equipping the defence forces adequately.

➢ The supreme commander of the Indian Armed Forces is the President of India. The responsibility for national defence, however, rests with the union cabinet. The Defence Minister is responsible to the Parliament for all matters concerning the defence of the country. Administrative and operational control of the armed force is exercised by the Ministry of Defence and the three Service Headquarters.

➢ The Defence Ministry consists of 4 departments : (i) Department of Defence (ii) Department of Defence Production (iii) Department of Defence Research and Development (iv) Department of Ex-Serviceman Welfare.

➢ In 2002, the Defence Ministry given a new name—'Integrated Headquarters of Ministry of Defence'. Indian Armed Forces are divided into three Services Army, Navy and Air Force. The three services function under their respective Chiefs of Staff. These three chiefs of staff constitute the Chief of staff Committee, the chairmanship of which rotates among the service chiefs according to seniority.

➢ In the contemporary world India has the fourth largest army in the world, the fifth largest air force and the seventh largest navy.

Indian Armed Forces are divided into three services :

1. **Army** :The Chief is 'Chief of the Army Staff'. Its headquarters is in New Delhi. The army is organised into the following seven commands :

Command	Headquarters	Command	Headquarters
Western Command	Chandigarh	Eastern Comm.	Kolkata
Northern Command	Udhampur	Southern Comm.	Pune
Army Training Comm.	Shimla	Central Comm.	Lucknow
South Western Comm.	Jaipur		

Note : *Each Command of Indian Army is commanded by a General Officer Commanding in Chief of the rank of Lieutenant General.*

2. **Navy** :The Chief is an Admiral ranked " Chief of the Naval Staff". The headquarters is in New Delhi. The Navy has three Naval Commands, commanded by Flag Officers Commanding-in-Chief of the rank of Vice-Admiral. They are :

Command	Headquarters	Command	Headquarters
Eastern Command	Visakhapatnam	Southern Command	Kochi
Western Command	Mumbai		

3. **Air Force :** The Chief is an Air Chief Marshal ranked 'Chief of the Air Staff'. Its headquarters is in New Delhi. The Air force is organized into seven commands (five Operational and two Functional Commands) :

Command	Headquarter	Command	Headquarter
Operational Commands			
Eastern Air Comd.	Shillong	Western Air Comd.	New Delhi
South-Western Air Comd.	Gandhinagar	Central Air Comd.	Allahabad
Southern Air Comd.	Tiruvananthpuram		
Functional Commands			
Maintenance Comd.	Nagpur	Training Comd.	Bangalore

4. **Commissioned Ranks**

Army	Air Force	Navy
General	Air Chief Marshal	Admiral
Lieutenant General	Air Marshal	Vice-Admiral
Major General	Air Vice-Marshal	Rear Admiral
Brigadier	Air Commodor	Commodor
Colonel	Group Captain	Captain
Lieutenant Colonel	Wing Commander	Commander
Major	Squadron Leader	Lieutenant Commander
Captain	Flight Lieutenant	Lieutenant
Lieutenant	Flying Officer	Sub Lieutenant

27. Internal Security of India

Organization	Year	Headquater
Assam Rifles (AR)(former Catchar Levy)	1835	Shillong
Central Reserve Police Force (CRPF)	1939	New Delhi
National Cadet Corps (NCC)	1948	New Delhi
Territorial Army (TA)	1949	In different states
Indo-Tibetan Border Police (ITBP)	1962	New Delhi
Home Guards (HG)	1962	In different states
Border Security Force (BSF)	1965	New Delhi
Central Industrial Security Force (CISF)	1969	New Delhi
Coast Guards (CG)	1977	New Delhi
National Security Guards (NSG)	1984	New Delhi

28. Defence Training Institutions of India

Army

- National Defence Academy (NDA), Khadakwasla (near Pune)
- National Defence College (NDC), New Delhi
- College of Defence Management (CDM), Secunderabad (A.P.)
- College of Military Engineering (CME), Pune (Maharashtra)
- Rashtriya Indian Military College (RIMC), Dehradun

- ➢ Armed Forces Medical College (AFMC), Pune
- ➢ Officer's Training School (OTS), Chennai
- ➢ High Altitude Warfare School Gulmarg (J&K)
- ➢ Counter Insurgency and Jungle Warfare School, Vairengte
- ➢ Infantry Schools, Mhow and Belgaum
- ➢ Armoured Corps Centre and School, Ahmednagar (Maharashtra)
- ➢ School of Artilary, Deolali

Air Force

- ➢ Air Force School, Sambra (Belgaum)
- ➢ Flying Instructors' School, Tambaram,
- ➢ Helicopter Training School, Avadi
- ➢ College of Air Warfare, Secunderabad
- ➢ Air Force Administrative College, Coimbatore
- ➢ Air Force Academy, Hyderabad
- ➢ Air Force Technical College, Jalahalli (Bangalore)
- ➢ Elementary Flying School, Bidar
- ➢ Paratroopers Training School, Agra (UP)
- ➢ Institute of Aviation Medicine, Banglore

Navy

- ➢ I.S.S. Chilka, Bhubaneswar (Orissa)
- ➢ I.N.S. Hansa, Goa
- ➢ Navy Shipwright School, Vishakhapatnam
- ➢ I.N.S. Satavahana, Visakhapatnam (AP)
- ➢ I.N.S. , Garuda, Kochi (Cochin)
- ➢ I.N.S. Shivaji, Lonavala
- ➢ I.N.S. Valsura, Jamnagar (Gujarat)
- ➢ I.N.S. Hamla, Mumbai
- ➢ I.N.S. kunjai, Mumbai
- ➢ I.N.S. Ashwini (INM), Mumbai
- ➢ I.N.S. Agrani, Coimbator
- ➢ Naval Academy, Goa

29. Foundation day of some States

Jan. 1	Nagaland Day
Jan. 21	Manipur, Meghalaya and Tripura Day
Feb. 6	Jammu-Kashmir Day
Feb. 20	Mizoram and Arunachal Pradesh Day
Mar. 11	Andaman & Nicobar Islands Day
Mar. 22	Bihar Day (Bihar Diwas)
Mar. 30	Rajasthan Day
Apr. 1	Utkal (Orissa), Day
Apr. 14	Tamil Nadu Day
Apr. 15	Himachal Pradesh Day
May 1	Gujarat and Maharashtra Day
May 16	Sikkim Day

Nov. 1	Chhattisgarh, Uttar Pradesh, Punjab, Haryana, Madhya Pradesh, Karnataka, Kerala & Andhra Pradesh Day
Nov. 9	Uttaranchal (Now Uttarakhand) Day
Nov. 15	Jharkhand Day (Jharkhand Diwas)
Dec. 19	Goa Day

30. Research Centres of India

1.	Indian Agricultural Research Institute	*New Delhi*
2.	Central Rice Research Institute	*Cuttack*
3.	Central Sugarcane Research Institute	*Coimbatore*
4.	Central Potato Research Institute	*Shimla*
5.	Central Tobacco Research Institute	*Rajamundry*
6.	Central Forest Research Institute	*Dehradun*
7.	National Sugar Research Institute	*Kanpur*
8.	Indian Lac Research Institute	*Ranchi*
9.	National Dairy Research Institute	*Karnal*
10.	Central Fuel Research Institute	*Dhanbad*
11.	Central Leather Research Institute	*Chennai*
12.	Central Mining Research Institute	*Dhanbad*
13.	Central Drug Research Institute	*Lucknow*
14.	Indian Meteorological Observatory	*Pune and Delhi*
15.	Raman Research Centre	*Bangalore*
16.	Central Scientific Instruments Organisation	*Chandigarh*
17.	National Metallurgical Laboratory	*Jamshedpur*
18.	Central Salt & Marine Chemical Research institute	*Bhavnagar*
19.	Archaeological Survey of India, India Museum	*Kolkata*
20.	Central Jute Technological Research Institute	*Kolkata*
21.	Central Coconut Research Institute	*Kasergod, Kerala*
22.	Textile Research Institute	*Ahmedabad*
23.	All India Institute of Medical Sciences (AIIMS)	*New Delhi*
24.	National Aeronautical Laboratory	*Bangalore*
25.	National Institute of Oceanography	*Panaji*
26.	National Geophysics Research Institute	*Hyderabad*
27.	Indian Institute of Petroleum	*Dehradun*
28.	Central Building Research Institute	*Roorkee*
29.	Central Road Research Institute	*New Delhi*
30.	Tata Institute of Fundamental Research	*Mumbai*
31.	High Altitude Research Laboratory	*Gulmarg*
32.	National Botanical Research Institute	*Lucknow*
33.	Central Food Technological Research Institute	*Mysore*

34.	Central Glass and Ceramic Research Institute	*Kolkata*
35.	National Enviornmental Engineering Research Institute	*Nagpur*
36.	Central Electro - Chemical Research Institute	*Karaikudi*
37.	Indian Institute of Chemical Biology	*Kolkata*
38.	Industrial Toxicology Research Centre	*Lucknow*
39.	Central Mechanical Engineering Research Institute	*Durgapur*
40.	Centre for Cellular and Molecular Biology	*Hyderabad*

31. Nuclear And Space Research Centres in India

1.	India Rare Earths Limited	Alwaye (Kerela)
2.	Uranium Corporation of India	Jadugoda
3.	Atomic Energy Commission (AEC)	Mumbai
4.	Electronics Corporation of India	Hyderabad
5.	Bhabha Atomic Research Centre (BARC)	Trombay (Mumbai)
6.	Radio Astronomy Centre	Ootacamund
7.	Tata Institute of Fundamental Research	Mumbai
8.	Saha Institute of Nuclear Physics	Kolkata
9.	Nuclear Fuel Complex	Hyderabad
10.	Nuclear Power Complex	Mumbai
11.	Centre of Earth Science's studies	Trivendrum (Kerala)
12.	Physical Research Laboratory	Ahmedabad
13.	Space Commission	Bangalore
14.	Vikram Sarabhai Space Centre	Thiruvananthpuram
15.	Indian Space Research Organisation (ISRO)	Bangalore
16.	Space Application Centre	Ahmedabad
17.	Thumba Equatorial Rocket Launching Station	Thumba (Kerala)
18.	Indian Scientific Satellite Project	Bangalore
19.	College of Satellite Communication Technology	Ahmedabad
20.	Saha Institute of Nuclear Physics	Kolkata

32. Health and Medicinal Research Centres in India

All India Malaria Research Institute	New Delhi
National Tuberculosis Institute	Bangalore
Indian Cancer Research Centre	Mumbai
Indian Veterinary Research Institute	Mukteshwar (H.P.), Izzatnagar (U.P.)
Institute of Ayurvedic Studies and Research	Jamnagar (Gujarat)
Vallabh Bhai Patel Chest Institute	Delhi
Haffkine Institute	Mumbai
National Institute of Communicable Diseases	Delhi

School of Tropical Medicine	Kolkata
Central Leprosy Training and Research Institute	Chingelpet
P.G.I. Medical Education and Research	Chandigarh
National Institute of Nutrition	Hyderabad
National Institute of Occupational Health	Ahmedabad
King Institute of Preventive Medicine	Guindy (Chennai)
All India Institute of Hygiene & Public Health	Kolkata

33. Defence Institutes in India

Air Defence Guided Missiles School	Gopalpur (Orissa)
Aircraft And System Training Establishment	Bangalore (Karnataka)
Airforce Academy	Hyderabad (A.P.)
Airforce Technical College	Jalahali (Bangalore)
Armed Forces Medical College (AFMC)	Pune (Maharashtra)
Defence Services Staff College (DSSC)	Wellington (Tamil Nadu)
Indian Millitary Academy (IMA)	Dehradun (Uttarakhand)
Defence Science Laboratory	Dehradun (Uttarakhand)
College of Millitary Engineering (CME)	Kirki (Pune)

34. Government Industrial Undertaking

Bharat Electronics Limited	Jalahalli (Bangalore)
Heavy Engineering Corporation Ltd.	Ranchi
Heavy Machine Building Plant	Ranchi
Heavy Vehicles Factory	Avadi (Chennai)
Hindustan Aeronautics Ltd.	Bangalore
Hindustan Aircraft Factory	Bangalore
Hindustan Cables Ltd.	Rupnarayanpur (W.B.)
Hindustan Housing Factory Ltd.	New Delhi
Hindustan Latex Ltd.	Peroorkada (Kerala)
Hindustan Organic Chemicals Ltd.	Kolaba (Maharashtra)
Hindustan Photo Films Manufacturing Company Ltd.	Ooti
Hindustan Zinc Ltd.	Udaipur (Rajasthan)
Hindustan Teleprinters Ltd.	Chennai
Integral Coach Factory	Perambadur (T.N.)
Security Paper Mill	Hoshangabad (M.P.)
Neyveli Lignite Corporation Ltd.	Neyveli (Tamil Nadu)

35. Famous Musical Instruments and their Exponents

Sitar	Pt. Ravi Shankar, Nikhil Banerjee, Ustad Vilayat Khan, Shujaat Khan, Jaya Biswas, Debu Choudhary, Nishaat Khan, Bande Hasan, Shahid Parvez, Uma Shankar Mishra, Buddhaditya Mukherjee,Anushka Shankar etc.

Tabla	Ustad Shafat Ahmed Khan, Sapan Choudhary, Zakir Hussain, Latif Khan, Allah Rakha Khan, Gudai Maharaj, Kishan Maharaj, Fayaz Khan, Sukhbinder Singh etc.
Flute	Pannalal Ghosh, Hari Prasad Chaurasia, Raghunath Seth, B.Kunjamani, N. Neela, Rajendra Prasanna, Rajendra Kulkarni, Prakash Saxena etc.
Sarod	Ustad Amjad Ali Khan,Ustad Ali Akbar Khan, Ustad Alauddin Khan, Hafiz Khan, Zarin Daruwala, Mukesh Sharma, Chandan Rai, Biswajit Roy Chaudhury, Sharan Rani etc.
Shehnai	Ustad Bishmillah Khan, Daya Shankar, Jagannath, Hari Singh, Shailesh Bhagwat,Ali Ahmad, Hussain Khan etc.
Violin	Dr. Smt. N. Rajan, Vishnu Gobind (VG) Jog, L. Subramaniam, Sangitha Rajan, Kunakkadi Baidyanathan, Shishir Choudhary, Lalgudi Jayaraman, R.P. Shastri, Suryadev Pawar, Govind Swami Pillai, T.N. Krishnan etc.
Veena	S. Balachandran, Badruddin Dagar, Kalyan Krishna Bhagavatar, B. Doraiswami Iyengar Gopal Krishna, Asad Ali etc.
Santoor	Pt. Shiv Kumar Sharma, Tarun Bhattacharya, Bhajan Sopori, etc.
Pakhawaj	Ustad Rehman Khan, Gopal Das, Chhatrapati Singh, Ramakant Pathak, Arun Saiwal etc.
Rudra Veena	Ushtad Sadiq Ali Khan, Zia Moinuddin Dagar Asad Ali Khan, etc.
Mridang	Thakur Bhikam Singh, Palghat Raju, Dr. Jagdish Singh, T.K. Moorthy, U.K. Sivaram, K.R. Mani etc.
Sarangi	Ustad Bendu Khan, Pt.Ramnarayanji, Aruna Kale, Santosh Mishra, Indralal, Ashiq Ali Khan etc.
Nadaswaram	Sheikh Chinna Maulana, Rajaratna Pillai, Niru Swami Pillai, N. Krishna etc.
Simphoni	Zubin Mehta.
Guitar	Vishwa Mohan Bhatt, Jatin Mazumdar, Brij Bhushan Kabra, Sri Krishna Nalin, Keshav Jalegaonkar etc.
Mandolin	U. Srinivas, Khagen Dey, Nagen Dey, etc.
Vichitra Veena	Ahmed Raza Khan, Abdul Aziz Khan etc.
Piano	V. Balsara
Ghatam	T.H. Vinayakaram
Harmonium	Jnan Prakash Ghosh, Shri Purushottam Walawalkar, Appa Jalgaonkar etc.
Jal Tarang	Himanshu Biswas, Jagdish Mohan, Ghasiram Nirmal, Ram Swaroop Prabhakar etc.
Surbahar	Imrat Khan, Anapurna Devi etc.
Israj	Alauddin Khan.
Mohan Veena	Pt. Vishwa Mohan Bhatt

36. States and their Folk Dances

Jharkhand	Chhau, Sarahul, Jat-Jatin, Karma, Danga, Bidesia, Sohrai.
Uttarakhand	Gadhwali, Kumayuni, Kajari, Jhora, Raslila, Chappeli.
Andhra Pradesh	Kuchipudi (Classical), Ghantamardala, Ottam Thedal, Mohiniattam, Kummi, Siddhi Madhuri, Chhadi.
Chhattisgarh	Goudi, Karma, Jhumar, Dagla, Pali, Tapali, Navrani, Diwari, Mundari.
Arunachal Pradesh	Mask dance (Mukhauta Nritya), War dance.
Himachal Pradesh	Jhora, Jhali, Chharhi, Dhaman, Chhapeli, Mahasu, Nati, Dangi, Chamba, Thali, Jhainta, Daf, Stick dance etc.
Goa	Mandi, Jhagor, Khol , Dakni etc.
Assam	Bihu, Bichhua, Natpuja, Maharas, Kaligopal, Bagurumba, Naga dance, Khel Gopal,Tabal Chongli, Canoe, Jhumura Hobjanai etc.
West Bengal	Kathi, Gambhira, Dhali, Jatra, Baul, Marasia, Mahal, Keertan etc.
Kerala	Kathakali (Classical), Ottam Thulal , Mohini-attam, Kaikottikali, Tappatikali, Kali Auttam.
Meghalaya	Laho, Baagla etc.
Manipur	Manipuri (Classical), Rakhal, Nat Rash, Maha Rash, Raukhat etc.
Nagaland	Chong, Khaiva, Lim, Nuralim etc.
Orissa	Odissi (Classical), Savari, Ghumara, Painka, Munari, Chhau, Chadya Dandanata etc.
Maharashtra	Lavani, Nakata, Koli, Lezim, Gafa, Dahikala Dasavtar or Bohada, Tamasha, Mauni, Powara, Gouricha etc.
Karnataka	Yakshagan, Huttari, Suggi, Kunitha, Karga, Lambi
Gujarat	Garba, Dandiya Ras,Tippani Juriun, Bhavai.
Punjab	Bhangra, Giddha, Daff, Dhaman etc.
Rajasthan	Ghumar, Chakri, Ganagor, Jhulan Leela, Jhuma, Suisini, Ghapal, Panihari, Ginad etc.
Mizoram	Khanatm, Pakhupila, Cherokan etc.
Jammu & Kashmir	Rauf, Hikat, Mandjas, Kud Dandi nach, Damali.
Tamil Nadu	Bharatnatyam, Kumi, Kolattam, Kavadi,
Uttar Pradesh	Nautanki, Raslila, Kajri, Jhora, Chappeli, Jaita.
Bihar	Jata-Jatin, Bakho-Bakhain, Panwariya, Sama-Chakwa, Bidesia, Jatra etc.
Haryana	Jhumar, Phag Dance, Daph, Dhamal, Loor, Gugga, Khor, Gagor etc.

37. Famous Places associated with eminent Persons

Place	Person	Place	Person
Corsica	Nepoleon Bonaparte	Jerusalem	Jesus Christ
Kapilvastu	Gautam Buddha	Lumbini	Gautam Buddha
Macedonia	Alexander, the Great	Mecca	Prophet Mohammed
Jeeradei	Dr. Rajendra Prasad	Waterloo	Nepoleon Bonaparte
Jalianwala Bagh	General Dyer	Porbundar	Mahatma Gandhi
Anand Bhawan	Jawaharlal Nehru	Bardoli	Sardar Patel
Chittore	Maharana Pratap	Fatehpur Sikri	Akbar, the Great
Haldi Ghati	Maharana Pratap	Puducherry	Aurobindo Ghosh
Sabarmati	Mahatma Gandhi	Talwandi	Guru Nanak
Sitab Diyara	Jai Prakash Narayan	Pawanar	Vinoba Bhave
Shantiniketan	Rabindra Nath Tagore	Seringapatnam	Tipu Sultan
Belur Math	Rama Kris. Paramhans	Kundgram	Mahavir
Sevagram	Mahatma Gandhi	Trafalgar	Nelson
Cuttack	Subhash Chandra Bose	Pawapuri	Mahavir
Kushi Nagar	Gautam Buddha	Trimurti Bhawan	Jawaharlal Nehru

38. Crematorium of Famous Persons

Raj Ghat	Mahatma Gandhi	Shanti Van	Jawahar Lal Nehru
Vijay Ghat	Lal Bahadur Shastri	Shakti Sthal	Indira Gandhi
Kishan Ghat	Ch. Charan Singh	Abhay Ghat	Morarji Desai
Veer Bhumi	Rajiv Gandhi	Samata Asthal	Jagjeevan Ram
Ekta Asthal	Giani Zail Singh, Chandra Shekhar	Karma Bhumi	Dr. Shankar Dayal Sharma
Uday Bhoomi	K.R. Narayanan	Mahaprayan Ghat	Dr. Rajendra Prasad

39. Famous Nicknames of Eminent Persons

Nickname	Person	Nickname	Person
Father of the Nation; Bapu	Mahatma Gandhi	*Grandfather of Indian Films*	Dhundiraj Govind Phalke
Frontier Gandhi; Badshah Khan	Khan Abdul Ghaffar Khan	*Grand Old Man of India*	Dadabhai Naoroji
Strong (Iron) Man	Sardar Vallabhbhai Patel	*Mahamana*	Pt. Madan Mohan Malaviya
Sher-e-Kashmir	Sheikh Abdullah	*Andhra Kesari*	T. Prakasam
Napoleon of India	Samudra Gupta	*Sahid-e-Azam*	Bhagat Singh
Shakespeare of India	Mahakavi Kalidas	*Deshbandhu*	Chitta Ranjan Das
Machiavelli of India	Chanakya	*Deenbandhu*	C.F. Andrews
Akbar of Kashmir	Jainul Abdin	*Lokmanya*	Bal Gangadhar Tilak

Nickname	Person	Nickname	Person
Vishwa Kavi; Kaviguru; Gurudev	Rabindranath Tagore	*Loknayak*	Jayaprakash Narayan
Rajaji / C.R.	Chakravarti Rajagopalachari	*Bangabandhu*	Sheikh Mujibur Rahman
Bihar Kesari	Dr. Srikrishna Singh	*Chacha*	Jawaharlal Nehru
Bengal Kesari	Ashutosh Mukherji	*Man of Peace*	Lal Bahadur Shastri
Punjab Kesari	Lala Lajpat Rai	*Guruji*	M.S. Golvalkar
Desh Ratna; Ajatshatru	Dr. Rajendra Prasad	*Sparrow*	Major General Rajinder Singh
Father of Gujarat	Ravi Sankar Maharaj	*Swar Kokila*	Lata Mangeshkar
Tau	Chaudhury Devi Lal	*Udanpari*	P.T. Usha
King Maker	Earl of Warwick	*Mother*	Mother Teresa
Nightingale of India	Sarojini Naidu	*Sardar*	Vallabhbhai Patel
Lady with the lamp	Florence Nightingale	*Young Turk*	Chandra Shekhar
Lal, Bal, Pal	Lala Lajpat Rai, Bal Gangadhar Tilak and Bipin Chandra Pal	*G.B.S.*	George Bernard Shaw
Bihar Vibhuti	Dr. Anugrah Narayan Singh	*Deshpriya*	Yatindra Mohan Sengupta
Babuji	Jagjeevan Ram	*Kuvempu*	K.V. Puttappa
Morning Star of India Renaissance	Raja Ram Mohan Roy	*Little Corporal; Man of Destiny*	Napoleon Bonaparte
King maker of Indian History	Sayyed Bandhu	*Father of English Poetry*	Geoffery Chaucer
Rajarshee	Purushottam Das Tandon	*Netaji*	Subhash Chandra Bose
Haryana Hurricane	Kapil Dev	*Uncle Ho*	Ho Chi Minh
Magician of Hockey	Dhyanchand	*Li- Kwan*	Pearl Buck
Jana Nayak	Karpuri Thakur	*Grand Old Man of Britain*	Willium E. Gladstone
II Duce	Benito Mussolini	*Desert Fox*	Gen. Ervin Rommel
Tota-e-Hind	Amir Khushro	*Quaid-i-Azam*	Md. Ali Jinnah
Maiden Queen	Queen Elizabeth I	*Little Master*	Sunil Gavaskar
Maid of Orleans	Joan of Arc	*Anna*	C.N. Annadurai
Man of Blood and Iron	Otto Van Bismark	*Bard of Avon*	William Shakespeare
Fuehrer	Adolf Hitler		

40. Some Great Works associated with Famous Persons

1.	Foundation of Red Cross	Henery Dunant
2.	Foundation of Scout	Baden Powell
3.	Foundation of Red Gaurds	Garrywaldy
4.	Founder of Socialism	Acharya Narendra Dev

5.	Father of Sanskrit Grammar	Panini
6.	Founder of Anand Van	Baba Amte
7.	Founder of 'Auroville Ashram' (Puducherry)	Aurobindo Ghosh
8.	Founder of Shantiniketan	Rabindra Nath Tagore
9.	Founder of Vishwabharati	Rabindra Nath Tagore
10.	Founder of Pawnar Ashram	Vinoba Bhave
11.	Founder of Bhudan Movement	Vinoba Bhave
12.	Founder of League of Nations	Woodrow Willson
13.	Founder of Golden Temple	Guru Arjun Dev
14.	Founder of Khalsa Panth	Guru Gobind Singh

41. Awards and Honours

Prize	Field
Nobel Prize	Peace, Literature, Medicine, Physics, Chemistry, (From 1901)and Economics (From 1969)
Pulitzer Prize	Journalism (From 1917)
Academy (Oscar) Awards	Film (From 1929)
Kalinga Award	Science (From 1952)
Booker Prize	Literature (From 1929)
Grammy Award	Music (From 1958)
Ramon Magasaysay Award	Government (Public) Service, Social Service, Journalism, Literature, Communication and International Understanding (From 1957)
Bharat Ratna	For outstanding contributions in the field of Art/Literature/Science and Public Service
Dada Saheb Phalke Award	Film (From 1969)
Jnanpith Award	Literature (From 1965)
Saraswati Samman	Literature (From 1991)
Vachaspati Samman	Sanskrit Literature (From 1992)
Shankar Award	Indian Philosophy , Culture and Art
Vyasa Samman	Literature
Kabir Samman	Socio - communal Harmony
Dronacharya Award	Sports Coaching / Training (From 1985)
Arjuna Award	Sports (From 1961)
Bhatnagar Award	Science (From 1957)
Dhanwantari Award	Medical Science (From 1971)
Bourlog Award	Agriculture (From 1992)

42. National Awards

Republic Day Awards : Bharat Ratna, Padma Vibhushan and Padma Shree are given for exceptional service towards the advancement of Art, Literature and Science and in recognition of public service of a high (or the highest) order.

Param Vir Chakra : It is the highest Gallantry Award. It is given for extraordinary act of bravery in the field of Naval, Air and Army.

Mahavir Chakra : It is the second highest Gallantry Award.

Vir Chakra : It is the third highest Gallantry Award.

Bharat Ratna

Bharat Ratna : The highest-civilian award is given for exceptional service the advancement of art, literature and science, and in recognition of public service of the highest order.

- The decoration is in the form of a *peepal leaf*, about 5.8 cm long, 4.7 cm wide and 3.1 mm thick. It is of toned bronze. On its obverse is embossed a replica of the sun, 1.6 cm in diameter, below which the words "Bharat Ratna" are embossed in Hindi. On the reverse are State emblem and the motto, also in Hindi. The emblem, the sun and the rim are of platinum. The inscriptions are in burnished bronze.
- The first three recipients of Bharat Ratna were C. Rajagopalchari, Dr. S. Radhakrishnan and Dr. C.V. Raman in 1954 while Khan Abdul Ghaffar Khan was the *first foreigner* to be honoured with this award in 1987.

Year	Recipients
1954	Chakravarti Rajagopalachari Dr. Sarvepalli Radhakrishnan, Dr. Chandrasekhar Venkat Raman
1955	Dr. Bhagwan Das, Dr. Mokshagundam Visvesvaraiya, Pt. Jawaharlal Nehru.
1957	Pt. Govind Ballabh Pant
1958	Dr. Dhondo Keshave Karve
1961	Rajarshi Purushottam Das Tandon, Dr. Bidhan Chandra (B.C.) Roy
1962	Dr. Rajendra Prasad
1963	Dr. Zakir Hussain, Dr. Pandurang Vaman (P. V.) Kane
1966	Lal Bahadur Shastri (Posthumous)
1972	Mrs. Indira Gandhi
1975	Varahagiri Venkat (V.V.) Giri
1976	Kumaraswami (K.) Kamraj (Posthumous)
1980	Mary Teresa Bojaxhiu (Mother Teresa)
1983	Acharya Vinoba Bhave (Posthumous)
1987	Khan Abdul Ghaffar Khan
1988	Marudur Gopalan (MG) Ramachandran (Posthumous)
1990	Dr. Bhim Rao Ramji Ambedkar (Posthumous), Dr. Nelson Rolihlahla Mandela
1991	Rajiv Gandhi (Posthumous), Sardar Vallabh Bhai Patel (Posthumous), Morarji Ranchhodji Desai

1992 Jehangir Ratanji Dadabhai (J.R.D.) Tata, Maulana Abul Kalam Azad (Posthumous), Satyajit Ray (Posthumous)

1997 Aruna Asaf Ali (Posthumous), Guljarilal Nanda (Posthumous), Dr. Avul Pakir Jainulabdeen (A.P.J.) Abdul Kalam

1998 Madurai Sanmukhavadivu (M. S.) Subbulakshmi, Chidambaram (C.) Subramaniam

1999 Prof. Amartya Sen, Pt. Ravi Shankar, Loknayak Jay Prakash Narayan (Posthumous) and Gopinath Bordoloi (Posthumous)

2001 Lata Dinanath Mangeshkar, Ustad Bismillah Khan

2009 Pt. Bhimsen Gururaj Joshi

2014 Prof. C.N.R. Rao, Sachin Ramesh Tendulkar* (*1st player and the youngest one to get 'Bhart Ratna')

Note : *Lal Bahadur Shastri was the first person to be honoured with Bharat Ratna posthumously and Indira Gandhi was the first woman recipient of Bharat Ratna.*

Padma Vibhushan : The award is given for exceptional and distinguished services in any field including service ·endered by government servants.

➢ The decoration is circular in design, with a geometrical pattern superimposed on the circle. The diameter of the circular portion is 4.4 cm and the thickness about 0.6 mm. On the obverse, there is a lotus flower embossed on the circular space. The word "Padma" is embossed in Hindi above the word "Vibhushan" below the lotus flower. On the reverse are the State emblem and the motto in Hindi. It is of *toned bronze*. The inscription "Padma Vibhushan" on the obverse, the geometrical pattern on either side and the border around periphery are in *burnished bronze*. All embossing on either side of decoration is in *white gold*.

Padma Bhushan : The award is given for distinguished service of a high order in any field, including service rendered by government servants.

➢ It has the same design as the "Padma Vibhushan". On its obverse the word "Padma" appears above and the word "Bhushan" below the lotus flower. The inscription "Padma Bhushan" on the obverse, the geometrical pattern on either side and the border around periphery are in *burnished bronze*. All embossing either side of the decoration is in *standard gold*.

Padma Shri : The award is given for distinguished service in any field including service rendered by government servants.

➢ The name of the decoration is embossed in Hindi with the word "Padma" above and the word "Shri" below the lotus flower on the obverse. The inscription "Padam Shri" on the obverse, the geometrical pattern on either side and the border around the periphery are in *burnished bronze*. All embossing on either side of the decoration is in *stainless steel*.

Other National Awards

Appan Menon Memorial Award : The award which carries a cash prize of Rs. 1 lakh aims at providing financial assistance to journalists interested in undertaking projects related to international affairs and developmental issues relevant to India and South Asia.

Aditya Vikram Birla Kalashikhar Puraskar : The award is conferred on an artiste in the field of visual and performing arts for lifetime achievement carries Rs. 1.5 lakh in cash, a momento and scroll of honour. Previous recipients of the award include Lata Mangeshkar, M. F. Hussain, Guru Kelucharan Mohapatra, Pandit Ram Narayan, Pandit Bhimsen Joshi.

43. Gallantry Awards

Param Vir Chakra : The highest decoration for valour is the Param Vir Chakra which is awarded for the most conspicuous bravery or some daring or pre-eminent act of valour or self-sacrifice in the presence of the enemy, whether on land, at sea or in the air.

- The decoration is made of bronze and is circular in shape. It has, on the obverse, four replicas of "Indra's Vajra" embossed round the State emblem in the centre. On the reverse the words "Param Vir Chakra" are embossed both in Hindi and English with two lotus flowers in the middle.
- the decoration is worn on the left breast with a plain purple coloured riband about 3.2 cm in width.

Mahavir Chakra : Mahavir Chakra is the second highest decoration and is awarded for acts of conspicuous gallantry in the presence of enemy, whether on land, at sea or in the air.

- It is made of standard silver and is circular in shape. Embossed on the obverse is a five pointed heraldic star with domed centre-piece bearing the gilded State emblem in the centre. The words "Mahavir Chakra" are embossed both in Hindi and English on the reverse with two lotus flowers in the middle. The decoration is worn on the left breast with a half-white and half-orange riband about 3.2 cm in width, the orange being near the left shoulder.

Vir Chakra : Vir Chakra is third in the order of awards given for act of gallantry in the presence of the enemy, whether on land, at sea or in the air.

- The decoration is made of standard silver and is circular in shape. Embossed on the obverse is a five pointed heraldic star which has an Ashoka Chakra in the centre. Within this chakra is a domed centre-piece bearing gilded State emblem. On the reverse, words "Vir Chakra" are embossed, both in Hindi and English, with two lotus flowers in the middle. The Chakra is worn on the left breast with a half-blue and half-orange riband, about 3.2 cm in width, the orange being nearer the left shoulder.

Ashok Chakra : Ashok Chakra is the country's highest peacetime gallantry award equivalent to Param Vir Chakra.

- The Chakra is made of *gilt gold* and is circular in shape. Embossed on the obsverse is a replica of Ashok Chakra surrounded by a lotus wreath. Along the edge is pattern of lotus leaves, flowers and buds. On the reverse, the words "Ashok Chakra" are embossed both in Hindi and English, with lotus flowers in the intervening space.
- The Chakra is worn on the left breast with a green silk riband, about 3.2 cm in width and divided into two equal segments by an orange vertical line.

Kirti Chakra : The decoration is awarded for conspicuous gallantry. It is made of *standard silver* and is circular in shape. The obverse and the reverse are exactly the same as in Ashok Chakra.

➢ The Chakra is worn on the left breast with a green silk riband, about 3.2 cm in width and divided equally into two by orange vertical lines.

Shaurya Chakra : The decoration is awarded for an act of gallantry. It is exactly like Ashok Chakra, except that it is made of *bronze*.

➢ The Chakra is worn on the left breast with a green silk riband, about 3.2 cm in width and divided into four equal segments by three orange vertical lines.

Param Vishisht Seva Medal (PVSM), Ati Vishisht Seva Medal (AVSM), Vishisht Seva Medal (VSM) : The Vishist Seva Medals are awarded to personnel of all the three services in recognition of distinguished service of the "most exceptional", "exceptional" and "high" order respectively. Param Vishisht Seva Medal is made of *gold*, Ati Vishisht Seva Medal of *standard silver* and Vishisht Seva Medal of *bronze*, all circular in shape and 3.5 cm in diameter. Each medal has on its obverse five pointed stars and on its reverse the Lion Capitol. Its ribbon is golden with *one dark-blue stripe* down the centre for Param Vishisht Seva Medal, *two dark-blue stripes* dividing it into three equal parts for Ati Vishisht Seva Medal and *three dark-blue stripes* dividing it into four equal parts for Vishisht Seva Medal.

44. Recipients of the Bharatiya Jnanpith Award

➢ The first Jnanpith Award was given in 1965.

➢ The Jnanpith Award carries a citation, shawl, srifal, a bronze idol of Vagdevi Saraswati and a cash prize of ₹ 7,00,000

Sl.	Year	Recipient	Work
1st	1965	G. Shankar Kurup	Auda Kujai (Malayalam)
2nd	1966	Tara Shankar Bandyopadhyay	Ganadevata (Bengali)
3rd	1967	K.V. Putappa, Uma Shankar Joshi	Ramayan Darshanam (Kannada), Nisheeth (Gujarati)
4th	1968	Sumitra Nandan Pant	Chidambara (Hindi)
5th	1969	Prof. Raghupati Sahay 'Firaq Gorakhpuri'	Gul-e-Naghma (Urdu)
6th	1970	Vishwanath Satyanarayana	Shreemad Ramayan Kalpavriksham (Telugu)
7th	1971	Vishnu Dey	Smriti Satta Bhavishya (Bengali)
8th	1972	Ramdhari Singh 'Dinkar'	Urvashi (Hindi)
9th	1973	Gopinath Mohanty, D.R Bendre	Mati Matal (Oriya) Naku Thanthi (Kannada)
10th	1974	Vishnu Sakharam Khandekar	Yayati (Marathi)
11th	1975	P.V. Akilandam	Chittirappavai (Tamil)
12th	1976	Smt. Ashapurna Devi	Pratham Pratishruti (Bengali)
13th	1977	Dr.K. Shivram Karanth	Mukajjiya Kanasugalu (Kannada)

Sl.	Year	Recipient	Work
14th	1978	Dr Sachidananda Hiranand Vatsyayana 'Agyeya'	Kitni Nawon Mein Kitni Bar (Hindi)
15th	1979	Dr. Virendra Kumar Bhattacharya	Mrityunjay (Assamia)
16th	1980	S.K Pottekat	Oru Dishatinte Katha (Malayalam)
17th	1981	Amrita Pritam	Kagaz te Canvas (Punjabi)
18th	1982	Mahadevi Verma	Yama (Hindi)
19th	1983	Masti Venkatesh Iyengar	Chikaveer Rajendra (Kannada)
20th	1984	T. Shiv Shankar Pillai	Kayar (Malayalam)
21st	1985	Pannalal Patel	Manvini Bhavai (Gujarati)
22nd	1986	Sachida Nanda Routroy	Oriya Literature
23rd	1987	Vishnu Vaman Shirwadkar	Marathi Literature
24th	1988	Dr. C. Narayana Reddy	Telugu Literature
25th	1989	Qurrtul - ain - Hyder	Urdu Literature
26th	1990	Prof. Vinayak Krishna Gokak	Kannada Literature
27th	1991	Subhash Mukhopadhyay	Bengali Literature
28th	1992	Naresh Mehta	Hindi Literature
29th	1993	Dr. Sitakant Mahapatra	Oriya Literature
30th	1994	Prof. U. R. Ananthamurthy	Kannada Literature
31st	1995	M.T. Vasudevan Nair	Malayalam Literature
32nd	1996	Mrs. Mahashweta Devi	Bengali Literature
33rd	1997	Ali Sardar Jafri	Urdu Literature
34th	1998	Girish Karnad	Kannada Literature
35th	1999	Nirmal Verma, Gurdayal Singh	Hindi Literature, Punjabi Literature
36th	2000	Dr. Indira Goswami	Assamese Literature
37th	2001	Rajendra Keshavlal Shah	Gujarati Literature
38th	2002	D. Jayakanthan	Tamil Literature
39th	2003	Vinda Karandikar	Marathi Literature
40th	2004	Rehman Rahi	Kashmiri
41th	2005	Kunwar Narayan	Hindi Literature
42nd	2006	Satyavrat Shastri, Ravindra Kelekar	Sanskrit Literature, Konkani Literature
43rd	2007	O.N.V. Kurup	Malayalam Literature
44th	2008	Akhlaq Mohammad Khan 'Shaharyar'	Urdu Literature
45th	2009	Amarkant and Shrilal Shukla (jointly)	Hindi Literature
46th	2010	Chandrashekhar Kambar	Kannada Literature
47th	2011	Pratibha Ray	Odiya Literature
48th	2012	Ravuri Bharadhwaja	Telugu Literature
49th	2013	Kedar Nath Singh	Hindi Literature

45. Recipients of Dada Saheb Falke Award

- Phalke award carries a 'Swarna Kamal', a shawl and a cash prize of Rs. 2 lakh.
- Introduced in 1969, the Dada Saheb Phalke award was first given to actress Devika Rani.

Year	Recipient	Year	Recipient
1969	Devika Rani Roerich	1970	Birendra Nath Sircar
1971	Prithvi Raj Kapoor (Posthumously)	1972	Pankaj Mallick
1973	Sulochana (Rubi Myers)	1974	B.N. Reddi
1975	Dhiren Ganguli	1976	Kanan Devi
1977	Nitin Bose	1978	Ray Chandra (R.C.) Boral
1979	Sohrab Modi	1980	P. Jairaj
1981	Naushad Ali	1982	L.V. Prasad
1983	Durga Khote	1984	Satyajit Ray
1985	V. Shantaram	1986	B. Nagi Reddi
1987	Raj Kapoor	1988	Ashok Kumar
1989	Lata Mangeshkar	1990	Akkineni Nageshwar Rao
1991	Bhalji (Bhalchandra Govind) Pendharkar	1992	Dr. Bhupen Hazarika
1993	Majrooh Sultanpuri	1994	Dilip Kumar
1995	Dr. Rajkumar	1996	Sivaji Ganesan
1997	Kavi Pradeep	1998	B.R. Chopra
1999	Hrishikesh Mukherjee	2000	Asha Bhonsle
2001	Yash Chopra	2002	Dev Anand
2003	Mrinal Sen	2004	Adoor Gopalkrishnan
2005	Braj Bhushan Chaturvedi	2006	Shyam Benegal
2007	Manna Dey	2008	V.K.Moorthy
2009	D. Rama Naidu	2010	K. Balachander
2011	Soumitra Chatterjee	2012	Praan Krishan Sikand
2013	Gulzar (Sampooran Singh Kalra)		

46. Important Books and Authors

[A] Indian writers and their books :

Writer	Books
Pt. Vishnu Sharma	Panchatantra
Vishakhadatta	Mudra Rakshas
Raskhan	Prem Vatika
Panini	Ashtadhyayi
Shudrak	Mrichhakatikam
Kalidasa	Raghuvansham, Kumarsambhavam, Meghdootam, Abhigyanshakuntalam
Vatsyayana	Kama Sutra

Writer	Books
Vigyaneshwar	Mitakshara
Jeemootwahan	Daybhag
Kalhana	Rajtarangini
Plini	Natural History
Kautilya	Arthashastra
Dandi	Avanti Sundari, Dashkumaracharitam
Ved Vyas	Bhagwat Gita, Mahabharata
Ashwaghosh	Buddha Charitam
Jayadev	Geet Govind
Bana Bhatt	Kadambari
Bhavabhuti	Malti Madhav
Amar Singh	Amar Kosh
Bhartrihari	Niti-Shatak, Shringar Shatak, Vairagya Shatak
Firdausi	Shahnama
Abul Fazal	Ain-i- Akbari, Akabarnama
Surdas	Sahityalahari, Sursagar
Kabirdas	Bijak, Ramayani, Sabar
Gulbadan Beghum	Humanyunama
Al-Beruni	Kitab-ul-Hind
Malik Mohammed Jayasi	Padmavat
Mulk Raj Anand	Coolie, Confession of a Lover, Two leaves and a bud
Nirad C. Chaudhury	Hinduism, Autobiography of an Unknown Indian, A Passage to England, Culture in the Vanity Bag, Continent of Crime
Rabindra Nath Tagore	Chitrangada, Gitanjali, Gora, Chandalika, Visarjana, Hungry Stones
Sumitranandan Pant	Jyotsana, Yugwani, Chidambara
Kuldip Nayyar	The Judgment, Distant Neighbours; India, The Critical Years; In Jail, India after Nehru, Between the Lines
Sri Aurobindo Ghosh	Life Divine, Essays on Gita
Swami Shivanand	Divine Life
Amrita Pritam	Death of a City, Kagaz te Canvas, Forty nine Days

Writer	Books
Munsi Premchand	Godan, Gaban, Karmabhumi, Rangbhumi
Khushwant Singh	Indira Gandhi Returns, Indira Gandhi : Badhate Kadam, The Company of Women
B. M. Kaul	Untold Story, Confrontation with Pakistan
Vijay Tendulkar	Sakharam Binder
R. K. Narayanan	The Dark Room, Malgudi Days, Guide, My Days, Swami and Friends
Dr. S. Radhakrishnan	Indian Philosophy
Sarojini Naidu	Golden Threshold, Broken Wings
Suryakant Tripathi Nirala	Anamika, Parimal, Gunjan, Juhi Ki Kali
Yashpal	Jhootha Sach
Jai Shankar Prasad	Kamayani, Aansoo, Skandagupta, Ajatshatru
Kazi Nazrul Islam	Agni Veena
Maithilisharan Gupt	Bharat Bharati
Ramdhari Singh Dinkar	Kurukshetra, Urvashi
Mrs. Indira Gandhi	Eternal India
S.H.Vatsyayan 'Agyeya'	Kitni Nawon Mein Kitnee Bar, Aangan Ke Paar, Dwar, Shekhar: Ek Jivani, Nadi Ke Dweep
Mahadevi Verma	Yama, Niharika, Neeraja
Amrit Lal Nagar	Amrit Aur Vish
Nayantara Sehgal	A Voice of Freedom
V. S. Naipal	Area of Darkness, A House for Mr. Biswas, A Million Mutinies Now, A Bend in the River
Devkinandan Khatri	Chandrakanta Santati
Sharat Chandra Chattopadhyay	Devdas, Charitraheen, Shrikant, Parineeta
Vrindavanlal Verma	Jhansi Ki Rani
Jainendra Kumar	Sunita, Tyagpatra
Bhagwati Charan Verma	Chitralekha
Phanishwar Nath 'Renu'	Maila Aanchal, Mare Gaye Gulfam
Gajanan Madhav 'Muktibodh'	Chand Ka Munh Tedha Hai
Bhartendu Harischandra	Bharat Durdasha, Satya Harischandra

[B] Some Important Foreign Writers and their Books

Writer	Book
Adam Smith	Wealth of Nations
Adolf Hitler	Mein Kamph
Albert Einstein	The World as I See it
Alexander Solzhenitsyn	August 1914
A. L. Basham	The Wonder that was India
Anton Chekhov	Cherry Orchard
Arther Hele	Airport
Aristotle	Politics
Boris Pasternak	Dr. Zhivago
David Baldacci	Absolute Power
Dante	Divine Comedy
E. M. Forster	A Passage to India, Maurice
Homer	Odyssey, Illiad
H. G. Wells	Shape of Things to Come
Harold Evans	Good Times, Bad Times
Henry Miller	Tropic of Cancer
Issac Newton	Principia
Katherine Mayo	Mother India
Machiavelli	The Prince
Maxim Gorky	Mother
Plato	Republic
Jean J. Rousseau	The Social Contract
John Milton	Paradise Lost, Lycidas
Winston Churchill	Gathering Storm
George Orwell	Farm House, Animal Farm
Charles Darwin	Descent of Man, Origin of Species
William Shakespeare	Commedy of Errors, As You Like It, A Mid Summer Night's Dream, Merchant of Venice, Hamlet, King Lear, Othello
George Bernard Shaw	Major Barbara, Man and Superman, Apple Carte, Arms and the Man, Pygmalion, Caesar and Cleopatra, Candida
Charles Dickens	A Tale of Two Cities, Oliver Twist, David Copperfield
J. K. Galbraith	Affluent Society, Ambassador's Journal, The Triumph
Herold Joseph Laski	Grammar of Politics, Dilema of Our Time
J. M. Barrie	Hindu Civilization, Peter Pan
Gunnar Myrdal	Against the Stream, Asian Drama
Leo Tolstoy	War and Peace
Z. A. Bhutto	Great Tragedy
Vladimir Nabakov	Lolita
Mao-tse Tung	On Contradiction

[C] Some Latest Books and Authors

Book	Writer
My Journey : Trasnforming Dreams into Actions	A. P. J. Abdul Kalam
Fractured Times	Eric Hobsbawm
The Competent Authority	Shovon Choudhury
The Sergeant's Son	Ashim Choudhury
The Cuckoo's Calling	Robert Galbraith
How The Light Gets in	Louise Penny
Gone Girl	Gilian Flynn
And The Mountains Echoed	Khaled Hosseini
The Liberty Amendments	Mark Levin
This Town	Mark Leibovish
Happy, Happy, Happy	Phil Robertson, Mark Schlabach
Zealot	Reza Asian
Shiva Triology 1. The Immortals of Meluha, 2. The Secrets of Nagas and 3. The Oath of Vayuputras)	Amish Tripathi
Romancing with Life	Dev Anand
Saurabh Ganguli : The Maharaja of Cricket	Debasheesh Dutta
Mohan Das : A True Story of a man, his People and Empire	Raj Mohan Gandhi
Lets Kill Gandhi	Tushar Gandhi
Eat, Prey, Love	Elizabeth Gilbert
Manzilon se Jyada Safar	V.P. Singh
A Call To Honour : In Service of Emergent India	Jaswant Singh
Guiding Souls	Dr. A.P.J. Abdul Kalam
Collected Plays	Girish Karnad
All My Sisters	Zudith Lenox
The Longest Race	Tom Alter
Gulab Bai : The Queen of Nautanki Theatre	Deepti Priya Mehrotra
Touch Play (Biography of Prakash Padukone)	Dev Sukumar
Out of My Comfort Zone : The Autobiography	Steev Waugh
Honeymoon	James Petterson
Da Vinci Code	Don Brown
The Broker	John Greeson
God of Small Things	Arundhati Rai
Speed Post	Shobha De
The Better Man	Anita Nayyar
Bookless in Baghdad	Shashi Thiroor
The Argumentative Indians	Dr. Amartya Sen
The Algebra of Infinite Justice	Arundhati Rai
Fire fly : A Fairy Tale	Ritu Beri
Two Lives	Vikram Seth
Glass Palace	Amitav Ghosh
The Brief History of Time	Stephen Hawking

Book	Writer
Freedom from Fear	Aung San Suu Kyi
Fasting, Feasting	Anita Desai
The Lord of the Flies	William Goldings
Struggle for Change	K.B. Lal
My Life	Bill Clinton
Life of Pi	Yann Martel
India in Slow motion	Mark Tully
Ignited Minds	Dr. A.P.J. Abdul Kalam
Wings of Fire	Dr. A.P.J. Abdul Kalam
Envisioning an Empowered Nation	Dr. A.P.J. Abdul Kalam
Interpreter of Maladies	Jhumpa Lahiri
One Day Cricket, The Indian Challange	Ashish Roy
A View from Outside	P. Chidambaram
Harry Potter and the Deathly Hallows	J.K. Rawlling
The Year of the Roester	Guy Sorman
Above Average	Amitabh Bagchi
Dalits in India : A Profile	Sukhdeo Thorat
The Top of the Raintree	Kamalini Sengapta
Terrifying Visions : Golwalkar,the RSS and India	Jyotirmay Sharma
Frontline Pakistan : The Struggle with Millitant Islam	Zahid Hussain
The Lowland	Jhumpa Lahiri
The Splender of Silence	Indu Sundaresan
The Leopard and the Fox : A Pakistani Tragedy	Tariq Ali
A Time of Transition : Rajiv Gandhi To The 21st Century	Mani Shankar Aiyer

47. Games and Sports

Olympic Games

The origin of the ancient Olympic Games is lost in the midst of pre-history, but for many centuries they were only a festival of the Greek people. The Games were first held in honour of the Greek god, Zeus in 776 BC in the plain of the kingdom of Elis, nestled in a lush valley between the Alpheus River and Mount Kronion, 15 km from the Ionian Sea. The Olympiad celebrated that year was considered as the first and was used to date subsequent historic events. But religious ceremonies and games were held in Olympia before that time. The oldest sanctuary of Greece was there, the altar of the Great Mother of Gods, Rhea (Earth). On the day of the feast, the priest stood in front of the altar, ready to perform a sacrifice. Women were forbidden to be present and the male contestants were naked. Young men waited at a distance on one stadium (about 200 yds). As soon as a signal was given they ran and the first to arrive at the altar received the torch from the priest's hand and lit the sacrificial fire.

The old Olympiads were held after every four years and the Greeks measured time in terms of Games started on the first new moon after the summer solstice, around mid-July. The ancient Olympic Games lasted for five days and the events took place in a precise order. On the first day, there were sacrifices and opening ceremonies. On the second day there were special competitions for the "ephebians". The third day was devoted to events for adult competitors : dromos, diaulos, dolichos, pugilism, wrestling, pancratium. On the fourth day, there were equestrian events, pentathlon, race with arms. On the fifth and the final day, there were closing ceremonies and proclamation of the heroes.

During the first six Olympic Games, however, the prize had been a portion of meat or 'meria' taken from an animal sacrificed to the gods. It was only after the VII Games that the olive crown was given to the winners and the moral significance of this prize was considerable. Once the prize were awarded, a flock of pigeons was released to carry the names of the champions to all the corners of Greece.

The Games came to a sudden end when the *Roman Emperor Theodosius* banned the competitions and their attendant sacrificial offerings as pagan manifestations. From 395 AD onwards the fall of Olympia was very rapid. In that year the first damage was caused by the invasion of Alaric's barbarians. A year earlier the famous crysele-phantide statue of Zeus had been taken to Constantinople. It was destroyed in 475 AD during the great fire. Following the attacks of the Goths, a fire destroyed the temple of Zeus; earthquakes from 522 to 551 and the most severe of all in 580 brought down whatever had remained standing. Glory had vanished and of the vast riches there were now left but a few ruins and the name of Olympia. Something immortal remained, however, and that was the Olympic spirit.

Modern Olympic Games

The revival work of the Games was undertaken by Baron Pierre de Coubertin nearly 1,500 years after the last of the ancient Games. He was born into a family of Italian origin which had settled in France. It was on November 25, 1892, during a conference at Sorbonne about the history of physical exercises, that he first pronounced those famous six words in public "The Restoration of the Olympic Games!" He said that the Games would ennoble and strengthen amateur sports to give them strength and lasting quality for an essential role in the world of modern education.

It was at the International Congress for the Study of the Propagation of the Principles of Amateurism held in Paris in June 1894 that the delegates led by Baron Pierre de Coubertin and associates unanimously voted to restore the Olympic Games and to create an International Olympic Committee to oversee them. De Coubertin had planned to propose Paris for the site of the first modern Olympics in 1900 but the enthusiasm and zeal of the delegates was so great that they insisted the first Games to be held in 1896. Athens was, therefore, the venue for the 1896 Games. Since then these Games are held every four years.

Olympic Symbol : It comprises five rings or circles, linked together to represent the sporting friendship of all people. The rings also symbolise the continents—Europe, Asia, Africa, Australia and America. Each ring is of a different colour, i.e., blue, yellow, black, green and red. The rings are meant to represent five continents viz., Africa (black), America (red), Asia (yellow), Australia (green) and Europe (Blue).

Olympic Flag : The Olympic flag, created in 1913 at the suggestion of Baron Pierre de Coubertin, was solemnly inaugurated in Paris in June 1914 but it was riased over an Olympic stadium for the first time at the Antwerp Games (Belgium) in 1920. There is also a second Olympic flag, which is used for the Winter Games. These flags are made of white silk and contain above mentioned five interwined rings. From left to right the rings are blue, yellow, black, green and red.

Olympic Flame : It was at the Amsterdam Games in 1928 that for the first time an Olympic flame was ceremonially lighted and burned in a giant torch at the entrance of the stadium. The modern version of the flame was adopted in 1936 at the Berlin Games. The Olympic flame symbolises the continuity between the ancient and modern Games. The torch, used to kindle the flame, is first lit by the sun's rays at Olympia, Greece, and then carried to the site of the Games by relay of runners. Ships and planes are used when necessary. On July 15, 1976, space age technology was used to transport the flame from one continent to another.

Olympic Motto : The Olympic motto is *"Citius-Altius-Fortius"* (faster, higher, stronger). Rev. Father Didon (1840-1900), headmaster of a school near Paris and a great promoter of sports in the French Catholic colleges first used the *motto* and had it embroidered on the pennants of his school clubs. This succinct definition of the philosophy of sport appealed to father Didon's friend, Baron Pierre de Coubertin who was responsible for the revival of the Olympic Games nearly 1,500 years after the last of the ancient Games. It was adopted at his suggestion at the International congress for the "Study and Propagation of the Principles of Amateurism" on June 23, 1894, the same day on which the restoration of the Olympic Games and the creation of the International Olympic Committee were also decided.

Olympic Prizes, Medals and Certificates : While in ancient times the Olympic heroes received a crown of olive branches for their exploits, modern Olympic champions are rewarded with medals and certificates. The winning athlete now receives a Gold medal, the athlete in the second place is awarded a Silver medal and the third placed athlete wins a Bronze medal. In addition, all athletes ranking from first to sixth receive a certificate. Each medal is 60 mm in diameter and 3 mm thick. The first and second place medals are made of 92.5 per cent silver and the medals for the first winner is then plated with 6 gram of fine gold. Thus this medal is not of full gold. The thrid place medal is of bronze.

➢ Olympic games were started in 776 B.C. on Mount Olympus in the honour of Greek God 'Zeus'.

➢ The modern Olympic games started in Athens, the capital of Greece on 6th April, 1896 with great efforts made by Pierre de Coubertin of France.

➢ The Olympic games are organised after every four years.

- In the flag of Olympics, there is a symbol of five coloured circles joining each other.
- The flag of Olympic Games was recognised in the year 1913 and was hoisted first time in the Antwerp Olympic Games in 1920.
- The tradition to lit the Olympic flame was started in Amsterdom Olympic Games in 1928.
- The Head office of International Olympic Committee is in Lusane (Switzerland).
- Participation of women in the Olympic games started in the Second Olympic Games in 1900.
- First Indian player who participated in the Olympic games was an Anglo Indian 'Norman Prichard', who took part in the Second Olympic Games in 1900 and won two Silver medals in Athletics.
- Marrie Lila Ro is 1st Indian woman participant in the Olympic games.
- International Olympic Committee was founded in 1894 at "Chakhon".
- Generally, in the inaugural ceremony of Olympic games the team of Greece got first place and host team is placed in the last in March Past parade. The teams of other places are placed in the alphabetical order of English alphabets.
- The first woman referee in the football was a Canadian lady Sonia Denancord in (Atlanta Olympics).
- The maximum no. of gold medal winner sports woman is Larina Lavyanina. She won 18 medals including 9 gold medals.
- The maximum gold medal winner sports woman is Christina Otty. She got 6 gold medals in swimming in Seoul Olympic of 1986.
- The maximum gold medal winner male player in an Olympic is Michael Phelps of USA. He won 8 gold medals in swimming in the Beijing Olympics 2008.

London Olympics 2012

Mascot : Wenlock and Mandeville

- India ranked 55th in the medals tally with a total of 6 medals (2 Silver and 4 Bronze).
- The London Olympic Games were inaugurated by Queen Elizabeth II on July 27, 2012 in the Olympic Stadium, London.
- London is the first city in the world to stage Olympic Games thrice, after the 1908 and 1948 Summer Olympics. Entitled *Isles of Wonder*, the opening ceremony was devised by Oscar Award – winning director Daniel Boyle of *Slumdog Millionaire* fame with music directors Rick Smith and Karl Hyde of the electronic music duo *Underworld*.
- The inaugural ceremony of the London Olympic 2012 also had an Indian flavour in the form of music composers Ilayaraja and A. R. Rahman.
- The theme for the night, *Isles of Wonder* was inspired by William Shakespeare's play *'The Tempest'*.
- The 2012 Olympic programme featured 26 sports disciplines. For the first time, women's boxing is included in the programme. In tennis, mixed doubles event returns to the Olympic progamme for the first time since 1924.

- Under the slogan "Inspire a Generation", the 30th edition of the Olympic Games will also be recorded as the first in which all participating delegations have female athletes. Brunei, Qatar and Saudi Arabia have included women for the first time, and Qatar named the female shooter, Bahiya–al–Hamad, as its flag-bearer.
- Yi Siling of China took the honour of claiming the first Gold Medal of the London Olympics when she won the women's 10 metre Air Rifle event on July 28, 2012.
- Wrestler Sushil Kumar led the Indian contingent holding the Indian tricolour in the opening ceremony, while female boxer M. C. Mary Kom was the flag bearer in the closing ceremony.
- The Indian Olympic Association (IOA) had sent a total of 83 athletes to compete in 13 sports, making it the largest contingent India has ever sent to the Olympic Games.
- In London Olympics India bagged a total of 6 medals with 1 Silver of Vijay Kumar in Shooting (Men's 25m Rapid Fire Pistol) and the second Silver medal of Sushil Kumar in Wrestling (Men's 66kg Freestyle), alongwith one Bronze each of Gagan Narang in Shooting (Men's 10m Air Rifle), Yogeshwar Dutt in Wrestling (Men's 60kg Freestyle), Saina Nehwal in Badminton (Women's Singles) and M. C. Mary Kom in Boxing (Women's Fly, 51 kg).
- Sushil Kumar's historic feat of winning back-to-back Olympic medals on the very last day of London Olympics 2012 turned out to be the high point of country's compaign. His Silver was India's fourth Wrestling medal in the Olympics and second in London after Yogeshwar Dutt, who won a Bronze in the 60 kg Freestyle event.
- KD (Khashaba Dadasaheb) Jadhav had won the country's first medal in Wrestling in 1952 Olympics at Helsinki.
- American swimmer Michael Phelps, the greatest Olympian of all time with his record 22 Olympic Medals, out of which 6 are from London Olympics, retired from the game after winning his fourth consecutive Gold on August 4, 2012. He also holds the all time records for Gold Medals (18, double that of the next highest record holders), Gold Medals in individual events (11), and Olympic medals in individual events for a male (13).
- Jamaica was dominant on the track again in London; highlighted by the men's 4 × 100m relay record. This record-breaking race marked the third time since 2008 that the Jamaican team had broken the record. Bolt also became an Olympic legend by repeating as champion in both the 100 metre and 200-metre sprints.

Medals Tally (Top Ten Nations and India) **of London Olympics, 2012**

S.No.	Coutnry	Gold	Silver	Bronze	Total
1.	USA	46	29	29	104
2.	China	38	27	23	88
3.	Britain	29	17	19	65
4.	Russia	24	26	32	82
5.	S. Korea	13	08	07	28

S.No.	Coutnry	Gold	Silver	Bronze	Total
6.	Germany	11	19	14	44
7.	France	11	11	12	34
8.	Italy	08	09	11	28
9.	Hungary	08	04	05	17
10.	Australia	07	16	12	35
55.	India	00	02	04	06

Some important results of Team events in London Olympics

Sport	Male		Female	
	Winner	Runner	Winner	Runner
Hockey	Germany	Netherlands	Netherlands	Argentina
Football	Mexico	Brazil	U.S.A.	Japan
Volleyball	Russia	Brazil	Brazil	U.S.A.
Basketball	U.S.A.	Spain	U.S.A.	France
Water Polo	Croatia	Italy	U.S.A.	Spain

First Olympics

- Year – 1896
- Date – April 4 to 15
- Place – Athens (Greece)
- Participating Countries – 13
- Players – 311 (all males)
- Game Competitions – 42
- India's position – *Not participated*

Second Olympics

- Year – 1900
- Date – May 20 to October 28
- Place – Paris (France)
- Participating Countries – 22
- Players – 1330 (11 females)
- Competitions – 60
- India's position – 2 Silver medals (Won by Norman Prichard – Athletics)

Third Olympics

- Year – 1904
- Date – July 1 to November 23
- Place – St. Louis (America)
- Participating Countries – 12
- Players – 625 (8 females)
- Competitions – 67
- India's position – *Not participated*

Fourth Olympics

- Year – 1908
- Date – April 27 to October 31
- Place – London (Britain)
- Participating Countries – 22
- Players – 2035 (36 females)
- Competitions – 104
- India's position – *Not participated*

Fifth Olympics

- Year – 1912
- Date – May 5 to July 22
- Place – Stockholm (Sweden)
- Participating Countries – 28
- Players – 2547 (57 females)
- Competitions – 106
- India's position – *Not participated*

Sixth Olympics

- Year – 1916
- Date – Cancelled due to World War I
- Place – Berlin (Germany)

Seventh Olympics

- Year – 1920
- Date – April 20 to Sept. 12
- Place – Antwerp (Belgium)

- Participating Countries – 29
- Players – 2607 (64 females)
- Competitions – 104
- India's position – Did not win any medal

Eighth Olympics

- Year – 1924
- Date – May 4 to July 27
- Place – Paris (France)
- Participating Countries – 44
- Players – 3092 (136 females)
- Competitions - 126
- India's position – Did not win any medal

Ninth Olympics

- Year – 1928
- Date – May 17 to August 12
- Place – Amsterdam (Holland)
- Participating Countries – 46
- Players – 3014 (290 females)
- Competitions – 109
- India's position – 1 Gold medal (in hockey)

Tenth Olympics

- Year – 1932
- Date – July 30 to August 14
- Place – Los Angels (USA)
- Participating Countries – 37
- Players – 1408 (127 females)
- Competitions – 117
- India's position – 1 Gold medal (in hockey)

Eleventh Olympics

- Year – 1936
- Date – August 1 to 16
- Place – Berlin (Germany)
- Participating Countries – 49
- Players – 4066 (328 females)
- Competitions – 129
- India's position – 1 Gold medal (in hockey)

Twelfth Olympics

- Year – 1940
- Date – Cancelled due to World War II
- Place – Tokyo, later on Helsinki

Thirteenth Olympics

- Year – 1944
- Date – Cancelled due to World War II
- Place – London (Britain)

Fourteenth Olympics

- Year – 1948
- Date – July 29 to August 14
- Place – London (Britain)
- Participating Countries – 59
- Players – 4099 (385 females)
- Competitions – 136
- India's position – 1 Gold medal (in hockey)

Fifteenth Olympics

- Year – 1952
- Date – July 19 to August 3
- Place – Helsinki (Finland)
- Participating Countries – 69
- Players – 4925 (518 females)
- Competitions – 149
- India's position – 1 Gold medal (in hockey) and 1 Bronze medal (in wrestling)

Sixteenth Olympics

- Year – 1956
- Date – Nov. 22 to Dec. 8
- Place – Melbourne (Australia)
- Participating Countries – 71
- Players – 3342 (384 females)
- Competitions – 145
- India's position – 1 Gold medal (in hockey)

Seventeenth Olympics

- Year – 1960
- Date–August 25 to September 11
- Place – Rome (Italy)
- Participating Countries – 83
- Players – 5348 (61 females)
- Competitions – 150
- India's position - 1 Silver medal (in hockey)

Eighteenth Olympics

- Year – 1964
- Date – October 10 to 24

- Place – Tokyo (Japan)
- Participating Countries – 93
- Players – 5140 (683 females)
- Competitions – 163
- India's position – 1 Gold medal (hockey)

Nineteenth Olympics

- Year – 1968
- Date – October 12 to 27
- Place – Mexico City (Mexico)
- Participating Countries – 112
- Players – 5531 (781 females)
- Competitions – 182
- India's position – 1 Bronze medal (in hockey)

Twentieth Olympics

- Year – 1972
- Date – August 26 to Sept. 10
- Place – Munich (W. Germany)
- Participating Countries – 122
- Players – 7147 (1070 females)
- Competitions – 195
- India's position – 1 Bronze medal (in hockey)

Twenty First Olympics

- Year – 1976
- Date – July 17 to August 1
- Place – Montreal (Canada)
- Participating Countries – 92
- Players – 6152 (1261 females)
- Competitions – 198
- India's position - Did not win any medal, were at position 7th in hockey

Twenty Second Olympics

- Year – 1980
- Date – July 19 to August 3
- Place – Moscow (Soviet Union)
- Participating Countries – 81
- Players – 5326 (1088 females)
- Competitions – 203
- India's position – 1 Gold medal (in hockey)

Twenty Third Olympics

- Year – 1984
- Date – July 28 to August 12
- Place – Los Angeles (U.S.A.)
- Participating Countries – 140
- Players – 7078 (1620 females)
- Competitions – 221
- India's position – Did not win any medal, 5th position in hockey

Twenty Fourth Olympics

- Year – 1988
- Date – September 17 to October 2
- Place – Seoul (S. Korea)
- Participating Countries – 159
- Players – 8,465
- Competitions - 237
- India's position – Did not win any medal, ranked sixth in hockey

Twenty Fifth Olympics

- Year – 1992
- Date – July 25 to August 9
- Place – Barcelona (Spain)
- Participating Countries – 169
- Players – 9,367
- Competitions - 257
- India's position – Did not win any medal

Twenty Sixth Olympics

- Year – 1996
- Date – July 19 to August 4
- Place – Atlanta (U.S.A.)
- Participating Countries – 197
- Players – 10,310
- Competitions – 271
- India's position – Leander Paes won a Bronze medal (in Lawn Tennis).

Twenty Seventh Olympics

- Year – 2000
- Date – Sept. 15 to Oct. 1
- Place – Sydney (Australia)
- Participating Countries – 200
- Number of players – 10,321
- Competitions – 300
- India's position – Karnam Malleshwari won a Bronze medal in the Weight lifting (in the 69 kg category).

Twenty Eighth Olympics

- Year – 2004
- Date – August 13 to August 29
- Place – Athens (Egypt)
- Participating Countries – 201
- Number of players – 10,500
- Competitions – 301
- India's position – Major Rajyavardhan Singh Rathore won a Silver medal (Shooting)

Twenty Ninth Olympics

- Year – 2008
- Place – Beijing (China)
- Participating Countries – 204
- Players – 10,708
- Competitions – 302
- India's position - 50th (with 1 Gold and 2 Bronze medals)

Thirtyth Olympics

- Year – 2012 (July. 27 – Aug. 12)
- Place – London
- Participating Countries – 204
- Players – 10,500
- Competitions (events) – 302
- India's position - 55th (with 2 Silver and 4 Bronze medals)

Thirty-first Olympics

- Year - 2016 (Aug. 05 – Sep. 21)
- Place (Proposed)- Rio de Janerio (Brazil)

Thinty-second Olympics

- Year—2020
- Place (Proposed)—Tokyo (Japan)

Paralympics and Winter Olympics

- London Paralympics 2012 (Aug. 29-Sept. 09, 2012) : London, the host city welcomed the 14th Paralympic Games with a spectacular Opening Ceremony, held in the Olympic Stadium. A total of 4294 athletes from 164 countries participated in the Games. China won the most medals – 231 (95 Gold, 71 Silver, 65 Bronze) followed by Russian Federation - 102 (36 G, 38S, 28 B) and Great Britain- 120 (34 G, 43 S, 43 B).
- In London Paralympics 2012 : Girisha H. Nagarajegowda (Karnataka) clinched the only medal after bagging the Silver in the Men's High Jump F42 event.
- Girisha is the third Indian after Javelin thrower Bhimrao Kesarkar and Shot put thrower Joginder Singh Bedi to claim Silver at the Paralympic Games. Kesarkar and Bedi won Silver at the 1984 Paralympics.
- First Ever Gold for India : India's Devendra created history by winning the first ever gold for the country in Athens Paralympics 2004. He claimed gold in Javelin throw.
- The first Games for disabled athletes were held in 1948 in Stoke Mandeville, England. On the day of the Opening Ceremony of the 1948 Olympic Games in London, the Stoke Mandeville Games were also launched and the first competition for wheelchair-bound athletes was organized.
- Olympic style Games for athletes with disability were organized for the first time in Rome in 1960, immediately after the Olympic Games. They are considered the first Paralympic Games.
- Since then, Paralympic Games have been organized after every four years. The Paralympic Games have always been held in the same year as the Olympic Games.
- Other disability groups were added in Toronto (Canada) in 1976 and the idea of merging together different disability groups for international sports competitions, was conceived. In the same year, the first Paralympic Winter Games took place in Sweden.

The next Paralympic Games will be held in 2016 in Rio de Janerio.

Winter Olympic Games : The Winter Olympic Games started in 1924 AD when the first Games were held at Chamonix, France followed by St. Moritz, Switzerland (1928 & 1948); Lake Placid, New York (1932 & 1980); Garmisch-Parthenkirchen, Germany (1936); Oslo, Norway (1952); Cortina d'Ampezzo, Italy (1956); Squaw Valley, California (1960); Innsbruck, Austria (1964 & 1976); Grenoble, France (1968); Sapporo, Japan (1972); Sarajevo, Yugoslavia (1984); Calgary, Canada (1988) and Albertville, France (1992). The XVII Winter Olympic Games were held in Lilleharnmer (Norway) in February 1994. Incidentally, the 1994 Games were the first in accordance with the International Olympic Committee's new cycle of having Winter Games and Summer Games two years apart, instead of in the same year, as had been the tradition since the commencement of these Games in 1924.

The XIX Winter Games were held in Salt Lake City (USA) from February 9 to 24, 2002. Germany topped in the Medals Tally winning 35 medals (including 12 Golds) while Norway finished as runner-up bagging 24 medals (11 Golds).

The XX Winter Olympics 2006 were held in Turin (Italy) from February 10-26, 2006. Germany once again topped the medals tally, after the 2002 Salt Lake Winter Olympics. The four-member Indian team was led by luge athlete Shiva Keshavan.

XXI Winter Olympics 2010 (February 12-28, 2010) : The 21st Winter Olympic was held in Vancouver, Canada from February 12 to 28, 2010. Total 2700 players of 82 countries participated in this 17 days sports festival.

XXII Winter Olympics 2014 (February 7-23, 2014) : 22nd Winter Olympic Games at Sochi (Russia), the 17 day costliest Olympics ever ($51 billion) of sport-driven global unity concluded on February 23, 2014.

Sochi Winter Olympics 2014 saw three athletes from India, luger Shiva Keshavan (fifth consecutive participation in the Winter Olympics), Alpine skier Himanshu Thakur and cross-country skier Nadeem Iqbal represent the country, but their performance was dismal.

Medals Tally of Top Five Countries in the 22nd Winter Olympics 2014

Country	Gold	Silver	Bronze	Total
Russia	13	11	09	33
Norway	11	05	10	26
Canada	10	10	05	25
USA	09	07	12	28
Netherlands	08	07	09	24

Sites of Winter Olympic Games

Year	Place	Year	Place
1924	Chamonix, France	1928	St. Moritz, Switzerland
1932	Lake Placid, New York	1936	Garmisch-Partenkirchen, Germany
1948	St. Moritz, Switzerland	1952	Oslo, Norway
1956	Cortina d'Ampezzo, Italy	1960	Squaw Valley, California
1964	Innsbruck, Austria	1968	Grenoble, France
1972	Sapporo, Japan	1976	Innsbruck, Austria
1980	Lake Placid, New York	1984	Sarajevo, Yugoslavia
1988	Calgary, Alberta	1992	Albertville, France
1994	Lillehammer, Norway	1998	Nagano, Japan
2002	Salt Lake City, USA	2006	Turin, Italy
2010	Vancouver, Canada	2014	Sochi, Russia
2018	Pyeong Chang, S. Korea (Scheduled)		

Commonwealth Games

After Olympics, Commonwealth Games is the second largest sports festival in the world. The Games are held once in four years but only in between the Olympic years. The Games were originally known as the British Empire Games.

- ➢ The 1st Commonwealth Games were held in 1930 at Hamilton, Canada.
- ➢ The 10th Commonwealth Games were held at Christchurch, New Zealand in 1974 and the 15th in Victoria (Canada) in 1994, where about 3,350 athletes from 64 nations (including South Africa, which joined the family of Commonwealth athletes after 36 years) participated.
- ➢ Namibia also, which gained its independence in 1990, made its debut while Hong Kong made its final appearance in the Games before being ceded to China in 1997.
- ➢ XVI Commonwealth Games were held in 1998 in Kuala Lumpur (Malaysia) while XVII Commonwealth Games were hosted by UK with Manchester as their venue.
- ➢ India, for the first time, participated in the second Commonwealth games held in London in 1934.

Commonwealth Games since 1930

Year	Places	Countries	Events	First	India's Medals
1930	Hamilton (Canada)	11	6	England	N. P.
1934	London (England)	16	6	England	B–1
1938	Sydney (Australia)	15	7	Australia	No medal
1950	Auckland (New Zealand)	12	7	Australia	N. P.
1954	Vancouver (Canada)	24	9	England	No medal
1958	Cardiff (Britain)	35	9	England	G–2, S–1
1962	Perth (Australia)	35	9	Australia	N. P.
1966	Kingston (Jamaica)	34	9	England	G–3, S–4, B–5
1970	Edinburgh (U.K.)	42	9	Australia	G–5, S–3
1974	Christchurch (N. Zealand)	38	9	Australia	G–4, S–8, B–3
1978	Edmonton (Canada)	48	10	Canada	G–5, S–4, B–6
1982	Brisbane (Australia)	47	10	Australia	G–5, S–5, B–3
1986	Edinburgh (U.K.)	26	10	England	N. P.
1990	Auckland (New Zealand)	55	10	Australia	G–13, S–8, B–7
1994	Victoria (Canada)	64	—	Australia	G–6, S–11, B–10
1998	Kuala Lumpur (Malaysia)	70	16	Australia	G–7, S–10, B–8
2002	Manchester (England)	72	17	Australia	G–32, S–21, B–19 (3rd)
2006	Melbourne (Australia)	71	—	Australia	G–22, S–17, B–11 (4th)
2010	Delhi (India)	71	—	Australia	G–74, S–55 B–48 (2nd)
2014	Glassgow (Scottland)		Scheduled		
2018	Gold Coast City (Australia)		Scheduled		

XIX Commonwealth Games (October 3-14, 2010)

- The XIX Commonwealth Games were held in Delhi (India) from October 3-14, 2010. Around 6,081 athletes from 71 nations participated in this 12-day sports extravaganza.
- Australia topped the medals tally with 177 (74 Gold, 55 Silver and 48 Bronze) medals, while the hosts India finished second with 101 (38 Gold, 27 Silver and 36 Bronze) medals. England was placed third with 142 medals (37 Gold, 60 Silver and 45 Bronze).
- The first Gold medal of the Games was won by India's N. Kunjarani Devi in the 48 kg category weightlifting contest. India put up a spectacular performance in shooting, table tennis, boxing and weightlifting.
- A 19-year old gymnast from Canada, Alexandra Orlando, won the maximum number of Gold medals (six) in the Games.

MEDALS TALLY (Top Ten Countries)

Country	Gold	Silver	Bronze	Total
Australia	74	55	48	177
India	38	27	36	101
England	37	60	45	142
Canada	26	17	33	76
South Africa	12	11	10	33
Kenya	12	11	09	32
Malaysia	12	10	13	35
Singapore	11	11	09	31
Nigeria	11	08	14	33
Scotland	09	10	07	26

Best Athlete : *Jamaican athlete Trecia Smith was honoured with the David Dixon Award after being adjudged the 'Best Athlete of the 19th Commonwealth Games'.*

- **'Shera'** was the **mascot** of the 2010 Commonwealth Games.
- Moto of 2010 Commonwealth Games : 'Come out and play'.
- No. of Commonwealth countries : 53
- No. of exhisting teams : 71
- Inauguration : 3rd October 2010
- Closing : 14th October 2010
- Events : 272 events in 21 disciplnes
- Officially opened by : Prince Charles (Britain) and the President of India Ms. Pratibha Devi Singh Patil.
- Athlete's Oath : Abhinav Bindra
- Queen's Baton last runner : Sushil Kumar

ASIAN Games

- The first Asian Games began on March 4, 1951 in New Delhi.
- The Asian Games Association has choosen shining sun as its symbol.
- The AGF (Asian Games Federation) adopted *'Ever Onward'*, given by Pt. Jawaharlal Nehru, as the *motto* of the Asian Games.
- The emblem of Asian Games is a 'bright full rising sun' with interlocking rings.
- The Maharaja of Patiala presented the Torch and the Flag for the first Asian Games and since then they have been carried from country to country.

ASIAN Games since 1951

Game Serial	Year	Places	Number of countries	Number of sports	Number of players
1st	1951	New Delhi (India)	11	6	491
2nd	1954	Manila (Philippines)	18	8	1021
3rd	1958	Tokyo (Japan)	20	13	1422
4th	1962	Jakarta (Indonesia)	16	13	1545
5th	1966	Bangkok (Thailand)	18	14	1945
6th	1970	Bangkok (Thailand)	18	13	1752
7th	1974	Tehran (Iran)	25	16	2869
8th	1978	Bangkok (Thailand)	25	19	3000
9th	1982	New Delhi (India)	33	21	3447
10th	1986	Seoul (S. Korea)	27	25	3883
11th	1990	Beijing (China)	37	27	4500
12th	1994	Hiroshima (Japan)	42	34	7300
13th	1998	Bangkok (Thailand)	41	38	7000
14th	2002	Busan (S. Korea)	44	38	9919
15th	2006	Doha (Qatar)	45	39	10000+
16th	2010	Guangzou (China)	45	42	9704

- 16th (2010) Asian Games were held in Guangzhou, China.
- In the 16th Asian Games Twenty-20 Cricket was one of the debut sport.
- Dance sport, Dragon boat, Roller sport and Weiqui (a form of chess) were other new entrants into the 16th Asian Games.
- 17th Asian Games will be held in Incheon, South Korea in 2014.

Position of India in Asian Games Medal Tally

Year	Gold	Silver	Bronze	Total	Position
1951	15	18	21	54	2nd
1954	5	4	9	18	5th
1958	5	4	4	13	7th
1962	10	13	11	34	3rd
1966	7	5	11	23	5th
1970	6	9	10	25	5th
1974	4	12	12	28	7th
1978	11	11	6	28	5th
1982	13	19	25	57	5th
1986	5	9	23	37	5th
1990	1	8	14	23	11th
1994	4	3	15	22	8th
1998	7	11	17	35	9th
2002	11	12	13	36	8th
2006	10	18	26	54	8th
2010	14	17	33	64	6th

XVI Asian Games (12–27 Nov. 2010)

- 16th Asian Games (2010) get off with a grand begining at Haixinsha Island, Guangzhou on 12th November 2010.
- India bagged the first gold medal at Guangzhou, when Pankaj Advani won Gold in the men's English Billiards.
- China, South Korea and Japan came first, second and third respectively in the 16th Asian Games.
- XVI Asiad came to a close on Nov. 27, 2010 with China (199 Gold, 119 Silver and 98 Bronze) topping the overall medals tally.

16th ASIAN GAMES : (Final Medals Tally of Top 10 Countries)

Country	Gold	Silver	Bronze	Total
China	199	119	98	416
S. Korea	76	65	91	232
Japan	48	74	94	216
Iran	20	14	25	59
Kazakhastan	18	23	38	79
India	14	17	33	64
Chinese Taipei	13	16	38	67
Uzbekistan	11	22	23	56
Thailand	11	09	32	52
Malaysia	09	18	14	41

- India won 14 gold, 17 silver and 33 bronze medals and managed to occupy the 6th position.

XVI ASIAN GAMES (12 – 27 November, 2010)

★ Motto : Thrilling Games, Harmonious Asia. ★ Mascots : Le Yangyang (5 rams) ★ Openning Ceremony : 12th Nov., 2010 ★ Closing Ceremony : 27th Nov., 2010 ★ Official opened by : Wen Jiabao, the Chinese Premier ★ Main Stadium : Haixinsha Island ★ Host City : Guangzhou, China ★ Participating Nations : 45 ★ Events : 476 in 42 sports ★ Athletes participating : 9704 ★ Athletes Oath : Fu Haifeng ★ Jndge's Oath : Yan Ninan ★ Torch Lighter: He Chong (Diver and the last Torch bearer) ★ Most Valuable Player : Lin Dan (the Chinese shuttler)

- The 16th Asian Games kicked off in style at Guangzhou, China with an eye-catching water themed opening ceremony involving 'set sail', a boat parade on the Zhujiang (Pearl) river on 12th Nov. 2010.
- This was the first occasion that an Asian Games inaugural gala was held outside a stadium.
- The Chinese Premier, Wen Jiabao, declared the Games open.
- Badminton star Fu Haifeng took the Oath of honour on behalf of the athletes while gymnastics referee Yan Ninan took the oath on behalf of the refrees.
- Gagan Narang, world record holder in shooting, carried the flag for India in the opening ceremony at Guangzhou.

- Participants from 45 countries participated in 476 events in the following 42 sports :
  1. Aquatics (Diving, Swimming, Sync. Swimming, Water Polo), 2. Archery, 3. Athletics, 4. Badminton, 5. Baseball, 6. Basketball, 7. Billiards, 8. Bowling, 9. Boxing, 10. Canoe/Kayak, 11. Chess, 12. Cricket, 13. Cycling (Track, Road, Mountain Bike, BMX), 14. Dance sport, 15. Dragon Boat, 16. Equestrian, 17. Fencing, 18. Football 19. Golf, 20. Gymnastics (Artistics Rhythmic, Trampoline), 21. Handball, 22. Hockey, 23. Judo, 24. Kabaddi, 25. Karate, 26. Modern Pantathlon, 27. Roller sport 28. Rowing, 29. Rugby, 30. Sailing, 31. Sepaktakraw, 32. Shooting, 33. Softball, 34. Squash, 35. Tackwando, 36. Table Tennis, 37. Tennis (Tennis soft Tennis), 38. Triathlon, 39. Volleyball (Beach, Volleyball), 40. Weightlifting 41.Wrestling, 42. Wushu.
- Pankaj Advani was one of the rare players to defend his Gold medal won in Billiards in the Doha Asiad 2006. He was also the one who opened the Gold count for India.
- Vijender Singh (Boxing), the World and Olympic medalist, helped India finish on a high by beating the two time World Champion Abbos Atoev of Uzbekistan.
- Vikas Krishnan also won a Gold medal in Boxing.
- The 13 boxers returned with nine medals, though the five-time World Champion Mary Kom had to settle for Bronze.
- However, a collection of one Gold, three Silver and four Bronze medals was to some extent a reflection of the strength of Indian shooting.
- The rowers won one Gold, three Silver and a Bronze.
- In Kabaddi, India won both the Golds for Men's and Women's events.
- Virdhawal Khade won the first swimming medal since 1986.
- Golf and Saling provided precious Silver medals, while other sports, viz. Badminton, Basketball, Table Tennis, Volleyball and Weightlifting drew a blank.
- Indian Hockey team won just the Bronze medal.
- Squash was as good as Wrestling with three Bronze medals.
- The events where India won Gold medals are — Men's Tennis Singles (Somdev Devvarman) and Men's Tennis Doubles (Somdev Varman and Sanam Kr. Singh); Billiards (Pankaj Advani); Women's 400 m Hurdles (Ashwini C. Akkunji); Women's 4 × 400 m relay (Ashwini C. Akkunji, Mandeep Kaur, Manjeet Kaur and Sini Jose); Men's 400 m Hurdles (Joseph Abraham); Men's 75 kg boxing (Vijender Singh); Men's 60 kg boxing (Vikas Krishan); Mens' Rowing (Bajrang Lal Takhar); Women's 3,000 m Steeplechase (Sudha Singh); Men's Double Trap Shooting (Ranjan Sodhi); Women's 10,000 m (Preeja Sridharan); Men's Kabaddi and Women's Kabaddi.

SAF Games

The South Asian Federation Games (SAF Games) is a sport festival of South Asian countries. The South Asian Sports Federation comprising India, Pakistan, Sri Lanka, Bangladesh, Nepal, Bhutan and Maldives was formed in New Delhi on November 26, 1982.

- The first SAF Games were held in Kathmandu in 1984 followed by Dhaka (1985), Kolkata (1987), Islamabad (1989), Colombo (1991), Dhaka (1993) and Chennai (1995).
- The Eighth SAF Games (Septemebr 25-October 4, 1999) were held in Kathmandu.
- As hitherto, India notched the top position winning 197 medals including 102 Gold. Nepal with 65 medals including 31 golds and Sri Lanka 119 medals (16 golds) finished on the second and third places, respectively.
- The 10th South Asian Federation Games (18-28 August, 2006) were held in Sri Lanka and India retained the crown, with 118 Gold, 69 Silver and 47 Bronze. Pakistan (43 – 44 – 71) and hosts Sri Lanka (37–63–78) came on the second and third positions respectively in the medals tally.

Flag and Motto of the SAF Games : The SAF Games flag includes a dove, suggesting the desire for peace in the area. The motto of the SAF Games is 'Peace, Propersity and Progress'.

New Name for SAF Games : The SAF Games have been rechristened as South Asian Games, according to a decision taken by the South Asian Sports Federation at its 32nd meeting held in Islamabad (Pakistan) on April 2, 2004.

11th South Asian Games

- India retained the crown at the 11th SA Games (January 29 - February 09, 2010) played in Dhaka, Bangladesh.
- It finished on top of the medals tally with 90 gold, 55 silver and 30 bronze medals.
- Pakistan came second and the hosts Bangladesh third.
- India dominated the events in badminton, swimming, T.T. and shooting.

Medals Tally

S. No.	Country	Gold	Silver	Bronze	Total
1.	India	90	55	30	175
2.	Pakistan	19	25	36	80
3.	Bangladesh	18	23	56	97
4.	Sri Lanka	16	35	54	105
5.	Nepal	08	09	19	36
6.	Afghanistan	07	09	16	32
7.	Bhutan	0	02	03	05
8.	Maldives	0	0	02	02

12th South Asian Games : India will be the host for the 12th South Asian Games was rescheduled to be held in 2013, but not held till now.

AFRO-ASIAN Games

- The first Afro-Asian Games (Octoebr 24 - November 1, 2003) concluded on November 1, 2003 in Hyderabad (India).
- China topped the medals tally bagging a total of 41 medals (including25Gold,11Silverand5Bronze).Indiagot80medals(19Gold,32 Silver and 29 Bronze) and Japan with 23 medals (15 Gold, 6 Silver and 2 Bronze) and occupied the second and third places, respectively.

Medals Tally (Top Five)

Country	Gold	Silver	Bronze	Total	Country	Gold	Silver	Bronze	Total
China	25	11	5	41	Nigeria	10	12	13	35
India	19	32	29	80	S. Africa	10	11	15	36
Japan	15	6	2	23					

The Second Afro-Asian Games were to be held in Algiers (Algeria) in July-August 2007, but the Games were indefinitely postponed.

Some Important Sports And Related Information

Cricket

- ➢ It is believed that Cricket was started in England in 1300 A.D.
- ➢ It started as a game of shepherds and became popular among other classes in 18th century A.D.
- ➢ After some time a club known as "Merylebone Cricket Club" (M.C.C.) was formed at Lords in London.
- ➢ Cricket became popular in Australia due to British influence there.
- ➢ The first official cricket test match was played in the year 1877 between Australia and England in Melbourne.
- ➢ When some other countries started playing Cricket Imperical Cricket Conference was formed in 1909 which gave birth to International Cricket Conference in 1956.
- ➢ The first One Day International cricket match was played in the year 1971 between England and Australia in Melbourne.
- ➢ The first World Cup of one day matches was played in 1975 in London. West Indies won the World Cup beating Australia by 17 runs.
- ➢ The apex institution of world cricket is the 'International Cricket Council' (ICC) and its headquarters is now in Dubai from August 1, 2005. Earlier it was in Lords (England).
- ➢ The President of the ICC is Mr. Percy Sonn of South Africa.
- ➢ Australia has won maximum of four World Cups till date.
- ➢ In India Cricket was introduced by British royalty. Parsee community of India was the first to take part in Cricket in 1848.
- ➢ Later on Parsee team visited England in 1886. Matches between European and Parsee teams, called Presidency matches, were started in Poona (now Pune) and Bombay (now Mumbai).
- ➢ Raja Bhupindra Singh of Patiala donated the Ranji Trophy in 1934 for the national championship of Cricket.
- ➢ The Board of Control for Cricket in India was formed in 1927.

The ICC World Test Championship

- ★ The ICC World Test Championship is intended to become the premier championship for Test cricket run by International Cricket Council (ICC).
- ★ The first ICC World Test Championship is to be held in 2017 in England.
- ★ The original plans to hold the competition in 2013 were abandoned due to financial problems.
- ★ It will replace the One-day International competition the ICC Champions Trophy, which was held in 2013 for the last time.

Measurements in cricket :

Length of the Pitch – 22 yards (20.11metres)

Length of the Crease – 1.22 – 1.83 metres (4 ft.)
Weight of the Ball – 155 to 163 gram
Circumference of the Ball – 22.4 -22.9 cm (9 Inch)
Length of the Bat – 96.5 cm (38 inch)
Width of the Bat – 10.8 cm (4.25 inch)
Length of the Stumps – 71.1 cm (28 inch)
Length of Bells – 11.1cm (each bail)

Winners of World Cup Cricket since 1975

Year	Place	Winner	Runners up
1975	England	West Indies	Australia
1979	England	West Indies	England
1983	England	India	West Indies
1987	India and Pakistan	Australia	England
1991	Australia and New Zealand	Pakistan	England
1996	India, Pakistan and Sri Lanka	Sri Lanka	Australia
1999	England	Australia	Pakistan
2003	South Africa	Australia	India
2007	West Indies	Australia	Sri Lanka
2011	India, Sri Lanka & Bangladesh	India	Sri Lanka
2015	Australia & New Zealand	Scheduled	
2019	England	Scheduled	
2023	India	Scheduled	

Cricket World Cup 2011, 2015 and 2019

- Initially India, Pakistan, Sri Lanka and Bangladesh were to host jointly the 2011 cricket World Cup, which comes to the sub continent after a gap of 15 years, but after the terrorist attack on Sri Lankan cricket team in Pakistan, Pakistan's name has been canceled from the hosts' list by the ICC.
- India was the main host of World Cup 2011.
- Inauguration ceremony was held at Sheikh Muzib Statidum, Dhaka, Bangladesh on 17th Feb., 2011, while the final match was held at Wankhede Stadium, Mumbai on April 2, 2011.
- M.S. Dhoni, the Captain of Indian Team was adjudged the 'Man of Match', while Yuvraj Singh was declared the 'Man of Tournament' in ICC Cricket World Cup 2011.
- India, Pakistan and Sri Lanka were the co-hosts for the 1996 world cup.
- Out of total 49 matches India hosted 29 matches (including the final), Sri Lanka 12 and Bangladesh 8 matches respectively.
- The matches of Cricket World Cup 2011 held in 12 cities of *three host countries* (India, Sri Lanka and Bangladesh and total 14 teams participated in two groups, i.e. Group 'A' and Group 'B'. India was in Group 'B'.

- India beat Australia in Quarter Final (QF), Pakistan in Semi Final (SF) and Sri Lanka in Final match.
- Jumbo (the elephant) : The mascot of 2011 World Cup Cricket was unveiled in Colombo on April 02, 2010.
- The 2015 World Cup has been awarded jointly to Australia and New Zealand, while England will be the host for the 2019 edition of the Cup.
- Some important Terminologies of Cricket : Played on, Appeal, Bye, Leg Bye, Power Play, Follow on, Dusara, Beamer, Hoober Shot, Lost Ball, Duck worthLuis, Retired Hurt, Chinaman, Batsman, Bowler, Wicket Keeper, Fielder, LBW (Leg Before Wicket), Catch, Hit wicket, Throw, Maiden over, Four, Sixer, Wide, Swing, Stroke, Cover, Mid on, Mid Off, Mid wicket, Over the wicket, Round the wicket, Leg spinner, Off spinner, Over throw, Over Slip, Gulley, Cover point, Silly point, Long off, Long on, Third man, Short pitch, Hook, Dead ball, Run out, Popping crease, Pitch, Bouncer (or Bumper), Full Toss, Yorker, Yorked, Googly, Wicket Maiden, Snick, Duck, Hat -Trick, Rubber, The Ashes, Scoring a Ton etc.

ICC Twenty-20 Cricket World Cup

- The first ICC Twenty-20 (T–20) World Cup Cricket held in South Africa in September 11-24, 2007. In the final match played at Wanderers stadium in Johannesburg, India thrashed Pakistan by 5 runs and clinched the first T-20 world cup trophy.
- Pakistan emerged winners of the second (2009) edition of the ICC Twenty-20 World Cup Cricket, beating Sri Lanka by 8 wickets in the final in London, England on June 21, 2009.
- In the third (2010) edition of the ICC T-20 World Cup Cricket England clinched the cup, defeating Australia by 7 wickets in the final in Bridgetown, Barbados (West Indies), on May 16, 2010.
- In the fourth ICC T-20 World Cup (2012) West Indies defeated the host Sri Lanka in the final at Colombo on Oct. 7, 2012.
- The fifth (ICC T-20 World Cup) was hosted by Bangladesh in 2014, from March 16 to April 6. Sri Lanka defeated India in the final by 6 wickets at Sher-e-Bangla Stadium in Dhaka (Bangladesh). Virat Kohli was declared 'Man of the Series'
- India will host its sixth edition in 2016.
- In all the five ICC T-20 World Cup held till now, M.S. Dhoni was the Captain of Indian team.

4th ICC Women's World Twenty-20

- Two time defending champion Australia won ICC Women's World Twenty-20 Championship 2014, defeating England by 6 wickets, in the final at Mirpur (Bangladesh) on April 06, 2014.

Football

- It is believed that Football is also of British origin. However, it is said that a game similar to Football was played in 500 B.C. by the Greeks of Sparta and they called this game 'Harpaston'. The first football club of the world 'Sheffield Football Club' was founded in the year 1857 in

England. Football was introduced in India by the Britishers in 1848 and the first football club of India was 'Dalhousie Club'. The Indian Football Association, the oldest football association in the east, was formed in 1878. The apex institution of football is 'Federation of International de Football Association' (FIFA), which was formed by seven countries on May 21, 1904. The headquarters of FIFA is in Paris (France). In order to distinguish this game from the carrying cum kicking game i.e. Rugby, it was given the name of "Soccer". This name was given to this game (Football) by an association named London Football Association which was formed in 1863 in England. The Football World Cup, organized by the FIFA, is the biggest competition.

- Football was included as a competitive game in Olympic Games officially in 1908.
- India took part in the World Olympic Football Competition in 1948 in London.
- Besides Olympic competitions, World Cup Football Championships were planned by two Frenchmen i.e. M Jules Rimet and Henry Delaunay.
- Jules Rimet was president of the French Football Federation and remained president of FIFA from 1924 to 1954.
- The first World Cup was organised at Monte Video (Uruguay) in 1930.
- The Trophy for this championship was named as "Jules Rimet Cup". This trophy became the permanent property of Brazil, as this country had won the world title for the third time (1958, 1962 and 1970).
- From 1974 (Xth championship of Germany) onwards, the trophy was named as "The FIFA World Cup". This was a new trophy cast in 18 ct. gold.
- In India Indian Football Association (IFA) organises National Football Championship.
- The trophy awarded in their competition is called Santosh Trophy, which was donated in the memory of Manmath Nath Roy Chaudhary of Santosh (now a part of Bangladesh).
- Durand Cup tournament, the oldest football tournament of India and the second oldest tournament of the world was started in 1888.
- Durand Cup tournament was first organised at Shimla and is being held in Delhi since 1940.
- A new chapter was added to the annals of the country's (India's) soccer with the launch of the Football Players' Association (FPA) of India in Kolkata on August 13, 2006.
- FIFA announced (in April 17, 2007) an assistance of $ 1 million to Indian football by launching 'Win in India with India' project that will initially run for a period of four year.
- FIFA President Joseph S. Blatter (during his visit to India in April, 2007) hinted that India could gain another grant of $ 400,000 for the third 'FIFA Goal Project' it was entitled to.

➢ The All India Football Federation (AIFF) has started the 'Goal Project' in Manipur and the second was launched in Delhi.

➢ FIFA and the Asian Football Confederation (AFC) have identified Sikkim as the third site of the project.

➢ According to Mr. Blatter the new project that the FIFA has specially launched for India will get annual grant of $ 250,000 for four years.

➢ FIFA World Cup is played after every four years.

Winners of World Cup Football

Year	Place	Mascot	Winner	Runners up
1930	Uruguay	—	Uruguay	Argentina
1934	Italy	—	Italy	Czechoslovakia
1938	France	—	Italy	Hungary
1942	Cancelled	—	—	—
1946	(2nd World War)			
1950	Brazil	—	Uruguay	Brazil
1954	Switzerland	—	West Germany	Hungary
1958	Sweden	—	Brazil	Sweden
1962	Chile	—	Brazil	Czechoslovakia
1966	England	Willie	England	West Germany
1970	Mexico	Juanito	Brazil	Italy
1974	West Germany	Tip and Tap	West Germany	Holland
1978	Argentina	Gauchito	Argentina	Holland
1982	Spain	Naranjito	Italy	West Germany
1986	Mexico	Pique	Argentina	West Germany
1990	Italy	Ciao	West Germany	Argentina
1994	U. S. A.	Striker	Brazil	Italy
1998	France	Footix	France	Brazil
2002	Japan and S. Korea	Ato, Kaz & Nik	Brazil	Germany
2006	Germany	Goleo	Italy	France
2010	South Africa	Zakumi	Spain	Netherlands (Holland)
2014	Brazil	—	Germany	Argentina
2018	Russia	—	(Scheduled)	—

➢ The measurements of the playground :

Length of the ground (Field)– 91 to 120 metres

Width of the ground (Field) – 45 to 91 metres

Weight of the ball – 396 to 453 grams

Circumference of the ball – 68 to 71 cm

➢ Some important Terminologies of Football : Abbey, Dribble, Extra time, Full back, Half back, Striker, Centre, Forward, Penalty kick, Free kick, Scissor Kick, Goal Kick, Direct Kick, Corner Kick, Referee, Tie breaker, Hat trick, Hand ball, Sweeper, Back, Throw in, Hand-ball (fault), Touch line, Place Kick or Kick off, Direct Free Kick, Indirect Free Kick, Tackle, Off side, Sliding Tackle, Drop Ball, Sudden death, Penalty shoot out etc.

20th Offical Logo FIFA World Cup Football–2014

Juntos num so ritmo (all in one rhythm)

➢ Mascot—Fuleco

➢ Started—June 12, 2014 in Sao Paulo (Brazil)

➢ Final Match held—July 13, 2014 in Maracana, Rio de Janerio (Brazil)

➢ Winner—Germany

➢ Runners up—Argentina

➢ Third Position—Netherlands

➢ Total—64 matches

➢ Golden Ball Award Winner (for best player)—Lionel Messi (Argentina)

➢ Golden Boot Award Winner (for top scorer)—James Rodriguez (Columbia)

➢ Golden Glove Award Winner (for best goalkeeper)—Manuel Neuer (Germany)

Hockey

➢ 'Blackheath Rugby and Hockey Club' is the first hockey club in the world which was set up in the year 1861 in England.

➢ London was the first city in England to popularize this game in the 1870s.

➢ In the year 1886, Hockey Association of England was formed in London.

➢ The apex institution of hockey is *'Federation Internationale de Hockey'*, established on January 7, 1924, with headquarters at Vienna (Austria) and later shifted to Paris (France). The first International Hockey Match was played between Wales and Ireland in Rayle on June 26, 1895.

➢ Hockey was introduced in the Olympic games for the first time in 1908 in London.

➢ Indian Hockey Federation (IHF) was formed on the 7th November, 1925 at Gwalior.

➢ Since 1944, National Hockey Championship is organised by the I.H.F. every year.

➢ All India Women's Hockey Federation was formed in 1947.

➢ India took that part in Olympics for the first time in 1928 (in Amsterdam Olympics).

➢ In Olympics, India has won the hockey title a maximum of 8 times. The first World Cup Hockey was played in Barcelona in 1971.

World Cup Hockey

Year	Place	Winner	Runners up	India's position
1971	Barcelona	Pakistan	Spain	Third
1972	Amsterdam	Holland	India	Second
1975	Kuala Lumpur	India	Pakistan	First
1978	Buenos Aires	Pakistan	Holland	Sixth
1982	Mumbai	Pakistan	West Germany	Fifth
1986	London	Australia	England	Twelfth
1990	Lahore	Holland	Pakistan	Tenth
1994	Sydney	Pakistan	Holland	Fifth
1998	Utrecht	Holland	Spain	Ninth
2002	Kuala Lumpur	Germany	Australia	Tenth
2006	Monchengladbach (Germany)	Germany	Australia	Eleventh
2010	New Delhi	Australia	Germany	Eighth
2014	The Hegue	Australia	Netherlands	Ninth

➢ The next World Cup Hockey (Mens) is proposed to be held in 2018 in Bhubneshwar (India).

➢ Measurements (Hockey) :

No. of Players – 11 players in each team

Length of the Playing field – 91.44 metres

Width of the Playing field – 50 to 55 metres

Weight of the Ball – 155 to 163 grams

Circumference of the Ball – 223 - 224 cm.

Colour of the Ball – White

Weight of the Hockey (Stick) – 280 grams (max)

➢ Terminology – Advantage, Back -stick, Bully, Carry, Dribble, Dodge, Goal line, Green Card, Flick, Free hit, Face of stick, Jab Stroke, Lung Stroke, Melee, Off side, Penalty shoot out, Short Corner, Striking circle or Shooting circle, Square pass, Tackling, Through pass, Under cutting, Stick, Penalty stroke, Scoop, Side line, Tie breaker, Penalty, Under cutting, Volley, Centre forward, Roll in, Push in, Shooting, Half volley, Full back etc.

Volleyball

➢ Volleyball, the game played with an inflated bladder and a high net was invented in 1895 at Holyoke Y.M.C.A. Gymnasium in United States of America by a Physical Director William J. Morgan.

➢ Its first name was 'MINTONNETTE' which was later named as Volleyball by Dr. A.T. Halsted of Springfield College because the ball had to be volleyed with hands from one side to the other.

➢ 'International Volleyball Association' was formed in 1947 with its headquarters in Paris (France).

➢ The first World Volleyball Championship was held in 1949 at Prague.

➢ The first Asian Volleyball Championship was held at Tokyo (Japan) in 1955 (India beats Japan in the final).

➢ The Volleyball Federation of India was formed in 1950.

➢ Measurements (Volleyball) – Length of the court - 18 metre, Width of the court – 9 metre, Weight of the ball – 250 to 260 grams, Circumference of the ball – 65-67 cm, Net – 1m (± 3 cm) wide and 9.5 m long, Net's height – 2.43m

(for men) and 2.24 m (for women)

Ball's internal pressure – 0.40 - 0.45 Kg/cm.

➢ Terminology (Volleyball) – Antennae, Attack hit, Back zone players, Dribbling, Libero, Front zone players, Blocking, Smash, Rotation, Boosting, Net fault, Volley pass, Forearm pass, Service, Hook serve, Set up, Referee etc.

Table Tennis

➢ This game was started in England in 1880s. 'International Table Tennis Association' was established in 1926.

➢ The first match of The Table Tennis World Championship was played in 1927.

➢ Table Tennis was introduced in the Olympic games much later in 1988 at Seoul (S. Korea).

➢ Table Tennis Association of India was formed in 1938.

➢ Measurements (Table Tennis) : Length of the table – 2.74 metre (9 feet), Width of the table – 1.52 metre (5 feet), Height of the table – 76 cm, Weight of the ball – 2.4 to 2.53 gram, Diametre of the ball – 37.2 -38.2 mm, Colour of the ball – white or yellow.

➢ Terminologies (Table Tennis) : Foil , End line, Late control, Flat hit, Block stroke, Service, Penholder grip, Back spin, Centre line, Half court, Side spin, Swing stroke, Push stroke, Rally, Let, Reverse, Top spin, Drop shot, Lob, Chopped return,Counter hitting etc.

Basketball

➢ The game Basketball was invented by Dr. James Naismith of U.S.A. in 1891 at Springfield College.

➢ International Basketball Federation was set up in 1932.

➢ Basketball Federation of India was formed in 1950. Its first World Championship was played in 1950.

➢ Measurements (Basketball) : Length of the court – 28 metre, Width of the court – 15 metre, Height of the basket from ground – 3.05 metre, Weight of the ball – 600 to 650 grams.

➢ Terminology (Basketball)– Dribbling, Front court, Second dribble, Two count stop, Travelling or shifting, Pivoting, Held ball, Jump ball, Violation, Foul, Feinting or Dodging, Shooting, Set shot, Ring, Guard point, Dead ball, Basket Rudnick, Hook pass, Goal, Centre line, Free throw line, Onsted, Fast break, Lay-up shot, Man to man defence, Pack, Three point, Turn over, Assist, Throw, Goal Tending, Steal, Tap etc.

Badminton

➢ Modern Badminton was probably developed in the 17th century and named from the place 'Badminton' in Gloucestershire (England).

➢ The International Badminton Federation (IBF) was established in 1934.

➢ Badminton Association of India was formed in 1934.

➢ The trophy for the international matches was named Thomas Cup after the name of the first president of the IBF Sir George Thomas. Thomas Cup competition (for men) started in 1948 - 49. Uber Cup Championship (for women) started in 1956.

➢ World Badminton Championship started in 1977.

➢ Measurements (Badminton) : Length of the court – 44 feet, Width – 20 feet (for Doubles) and 17 feet (for Singles), Height of the net – 5 feet, Weight of the Shuttle cock – 4.74 to 5.50 gram, Overall length of the Racket – 680 mm (2.5 ft.) maximum, Overall width of the Racket – 230 mm (9 inches) maximum, Overall length of the racket head – 290 mm (11.5 inches) maximum, Weight of the racket – between 85 to 140 grams.

➢ Terminology (Badminton) : Badminton Court, End, Trans Lines, Back gallery, Service Court, Let, Forward Stroke, Backward Stroke, Toss or Lob, Clear, Smash, Net strokes, Rally, Setting, First hand or Second hand, Side out, Base of operation, Rotation, Long service, Net fault, Double fault, Foot Fault, Service break, Match point, Set point, High service, Cross shot, Service change, Drive, Drop shot, Duce, Advance etc.

Lawn Tennis

➢ Tennis was introduced by Major Wingfeild in Wales in 1870.

➢ All England Championship (popularly known as Wimbledon Championship) started in 1877 for men only. Tennis competitions for women (in Wimbledon Championship) were introduced in 1884.

➢ Measurements (Tennis) : Length of the court – 78 feet or 23.77 m (singles), Width of the court – 27 feet or 8.23 m (singles), 36 feet or 10.97 m (doubles), Height of the net – 3 feet (0.914 m) , Weight of the ball – 56.0 to 59.4 gram, Maximum length of the frame of the racket – 32 inches (81.28 cm), Colour of the ball – white or yellow

➢ Terminology (Tennis) : Ace, Advantage, A Let, Back hand drive, Deuce, Chip Shot, Volley, Half volley, Let fault, Foot fault, Double fault, Smash, Service, Grand slam, Singles sticks, Love, Slice.

Polo

➢ Measurements (Polo) : Length of the field – 300 yards, Width of the field – 150 yards, Distance between the goals – 250 yards, Distance between the goal posts – 8 yards.

➢ Terminology : Bunker, Chuker, Mallet etc.

Wrestling

➢ Measurements (Wrestling) : In International Competitions there is a circular area with 9 metre diameter with circle in the centre of 1 metre diameter . Competitions played on a mattress, the mattress is 1:1 metre diameter high.

➢ Terminology : Heave, Half, Nelson, Rebuts, Hold sager etc.

Chess

- ➢ The number of squares on a chessboard : 64, Colour of the squares – White and black, Number of same colour Chess - 16
- ➢ Terminology : Bishop, Gambit, Checkmate, Stalemate, Pawn, Grandmaster etc.

Golf

- ➢ Diameter of the hole : 4 inches
- ➢ Terminology : Bogie, Fore some, Stymie, T, Put hole, Nib lick, Caddy, Limns, Iron, Putting, The green, Bunker etc.

Water Polo

- ➢ The length and width of the field : 30 X 20 yards
- ➢ Terminology : 2 metre line, 4 metre line, Goal line, Caps, Personal, Fault, Ball under etc.

Baseball

- ➢ The distance of each base is 90 feet, The distance of the base along with its hypotenuse – 127 feet
- ➢ Terminology : Home, Diamond, Pitcher, Put out, Home run, Strike, Ant rubber etc.

Billiards

- ➢ Terminology : Cue, Jigger, Pot, Break Pot, In luck, In off, Cans, Bolting, Hazard, Long etc.

Rifle Shooting

- ➢ Terminology : Target, Bulls eye, Muzzle flub etc.

Kho-Kho

- ➢ Terminology : Chasers, Active Chaser, Runners, Diving, Taking a direction, To recede, Tapping, Trapping, Dupe turn, Late Kho, Giving Kho, Fake Kho etc.

Swimming

- ➢ Terminology : Crawl, Breast Stroke, Spring Board, Twist, Butter fly.

Boxing

- ➢ Length and width of the ring : Minimum 4.9X4.9 m² and maximum 6.10X6.10 m²
- ➢ Terminology : Punch, Upper cut, Round, Jab, Hook, Knock down, Knock out, Hitting willow, Ring, Break, Bell, Belt, Blow, Bounce, Bout.

Marathon

- ➢ The distance of the marathon run : 26 mile 385 yards or 42.195 km.

Cups and Trophies (Associated with Sports /Games)

Sport	Cups and Trophies
Hockey	Aga Khan Cup, Begam Rasul Trophy (women's), Maharaja Ranjit Singh Gold Cup, Lady Ratan Tata Trophy (women's), Gurunanak Championship (women's) Dhyanchand Trophy, Nehru Trophy, Sindhia Gold Cup, Murugappa Gold Cup, Wellington Cup etc.

Sport	Cups and Trophies
Football	Beghum Hazarat Mahal Cup, BILT Cup, Bordoloi Trophy, Colombo Cup, Confederation Cup, D C M Trophy, Durand Cup, Rovers Cup, B.C. Rai Trophy (National Championship), FIFA World Cup, Jules Rimet Trophy, Kalinga Cup, Santosh Trophy (National Championship), IFA Shield, Scissor Cup, Subroto Mukherjee Cup, Sir Ashutosh Mukherjee Trophy, Todd Memorial Trophy, Vittal Trophy, etc.
Cricket	Anthony D' Mellow Trophy, Ashes, Asia Cup, Benson and Hedges Cup, Bose Trophy, Champions Trophy, Charminar Challenger Cup, C.K. Naidu Trophy, Cooch - Behar Trophy, Deodhar Trophy, Duleep Trophy, Gavaskar - Border Trophy, G.D. Birla Trophy, Gillette Cup, Ghulam Ahmad Trophy, Hakumat Rai Trophy, ICC World Cup, Irani Trophy, Interface Cup, Jawaharlal Nehru Cup, Lomboard World Challenge Cup, Mc Dowells Challenge Cup, Merchant Cup, Moin - ud - Dowla Cup, Nat West Trophy, Prudential Cup (World Cup), Rani Jhansi Trophy, Ranji Trophy, Rohinton Baria Trophy, Rothmans Cup, Sahara Cup, Sharjah Cup, Sheesh Mahal Trophy, Sheffield Shield, Singer Cup, Sir Frank Worrel Trophy, Texaco Cup, Titan Cup, Vijay Hazare Trophy, Vijay Merchant Trophy, Vizzy Trophy, Wisden Trophy, Wills Trophy, World Series Cup.
Table Tennis	Berna Bellack cup (men), Corbillion Cup (women), Jai Laxmi cup (women), Rajkumari Challenge Cup (women junior), Ramanuja Trophy (men junior), Travancore Cup (women), Swathling Cup (men)etc.
Badminton	Aggrawal Cup, Amrit Diwan Cup, Asia Cup, Australasia Cup, Chaddha Cup, European Cup, Harilela Cup, Ibrahim Rahimatollah Challenger Cup, Konica Cup, Narang Cup, S.R. Ruia Cup, Sophia Cup, Kitiakara Cup, Thomas Cup, Tunku Abdulrahman Cup, Uber Cup, World Cup, Yonex Cup etc.
Basket ball	Basalat Jha Trophy, B.C. Gupta Trophy, Federation Cup, S.M. Arjuna Raja Trophy, Todd Memorial Trophy, William Jones Cup, Bangalore Blues Challenge Cup, Nehru Cup, Federation Cup
Bridge	Basalat Jha Trophy, Holkar Trophy, Ruia Gold Cup, Singhania Trophy. etc
Polo	Ezra Cup, Gold Cup, King's Cup, Prithi Pal Singh Cup, Radha Mohan Cup, Winchester Cup etc.
Athletics	Charminar Trophy, Federation Cup etc.
Air Racing	Jawaharlal Challenge Trophy, King's Cup, Schneider Cup
Billiards	Arthur Walker Trophy, Thomas Cup etc.
Boxing	Aspy Adjahia Trophy, Federation Cup , Val Baker Trophy etc.
Golf	Canada Cup, Eisenhower Trophy, Muthiah Gold Cup, Nomura Trophy, President's Trophy, Prince of Wales Cup, Ryder Cup, Solheim Cup, Topolino Trophy, Walker Cup, World Cup etc.

Sport	Cups and Trophies
Chess	Naidu Trophy, Khaitan Trophy, Limca Trophy, Lin Arec City Trophy, World Cup etc.
Horse Racing	Beresford Cup, Blue Riband Cup, Derby, Grand National Cup etc.
Netball	Anantrao Pawar Trophy etc.
Rugby Football	Bledisloe Cup, Calcutta Cup, Webb Ellis Trophy, etc.
Shooting	North Wales Cup, Welsh Grand Prix etc.
Volleyball	Centennial Cup, Federation Cup, Indira Pradhan Trophy, Shivanthi Gold Cup, etc.
Yatching	America Cup etc.

Famous Stadia and Sports

➢ Government of India has recently constituted "National Playing Fields Association of India (NPFAI)" under an ambitious scheme of 'Kendriya Yuva Karya Evam Khel Mantralay' to sater to tne development of Games & Sport and the players as well.

Stadium	Sports	Place
Indraprastha Stadium	Indoor Games	Delhi
Jawaharlal Nehru Stadium	Athletics	Delhi
Ferozeshah Kotla Ground	Cricket	Delhi
Ambedkar Stadium	Football	Delhi
Shivaji Stadium	Hockey	Delhi
National Stadium	Hockey	Delhi
National Stadium	Hockey & others	Mumbai
Wankhede Stadium	Cricket	Mumbai
Brabourne Stadium	Cricket	Mumbai
Eden Gardens	Cricket	Kolkata
Green Park Stadium	Cricket	Kanpur
Keenan Stadium	Cricket	Jamshedpur
Nehru (Chepak) Stadium	Cricket	Chennai
Varabati Stadium	Cricket	Cuttack
Aintree, Doncaster, Epsom	Horse racing	England (U.K.)
Flemington	Horse racing	Melbourn (Australia)
Headingley Manchester	Cricket	England (U.K.)
Lords, Oval, Leeds	Cricket	England (U.K.)
Black Heath	Rugby Football	London (U.K.)
Wimbledon	Lawn Tennis	London (U.K.)
Wembley Stadium	Football	London (U.K.)

Stadium	Sports	Place
Brookland	Football	England (U.K.)
Twickenham	Rugby Football	England (U.K.)
Putney Mart Lake	Boat race	England (U.K.)
Trent Bridge	Cricket	England (U.K.)
White City	Dog race	England (U.K.)
Hurlington	Polo	England (U.K.)
Henlay	Regata	England
Brisbane, Melbourne, Perth, Sydney	Cricket	Australia
Yankee Stadium	Boxing	New York (USA)
Brooklyn	Baseball	New York (USA)
Forest Hill	Tennis	USA
Sendy Lodge	Golf	Scotland

National Games and Sports of Some Countries

Country	Sports	Country	Sports
United States of America	Baseball	England	Cricket
Spain	Bull -fighting	Japan	Ju-Jitsu
Canada	Ice Hockey	Australia	Cricket
India	Hockey	Pakistan	Hockey
Russia	Chess	China	Table Tennis
Scotland	Rugby Football		

Court, Campus or Field Associated with Sports

Court / Campus / Field	Games / Sports
Court	Tennis, Badminton, Net Ball, Handball, Volleyball, Squash, Kho – kho, Kabaddi
Diamond	Baseball
Ring	Sketing, Boxing
Course	Golf
Pool	Swimming
Board	Table tennis
Mat	Judo, Karate, Taikwondo
Arena	Horse riding
Vellodrome	Cycling
Field	Polo, Football, Hockey
Track	Athletics
Pitch	Cricket
Greens	Bowls
Rink	Curling, Ice hockey
Range	Shooting, Archery

Number of Players in Some Popular Sports/Games

Sports	Number of Players (on each side or in each team)
Baseball	9
Rugby football	15
Polo	4
Water polo	7
Kho Kho	9
Kabaddi	7
Hockey, Football and Cricket	11
Netball	7
Volleyball	6
Badminton, Tennis and Table tennis	1 or 2 (Singles & Doubles respectively)
Basketball	5
Gymnastic	Several individuals compete simultaneously
Billiards / Snooker	1
Boxing / Chess	1
Bridge	2
Croquet	13 or 15
Golf	Several individuals compete simultaneously
Lacrosse	12

★★★

COMPUTER

10

Introduction

➢ The era of 20th and 21st century has witnessed rapid developments in science and technology influencing every aspect of human life. One of the greatest things that man has ever created is, perhaps, 'the Computer'. The computer is truly an amazing machine. Computer is being used in areas of administration, medicine, education, sports, defence, shops, home, markets and many more. Computer and Information Technology (IT), in recent years, has become an integral part of our life. We can see it almost everywhere.

➢ A computer is an electronic machine that helps to process data. It is used to solve problems relating to almost all fields such as education, home, medicine, science and technology, research, designing, publishing, communication etc.

➢ A computer is an information-processing and information-accessing tool. This means that a computer accepts some information or data from the outside world. It processes it to produce a new information.

➢ Information processing is the essence of computing.

➢ Meaning of Computer : The word computer has derived from an English word 'Compute', which means 'to calculate'.

➢ Computer is an electronic device which processes the input informations according to the given set of instructions, called program.

➢ Blaise Pascal had developed the first mechanical calculator in 1642 AD, which is called 'Pascalene'.

➢ British scientist Charles Babbage was the first person to conceive an automatic calculator or a computer in 1833. He is called the 'Father of modern computer'.

➢ The credit of developing first computer program goes to Lady Ada Augusta, a student of Babbage.

➢ Herman Holorith prepared an electronic tabulating machine in 1880, which was automatically functional with the help of Punch Card. This Punch Card is used in computer even today.

➢ Howard Ekin developed the first Mechanical Computer 'Mark - I' in 1937.

➢ J.P. Ekart and John Moschley invented world's first electronic computer 'ENIAC-I' in 1946 and paved the way for first revolution in the field of calculating machine or computer. Electronic Valve or Vaccum Tube was used as a switch in the computer.

➢ John Van Newman invented EDVAC (Electronic Descrete Variable Computer) in 1951, in which he used Stored Program. The credit of using Binary System in computers also goes to him. Indeed Mr. Newman contributed most in the development of computer and thus gave a right direction to the Computer Revolution (Second Revolution).

Five Generations of Computer

Generation	Period	Main Electronic components	Main Computers
I	1940 - 52	Electronic Valve Vaccum Tube	EDSAC, EDVAC, UNIVAC
II	1952 - 64	Transistor	IBM–700, IBM–1401, IBM–1620, CDC–1604, CDC–3600, ATLAS, ICL–1901
III	1964 - 71	Integrated Circuit	IBM–360, IBM–370, NCR–395, CDC–1700, ICL–2903
IV	1971 -	Largely Integrated Circuit	APPLE, DCM
V	—	Optical Fibre	

Types of Computer : According to size and capacity these are following types of Computer —

1. Micro Computer : These computers are used by individual, thus also called PC or Personal Computer. These days P.Cs are largely used for domestic and official purposes etc.
2. Mini Computer : This type of computer is comparatively larger than that of micro computer. This is 5 to 50 times more powerful than that of a Micro Computer.
3. Main Frame Computer : These are large sized computers. By Time Sharing and Multi Tasking techniques many people rather more than 100 people can work at a time on different terminals of this computer.
4. Super Computer : These are very powerful computers and have more storage capacity. These are the most expensive and the fastest computers, able to process most complex jobs with a very high speed.
5. Quantum Computer : The development of this type is in final stage. Probably Quantum Computers will be more advanced than that of human brain. In Quantum Computers Q -Bit will be used in lieu of Binary Bits.

Programming Languages of different generations

Generation	Languages
1st Generation (1940-52)	FORTRAN- i
2nd Generation (1952-64)	FORTRAN-ii, ALGOL - 60, COBOL, LISP
3rd Generation (1964-71)	PL / I, ALGOL - W, ALGOL - 68, Pascal, SIMULA - 67, APL, SNOBOL, 4 BASIC, C
4th Generation (1971- —)	CLUE, ALFARD, UCLID, Reformed Pascal, MODULA, EDA, ORACLE
5th Generation (For future)	Artificial Intelligence Languages.

Some Important Facts related to Computers

- ➢ December 2 is observed as Computer Literacy Day.
- ➢ India has announced New Computer Policy in 1984.

Super Computers developed in the World	
Name	Manufacturer
CRAY KIS	CRAY K Research Co., USA
Deep Blue	IBM Co., USA
Blue Gene	IBM Co., USA
COSMOS	Cambridge University, UK.

Super Computers developed in India	
Name	Manufacturer
FLO SOLVER	NAL, Bangalore
PACE	DRDO
PARAM-10000	C - DAC, Pune
CHIPP - 16	C-Dot, Bangalore
MULTIMICRO	IIS, Bangalore
MACH	IIT, Bombay

- First computer (made in India) is 'Siddharth', which was manufactured by Electronics Corporation of India.
- First computer in India was installed in the *Main Post Office of Bangalore* on August 16, 1986.
- First Pollution Free Computerized Petrol Pump of India is in Mumbai.
- First Computer University (in Private Sector) in India is Rajeev Gandhi Computer University.
- Bangalore (now Bangaluru) is also known as the Silicon Valley of India.
- First Indian News Paper to be available on Internet is 'The Hindu'.
- First Indian magazine to be available on Internet is 'India Today'.
- First Indian political party which has created its website on internet is 'Bhartiya Janata Party (BJP)'.
- Mainly there are three types of Computer, Digital, Analog and Hybrid.
- First Super Computer of the world is CRAY K-1-S, developed by Cray K Company of U.S.A.
- 'Deep Blue' is a Super Computer which had defeated World Chess Champion Garry Kasparov. This Super Computer is able to do the work equivalent to the work of 32 computers and can think 20 crore steps of chess in 1 second.
- First Electronic Digital Computer of the world is 'ENIAC'.
- Most popular Operating System in the world is WINDOWS.
- USENET is a link to connect all the universities.
- First book on Personal Computer was written by Ted Nelson.
- The book of Ted Nelson 'Soul of New Machine', won Pulitzer Prize.
- First magazine on Computer is 'Computer and Automotion'.
- First home Computer is Comodor VIC / 20.
- First Practical Digital computer is UNIVAC.
- FORTRAN is the first Programming Language.
- PROLOG is the language of the fifth generation of computer.
- J.S. Kilbi developed the IC chips.
- A computer error is known as Bug.
- C -DAC (Centre for Development and Advanced Computing) was established in Pune in 1988.
- Super computer PARAM - 10000, having the capacity of 1 billion calculations per second, was made by the scientists of C - DAC of

Pune on March 28, 1998. The main credit for the development of the PARAM-10000 goes to Dr. Vijay P. Bhaskar, Executive Director of C-DAC, Pune.

- National Aeronautics Laboratories, Bangalore was the first in India to develop a Super Computer named FLO SOLVER.
- Laser Printers are the fastest printers.
- IBM (International Business Machine) is an American computer company.
- Computer virus is a man made digital parasite, which corrupts (infects) the file and known as 'File corrupter'.
- Modem is a device which connects the computers and works based on telephone lines.
- Y-2 K was a technical problem, associated with the calendar (Date, Month and Year) known as 'Millenium Bug'.
- The development of computer started in India since 1955.
- Indian Institute of Science, Bangalore has developed 'Simputer', which is a small palm sized touch screen computer.
- First computerarium in India is in Bangaluru (Karnataka).
- Vellanad of Thiruvananthpuram district in Kerala has been declared the first fully computerised village of India.
- PC, Home computer, Electronic notebook etc. are the examples of micro computer.
- Some Operating Systems, used in micro computers are — CP / M, Mac OS (Apple), DOS, Pro DOS, MS DOS / PC DOS, XENIX, WINDOWS, LINUX etc.
- *Linus Benedict Torvalds,* creator and coordinator of the Unix like Operating System. Linus was born in Helsinki, Finland on December 28, 1969.
- On Sept. 17, 1991 Linus completed the first version of Linux. He made the wisest decision in Operating System history by releasing Linux under General Public Licence, thereby making it open and free to all.
- He is one of the pioneers who advocated the idea of free software and thereby changed the software market.
- A computer may be used to control purely mechanical action. It has two main parts : (i) Hardware and (ii) Software.

Hardware

Computer performs some operations to solve problems. For this the various units of a computer system must perform and co-ordinate all operations.

- A computer has three main units : 1. Input unit, 2. Processing unit and 3. Output unit. These are the physical units of a computer system. These units constitute the hardware of a computer.
- The computer has its own internal 'language'.
- The computer is essentially made of electronic components. All these components are capable of generating any one of the two states, either a low (or a 0 volt) or a high (say 5 volts).

- It is difficult to talk always in terms of currents and voltages to represent information. Therefore, computer scientists use a special convention. A high is symbolically represented by a '1' and a low is represented by a '0'. The 1s and 0s are known as binary digits, or in short 'bits' (the term 'binary' refers to something that has two parts).
- Computers always work with bits. They do not understand any other form.
- Computer scientists use combination of 8 bits taken together to represent various symbols.
- Because every bit can take one of 2 possible values, the total number of combinations possible, using 8 bits, the computer can represent 256 different symbols.
- This is enough to cover our entire range of alphabets, numbers and other special characters like $, @, +, ₹ etc. Such a combination of 8 bits is called a byte.
- To build complex information like paragraphs and mathematical equations, we would need a larger number of bytes or characters. Thus we have the kilobyte, megabyte and gigabyte.
- 1 kilobyte = 1024 bytes.
- In computers information is represented using multiples of 8 (2^3) bits, since 8 bits are the smallest unit of information. Therefore, higher units are expressible in multiples of 2^3.
- The power of two closest to a kilo (1000) is $2^{10} = 1024$.
- Megabytes is used in a more conventional sense and is equal to 1 million bytes or 1000 kilobytes.
- 1 MB = 1000 KB
- A gigabyte refers to 1000 megabytes or 1 million kilobytes.
- 1 GB = 1000 MB
- The earliest computers were designed so that there components could work with 8 bits at a time.
- While the earliest machine were 8-bit machines, contemporary computers can work with 16, 32 and even 64 bits. This is called the data width of the computer.
- The basic elements of computers that can signal a 1 or a 0 are called flip-flops. It is a simple electrical device and can either be a '0' or a '1', which means that the flow of current is either inward or outward.
- Modern computers use a very tiny set of flip-flops known as a register. The most important characteristic of these registers is that the binary digits can be stored in them using certain voltages.
- The entire independent circuits can be designed on a small piece of a semi conductor material like silicon.
- Silicon is obtained from sand and is a poor conductor of electricity. But, by chemical processes, the surface and the enterior of a silicon 'chip' are modified to give it electronic capabilities. Such miniature circuits are called Integrated Circuits (IC).

➢ By 1971, engineers were able to put a few component switches — necessary to build a complete computer on a single chip of silicon. This tiny silicon chip was called the microprocessor.

➢ Because the computer is a binary machine, it performs mathematical operations using the binary number system.

➢ The binary number system is similar to the decimal system where we use ten digits, 0, 1, 2, 3.... 8, 9 to represent all numerical values. The only difference is in the number of digits used.

➢ The computer converts all decimal numbers into binary numbers or combinations of bits. Then by acting upon individual bits, it can perform the required mathematical operation addition, subtraction, etc.

➢ The internal circuits that can perform mathematical operations on bits are usually made of two or more logic gates. Logic gates are components that generate a 1 or a 0 depending on the input.

➢ The three basic logic gates are AND, OR and NOT.

➢ A computer is organized into three basic units :
(i) the Central Processing Unit (CPU)
(ii) the Memory Unit (MU) and
(iii) the Input / Output Unit

(i) Central Processing Unit (CPU)

The CPU is the part of a computer that performs the main function of information processing. The memory unit stores data. The computer supplies processed information back to the users using special output devices.

➢ The Central Processing Unit or CPU, is the most important part of the computer. It is called the brain of the computer. It makes all the required calculations and processes data.

➢ The CPU can be divided into three main components : (a) ALU (b) CU and (c) Registers.

(a) *The Arithmetic and Logic Unit (ALU)* : ALU performs all the mathematical and logical operations on the information supplied to the CPU.

(b) *Control Unit (CU)* : This unit directs the working of the CPU. It fetches instructions (Programs) from the memory and according to the instructions, controls the flow of data between the ALU and other parts of the computer.

(c) *Registers* : Registers are storage locations that hold instructions or data while the CPU is using them. The registers consist of flip-flops and the registers used by the CPU are the fastest memory elements in the computer. In contrast, the memory unit holds instructions and data before or after the CPU processes these.

Main attributes of CPU

(a) *Data Width* : It refers to the number of bits of data that can be manipulated within the CPU at one given time.

➢ The data width of a computer is also called its word size.

- ➢ Computers have data widths ranging from 8 to 64 bits.
- ➢ A higher data width means the CPU is capable of processing data faster. A CPU with a higher data width is more powerful.

(b) *Address Range* : Address range refers to the amount of memory that can be directly read or written by the CPU.

(c) *Clock Speed* : The speed of CPU is known as Clock Speed. The computer is essentially composed of tiny devices that can be put on or off to indicate 1 or 0.

- ➢ At any moment several thousand such devices change their state. To synchronize the change of all these components the CPU uses an internal clock.
- ➢ With every tick of this clock all switches that need to change their position do so in perfect harmony.
- ➢ The larger the number of ticks per second the faster is the speed of the CPU.
- ➢ The ticks per second of the internal clock are measured in megahertz and gigahertz.
- ➢ Hertz is a unit of frequency .
- ➢ 1 MHz = 1million 'ticks' per second, 1 GHz = 1000 MHz
- ➢ Higher the clock-speed, faster the computer.

(ii) Memory Unit (MU)

The memory unit stores all instructions and data for the CPU. Memory Unit is an important part of the computer system. The storage device of a computer system is known as memory. Memory Unit can receive data, hold it and deliver according to the instructions from the control unit.

- ➢ Memory is of two kinds : (a) Primary and (b) Secondary.

(a) *Primary Memory* : It is often referred to as the working memory or the main memory of a computer system. It is capable of sending and receiving data at a very high speed. It is temporary in nature i.e. Data stored in primary memory are lost when the computer is switched off. So it is also called volatile memory. Example of primary memory is RAM.

- ➢ Primary memory is directly accessible to the CPU. It must be able to provide data very quickly.
- ➢ The two basic kinds of primary memory are the Random Access Memory (RAM) and the Read Only Memory (ROM).
- ➢ The RAM is a read/write memory.
- ➢ The CPU can change the contents of the RAM at any time. In addition, RAM is volatile.
- ➢ The RAM capacity greatly influences the computing ability of the computer. Capacity is usually measured in kilobytes and megabytes.
- ➢ The ROM can not be altered.
- ➢ Informations is stored on the ROM at the time of its manufacture. The

information might be in the form of crucial instructions that govern the working of the computer.

- ➢ The ROM is non-volatile and retains its information even after the power is turned off.
- ➢ The PROM (Programmable Read Only Memory), however, has the option of being programmed, i.e. the manufacturer of the computer may choose to load a program designed by his company into this PROM, and then the computer would use this PROM like any other ROM.

(b) *Secondary Memory* : It is used to store data for a long term. It operates at a much slower rate than primary memory. Secondary memory is permanent in nature, so it is also called non-volatile. It is also cheaper than primary memory. Examples of secondary memory are floppy disks, hard disks, magnetic tapes etc.

- ➢ Primary memory is fast but expensive. To reduce storage costs, computers also use secondary memory.
- ➢ It is not directly accessible to the CPU. Information is moved from the secondary memory to the primary memory first and then to the CPU.
- ➢ Common examples of secondary memory are floppy diskettes, hard (fixed) discs and magnetic tapes.
- ➢ A floppy diskette is a plastic disk coated with magnetic material.
- ➢ Special devices known as disk drives are capable of reading from and writing to floppies using special magnetic 'head'.
- ➢ Any piece of information stored on a floppy diskette can be directly accessed.
- ➢ Magnetic tapes are long plastic tapes coated with magnetic material.
- ➢ Magnetic tapes can store far larger amounts of data than the floppy diskette. But a problem with magnetic tapes is that information can not be accessed directly as in the case of floppy diskettes.
- ➢ The third type of medium, called fixed or hard disks, are more or less similar to the floppy diskette. But one hard disk drive contains several discs of a hard material.
- ➢ Another popular storage medium is the compact disk (CD). Unlike the media described above, CDs are an 'optical' medium.
- ➢ An optical medium is one where the properties of light is used for the medium to perform its basic functions.
- ➢ Conventional CDs are made of a special kind of plastic.
- ➢ The CD is read using a laser beam .
- ➢ Secondary memory is much slower, but it is non-volatile and can be used to store information for long periods of time.

(iii) Input/Output

- ➢ There has to be a physical channel that permits users to supply informations to the computer.
- ➢ Devices that permit users to supply information to the computer are called 'input' devices.

- Input unit enables us to enter (or "Input") data into a computer. The common input devices are keyboard and mouse.
- Similarly, a physical channel that permits a computer to convey the processed information to the outside world. Devices that permit such a function are called 'output' devices.
- Output unit enables the computer to show us the result and the information that we want. The common output devices are monitor, printer and speakers.
- Input and output devices are indispensable, but are not a part of the CPU. They are also called peripheral devices, suggesting that they lie on the periphery of the CPU.
- These devices are also called an interface, because they translate informations for man and machine.
- The most popular input device used in contemporary computers is the keyboard.
- Another way to input information into a computer is to use an Optical Mark Reader (OMR). Optical Mark Readers are capable of reading specially prepared forms. These forms have a provision for black marks to be made using a pen or a pencil in a specific position.
- Most competitive examinations that deal with a large number of students usually use this system.
- Banks use another input device called a Magnetic Ink Character Reader (MICR).
- Special numbers are written on bank cheques using magnetic ink and in a particular style to write different numbers. The MICR passes over the words or characters, examines the shape of the magnetic field created by the character, and is thus able to recognize it.
- Bar codes are often imprinted on products in merchandise stores. A bar code consists of several parallel vertical lines of different thickness that represent the binary digits.
- The bits form a code that can be used to identify the object on which the bar code is imprinted. A bar code reader is used to read the bar codes by detecting the bars by using light.
- The bar code can represent information like the price of the product or its date of expiry etc.
- Menu-driven programs, where the user sees the host of on-screen choices, sometimes use another input devices called the mouse.
- The mouse is a pointing device. It can be gripped in the palm of the hand and moved over a horizontal surface. The motion of the mouse can be monitored by the computer in different ways.
- The movement is measured and transmitted to the computer. This generates a corresponding movement of an on-screen marker called a cursor from one option to another.
- To select an option, the user presses one of the mouse's buttons.
- Another, input device is a digital camera. A digital camera has a circuit that is sensitive to light.

- The two most common devices are the Visual Display Unit (VDU) and the printer.
- A Visual Display Unit (VDU) uses a cathode ray tube to display informations.
- To represent any character, VDU illuminates a particular pattern of these dots. These dots are also known as pixels, a short form for picture - elements.
- Printers print characters on paper or other similar medium.
- Printers come in three popular versions : dot matrix printers, ink-jet printers and laser printers.
- Dot matrix printers print characters in the form of combinations of very tiny dots. The printing head aligns its 'pins' to match a particular pattern of dots.
- Ink-jet printers spray jets of ink on to the paper to print any character. The characters are absolutely smooth as ink is sprayed in a continuous flow.
- Laser printer, uses a laser beam to actually 'burn' the characters on to the paper.
- We need to issue the computer a detailed sequence of instructions that it needs to follow to operate upon any data. Such a sequence is called a program.
- A program may directly be written to the RAM or may be stored in some form of secondary memory.
- It may be transferred from the secondary memory to the RAM as and when required.
- Execution of a program means that data is moved around in the CPU according to a well-detailed sequence by the programme.
- Computer programs are written using special languages called programming languages.
- There are several programming languages. Each language has its own 'grammar' called its syntax.

Types of Programming Languages

- Machine language and the assembly language are examples of low-level languages.
- A special program called Assembler converts all instructions into the binary format.
- Because all such instructions must finally be converted to the binary form, all high - level languages have their own translation programs called compilers or interpreters.
- Examples of popular high - level languages are C, C++, JAVA, Pascal, Fortran etc.

Software

- Software relates to set of programs. The software controls the computer hardware parts and make them operational. In other words, it governs the operations of a computer system.

- Software is a general term used for all computer programs. This distinguishes programs from the physical components of the computer, which are collectively called the hardware.
- Software is generally divided into two kinds of programs : Application programs and System's programs.
- Applications programs are programs that permit the computer to be used as a tool for some specific tasks.
- A common term used for special text editors is word processors.
- Another popular type of application programs is the Data Base Management Systems (DBMS).
- The most important system's program is an operating system.
- Operating systems help users interact with the computer.
- Unix, MS - DOS, Linux, Windows, Mac OS are some of the most popular operating systems used by contemporary computers.

Glossary

Active Cell : The cell in MS Excel with dark boundary is called the active cell.

ALU : It stands for Arithmetic Logic Unit. All calculations in computer are done here.

Application Software : It is designed to perform some specific applications such as payroll, word processing, graphics etc.

Batch Processing : Data are processed in a batch.

BIOS : It stands for Basic Input Output System. This program is stored in ROM.

Bit : It is the short form of Binary Digit.

Boot Loader : It reads the main portion of the operating system from secondary memory.

Byte : One byte is a collection of 8 bits.

Cell : Cells are boxes created by the interaction of rows and columns.

Cell Pointer : The boundary of active cell is called cell pointer.

Copyright : It means the material and information are the personal property of the owner or producer.

Counter feiting : It is a process of making and distributing illegal copies of software packages.

Cracker : A cracker is a person who breaks into a computer system to steal the information as programs for unauthorized use.

CU : It stands for Control Unit. It controls the computer system.

Data : Data are raw facts and figures.

Database : It is a collection of files. Data remains in an organized form in a database.

Data Capture : It is a process of collecting or capturing data from a site or a source.

Data Manipulation : Captured data are manipulated to produce information.

Data processing : It is the process to get meaningful information from data.

DBMS : It stands for Database Management System. It is a software package to manage database.

DHTML : It stands for Dynamic Hyper Text Markup Language. It is used to create dynamic content on web pages.

Dial Up Networking : It is the method by which a computer is connected to the Internet using telephone.

DOS : It stands for Disk Operating System. It is an operating system.

Ethics : Ethics are rules and beliefs.

Fields : A field in database is a collection of bytes that contain data about an item.

File : A file is a collection of related records.

GML : It stands for General Mark-up Language.

Hacker : A hacker is a person who breaks into a computer system to get access the information stored there.

HTML : It stands for Hyper Text Markup Language. It is used to create web-pages.

IAB : It stands for Internet Activities Board which was formed in 1983. It is now called as Internet Architectural Board.

IAS : It stands for Internet Application Software also known as Browsers.

IETF : It stands for Internet Engineer Task Force.

IRTF : It stands for Internet Research Task Force.

ISP : It stands for Internet Service Provider.

Internet Society : It was formed in 1992 to promote the use of Internet.

Input Unit : It is a part of computer system and used to enter data.

Linux : It is a Unix like Operating System with graphical user interface.

MAC OS : It is an Operating System used in Macintosh Computer, developed by Apple.

Modem : It is a device to connect different computer systems to the internet using telephone or cable lines.

MU : It stands for Memory Unit. It is used to store data.

Online Processing : It is used when data are coming continuously without delay.

Operating Unit : It is used to take output from the computer.

Operating System : It is an interface between the human user and the computer hardware.

Piracy : It is the illegal reproduction and distribution of software application.

Primary Key : It is a field with unique value for each record.

Primary Memory : It is the main memory of a computer system.

Query : It is used to extract information from a database.

Range of Cells : It is group of neighbouring cells that touch each other.

RDBMS : It stands for Relational Database Management System.

Record : It is the collection of related fields.

Secondary Memory : It is the permanent memory of the computer.

Software : It relates to sets of programs.

SOLARIS : It is a Unix like Operating System developed by Sun Microsystems.

Sorting : It is arranging of data in order.

System Software : It performs the basic functions that are necessary to operate a computer system.

Tag : It is part of HTML. It determines the way, the browser displays text in a Web Page.

Unix : It is a powerful multiuser operating system. It uses command line user interface.

Virus : It is a harmful computer program.

Some Memorable Facts

- A computer is a data processing machine.
- It has two main parts: hardware and software.
- Hardware comprises of the physical units of a computer system.
- Software is a set of programs.
- Both hardware and software together make a computer system functional.
- Data are raw facts and figures.
- An operating system is an interface between the user and the computer hardware.
- An operating system manages computer resources.
- An operating system performs different functions.
- An operating system is responsible for process management, file management, etc.
- There are many kinds of operating system.
- Some popular operating systems are DOS, UNIX, Windows, LINUX, Mac OS, etc.
- The Windows Explorer program is more efficient for viewing folders in Windows.
- Windows Explorer is divided vertically into two parts or two panes.
- The left side pane displays disk drives and folders in a hierarchical order.
- The right pane displays the contents of the folder / drive that is selected on left side pane.
- The process of linking text values in a series within a formula is called 'concatenation'.
- The computer is a data processing machine.
- Data processing involves some activities like data comptuing data manipulation and information management.
- A database is a collection of interrelated data.
- Computers are very useful for maintaining databases.
- A relational database is a collection of data items organized as a set of formally described tables from which data can be accessed or reassembled in many different ways without having to reorganize the database tables.

- MS Access is a powerful program to create and manage our databases.
- A table is a collection of data about a specific topic.
- A form is a graphical representation of a table.
- A report is a presentation of data in a printed format.
- We can create mailing labels for your database using MS Access.
- Internet is the network of computer networks with millions of computer attached to it.
- Websites are files in servers, which are powerful computers.
- Websites contain pages called Web Pages.
- The collection of all websites is called World Wide Web or WWW.
- Hyper text was first coined by Ted Nelson in 1960s.
- HTML is a markup language. It is used to create Web Pages. It uses commands called Tags.
- Text editors are used to compose HTML documents. HTML documents are viewed in Web browsers.
- In the Photoshop toolbox, the tools are grouped by type.
- Some of the tool icons have a tiny black triangle in the lower - right corner of their icons. This means that there are more tools of the same general kind available on a pop-up menu.

Abbreviations associated with Computer

CDAC	Centre for Development of Advanced Parallel Computing
C-DOT	Centre for Development of Telematrics
HTTP	Hyper Text Transfer Protocol
ROM	Read Only Memory
RAM	Random Access Memory
BIOS	Basic Input-Output System
MODEM	Modulation-Demodulation
CAD	Computer Aided Design
PSTN	Public Switched Telephone Network
PSPDN	Pocket Switched Public Data Network
RABMN	Remote Area Business Message Network
LAN	Local Area Network
WAN	Wide Area Network
MAN	Metropolitan Area Network
CDMA	Code Division Multiple Access
GAIS	Gateway Internet Access Service
E-Mail	Electronic Mail
CD	Compact Disc
LDU	Liquid Display Unit
CPU	Central Processing Unit
CAM	Computer Aided Manufacturing
CATScan	Computerised Axial Tomography Scan
COBOL	Common Business Oriented Language

COMAL	Common Algorithmic Language
DOS	Disc Operating System
DTS	Desk Top System
DTP	Desk Top Publishing
E-Commerce	Electronic Commerce
ENIAC	Electronic Numerical Integrator And Calculator
FAX	Fascimile Automated Xerox
FLOPS	Floating Operations Per Second
FORTRAN	Formula Translation
HLL	High Level Language
HTML	Hyper Text Markup Language
IBM	International Business Machine
IC	Integrated Circuit
ISH	International Super Highway
LISP	List Processing
LLL	Low Level Language
MICR	Magnetic Ink Character Recognition/Reader
MIPS	Millions of Instructions Per Second
MOPS	Millions of Operations Per Second
MPU	Micro Processor Unit
NICNET	National Informatics Centre Network
OMR	Optical Mark Reader/Recognition
PC-DOT	Personal Computer Disk Operation System
PROM	Programmable Read Only Memory
SNOBOL	String Oriented Symbolic Language
UPS	Uninterruptable Power Supply
VDU	Visual Display Unit
VLSI	Very Large Scale Integrated
WWW	World Wide Web

Abbreviations

A.V.E.S.	Acute Viral Encephalitic Syndrome
B.C.T.T.	Bank Cash Transaction Tax
B.C.S.B.I.	Banking Codes and Standard Board of India
C.I.C.	Central Information Commission
C.S.T.O.	Collective Security Treaty Organization
CNLU	Chanakya National Law University
D.I.I.	Domestic Institutional Investor
DTH	Direct to Home
E.C.G.C.	Export Credit Guarantee Corporation
F.D.I.	Foreign Direct Investment

F.I.I.	Foreign Institutional Investor
GANDHI	Green Action for National Dandi Heritage Initiative
GUAM	Georgia, Ukraine, Azerbaijan and Moldova
GAGAN	GPS Aided Geo-Augmented Navigation
H.P.A.I.	Highly Pathogenic Avian Influenza
IAEA	International Atomic Ener gy Agency
IITF	India International Trade Fair
I.M.O.	Instant Money Order
IBSA.	India, Brazil, South Africa
IRDA	Insurance Regulatory Authority
KYC	Know Your Customer
M.R.O.	Mars Recconnaissance Orbiter
N.A.D.T.	National Authority on Drugs and Therapeutics
N.C.C.E	National Council for Clinical Establishments
N.C.H.	National Consumer Helpline
N.E.I.A.	National Export Insurance Account
N.M.D.P.	National Maritime Development Programme
M.N.R.E.G.A.	Mahatma Gandhi National Rural Employment Guarantee Act
N.J.C.	National Judicial Council
NOTE	National Organization for Tobacco Eradication
O.C.I.	Overseas Citizen of India
PETA	Peoples for Ethical Treatment of Animal
PURA	Providing Urban Amenities in Rural Areas
P.H.F.I.	Public Health Foundation of India
QIB	Qualified Institutional Buyer
QIP	Qualified Institutional Placement
R.L.D.A	Railway Land Development Authority
RTA	Railway Territorial Army
RTC	Round Table Conference
RTG	Radio-isotope Thermo-electric Generator
SCRAMJET	Supersonic Combustion Ramjet
SIM	Subscriber Identification Module
SWIFT	Society for World-Wide International Financial Transactions
SWOT	Strengths, Weaknesses, Opportunities, Threats
SYL	Sutlej-Yamuna Link (canal)
YWCA	Young Women's Christian Association
UID	Unique Identity Number
UIDAI	Unique Identification Authority of India
VAT	Value Added Tax
ZSI	Zoological Survey of India
ZUPO	Zimbabwe United People's Organization

★★★